EVENING THOUGHTS

GREAT CHRISTIAN BOOKS
LINDENHURST, NEW YORK

EVENING THOUGHTS

OCTAVIUS WINSLOW

Great Christian Books
is an imprint of Rotolo Media
160 37th Street Lindenhurst, New York 11757
(631) 956-0998

Winslow, Octavius, 1808 – 1878
Evening Thoughts / by Octavius Winslow
p. cm.
A "A Great Christian Book" book
GREAT CHRISTIAN BOOKS an imprint of Rotolo Media
ISBN 978-1-61010-003-8
Recommended Dewey Decimal Classifications: 200, 202, 230, 234
Suggested Subject Headings:
1. Religion—Christianity & Christian theology—Devotional
2. Christianity—Bible—Christian Living
I. Title

Book and cover design are by Michael Rotolo, www.michaelrotolo.com. This book is typeset in the Minion typeface by Adobe Inc. and is quality-manufactured on acid-free paper stock. To discuss the publication of your Christian manuscript or out-of-print book, please contact us.

Manufactured in the United States of America

CONTENTS

JANUARY	7
FEBRUARY	43
MARCH	79
APRIL	117
MAY	154
JUNE	194
JULY	232
AUGUST	273
SEPTEMBER	318
OCTOBER	369
NOVEMBER	415
DECEMBER	456

JANUARY

JANUARY 1

As your days, so shall your strength be. Deut. 33:25

CHRISTIAN, consider this new epoch of time, unfold a new page of your yet unwritten history, with the full, unwavering conviction that God is faithful; that in all the negotiations, transactions, and events of the unknown future, in all the diversified and fluctuating phases of experience through which you may pass, it will be your mercy to do with Him of whom it is said, "It is impossible for God to lie." Oh, take this precious truth into your heart, and it will shed a warm sunlight over all the landscape of your yet shadowy existence. "He abides faithful: He cannot deny Himself." Standing yet within the solemn vestibule of this new and portentous year, could our fluttering hearts find repose in a more appropriate or sweeter truth than the Divine faithfulness of Him, "with whom there is no variableness neither shadow of turning"? As a new period of time slowly rises from the depths of the unknown and mysterious future, shrink we from its stern and solemn duties, its bosomed sorrows, its deep and impenetrable decrees? Why shrink we? Infinite resources unveil their treasures upon its threshold. Christ's atoning merits confront our vast demerit. Christ's boundless grace confronts our deep necessities. Christ's promised presence confronts our sad and gloomy loneliness. Jesus thus filled with grace so overflowing, with love so tender, with sympathy so exquisite, with power so illimitable, with resources so boundless, with a nature so changeless, stands before us and says to each trembling heart, "Fear not!" We commence a new march under his convoy. We prepare for a new conflict with his armor. We renew our pilgrimage with fresh supplies of 'angels' food,' affording nourishment for the present and pledges for the future. For that future do not be needlessly, unbelievingly anxious. It is all in God's hands. He would that you should live each day upon Him as a little child—simple in your faith, unshaken in your confidence, clinging in your love. Let each morning's petition be—ever linking it with the precious name of Jesus—"My Father! give me this day my daily bread." Then shall the promise be fulfilled, and its fulfillment shall be the immediate answer to your prayer—"As your days so shall your strength be."

And let us, on this birthday of the year, renew each his personal and solemn dedication to God; supplicating forgiveness for the past, and invoking grace to help in every time of need for the future. The atoning blood of Jesus! How solemn and how precious is it at this moment! Bathed in it afresh, we will more supremely, unreservedly, and submissively yield ourselves unto God, as those that are alive from the dead. We will travel to the open fountain, wash, and be clean. Christ loves us to come as we are. We may approach all clothed with shame for the past, but not a reproving look will dart from His eye, nor an upbraiding word will breathe from his lips. Nor shall abused and ill-requited mercies past seal our lips from supplicating blessings for the future. "Open your month wide, and I will fill it," is still the Divine promise and He who gave it has added a supplementary one, if possible, yet ampler and richer, "Call unto me, and I will answer you, and show you great and mighty things which you know not."

JANUARY 2

Yet the Lord will command his loving-kindness in the daytime, and in the night his song shall be with me, and my prayer unto the God of my life. Psalm 42:8

SONGS in the night!—who can create them? Midnight harmony!—who can inspire it? God can, and God does. The "God of all consolation," the "God who comforts those who are cast down;" the "God of hope," who causes the "bright and morning star" to rise upon the dreary landscape; the "God of peace, who Himself gives peace, always and by all means;" even He, our Maker and Redeemer, gives songs in the night. Music, at all times sweet, is the sweetest amid the sublimity of night. When in the solemn stillness that reigns—not a breath rustling the leaves, and Echo herself slumbers—when in the darkness that enshrouds, the thoughts that agitate, the gloomy phantoms that flit before the fancy like shadows dancing upon the wall, there breaks upon the wakeful ear the soft notes of skillfully touched instruments, blending with the melting tones of well—tuned voices, it is as though angels had come down to serenade and soothe the sad and jaded sons of earth. But there are songs richer, and there is music sweeter still than theirs—the songs which God gives, and the music which Jesus inspires, in the long dark night of the Christian's pilgrimage. A saint of God is, then, a happy man. He is often most so when others deem him most miserable. When they, gazing with pity upon his adversities and his burdens, and silently marking the conflict of thought and feeling passing within—compared with which external trial is but as the bubble floating upon the surface—deem him a fit object of their commiseration and sympathy, even then there is a hidden spring of joy, an under-current of peace, lying in the depths of the soul, which renders him, chastened and afflicted though he is, a happy and an enviable man. "Blessed are those who mourn now, for they shall be comforted."

JANUARY 3

Jesus Christ, and him crucified. 1 Co2. 2:2.

FAITH, picturing to its view the cross, the Holy Spirit engraving it on the heart in spiritual regeneration, the whole soul receiving Him whom it lifts up, as its "wisdom, and righteousness, and sanctification, and redemption," gently and effectually transforms the spirit, that was chafed and restless, into the "meekness and gentleness of Christ." Oh what calmness steals over his ruffled soul! oh what peace flows into his troubled heart! oh what sunshine bathes in its bright beams his dark spirit, who, from the scenes of his conflict and his sorrow, flees beneath the shadow and the shelter of the cross! The storm ceases—the deluge of his grief subsides—the Spirit, dove-like, brings the message of hope and love—the soul, tempest-tossed, rests on the green mount, and one unbounded spring clothes and encircles the landscape with its verdure and its beauty. Child, chastened by the Father's love, look to the cross of your crucified Savior; and as you fix upon it your believing, ardent, adoring gaze, exclaim—

"Wearily for me you sought,
On the cross my soul you bought;
Lose not all for which you wrought."

What is your sorrow compared with Christ's? What is your grief gauged by your Lord's? Your Master has passed before you, flinging the curse and the sin from your path, paving it with promises, carpeting it with love, and fencing it around with the hedge of His divine perfections. Press onward, then, resisting your foe resolutely, bearing your cross patiently, drinking your cup submissively, and learning, while sitting at the Savior's feet, or leaning upon His bosom, to be like Him, "meek and lowly in heart."

JANUARY 4

Let my prayer be set forth before you as incense; and the lifting up of my hands as the evening sacrifice. Psalm 141:2

THIS passage presents the Christian to our view in his holiest and most solemn posture—drawing near to God, and presenting before the altar of His grace the incense of prayer. The typical reference to this is strikingly beautiful. "You shall make an altar to burn incense upon..... And Aaron shall burn thereon sweet incense every morning; when he dresses the lamps, he shall burn incense upon it. And when Aaron lights the lamps at even, he shall burn incense upon it, a perpetual incense before the Lord throughout your generations." That this incense was typical of prayer would appear from Luke 1:10, "And the whole multitude of the people were praying without at the time of incense." And David, though dwelling in the more shadowy age of the church, thus correctly and beautifully interprets this type: "Let my prayer be set before you as incense."

But from where arises the incense of prayer ascending to the throne of the Eternal? Oh, it is from the heart. The believer's renewed, sanctified heart is the censer from where the fragrant cloud ascends. True prayer is the incense of a heart broken for sin, humbled for its iniquity, mourning over its plague, and touched, and healed, and comforted with the atoning blood of God's great sacrifice. This is the true censer; this it is at which God looks. "For the Lord sees not as man sees; for man looks on the outward appearance, but the Lord looks on the heart." Precious censer! molded, fashioned, beautified by God. There exists not upon earth a more vile and unlovely thing, in the self-searching view of the true believer, than his own heart. And yet —oh wondrous grace!—God, by his renewing Spirit, has made of that heart a beautiful, costly, and precious censer, the cloud of whose incense ascends and fills all heaven with its fragrance. With all its indwelling evil and self-loathing, God sees its struggles, watches its conflict, and marks its sincerity. Not a feeling thrills it, not an emotion agitates it, not a sorrow shades it, not a sin wounds it, not a thought passes through it, of which He is not cognizant. Believer! Jesus loves that heart of your. He purchased it with his own heart's blood, agonies, and tears—and He loves it. It is His temple, His home, His censer, and never can it approach Him in prayer, but He is prepared to accept both the censer and incense with a complacency and delight which finds its best expression in the language of His own word, "I will accept you with your sweet savor." And what shall we say of the fragrance of this incense? Oh, how much have we yet to learn of the intrinsic sweetness of real prayer! We can but imperfectly conceive the fragrance there must be to God in the breathing of the Divine Spirit in the heart of a poor sinner. It is perhaps but a groan—a sigh—a tear—a look—but it is the utterance of the heart; and God can hear the voice of our weeping, and interpret the language of our desires, when the lips utter not a word; so fragrant to Him is the incense of prayer. "Lord, all my desire is before You, and my groaning is not hid from You."

JANUARY 5

And another angel came and stood at the altar, having a golden censer; and there was given unto him much incense, that he should offer it with the prayers of all saints upon the golden altar which was before the throne. And the smoke of the incense, which came with the prayers of the saints, ascended up before God out of the angel's hand. Rev. 8:3-4

THIS angel is none other than the Angel of the Covenant, Jesus, our great High Priest, who stands before the golden altar in heaven, presenting the sweet incense of His divine merits and sacrificial death; the cloud of which ascends before God "with the prayers of the saints." Oh, it is the merit of our Immanuel, "who gave Himself for us, an offering and a sacrifice to God for a sweet—smelling savor," that imparts virtue, prevalence, and acceptableness to the incense of prayer ascending from the heart of the child of God. Each petition, each desire, each groan, each sigh, each glance, comes up before God with the "smoke of the incense" which ascends from the cross of Jesus, and from the "golden altar which is before the throne." All the imperfection and impurity which mingles with our devotions here is separated from each petition by the atonement of our Mediator, who presents that as sweet incense to God. See your Great High Priest before the throne! See Him waving the golden censer to and fro! See how the cloud of incense rises and envelopes the throne! See how heaven is filled with its fragrance and its glory! Believer in Jesus, upon the heart of that officiating High Priest your name is written; in the smoke of the incense which has gone up from that waving censer your prayers are presented. Jesus' blood cleanses them, Immanuel's merit perfumes them, and our glorious High Priest thus presents both our person and our sacrifice to his Father and our Father, to His God and our God. Oh wonderful encouragement to prayer! Who, with such an assurance that his weak, broken, and defiled, but sincere petitions shall find acceptance with God, would not breathe them at the throne of grace. Go, in the name of Jesus; go, casting yourself upon the merit which fills heaven with its fragrance; go, and pour out your grief, unveil your sorrow, confess your sin, sue out your pardon, make known your needs, with your eye of faith upon the Angel who stands at the "golden altar which is before the throne," and the incense which breathes from your oppressed and stricken heart will ascend up before God out of the Angel's hand, as a cloud, rich, fragrant, and accepted.

JANUARY 6

Lo, he goes by me, and I see him not: he passes on also, but I perceive him not. Behold, he takes away, who can hinder him? who will say unto him, What do you? Job 9:11-12

AND is this the way of the Lord with you, my beloved? Are you bewildered at the mazes through which you are threading your steps; at the involved circumstances of your present history? Deem yourself not alone in this. No mystery has lighted upon your path but what is common to the one family of God: "This honor have all his saints." The Shepherd is leading you, as all the flock are led, with a skillful hand, and in a right way. It is yours to stand if He bids you, or to follow if He leads. "He gives no account of any of His matters," assuming that His children have such confidence in His wisdom, and love, and uprightness, as in all the wonder-working of His dealings with them, to "be still and know that He is God." Throw back a glance upon the past, and see how little you have ever understood of all the way God has led you. What a mystery—perhaps now better explained—has enveloped His whole proceedings! When Joseph, for example, was torn from the homestead of his father, sold, and borne a slave into Egypt, not a syllable of that eventful page of his history could he spell. And yet God's way with this His servant was perfect. And could Joseph have seen at the moment that he descended into the pit, where he was cast by his envious brethren, all the future of his history as vividly and as palpably as be beheld it in after years, while there would have been the conviction that all was well, we doubt not that faith would have lost much of its vigor, and God much of His glory. And so with good old Jacob. The famine, the parting with Benjamin, the menacing conduct of Pharaoh's prime minister, wrung the mournful expression from his lips, "All these things are against me." All was veiled in deep and mournful mystery. Thus was it with Job, to whom God spoke from the whirlwind that swept every vestige of affluence and domestic comfort from his dwelling. And thus, too, with Naomi, when she exclaimed, "Call me not Naomi, call me Mara: for the Almighty has dealt very bitterly with me. I went out full, and the Lord has brought me home again empty." That it is to the honor of God to conceal, should in our view justify all His painful and humiliating procedure with us. "It is the glory of God to conceal a thing," as it will be for His endless glory, by and by, fully to reveal it all. But there is one thing, Christian sufferer, which He cannot conceal. He cannot conceal the love that forms the spring and foundation of all His conduct with His saints. Do what He will, conceal as He may, be His chariot the thick clouds, and His way in the deep sea, still His love betrays itself, disguised though it may be in dark and impenetrable providence. There are under-tones, gentle and tender, in the roughest accents of our Joseph's voice. And he who has an ear ever hearkening to the Lord shall often exclaim, "Speak, Lord, how and when and where you may—it is the voice of my Beloved!"

JANUARY 7

The Lord is near unto those who are of a broken heart; and saves such as be of a contrite spirit. Psalm 34:18

A broken and a contrite heart, O God, you will not despise. Psalm 51:17

THERE are those by whom a broken heart is despised. Satan despises it—though he trembles at it. The world despises it—though it stands in awe of it. The Pharisee despises it—though he attempts its counterfeit. But there is one who despises it not. "you will not despise it," exclaims the penitent child, with his eye upon the loving heart of his God and Father. But why does God not only not despise it, but delights in and accepts it? Because He sees in it a holy and a fragrant sacrifice. It is a sacrifice, because it is offered to God, and not to man. It is an oblation laid upon His altar. Moses never presented such an oblation—Aaron never offered such a sacrifice in all the gifts which he offered, in all the victims which he slew. And while some have cast their rich and splendid gifts into the treasury, or have laid them ostentatiously upon the altar of Christian benevolence, God has stood by the spot to which some poor penitent has brought his broken heart for sin, the incense of which has gone up before Him as a most precious and fragrant sacrifice. Upon that oblation, upon that gift, His eye has been fixed, as if one object, and one only, had arrested and absorbed His gaze—it was a poor broken heart that lay bleeding and quivering upon His altar. It is a sacrifice, too, offered upon the basis of the atoning sacrifice of His dear Son—the only sacrifice that satisfies Divine justice—and this makes it precious to God. So infinitely glorious is the atonement of Jesus, so divine, so complete, and so honoring to every claim of His moral government, that He accepts each sacrifice of prayer, of praise, of penitence, and of personal consecration, laid in faith by the side and upon that one infinite sacrifice for sin. He recognizes in it, too, the work of His own Spirit. When the Spirit of God moved upon the face of unformed nature, and a new world sprang into life, light, and beauty, He pronounced it very good. But what must be His estimate of that new creation which His Spirit has wrought in the soul, whose moral chaos He has reduced to life, light, and order!

But in what way does God evince His satisfaction with, and His delight in, the broken and contrite heart? We answer—first by the manifestation of His power in healing it. "He heals the broken in heart, and binds up their wounds." "The Spirit of the Lord God is upon me; because the Lord has anointed me to preach good tidings to the meek: He has sent me to bind up the brokenhearted." Never did a physician more delight to display his skill, or exercise the benevolent feelings of his nature in the alleviation of suffering, than does Jesus in His work of binding up and healing the heart broken for sin, by speaking a sense of pardon, and applying to it the balsam of His own most precious blood. But our Lord not only heals the contrite heart, but, as if heaven had not sufficient attraction as His dwelling-place, He comes down to earth, and makes that heart His abode. "Thus says the high and lofty One, that inhabits Eternity, whose name is Holy, I dwell in the high and holy place, with him also who is of a contrite and humble spirit, to revive the spirit of the humble, and to revive the heart of the contrite ones." What, dear, humble penitent, could give you such a view of the interest which Christ takes in your case—the delight with which He contemplates your contrition, and the welcome and the blessing which He is prepared to bestow upon you, on your casting yourself down at His feet, as this fact, that He waits to make that sorrow-stricken heart of yours His chief and loved abode—reviving it, healing it, and enshrining Himself forever within its renewed and sanctified affections.

JANUARY 8

What must I do to be saved? And they said, Believe on the Lord Jesus Christ, and you shall be saved, and your house. Acts 16:30-31

THE faith of the child of God stands in the righteousness of the God-man Mediator—"the righteousness which is of God by faith." This faith has not been inappropriately termed the "poor man's grace." It is so because it comes to Jesus empty-handed. It travels to Christ in poverty and rags, in want and in woe. It is the grace of him who, feeling the working of an inward plague, and repudiating all idea of human merit, appears at the door of mercy, "poor in spirit," humbly knocking, and earnestly suing, and freely receiving, as a pensioner, the blessing of sovereign grace. Oh, how glorious to the eye of such an one appears the righteousness of the Incarnate God! How precious to his heart the atoning blood of Jesus! How suitable and attractive to his view the foundation to which he is invited, and upon which, with the confidence of faith, he is encouraged to build his assured hope of future glory! Who would not desire, and who would not seek, establishment in a faith like this? a faith that can read its pardon in the blood—its justification in the righteousness—its sanctification in the grace, and its security in the resurrection, life, and intercession of the great High Priest enthroned in heaven. Oh, let a man's faith cling to this, and he is a saved man! And to be saved! Oh, how will eternity prolong the swelling chant!—"Saved, for ever saved! A sinner the very chief—a saint the very least—a child the most unworthy! yet here, through grace, I am saved, forever saved!" Before the glory and importance of this salvation, oh, how do fade and disappear the grandeur and the significance of all other objects! "How shall we escape, if we neglect so great salvation?" "This is the record, that God has given to us eternal life, and this life is in His Son. He that has the Son has life, and he that has not the Son has not life." But the faith of the true believer is built upon Christ. It has Christ for its basis, Christ for its object, Christ for its beginning and its end. It is built upon the Godhead of His person, the obedience of His life, and the vicariousness of His death. He who builds his faith short of Deity, builds upon the treacherous sand which the first heaving billow sweeps from beneath his feet. We want, in the great matter of our salvation, Deity to become incarnate—Deity to obey—Deity to atone—Deity to justify—Deity to uphold—Deity to comfort—and Deity to bring us at last to the glorious abode of Deity, to dwell amid its splendors forever.

JANUARY 9

Jesus only. Matthew 17:8

Is not this the motto of every true believer? Whom does his heart in its best moments, and holiest affections, and intentest yearnings, supremely desire? The answer is, "Jesus only." Having by His Spirit enthroned Himself there, having won the affections by the power of His love and the attractions of His beauty, the breathing of the soul now is, "Whom have I in heaven but You, and who is there on earth that I desire beside You?" Blessed is that soul, the utterances of whose heart are the sincere and fervent expressions of a love of which Christ is the one and supreme object! Oh, to love Him more! Worthy, most worthy is He of our first and best affections. Angels love Him ardently and supremely; how much more should we, who owe to Him a deeper debt of love than they! Let the love of Christ, then, constrain us to love Him, in return, with an affection which shall evince, by the singleness of its object and the unreserved surrender of its obedience, that He who reigns the sovereign Lord of our affections is—"Jesus only."

In all the spiritual circumstances of the believer's history, it is still "Jesus only." In the corrodings of guilt upon the conscience, in the cloud which veils the reconciled countenance of God from the soul, where are we to look, save to "Jesus only"? In the mournful consciousness of our unfaithfulness to God, of our aggravated backslidings, repeated departures, the allowed foils and defeats by which our enemies exult, and the saints hang their heads in sorrow, to whom are we to turn, but to "Jesus only"? In the cares, anxieties, and perplexities which gather around our path, in the consequent castings-down of our soul, and in the disquietude of our spirit within us, to whom shall we turn, but to "Jesus only"? In those deep and mysterious exercises of soul-travail, which not always the saints of God can fully understand—when we see a hand they cannot see, and when we hear a voice then cannot hear; when we seem to tread a lone path, or traverse a sea where no fellow-voyager ever heaves in sight; the days of soul-exercise wearisome, and its nights long and dark—oh! to whom shall we then turn, save to "Jesus only"? Who can enter into all this, and sympathize with all this, but Jesus? To Him alone, then, let us repair, with every sin, and with every burden, and with every temptation, and with every sorrow, and with every mental and spiritual exercise, thankful to be shut up exclusively to "Jesus only."

And when the time draws near that we must depart out of this world, and go unto the Father, one object will fix the eye, from which all others are then receding—it is "Jesus only." Ah! to die, actually to die, must be a crisis of our being quite different from reading of death in a book, or from hearing of it in the pulpit, or from talking of it by the way-side. It is a solemn, an appalling thing to die! But to the believer in Jesus, how pleasant and how glorious! "Absent from the body," he is "present with the Lord." Jesus is with him then. The blood of Jesus is there, cleansing him from all his guilt; the arms of Jesus are there, supporting him in all his weakness; the Spirit of Jesus is there, comforting him in all his fears; and now is he learning, for the last time on earth, that as for all the sins, all the perils, all the trials, and all the sorrows of life, so now as that life is ebbing fast away, and death is chilling, and eternity is nearing, "Jesus only" is all—sufficient for his soul. Believer! look to "Jesus only"—lean upon Him, cleave to Him, labor for Him, suffer for Him, and, if need be, die for Him; thus loving and trusting, living and dying for, "JESUS ONLY."

JANUARY 10

This is my beloved, and this is my friend. Song 5:16

THE object of the believer's trust is Jesus, his Beloved. He is spoken of by the apostle as "THE Beloved," as though he would say, "There is but one beloved of God, of angels, of saints—it is Jesus." He is the beloved One of the Father. "Behold my servant, whom I uphold; mine elect, in whom my soul delights." "This is my beloved Son, in whom I am well pleased." But Jesus is also the church's beloved, the beloved of each member of that church. His person is beloved, uniting all the glories of the Godhead with all the perfections of the manhood. His work is beloved, saving His people from the entire guilt, and condemnation, and dominion of their sins. His commandments are beloved, because they are the dictates of His love to us, and the tests of our love to Him. O yes! you have but one beloved of your heart, dear believer. He is "white and ruddy, the chief among ten thousand;" He is all the universe to you; heaven would be no heaven without Him; and with His presence here, earth seems often like the opening portal of heaven. He loved you, He labored for you, He died for you, He rose for you, He lives and intercedes for you in glory; and all that is lovely in Him, and all that is grateful in you, constrain you to exclaim—"I am my Beloved's, and any Beloved is mine."

And where would you lean in sorrow but upon the bosom of your Beloved? Christ's heart is a human heart, a sinless heart, a tender heart; a heart once the home of sorrow, once stricken with grief; once an aching, bleeding, mournful heart. Thus disciplined and trained, Jesus knows how to pity and to support those who are sorrowful and solitary. He loves to chase grief from the spirit, to bind up the broken heart, to staunch the bleeding wound, and to dry the weeping eye, to "comfort all that mourn." It is His delight to visit you in the dark night-season of your sorrow, and to come to you walking upon the tempestuous billows of your grief, breathing music and diffusing calmness over your scene of sadness and gloom. When other bosoms are closed to your sorrow, or are removed beyond your reach, or their deep throbbings of love are stilled in death—when the fiery darts of Satan fly thick around you, and the world frowns, and the saints are cold, and your path is sad and desolate—then lean upon the love, lean upon the grace, lean upon the faithfulness, lean upon the tender sympathy of Jesus. That bosom will always unveil to welcome you. It will ever be an asylum to receive you, and a home to shelter you. Never will its love cool, nor its tenderness lessen, nor its sympathy be exhausted, nor its pulse of affection cease to beat. You may have grieved it a thousand times over, you may have pierced it through and through, again and again—yet returning to its deathless love, penitent and lowly, sorrowful and humble, you may lay within it your weeping, aching, languid head, depositing every burden, reposing every sorrow, and breathing every sigh upon the heart of Jesus. Lord! to whom shall I go? yes, to whom would I go, but unto You?

We lean truly upon Jesus that we may advance in all holiness, that the graces of the Spirit may he quickened and stimulated, that we may cultivate more heavenly-mindedness, and be constantly coming up from the world, following him without the camp, bearing His reproach. Let our path, then, be upward; let us gather around us the trailing garment, casting away whatever impedes our progress; and leaning upon our Beloved and our Friend, hasten from all below, until we find ourselves actually reposing in the bosom upon which, in faith and love, in weakness and sorrow, we had rested amid the trials and perils of the ascent. There is ever this great encouragement, this light upon the way, that it is a heaven-pointing, a heaven-conducting, a Heaven-terminating path; and before long the weary pilgrim will reach its sunlit summit; not to lie down and die there, as Moses did upon the top of Pisgah, but to commence a life of perfect purity and of eternal bliss.

JANUARY 11

For none of us lives to himself, and no man dies to himself. For whether we live, we live unto the Lord; and whether we die, we die unto the Lord: whether we live therefore, or die, we are the Lord's. Romans 14:7-8

THE Lord Jesus can only erect and carry forward His kingdom in the soul upon the ruins of self: and as this kingdom of grace is perpetual in its growth, so the demolition of self is a work of gradual advancement. As the inner life grows, Christ grows more lovely to the eye, more precious to the heart. His blood is more valued, His righteousness is more relied on, His grace is more lived upon, His cross is more gloried in, His yoke is more cheerfully borne, His commands are more implicitly obeyed. In all things Christ is advanced, and the soul by all means advances in its knowledge of, and in its resemblance to, Christ. Reader, is Christ advanced by you? Is His kingdom widened, is His truth disseminated, is his fame spread, is His person exalted, is His honor vindicated, is His glory promoted, by the life which you are living? Oh, name not the name of Christ, if it do not be to perfume the air with its fragrance, and to fill the earth with its renown.

This "living unto the Lord" is a life of self-denial; but have the self-denying, the self-renouncing, no reward? Oh yes! their reward is great. They are such as the King delights to honor. When John the Baptist declared, "He must increase, but I must decrease," and on another occasion, "whose shoe-latchet I am not worthy to unloose," Christ pronounced him "the greatest born of women." When the centurion sent to say, "Lord, I am not worthy that you should come under my roof," our Lord places this crown upon his faith, "I tell you, I have not found so great faith, no, not in Israel." When the publican exclaimed, "God be merciful to me a sinner," he descended from the temple "justified rather" than the self-vaunting Pharisee. Yes, "when men are cast down, then there is lifting up." And what tongue can describe the inward peace, satisfaction, and contentment of that soul in whom this self-denying life of Christ dwells! Such a one has a continual feast. He may be deeply tried, sorely tempted, heavily afflicted, severely chastened, but his meek and submissive spirit exclaims, "It is the Lord, let Him do as seems good in His sight." Another characteristic of this life is—it is a conflicting life. It always wears the harness, and is ever clothed with the armor. Opposed by indwelling sin, assailed by Satan, and impeded by the world, every step in advance is only secured by a battle fought, and a victory achieved. It is also a holy life: springing from the indwelling of the Holy Spirit, it must necessarily be so. All its actings are holy, all its breathings are holy, all its fruits are holy, and without holiness no man has this life, or can be an in heritor of that life to come, of which this is the seedling and the germ, the foretaste and the pledge. Need we add, that happiness, progression, and deathlessness are equally its characteristics? Happiness is but a phantom and a name, where Christ dwells not in the heart. Progression is but an advance towards eternal woe, where the love of God is not in the soul. And death is an eternal, lingering despair, where the Spirit of life has not quickened the inner man, creating all things new.

Christian reader, that was a blissful day that witnessed your resurrection from a grave of sin to walk in newness of life! Happy hour when you left your soul's shroud in the tomb, exchanging it for the robe of a glorious deathlessness—when your enmity was conquered, and you were led in willing and joyous captivity, amid the triumphs of your Lord, to the altar where He bled—self-consecrated to His service! Ever keep in mind your deep indebtedness to sovereign grace, your solemn obligation to Divine love, and the touching motives that urge you to "walk worthy of the vocation with which you are called." And welcome all the dealings of God, whatever the character of those dealings may be, designed as they are but to animate, to nourish, and to carry forward this precious life in your soul.

JANUARY 12

I give myself unto prayer. Psalm 119:4

OH, give yourself to prayer! Say not that your censer has nothing to offer; that it contains no sweet spices, no fire, no incense. Repair with it, all empty and cold as it is, to the great High Priest, and as you gaze in faith upon Him who is the Altar, the slain Lamb, and the Priest, thus musing upon this wondrous spectacle of Jesus' sacrifice for you, His Spirit will cast the sweet spices of grace, and the glowing embers of love, into your dull, cold hearts, and there will come forth a cloud of precious incense, which shall ascend with the "much incense" of the Savior's merits, an "offering and a sacrifice to God of a sweet-smelling savor." Nor forget that there is evening as well as morning incense. "When Aaron lights the lamps at even, he shall burn incense." And thus, when the day-season of your prosperity and joy is passed, and the evening of adversity, sorrow, and loneliness draws its somber curtains around you, then take your censer and wave it before the Lord. Ah! methinks at that hour of solemn stillness and of mournful solitude—that hour when all human support and sympathy fails—that then the sweetest incense of prayer ascends before God. Yes, there is no prayer so true, so powerful, so fragrant, as that which sorrow presses from the heart. Oh, betake yourself, suffering believer, to prayer. Bring forth your censer, sorrowful priest of the Lord! Replenish it at the altar of Calvary, and then wave it with a strong hand before God, until your person, your sorrows, and your guilt are all enveloped and lost in the cloud of sweet incense as it rises before the throne, and blends with the ascending cloud of the Redeemer's precious intercession. Prayer will soothe you—prayer will calm you—prayer will unburden your heart—prayer will remove or mitigate your pain—prayer will heal your sickness, or make your sickness pleasant to bear—prayer will expel the tempter—prayer will bring Jesus sensibly near to your soul—prayer will lift your heart to heaven, and will bring heaven down into your heart. Mourning Christian, give but yourself unto prayer in the hour of your sorrow and loneliness, and your breathings, sent up to heaven in tremulous accents, shall return into your own disconsolate and desolate heart, all rich and redolent of heaven's sweet consolations. The holy breathings which ascend from a believer's heart gather and accumulate in the upper skies, and when most he needs the refreshing, they descend again in covenant blessings upon his soul. That feeble desire, that faint breathing of the soul after God, and Jesus, and holiness, and heaven, shall never perish. It was, perhaps, so weak and tremulous, so mixed with grief and sorrow, so burdened with complaint and sin, that you could scarcely discern it to be real prayer, and yet, ascending from a heart inhabited by God's Holy Spirit, and touched by God's love, it rose like the incense-cloud before the throne of the Eternal, and blended with the fragrance of heaven.

JANUARY 13

For there is one God, and one mediator between God and men, the man Christ Jesus. 1 Tim. 2:5

THE salvation of man is an embodiment of God Himself. The essence, the heart, the mind, the attributes, the character, the government of God, are all embarked, embodied, and exhibited in the salvation of man. It is a work so surpassingly stupendous, glorious, and divine, we can account for its vast and unique character, and its transcendent results, upon no other principle than its essential demonstration of Deity—"God manifest in the flesh." To mix, then, anything extraneous with this great and finished work, to add to it anything of human device, would seem a crime of deepest dye—a sin, the pardon of which might well extend beyond the provision of its mercy. God has, at every point, with a jealous regard for His own glory, exhibited and protected this great truth. Over the cross beneath which as a sinner I stand—inscribed upon the portal of the refuge into which as a sinner I flee—above the fountain within which as a sinner I bathe—upon every object on which as a sinner I believingly gaze, God has written one sentence—solemn, pregnant, and emphatic—"Jesus only!"

Jesus alone could stoop to our low estate. He only could stand between justice and the criminal—the Day's-man between God and us. He only had divinity enough, and merit enough, and holiness enough, and strength enough, and love enough to undertake and perfect our redemption. None other could embark in the mighty enterprise of saving lost man but He. To no other hand but His did the Father from eternity commit His church—His peculiar treasure. To Jesus only could be entrusted the recovery and the keeping of this cabinet of precious jewels—jewels lost and scattered, and hidden in the fall, yet predestinated to a rescue and a glory great and endless as God's own being. Jesus only could bear our sin, and sustain our curse, endure our penalty, cancel our debt, and reconcile us unto God. In His bosom only could the elements of our hell find a flame of love sufficient to extinguish them; and by His merit only could the glories of our heaven stand before our eye palpable and revealed. Jesus must wholly save, or the sinner must forever perish. Listen to the language of Peter, uttered when "filled with the Holy Spirit," and addressed with burning zeal to the Christ-rejecting Sanhedrin: "This is the stone which was set at nothing of you builders, which is become the head of the corner. Neither is there salvation in any other: for there is none other name under heaven given among men whereby we must be saved." Thus, in the great and momentous matter of our salvation, Jesus must be all.

JANUARY 14

O Israel, you shall not be forgotten of me. I have blotted out, as a thick cloud, your transgressions, and, as a cloud, your sins: return unto me; for I have redeemed you. Isaiah 44:21-22

I KNOW not a truth more calculated to light up the gloom of a lone chamber, to lift up the drooping spirit of a heart-sick child of God, than the announcement that God, for Christ's sake, has pardoned all his transgressions and his sins, and stands to him in the relation of a reconciled Father. What has all the restoring conduct of our Lord been towards us, but just this turning to us, when we had turned from Him? We have wandered, He has gone after us; we have departed, He has pursued us; we have stumbled, He has upheld us; we have fallen, He has raised us up again; we have turned from Him, He has turned to us. Oh! the wonderful love and patience of Christ! And what is still His language? "Return unto me; for I have redeemed you." And what should be the response of our hearts? "Behold, we come unto you; for you are the Lord our God." Then "let us search and try our ways, and turn again unto the Lord." What! after all my backslidings and recoveries, my departures and returns, may I turn again to the Lord? Yes! with confidence we say it, "turn AGAIN unto the Lord." That look of love beaming from the eye of Jesus invites you, woos you, to return AGAIN yet this once more to the shelter to His pierced side, to the home of His wounded heart. Press to your heart the consolation and joy of this truth—the glance of Jesus falling upon His accepted child ever speaks of pardoned sin. Chastened, sorrowful, and secluded you may be, yet your sins are forgiven you for His name's sake. Oh! that the Spirit, the Comforter, may give you this song to sing—"Bless the Lord, O my soul! and do not forget all his benefits; who forgives all your iniquities, who heals all your diseases, who redeems your life from destruction, and crowns you with loving-kindness and tender mercies."

JANUARY 15

I am the resurrection, and the life: he that believes in me, though he were dead, yet shall he live. John 11:25

EVERY truly gracious man is a living soul. He is in the possession of an inner, spiritual life. The first important characteristic of this spiritual life is its engrafting upon a state of death. The words of the apostle will explain our meaning: "For I through the law am dead to the law, that I might live unto God." "I am crucified with Christ; nevertheless I live." The simple meaning of these declarations is—the living soul is dead to the law of God as an instrument of life, and to its works as a ground of salvation. It is dead, too, to the curse and tyranny of the law, and consequently to its power of condemning. To all this the soul made alive by Christ is dead with Christ. Thus is it most clear that a man, dead already though he originally is in trespasses and in sins, must morally die before he can spiritually live. The crucifixion with Christ must precede the living with Christ. He must die to all schemes and hopes of salvation in or by himself, before he can fully receive into his heart Christ as the life of his soul. This spiritual mystery the natural man cannot understand or receive: he only can who is "born of the Spirit." Has the law of God been brought into your conscience with that enlightening, convincing, and condemning power, as first to startle you from your spiritual slumber, and then to sever you from all hope or expectation of salvation in yourself? If so, then will you know of a truth what it is first to die before you live. Dying to the law, dying to self, you will receive Him into your heart, who so blessedly declared, "I am come that you might have life, and that you might have it more abundantly."

The Lord Jesus is ESSENTIAL LIFE. Standing by the grave that entombs the soul dead in sin, ESSENTIAL LIFE exclaims, "I am the resurrection and the life—come forth!" and in a moment the soul is quickened, and rises to newness of life. What but Deity could accomplish this? Take off your shoes from your feet; for you stands upon holy ground! Jesus is the TRUE GOD, and ESSENTIAL LIFE. The smallest seed, the meanest insect, the lowest creature on earth, and the mightiest angel and the brightest saint in heaven, draw their life from Christ. What a mighty and glorious Being, then, is the Son of God, the ceaseless energy of whose essence prevents each moment everything that has life from being destroyed, and from accomplishing its own destruction! Who would not believe in, who would not love, who would not serve such a Being? Who would not crown Him Lord of all?

JANUARY 16

Examine yourselves, whether you be in the faith; prove your own selves. Know you not your own selves, how that Jesus Christ is in you, except you be reprobates? 2 Cor. 13:5

ALAS! how is this precept overlooked! How few are they who rightly and honestly examine themselves! They can examine others, and speak of others, and hear for others, and judge of others; but themselves they examine not, and judge not, and condemn not. To the neglect of this precept may be traced, as one of its most fruitful causes, the relapse of the inner life of the Christian. Deterioration, and eventually destruction and ruin, must follow in the steps of willful and protracted neglect, be the object of that neglect what it may. The vineyard must become unfruitful, and the garden must lose its beauty, and the machinery must stand still, and the enterprise must fail of success, and the health must decline, if toilsome and incessant watchfulness and care has not its eye broad awake to every symptom of feebleness, and to every sign of decay. If the merchantman examine not his accounts, and if the husbandman examine not his field, and if the nobleman examine not his estate, and if the physician examine not his patient, what sagacity is needed to foresee, as the natural and inevitable result, confusion, ruin, and death? How infinitely more true is this of the soul! The want of frequent, fearless, and thorough searching into the exact state of the heart, into the real condition of the soul, as before God, in the great matter of the inner life, reveals the grand secret of many a solemn case, of delusion, shipwreck, and apostasy. Therefore the apostle earnestly exhorts, "Examine yourselves;" do not take the state of your souls for granted, prove your own selves by the word, and rest not short of Christ dwelling in your hearts—your present life, and your hope of glory.

But how does Christ dwell in the believer? We answer—by his Spirit. Thus it is a spiritual, and not a personal or corporeal, indwelling of Christ. The Scripture testimony is most full and decisive on this point. "Know you not that your body is the temple of the Holy Spirit? If Christ be in you, the body is dead, because of sin; but the Spirit is life, because of righteousness. But if the Spirit of Him that raised up Jesus from the dead dwell in you, He that raised Christ from the dead shall also quicken your mortal bodies by His Spirit that dwells in you." And that this inhabitation of Christ by the Spirit is not the indwelling of a mere grace of the Spirit, but the Spirit Himself, is equally clear from another passage—"Hope makes not ashamed; because the love of God (here is a grace of the Spirit) is shed abroad in our hearts by the Holy Spirit which He has given us"—(here is the possession of the Spirit himself). This is the fountain of all the spiritual grace dwelling in the soul of the truly regenerate, and at times so blessedly flowing forth in refreshing and sanctifying streams. Thus, then, is it most clear, that by the indwelling of the holy Spirit, Christ has His dwelling in the hearts of all true believers.

JANUARY 17

And I will bring the blind by a way that they knew not; I will lead them in paths that they have not known: I will make darkness light before them, and crooked things straight. These things will I do unto them, and not forsake them. Isaiah 42:16

THESE words imply a concealment of much of the Lord's procedure with His people. With regard to our heavenly Father, there can be nothing mysterious, nothing inscrutable to Him. A profound and awful mystery Himself, yet to His infinite mind there can be no darkness, no mystery at all. His whole plan—if plan it may be called—is before Him. Our phraseology, when speaking of the Divine procedure, would sometimes imply the opposite of this. We talk of God's fore-knowledge, of His foresight, of His acquaintance with events yet unborn; but there is, in truth, no such thing. There are no tenses with God—no past—nor present—nor future. The idea of God's eternity, if perfectly grasped, would annihilate in our minds all such humanizing of the Divine Being. He is one ETERNAL NOW. All events, to the remotest period of time, were as vivid and as present to the Divine mind from eternity, as when at the moment they assumed a real existence and a palpable form.

But all the mystery is with us, poor finite creatures of a day. And why, even to us, is any portion of the Divine conduct thus a mystery? Not because it is in itself so, but mainly and simply because we cannot see the whole as God sees it. Could it pass before our eye, as from eternity it has before His, a perfect and a complete whole, we should then cease to wonder, to cavil, and repine. The infinite wisdom, purity, and goodness that originated and gave a character, a form, and a coloring to all that God does, would appear as luminous to our view as to His, and ceaseless adoration and praise would be the grateful tribute of our loving hearts. Let us, then, lie low before the Lord, and humble ourselves under His mysterious hand. "The meek will He guide in judgment, and the meek will He teach His way. All the paths of the Lord are mercy and truth unto such as keep His covenant and His testimonies." Thus writing the sentence of death upon our wisdom, our sagacity, and our strength, Jesus—the lowly one—seeks to keep us from the loftiness of our intellect and from the pride of our heart—prostrating us low in the dust at His feet. Holy posture! blessed place! There, Lord, would I lie; my trickling tears of penitence and of love falling upon those dear feet that have never misled, but have always gone before, leading me by a right way, the best way, to a city of rest. Wait, then, suffering believer, the coming glory—yielding yourself to the guidance of your Savior, and submitting yourself wholly to your Father's will.

JANUARY 18

For I will declare mine iniquity; I will be sorry for my sin. Psalm 38:18
The blood of Jesus Christ his Son cleanses us from all sin. 1 John 1:7

SEEK, cherish, and cultivate constantly and habitually a broken heart for sin. Do not think that it is a work which, once done, is to be done no more. Deem it not a primary stage in your spiritual journey, which, once reached, never again occurs in your celestial progress. Oh no! As in the natural life we enter the world weeping, and leave it weeping, so in the spiritual life—we begin it in tears of godly sorrow for sin, and we terminate it in tears of godly sorrow for sin—passing away to that blessed state of sinlessness, where God will wipe away all tears from our eyes. The indwelling of all evil—the polluting nature of the world along which we journey—our constant exposure to temptations of every kind—the many occasions on which we yield to those temptations, the perpetual developments of sin unseen, unknown, even unsuspected by others—the defilement which attaches itself to all that we put our hands to, even the most spiritual and holy and heavenly, the consciousness of what a holy God must every moment see in us—all, all these considerations should lead us to cherish that spirit of lowliness and contrition, self-abhorrence and self-renunciation, inward mortification and outward humility of deportment, which belong to and which truly prove the existence of the life of God in our souls.

And what, too, prompts a constant traveling to the atoning blood?—what endears the Savior who shed that blood?—what is it that makes His flesh food indeed, and His blood drink indeed?—what is it that keeps the conscience tender and clean?—what enables the believer to walk with God as a dear child? Oh, it is the sacred contrition of the lowly spirit, springing from a view of the cross of Jesus, and through the cross leading to the heart of God. Backsliding Christian! do you feel within your heart the kindlings of godly sorrow? Are you mourning over your wandering, loathing the sin that drew you from Christ, that grieved the Spirit, and wounded your own peace? Are you longing to feed again in the green pastures of the flock, and by the side of the Shepherd of the flock, assured once more that you are a true sheep, belonging to the one fold, known by, and precious to, the heart of Him who laid down His life for the sheep? Then approach the altar of Calvary, and upon it lay the sacrifice of a broken and a contrite heart, and your God will accept it. The door of your return stands open—the pierced heart of Jesus. The golden scepter that bids you approach is extended—the outstretched hand of a pacified Father. The banquet is ready, and the minstrels are tuning their harps to celebrate the return from your wanderings to your Father's heart and home, with the gladness of feasting, and with the voice of thanksgiving and of melody.

JANUARY 19

Giving all diligence, add to your faith virtue; and to virtue knowledge; And to knowledge temperance; and to temperance patience; and to patience godliness; And to godliness brotherly kindness; and to brotherly kindness charity. For if these things be in you, and abound, they make you that you shall neither be barren nor unfruitful in the knowledge of our Lord Jesus Christ. 2 Peter 1:5-8

HOW many Christian professors limit their spiritual knowledge to the first elements of truth! They seem never to pass beyond the alphabet of the gospel. But if we desire the advancement of the Divine life within us, we must know more of Jesus—we must discern more beauty in our Beloved—we must see more of the glory of our Incarnate God—we must know more of the love and grace of the Father in the gift of His dear Son—we must, in a word, grow in the knowledge of God and of Christ. Thus the soul will be established. Every step within the great sanctuary of truth will confirm the believing heart in the divinity and the vastness, the riches and the glory, of its treasures. That no such affluence of wisdom and knowledge, and truth and holiness, could flow from any other source than Deity, would be a reflection disarming every assault upon the faith of the Christian of its virulence and power. There can be no real establishment apart from growth in spiritual knowledge. Oh seek to be rooted and grounded in the faith! Do not be always a babe in knowledge, a mere dwarf in understanding, but go forward in the use of all God's ordained means of faith, until you "come in the unity of the faith, and of the knowledge of the Son of God, unto a perfect man, unto the measure of the stature of the fullness of Christ."

And overlook not your individual responsibility in this matter of establishment. The Christian is here cast upon his own endeavor. He is to rouse himself to the great task; to labor as though the achievement of that task were of a power solely his own. "Work out your oven salvation"—"It is God that works in you"—are words which at once link human accountability and individual responsibility with Divine power and accomplishment. Let every Christian professor feel that God has given him this work to do—that he is responsible for its being done and that all grace is laid up in Jesus for its performance, and the church of God would go forth in the great work of her Head, "fair as the moon, clear as the sun, and terrible as an army with banners." Christian reader, persevere! Angels whisper—persevere! Saints, bending from their thrones in glory, whisper—persevere! God bids you—persevere! The Holy Spirit earnestly speaks—"Be you steadfast, immoveable, always abounding in the work of the Lord; forasmuch as you know that your labor is not in vain in the Lord."

JANUARY 20

For in Him dwells all the fullness of the Godhead bodily. Col. 2:9.

WHAT a glorious declaration is this! How should our hearts leap for joy and our souls thrill with gladness at its very sound! All the "fullness of the Godhead bodily," all the fullness of the Church graciously, all the fullness of the sinner savingly, all the fullness of the Christian sanctifyingly—in a word, all that a poor, fallen, tried son of Adam needs, until he reaches heaven itself, where this fullness has come, is, by God's eternal love and wisdom, treasured up in the "second Adam, the Lord from heaven." God, the "Fountain of life," light, and grace, has ordained that the Lord Jesus Christ, his own beloved Son, should be the one source of supply from where all the salvation of the sinner, all the sanctity of the saint, and all the grace and truth of the Church, collectively and individually, should be derived—"of whose fullness all we have received, and grace for grace."

How precious ought Jesus to be to us, who has condescended to pour this heavenly treasure into our hearts, and to undertake its constant supply! In what way can we best prove our sense of His goodness, but by drawing largely from this fullness, and by glorifying Him in what we receive. Our resources are inexhaustible, because they are infinite. Nor can we come too frequently, nor draw too largely. Spring up, O well of grace and love, into our hearts! Oh, for more depth of indwelling grace! Oh, for more fervor of holy love! Oh, for richer supplies from the fullness of Christ! Oh, for a gracious revival in our souls! "Come down," blessed Jesus, "as rain upon the mown grass!" Breathe, O south wind of the Spirit, upon the garden of our souls, that the spices may flow out! Truly the well is deep, from where we have this living water; but faith can reach it, and in proportion to the strength of our faith, and the directness and simplicity with which it deals with Christ, will be the plenitude of our supply. "Drink, yes, drink abundantly, O beloved," is our Lord's gracious invitation to His Church.

JANUARY 21

I in them. John 17:23

OBSERVE, these are not the words of the apostle, whose ardent mind and glowing imagination might be supposed to exaggerate a truth beyond its proper limits; but they are the words of Jesus himself— of Him who is the Truth, and who therefore cannot lie. "I in them." Christ, dwelling in the soul, forms the inner life of that soul. The experience of this blessing stands connected with the lowest degree of grace, and with the feeblest faith; the lamb of the flock, the soul that has but touched the hem of the Savior's garment, prostrate as a penitent at the feet of the true Aaron, in each and in all Christ alike dwells. He has a throne in that heart, a temple in that body, a dwelling in that soul; and thus, as by a kind of second incarnation, God is manifest in the flesh, in Christ's manifestation in the believer.

You are, perhaps, a severely tried, a sorely tempted, a deeply afflicted believer. But cheer up! you have Christ living in you, and why should you yield to despondency or to fear? Christ will never vacate His throne, nor relinquish His dwelling. You have a suffering Christ, a humbled Christ, a crucified Christ, a dying Christ, a risen Christ, a living Christ, a triumphant Christ, a glorified Christ, a full Christ, dwelling in you by His Spirit. Yes; and you have, too, a human Christ, a feeling Christ, a sympathizing Christ, a tender, loving, gentle Christ, spiritually and eternally reposing in your heart. Why, then, should you fear the pressure of any want, or the assault of any foe, or the issue of any trial, since such a Christ is in you? "Fear not!" They are His own familiar and blessed words—"It is I, do not be afraid." You cannot want for any good, since you have the Fountain of all good dwelling in you. You cannot be finally overcome of any spiritual evil, since you have the Conqueror of sin, and Satan, and the world enthroned upon your affections. Your life—the divine and spiritual life—can never die, since Christ, ESSENTIAL LIFE, lives and abides in you. Like Him, and for Him, you may be opposed; but like Him, and by him, you shall triumph. The persecution which you meet, and the trials which you endure, and the difficulties with which you cope, shall but further your well-being, by bringing you into a closer communion with Jesus, and by introducing you more fully into the enviable state of the apostle—"Always bearing about in the body the dying of the Lord Jesus, that the life also of Jesus might be made manifest in our body....For which cause we faint not; but though our outward man perish, yet the inward man is renewed day by day. For our light affliction, which is but for a moment, works for us afar more exceeding and eternal weight of glory."

JANUARY 22

Now he which establishes us with you in Christ, and has anointed us, is God; Who has also sealed us, and given the earnest of the Spirit in our hearts. 2 Cor. 1:21-22

THE Holy Spirit renews, sanctifies, and inhabits the believer as a Divine person. It is not the common light of nature, nor the ordinary teaching of man, nor the moral suasion of truth, which has made him what he is—an experimental CHRISTIAN: all his real grace, his true teaching, flows from the Divine Spirit. His light is divine, his renewing is divine, his sanctification is divine. There is more real value in one ray of the Spirit's light, beaming in upon a man's soul, than in all the teaching which books can ever impart! The Divine Spirit, loosing the seals of the written Word, and unfolding to him the mysteries of the kingdom, the glories of Christ's person, the perfection of Christ's work, the fullness of Christ's grace, the revealed mind and will of God, has in it more wealth and glory than all the teaching the schools ever imparted. How precious the grace of the Holy Spirit, what tongue is sufficiently gifted to describe! How precious is his indwelling—an ever-ascending, heaven-panting, God-thirsting, Christ-desiring Spirit! How precious are all the revelations He makes of Christ! How precious are the consolations He brings, the promises He seals, the teachings He imparts, all the emotions He awakens, the breathings He inspires, and the affections He creates! How precious are those graces in the soul of which He is the Author—the faith that leads to a precious Savior, the love that rises to a gracious God, and the holy affections which flow forth to all the saints!

But through what channel does this Divine anointing come? Only through the union of the believer to Christ, the Anointed One. All the saving operations of the Spirit upon the mind are connected with Jesus. If He convinces of sin, it is to lead to the blood of Jesus; if He reveals the corruption of the heart, it is to lead to the grace of Jesus; if He teaches the soul's ignorance, it is to conduct it to the feet of Jesus: thus all His operations in the soul are associated with Jesus. Now, in conducting this holy anointing into the soul, He brings it through the channel of our union with the Anointed Head. By making us one with Christ, He makes us partakers of the anointing of Christ. And truly is the weakest, lowliest believer one with this anointed Savior. His fitness, as the Anointed of God, to impart of the plenitude of His anointing to all the members of his body, is a truth clearly and beautifully set forth. Thus is He revealed as the Anointed Head of the Church, the great High Priest of the royal priesthood: "You loves righteousness, and hate wickedness: therefore God, your God, has anointed You with the oil of gladness above your fellows." "The Spirit of the Lord God is upon me; because the Lord has anointed me to preach good tidings unto the meek." In the Acts of the Apostles a distinct reference is made to this truth: "how God anointed Jesus of Nazareth with the Holy Spirit and with power." His human soul filled with the measureless influence of the Divine Spirit, the fullness of the Godhead dwelling in Him bodily, He became the true Aaron, of whose anointing all the priests were alike to partake. One, then, with Jesus, through the channel of his union to the Head, the lowest member is anointed with this Divine anointing.

JANUARY 23

He that has the Son has life. 1 John 5:12.

A living Christ dwelling in a living soul. This implies permanency. The religion of some is a religion of the moment. Like the gourd of the prophet, it appears in a night, and it withers in a night. It is the religion of impulse and of feeling. It comes by fits and starts. It is easily assumed, and as easily laid aside. But here is the grand characteristic of a truly converted man—Christ lives in him, and lives in him never to die. He has entered his heart never to retire. He has enthroned Himself, never to abdicate. And although the fact of His permanent indwelling may not always appear with equal clearness and certainty to the mind of the believer himself, nevertheless Christ is really there by His Spirit. It is His home, His dwelling-place, His kingdom. He lives there, to maintain His government, to sway His scepter, and to enforce, by the mild constraint of His love, obedience to His laws. He lives there to guard and nourish His own work, shielding it when it is assailed, strengthening it when it is feeble, reviving it when it droops, restoring it when it decays; thus keeping, amid opposing influences, the life of God that it die not.

But perhaps it is a question of deep anxiety with you—"Would that I knew I were in reality a possessor of this spiritual life! My heart is so hard, my affections are so cold, my spirit is so sluggish, in everything that is spiritual, holy, and divine." Permit me to ask you, Can a stone feel its hardness, or a corpse its insensibility? Impossible! You affirm that you feel your hardness, and that you are sensible of your coldness. From where does this spring but from life? Could you weep, or mourn, or deplore, were the spiritual state of your soul that of absolute death? Again I say impossible. But rest not here; go to Jesus. What you really need is a fresh view of, a renewed application to, the Lord Jesus Christ. Take to Him the stone-like heart, the corpse-like soul. Tell him you want to feel more, and to weep more, and to love more, and to pray more, and to live more. Go and pour out your heart, with all its tremblings, and doubts, and fears, and needs, upon the bleeding, loving bosom of your Lord, until from that bosom life more abundant has darted its quickening energy, vibrating and thrilling through your whole soul. "I have come," says Jesus, "that they might have life, and that they might have it more abundantly." Jesus stands between you and God, prepared to present to God every sigh, and groan, and desire, and tear, and request; and to convey from God every blessing—covenant, blood-purchased blessing—which it is possible for Him to give, or needful for you to receive. Exult in the prospect of soon reaching heaven, where there are no frosts to congeal, where there is no blight to wither, and where no earthly tendencies will ever weigh down to the dust the life of God in your soul.

JANUARY 24

Let us draw near with a true heart in full assurance of faith. Heb. 10:22

THE principle of faith is altogether divine—created by no human power, commanded by no human authority, and sustained by no human resources. "Faith is the gift of God." Jesus is its author and its finisher. It is a free, unmerited, unpurchased bestowment. It is given to the poor because of their poverty, to the vile because they are unworthy, to the bankrupt because they have "nothing to pay." Such is the faith which the Bible enforces.

There can be no perfection of the Lord Jesus of more exalted glory in His eye than His faithfulness. If the truthfulness of Christ can be impeached, then no reliable confidence can be placed in anything that He is, that He does, or that He says. But because He is not only truthful, but truth, His word eternally fixed and unalterable—"righteousness the girdle of His loins, and faithfulness the girdle of His reins," veracity an essential perfection of His nature—He condescendingly appeals to our confidence, and says, "Only believe." And have we in any single instance ever had reason to doubt His word? Has He ever given us cause to distrust Him? No, never! He has often done more than He promised—never less. His word is truth. All the promises of God are yes and amen in Him. Has He promised to be a Father, a Husband, a Mother, and a Friend to those who put their trust in Him? Has He pledged to guide their steps, to supply their needs, to shield their souls, to do them good and not evil, to be with them down to old age, and even unto death? Then hear Him say, "Heaven and earth shall pass away, but my words shall not pass away."

As the Mediator and High Priest of His Church, it is one of Christ's especial prerogatives that He has to do with the prayers of His saints. Standing midway between God and the suppliant, He intercepts the petition, purifies it from all taint, divests it of all imperfections, supplies its deficiencies, and then blending it with His own merits, perfuming it with the much incense of His atoning sacrifice, He presents it to the Father endorsed with His name, and urged by His own suit. Thus the believer has an "Advocate with the Father," who ever "lives to make intercession." Oh, costly and precious privilege, that of prayer! Access to God—fellowship with the Most High—communion with the Invisible One—filial communion with our Heavenly Father—mighty privilege this, and yet, vast as it is, it is ours. Then, beloved, with the throne of grace accessible moment by moment—with the Holy Spirit disclosing each want, inditing each petition, and framing each request—with Christ at the right hand of God presenting the petition—and with a Father in heaven bowing down His ear, and hearkening but to answer, surely we may "trust and not be afraid." Why should we stand afar off? why doubt, and linger, and hesitate? "Having therefore, brethren, boldness (or liberty) to enter into the holiest by the blood of Jesus....let us draw near....in full assurance of faith."

JANUARY 25

Surely it is meet to be said unto God, I have borne chastisement, I will not offend any more: That which I see not teach you me: if I have done iniquity, I will do no more. Job 34:31-32

OH, what a detector of the secret state of our souls does the season of trial often prove! We are not aware of our impaired strength, of our weak faith, of our powerless grace—how feeble our hold on Christ is—how legal our views of the gospel are—how beclouded our minds may be—how partial our acquaintance with God is—until we are led into the path of trouble. The season of prosperity veils the real state of our souls from our view. No Christian can form an accurate estimate of his spiritual condition, who has not been brought into a state of trial. We faint in the day of adversity, because we then find—what, perhaps, was not even suspected in the day of prosperity—that our strength is small.

But seasons of trial are emphatically what the word expresses—they try the work in the souls of the righteous. The inner life derives immense advantage from them. The deeper discovery that is then made of the evil of the heart is not the least important result: "Foolishness is bound in the heart of a child; but the rod of correction shall drive it far from him." What folly still dwells in the hearts of the wise—bound up and half concealed—who can tell? Who would have suspected such developments in the life of Abraham, of David, of Solomon, of Peter? And so is it with all who yet are the possessors of that wisdom which will guide their souls to eternal glory. Folly is bound up in their hearts; but the sanctified rod of correction reveals it, and the discovery proves one of the costliest blessings in the experience of the disciplined child. Listen to the language of Moses, addressed to the children of Israel: "You shall remember all the way which the Lord your God led you these forty years in the wilderness, to humble you, and to prove you, to know what was in your heart, whether you would keep His commandments or no." And oh, what a discovery that forty years' marching and counter-marching in the wilderness was to them of the pride, and impatience, and unbelief, and ingratitude, and distrust that were bound up in their heart! And yet, though all this evil was deep-seated in their nature, they knew it not, and suspected it not, until trial brought it to the surface. Thus, beloved, is it with us. The latent evil is brought to light. God leaves us to try what is in our heart, and this may be the first step in the reviving of His gracious work in our souls. Oh, let us not, then, shrink from the probing, nor startle at its discovery, if it but lead us nearer to holiness, nearer to Christ, nearer to God, nearer to heaven!

The time of trouble is often, too, a, time of remembrance. and so becomes a time of reviving. Past backslidings—unthought of, unsuspected, and unconfessed—are recalled to memory in the season that God is dealing with us. David had forgotten his transgression, and the brethren of Joseph their sin, until trouble summoned it back to memory. Times of trial are searching times, remembering times. Then with David we exclaim, "I thought on my ways, and turned my feet unto Your testimonies: I made haste, and delayed not to keep Your commandments."

JANUARY 26

The Lord redeems the soul of his servants: and none of those who trust in him shall be desolate. Psalm 34:22.

AMID the many changes and vicissitudes of time, how precious becomes this truth! Out of God, "nothing is fixed but change." "Passing away" is inscribed upon all earth's fairest scenes. How the heart saddens as the recollections and reminiscences of other days come crowding back upon the memory! Years of our childhood, where have you fled? Friends of our youth, where are you gone? Hopes the heart once fondly cherished, joys the heart once deeply felt, how have you, like Syrian flowers, faded and died? All, all is changing but the Unchanging One. Other hearts prove cold, other friendships alter—adversity beclouds them—inconstancy chills them—distance separates them—death removes them from us forever. But there is One heart that loves us, clings to us, follows us in all times of adversity, poverty, sickness, and death, with an unchanged, unchangeable affection—it is the heart of our Father in heaven. Oh, turn you to this heart, you who have reposed in a human bosom, until you have felt the last faint pulse of love expire. You who have lost health, or fortune, or friends, or fame—be your souls' peaceful, sure asylum the Father's heart, until these calamities be overpast. And when from God we have strayed, and the Holy Spirit restores us to reflection, penitence, and prayer, and we exclaim, "I will arise!" who invites and woos us back to His still warm, unchanged, and forgiving affection? Who, but the Father?—that same Father thus touchingly, exquisitely portrayed: "And when he was a great way off his Father saw him, and had compassion, and ran, and fell on his neck, and kissed him." Oh, who is a God like unto You?

Do not forget that there is no needed, no asked blessing which God can refuse you. Never will God chide you for asking too much. His tender upbraiding is that you ask too little. "Open your mouth wide, and I will fill it." Oh, be satisfied with asking nothing less than God Himself. God only can make you happy, He only can supply the loss—fill the void—guide you safely, and keep you securely unto His eternal kingdom. God loves you! Oh embosom yourself in His love; and then, were all other love to wane and die—were it to chill in your friends—to cease its throbbings in a father's bosom—to quit its last and holiest home on earth—a mother's heart—still, assured that you had an interest in the love of God, a home in the heart of the Father, no being in the universe were happier than you. Let the grief you bear, the evil you dread, the sadness and loneliness you feel, but conduct you closer and yet closer within the loving, sheltering heart of God. No fear can agitate, no sorrow can sadden, no foe can reach you there! The moment you find yourself resting in child-like faith upon God, that moment all is peace!

JANUARY 27

But rejoice, inasmuch as you are partakers of Christ's sufferings; that, when his glory shall be revealed, you may be glad also with exceeding joy. 1 Peter 4:13

WITH the cross of Immanuel before us, and with the heaven of glory which that cross unveils, and to which it leads, can we properly contemplate our trials in any other view than as loving corrections? "He that spared not His own Son, but gave Hint up for us all," shall He send an "evil" which we refuse to interpret as a good? and shall not that good, though wearing its somber disguise, raise the soul to Him upon the outstretched and uplifted wing—as the wing of the "anointed cherub"—of adoration, thanksgiving, and praise? If, numbered among His saints—and, oh, be quite sure, beloved, of your heavenly calling—we stand before Him, objectively, the beings of His ineffable delight, and, subjectively, the recipients of his justifying righteousness. Thus loved and accepted—and we believe, and are sure, that this is the true and unchangeable condition of all His people—shall anything but a sentiment of uncomplaining gentleness—a submission not shallow but profound, not servile but filial—respond to the dealings, however severe, of our Father in heaven?

It is, beloved, in these disciplinary seasons that we become more thoroughly schooled in the knowledge, of the infinite worth, glory, and preciousness of the Savior. How much is involved in a spiritual and experimental acquaintance with the Lord Jesus! We are in the possession of all real knowledge when we truly know Christ. And we cannot know the Son, and not know also the Father. And it is utterly impossible to know the Father, as revealed in His Son, and not become inspired with a desire to love Him supremely, to serve Him devotedly, to resemble Him closely, to glorify Him faithfully here, and to enjoy Him fully hereafter. And oh, how worthy is the Savior of our most exalted conceptions—of our most implicit confidence—of our most self-denying service—of our most fervent love! When He could give us no more—and the fathomless depths of His love and the boundless resources of His grace would not be satisfied by giving us less—He gave us himself. Robed in our nature, laden with our curse, oppressed with our sorrows, wounded for our transgressions, and slain for our sins, He gave His entire self for us. And let it be remembered, that it is a continuous presentation of the hoarded and exhaustless treasures of His love. His redeeming work now finished, He is perpetually engaged in meting out to his Church the blessings of that "offering made once for all." He constantly asks our faith—woos our affection—invites our grief—and bids us repair with our daily trials to His sympathy, and with our hourly guilt to His blood. We cannot in our drafts upon Christ's fullness be too covetous, nor in our expectations of supply be too extravagant. Dwelling beneath His cross, our eye resting upon the heart of God, we will in all things desire and aim to walk uprightly, presenting our "bodies as a living sacrifice, holy and acceptable to God;" that "the trial of our faith may be found unto praise and honor and glory at the appearing of Jesus Christ."

JANUARY 28

The God of all comfort, who comforts us in all our tribulation. 2 Cor. 1:3-4

GOD'S family is a sorrowing family, "I have chosen you," He says, "in the furnace of affliction." "I will leave in the midst of you a poor and an afflicted people." The history of the Church finds its fittest emblem in the burning yet unconsumed bush which Moses saw. Man is "born to sorrows;" but the believer is "appointed thereunto." It would seem to be a condition inseparable from his high calling. If he is a "chosen vessel," it is, as we have just seen, "in the furnace of affliction." If he is an adopted child, "chastening" is the mark. If he is journeying to the heavenly kingdom, his path lies through "much tribulation." If he is a follower of Jesus, it is to "go unto Him without the camp, bearing His reproach." But, if his sufferings abound, much more so do his consolations. To be comforted by God may well reconcile us to any sorrow with which it may please our heavenly Father to invest us.

God comforts His sorrowful ones with the characteristic love of a mother. See the tenderness with which that mother alleviates the suffering and soothes the sorrow of her mourning one. So does God comfort His mourners. Oh, there is a tenderness and a delicacy of feeling in God's comforts which distances all expression. There is no harsh reproof—no unkind upbraiding—no unveiling of the circumstances of our calamity to the curious and unfeeling eye—no artless exposure of our case to an ungodly and censorious world; but with all the tender feeling of a mother, God, even our Father, comforts the sorrowful ones of His people. He comforts in all the varied and solitary griefs of their hearts. God meets our case in every sorrow. To Him, in prayer, we may uncover our entire hearts; to His confidence we may entrust our profoundest secrets;

upon His love repose our most delicate sorrows; to His ear confess our deepest departures; before His eye spread out our greatest sins. Go, then, and breathe your sorrows into God's heart, and He will comfort you. Blessed sorrow! if in the time of your bereavement, your grief, and your solitude, you are led to Jesus, making Him your Savior, your Friend, your Counselor, and your Shield. Blessed loss! if it be compensated by a knowledge of God, if you find in Him a Father now, to whom you will transfer your ardent affections—upon whom you will repose your bleeding heart. But let your heart be true with Him. Love Him, obey Him, confide in Him, serve Him, live for Him; and in all the unknown, untrodden, unveiled future of your history, a voice shall gently whisper in your ear—"As one whom his mother comforts, so will I comfort you."

JANUARY 29

I call to remembrance my song in the night. Psalm 77:6

IT is no small wisdom, tried Christian, to recall to memory the music of the past. Do not think that, like sounds of earth-born melody, that music has died away never to awake again. Ah, no! those strains which once floated from your spirit-touched lips yet live! The music of a holy heart never dies; it lingers still amid the secret chambers of the soul. Hushed it may be for a while by other and discordant sounds, but the Holy Spirit, the Christian's Divine Remembrancer, will summon back those tones again, to soothe and tranquillize and cheer, perhaps in a darker hour and in richer strains, some succeeding night of heart-grief: "I remember You upon my bed, and meditate on You in the night watches."

But this season of night is signally descriptive of some periods in the history and experience of a child of God. It reminds us of the period of soul-darkness which oftentimes overtakes the Christian pilgrim. "My servant that walks in darkness and has no light," says God. Observe, he is still God's servant, he is the "child of the light," though walking in darkness. Gloom spreads its mantle around him—a darkness that may be felt. God's way with him is in the great deep: "You are a God that hides Yourself," is his mournful prayer. The Holy Spirit is, perhaps, grieved—no visits from Jesus make glad his heart, he is brought in some small degree into the blessed Savior's experience—"My God, my God, why have You forsaken me?" But, sorrowful pilgrim, there is a bright light in this your cloud—turn your eye towards it; the darkness through which you are walking is not judicial. Oh no! You are still a "child of the day," though it may be temporary night with your spirit. It is the withdrawal but for "a little moment"—not the utter and eternal extinction—of the Sun of Righteousness from your soul. You are still a child, and God is still a Father. "In a little wrath, I hid my face from you for a moment; but with everlasting kindness will I have mercy on you, says the Lord your Redeemer." "Is Ephraim my dear son? is he a pleasant child? for since I spoke against him I do earnestly remember him still."

And what are seasons of affliction but as the night-time of the Christian. The night of adversity is often dark, long, and tempestuous. The Lord frequently throws the pall of gloom over the sunniest prospect—touching His loved child where that touch is the keenest felt. He knows the heart's idol—the temptation and the peril lying in our path. He knows better far than we the chain that rivets us to some endangering object; He comes and draws the curtain of night's sorrow around our way. He sends messenger after messenger. "Deep calls unto deep." He touches us in our family—in our property—in our reputation—in our persons. And, oh, what a night of woe now spreads its drapery of gloom around us!

But dark and often rayless for a time as are these various night-seasons of our pilgrimage, they have their harmonies. There are provided by Him who "divides the light from the darkness"—alleviations and soothings, which can even turn night into day, and bring the softest tones from the harshest discord. The strong consolations which our God has laid up for those who love Him are so divine, so rich, so varied, that to overlook the provision in the time of our sorrow seems an act of ingratitude darker even than the sorrow we deplore. It is in the heart of God to comfort you, His suffering child. Ah! my reader, there is not a single midnight of your history—never so dark as that midnight may be—for which God has not provided you a song, and in which there may not be such music as human hand never awoke, and as human lip never breathed—the music that God only can create: "In the night his song shall be with me."

JANUARY 30

Commit your way unto the Lord; trust also in him; and he shall bring it to pass. Psalm 37:5.

WHEN we consider the convolutions of life's future, how varied and undulating the path! It resembles in its windings and its changes the serpentine course of a river, as it pursues its way—now suddenly disappearing behind jutting rocks or towering headlands, now bursting into view again and rushing on, foaming and sparkling, through smiling meadows and sunny slopes—then by some sudden course lost again to view—surely the believer will feel the need of confidence in an invisible Hand to guide him through the labyrinth of his intricately tortuous way. This cloud of mystery, enshrouding all the future from our view, bids us trust. Not a step can we take by sight. We cannot even conjecture, much less decide, what the morrow will unfold in our history—what sweet sunbeam, shall illumine, or what somber cloud shall shade our path. How veiled from sight the next bend of our path! But, just as the dark, uncertain vista stands open to our view, our hearts all quaking for fear of what may transpire, Jesus meets us and says, "Only believe—only trust my love, wisely, gently, safely to guide you through the wilderness, into the good land that lies beyond."

The number, invisibility, and insidiousness of our spiritual foes—their combined power, and the surprisal of their incessant assaults—demands our trust in Jesus. Nothing is more unseen than the principalities and powers through which we have to force our way to heaven. Satan is invisible—his agents unseen—moral evil veiled—our hearts a great deep—the world masked; truly we have need to cling to, and confide in, Jesus, the Captain of our salvation, seeing that "we wrestle not against flesh and blood, but against principalities, against powers, against the rulers of the darkness of this world, against spiritual wickedness in high places," and that therefore we are to take to ourselves the whole armor of God, remembering that "this is the victory that overcomes the world, even our faith," or trust in Jesus.

The foreign source of all our supplies for the battle and the journey of life pleads for our trust in Jesus. In ourselves we have no resources. Grace is not natural to us, holiness is not innate, and our native strength is but another term for utter impotence. Where, then, are supplies? All in Jesus. "It has pleased the Father that in Him all fullness should dwell." "Who has blessed us with all spiritual blessings in heavenly places (things) in Christ." Christ is both the believer's armory and his granary. The weapons of our warfare, and the supplies of our necessities—all are in Christ. And the life we live as warriors and as pilgrims must be a life of continuous coming to, and trusting in, a full Christ, an all-sufficient Savior. If as each morning dawns, and before we gird ourselves for the conflict, the duties, and the trials of the day, we breathe from our hearts to our Heavenly Father the prayer, "Give me, my Father, this day my daily bread; I look to You for the wisdom that counsels me, for the power that keeps me, for the love that soothes me, for the grace that sanctifies me, and for the presence that cheers me, now supply my need, and do unto me as seems good unto You," we should experience the blessedness of living upon a

Father's bounty, upon the Savior's grace, and upon the Spirit's love.

JANUARY 31

And he that sent me is with me: the Father has not left me alone. John 8:29

OUR Lord's was a solitary life. He mingled indeed with man, He labored for man, He associated with man, He loved man; but He "trod the twine press alone, and of the people there was none with Him." And yet He was not all alone. Creatures, one by one, had deserted His side, and left Him homeless, friendless, solitary—but there was One, the consciousness of whose ever-clinging, ever-brightening, ever-cheering presence infinitely more than supplied the lack. "Behold, the hour comes, yes, is now come, that you shall be scattered every man to his own, and shall leave me alone; and yet I am not alone, because the Father is with me."

The disciples of Christ, like their Lord and Master, often feel themselves alone. The season of sickness, the hour of bereavement, the period of trial, is often the occasion of increased depression from the painful consciousness of the solitude and loneliness in which it is borne. The heavenly way we travel is more or less a lonely way. We have at most but few companions. It is a "little flock," and only here and there we meet a traveler, who, like ourselves, is journeying towards the Zion of God. As the way is narrow, trying, and humiliating to flesh, but few, under the drawings of the Spirit, find it. If, indeed, true religion consisted in mere profession, then there were many for Christ. But if the true travelers are men of broken heart, poor in spirit, who mourn for sin, who know the music of the Shepherd's voice, who follow the Lamb, who delight in the throne of grace, and who love the place of the cross, then there are but 'few' with whom the true saints journey to heaven in fellowship and communion.

But not from these causes alone springs the sense of loneliness which the saints often feel. There is the separation of loving hearts, and of kindred minds, and of intimate relationships, by the providential ordering and dealings of God. The changes of this changing world—the alteration of circumstances—the removals to new and distant positions—the wastings of disease, and the ravages of death, often sicken the heart with a sense of friendlessness and loneliness which finds its best expression in the words of the Psalmist, "I watch, and am as a sparrow alone on the housetop."

But should we murmur at the solitary way along which our God is conducting us? Is it not His way, and therefore the best way? In love He gave us friends—in love He has removed them. In goodness He blessed us with health—in goodness He has taken it away. And yet this is the way along which He is conducting us to glory. And shall we rebel? Heaven is the home of the saints; "here we have no continuing city." And shall we repine that we are in the right road to heaven? Christ, our heart's treasure, is there. And shall we murmur that the way that leads us to it and to Himself is sometimes enshrouded with dark and mournful solitude? Oh, the distinguished privilege of treading the path that Jesus walked in!

But the solitude of the Christian has its sweetness. The Savior tasted it when He said, "the Father has not left me alone;" and all the lonely way that He traveled, He leaned upon God. And you cannot be in reality alone, when you remember that Christ and you are one—that by His Spirit He dwells in the heart, and that therefore He is always near to participate in each circumstance in which you may be placed. Your very solitude He shares; with your sense of loneliness the sympathizes. You cannot be friendless, since Christ is your friend. You cannot be relationless, since Christ is your brother. You cannot be unprotected, since Christ is your shield. Want you an arm to lean upon? His is outstretched. Want you a heart to repose in? His invites you to its affection and its confidence. Want you a companion to converse with? He welcomes you to His fellowship. Oh sweet solitude, sweetened by such a Savior as this! always present to comfort, to counsel, and to protect in times of trial, perplexity, and danger.

FEBRUARY

FEBRUARY 1

Behold, the eye of the Lord is upon those who fear him, upon those who hope in his mercy; To deliver their soul from death. Psalm 33:18-19

A FATHER'S eye beaming with tenderness upon a rebellious, wandering child, inviting, welcoming his return—what adamant can resist it? The deepest, bitterest, truest grief for sin is felt and expressed beneath God's eye alone. When the wakeful pillow of midnight is moistened, when the heart unveils in secret to the eye of Jesus, when the chamber of privacy witnesses to the confidential confessions and pleadings of a contrite heart, there is then felt and expressed a sorrow for sin, so genuine, so touching, as cannot but draw down upon the soul a look from Christ the most tender in its expression, and the most forgiving in its language.

Let us always endeavor to realize the loving eye of Jesus resting upon us. In public and in private, in our temporal and spiritual callings, in prosperity and in adversity, in all places and on all occasions, and under all circumstances, oh! let us live as beneath its focal power. When our Lord was upon earth, "a man of sorrows," His eyes were dim with grief; but now that He is in heaven, they are as "a flame of fire,"—to His saints not a burning, consuming flame, but a flame of inextinguishable love. Deem not yourself, then, secluded believer, a banished and an exiled one, lost to all sight. Other eyes may be withdrawn and closed, distance intercepting their view, or death darkening their vision; but the eye of Jesus, your Lord, rests upon you ever, with unslumbering affection. "I will guide you with mine eye," is the gracious promise of your God. Be ever and intently gazing on that Eye—"looking unto Jesus." He is the Fountain of Light; and in the light radiating from His eye you shall, in the gloomiest hour of your life, see light upon your onward way. "By His light I walked through darkness."

"Bend not your light-desiring eyes below,
There your own shadow waits upon you ever;
But raise your looks to Heaven—and lo!
The shadeless sun rewards your weak endeavor.
Who sees the dark, is dark; but turns toward the light,
And you become like to that which fills your sight."

"We all, with open face, beholding, as in a glass , the glory of the Lord, are changed into the same image from glory to glory, even as by the Spirit of the Lord."

FEBRUARY 2

Until the day break, and the shadows flee away, I will get me to the mountain of myrrh, and to the hill of frankincense. Song 4:6

THAT we dwell so much in the region of present clouds, and so little in the meridian of future glory, entails upon us a serious loss. We look too faintly beyond the midnight of time, into the daylight of eternity. We are slow of heart to believe all that is revealed of the bliss that awaits us, and do not sufficiently realize that in a little while—oh how soon!—the day will break, the will flee away, and we shall bathe our souls in heaven's full, unclouded, endless light.

And when does this day begin to break, and the shadows to flee? Go, and stand by the side of that expiring believer in Jesus—the daybreak of glory is dawning upon his soul! He is nearing heaven; He will soon be there—in a few hours, perhaps moments—and oh! what wonders, what glories, what bliss will burst upon his emancipated spirit! Hark, how he exclaims to the loved ones who sincerely would detain him a little longer here—"Let me go, for the day breaks!" Oh blessed day now opening upon his view, as shadow after shadow is dispersed, revealing the wall of sapphire, and the gate of pearl, and the jasper throne, and Him who sits upon it, of the New Jerusalem, all inviting and beckoning him away.

But the noon-tide splendor of this day of glory will be at the SECOND COMING of our Lord in majesty and great power, to gather together His elect, and consummate the bliss of His Church. "He shall come to be glorified in His saints, and to be admired in all those who believe." Precious in the sight of the Lord as is the death of His saints, and blissful to the saints themselves as will be the time of their departure, yet not our death, but the Redeemer's glorious appearing, is the hope set before us in the Scriptures. "Looking for that blessed hope, and the glorious appearing of the great God and our Savior Jesus Christ." Suffering Christian! look rather to this blessed hope of the perfect day, than to the gloomy passage the dark valley. "I will come again," says your gracious Lord, "and receive you to myself; that where I am, there you may be also." Let our hearts respond, "Come, Lord Jesus, come quickly."

And where shall we resort until then? Listen to her words: "Until the day break, and the shadows flee away, I will get me to the mountain of myrrh and to the hill off frankincense." The Lord has fragrant places of safety and repose people until He comes to fetch them to glory. What a "mountain of myrrh" is Jesus!—in whom we may abide, to whom in all lowering clouds we may repair, "until the day break, and the shadows flee away." Closer and closer let us cling to Christ, whose name is "as ointment poured forth " to the Lord's faint and weary ones—until we see Him face to face. And oh! how fragrant are these "hills of frankincense," which the Lord has provided for His people, in the means of grace, to which He invites, and where He meets and communes with them "until the day break, and the shadows flee away." Such is the secret place of prayer—the place of social prayer—the place and public prayer, where the incense of devotion and love ascends, so precious, so cheering and strengthening to the weary. And what is the ministration of the truth, and what is the word of God, but the "hills of frankincense," to which we are privileged to betake ourselves until our Lord comes to us, or until we go to Him. To these fragrant hills of safety and repose let us constantly repair. "Not forsaking the assembling of ourselves together, as the manner of some is, but exhorting one another; and so much the more, as you see the day approaching."

FEBRUARY 3

But let every man prove his own work, and then shall he have rejoicing in himself alone, and not in another. Galatians 6:4

"OH that I were quite sure that I was more than a mere professor!" But why be in doubt? Never was so momentous a matter more easily and speedily settled. "He that believes in the Son of God has the witness in himself." Thus from yourself you need not travel in order to ascertain your true spiritual condition. No one can be a substitute in this great matter for yourself: It is a thing which has too close and personal a relation to you as an individual, to admit of a transfer of its obligations to another. You must feel for yourself—you must experience for yourself—and you must decide for yourself alone. Thus may you come to a right and safe decision in a question involving interests as solemn and as deathless as eternity. Seek the inward witness of the Spirit. Witnessing to what? that your heart has been convinced of sin—that you have renounced your own righteousness—that you have fled to the Lord Jesus Christ—and that your soul is breathing after personal holiness. Do not, I beseech you, rest short of this. Do not be concerned about others; let your first and chief concern be about yourself.

Give all diligence in the use of the means of grace, if you desire a flourishing state of soul. They are the Divinely appointed channels of conveyance from the Fountain. They are the tributary streams from the great Ocean. You cannot possibly maintain a healthy, vigorous state of the inner life without them. You cannot neglect with impunity private prayer, meditation, and self examination—or public ordinances—the ministry of the word, the services of the sanctuary, the assemblies of the saints. A slight thrown upon these must entail a severe loss to your soul. It is in the way of diligent, prayerful waiting upon the means, that the Christian "goes from strength to strength, until he appears before God." Search, oh search, for this living grace. No man shall wait upon the Lord in vain. "Those who wait upon the Lord shall renew their strength." They who plough deeply the fallow ground, and in its furrows sow the precious seed, shall not lack the Holy Spirit's descending influence, in silent dew by night, and in copious showers by day, to quicken and to fructify it. Only honor the God of grace in all the means of grace, and God will honor you by imparting to you grace through the means. "The diligent soul shall be made fat."

Reader, examine yourself, prove your own self, and ascertain truly if you have "Christ in you the hope of glory." Satisfy not yourself with external ceremonies, with the observance of days, of matins and vespers, and frequent communions—with alms-giving and charities. Is Christ dwelling in your heart by his Spirit? This, this is the great and momentous question which, in the near prospect of death, and of the judgment that follows death, it behooves you to decide. "He that has the Son has life, and he that has not the Son of God has not life. These things have I written unto you that believe on the name of the Son of God, that you may know that you have eternal life, and that you may believe on the name of the Son of God."

FEBRUARY 4

Which were born, not of blood, nor of the will of the flesh, nor of the will of man, but of God. John 1:13.

THE real believer in Jesus is a gracious man. He is a "living soul." He is the partaker of a new and a divine nature, and is the depository of a heavenly and a precious treasure. But grace is a thing foreign to the natural state of a man. His possession of it is not coeval with his birth, nor can it be his by right of hereditary law. No parent, however holy, can transmit a particle of that holiness to his posterity. But see how this mystery is cleared up in the conversation which Jesus held with the Samaritan woman, as He sat wearied upon the mouth of Jacob's well: "Jesus answered and said unto her, If you knew the gift of God, and who it is that says to you, Give me to drink, you would have asked of him, and he would have given you living water." This is the grace of which we speak, and this is the source from where it flows into the hearts of all the truly regenerate. It is in you, Christian reader, a "well of water," a springing well, mounting upward, and ascending to the source from where it rises. Blessed words—"springing up into everlasting life"! As the first blush of morning is a part of the day, so the least dawn of grace in the soul is a portion of heaven.

What an exalted character, and what an enviable man, is the true Christian! All the resources of the Triune God unite to replenish this earthen vessel. No angel in heaven contains a treasure half so costly and so precious as that poor believing sinner, who getting near to the Savior's feet, and bathing them with tears of penitence and love can look up and exclaim, "Whom have I in heaven but You? and there is none upon earth that I desire beside You." But what deep humility ought to distinguish the true Christian, as a real professor of the grace of Christ Jesus! The grace which you possess is a communicated grace. All that is really holy and gracious in us springs not from our fallen nature, but, like "every good and perfect gift, comes down from the Father of lights." It is the spontaneous outflowing of the heart of God—the free unmerited bestowment of his sovereign mercy. Then what meekness of heart, what profound humility of mind, ought to mark you! What a prostration of every form of self, self-confidence, self-seeking, self-boasting—should there be, as reasonably becomes those who have nothing but what they have received, and whom free and sovereign grace alone has distinguished from others!

FEBRUARY 5

Let us search and try our ways, and turn again to the Lord. Lamentations 3:40

LET the spiritual believer but take the history of a single week as the gauge of the general tenor of his life, and what a lesson does it read him of the downward, earthly tendency of his soul! Yes, in one short week how have the wheels lessened in their revolutions—how has the timepiece of his soul lost its power—how have the chords of his heart become unstrung! But his prayer is for Divine quickening. It is his anxious inquiry—What course am I to adopt when I find deadness in my soul, and cannot feel, nor weep, nor sigh, nor desire?—when to read and meditate, to hear and pray, seem an irksome task?—when I cannot see the Savior's beauty, nor feel Him precious, nor labor as zealously, nor suffer as patiently, for Him as I would? The answer is at hand—Look again to Jesus. This is the only remedy that can meet your case. Go direct to Christ; He is the Fountain-head, He is the living Well. May the Holy Spirit open your eyes to see, that while all emptiness exists in you, all fullness dwells in Jesus—there is a fathomless depth in the heart of Christ—of love unchangeable, of grace all-sufficient, of truth immutable, of salvation from all sin and trial and sorrow—commensurate with your need and vast as His own infinity. Never can your grace be too low, nor your frame too depressed, nor your path too perplexing, nor your sorrow too keen, nor your sin too great, nor your condition too extreme, for Christ; because He is both Divine and human: thus uniting the nature that can relieve with the nature that can sympathize. "Son of God! Son of man! how wondrous and glorious are You!"

Be very honest and diligent in ascertaining the cause of your soul's deadness. The correct knowledge of this is necessary to its removal; and its removal is essential to the effectual recovery of the inner life from its relapsed state. Is it indulged sin? Is it the neglect of private prayer? Is it worldliness, carnality, unwatchfulness? Any one of these would so grieve the Spirit of God within you, as to dry up the spirituality of your soul. Do not be beguiled with the belief that the real recovery has taken place, simply because that, conscious of your state, in meaningless regrets you acknowledge and deplore it. "The sluggard desires and has nothing." Observe, He has his desires, but nothing more, because with them he is satisfied. Let not this be your state. Seek earnestly, importunately, believingly, until you possess more abundantly life from Christ. Seek a gracious revival of the life of God in your soul. Seek a clearer manifestation of Christ, a renewed baptism of the Spirit, a more undoubted evidence of your conversion, a surer, brighter hope of heaven. Thus seeking, you will find it; and finding it, your "peace will flow like a river, and your righteousness as the waves of the sea." Oh the joy of a revived state of the inner life of God! It is the joy of spring succeeding to the gloom and chill of winter. It is the joy of the sunlight after a cloudy and dark day. "Lord, lift You up the light of Your countenance upon, us." " Turn us again, O Lord God of hosts; cause Your face to shine, and we shall be saved."

FEBRUARY 6

Unto you it is given in the behalf of Christ, not only to believe on him, but also to suffer for his sake. Philippians 1:29

Such is the nature of Christ's religion, and such the terms of His discipleship—suffering and self-denial. By those who are not initiated into the mysteries of the kingdom of grace, this is a truth hard to be understood. To them it is inexplicable how one whose person is loved by God, whose sins Christ has forgiven, whose life appears holy, useful, and honored, should be the subject of Divine correction, and perhaps in some instances should, more than others, seem smitten of God and afflicted. But to those who are students of Christ, who learn at the feet of Jesus, this is no insoluble problem. They understand, in a measure, why the most holy are frequently the most chastened. Ah! beloved, in the school where this truth is learned, all truth may be learned—at the feet of Jesus. In His light we shall see light. But men turn from the sun, and wonder that, in the study of divine truth, shadows should fall darkly upon their path. They study the Bible so little beneath the cross, with an eye intent upon Christ, from whom all truth emanates, of whom all truth testifies, and to whom all truth leads. What says "the Truth" himself? "This is life eternal, that they might know You, the only true God, and Jesus Christ whom You have sent." The crisis in your life speeds on, when all knowledge, save the knowledge of Christ loving you, pardoning you as a guilty, saving you as a lost, sinner, and reconciling you to God as a rebellious sinner, will prove as unsubstantial as a shadow, as unreal and fleeting as a dream. Oh, let this be the one desire and earnest resolve of your soul, "That I may know Him." "Yes, doubtless, and I count all things but loss, for the excellency of the knowledge of Christ Jesus my Lord."

Such, then, as have learned of Christ can understand why a child of God should be a child of affliction. Why "the Lord tries the righteous." Declarations such as these have a significance of meaning they can well comprehend—"I have chosen you in the furnace of affliction." "Whom the Lord loves He chastens, and scourges every son whom He receives." "As many as I love, I rebuke and chasten." And when the present and hallowed results of the Divine dealings are in a measure realized—when some sheaves of the golden fruit of the precious seed sown in weeping are sickled—the heart awakened to more prayer, Christ more precious, sin more hated, self more loathed, holiness more endeared, and the soul brought into greater nearness to God—when the suffering Christian reviews the Divine supports he has experienced in his affliction, how God encircled him with the everlasting arms, how Christ pillowed his languid head, how the Holy Spirit comforted and soothed his anguish, by unfolding the sweetness and fullness of the Scriptures, sealing promise upon promise upon his smitten heart, his chastened spirit can well exclaim, "You have dealt well with Your servant, O Lord, according to Your word." You have broken but to bind up, have wounded but to heal, have emptied but to replenish, have embittered but to sweeten, have removed one blessing but to bestow another and a greater.

"You do but take my lamp away,
To bless me with eternal day."

"Whom have I in heaven but You? and there is none upon earth that I desire beside You."

FEBRUARY 7

I shall be satisfied, when I awake, with your likeness. Psalm 17:15.

THE beatific vision has brought the believer's whole soul into the most perfect harmony with God. He is satisfied with the character and perfections of God, which now unfold their grandeur without a cloud, and fill the soul without a limit. "Now we see through a glass, darkly; but then face to face: now I know in part; but then shall I know even as also I am known." An angel's sight, and an angel's knowledge, enkindle an angel's fervor; and as growing discoveries and endless illustrations of the Divine perfections increase with eternity, glory, honor, and thanksgiving to Him who sits upon the throne will be the saint's undying song. He is satisfied, too, with all God's providential dealings with him in the world he has passed. The present is the repose of faith—and faith can say, amid scenes of perplexity and peril, of obscurity and doubt, "It is well", trusting in the wisdom and faithfulness of God. And yet how difficult often do we find it to trace God's design, or connect His strange dealings with a wise purpose or a gracious end. We cannot unravel the web. Is it not so, my reader? Let faith look back upon the past of your life, not to revive its painful emotions, but that with steadier wing and bolder flight it may bear you forward. That dark cloud of sorrow that settled upon your fair prospects—that blast of adversity that swept away riches—that stroke of providence that tore from your sight the wife of your youth, or hurried the child of your hopes prematurely to the grave, or that placed the friend of your bosom, the companion of your hours, into darkness—or that came near to your own person, and arrested you with disease—you pause and inquire, Why is it thus? Ah! the full answer you may never have in this world—for faith must have scope; but, by and by, if not here, yet from a loftier position and beneath a brighter sky, and with a stronger vision, you shall look back and know and understand, and admire it all, and "shall be satisfied." The glorified are satisfied, too, with the conduct of God's grace. If there is often inexplicable mystery in providence, there is yet profounder mystery in grace. Loving him as God does, yet that He should hide Himself from His child; hating sin, yet allowing its existence, and permitting His children to fall under its influence; leaving them often to endure the fiery darts of Satan, and to tread dreary paths, cheerless, starless—the sensible presence of the heavenly Guide withdrawn, and not a voice to break the solemn stillness or to calm the swelling wave—ah! this is trying indeed!—But all, before long, will be satisfactorily explained. Now the glorified see how harmonious with every principle of infinite holiness and justice, truth and wisdom, was God's scheme of redeeming mercy; and that it was electing love, and sovereign mercy, and free favor, that made him a subject of grace on earth, and an heir of glory in heaven. And as he bends back his glance upon all the way the Lord his God brought him the forty years' travel in the wilderness—traces the ten thousand times ten thousand unfoldings of His love—the love that would not and the power that could not let him go—the faithful rebukes, the gentle dealings, the unwearied patience, and the inexhaustible sympathy of Jesus, with what depth of emotion and emphasis of meaning does he exclaim, "I am satisfied!" The saints are satisfied, too, with the heaven of glory to which they are brought. They awake up in God's likeness. Positively and perfectly holy, positively and perfectly happy, actually with Christ, and contemplating, with an intellectual and moral perception all unclouded, the glory of God, how completely satisfied is he with the new world of purity and bliss, of light and splendor, into which his ransomed spirit sprung! The last earthly passion has died away, the last remnant of corruption is destroyed, the last moan of suffering and sigh of sorrow is hushed in the stillness of the tomb; the corruptible has put on incorruption, the mortal has put on immortality, and the glorified spirit stands amid the throng of holy and adoring ones who encircle the throne, and swells the universal an them—"He has done all things well."

FEBRUARY 8

That like as Christ was raised up from the dead by the glory of the Father, even so we also should walk in newness of life. Rom. 6:4

THE resurrection of Christ is a vital doctrine of Christianity. It sustains an essential relation to the spiritual life of the believer. Viewing it in connection with the union of Christ and His people, the two facts become identical—standing in the relation of cause and effect. Our Lord, in His great atoning work, acted in a public or representative character. He represented in His person the whole elect of God, who virtually were in Him, each step that he took in working out their redemption. In His resurrection from the grave this was preeminently so. The Head could not be resuscitated apart from the body. Christ could not rise without the Church. Thus, then, the new or the resurrection life of Christ, and the inner or spiritual life of the believer, are one and indivisible. Now, when the resurrection of the Head is spiritually realized, when it is fully received into the heart by faith, it becomes a quickening, energizing, sanctifying truth to each member of His body. It transmits a power to the inmost soul, felt in all the actings and manifestations of the spiritual life. Blessed are they who feel, and who feel daily, that they are indeed "risen with Christ," and who find every new perception of this great truth to act like a mighty lever to their souls—lifting them above this "present evil world"—a world passing away.

Perhaps no circumstance connected with the resurrection of Christ conveys to the mind a clearer idea of its bearings upon the happiness of the Church than the part which the Divine Father is represented as having taken in the illustrious event. His having committed Himself to the fact at once stamps it with all its saving interest. "Whom God has raised." "Like as Christ was raised up from the dead by the glory of the Father." "If the Spirit of Him that raised up Jesus from the dead." By this act of raising up His Son from the grave, the Father manifested His delight in, and His full acceptance of, the sacrifice of Christ, as a finished and satisfactory expiation for the sins of His people. So long as Jesus remained in the grave, there was wanting the evidence of the acceptance of His death; the great seal of heaven, the signature of God, was needed to authenticate the fact. But when the Father released the Surety from the dominion of death, he annihilated, by that act, all legal claim against His Church, declaring the ransom accepted, and the debt cancelled. "He was taken from prison,"—as the prisoner of justice—the prisoner of death—and the prisoner of the grave; the Father, in the exercise of His glorious power, opens the prison door, and delivers the illustrious Captive—and by the door through which He emerges again to life, enters the full justification of His whole Church; for it is written—"He was delivered for our offenses, and was raised again for our justification."

A more important truth—where all are of infinite moment to the happiness of man—is not found in the Word of God. As it forms the keystone to the mighty arch of Christianity, so it constitutes the groundwork of spiritual life, upon the basis of which the Holy Spirit of God quickens the souls of all, who are "the called according to His purpose." It was a knowledge of this truth which awoke the ardent desire of the apostle's soul, "That I may know Him, and the power of His resurrection."

FEBRUARY 9

And an highway shall be there, and a way, and it shall be called The way of holiness: the unclean shall not pass over it;....but the redeemed shall walk there. Isaiah 35:8, 9

HEAVEN is the abode of a renewed people; it is a holy place, and the home of the holy; and before the sinner can have any real fitness for heaven, any well-grounded hope of glory, he must be a partaker of a nature harmonizing with the purity, and corresponding with the enjoyments, of heaven. Heaven would be no heaven to a carnal mind, to an unsanctified heart. Were it possible to translate an unconverted individual from this world to the abodes of eternal glory, overwhelmed with the effulgence of the place, and having no fellowship of feeling with the purity of its enjoyments, and the blessedness of its society, he would exclaim—"Take me hence—it is not the place for me—I have no sympathy with it—I have no fitness for it—I have no pleasure in it." Solemn thought! But the Christian is a renewed creature—he is a partaker of the Divine nature; he has sympathies, affections, and desires, imparted to him by the Spirit, which assimilate him to the happiness and purity of heaven. It is impossible but that he must be there. He possesses a nature unfit for earth, and congenial only with heaven. He is the subject of a spiritual life that came from, and now ascends to, heaven. All its aspirations are heavenly—all its breathings are heavenly—all its longings are heavenly; and thus it is perpetually soaring towards that world of glory from where it came, and for which God is preparing it. So that it would seem utterly impossible but that a renewed man must be in heaven, since he is the partaker of a nature fitted only for the regions of eternal purity and bliss. But what is it that gives the Christian a valid deed, a right of possession, to eternal glory? It is his justification by faith through the imputed righteousness of Christ. This is the only valid title to eternal glory which God will admit—the righteousness of His dear Son imputed to him that believes. Here is the grand fitness of a poor, lost, polluted, undone sinner; the fitness that springs from the spotless righteousness of the Lord Jesus, "who of God is made unto us wisdom, and righteousness, and sanctification, and redemption." "He has made Him to be sin for us, who knew no sin, that we might be made the righteousness of God in Him." Behold, then, beloved, the high vantage-ground on which a saint of God stands, with regard to his hope of heaven. He stands out of his own righteousness in the righteousness of another. He stands accepted in the Accepted One, he stands justified in the Justified One, and justified, too, by God, the great Justifier.

The spiritual life which God has breathed into our souls will never rest until it reaches its full and perfect development. Deep as are its pulsations, holy as are its breathings, it is yet but in its infancy, compared with that state of perfection to which it is destined. The highest state of sanctification to which the believer can arrive here is but the first dawn of day, contrasted with the "far more exceeding and eternal weight of glory," which will burst upon him in a world of perfect holiness. Heaven will complete the work which sovereign grace has begun upon earth. Heaven is the consummation of the spiritual life of the believer.

FEBRUARY 10

To present you holy and unblameable and unreproveable in his sight: if you continue in the faith grounded and settled. Colossians 1:22, 23.

NEXT to an ardent desire to be assured that he possesses the truth—the believer in Jesus will feel anxious for establishment in the truth. It will not suffice for him to know, upon evidence he may not gainsay, that he is a converted man; He will aim to be an advancing Christian. Just to have touched the border of the Savior's righteousness, and obtained the healing, will not satisfy his conscience; with a strong and growing faith he will strive to wrap the robe more closely around him, in that full assurance of his "acceptance in the Beloved," of his "completeness in Christ," which supplies the strongest incentive to a walk worthy of his heavenly calling.

The Christian's faith includes not merely what we are to believe, but also what we are to practice. It embraces not only the doctrines of Christ, but equally the precepts and commandments of Christ. The true Christian desires to stand "complete in all the will of God." No longer under a covenant of works, but under the law of Christ, He aspires to be an obedient disciple, manifesting his love to Jesus by observing the commands of Jesus. He needs Christ to be his King, as he needs Him to be his Priest; to govern him, as to atone for him; to sanctify, as to save him. His faith is characterized by the apostle Jude as our "most holy faith." Its nature is holy, its principle is holy, its actings are holy, its tendencies are holy, its fruits are holy. It seeks to "bring every thought into obedience to Christ;" nor will it cease its mighty work—opposed, thwarted, and foiled, though it be—until the soul it sanctifies takes its place "without fault before the throne," perfected in the image of God and of the Lamb.

Establishment in the faith is a matter of great moment in the experience of a child of God. The relation of stability in the truth with progress in the Divine life, is the relation of cause and effect. It is impossible that there can be any progress of the inner life in connection with unsettledness and instability of opinion on the great points of the Christian faith. Hence the especial stress which the Spirit of truth has laid upon it. What says the Scripture? "As you have therefore received Christ Jesus the Lord, so walk you in Him: rooted and built up in Him, and established in the faith, as you have been taught." "Now He which establishes us with you in Christ, and has anointed us, is God." "I long to see you, that I may impart unto you some spiritual gift, to the end you may be established." Welcome all God's dealings, as designed and as tending to build you up on your most holy faith, and thus advance the life of God in your soul. A hallowed possession of trial is a great mean of soul-advancement. Affliction is God's school. Every true child of God has been placed in it. Every glorified saint has emerged from it. "Blessed is the man whom You chasten, O Lord, and teach him out of Your law." Chastening—the school; instruction—the end. Humbling and painful though the process be, who, to secure such an end, would not meekly welcome the discipline?

FEBRUARY 11

This is my comfort in my affliction: for your word has quickened me. Ps. 119:50

OH, how many a deeply-tried Christian has set his seal to this truth! What is the comfort sought by the worldling in his affliction? Alas! he seeks to drown his sorrow by plunging yet deeper into that which has created it. He goes to the world for his comfort; that world that has already belied him, betrayed him, and stung and wounded him more keenly and deeply than the adder. But turn to the man of God. What was the Psalmist's comfort in his sorrow? Was it the lightness of his affliction? Was it the soothing tenderness and sympathy of the saints? Ah, no! it was none of these. It was the spiritual quickening his soul received through the truth of God! This healed his sorrow-stricken heart; this poured a tide of richer comfort into his deeply afflicted soul than the sweetest human balm, or even the entire removal of his trial, could have done. Oh, favored soul, who, when in deep and dark waters—when passing through the fiery furnace—are led to desire spiritual quickening above all other comforts beside—sweetly testifying, "This is my comfort in my affliction, Your word has quickened me." That word, unfolding to us Jesus, leading us to Jesus, and transforming us into the image of Jesus, proves a reviving word in the hour of trial.

By bringing us into a closer acquaintance with the word, trial stimulates the inner life. We flee to the word for counsel or for comfort, and the word proves a quickening word. Divine correction not only teaches, but it stimulates our relish for the spiritual parts of God's truth. In times of prosperity we are tempted to neglect the word. The world abates the keenness of the soul's appetite. We taste no sweetness in its promises, and cannot receive its admonitions and rebukes. "The full soul loaths a honeycomb, but to the hungry soul every bitter thing is sweet." Replenished with created good, and surfeited with earthly comfort, the soul, in its pride and self-sufficiency, loathes the divine honey of God's word. But when the Lord removes the creature, and embitters the world—both proving cisterns that can hold no water—then how precious becomes the word of Jesus! Not its doctrines and its consolations only, but even its deepest searching and its severest rebukes—that which lays us the lowest in the dust of shame and self-abhorrence—are then sweet as the honey and the honeycomb to our renewed taste. Then in truth we exclaim—"How sweet are Your words to my taste! yes, sweeter than honey to my mouth!"

FEBRUARY 12

But God has revealed them unto us by his Spirit: for the Spirit searches all things, yes, the deep things of God. 1 Cor. 2:10

THERE is no darkness which God's own Spirit cannot scatter, no difficulty which He cannot remove, no portion of the word which He cannot explain. All that is necessary to your salvation is revealed in the word, all that can be known of Jesus is there discovered; and all this the blessed Spirit stands prepared to snake known to you. He it is who leads you to Jesus; Jesus lifts the veil and reveals the Father; and the Father, when revealed, appears full of love, mercy, and forgiveness, to the poor returning prodigal, who, in penitence and lowliness, seeks an asylum in His heart. And, oh! how ready is the Spirit to instruct you! Such love and grace has He in His heart, the Heavenly Dove seems ever poised upon the wing, ready to fly to that soul who but sighs for His inward teaching. Does He see one oppressed with a sense of guilt, He hastens to apply the atoning blood of Jesus. Does He mark one weary with his fruitless toil? He seals the promise of the Savior on the heart, "Come unto me, all you that labor and are heavy laden, and I will give yore rest." Does He observe one combating with temptation, tormented with fear, harassed with doubts, struggling with infirmity, halting through weakness? Oh, how ready is He to show that soul where its great strength, and comfort, and grace lie—even in the fullness of a most loving, precious, and all-sufficient Savior! Oh, then, in the name of Jesus, seek this glorious gift of God. Seek Him as a life-giving Spirit, as making Jesus known to you—as leading you into the deep things of God's word—as deeply sanctifying you—as imparting to you the love, confidence, and consolation of an adopted child—as comforting you in every sorrow—as strengthening the divine life in your soul—as being to you the earnest and the seal of eternal glory.

Let it be your encouragement to remember that God knows His own work in your heart; and not only does He know, but He acknowledges it; and not only does He acknowledge, but He delights in it. Your faith may be feeble, your strength small, your grace but little, your knowledge limited, your experience defective; yet, if by the Eternal Spirit you have been led out of yourself, to take refuge in Christ, you are one over whom God rejoices with joy. Beauteous to His eye, and dear to His heart, is that mark of holiness in your soul. What is it but the product of His own power, the germ of His own grace, the fruit of His own Spirit, the outline of His own image? Will He, then, despise, overlook, or turn His back upon it? Never! never! Have you been made willing in the day of His power? Have you laid upon His altar the richest and the best of the sacrifice? Oh, honored servant you! Oh, rich, costly, and acceptable offering! Your God delights in it; yes, delights in you! Ask, and you shall receive a fuller teaching and anointing of the Holy Spirit. Possessing Him, your path to glory will grow brighter and brighter unto the perfect day. "If you then, being evil, know how to give good gifts unto your children, how much more shall your Heavenly Father give the Holy Spirit to those who ask Him!"

FEBRUARY 13

Why let those who suffer according to the will of God commit the keeping of their souls to him in well-doing, as unto a faithful Creator. 1 Peter 4:19

THE God who is now dealing with you is love, all love—a God in Christ—your covenant God—your reconciled Father. All His thoughts towards you, peace; all His feelings, love; and all His dealings, mercy. Soon will you be in His heavenly presence, and behold His unveiled glory as it beams forth from the eternal throne. Soon will you be with Jesus, shall see Him, be like Him, and dwell with Him forever. Darkness, and conflict, and sickness, and death shall cease, because sin shall cease. Then, in your blessed experience, will be realized the beatific vision—"And God shall wipe away all tears from their eyes; and there shall be no more death, nor sorrow, nor crying, neither shall there be any more pain; for the former things are passed away." Let this prospect reconcile you patiently to wait all the days of your appointed time, until your change come. God is faithful. Christ, in whom you believe, is able to keep that which you have committed unto Him against that glorious day. He will perfect that which concerns you. Nothing shall be consumed in your present fiery trial, but the tin and dross. The precious and imperishable gold shall be "found unto praise, and honor, and glory, at the appearing of Jesus Christ." Not more safe were Noah and his family, when they sailed in the ark through the storm, than is that soul who is shut up in Christ. If you have come out of yourself, have left all, and have fled to Jesus, this is your encouragement—not a soul ever perished whom the Father gave in covenant to his Son—whom the Son redeemed—whom the Spirit has regenerated, and in whom He dwells. A threefold cord keeps that precious saint—the Father, the Son, and the Holy Spirit. "Kept by the power of God, through faith, unto salvation." Oh, precious declaration! Press it with a stronger faith to your heart; for if God be for you, who can be against you? In your present state of suffering you find it difficult to think or to pray. But He, who formed you, knows your frame, "He remembers that we are dust." There is One who thinks and prays for you. It is Jesus, your Elder Brother; the "brother born for adversity;" the great High Priest, wearing your nature, who has passed within the veil, "now to appear in the presence of God for us." Jesus intercedes for you moment by moment. Your faith shall not fail, your grace shall not decline, your hope shall not make ashamed; for He who came down to earth, and was wounded for your transgression, and was bruised for your iniquities, rose again from the dead, and ascended on high, now to appear in the presence of God for you. Christ prays for you, and that, when by reason of confusion of mind and weakness of body you cannot pray for yourself. Precious Jesus! You are that gentle Shepherd, who over-drives not Your little ones. When they cannot run, You do permit them to walk; and when, through feebleness, they cannot walk, You do carry them. You are He of whom it is said, "He shall feed his flock like a shepherd, he shall gather the lambs with his arm, and carry them in his bosom."

FEBRUARY 14

For every high priest taken from among men is ordained for men in things pertaining to God, that he may offer both gifts and sacrifices for sins: Who can have compassion on the ignorant, and on those who are out of the way; for that he himself also is compassed with infirmity. Hebrews 5:1-2

OVERLOOK not the fitness of the Lord Jesus to meet all the infirmities of His people. There are two touching and expressive passages bearing on this point. "Himself took our infirmities, and bare our sicknesses." Wondrous view of the Incarnate God! That very infirmity, Christian reader, which now bogs you to the earth, by reason of which you can in no wise lift up yourself— your Savior bore. Is it sin? is it sorrow? is it sickness? is it want? It bowed Him to the dust, and brought the crimson drops to His brow. And is this no consolation? Does it not make your infirmity even pleasant, to remember that Jesus once bore it, and in sympathy bears it still? The other passage is—"We have not an high priest which cannot be touched with the feeling of our infirmities." Touched with my infirmity! What a thought! I reveal my grief to my friend, I discern the emotions of his soul. I mark the trembling lip, the sympathizing look, the moistened eye—my friend is touched with my sorrow. But what is this sympathy—tender, soothing, grateful as it is—to the sympathy with which the great High Priest in heaven enters into my case, is moved with my grief, is touched with the feeling of my infirmity?

Let us learn more tenderly to sympathize with the infirmities of our brethren. "We that are strong ought to bear the infirmities of the weak, and not to please ourselves." Oh for more of this primitive Christianity! The infirmity of a Christian brother should by a heartfelt sympathy become in a measure our own. We ought to bear it. The rule of our conduct towards him should be the rule of our conduct towards our own selves. Who would feel bound or disposed to travel from house to house, proclaiming with trumpet tongue, and with evident satisfaction, his own weaknesses, failings, and infirmities? To God we may confess them, but no divine precept enjoins their confession to man. We unveil them to His eye, and He kindly and graciously veils them from all human eyes. Be this our spirit, and our conduct, towards a weak and erring brother. Let us rather part with our right hand than publish his infirmity to others, and thus wound the Head by an unkind and unholy exposure of the faults and frailties of a member of His body; and by so doing cause the enemies of Christ to blaspheme that worthy name by which we are called.

Honor and glorify the Spirit, who thus so graciously and so kindly sympathizes with our infirmities. Pay to Him divine worship, yield to Him divine homage; and let your unreserved obedience to His commands, your jealous regard for His honor, and your faithful hearkening to the gentle accents of His "still, small voice," manifest how deeply sensible you are of His love, His grace, and His faithfulness, in sympathizing with your sorrows, in supplying your need, and in making your burdens and infirmities all and entirely His own.

Nor let us forget that, so condescending is Jesus, He regards Himself as honored by the confidence which reposes our sorrows upon His heart. The infirmity which we bring to His grace, and the sin which we bring to His atonement, and the trials which we bring to His sympathy, unfold Jesus as He is—and so He is glorified. Consequently, the oftener we come, the more welcome we are, and the more precious does Jesus become.

FEBRUARY 15

You are the salt of the earth. Matthew 5:13

WHEN our Lord reminds His people that they are "the salt of the earth," He describes the gracious state of all real believers. The grace of God is that "salt," apart from which all is moral corruption and spiritual decay. Where Divine grace exists not, there is nothing to stunt the growth, or to check the progress, or to restrain the power, of the soul's depravity. The fountain pours out its streams of corruption and death, bidding defiance to all human efforts either to purify or restrain. But let one grain of the salt of God's grace fall into this corrupt fountain, and there is deposited a counteracting and transforming element, which at once commences a healing, purifying, and saving process. And what parental restraint, and the long years of study, and human law, had failed to do, one hour's deep repentance of sin, one believing glance at a crucified Savior, one moment's realization of the love of God have effectually accomplished. Oh the intrinsic preciousness, the priceless value, the sovereign efficacy of this Divine salt—God's converting, sanctifying grace! Effecting a lodgment in the most debased and corrupt heart, it revolutionizes the whole soul—changing its principles, purifying its affections, and assimilating it to the Divine holiness.

Thus all true believers in Jesus, from their gracious character, are denominated "the salt of the earth." And why so? Because all that is divine, and holy, and precious, exists in them, and in them only. It is found in that nature which the Holy Spirit has renewed, in that heart which Divine grace has changed, in that soul humbled in the dust before God for sin, and now, in the exercise of faith which He has given, reposing on the atoning work of Jesus, exclaiming—

"Other refuge have I none,
Hangs my helpless soul on you."

There, where God's love is felt—there, where the Holy Spirit is possessed—there, where the Savior's atonement is received, and His image is reflected—there is found the precious "salt of the earth." The world does not know it, and even the lowly grace may be veiled from the eye of the Church—few mark the silent tear, or see the deep prostration of the Spirit before the Lord, or are cognizant of its hidden joy, or measure the extent of the holy influence, noiselessly yet effectually exerted; but God, looking from His throne of glory through the ranks of pure intelligences that encircle Him, beholds it; and in that humble mind, and in that believing heart, He sees the divine and precious "salt," which beautifies, sanctifies, and preserves the world. He sees true holiness nowhere else; He recognizes His own moral image in no other. The Christian is emphatically "the salt of the earth."

FEBRUARY 16

But if the salt have lost its savor, with which shall it be salted? Matthew 5:13

THE indestructibility of the divine life in the soul of man, the imperishable nature of real grace, is a truth so deeply involving the holiness and happiness of the Christian, and—what is of still greater moment—the glory of God, that we would place it in the foreground of the statement we are about to advance. In the most searching investigation we would make into the state of religion in the soul, we would never forget, that where there exists real grace, that grace is as imperishable as the God who implanted it; that where true faith has led your trembling footsteps to Jesus, to receive Him as all your salvation, that faith is as deathless as its author.

But with this broad and emphatic statement of a great and holy truth, we must proceed to justify the affecting declaration of the Savior's words, that the salt may lose its savor. In what sense will this apply to the spiritual life of the believer? Most clearly and indisputably, in the sense of a relapsed state of grace, and of its consequent loss of vigorous influence. The first symptom of this state which appears may be a change which the individual detects in his own soul as to his actual, personal enjoyment of religion. Put to him the question—With all your observance of external religious duties and activities, what amount of spiritual enjoyment have you of vital religion in your soul? Have spiritual truths that holy savor and sweetness to your taste which indicate a healthy state of soul? Do you know habitually what close, filial, and confidential communion with God is?—the purifying power of confession?—the frequent sprinkling of the atoning blood?—the meek submissive temper of mind in trials sent by God, or under provocation received from man? Were he to reply to these close, searching interrogatories as a man honest with himself and to his God, he would perhaps unhesitatingly answer—"Alas! the salt has lost its savor! There was a period when all this was the happy experience of my soul. There was then a savor in the very name of Jesus—but it is gone! There was a reality in divine truth—but it is gone! There was an attraction in the throne of grace—but it is gone! I once walked filially with my Heavenly Father—I felt the power of godliness in my soul—I knew what heart religion was, what secret, closet religion was—but alas! the salt has lost its savor!"

But a solemn question is proposed—"With which shall it be salted?" In other words, how can such a relapsed state of the spiritual life be recovered? The recovery is not impossible, and the case, therefore, is not hopeless. The salt may again be salted; the waning strength may be restored. Impossible as this may be to man, with God it is possible. By infusing a new life into the renewed nature, a fresh impartation of grace to the heart, and thus by putting His hand again to the entire work of restoring and reviving the whole inner man, the salt, re-salted, may regain its former sweetness and power. The means by which this great and gracious recovery may be effected are such as His wisdom will suggest, and His sovereignty will adopt. But of this we may rest assured, all will be under the direction of unchangeable love. Whether it may be by the gentle gales of the Spirit, or by the severe tempest of trial, is but of little moment in comparison of the happy and glorious result. If the salt that has lost its savor be but re-salted, the mysterious process by which it is effected we will calmly and submissively leave in His hands. "This also comes forth from the Lord of Hosts, who is wonderful in counsel and excellent in working."

FEBRUARY 17

Give ear, O Lord, unto my prayer; and attend to the voice of my supplications. In the day of my trouble I will call upon you: for you will answer me. Psalm 86:6-7

THE grace that is brought into exercise in the season of affliction must necessarily tend greatly to promote the revival of the life of God in the soul of the believer. How liable is grace to decay, when all things smile upon a path smooth and unruffled! But God sends affliction, and the grace that lay concealed is brought to view, and the grace that remained dormant is summoned to arms; the whole soul is awakened, and inspired as with new life. "The trial of faith works, patience." Thus one tried grace stirs up another grace, until all the links in the golden chain feel the electric influence, and are set in motion. Oh blessed trouble, that so stirs up the life of God in the soul as to make each grace of the Spirit a "new sharp threshing instrument having teeth;" a weapon re-cast, and newly furbished in the furnace, and so coming forth with keener edge and more polished blade, to "fight the fight of faith" with mightier power and success.

But the influence of sanctified affliction upon the inner life is, perhaps, the most evident and powerful in the revival of the spirit of prayer. Strange, that to this, the highest, holiest, and sweetest privilege prepared for the Christian, he is often the most indifferent, and in its observance his feelings are the most chilled and sluggish. What an evidence—one more melancholy there cannot be—of the moral deadness of the soul by nature, that even after it is quickened with a life that brings it into union with the life of God, after the Spirit of God has entered and made it His abode there, ever dwelling and reigning and working in it, there should still remain so much deadness to that which is spiritual, especially the most spiritual of all duties, and the most precious of all privileges—communion with God.

But in the time of trouble we awake to the conviction that we are in possession of a mighty instrument, which when exerted brings all heaven and the God of heaven into our soul. We start as from a dream; and just at the identical moment when all creature assistance droops, and all earthly resources fail, we discover that we are furnished with a power of relief mightier than the mightiest angels—a power which, when exerted (we speak it with reverence), overcomes, like the wrestling patriarch, Omnipotence itself—the power of prayer! And what is prayer but God's power in the soul of a poor, feeble worm of the dust over himself? It was no human might of Jacob which enabled him to wrestle with, and prevail with, the Angel of the Covenant; it was the power of the Holy Spirit in his soul; and when the Divine Angel yielded, He yielded but to himself; and so God had all the glory—and shall have, of all that He has wrought for us, and of all that we have wrought by Him, through eternity. Oh costly and precious privilege, that of prayer! "You people, pour out your heart before him; God is a refuge for us."

FEBRUARY 18

I was dumb, I opened not my mouth, because you did it. Psalm 39:9.

THERE are few lessons taught in God's school more difficult to learn, and yet, when really learned, more blessed and holy, than the lesson of filial submission to God's will. There are some beautiful examples of this in God's word. "And Aaron held his peace." Since God was " sanctified and gloried," terrible as was the judgment, the holy priest mourned not at the way, nor complained of its severity, patient and resigned to the will of God. Thus, too, was it with Eli, when passing under the heavy hand of God: "It is the Lord, let Him do what seems Him good." He bowed in deep submission to the will of his God. Job could exclaim, as the last sad tidings brimmed his cup of woe, "The Lord gave, and the Lord has taken away; blessed be the name of the Lord." And David was "dumb and opened not his mouth, because God did it." But how do all these instances of filial and holy submission to the Divine will—beautiful and touching as they are—fade before the illustrious example of our adorable and blessed Lord: "O my Father, if this cup may not pass away from me, except I drink it, your will be done." Oh, how did Jesus, in the deepest depth of His unutterable sorrow, "behave and quiet himself as a child that is weaned of his mother: his soul was even as a weaned child." Such, beloved, be the posture of your soul at this moment. "Be still!" Rest in your Father's hands, calm and tranquil, quiet and submissive, weaned from all but Himself. Oh, the blessedness of so reposing!

"Sweet to lie passive in His hands,
And know no will but His."

"God's love!" It is written upon your dark cloud—it breathes from the lips of your bleeding wound—it is reflected in every fragment of your ruined treasure—it is penciled upon every withered leaf of your blighted flower—"God is love." Adversity may have impoverished you—bereavement may have saddened you—calamity may have crushed you—sickness may have laid you low—but "God is love." Gently falls the rod in its heaviest stroke—tenderly pierces the sword in its deepest thrust—smilingly bends the cloud in its darkest hues—for "God is love."

FEBRUARY 19

Until the day dawn. 2 Peter 1:19.

THERE awaits the believer such a day as earth never saw, but as earth will surely see—the daybreak of glory. Oh, what a day is this! It will be "as the light of the morning, when the sun rises, even a morning without clouds." Grace now yields its long-held empire, and glory begins its brilliant and endless reign. The way-worn "child of the day" has emerged from the shadows of his pilgrimage, and has entered that world of which it is said, "there shall be no night there." Contemplate some of the attributes of this day of glory.

It will be a day of perfect knowledge. When it is said that there will be no night in heaven, it is equivalent to the assertion that there will be no intellectual darkness in heaven; consequently there will be perfect intellectual light. It is said that we shall then "know every as also we are known." The entire history of God's government will then be spread out before the glorified saint, luminous in its own unveiled and yet undazzling brightness. The mysteries of providence, and the yet profounder mysteries of grace, which obscured much of the glory of that government, will then be unfolded to the wonder and admiration of the adoring mind. The misconceptions we had formed, the mistakes we had made, the discrepancies we had imagined, the difficulties that impeded us, the controversies that agitated us, all, all will now be cleared up—the day has broken, and the shadows have fled forever. Oh, blessed day of perfect knowledge, which will then give me reason to see that all the way along which my God is now leading me, through a world of shadows, is a right way; and that where I most trembled, there I had most reason to stand firm; and that where I most yielded to fear, there I had the greatest ground for confidence; and that where my heart was the most collapsed with grief, there it had the greatest reason to awaken its strings to the most joyous melody.

It will be a day of perfect freedom from all sorrow. It must be so, since it is written, that "God shall wipe away all tears from their eyes; and there shall be no more death, neither sorrow, nor crying, neither shall there be any more pain; for the former things are passed away." What a cluster of sweet hopes is there! What a collection of bright beams, throwing, in focal power, their splendor over that cloudless day! Child of sorrow! sick ones dear to Christ! bereaved mourners! hear you these precious words, and let music break from your lips! God will dry your tears. As the mother comforts her sorrowing one, so God will comfort His. Yes, child of grief, there will be no more weeping then; for—oh, ecstatic thought!—"God shall wipe away all tears from their eyes." And "there shall be no more death." No more rending asunder of affection's close and tender ties; no more separations from the hearts we love; the mourners no more go about the streets; for death is now swallowed up in victory! "Neither sorrow, nor crying." Grief cannot find existence or place in an atmosphere of such bliss. No frustrated plans, no bitter disappointments, no withered hopes, no corroding cares, there mingle with the deep sea of bliss, now pouring its tide of joyousness over the soul. "Neither shall there be any more pain." Children of suffering! hear you this. There will be no more pain racking the frame, torturing the limbs, and sending its influence through the system, until every nerve and fibre quivers with an indescribable agony. "The former things are passed away."

It will be a day of perfect freedom from all sins. Ah! this methinks will be the brightest and sweetest of all the joys of heaven. The Canaanite will no more dwell in the land. Inbred corruption will be done away; the conflict within us will have ceased; no evil heart will betray into inconsistencies and sorrows; not a cloud of guilt will tarnish the unsullied purity of the soul. You holy ones of God! weeping, mourning over indwelling and outbreaking sin, the last sigh you heave will be a glad adieu to pollution—to be tormented with it no more, to be free from it forever. "I shall be satisfied, when I awake, with your likeness." This is heaven indeed.

FEBRUARY 20

How sweet are your words unto my taste! Yes, sweeter than honey to my mouth. Psalm 110:103

THIS similitude is one of frequent occurrence in the Bible. Moses says, that the Lord made his people to "suck honey out of the rock, and oil out of the flinty rock." It is quite clear, then, that we may regard this species of food as the symbol of great spiritual blessings. The sources from where the Christian's nourishment is derived are various. We should be grateful to God that He has not limited us to one secondary source of spiritual nourishment. It was proper, it was wise and gracious in God, that there should be but one Plant of Renown, but one Rose of Sharon, but one Lily of the Valley, but one Living Vine, in other words, that there should be but one Savior and Redeemer, but one Head and Reservoir of the Church. But there are offshoots from this divine plant, there are streams issuing from this sacred fountain-head, from each of which the believer may, by faith, extract the nourishment that strengthens and revives hone?

And what is the word of God but this honey? And from where does this honey fall, but from the heart of God? It is the unfolding of the heart of God. His mind conveys the word, but His heart dictates the word. Take the promises; how "exceeding great and precious" they are. Have you not often found them sweet to your taste as the honey and the honeycomb? When some portion of the word suited to your present need has been brought home to your heart by the sealing power of the Holy Spirit, how have all other sweets become bitter to your taste compared with this! Your Heavenly Father saw your grief, your Divine Captain beheld your conflict and your exhaustion, and bade His Spirit go and drop that sweet promise into your sad heart, and you found the entrance of God's word gave light and comfort to your sad and gloomy spirit.

The love of God in Christ! Oh, it is sweeter than honey. The love that gave Christ—that chose us in Christ—that has blessed us in Christ—that gives us standing in Christ—surely it passes all knowledge. To see it traveling over all the opposition of our unbelieving minds, and the corruption of our depraved hearts, and meeting us at some peculiar stage of our journey, in some painful crisis of our history, in some bitter lonely trial through which we are passing, how does this exalt our views of its greatness, and bring us into the experience of its sweetness! Such too is the love of the Spirit, His love as tasted in His calling—in His comforting—in His sanctifying—in His witnessing, and in all His effectual and unwearied teaching. "God is love;" and on this truth—sweet in our present experience—we shall be living through eternity, "if so be we have tasted that the Lord is gracious."

FEBRUARY 21

For God so loved the world that he gave his only begotten Son, that whoever believes in him should not perish, but have everlasting life. John 3:16.

RICH is the provision which God has made for poor broken-hearted, humble, penitent sinners "God so loved the world." Oh what love was that! This is the love to which, as a trembling sinner, I invite you. And what has this vast and astounding love provided? A "Savior and a great one." Jesus is that Savior! Has the Spirit convinced you of sin? Do you feel guilt a burden, and does the law's curse lie heavy upon you? Then He is your Savior. Believe in Him, embrace and welcome Him. See, how He points to His atoning blood, and bids you bathe in it! See, how He shows you His wounded side, and invites you to take refuge in it! Hear Him say, "Come unto me, all you that labor, and are heavy laden, and I will give you rest. Him that comes to me, I will in no wise cast out." Oh come to Jesus! A full Christ, a willing and an able Christ, a precious Christ, a tender, compassionate, loving Christ is He. There is a fullness of pardon, a fullness of righteousness, a fullness off grace, a fullness of love in Jesus; enough for you, enough for me, enough for every poor, penniless comer.

Your vileness, your unworthiness, your poverty, your age, are no hindrance to your coming to Jesus. Where can you take your guilt, your burden, your sorrow, but to Him? Go, then, nothing doubting of a welcome. "Only believe," and you are saved. Free, free as God's grace can make it, is the blessing of salvation. Your own righteousness will avail you nothing in the procurement of Divine forgiveness. Coming, building on any work of your own, you will be as surely rejected, as he who comes building on Christ's work alone will be surely received. "Being justified freely by his grace, through the redemption that is in Christ Jesus." "By grace you are saved, through faith." Oh, glad announcement to a poor bankrupt sinner!—without works! without merit! without money! without worthiness! Of faith! By grace! The Spirit of comfort speaking these words to your broken heart, you may exclaim in an ecstasy of joy, "Then I am saved!" God is mine, Christ is mine, salvation is mine, heaven is mine! Such, my reader, is the Lord Jesus. Oh! for a thousand tongues to tell of His dying love to poor sinners—the readiness and the gentleness with which He heals a broken heart, binds up a wounded spirit, soothes a disconsolate mind, and gives the "oil of joy for mourning, the garment of praise for the spirit of heaviness." "Whoever believes on him shall not be ashamed."

FEBRUARY 22

Let a man examine himself. 1 Cor. 11:28.

THERE is nothing clearer than this, that man must be a new creature if he would enjoy heaven. God could not make you happy, unless He made you like Himself. God must make you divine—He must give you new desires, new principles—He must create you "new creatures in Christ Jesus." And you must ascertain whether this great change has passed over you. The question must be—Have I "passed from death unto life"? Has my heart been smitten for sin—broken by the Holy Spirit? Have I come as a poor guilty sinner to the Lord Jesus Christ? Do not take all this for granted, but examine yourself, and see whether your heart has been laid upon God's altar—whether it is a "broken and contrite heart, which He will not despise." Examine yourself to ascertain the existence of love to God, and faith in the Lord Jesus Christ. It is a most certain truth that "love is the fulfilling of the law." Enmity against God is the great characteristic of the carnal mind—love to God is the great characteristic of the renewed mind. Do you feel that the name of Jesus creates a thrill of joy in your soul? Do you love God because He is holy, and because He is righteous? Are you in love with His government and with His law? Is it your delight and do you desire to be conformed to its teachings? Is it the supreme wish of your heart that God should rule you—and that you should submit to Him? Do you love Him for sending Jesus—His "unspeakable gift"? Do you love God as your Father—and because He sent His dear Son to bleed and die for you? Examine your own heart on these matters.

Examine your heart also, as to its governing principles. There are many deceitful things in the world. The wind is deceitful—the ocean is deceitful; but the most deceitful thing of all is the human heart. God searches the heart, and looks at all the principles by which we are governed; and no service is acceptable in His sight which does not spring from right motives. And oh, what self-seeking, what self-complacency, what desire for human approval is there in all our actions! But ask yourself—Is my heart governed by love to the Lord Jesus, and by the fear of God? Can I unveil my heart in this transaction as under the eye of one who pierces my inmost thoughts? Can I appeal to God and say—Lord, sinful as I am, I desire to do all for Your glory, and to be governed only by love to You. Examine your heart then, and see what are the principles which actuate you. If they are false—oh cast them away, and ask God so to destroy the power of sin in you, and so to govern you by His love, that you shall only do that which is pleasing in His sight. No service can be acceptable, but that which springs from love to Him, and a simple desire for His glory. But oh how acceptable, then, is even the smallest offering! It may be only the "widow's mite"—or the "cup of cold water,"—but it is pleasing in the sight of God. It may be a service trying to yourself, and perhaps despised by others; but God sees your motives, and will accept your offering, if it springs from a principle in harmony with His will: "For the Lord sees not as man sees; for man looks on the outward appearance, but the Lord looks on the heart."

FEBRUARY 23

Commune with your own heart upon your bed, and be still. Psalm 4:4

How spiritual and solemn is the engagement of communing with our own hearts! The heathen nations have enunciated it as an essential principle, "Man, know yourself,"—but with how much greater power does the Gospel enforce the important duty of self-communion. Let me offer one or two suggestions, as to the manner of engaging in this great work.

There must be an earnest seeking of the Spirit's grace, in this spiritual duty; and if you thus seek, the Holy Spirit will be given to aid you. He will help, and guide, and teach you, and then it shall prove a most delightful exercise.

Oh, seek the influence of this promised Spirit—that Spirit of Light—that Spirit of Love—that Spirit of Jesus which is so ready to aid you—and you shall then reap the most blessed results.

"Commune with your own heart" in communion with the heart of God. Let this self-communion be maintained at the "mercy-seat," in earnest prayer. Feel that God loves you, and that though your love may have waned and become cold, yet that His is unalterably the same—that there is not one thought or pulsation in God's heart which is against you. Feel that you are communing with your Father in heaven, and that you are His child, who, though full of weakness and sin, are yet standing in the closest relationship to your God. "Commune with your own heart," with your eye of faith constantly fixed on the cross. You will find nothing in the bleeding heart of Jesus but love. And though you may feel burdened under a sense of guilt, yet look to Christ, and rest all your hope on His finished work.

The blessings which will result from this self-communion are many and great. Such a process of self-investigation will keep you acquainted with the exact state of your own soul. You will know how matters stand between God and your conscience. The creature cannot then encroach on that affection which is due to God, and you not know it. The world shall not make advances, and you not be aware of it. Come away, then, from the family circle—from all the turmoil of the world—seek your chamber—let no one intrude, and there "commune with your heart;"—not with your brother's, not with your sister's heart—but with your own heart; for this is a personal matter. Let the voice of conscience be heard—I must die alone—I must stand at the judgment-seat alone—I am to be searched alone. Let me then draw away my heart from all those I love, and who perhaps too fondly love me, and let me see how I stand with God. Another blessing which will follow this self-communion will be the great promotion of personal sanctity, and increase in holiness. It is impossible for a child of God thus to commune with himself, and not "grow in grace." Only converse with your own heart, and you will be prepared to meet all the temptations that surround you, to resist all the hindrances that beset you. This communion will endear Jesus to your soul. You cannot become more acquainted with your own heart, and not know more of His heart. He will become more precious who has said, "My blood has pardoned all your sin, my righteousness wraps you round, and I will present you faultless before my Father."

FEBRUARY 24

When he had by himself purged our sins, sat down on the right hand of the Majesty on high. Hebrews 1:3

WHAT a blessed declaration is this!—the words are inexpressibly sweet. Having finished His work, having made an end of sin, having brought in an everlasting righteousness, having risen from the grave, having ascended up on high, Christ has sat down at the right hand of God, reposing in the full satisfaction, glory, and expectancy of His redeeming work. And for what object is He there seated? Why is He thus presented to the eye of faith? That the Church of God might have visibly and constantly before its view a risen, living Christ. Oh how constantly is the Lord teaching us that there is but one Being who can meet our case, and but one Object on which our soul's affections ought to be supremely placed—even a risen Savior. We have temptations various; trials the world know nothing of, crosses which those who know and love us the most, never suspect; for often the heart's acutest sorrow is the least discoverable upon the surface.

But here is our great mercy—Christ is alive. What if we are unknown, tried, tempted, and sad; we yet have a risen Savior to go to, who, as Rutherford says, "sighs when I sigh, mourns when I mourn, and when I look up He rejoices." How can I want for sympathy, when I have a risen Christ? how can I feel alone and sad, when I have the society and the soothing of a living and an ever present Jesus—a Jesus who loves me, who knows all my circumstances, all my feelings, and has His finger upon my every pulse—who sees all my tears, hears all my sighs, and records all my thoughts—who, go to Him when I will, and with what I will, will never say to me no, nor bid me depart unblest—who is risen, exalted, and is set down at the right hand of His Father and my Father, His God and my God, to administer to me all the blessings of the everlasting covenant, and to mete out, as I need them, all the riches of His grace and the supplies of His salvation? Why then should I despond at any circumstance, why despair at any emergency, or sink beneath any trial, when I have a risen, a living Christ to go to? Oh the amazing power of the Lord's resurrection! Oh the preciousness of the fruit that springs from it! Communion with our heavenly Father, near walking with God, a life of faith in Christ, living on high—living not only on Christ's fullness, but on Christ himself; not only on what He has, but on what He is, in His godhead, in His humanity, in the tenderness of His heart, as well as the fullness of His salvation; living in the blessed anticipation of glory, and honor, and immortality; rising in the morning and saying, "This day, and every day, I would consecrate to my God;"—these are some of the fadeless flowers and precious fruits that grow around the grave of Jesus, when faith, listening to the voice that issues from the vacant sepulcher—"He is not here, but is risen"—looks up and beholds Him alive, "seated at the right hand of the Majesty on high." Then, oh then, it exclaims in a transport of joy, "Whom have I in heaven but you? and there is none upon earth I desire beside you," you risen, living, and glorious Redeemer!

"Oh, there is nothing in yon bright sky,
Worthy this worthless heart to own;
On earth there's nothing; friends, creatures, fly;
I pant, my Lord, for You alone."

FEBRUARY 25

Knowing this, that our old man is crucified with Him, that the body of sin might be destroyed, that henceforth we should not serve sin. Rom. 6:6

THE great evil and power of sin lies in the sin of our nature, the body of death which we bear about with us. And herein consists true mortification—the slaying of the principle from where all sin proceeds; the subduing of the original corruption, the strength of which weakens the actings of grace, by impairing the principle of grace. Oh, then, be earnest in seeking this attainment! Do not be content to arrest the stream while the fountain runs, nor to sever the branches while the root remains. But going to the source of the evil, descending to the depth of the corruption, begin the holy work where the potency of sin mainly lies. What is your predominant sin?—lay the axe at its root. Seek its death and destruction, or it will be death and destruction to you as long as it prevails. It must bring a deathliness into the life of God within you, and prove the ruin of your peace and joy and happiness. "Therefore, brethren, we are debtors, not to the flesh, to live after the flesh. For if you live after the flesh, you shall die; but if you through the Spirit do mortify the deeds of the body, you shall live." Oh, then, take this sin which seeks to have dominion over you, to the cross of Jesus, and transfix it there; and as it dies, your soul shall live. Nothing but the cross of Jesus will prove its death, and your life. "I am crucified with Christ, nevertheless I live." There must be the crucifixion before the life; Christ's death for sin must be our death unto sin: no mere outward mortification, no fastings, nor self-inflictions, nor painful austerities, will ever weaken the principle or mortify the root of sin; nothing but faith in the atoning blood of the Son of God can effectually meet the case. Far be it from me to speak indifferently of that aid to the mortification of in-being sin which God's word encourages. I would not lightly esteem, as auxiliary to faith in the atonement, the diligent reading of the word—frequent meditation upon its truths—seasons of retirement from others, and from surrounding objects—private communion with God—self-examination—self-judging—and honest, minute confession of sin. Nor would I overlook the immense blessing which often flows from deep affliction, from painful, bitter trial, traced in the deeper mortification of sin in the temper, spirit, and life of the true believer. But in this great and solemn work our constant motto must be, " Looking unto Jesus." Without the eye of faith upon the cross, apart from the efficacy of the atoning blood and the power of the grace that is in Jesus, there can be no effectual progress in the real work of sanctification. One sight of a crucified Savior imparted by the Holy Spirit will more effectually weaken the power of in-dwelling sin than all other means combined. Oh the might of the cross! Oh the virtue of the blood! Oh the power of the grace of Jesus to crucify, cleanse, and subdue our iniquities! Suffer not any sin, then, to have power over you, seeing Jesus can enable you to oppose it, and will crown your sincere and persevering opposition with a certain and glorious victory. "He will subdue our iniquities."

FEBRUARY 26

It is good for me that I have been afflicted; that I might learn your statutes. Psalm 119:71

THE believer, regarding all God's dispensations in the light of needed discipline, cheerfully acquiesces in the wisdom and righteousness of the Divine procedure. Discipline by trial is an essential element in the Christian's sanctification and instruction. Our adorable Lord, as man, exemplified this truth in His own personal history. We read that, "Though he were a Son, yet learned He obedience by the things which He suffered." The lesson which Christ learned—to Him a new one—was the lesson of obedience—obedience to the will of His Father in suffering. As the curse dilated before Him into more perfect and awful proportion, He came to learn more of the evil of sin and more of the difficulties of redemption, and so more deeply the lesson of obedience—doing and suffering the will of God. It was thus our blessed Lord was perfected through suffering. And this, beloved, is the school in which the "many sons" Christ is bringing to glory learn submission to the Father's will.

The discipline which was becoming in the case of the Head, cannot be without its need and its blessing in the case of the members. There is much—many deep truths of God, and many holy lessons of practical Christianity—to be learned in the pathway trodden by the Savior, which can be learned in no other path—the path of afflictive discipline! But, oh, how needful and how wholesome this discipline! Who would be exempt from it, that has once plucked and tasted the fruit which clusters so richly on the blossoming rod? If submission to the Divine will is ever learned, beyond all question it is where Christ learned it—by the things which we suffer. And, oh, what holy fruit is this—the will of God accomplished in us! The pathway may be through the furnace, whitened seven-fold with the heat, but your will has become more pliant with the will of your Heavenly Father. If the Christian character has become purified, and the graces of the Holy Spirit have become strengthened, and a wider and freer scope has been given to faith, and hope, and love, then ought we not to rejoice in tribulation? The canker-worm has perhaps been busy at the root of your pleasant gourd, the cold east wind has blown rudely over the long-nurtured buds, and the fell hand of death has laid the cedar low, and in the anguish of your soul you exclaim, "Is it nothing to you, all you that pass by? behold and see if there be any sorrow like unto my sorrow, which is done unto me, with which the Lord has afflicted me in the day of his fierce anger." But the Son of God drank a deeper and bitterer cup, and trod a more suffering path, than you, and yet could say, "My Father, not my will, but Your be done;" and shall you shrink from a training and a discipline through whose courses God led the Elder Brother and High Priest of our profession? "Oh, no!" you reply "the self-knowledge I have already attained unto has been so needful and so salutary, that I would not that the cup of sorrow had passed my lips untouched. I little thought I was so unbelieving until the Lord tried my faith. I little imagined that I was so impatient, self-willed, and restive, until God bade me wear the yoke and wait His will. I little supposed that my strength was so small, until the Lord laid upon me the burden. Little did I believe how limited was my knowledge of Christ, how deficient was my acquaintance with divine truth, and how estranged my heart was from true prayer, until the affliction of my God set me upon examining my resources to meet it. Then I discovered how shallow was my experience, and how low and meager was my Christianity. Thus when we trace the discipline to its necessity, the chastisement to the evil it was designed to correct, the meek and lowly heart can say, "It is good for me that I have been afflicted."

FEBRUARY 27

Say you to the righteous, that it shall be well with him. Isaiah 3:10

IN all the spiritual exercises through which the believer in Jesus passes, it must in truth be well with him as to his real standing in Christ. You may be walking in darkness, or in light. You may be mourning in the valley, or rejoicing on the mount; now conquering, now foiled; now weeping, now rejoicing; yet it is still well with you as a pardoned, justified, saved sinner. Nothing can touch your interest in the Savior, or expel you from the covenant, or change the love of God towards you. There are tides in the faith and comfort of a child of God, even as there are in the ocean. The believer has his ebb and flow, his fluctuations of spiritual feeling. It is often low tide with his soul. The waves of spiritual joy and peace ebb, and all looks barren and cheerless. And now he begins to question the reality of all his former experience, and the sincerity of all his past professions. He abjures his adoption, doubts his interest in Christ, puts from him the promises, appropriates the judgments, keeps back from the ordinances, and his soul refuses to be comforted. But, beloved saint of God, is there no flow, as well as ebb, in the spiritual joy and comfort of the believer? Is there no return of the tide of faith and consolation and hope, in the Christian's experience—the wave of love's infinite ocean, of the soul's perfect peace, of glory's anticipated joy, rolling back again upon the shore, in sweet heavenly cadence? Oh yes! Listen to the Divine assurances of this: "I have loved you with an everlasting love." "I have chosen you, and not cast you away." "I will never leave you, nor forsake you." "I have prayed for you, that your faith frill not." "I will restore comforts unto you." "I will not leave you comfortless." You have a little strength." "Therefore will the Lord wait that he may be gracious unto you." "He will be very gracious unto you at the voice of your cry: when he shall hear it, he will answer you." "He restores my soul." All these exceeding great and precious promises, beloved, are yours. They are your Father's epistles of love, and He bids you read, believe, and enjoy them.

Oh, it is, it must be, well with those whose sins are forgiven through Christ, whose people are accepted in the Beloved, whose God is the Lord, and upon whom His eye of love and delight rests from the beginning of the year to the end of the year. Say not it is ill with your soul, and not well, because the Holy Spirit is inserting the plough more deeply into your heart, thus discovering more of its hidden evil, detecting the lurking sin where its existence was not suspected, and discovering the flaw and the failure in the action, the principle, the motive, the end, which the fair surface, self-flattery, or specious reasoning had concealed. Oh say not that it is ill with your soul, and not well, because Jesus does not speak, God does not smile, and prayer is not answered. "For a small moment," says God, " have I hid myself from you; but with great mercies will I gather you." In the dreary, lonely, trying path you now tread, trace you not the footsteps of the flock, and, yet more distinct and blessed than all, the footprints of the Shepherd of the flock? Do not be, then, cast down. The Lord will bring you through this night of weeping into a morning of joy. And your knowledge will be the deeper, and your faith the stronger, and your joy the fuller, and your hope the brighter, and your song the sweeter and the louder, for all the painful exercises through which your soul has passed, and with deeper emphasis you shall exclaim, "It is well."

FEBRUARY 28

An inheritance among all those who are sanctified. Acts 20:32.

UNDER the figure of an inheritance, heaven is here presented to the mind. Nor is this the only passage in which the same similitude occurs. In the first chapter of the Ephesians, and the eleventh verse, we read—"In whom also we have obtained an inheritance, being predestinated according to the purpose of Him who works all things after the counsel of His own will:" and in the thirteenth verse of the same chapter, it will be observed, we have a pledge or an earnest of this inheritance—"In whom, also, after you believed, you were sealed with that Holy Spirit of promise, which is the earnest of our inheritance, until the redemption of the purchased possession, to the praise of His glory." And if it be inquired what the saints of God do thus inherit, the answer will be found in the twenty-first chapter of the Revelation by John, and the seventh verse: "He that overcomes shall inherit all things; and I will be his God, and he shall be my son." How vast, how illimitable, then, the inheritance of the saints—inheriting "all things"! It is a beautiful idea of heaven; it is a lovely picture, on which the eye of faith delights to dwell. The earthly heir looks at his inheritance, surveys it, walks through it, luxuriates amid its beauties, and anticipates its full possession. The heir of glory has his inheritance too; it is heaven. He looks to it, he longs for it; and soon the Savior will come in personal glory, and institute him into its full and eternal possession. But whose is this inheritance? It is the inheritance of the Lord's holy ones, of every nation and from every fold. They form the whole election of grace—the chosen, ransomed, called people of God, be their outward name among men what it may—all who are sanctified by God the Father—all who have been washed in the blood of the Lamb—all who are renewed by the Holy Spirit—all who have "the white stone" and the "new name" in that white stone—all who are living holy, godly lives, in whom dwells the Holy Spirit—and by whose grace the Lord is, day by day, step by step, carrying on that blessed kingdom of grace in their hearts, which will soon fit them for the full possession of eternal glory.

And what is the great end of all God's dealings with His people? For what purpose is the Lord's furnace in Zion, and His fire in Jerusalem? It is to purify, and sanctify, and fit the believer for "an inheritance among all those who are sanctified." All your heaven-blessed trials, all your sanctified temptations, all the covenant transactions of God with you, beloved, in the way of afflictive providences, are designed but to fit you more thoroughly for your inheritance. In this point of view, who would not welcome the severest chastisement? who would not drink willingly the bitterest cup? who would not be willing to have the fetter unbound, the chain snapped, the bond severed, that gives liberty to his struggling and ascending spirit, and brings him in a state of holy fitness nearer and still nearer to heaven?

FEBRUARY 29

Who is a wise man and endued with knowledge among you? let him show out of a good conversation his works with meekness of wisdom. James 3:13

THE knowledge and the grace that God has given You, though for yourself primarily, are not for yourself exclusively. God, in making you a possessor of Divine grace, designed that, through the consistency of your walk, the holiness of your life, and the personal activity of your grace in the cause of God and of truth, it might be dispersed abroad for the benefit of others.

To the true believer it is given to know the mysteries of the kingdom, while from others they are hidden. Where may we look for an understanding of the revealed mind of God but to him? Who knows the secret of the Lord, and to whom does he show His covenant, but to those who fear Him? Having an "unction from the Holy One," he knows all things. He knows something of that mystery, which no philosophy of man can teach him—the plague of his own heart. He knows something, too, of the value of Christ—His person, His work, His glory, His fullness, His tenderness, His sympathy, His preciousness. He knows something of the character and dealings of God—as a holy God, as a just God, and yet who blots out sin, and remembers it no more forever. He knows in some measure what the intricacies of the intricate way are; what the narrowness of the narrow path is; what are the difficulties of walking with God; what are the conflicts, the trials, the tribulations of the Christian life. The Spirit of holiness inhabiting him, despite the corrupt sediment of his fallen nature, he contains and dispenses abroad that stream of holy influence which carries with it a blessing wherever it flows. Where do we look for true holiness save in the soul born again of the Spirit? A holy man is earth's greatest blessing—is the world's richest ornament and shield. How full of compassion is the real Christian! He it is who, taught the priceless value of his own eternal happiness, has affections of compassion for the souls of others involved in like ruin with himself. "Oh that my head were waters, and mine eyes a fountain of tears!" says Jeremiah. "Rivers of water run down mine eyes, because they keep not Your law!" exclaims David. The Lord Jesus, the great Mourner, who wept not for Himself, but for others, has His bottle for the tears of those whose sympathies, prayers, and exertions flow forth for the conversion of sinners, for the salvation of souls. Full of charity, too, is the true Christian. Where shall we look for the Divine cement, the true bond, which unites the heart of man to man, but in the one Church of God? Who is the true peace-maker, the diligent sower of peace, the zealous promoter of love, charity, and good-will among men, but he in whose heart the love of God finds a home? Who has such sincere pity for the poor—whose hand is more ready to relieve their necessities, than he who himself is a conscious partaker of the benevolence of God? Such, dear reader, are some of the characteristics of true Christians.

MARCH

MARCH 1

For he says to Moses, I will have mercy on whom I will have mercy, and I will have compassion on whom I will have compassion. Romans 9:15

THERE is a sovereignty in all the works and dealings of God. If it be asked, what God's own definition of His sovereignty is, we refer the inquirer to His words, "I will have mercy on whom I will have mercy." Here is the Sovereign! How like Himself He speaks! He carries forward His gracious purposes of infinite wisdom and love—chooses or rejects—reveals or withholds, "working all things after the counsel of His own will," and "giving no account," either to angels or to men, "of any of His matters." We will not expand this part of the subject, by citing the numerous examples of this truth which abound in the Scriptures. We would urge the reader to examine the cases of Jacob and Esau—the Publican and Pharisee—Saul of Tarsus and the men who journeyed with him—the two thieves upon the cross—and mark, if the sovereignty of the Divine choice, and the operation of the Eternal Spirit, are not written out in their histories as with a sunbeam.

Is the reader a child of God? Then we will not confine him to the word of Divine truth. We summon him as a witness to the sovereignty of the blessed Spirit's operation. "You are my witnesses," says God. Who and what made you to differ? You have been taken out of your family, your kindred, your friends, your companions. From this circle you alone have been selected, called, and made a child of grace, an heir of glory. The others, where are they? Still dead in trespasses and sin. Where are they? Living in the world, and to the world—lovers of pleasure, lovers of self, lovers of sin, hating God, rejecting Christ, and warring against the Spirit speaking to them in the word, through providences, and by the conscience. Where are they? Bursting through every restraint, and bending their footsteps down to the doom of the lost. Where are they? Gone, many of them, into eternity—past the confines of mercy, "in hell lifting up their eyes, being in torments." And what are you? A sinner saved by grace—a sinner chosen and called, pardoned and justified, washed and clothed, adopted and sanctified—brought to the foot of the cross, constrained to welcome Jesus, to take up His cross, and to follow Him. Oh the electing love of God! Oh the distinguishing grace of Jesus! Oh the sovereign operation of the Eternal Spirit! "Who are you, O man, that replies against God?" Bow down to the sovereignty of His will—silently wonder, and adore Him who says, "Be still, and know that I am God."

Has my reader hitherto found this doctrine a "hard saying"? Has he been prone to cavil at it, or passed it by? I would with all meekness and affection urge him seriously, candidly, and prayerfully to examine it by the light of the Divine word—to cavil not at it, lest he be found to "fight against God;"—to pass it not by, lest he "grieve the Spirit," and rob his own soul of an inestimable blessing. Oh precious truth! It stains the pride of human merit—it lays the axe at the root of self—it humbles and abases—it empties and lays "low in a low place," and ascribes all the praise, honor, and glory, might, majesty, and dominion of the new creation in the soul to the Triune God.

MARCH 2

So then it is not of him that wills, nor of him that runs, but of God that shows mercy. Rom. 9:16

INTIMATELY connected with the sovereignty, is the free grace of the Spirit's operation. No worthiness of the creature allures Him to the sinner's breast. What worthiness can be supposed to exist—what merit in an adjudged criminal—an outlawed rebel—a poor insolvent—one whose mind is enmity, whose heart is swelling with treason against God, His government, and His Son—one who owes ten thousand talents, and has "nothing to pay"? None whatever. And that the Eternal Spirit should enter the heart of such an one—convincing of sin—subduing the hatred—breaking down the rebellion—leading to Jesus, and sealing pardon and peace upon the conscience—oh! what but free grace—unmerited mercy—sovereign love, could thus have constrained Him? In exercising his sovereignty in conversion, let none suppose that that which decides Him in the selection of His subject is anything more worthy, or more lowly He discovers in one than in another. Oh no! He often selects the poorest, the vilest, the most depraved and fallen, as if utterly to explode all idea of human merit, and to reflect in its richest luster the free grace of His heart.

Behold, then, the grace of the blessed Spirit's operation, He comes—He knocks—He unbars—He enters, and creates all things new, irrespective of any merit of the creature, if merit that may be called, which is so wretched and poor, that language fails adequately to describe it. Oh the riches of His grace! How it is magnified—how it is illustrated—how it shines in the calling of a poor sinner! "Lord, what did you see in me," exclaims the convinced soul, "that moved

You with compassion, that drew You to my breast, and that constrained You to make me Your temple?" Nothing, on my part, but poverty, wretchedness, and misery—on Your part, nothing but love, sovereignty, and unmerited favor." Reader, turn not from this glorious feature of the blessed Spirit's operation; it glorifies God, while it humbles man—it exalts Jesus on the ruins of the creature.

Poor in spirit, blessed are you! You are rich in your poverty—you are exalted in your lowliness. All the love that is in God—all the grace that is in Jesus—and all the tenderness that is in the Spirit, all, all is for you. Lift up your head, then, and let your heart sing for gladness. Though poor, though nothing, though despised, though worthless in your own eyes—ah! and in the eyes of the vaunting Pharisee—yet for you Jehovah pours out all the treasures of His grace—gave His well-beloved Son, and sent His blessed Spirit. "All things are yours," you poor in spirit, you broken in heart—"all things are yours." How vast the compass of your blessings! "All things are yours; for you are Christ's, and Christ is God's." Oh, could you know how dear you are to the heart of God—could you know with what tenderness Jesus yearns over you—how the blessed Spirit delights to make you His dwelling-place, you would rejoice in that you are made low. "For thus says the high and lofty One that inhabits eternity, whose name is Holy, I dwell in the high and holy place, with him also that is of a contrite and humble spirit, to revive the spirit of the humble, and to revive the heart of the contrite ones."

MARCH 3

I will never forget your precepts: for with them you have quickened me. Psalm119:93.

IT is no small attainment to arrive at the full belief of the heart in the truth of the Divine record. I speak not now of the historical credence which an enlightened judgment may yield—I speak of a higher faith than this. Nor do I confine myself to that entire assent of the mind, and trembling belief of the heart, upon the grounds of which the soul may have ventured an humble reliance upon Christ, although this is no small attainment; but I allude to that firm, unmoved, and immoveable belief of the truth, which is often an after-work—a work of time and of deep experience, before the heart becomes thoroughly schooled in it. Let me not be supposed to undervalue the smallest degree of faith. To believe that God's word is true, and on the strength of that belief to be willing to renounce all other dependence, and to rest simply and implicitly upon its revealed plan of salvation, is a blessed attainment—an attainment only to be realized by the power of the Holy Spirit; but, to know it from a deep experience of its sanctifying power, from the heartfelt preciousness and fulfillment of its promises, from its sustaining and soothing influence in sorrow, its all-sufficient light in darkness and perplexity—to be brought to trust the naked promise because God has spoken it—to believe, and to go forward, because he has said it, is a still higher step in faith's ladder, and a more illustrious display of the grace and power of the Spirit.

It is an unspeakable mercy to be well grounded in the belief of the truth. Let those speak who have thus been blessedly taught. Let them testify that God's word was, when they first believed, as a sealed book, compared with what it now is—that since they have advanced in the Divine life, led and instructed by the Spirit of truth, it has opened to their minds with all the light and freshness of a new revelation; doctrines, once mysterious, are now beautifully lucid—promises, once unfelt, are now sweetly consolatory—precepts, once insipid, are now powerfully persuasive. And to what is this maturity in the full belief of the truth to be ascribed? We unhesitatingly reply, the witness of the Spirit—the Holy Spirit deepening His work in the heart, teaching the soul more experimentally, and guiding it more fully into all truth—in a word, bringing the truth to the mind with a more realizing and convincing power.

MARCH 4

Whoever is born of God does not commit sin; for his seed remains in him: and he cannot sin, because he is born of God. 1 John 3:9

THESE words have received two interpretations, both of which we believe are equally true. The more general one is, that he who is born of God does not willingly sin, having "put on the new man, which after God is created in righteousness and true holiness," he cannot sin with the full consent and concurrence of the will. He hates it, he fights against it, he resists it. But it may be inquired, is not all sin an act of the will? We reply, not the renewed will. The apostle speaks of two wills in a believer, or rather, the same will under two opposite influences. Thus, Rom. 7:15: "That which I do, I allow not: for what I would, that do I not; but what I hate, that do I." Ver. 19: "For the good that I would, I do not: but the evil which I would not, that I do." Few will question that Paul here speaks of himself as a regenerate man. And yet he refers to two antagonist principles dwelling in him—the one on the side of holiness, the other on the side of sin. "What I hate, that I do." No man can possibly hate sin, unless he is "born of the Spirit." "The fear of the Lord is to hate evil." And still he says, “what I hate,” the sin that is so abhorrent to me—“that I do.” Is there volition in the act? True philosophy demands that we reply, “Yes.” Every sin must be voluntary; if not so, it cannot be sin. Is there the concurrence and consent of the renewed will in the act? True grace demands that we reply, “No.” “For what I hate,”—there is the mark of the regenerate man—“that do I,”—there is the act of the will under the influence of indwelling sin.

But there is another and a stronger interpretation of which the passage is susceptible. It is this—He that is born of God, as such, sins not at all—there is in him a regenerate soul, an indwelling, living principle of grace and holiness, whose natural and constant bias is to holiness. “He” (the new man) “cannot sin, because he is born of God.” “He cannot sin;”—why? “because his seed remains in him;” and what is that seed? “Incorruptible,”—“Being born again, not of corruptible seed, but of incorruptible.” In accordance with Christ’s own words, “That which is born of the flesh is flesh; and that which is born of the Spirit is spirit.” It is spiritual, holy, “from above,” “the Divine nature,”—it “cannot sin, because it is born of God.”

Again, we beg the reader to mark this great evidence of regeneration. “Whoever is born of God does not commit sin.” He does not commit it with the total, absolute, and complete assent and concurrence of the renewed will. He does not give himself over to sin “with greediness.” He “would do good.” He hates sin. Grace reigns, not sin. Sin dwells in him, but does not govern—it has power, but does not rule—it torments, but does not reign with a continued, unbroken supremacy; in accordance with the promise, “sin shall not have dominion over you.” It may for a moment triumph, as it did in David, in Solomon, in Peter, and in a host of other eminently holy men; yet still the promise is verified, as we see in the restorings of the blessed Spirit in their spirit and conduct, in their humblings and confessions, and their holy and upright walk with God in after-years. Reader, have you ever been made sensible of the inward plague? What do you know of the warfare within—of “the flesh lusting against the Spirit, and the Spirit against the flesh”? Your honest reply will decide the great question, whether you are born of God.

MARCH 5

For the law made nothing perfect, but the bringing in of a better hope did; by the which we draw near unto God. Hebrews 7:19

THE Holy Spirit teaches the believer to plead the atoning blood of Christ. He puts this great and prevailing argument in his mouth; and when sin seems a mountain, when unbelief would suppress the aspiration, and a deep consciousness of unworthiness would cause the soul to "stand afar of," He opens to his view this precious and encouraging truth, the prevalency of the blood of Jesus with God on behalf of His people. In a moment, the mountain is leveled, unbelief is checked, and the soul, unfettered and unrestrained, draws near to God, yes, to the bosom of its Father. What a view does this give us of the love of the Spirit, as the Author of prayer! Who has not experienced it who is not yet a stranger to the blessed exercise of communion with God? How often has guilt caused the head to hang down, and the sense of utter vileness and worthlessness has covered the soul with shame, and even the very destitution has kept back the believer, just as the penury, the wretched covering, the loathsomeness of the poor beggar have kept him from the door—then does the blessed Spirit, in the plenitude of His grace and tenderness, unfold Jesus to the soul, as being all that it needs to give it full, and free, and near access to God. He removes the eye from self, and fixes and fastens it upon the blood that pleads louder for mercy than all his sins can plead for condemnation; he brings, too, the righteousness near, which so clothes and covers the soul, as fits it to appear in the presence of the King of kings, not merely with acceptance, but with delight. Beholding him thus washed and clothed, God rests in his love, and rejoices over him with singing.

Nor must we overlook the understanding which subsists between God the Father and the Spirit. The Father, the searcher of hearts, knows the mind of the Spirit. He understands the desire and the meaning of the Spirit in the souls of His saints. He understands the "groanings which cannot be uttered." He can interpret their sighs, yes, He can read the meaning of their very desires. And, when feeling has been too deep for utterance, and thought too intent for expression, when the soul could but groan out its needs and requests, then has God understood the mind of the Spirit. Oh the inconceivable preciousness of a throne of grace! To have a God to go to, who knows the mind of the Spirit—a God who can interpret the groan, and read the language of desire—to have promise upon promise bidding the soul draw near; and when, from the fullness of the heart, the mouth has been dumb, and from the poverty of language, thought could not be expressed—that then, God, who searches the hearts, and knows what is the mind of the Spirit, should say, "Never did you, my child, pray to me as you did then—never was your voice so sweet, so powerful, so persuasive, never were you so eloquent as when my Spirit made intercession for you with groanings which you could not utter." It was, perhaps, your last resource; refuge failed you, no man cared for your soul; friends failed you, your heart failed you, all forsook you and fled; and, in your extremity, you did betake yourself to God, and He failed you not. You did find the throne of grace accessible; you did see a God of grace upon it, and the sweet incense of the Redeemer's precious merits going up; and you did draw near, and sigh, and groan, and breathe out your needs, and did say, "It is good for me to draw near to God." Yes! "He knows the mind of the Spirit." The secret desire for Jesus, the longing for Divine conformity, the hidden mourning over the existence and power of indwelling sin, the feeblest rising of the heart to God, the first sigh of the humble and contrite spirit, all are known to God. Oh let this encourage you, dear reader, when you feel you cannot pray by reason of the weakness of the flesh, or the depth of your feeling; if the Spirit is interceding in you, your heavenly Father knows the mind of the Spirit, and not a sigh or a groan can escape His notice.

MARCH 6

For the Father himself loves you, because you have loved me, and have believed that I came out from God. John 16:27

THERE is in us a secret tendency to partiality in our estimate of the cost of redemption. There is a proneness to keep out of sight the interest which the Father took in the salvation of His Church; and to look upon the work of the Son as though it originated and purchased all the love, the benevolence, and the allurings which God the Father is represented as manifesting towards His revolted but recovered family. You have studied but imperfectly the wonders of redemption—have but partially seen its glories—with shallow line have fathomed its depth—and with feeble pinion have soared to its height, if you have not been accustomed to associate the Father's purpose of grace and love with every step which the Son took in working out the recovery of a lost Church. So used are we to fix our admiring and adoring gaze upon the incarnate Son—so used to attach our exclusive affections around Him who for us "loved not His life unto the death," as to come short of the stupendous and animating truth, that all the love, grace, and wisdom, which appear so conspicuous and so resplendent in salvation, have their fountain-head in the heart of God the Father!

May we not trace to the holding of this partial view, those hard and injurious thoughts of His character, and those crude and gloomy interpretations of His government, which so many of us bear towards Him? And was it not this contracted and shadowy conception of the Father, which Jesus so pointedly, yet so gently, rebuked in His disciples, "If you had known me, you should have known my Father also: and from henceforth you know Him, and have seen Him." To this, His incredulous disciple still objected, "Lord, show us the Father, and it suffices us. Jesus says unto him, Have I been so long time with you, and yet have you not known me, Philip? He that has seen me, has seen the Father; and how say you then, Show us the Father?" What further testimony, and what more conclusive proof, need we? "He that has seen me, has seen the Father." Do we see the glory of Jesus beaming through the attempted concealment of His humanity?—it is the glory of the Father shining. Do we follow Jesus in His walks of mercy, and behold Him lavishing the exuberance of His tenderness and sympathy, upon the objects of misery and want, who thronged His way?—strange though it may seem, yet, in those displays of love, in those meltings of compassion, in that voice of mercy, and in those tears of sympathy, we see and hear the Father Himself. Do we contemplate the love of Jesus, laboring, suffering, dying?—we see the Father's love in equal vastness, strength, and intensity. He that has thus seen the Son, path seen the Father also.

MARCH 7

And we have seen and do testify that the Father sent the Son to be the Savior of the world. 1 John 4:14

WOULD we breathe a syllable, or pen a line, tending to lessen your attachment to the Son? God forbid! Rather would we heighten your love, and elevate it to a standard never reached before. We claim for Christ your highest admiration and your supremest affection; and unhesitatingly declare, that there is not an object in the universe so worthy of them as He. But we are jealous of the Father's glory; and we wish to guide you through the channel to the Fountain from where it flows—even the eternal purpose, the everlasting love, the covenant mercy of God the Father. Here is the grand secret revealed, of God so loving the world. His love originated the salvation of His Church—the salvation of the Church did not originate His love. Do not think, then, that the work of Jesus was the procuring cause of God's love to sinners! Oh no! You do Him sore injustice and wrong if so you interpret His affection. He loved the Church long before He tore His Son from His bosom to die for it. There was the love, thirsting, panting, and longing for an outlet, and only finding it through the riven heart of Jesus. Oh! to see that every step which Jesus took to work out our redemption from the curse was in perfect harmony with the purpose, the mind, and the heart of the Father! He could, with all truth, say, as He travailed in soul, "I and my Father are one." "I do always those things which please Him." "The Father that dwells in me, He does the work." "I am in the Father, and the Father in me."

Behold, then, the Fountain of living waters! the infinite, the eternal, and inexhaustible Fountain—the Father's love! Do you now marvel at redemption? Do you now wonder at His un speakable gift? The mystery is explained in the Father's love. "In this was manifested the love of God toward us, because that God sent His only-begotten Son into the world, that we might live through Him." "Herein is love, not that we loved God, but that He loved us, and sent His Son to be the propitiation for our sins."

Learn, dear Christian reader, to include the Father in the affections that cluster around the Son. Eternally welled in His infinite heart was the love which constrained Him not to spare His own Son that He might spare you. Give to Him an equal place in your thoughts, your affections, your worship, and your service. Blend Him with every view which you take of Jesus. Associate His love who gave with every hallowed remembrance of His love who was given. And when you see the heart of the Son impaled upon the Roman's spear, think that it "pleased Jehovah to bruise Him, and to put Him to grief," for the love which He bore the Church.

MARCH 8

But as he which has called you is holy, so be you holy in all manner of conversation; because it is written, Be you holy; for I am holy. 1 Peter 1:15, 16

IF this motive to sanctification came clothed with such solemnity and power, and was so felt by the Jewish Church, what should be its authority and influence with the Church as it now exists! The increased power and solemnity of this motive is drawn from the more resplendent exhibition of God's holiness in the cross of Christ. With no such development of the Divine purity, as an argument to sanctification, were the saints of the Old Testament favored. But we possess it; so that if we continue in sin, after we have believed, we are "without excuse," and God is "clear when He judges." Here, in the cross, is God's grand demonstration of His holiness. Here has He, as it were, unveiled His great perfections, and shown what a sin-hating, holiness-loving God He is. What! could He not pass by His dear Son—did He give Him up to the "shame and the spitting,"—did He not withhold His "darling from the potter of the dog,"—did justice sheathe its sword in the heart of Jesus—did it smite the Shepherd? And why all this? The answer comes from Calvary, "I, the Lord, am a holy God." And then follows the precept—oh how touching!—"Be you holy, for I am holy." See how the justice of God (and what is the justice of God but His holiness in exercise?) revealed itself as a "consuming fire" on Calvary. Our dear Lord was "a whole burned-offering" for His people; and the fire that descended and consumed the sacrifice was the holiness of God in active and fearful process. Here, then, springs the solemn necessity for sanctification in the believer. The God he loves is holy—his Father is holy, and He has written out that holiness, in awful letters, in the cross of His well-beloved Son. "Be you holy, for I am holy." We must study God in Christ. There we see His holiness, justice, wisdom, grace, truth, love, and mercy, all unfolded in their richest glory and most benevolent exercise.

The necessity for sanctification also springs from the work of Christ. The Lord Jesus became incarnate and died as much for the sanctification as for the pardon and justification of His Church; as much for her deliverance from the indwelling power of sin as from the condemnatory power of sin. His work had been but partial and incomplete, had no provision been made for the holiness of the believer. But He came not only to blot out sin, but to rend asunder its chain—not only to remove its curse, but to break its scepter. The believer in Jesus may be but imperfectly aware how closely associated his sanctification is with the obedience and death of Christ. Yes, that the very death of Christ for sin out of him, is the death of sin in him—that no inroads are made upon the dominion of indwelling sin, no conquests obtained, no flesh crucified, no easy-besetting sin laid aside, save only as the believer hangs daily upon the cross. Observe how the Holy Spirit connects the two—the death of Christ and the holiness of the believer "And for their sakes," says Jesus, "I sanctify myself, that they also might be sanctified through the truth." As their High Priest to atone and purify, He set Himself apart as a holy sacrifice to the Lord God for the Church's sake: "For their sakes I sanctify myself," or set apart myself. Oh, what a motive to holiness is this! Saint of God! can you resist it?

MARCH 9

But we are bound to give thanks aways to God for you, brethren beloved of the Lord, because God has from the beginning chosen you to salvation through sanctification of the Spirit and belief of the truth. 2 Thess. 2:13

THE work of sanctification is preeminently the product of the Spirit. He is the great Sanctifier of the soul. The implantation of the germ of holiness in regeneration is of Him. For let it still be borne in mind, that a renewed soul has within him the "incorruptible seed" of holiness; and although its growth, in many instances, may be slow, and scarcely perceptible; though, during a long period of his journey, the believer may be the subject of strong corruptions and clinging infirmities, which in a degree act like frosts upon the tender scion, checking its advance to maturity, yet the seed is there, and indwelling sin cannot destroy it, the frosts cannot kill it; it is "incorruptible," cannot be corrupted; and in process of time, under the tender and faithful culture of the Eternal Spirit, it shall deepen and expand its roots, and put forth its branches and its boughs, and then shall appear the fruit, "first the blade, then the ear, after that the full corn in the ear;" varying in its degree of fruitfulness among the saints, "in some twenty, some sixty, some an hundredfold," but in all, of the same nature, and the product of the same Spirit.

It has been the constant effort of Satan to divert men from the great point we are now considering. In two ways has he proved successful. First, in setting them upon the work of mortification of sin before regeneration; and second, in setting them upon the same work after conversion, in their own strength. With regard to the first, sanctification is not the antecedent work of an unbeliever: although it is awfully true that "without holiness no man shall see the Lord," yet the attainment of holiness is an utter impossibility so long as the heart remains a stranger to the regenerating operation of the Holy Spirit. Repentance and faith are the first duties in the order of time, with an unconverted man. And with regard to the second effort of Satan to deceive the soul, equally ruinous is it to all true mortification of sin. No child of God can accomplish this mighty work in his own strength. Here lies the secret, be assured, of all our failure and disappointment in the work. Forgetting that he who would prove victorious in this warfare must first learn the lesson of his own weakness and insufficiency, and, thus schooled, must go forth in the strength that is in Christ Jesus, and in the "power of His might," girt with the shield of faith, the helmet of salvation, and the sword of the Spirit—forgetting this important truth, we march to the overthrow of our giant corruptions in our own fancied wisdom and power; and the result always has been, and with the same means ever will be, our complete discomfiture. Oh! when shall we learn that we are nothing, that we have "no might," and that our feeblest enemy will triumph if his subjection be attempted in our own insufficiency?

The Holy Spirit is the efficient cause of all holiness in the believer. If we look into the prophecy of Ezekiel, we find clear intimations of the promise of the Spirit to this effect. There God unfolds what may be regarded as the foundation of all sanctification—the removal of the stony heart, the implantation of a new spirit. "I will give them one heart, and I will put a new spirit within you." "A new heart also will I give you, and a new spirit will I put within you." Let us see the doctrine as more clearly unfolded in the writings of the apostles. "And such were some of you but you are sanctified, but you are justified, in the name of the Lord Jesus, and by the Spirit of our God." "Elect according to the foreknowledge of God the Father, through sanctification of the Spirit." We are far from excluding the Father and the Son from any part in this great work—we believe they are deeply interested in it, as the Divine word shows: "Those who are sanctified by God the Father," Jude 1. "Those who are sanctified in Christ Jesus," 1 Cor. 1:2. But the Holy Spirit is the special and immediate Agent to whom the work of sanctifying the believer is assigned.

MARCH 10

Then drew near unto him all the publicans and sinners for to hear him. And the Pharisees and scribes murmured, saying, This man receives sinners, and eats with them. Luke 15:1, 2.

NEVER was there a tongue like Christ's—so learned, so eloquent, and so skilled. "Never man spoke like this man." Greece and Rome, in their "high and palmy state," never exhibited such philosophy as He taught, such erudition as He displayed, or such eloquence as He breathed. Had He so chosen it, He could have placed Himself al the head of a school of His own, and with a beck might have allured to His feet all the poets and the philosophers of His day, proud to own Him as their Master. But no! the wisdom and the eloquence of this world possessed no charm for Jesus. He drew the learning and the melting power with which He spoke from a higher, even a heavenly, source. His was Divine philosophy; His was the eloquence of God! "The Lord Jehovah has given me the tongue of the learned."

And to whom did He consecrate this learning, this wisdom, and this eloquence? To the very objects whom the proud philosophers and the doctors of His day despised and neglected—even the weary. What a field was here for the exercise of His skill, and for the play of His benevolence! How fully would he demonstrate that He truly possessed the "tongue of the learned"! If to interest the feelings of the exhausted—if to enchain the attention of the weary—if to concentrate upon one subject the powers of a mind jaded and burdened—if to awaken music from a heart whose chords were broken and unstrung, mark the loftiest reach of eloquence, then His was eloquence unsurpassed—for all this He did. The beings whom He sought out, and drew around Him, were the burdened, the bowed, the disconsolate, the poor, the friendless, the helpless, the ignorant, the weary. He loved to lavish upon such the fullness of His benevolent heart, and to exert upon such the skill of His wonder-working power. Earth's weary sons repaired to His out-stretched arms for shelter, and the world's ignorant and despised clustered around His feet, to be taught and blessed. Sinners of every character, and the disconsolate of every grade, attracted by His renown, pressed upon Him from every side. "This man receives sinners," was the character and the mission by which He was known. It was new and strange. Uttered by the lip of the proud and disdainful Pharisee, it was an epithet of reproach, and an expression of ridicule. But upon the ear of the poor and wretched outcast, the sons and daughters of sorrow, ignorance, and woe, it fell sweeter than the music of the spheres. It passed from lip to lip, it echoed from shore to shore—"This man receives sinners." It found its way into the abodes of misery and want; it penetrated the dungeon of the prisoner and the cell of the maniac; and it kindled a celestial light in the solitary dwelling of the widow and the orphan, the unpitied and the friendless. Thus received its accomplishment the prophecy that predicted Him as the "Plant of renown," whom Jehovah would raise up. Thousands came, faint, weary, and sad, and sat down beneath His shadow; and thousands more since then have pressed to their wounded hearts the balsam that exuded from His bleeding body, and have been healed.

MARCH 11

And Jesus was left alone, and the woman standing in the midst. John 8:9

WHAT an object was here, befitting the Savior's sympathy and power! Do you think, reader, that from it His pure and gentle spirit shrunk? Would He feel terrified or polluted by so close a proximity to an object of guilt and wretchedness? Ah, no! Come, you vaunting philanthropists of poetry and romance, who dissolve over a fiction, and petrify at a reality—come, you who have your tears for imaginary woe, and recoil from contact with true misery—who deem it pollution to take kindly the hand of a poor wanderer, exclaiming, "Stand by yourself, come not near to me; for I am holier than you!"—come you, and learn what true philanthropy and sensibility mean. Our Lord's was no mawkish, sentimental humanity, standing aloof from the fallen and the despised, and attracting to itself only the virtuous and the worthy. It was a humanity that identified itself with our fall, and with all its consequent miseries. Itself pure, it yet took our impurity; itself happy, it yet took our sicknesses and our sorrows. He came as the Savior, and sinners were the objects of His love and compassion. He was a man, and to nothing that was human, but its essential taint, was he a stranger. He even carried our sins, as a crushing weight, upon that sinless frame; and that heart, to which sorrow was unknown, became "acquainted with grief."

Oh, it is wondrous to see how closely the Son of God linked Himself with fallen, suffering man. Touch what chord you may of the human heart, and there comes up from the depths of His an instantaneous and harmonious response. With what effect would some of these hidden springs of feeling in the human soul of Jesus now be touched! He would remember, as His eye fell upon this trembling object of His sympathy, that He Himself was born of a woman, amid her perils and her pangs. He would remember, too, that there still was one who bore to Him the endearing appellation of mother, and that yet others stood to Him in the sweet relation of sisters, and all that was tender in His heart would be moved. Looking at her humiliation, and thinking of His own, pity would melt His heart; and while listening to the voice of her clamorous accusers, with the garden of Gethsemane and Calvary full in view, her sin would stir to its center the deep fountain of His mercy. Then was fulfilled the Messianic prediction of the Psalmist, "He shall deliver the needy when he cries: the poor also, and him that has no helper; for He shall stand at the right hand of the poor, to save him from those who condemn his soul."

MARCH 12

And the servant of the Lord must not strive; but be gentle unto all men, apt to teach, patient. 2 Timothy 2:24

ONE exercise of Christian love will be its endeavor to avoid all occasions of offence. These, through the many and fast-clinging infirmities of the saints of God, will often occur. But they are to be avoided, and, in the exercise of that love which proves our Christian character, they will be avoided. The child of God will desire to "keep the unity of the Spirit in the bond of peace." Whatever tends to weaken that bond he will endeavor to lay aside. Whatever He may discover in his communion with the saints calculated to wound, to distress, to alienate, to offend, either in his manner or in his spirit, the healthy exercise of holy love will constrain him to overcome. He will avoid "giving offence." He will be modest in the expression of his own opinion, respectful and deferential towards the opinion of others. He will avoid that recklessness of spirit which, under the cover of faithfulness, cares not to estimate consequences; but which, pursuing its heedless way, often crushes beneath its rough-shod heel the finest feelings of the human heart; saying and doing what it pleases, regardless of the wounds which, all the while, it is deeply and, irreparably inflicting. How sedulous, too, will he be to avoid anything like a dictatorial manner in enunciating his judgment, and all hard words and strong expressions in differing from authorities of equal, perhaps of greater, weight than his own. Oh! were this divine affection but more deeply lodged in the hearts of all those who "profess and call themselves Christians," what courtesy of manner—what grace of deportment—what tender regard of each other's feelings—what kindness in word and in action—what carefulness to avoid inflicting even a momentary pain—what putting away, as becomes saints, all wrath, anger, evil speaking, and malice—and what constant remembrance of His solemn words who said, "Whoever shall offend one of these little ones which believe in me, it were better that a mill-stone were hanged about his neck, and that he were drowned in the depths of the sea," would each believer exhibit! Lord, fill our souls more and more with this lovely grace of love!

Especially in Church communion will the grace of forbearance be called in requisition. When the providence of God has thrown together a community of individuals, composed of a great variety of character, of mind, and of constitutional temperament, although each grade may be more or less modified by the renewing of the Spirit, there will still be a broad field for the passive exercise of love. In a Church, necessarily imperfect, there may exist many things, in which taste as well as judgment will be found at fault, calculated to engender a feeling of dislike, and even of disgust, in a mind refined and delicate. But here Christian forbearance must be exercised. They are the infirmities of the weak of Christ's flock, and they who are stronger in grace should kindly and patiently bear them. In pursuing a different course, we may wound some of the most gracious, humble, and prayerful saints of God. We may be but little aware with what frequent and deep humiliation in secret their conscious failings may overwhelm them. And we ought to bear in mind, that if we sometimes might wish to see in them less that was rough in speech, abrupt and forward in manner, and fault-finding in disposition, they may detect in us a loftiness of spirit, a coldness of demeanor, and an apparent haughtiness of carriage, which may be an equal trial to them, demanding the exercise on their part of the same grace of forbearance towards us. How watchful, how tender, how kind, then, should we be, ever standing with the broad mantle of charity in our hands, prepared to cast it over the failings of a Christian brother, the moment it meets the eye!

MARCH 13

You have ascended on high, you have led captivity captive. Psalm 68:18

As a victorious King, our Lord is now enthroned in glory. He went back to heaven as a Conqueror over sin, hell, and death. Never did a Roman victor return from the battle-field, bearing such spoil; or amid such glory and acclamation, as that with which Jesus reentered His kingdom. The Captain of our salvation had gotten Him the victory over every foe of His Church. He met and battled, single-handed and alone, the combined hosts of His enemies and hers. And although He fell in the conflict, He yet won the battle. He conquered by submitting to conquest; He overcame in being overcome. He slew death in being slain by death. Want you a confirmation to your belief in the essential Deity of your Lord? Behold it, beloved. Where will you turn to the record of a battle so strange, between combatants so opposite, and attended by results so wondrous? That, in the greatest weakness, our Lord should demonstrate His greatest strength; that, by a decided defeat, He should prove the victor; and that in succumbing to the power and dominion of death, He should be the death of Death—oh, how truly Divine does He appear!

Believer in Jesus! the King, whose banner waves over you, has fought and won all your battles. One with Him, every believer is victorious. Treading in his Lord's footsteps, he overcomes, even as Christ overcame. It is impossible but that the weakest believer must obtain the victory in the severe conflict which he is waging with the foe. He may at times be foiled, embarrassed, and overcome, but he will ultimately triumph. The battle may go against us, but not the war. Faith, realizing its union with the Lord, obtains the victory. And never does the believer go forth to face the enemy in the name of Jesus, but with the disciples he may exclaim, "Lord, even the devils are subject unto us through Your name." Come, you faint and exhausted warriors! refresh your spirits and renew your strength with this precious truth—your Captain is victorious! He who lives for you upon the throne, He who dwells in you by His Spirit, is He who rose to glory with your every foe chained in defeat and humiliation to His chariot, carrying "captivity captive." Do you still hesitate to believe so great a truth? Hark how His angelic escort heralded His approach to glory. "Lift up your heads, O ,you gates; and be you lift up, you everlasting doors; and the King of glory shall come in. Who is this King of glory? The Lord strong and mighty, the Lord mighty in battle."

MARCH 14

Then comes the end, when he shall have delivered up the kingdom to God, even the Father; when he shall have put down all rule and all authority and power. For he must reign until he has put all enemies under his feet. 1 Cor. 15:24, 25.

OUR Lord, although a victorious, is not a triumphant King. Nor will He be, until He comes the second time to receive His kingdom, and to reign in undisputed and universal supremacy in the bosom of a gathered Church, and over a subdued and renovated world. He will then appear "more than a conqueror,"—even triumphant. He is represented as having, "after He had offered one sacrifice for sins, forever sat down on the right hand of God; from henceforth expecting until his enemies be made his footstool." What are we to gather from this statement? Much that is deeply and gloriously significant. It describes the Redeemer in the interval between the victory and the triumph—the victory which signalized His past humiliation, and the triumph which will aggrandize His coming glory. It defines His position of repose and His attitude of expectation. It is impossible not to perceive, in these remarkable words, a reference to another and a final conflict—the issue of that conflict being the crowning act of His glory.

Are His enemies yet His footstool? Are all things yet subdued under Him? Is the world subdued? Is sin subdued? Is Antichrist subdued? Are the powers of darkness subdued? Is Death subdued? No! But they shall be. At what time? When Christ "shall appear the second time without sin,"—or a sin-offering, and therefore no more as a Priest who is to die; "unto salvation"—and therefore as a King who is to reign. "For He must reign, until He has put all enemies under His feet." Then, then will our Lord appear as a triumphant King to your eye. Picture the scene! Every foe now falls before Him. Death, the last enemy, is destroyed. All His enemies are "consumed with the spirit of His mouth"—the universal diffusion of His gospel—"and with the brightness of His coming"—the kingly power of His advent. All antichrists retire—their imposture exposed, their pretensions confounded—and Christ remains in triumph. All earthly kingdoms are dissolved—their dominion destroyed, and their glory passed away—and the kingdom of Messiah fills the world. All principalities and powers lay down their sovereignty at His feet, and Immanuel triumphantly reigns, having on his vesture and on his thigh a name written—"King of kings, and Lord of lords."

MARCH 15

Let us be glad and rejoice, and give honor to Him: for the marriage of the Lamb is come, and his wife has made herself ready. Rev. 19:7

"Behold, the Bridegroom comes!" Jesus sustains no relation to His Church more expressive than this. From all eternity He betrothed her to Himself, and forever. He asked her at the hands of her Father, and the Father gave her to Him. He entered into a covenant that she should be His. The conditions of that covenant were great, but not too great for His love to undertake. They were, that He should assume her nature, discharge her legal obligations, endure her punishment, repair her ruin, and bring her to glory. He undertook all, and He accomplished all—because He loved her. The love of Jesus to His Church, is the love of the most tender husband. It is single, constant, affectionate, matchless, wonderful. He sympathizes with her, nourishes her, provides for her, clothes her, watches over, and indulges her with the most intimate and endearing communion. "Christ also loved the Church, and gave Himself for it; that He might sanctify and cleanse it with the washing of water by the word, that He might present it to Himself a glorious Church, not having spot, or wrinkle, or any such thing; but that it should be holy and without blemish." Reader, know you what this union with Jesus is? Apart from its experience, pride not yourself upon any other union. The dearest, choicest ties of human affection are but as brittle glass. They are easily broken, and soon destroyed. No union, but that which is with Jesus, and in Jesus, extends beyond the grave. He must share in every tie of creature love, if it be holy and permanent. Do not think that the union of holy hearts is dissolved by death. Oh no!—death does not sever, death unites the sanctified. The bonds of the holy are beyond his ruthless power to break. The love which the image of Jesus, reflected in His people, inspires, is as deathless as the love of Jesus Himself; it is as immortal as their own redeemed, transformed, and glorified nature. But the Lord Jesus will come in the clouds of heaven, and this will be the occasion of His public espousal of His Church. Her present union to Him is secret and unknown—invisible to the world, and often concealed to herself. But He will appear, openly and visibly to take her to Himself; and before His Father and the holy angels He will solemnize her eternal union. Oh what a time of splendor and of rejoicing will that be! Arrayed in His nuptial robes, Jesus will descend to make her His own; and she, "prepared as a bride adorned for her husband," will go forth to meet Him. Then will be heard the song of angels, "Let us be glad and rejoice, and give honor to Him; for the marriage of the Lamb is come, and His wife has made herself ready." Yes! "Blessed are they which are called unto the marriage supper of the Lamb." May the writer and the reader, through grace, sit down together there!

MARCH 16

How can you believe, which receive honor one of another, and seek not the honor that comes from God only? John 5:44

THE life of the renewed soul, springing from the indwelling of Christ by the Spirit, includes the crucifixion of self in us. "I live, yet not I." What a depth of meaning is contained in these words! We may not in this life be able fully to measure its depth, but we may in some degree fathom it. There is not—indeed there cannot be—a more sure evidence of the life of Christ in the soul, than the mortifying of that carnal, corrupt self-boasting that is within us. For its utter annihilation, in this present time-state, we do not plead. This would be to look for that which the word of God nowhere warrants. But we insist upon its mortification; we plead for its subjection to Christ. Who has not detected in his heart its insidious working? If the Lord has given us a little success in our work, or put upon us a little more honor than another, or has imparted to us a degree more of gift or grace, oh what fools do we often make of ourselves in consequence! We profess to speak of what He has done—of the progress of His work—of the operation of His grace, when, alas! what burning of incense often is there to that hideous idol self! Thus we offer "strange fire" upon the altar.

But the most gracious soul is the most self-denying, self-crucifying, self-annihilating soul. "I live, yet not I. I believe, and am comforted—yet not I. I pray, and am answered—yet not I. I preach, and sinners are converted—yet not I. I labor, and good is done—yet not I. I fight, and overcome—yet not I, but Christ in me." Beloved, the renewed life in us will be ever striving for the mastery of self in us. Self is ever seeking to take the glory from Jesus. This is one cause of the weakness of our faith. "How can you believe," says the Savior, "which receive honor one of another, and seek not the honor which comes from God only?" "We know but little of God," remarks an eminently holy man, "if we do not sicken when we hear our own praise." And if we have kept the glory of God in view, rather than our own, remember, it is the gift of God, the work of His Spirit, which has gained a victory over self, through faith in Christ. Oh that the life of Christ within us may more and more manifest itself as a self-denying, self-mortifying, self-annihilating life—willing to be a fool for Christ, yes, to be nothing, that Christ may wear the crown.

MARCH 17

In all their a action he was afflicted. Isaiah 63:9

HERE is open the true and blessed source of comfort, in the hour and the circumstance of sorrow. The Lord's people are a tried people—Jesus was a tried Savior. The Lord's people are an afflicted people—Jesus drank deep of its bitter cup. The Lord's people are a sorrowing family—Jesus was a "man of sorrows and acquainted with grief." He brought Himself down to a level with the circumstances of His people. He completely identified Himself with them. We are not however to suppose that in every peculiarity of trial there is an identity with our dear Lord. There are trials growing out of peculiar circumstances and relations in life, to which He was a stranger. But Jesus took upon Him pure humanity in its suffering form, was deeply acquainted with sorrow as sorrow; and from these two circumstances, became fitted in all points to support, to sustain, and to sympathize with His afflicted, sorrowing people, whatever the cause of that affliction or sorrow was. It is enough for us that He was "bone of our bone, and flesh of our flesh." It is enough for us that His heart was composed of all the tenderness, sympathy, and gentleness of our nature, and that, too, freed from everything growing out of the infirmity of sin, that could weaken, and impair, and blunt His sensibilities. It is enough for us that sorrow was no stranger to His heart, that affliction had deeply furrowed His soul, and that grief had left its traces upon every line of His countenance. What more do we require? What more can we ask? Our nature?—He took it. Our sicknesses?—He bore them. Our sorrows?—He felt them. Our crosses?—He carried them. Our sins?—He pardoned them. He went before His suffering people; trod out the path; left His foot-print; and now invites them to walk in no way, to sustain no sorrow, to bear no burden, and to drink no cup, in which He has not Himself gone before. It is enough for Him that you are a child of grief, that sorrow is the bitter cup you are drinking. He asks no more. A chord is in a moment touched in His heart, which vibrates to that touched in yours, whether its note be a pleasing or mournful one. For let it be ever remembered that Jesus has sympathy for the joys, as for the sorrows, of His people. He rejoices with those that rejoice, and He weeps with those that weep.

But how does Jesus sympathize? Not in the sense in which some may suppose—that when we weep He actually weeps, and that when we suffer He actually suffers. This may at one time have been so, but we no more know Christ in the flesh, as He was once known. Ah! there was a period when "Jesus wept"! There was a period when His heart was wrung with anguish, and when

His body agonized in pain. That period is no more. There yet is a sense, and an important one, in which Jesus feels sympathy. When the believer suffers, the tenderness of Jesus is drawn forth. His sustaining strength, His sanctifying grace, His comforting love, are all unfolded in the experience of His child, while passing through the furnace. The Son of God is with him in the flames. Jesus of Nazareth is walking with him on the billows. He has the heart of Christ. And this is sympathy—this is fellowship—this is to be one with Christ Jesus.

MARCH 18

For this God is our God forever and ever: he will be our guide even unto death. Psalm 47:14

THE natural man is a god to himself. Yes, he has his gods many. Whether it be self-righteousness, self-gratification, the world, wealth, family, in whatever form it appears, "other lords have dominion over him," to the exclusion of the one true and living God. The nature of the human mind is such, that it must love and worship some object supremely. In his state of innocence, Jehovah was the one and supreme object of the creature's love and adoration. Seduced from that state of simple and supreme affection by the tempter's promise, that if they ate of the fruit, forbidden of God, "they should be as gods," in one moment, they threw off their allegiance to Jehovah; renounced Him as the object of their supreme love, the center of their holiest affections, and became gods to themselves. The temple was ruined, the altar was thrown down, the pure flame was extinguished; God departed, and "other lords" entered and took possession of the soul. But what a change does grace produce! It repairs the temple, rebuilds the altar, rekindles the flame, and brings God back to man! God in Christ is now the supreme object of his love, his adoration, and his worship. The idol self has been cast down, self-righteousness renounced, self-exaltation crucified. A stronger than it has entered, cast out the usurper, and, "creating all things new," has resumed His rightful supremacy. The affections, released from their false deity, and renewed by the Spirit, now turn to, and take up their rest in, God. God in Christ! how glorious does He now appear! Never did the soul see in Him such beauty, such excellence, such blessedness as it now sees. All other glory fades and dies before the surpassing glory of His character, His attributes, His government, and His law. God in Christ is viewed as reconciled now; enmity ceases; hatred has passed away; opposition grounds its weapons; hard thoughts of His law, and treason thoughts of His government, subside; love kindles in the soul, and in one precious Christ, the one Mediator, God and the sinner meet, embrace, and blend. Truly they become one. God says, "You are mine." The soul responds, "You are my God. Other lords have had dominion over me, but henceforth You only will I serve, You only will I love. My soul follows hard after You; Your right hand upholds me."

God in Christ is his Father now. "I will arise and go unto my Father," is the first motion of a renewed soul. "Father, I have sinned against You," is the first confession rising from the broken heart. The Father hastens to meet and embrace his child, and clasping him to his bosom exclaims, "This my son was dead, and is alive again." Reconciled, he now looks up to Him truly as his father. "You shall call me My Father; and shall not turn away from me." Does God speak? it is the voice of a Father he hears. Does God chasten and rebuke? it is from his Father he feels. Are his hopes disappointed, his plans crossed, his cisterns broken, his gourds withered? "My Father has done it all," he exclaims. Blessed spirit of adoption! sweet pledge and evidence are you of the new creature.

God in Christ is now the object of confidence and trust. Trust in a reconciled God and Father was no mark and portion of his unrenewed state. It was then trust in self, in its imagined wisdom and strength and goodness. It was then trust in the arm of flesh, in second causes. Now the soul trusts in God; trusts him at all times and under all circumstances; trusts Him in the darkest hour, under the gloomiest dispensation; trusts Him when His providences look dark and lowering, and God seems to hide Himself; yes, trusts Him "though he slay." Oh, how safe he feels in God's hands and under His government now! His soul, his body, his family, his business, his cares, are completely surrendered, and God is all in all. Reader, this is to be born again.

MARCH 19

And I will pray the Father, and he shall give you another Comforter, that he may abide with you forever; Even the Spirit of truth; whom the world cannot receive, because it sees him not, neither knows him: but you know him; for he dwells with you, and shall be in you. John 14:16-17

GOD has never revoked this gift. He has never removed His Spirit from the Church—He is still her Divine, personal, and abiding Resident. All that we spiritually know of ourselves—all that we know of God, and of Jesus, and His word, we owe to the teaching of the Holy Spirit; and all the real light, sanctification, strength, and comfort, we are made to possess on our way to glory, we must ascribe to Him. To be richly anointed with the Spirit is to be led into all truth; and to be filled with the Spirit is to be filled with love to God and man. To plead for the bestowment of that which God has already so fully and graciously given, seems to mark an unbelief in, and an overlooking of, the mercy, as ungrateful to the Giver as it is dishonoring to the gift.

But for a larger degree of His reviving, anointing, and sanctifying influences we do most earnestly plead. The Spirit, though the ever-blessed and abiding occupant of the Church of Christ and of the individual believer, may not always be manifestly present. The prayerless, unholy, and trifling walk of a believer will cause Him to withdraw His sensible presence. The coldness, formality, worldliness, and divisions of a church will compel Him to withhold the plentiful rain or the gentle dew of His precious influence. He may be so disowned, dishonored, wounded, and grieved, as to retire within the curtains of His secret glory, leaving for a while the scene of worldliness and strife to the curse and the reproach of barrenness. All we want is a richer and more enlarged degree of the reviving, sealing, and witnessing influence of the Holy Spirit. This will sanctify and bless the learning, the wealth, and the influence, now so rich an endowment of Christ's redeemed Church; and without which, that learning, wealth, and influence will but weaken her true power, impede her onward progress, and beget in her a spirit of human trust and vain-glory. This, too, will consume in its holy fire the unhallowed spirit of jealousy and party strife, now the canker-worm of the one body; and without asking for the compromise of truth, will yet, in the love it shall enkindle, so cement the hearts of the brotherhood, and so throw around them the girdle of a heaven-born and uniting charity, as will establish an evidence of the truth of Christianity—the last that Christ will give—which all its enemies shall not be able to gainsay or resist. Descend, holy and blessed Spirit, upon all Your churches, Your ministers, and Your people! Descend You upon Jew and Gentile; everywhere and among all people manifest Your glory, until the Church scattered up and down the earth shall acknowledge, receive, and welcome You, her ever-blessed and ever-abiding Indweller, Sanctifier, and Comforter!

MARCH 20

According as he has chosen us in him before the foundation of the world, that we should be holy and without blame before him in love. Ephesians 1:4

THE very election of the believer to eternal life provides for and secures his holiness. There could possibly be no holiness without election, because election provides the means of its attainment. Thus clearly does the Spirit of truth unfold it in our motto, and in 2 Thess. 2:13, "We are bound to give thanks aways to

God for you, brethren, beloved of the Lord, because God has from the beginning chosen you to salvation through sanctification of the Spirit and belief of the truth." Let us be clearly understood. On the ground of no foreseen holiness in the creature, did God thus purpose to save him; but seeing the indispensable necessity of sanctification in order to eternal glory—the impossibility of the one without the other—He chose us in Christ "that we should be holy."

Let not the Christian reader turn away from, or treat lightly, this precious revealed truth of God's word—an election of a people unto holiness here and glory hereafter. The prejudice of education—early modes of thought—a preconceived system—and more than all besides, the neglect of a close and prayerful investigation of God's word for himself, may lead to the rejection of the doctrine. But He who first cavils, and then renounces it, without a thorough and prayerful sifting of its scriptural claims to belief, stands on solemn ground, and assumes a fearful attitude. What God has revealed. "that call not you common." What He has commanded, that turn not from, lest you be found to have turned from God Himself. Why it has so pleased the Lord to choose a people, it is not our province to inquire, nor, we believe, would it be for our happiness to know. We attempt not to explain the doctrine, much less to account for it. We simply, and we trust scripturally, state it, leaving God to vindicate and bless it. He is the best defender and apologist of His own sacred truth. "Secret things belong unto the Lord our God: but those things which are revealed belong unto us and to our children forever, that we may do all the words of this law." The secret thing in the doctrine of election is, why God has done it—the thing which is revealed is, that He has done it. Let us not, then, seek to be wise above what is written, though it is our duty, as an acute writer has remarked, to be wise up to what is written; leaving the more perfect knowledge of the things that are now seen as "through a glass darkly" to that period of perfect illumination when we shall "know, even as we are known." But thus much we know, that it is the eternal purpose of God, revealed and provided for in the covenant of grace, that all who are chosen, called, and justified, shall, with a view to their being glorified, be "partakers of his holiness." Heaven is a holy place, its inhabitants are a holy people, and He whose glory fills the temple is a holy God. Behold, then, the provision God has made for the sanctification of the believer in the everlasting covenant of grace. The foundation is laid in the death of Christ, it commences in the effectual calling of the Spirit—and by all the precious assurances of grace, and wisdom, and strength, provided in the covenant, it is carried forward to a glorious completion.

MARCH 21

Also, you son of man, shall it not be in the day when I take from them their strength, the joy of their glory, the desire of their eyes, and that whereupon they set their minds, their sons and their daughters, That he that escapes in that day shall come unto you, to cause you to hear it with your ears? Ezekiel 24:25-26

WHAT is the history of creature idolatry, but a mournful record of beautiful and inviting cisterns of happiness, which, nevertheless, God has destroyed. This is a wide and an affecting circle. We enter it cautiously, we allude to it feelingly and tenderly. We touch the subject with a pen that has often sought (though in much feebleness it is acknowledged), to comfort the mourner, and to lift the pressure from the bowed spirit. We enter the domestic circle—oh! what beautiful cisterns of creature good, broken and empty, meet us here! The affectionate husband, the fond wife, the devoted parent, the pleasant child, the faithful friend, laid low in death. They were lovely cisterns, and the heart loved to drink from them its bliss. But lo! God has smitten, and they are broken, and the sweet waters have passed away! Was there not a worshiping of the creature, rather than the Creator? Was not the object deified? Was not the attachment idolatrous? Did not the loved one occupy Christ's place in the heart? Ah! the wound, the void, the desolateness, the lonely grief of that heart, but too truly tell who was enthroned upon its strongest and its best affections.

Turn every loss of creature-good into an occasion of greater nearness to Christ. The dearest and loveliest creature is but a cistern—an inferior and contracted good. If it contains any sweetness, the Lord put it there. If it is a medium of any blessing to your soul, Jesus made it so. But do not forget, beloved, it is only a cistern. And what more? Shall I wound you if I say it? Tenderly do I speak—and if, instead of leading you to, it draws you from, the Fountain, in unerring wisdom, in tender mercy, and in faithful love, the Lord will break it, that you might learn, that while no creature can be a substitute for Him, He Himself can be a substitute for all creatures. Thus His friendship, His love, and His presence are frequently the sweetest, and the most fully enjoyed, when He has taken all things else away. Jesus loves you far too much to allow another, however dear, to eclipse and rival Him. "The day of the Lord will be upon all pleasant pictures," and then the poor, imperfect copy will retire, and give place to the divine and glorious Original; and God in Christ will be all in all.

MARCH 22

Not by might, nor by power, but by my Spirit, says the Lord of hosts. Zech. 4:6

WHAT a mystery is the operation of the Holy Spirit in the soul! That a work so renewing, so gracious, and so holy, should ever transpire in the heart of a poor sinner, is itself a wonder. What a marvelous view of the power, nor less of the grace, of God does it present! Every step in the mighty process awakens new amazement. The first conviction of sin that saddens the heart—the first beam of light that illuminates the mind—the first touch of faith that heals the soul, possesses more that is truly wonderful than the most sublime mystery, or the profoundest secret, in nature. There is more of God in it; and the more of God, the more of wonder; and the more of wonder we see in His work and operations, the more readily should reason assent, and the more profoundly should faith adore. The mystery of grace is illustrated by the mystery of nature. "The wind blows where it wills, and you hear the sound thereof, but can not tell where it comes, and where it goes: so is every one that is born of the Spirit." I saw one but as yesterday, living without God, in total neglect of his soul's salvation. The solemn eternity to which he was hastening gave him not a moment's serious concern. His heart was filled with pharisaical pride, worldly ambition, and covetous desires. Self was his god—the only deity he worshiped; the world was his paradise—the only heaven he desired. Today I see him the subject of deep and powerful emotion, a humble suppliant, in the spirit of self-abasement, pleading for mercy as the chief of sinners. What a change has come over him! How in a moment have old things passed away, and all things become new! And he who but as yesterday was dwelling among the tombs, himself dead in trespasses and sins, today is sitting as a lowly disciple and an adoring worshiper at the feet of Jesus. Where this wondrous transformation—this new creation? Oh, it was the Spirit of God who wrought it, and the work is marvelous in our eyes.

Nor does the sustaining and the carrying forward of this work of grace in the soul unfold less of the wonderful power of God the Holy Spirit. When we take into consideration the mass which the little leaven of grace has to transform—the extent of that revolted territory which the new kingdom has to subjugate to itself—then the sustaining and the perfecting of this work is one continued miracle of wonder. To see one strong in conscious weakness—maintaining his position in the face of much opposition—buoyed up amid billows of sorrow—growing in grace in the midst of circumstances the most unfavorable—witnessing for God and His truth at the loss of family affection and long-endeared friendship—is a spectacle that must fill the mind with adoring thoughts of the love and faithfulness and power of that divine Spirit whose work it is.

MARCH 23

I have fought a good fight, I have finished my course, I have kept the faith. 2 Tim 4:7

WE are here invited to contemplate the Christian in the character of a conqueror. The battle consists of a moral conflict with inward and outward enemies, all leagued in terrible force against the soul. To this is added—what, indeed, was most peculiar to the early Church—a war of external suffering, in which penury, persecution, and martyrdom constituted the dark and essential elements. Now it will be instructive to observe in what way Christ provides for the holy warrior's passage through this fiery contest. It will be perceived that it is not by flight, but by battle; not by retreat, but by advance; not by shunning, but by facing the foe. The Captain of their salvation might have withdrawn His people from the field, and conducted them to heaven, without the hazard of a conflict. But not so. He will lead them to glory, but it shall be by the path of glory. They shall carve their way to the crown by the achievements of the sword. They shall have privations, and distress, and suffering, of every kind; yet while beneath the pressure, and in the very heat of the battle, victory shall crown their arms, and a glorious triumph shall heighten the splendor of their victory. And what spiritual eye does not clearly see, that in conducting His people across the battle-field, the Lord wins to Himself more renown than though He had led them to their eternal rest with entire exemption from conflict and distress?

But in what sense are we conquerors? Just in that sense in which the Holy Spirit obtains the victory. It is not the believer himself who conquers; it is the Divine Spirit within the believer. No movement is seen, no tactics are observed, no war-cry is heard, and yet there is passing within the soul a more important warfare, and there is secured a more brilliant victory, than ever the pen of the historian recorded. In the first place, there is the conquest of faith. Where do the annals of war present such a succession of victories so brilliant, achieved by a weapon so single and simple, as is recorded in the eleventh chapter of the Epistle to the Hebrews? And what was the grace that won those spiritual and glorious victories? It was the grace of faith! "This is the victory that overcomes the world, even your faith." Faith in the truth of

God's word faith in the veracity of God's character—faith in the might, and skill, and wisdom of our Commander and Leader—faith, eyeing the prize, gives the victory to the Christian combatant, and secures the glory to the Captain of his salvation. Then there is the triumph of patience. "That you do not be slothful, but followers of them who through faith and patience inherit the promises." "And so, after he had patiently endured, He obtained the promise." Oh, is it no real victory of the Holy Spirit in the believer, when beneath the pressure of great affliction, passing through a discipline the most painful and humiliating, the suffering Christian is enabled to cry, "Though He slay me, yet will I trust in him"? "The cup which my Father has given me, shall I not drink it"? "Not my will, but your, be done"? Suffering child of God, "let patience have her perfect work, that you may be perfect and entire, wanting nothing." And then there is the conquest of joy. "Having received the word in much affliction, with joy of the Holy Spirit." "My brethren, count it all joy when you fall into diverse temptations," or trials. Why is trial an occasion of joy? Because it is the triumph of the Holy Spirit in the soul. And does not Christ say, "You shall be sorrowful, but your sorrow shall be turned into joy"? Who but Jesus can turn our sorrow into joy?—not only assuaging our griefs, alleviating our sufferings, and tempering the furnace-flame, but actually making our deepest, darkest sorrows the occasion of the deepest gladness, praise, and thanksgiving. Oh, yes! it is a glorious victory of the Holy Spirit, the Comforter, in the soul, when it can enable the believer to adopt the words of the suffering apostle, "I am filled with comfort, I am exceedingly joyful in all our tribulation." Suffering reader! Jesus knows how to turn your sorrow into joy. Confide your grief to Him, and He will cause it sweetly to sing.

MARCH 24

For this corruptible must put on incorruption, and this mortal must put on immortality. 1 Cor. 15:53

OUR present existence is one of deep humiliation and certain decay. In the strong and emphatic language of Scripture, this physical structure, which we adorn with so much care, and which others so extravagantly admire, is described as a "vile body," as "corruption," as "mortal." Has the fact with many—perhaps, my reader, with you—become so common-place as to have changed its character, from one of the most affecting and humbling, to one the existence and contemplation of which awakens in the mind no deep and serious reflection? Have you grown so familiar with disease, and become so conversant with death—the inanimate clay, the shroud, the coffin, the hearse, the grave—those sad emblems of our mortality, as to feel sensible of no solemn emotions when the Holy Spirit brings the fact before the mind? Is it with you a light matter to die? Ah! death is no trifle; and he will find it so who knows not Him who is the "Resurrection and the Life."

But, display the Stoic and act the philosopher as you may, give place to mirth and hilarity and thoughtlessness as you will, in all your vivacity, your pomp and power, you are mortal, and must die. "Dust you are, and unto dust shall you return." You shall "say to corruption, You are my father; and to the worm, You are my mother and any sister." To this humiliating end all are tending: and although some of our race move to the tomb in greater state and luxury than others, yet "The grave is my house" is the affecting exclamation of all. There the rich and the poor meet together—Dives and Lazarus side by side. "There the wicked cease from troubling, and the weary are at rest." Yet how few feel the solemnity and admit the force of this truth! How few pause to consider, that this body which they now pamper with such studied luxuriousness, and adorn with such refinement of taste, will before long need no clothing but the winding-sheet, no house but the coffin, and no home but the grave! And that so changed will be the countenance, once lined with beauty and radiant with thought—and so decayed the body, once so graceful and athletic—that those who regarded it with the fondest love, and even worshiped it with the deepest devotion, will be the first to exclaim, "Bury my dead out of my sight." Oh, how dire the humiliation of our present existence! "The body is dead because of sin." But there glows around the grave of the believer in Jesus the halo of a blessed hope. "He that raised up Christ rom the dead shall also quicken your mortal bodies." No pomp or circumstance may attend him to the tomb, no marble monument may rear its chiseled form to record his virtues, to perpetuate his name, or mark the spot where his ashes repose. Those ashes the ocean's cave may contain; his only tombstone the crested billows; his only requiem, chanted to the wild sea-bird, the solemn music of the waves as they dash and die upon the shore—but He sleeps in Jesus, and slumbering thus, his flesh rests in hope of a glorious resurrection and a blissful immortality. What a new and impressive character does Christianity give to the entire scene of the believer's departure out of this world to go unto the Father! To the eye of sense, the outer door of the tomb appears hideous and for bidding. The deadly nightshade and the overshadowing ivy entwine darkly and thickly over its dismal arch, while the trail of the worm and the time-gathered mold upon its bars deepen the air of its repulsiveness.

But viewed by faith, how changed that tomb! As seen by its piercing eye, it is all radiant around, and all refulgent within. The Redeemer has been there, touching and gilding all with life and glory. And when the inner door opens upon heaven, what a scene of grandeur bursts upon the spirit's view! Glory, streaming from above, bathes it in its celestial beams, and lights its pathway to the skies. This is the tomb of a believer in Jesus. No; it is no longer a tomb—it is a triumphal arch, all radiant and garlanded, through which the spiritual conqueror, laden with the spoils off his last victory, passes, amid the acclaim of angels and the welcomings of kindred spirits, to his crown and his rest.

MARCH 25

I will sing of mercy and judgment: unto you, O Lord, will I sing. Ps. 101:1

How shall we enumerate all the blessings which result from the chastening of love? We might tell how prayer is quickened, how pride is abased, how weanedness is attained, how charity is increased, how character is formed, how meditation and solitude are sweetened, how Christ is endeared, and how God is glorified. It will be recollected, that in the ark of the covenant there was "Aaron's rod that budded." Our glorious covenant of grace has, too, its rod—its budding, its blossoming rod—and precious is the nature and rich the variety of the fruit which it bears. But in that ancient ark there was also the "pot of manna." "Mercy and judgment," bitter and sweet, light and shade, are blended in the covenant dealings of God with His people. The rod and the pot of manna go together. If the one is bitter, the other is sweet. God will never send the rod unaccompanied with the manna. Jesus, exhibited in the word, and unfolded by the Spirit, in the sweet sympathy of His nature, in the tenderness of His heart, as the "Brother born for adversity," is the manna—sustaining and strengthening the believer, passing under the covenant-rod of God. Thus, if afflictions be grievous, the fruit they bear is gracious.

In the history of the Jewish Church there is yet another type, beautifully illustrative of God's dealings with the chastened Christian. I allude to the pillar, which guided the pilgrimage of the Church in the wilderness. By night it was a pillar of fire, and by day it was a pillar of cloud. The darkest night of weeping that can possibly enshroud the child of God has its bright light—its alleviation, its promise, its guiding. And in the most prosperous period in the Christian's experience, it is ordered by unerring wisdom and infinite love that there should be some counter-dispensation of trial, to preserve the just balance of the soul. It has been well remarked, that "Things never go so well with God's children, but they have still something to groan under; nor so ill, but they have still some comfort to be thankful for."

I would have you, then, my reader, not overlook the truth, that the covenant of grace has made provision for everything in the life of a child of God, especially for the life of suffering. It strews the richest blessings and the most profusely upon the chequered path—the path inlaid with stones of various colors, and yet each one most needful and most precious. "Oh you afflicted, tossed with tempest, and not comforted, behold I will lay your stones with fair colors, and lay your foundations with sapphires." It is true that the covenant has anticipated as much the perilous season of prosperity, as the dark hour of adversity; but it always supposes the way to glory to be one of trial and of danger. A heavenly-minded man will learn to look upon the earthly distinction and wealth which the world, so lavish sometimes of its favors, may confer upon him, as a trial and a snare, to one desirous of bearing the cross daily after his crucified Lord; and yet for this specific form of danger the covenant of grace amply provides. Be satisfied, my reader, with any station your God may assign you; believing that for every station in which He places His child, there is the grace peculiar to its exigencies treasured up for him in the everlasting covenant.

MARCH 26

Beloved, think it not strange concerning the fiery trial which is to try you, as though some strange thing happened unto you; but rejoice inasmuch as you are partakers of Christ's sufferings. 1 Peter 4:12,13

IF, dear reader, you are in possession of real faith, even in the smallest degree, expect its conflict and its trial. It is truly remarked by the holy Leighton, that God never had but one Son without sin, and never one without suffering. The existence of faith seems necessarily to imply the endurance of suffering—not because of any intrinsic defect in faith, but in consequence of the impurity of the heart in which that faith is lodged; its perpetual admixture with the alloy of a mind but partially renewed, its constant contact with the objects and scenes of sense and of earth, render trial as essential to the purification of faith, as the flail to the pure wheat, and as the crucible to the precious metal.

The trials and temptations, therefore, with which God visits His people, are designed as tests of faith. Without them we should lack some of the strongest evidences of experimental Christianity. Who would wish the stubble and the chaff to render doubtful the existence of the true grain, or the tin and the dross to obscure the luster of the fine gold? Welcome, then, every trial and test of your faith. Welcome whatever stamps its reality, increases its strength, and heightens its luster. Nor be surprised that this, above all the graces of the Holy Spirit, should be a mark for the great enemy of God. As faith is the grace which most glorifies God, which brings the greatest degree of joy and peace into the soul, and which constitutes its mightiest shield in the conflict, it becomes an especial object of Satan's malignant attack. The most Christ-exalting, God-honoring, and sanctifying of all the Spirit's graces must not expect to escape his fearful assaults. If this "gold " was "tried in the fire" in the sinless person of Jesus, is there not a greater necessity that in our fallen and corrupt nature it should be subjected to a second process of trial? It was tried in the Head, to show that it was real gold; it is tried in the members, to separate it from the alloy with which t becomes mixed in its contact with our hearts. In the one case, the trial was to stamp its divine nature; in the other case, the trial is to purify it from the human nature. Thus are we honored to suffer, in some small degree, as our Lord and Master suffered. Therefore, beloved, "rejoice, inasmuch as you are partakers of Christ's sufferings, that when His glory shall be revealed, you may be glad also with exceeding joy."

MARCH 27

Who is even at the right hand of God, who also makes intercession for us. Romans 8:34

THE exaltation of Jesus in heaven is associated with the dearest interests of His people on earth. Joseph was forgotten when Pharaoh lifted up the head of the chief butler. But our Lord, amid the honors and splendors to which God has highly exalted him, still remembers his brethren in bonds, and makes intercession for them. How expressive is the type of our Lord's present engagement on behalf of His people. "And he (Aaron) shall take a censer full of burning coals of fire from of the altar before the Lord, and his hands full of sweet incense beaten small, and bring it within the veil: and he shall put the incense upon the fire before the Lord, that the cloud of the incense may cover the mercy-seat that is upon the testimony." The passing of Aaron into the holy of holies was the shadowing forth of our Lord's entrance into heaven. The blood sprinkled at the mercy-seat was the presentation of the great Atonement within the veil. And the incense overshadowing with its fragrant cloud the mercy-seat, thus touched with blood, was the figure of the ceaseless intercession of our great High Priest in the holiest. "For Christ is not entered into the holy places made with hands, which are the figures of the true: but into heaven itself now to appear in the presence of God for us."

It is an individual, an anticipative, and a present intercession. It embraces all the personal needs of each believer, it precedes each temptation and each trial, and at the moment that the sympathy and the prayers of the Savior are the most called for, and are felt to be the most soothing, it bears the saint and his sorrow on its bosom before the throne. Just at a crisis of his history, at a juncture, perhaps, the most critical in his history, the heart, oppressed with its emotions, cannot breathe a prayer—Jesus is remembering him, sympathizing with him, and interceding for him. Oh, who can fully describe the blessings that flow through the intercession of the Son of God? The love, the sympathy, the forethought, the carefulness, the minute interest in all our concerns, are blessings beyond description.

Tried, tempted believer! Jesus makes intercession for you, Your case is not unknown to Him. Your sorrow is not hidden from Him. Your name is on His heart; your burden is on His shoulder; and because He not only has prayed for you, but prays for you now, your faith shall not fail. Your great accuser may stand at your right hand to condemn you, but your great Advocate is at the right hand of God to plead for you. And greater is He that is for you, than all that are against you. The mediatorial work of Christ shuts every mouth, meets every accusation, and ignores every indictment that can be brought against those for whom He died, rose again, ascended up on high, and makes intercession.

MARCH 28

He has filled the hungry with good things; and the rich he has sent empty away. Luke 1:53

BEWARE of placing any limit whatever to the grace of Jesus. Be your circumstances what they may, remember that "God is able to make all grace abound towards you; that you always, having all sufficiency in all things, may abound to every good work." Make no allowance for sin, frame no excuses for inactivity, shrink from no cross, be dis-heartened by no difficulty, give place to no temptation, yield to no excessive grief; for Jesus has spoken it, and He now speaks it to you, "My grace is sufficient for you." Since, then, the grace of Jesus is illimitable, take with you in your journeyings to the one Source of supply a vessel of large capacity, that you may receive abundantly. Remember that, as a believer in the Lord Jesus, "All things are for your sake, that the abundant grace might, through the thanksgiving of many, redound to the glory of God." Let your life be a perpetual traveling to this grace. Do not be satisfied with what you have already received. Go, again and yet again, to this Divine Fountain, taking every corruption as it is developed, every sin as it is felt, every sorrow as it rises, to Jesus; remembering for your encouragement, that though you have received much, yet "He gives more grace," and is prepared to give you much more than you have yet received.

Rejoice that the emptiness of the vessel is no plea against the filling of the vessel. If the Spirit of God has made you "poor in spirit," has wrought in you a "hungering and thirsting for righteousness," betake yourself to the grace of Jesus. The full vessel He needs not, nor does the full vessel want Him. He invites, He draws, He receives none save the empty. He will have all the honor of our salvation. He will magnify His grace in the creature's nothingness. Your emptiness shall eternally glorify His fullness. With the example and the words before me of him who styled himself the 'chief of sinners,' I hesitate not to encourage the greatest sinner to come to Christ. "Who was before a blasphemer, and a persecutor, and injurious: but I obtained mercy... And the grace of our Lord was exceeding abundant with faith and love which are in Christ Jesus. This is a faithful saying, and worthy of all acceptation, that Christ Jesus came into the world to save sinners, of whom I am chief." Truly might he exclaim, "By the grace of God I am what I am." Beware, then, I beseech you, of going to Christ for salvation in any other character than as an empty sinner. Had the vessels been brought other than empty, to receive the miraculous oil, they would have been refused, filled though they had been with ambrosia itself. Nothing should mingle with the oil. Nothing should shade the luster of the miracle. And so is it with the grace of Jesus. Brilliant genius, profound erudition, costly benevolence, and the purest ethics of natural religion, avail nothing in the matter of the soul's salvation. These are the ambrosia, of which the vessel must be emptied before it comes to Christ. It must all be laid aside as constituting a plea of acceptance. The only plea admissible with Christ is, that without His grace you perish forever. "Lord, save, or I perish."

MARCH 29

For what nation is there so great, who has God so near unto them, as the Lord our God is in all things that we call upon him for? Deut. 4:7

ARE you not ready to exclaim, "What a glorious privilege is prayer?" Ah, yes! and you may add, "What mighty power, too, it possesses!" The power of a holy wrestler with God approaches the nearest to an act of omnipotence of any display of finite might whatever. Angelic mightiness must be weakness itself in comparison. What eloquence in that one word 'Father,' lisped in believing prayer! Demosthenes and Cicero, in the glory of their eloquence, never surpassed, no, never equaled it. It is breathed—and heaven's door expands; it is uttered again—and the heart of God flies open. With such a key in the hands of faith, which may at any moment unlock the treasury of God, as prayer, why do we not oftener use it! Oh that the Spirit of God might stir us up to more earnest prayer!—teaching us to enshrine everything, to pervade and saturate everything, in the heart and with the spirit of humble, importunate, believing prayer. What real and immense gainers should we be, did we "in everything, by prayer and supplication, with thanksgiving, let our requests be made known unto God." "For what nation is there so great, who has God so near unto them, as the Lord our God is in all things that we call upon Him for?"

In a word, my Christian reader, "have faith in God" at all times, and in all things. This is the utmost that He asks at your hands—no unreasonable or impossible requirement. Would Jesus have limited you to this single duty, making your whole happiness for both worlds dependent upon it, were it so? Never! Relinquishing your own wisdom, resting from your own toil, and ceasing from man, God would have you now cast yourself upon Him in simple faith for all things. You have had faith in the creature, and it has disappointed you; in earthly good, and it has faded away; in your own heart, and it has deceived you. Now, have faith in God! Call upon Him in your trouble, try Him in your trial, trust Him in your need, and see if He will not honor the faith that honors Him. "Have faith in God,"—words of Jesus, oh how sweet! spoken to allure your chafed and weary spirit to its Divine and blessed rest. Press the kind message to your grateful heart, responding, in a strain of blended praise and prayer, "Lord, I believe; help You my unbelief."

By this grace you may be assimilated with the Divine will, may be transformed into the Divine image, may be trained for active toil or for passive endurance. Limit not a Divine blessing so inexhaustible in its resources, and so free in its bestowment; but out of the Savior's fullness receive grace for grace, that in all things "the name of our Lord Jesus may be glorified in you, and you in Him, according to the grace of our God and the Lord Jesus Christ."

MARCH 30

And he said unto them, Come you yourselves apart into a desert place, and rest awhile." Mark 6:31.

SUFFER me, dear reader, to urge upon you the daily and diligent cultivation of that Christianity which derives its freshness, its vigor, and its radiance, from much hidden communion with Jesus. We plead not for the religion of the recluse. A monkish Christianity is not the Christianity of the Bible. When God, in the exercise of His sovereign grace, converts a man, He converts him, not for himself only, but also for others. He converts him, not for the Church alone, but also for the world. He is to be a monument, whose inscription all may read—a city whose beauty all may admire—a burning and a shining light, in whose radiance all may rejoice. He is to live and labor, and, if need be, die for others. But we plead for more of that Christianity which is often alone with God: which withdraws at periods from the fatigue of labor and the din of strife, to renew its strength, and to replenish its resources, in a secret waiting upon the Lord. Christians must be more alone with Jesus. In the midst of what a whirlpool of excitement and of turmoil do numbers live! How few withdraw from domestic and public enjoyments—the calls of business, the duties of committees, of secretaryships, and of agencies—to hold communion alone with God! This must not be. The institutions which they serve, the calling at which they toil, the families for whom they labor, would be the gainers, rather than the losers, by their occasional sequesterment from the world, to be alone with God. And were our Lord still upon the earth, contemplating their incessant action, their little devotional retirement, and consequent leanness of spirit, would He not be constrained to address them as He once tenderly did His jaded and exhausted disciples, "Come you yourselves apart into a desert place, and rest awhile." He would allure them from others to Himself.

Do not be surprised at any way which the Lord may take to bring your weary soul to rest in Himself. It is not always in the crowd that He speaks most tenderly to the heart. More frequently He leads His people out, and takes them apart by Himself alone. It is often in the privacy of separation and retirement, when the soul is curtained within his pavilion, that the greatest and the sweetest nearness to Jesus is experienced. "Behold, I will allure her into the wilderness, and speak comfortably to her,"—(margin, speak friendly to her heart). Has the Lord been leading you about—severing this tie, and breaking up that repose; disappointing you here, and thwarting you there? Amazed, you have asked, "Lord, why this?" And the only reply has been the comfort which He has spoken to your weary, desolate heart. Thus does He make good in your experience His own exceeding great and precious promise—"I have satiated the weary soul, and I have replenished every sorrowful soul."

MARCH 31

For the Lord takes pleasure in his people: he will beautify the meek with salvation. Psalm 149:4

YES, God delights in the people of His love. They are precious, inconceivably precious, to His heart. He keeps them as the apple of His eye. Their people in their own view may be vile, polluted, worthless; but seen by Him in Jesus, He can, and He does, say to each one, "You are all fair, my love; I see no spot in you." Resting in Jesus, the Son of His love, He rests in His people, the objects of His love. He may afflict and chasten, rebuke and try them, or permit them to be severely assailed; He may even hide His face from them for a little moment, and speak harshly to them, like Joseph to his brethren; He may disturb their resting-places, and scatter their creature-mercies to the winds—nevertheless, you saints of God, "The Lord your God in the midst of you is mighty; He will save, He will rejoice over you with joy; He will rest in His love, He will joy over you with singing." Nor will He be satisfied until He has gathered them all around Him within His house in heaven—Jesus presenting to Him the whole body, "a glorious Church," exclaiming, "Behold I and the children whom You have given me." Then, and not until then, will the joy of the Lord over His Church be full. Then, and not until then, will His rest in the people of His love be complete.

God delights in the manifestation of His love. Even in our fallen state, with our impaired affections clinging to us, like the green ivy around a splendid ruin, we can understand something of this feeling. If love exists, where is the heart that can conceal the affection? It must, in some mode or other, express the sentiment it feels. If revealed only to God, the heart must unburden itself of its hidden, trembling emotion. But how delightful is the expression of affection! The parent feels it when he presses his little one to his fond heart; the mother, when she clasps her infant to her thrilling bosom; the friend, when he communes with his friend. But if this principle be so strong, and its expression so delightful, in such a nature as ours, all of whose affections are so sinful and selfish, what must it be in God! Conceive, if it is possible, what must be the holy delight of God's heart in lavishing its affection upon His people; what must be the joy of Christ when He comes and manifests Himself to His saints, as He does not unto the world. A benevolent mind delights in the exercise of benevolence. God is infinitely so. Infinite, therefore, must be the satisfaction of His heart, intense the delight of His soul, when He sheds abroad His love in the hearts of His people, when he draws near in the day that they call upon Him, and manifests Himself as a loving, tender, faithful Father. "You meet him that rejoices and works righteousness, those that remember You in Your ways." Since then the Father delights to unlock the springs of His love, and to fill the heart to overflowing, take your poor, timid, doubting heart, and place it beneath those springs, that it may be perfect in love—and perfected in love, all slavish fear will be expelled.

APRIL

APRIL 1

Behold, God is great, and we know him not, neither can the number of his years be searched out. Job 36:26

THERE is a state of mind often enfeebling to the exercise of prayer, arising from the difficulty of forming proper views of the spiritual nature of the Divine object of prayer. The spirituality of God, through the weakness of our nature, has been felt to be, by some, a stumbling-block in the approach of the soul. "God is a Spirit," is a solemn announcement that meets it at the very threshold, and so completely overawes and abashes the mind, as to congeal every current of thought and of feeling, and well-near to crush the soul with its inconceivable idea. Nor is this surprising. Prayer is the approach of finity to Infinity; and although it is the communing of spirit with Spirit, yet it is the finite communing with the Infinite, and that through the organs of sense. Is it any marvel, then, that at periods a believer should be baffled in his endeavor to form some just conception of the Divine existence, some faint idea of the nature of that God to whom his soul addresses itself; and, failing in the attempt, should turn away in sadness, sorrow, and despair?

The remedy for this state of mind, we believe, is at hand. It is simply scriptural. That we can enlarge our thoughts with any adequate idea of the nature and the appearance of the Divine Spirit is an utter impossibility. He that attempts it, and thinks he has succeeded, lives in the region of fancy, and opposes himself to the revelation of God Himself, which expressly declares, "No man has seen God at any time." "Who only has immortality, dwelling in the light which no man can approach unto; whom no man has seen, nor can see." This being then admitted, as it must be by all reflective minds, the question arises, "How am I to view God? what idea am I to form of His existence in approaching Him in prayer?" In reply, two things are necessary in getting proper thoughts of God as the object of prayer. First, that the mind should resign all its attempts to comprehend the mode of the Divine existence, and should concentrate all its powers upon the contemplation of the character of the Divine existence. In what relation God stands to the creature, not in what way He exists in Himself, is the point with which we have to do in approaching Him. Let the mind be wrapped in devout contemplations of His holiness, benevolence, love, truth, wisdom, justice, &c., and there will be no room for vain and fruitless imaginations respecting the fathomless and inconceivable mode of His existence. The second thing necessary is, that the mind should view God in Christ.

APRIL 2

He that has seen me has seen the Father; and how say you then, Show us the Father? John 14:9.

IF the mind is baffled and perplexed, as it surely will be, in its attempts to unravel the spiritual nature of God, let it seek a resting-place in the "incarnate mystery." This was one part of the gracious design of God in assuming human nature. It was to bring, so to speak, the Infinite in a direct angle with the finite, so that the two lines should not merely run parallel, but that the two extremes of being should meet. It was so to embody His essential and surpassing glories, as would present an object which man could contemplate without fear, worship without distraction, and look upon and not die. The Lord Jesus Christ is "the image of the invisible God," "the brightness of His glory, the express image of His person." "He that has seen me (His own declaration), has seen the Father." Wondrous stoop of the great God! In all approach to God then, in prayer, as in every other kindred exercise, let the eye of faith be fixed upon Him who fills the middle seat upon the throne—the Day's-Man—the Mediator—the incarnate Son of God! How quieting to the mind of a praying soul is this view of God! What a mildness invests the throne of grace, and what an easy access to it presents itself, when the eye of faith can behold "the glory of God in the face of Jesus Christ" If the mind be embarrassed in its attempt to conceive an idea of His spiritual nature, it can soothe itself to repose in a believing view of the glorified humanity of Jesus, "God manifest in the flesh." To this resting-place He Himself invites the soul, "I am the way, the truth, and the life: no man comes unto the Father, but by me." And thus, too, He calmed the fears of His exiled servant, who, when the splendor of His glorified humanity broke upon his view, fell prostrate to the earth: "And when I sate Him," says John, "I fell at his feet as dead, and He laid His right hand upon me, saying unto me, Fear not; I am the first and the last: I am He that lives, and was dead; and behold, I am alive for evermore, Amen; and have the keys of hell and of death."

There is no access to God but through Jesus. If there do not be an honoring of Christ in His person, blood, righteousness, intercession, in prayer, we can expect no answer to prayer. The great encouragement to draw near to God is Jesus at the right hand of God. Jesus is the door. Coming through Him, the poorest, the vilest, the most abject, may approach the throne of grace, and ask what He will. The glorious Advocate is on the throne, to present the petition, and urge its acceptance, and plead for its answer on the basis of His own infinite, atoning merits. Come then, you poor; come, you disconsolate; come, you tried and afflicted; come, you wounded; come, you needy; come and welcome to the mercy-seat; for Jesus waits to present your petition and press your suit. Ask nothing in your own name, but ask everything in the name of Jesus; "ask and you shall receive, that your joy may be full." The Father may reject you, but His Son He cannot reject.

APRIL 3

And that he died for all, that they which live should not henceforth live unto themselves, but unto him which died for them, and rose again. *2 Cor. 5:15.*

How high the obligation to live to God! Are we born again? Can we think of the "horrible pit, the miry clay,"—the "valley of bones,"—the "rock where we were hewn,"—and then remember that if we are born again, we have in our souls, at this moment, the buddings of eternal life?—oh, can we think of this, and not desire an unreserved surrender of all we are, and all we have, to God? Christian! watch over your principles—your daily walk—your communion with the world, and see that the evidences of the new birth signalize every action of your life. The world is a close observer. Narrowly and vigilantly are you watched. It weighs your actions, scrutinizes your motive, sifts your principles, and ponders all your steps, waiting for your halting. Disappoint it! Live out your religion, carry out your principles; they are designed not merely for the Sabbath, but for the week—not merely to be exhibited in the place and at the hour of prayer and social Christian communion, but they are to be carried into Four haunts of business, into your shop, your countinghouse, your study, your profession; you are to exhibit them, not in a spirit of vain-glory, but in "lowliness of mind," in all your communion with a world lying in wickedness. To be born again! oh, it is a mighty work! Let the evidences of its reality in you be such as shall compel the gain-sayer to admire the work, though He may hate the change. Oh, be in spirit—in temper—in life—like Jesus.

What have you not to praise God for, tried and afflicted reader! Born again! Now light are your afflictions, when compared with this! Take the scales, and weigh the two. Place in one your every sorrow. Is it domestic?—place it there. Is it personal—a nervous frame, a feeble constitution, trying circumstances?—place it there. Are friends unfaithful, are saints unkind, does the world frown?—place it all there. Then in the other cast your hidden life—your sense of pardon—your hope of heaven; these outweigh them all. "For I reckon," says Paul, "that the sufferings of this present time are not worthy to be compared with the glory which shall be revealed in us."

APRIL 4

Because you say, I am rich, and increased with goods, and have need of nothing; and know not that you are wretched, and miserable, and poor, and blind, and naked: I counsel you to buy of me gold tried in the fire, that you may be rich; and white clothing, that you may be clothed, and that the shame of your nakedness do not appear; and anoint your eyes with eye salve, that you may see. Rev. 3:17-18

SUCH is the fallen condition of the soul—such its poverty, ignorance, and infirmity, it knows not its real weakness and deep necessity—until taught it by the Holy Spirit. This is even so after conversion. A dear child of God (and it is awfully true, without any qualification, of an unrenewed man) may fall into the state of the Laodicean church; a believer may not know his real condition, his absolute need. There may be a secret declension in his soul—the enfeebling and decay of some spiritual grace—the slow but effectual inroad of some spiritual enemy—the cherishing of some Achan—the feeding of some worm at the root of his holiness, and all the while he may remain ignorant of the solemn fact. And how is he to know it, unless some one teach him? And who is that teacher but the Spirit? As He first convinced of sin, so, in each successive stage of the believer's experience, He convinces of the daily want, the spiritual necessity, the growing infirmity, the increasing power of sin, and the deepening poverty. Overlook not this important part of His work. To go to the throne of grace, we must have something to go for—some errand, to take us there, some sin to confess, some guilt to mourn over, some want to supply, some infirmity to make known, nor would we leave out—some blessing to acknowledge. How is all this to be effected, but by the blessed Spirit? Oh what an unspeakable mercy to have One who knows us altogether, and who can make us acquainted with ourselves!

It is a far advanced step in grace, when we know our real undisguised condition. A man may lose a grace, and may travel far, and not be sensible of his loss. The world has come in, and filled up the space. Some carnal joy or pursuit has occupied the mind, engrossed the affections and the thoughts; and the soul has not been sensible of the loss it has sustained. Thus have many lost the sense of adoption, and pardon, and acceptance—and the graces of faith, of love, of humility, have become enfeebled, until the description of Ephraim may truly and painfully apply to them—"Ephraim he has mixed himself among the people; Ephraim is a cake not turned. Strangers have devoured his strength, and he knows it not; yes, grey hairs are here and there upon him, yet he knows it not." But the blessed Spirit at length discovers to the soul its loss, convinces it of its departure, makes known its real condition, and in this way leads it to the throne of grace. Dear reader, cherish high views of this work of the Spirit. To have One near at hand, yes, in you, as He is, to detect so faithfully and lovingly, as He does, the waning grace, the feeble pulse, the spiritual decay; to awaken sensibility, godly sorrow, and draw out the heart in confession, is to possess one of the most costly blessings. Honor the blessed Spirit, laud Him for His work, extol His faithfulness and love, and treat Him as your tenderest, dearest Friend.

APRIL 5

If a man say, I love God, and hates his brother, he is liar: for he that loves not his brother whom he has seen, how can he love God whom he has not seen? 1 John 4:20.

HERE is a test of relationship to the family of God which never fails. "We know that we have passed from death unto life, because we love the brethren." From this the weakest believer may extract the greatest consolation. Other evidences, beloved, may be beclouded. Divine knowledge may be deficient, Christian experience may be limited, and the question, "Am I a child of God?" may long have been one of painful doubt; but here is an evidence which cannot deceive. You may doubt your love to God, but your love to His people, as such, proves the existence and the reality of your love to Him. Your attachment to them, because they are holy, is an evidence of your own holiness, which no power can invalidate or set aside. Since the Holy Spirit has constituted it as evidence, and since God admits it as such, we press its comfort, with all the energy which we possess, upon the heart of the doubting, trembling child of God.

You may often have questioned the reality of your love to God, scarcely daring to claim an affection so great as this. Your attachment to Jesus, so inconstant, so wavering, and so cold, may often have raised the anxious fear and the perplexing doubt. But your love to the people of God has been like a sheet-anchor to your soul. This you have not questioned, and you could not doubt. You have loved them because they were the people of God; you have felt an attachment to them because they were the disciples of Christ. What does this prove, but your love to God, your affection to Jesus, and your own participation in the same Divine nature? It were a thing impossible for you to love that which is holy, without a corresponding principle of holiness in yourself. Speaking of the enmity of the ungodly against His people, our Lord employs this language; "If you were of the world, the world would love his own; but because you are not of the world, but I have chosen you out of the world, therefore the world hates you." Now, if there is the opposite feeling to this glowing in your hearts, be sure that, as the hatred of the world to the saints proves that it loves only its own, so your love to the saints places the fact of your union with them beyond all doubt. Try your heart, beloved, by this test. Do you not love the people of God, because they are His people? Is not Christ's image in those who upon which you so delight to gaze, and gazing upon which, often enkindles your soul with love to Christ Himself? Do you not love to cull the choicest flowers of grace in the Lord's garden—growing in what bed they may—as those in whom your soul has the greatest delight—their different tints, their varied beauties and odors, rather increasing, than diminishing, the pleasure which they afford you? Then, let every Christian professor test his religion by this grace. Let him who has been used to retire within his own narrow enclosure ask himself the question, "If I love not my brother whom I have seen, how can I love God whom I have not seen?"

APRIL 6

And whether one member suffer, all the members suffer with it; or one member be honored, all the members rejoice with it. Now you are the body of Christ, and members in particular. 1 Cor. 12:26, 27.

IN this exercise of Christian sympathy "the members have the same care one for another." The Church of God is a suffering Church. All the members are more or less and variously tried. Many are the burdens of the saints. It would be impossible, we think, to find one whose lip has not touched the cup of sorrow, whose spirit has not felt the pressure of trouble. Some walk in doubt and darkness—some are particularly set up as a mark for Satan—some suffer from a nervous temperament, discoloring every bright and beautiful picture of life—some are the subjects of personal affliction, pining sickness excluding them from all participation in the songs of Zion and the solemn assemblies of the saints—some are bereaved, sorrowing like Rachel for her children, or mourning like the sisters of Bethany for their brother. Some are suffering from narrowed and exhausted resources; and there may do not be a few suffering even from actual want itself. Ah! how many will say, "You have touched upon every sorrow but mine,"—so extensive is the field of Christian sympathy! But what scope for the play of those heaven-born affections exists in the heart of each true believer! "A new commandment give I unto you," says Christ, "that you love one another." And how is this commandment to be obeyed? The apostle answers, "Bear you one another's burdens, and so fulfil the law of Christ." Therefore the bearing of one another's burdens is a necessary effect and proper exercise of this holy love. It will delight to recognize the suffering Savior in His suffering members. It will go and lift the pressure from the spirit, chase the sorrow from the heart, dry the tear from the eye, and supply the pressing need. Or if it cannot accomplish this, it will take its place by the side of the sufferer, sharing the sorrow and the want it has no power to comfort or remove. Is this law of Christ—the law of love—thus exhibited in you?

Christian forbearance is another beautiful exhibition of this feeling. The image of God is but imperfectly restored in the renewed soul. The resemblance to Christ, in the most matured believer, is at best but a faint copy. In our communion with the saints of God, we often meet with much that calls for the exercise of our indulgence; many weaknesses of the flesh and of the spirit, and many peculiarities of thought and of manner. There are, too, diversities of gifts and degrees of grace. Some are more deeply taught than others—some are strong and some are weak—some travel rapidly, and others slowly—some are fearless and intrepid, others are timid and scrupulous. Now all these things call for the exercise of Christian forbearance. The apostle clearly defines the rule that should guide us here: "We that are strong ought to bear the infirmities of the weak, and not to please ourselves."

APRIL 7

I know your works, that you have a name that you live, and are dead. Rev.3:1.

IN a land where the institutions and the ordinances of religion are so strictly and so properly observed—where religious training from infancy, the habit of an early connection with the visible Church, and the consequent observance of the Lord's Supper expected and enjoined, are such marked characteristics—would it be overstepping the bounds of propriety and delicacy, if we press upon the professing reader the importance of close self-examination, and of trial by the word of God, touching the great change, apart from which the most splendid

Christian profession will but resemble the purple robes and the fine linen with which Dives moved in grandeur and in state to the torments of the lost. Professors of religion!—Church communicants!—office-bearers!—have you the root of the matter in you? Have you Christ in you? Are you temples of the Holy Spirit? Are you walking humbly with God? Are you born from above? Rest not short of the great change—the heavenly, the divine birth. Place no reliance upon your external relation to the Church of God. Do not be deceived by a false semblance of conversion. You may go far in a Christian profession, and even may live to see the Lord come in the air, and yet have not one drop of "oil in your vessel with your lamp."

Have you sometimes trembled under the powerful exhibition of the truth? so did Felix, and yet he never truly repented! Have you heard the Gospel gladly, and under its momentary influence have done many things? so did Herod, and yet he kept Herodias, and beheaded John! Do you show much apparent zeal for the Lord? so did Jehu, but it was zeal for himself! Are you the associate and the companion of good and holy men? so was Demas, and yet he loved this present evil world. Have you been united to the Church upon a profession of faith and by baptism? so was Simon Magus, and yet he was in the gall of bitterness and in the bond of iniquity. Do you desire to die the death of the righteous? so did Balaam, and yet he died as the fool dies! Oh, look well to your religion. Take nothing for granted. Think less of burnishing your "lamp," than of having a large supply of oil, that when the Lord sends or comes, you may not be found in darkness, not knowing where you go. Without converting grace in your heart, your Church relation is but the union of a dead branch to a living stem; and your partaking of the Lord's Supper, an "eating and drinking of the Lord's body and blood (as symbolically represented therein) unworthily." Receive in love these faithful admonitions, penned by one whose only hope, as the chief of sinners, is in the finished work of Immanuel, and let them take you to prayer—to the Word—to Christ.

APRIL 8

For our conversation is in heaven; from where also we look for the Savior, the Lord Jesus Christ. Philip. 3:20.

HEAVENLY-MINDEDNESS can only be maintained by the strictest vigilance. It is a delicate and fragile flower, susceptible of every variation of the spiritual atmosphere. Guard against that which checks its growth. Many are not aware how much great exuberance of spirits, light conversation, foolish jesting, witticisms at the expense of Scripture sanctity, novel reading, carnal music, unfit the heart for communion with God, and lessen the tone of its spirituality. Close communion with mere nominal religious professors is particularly to be avoided. Much more injury to spiritual-mindedness accrues from intimate friendship with such, than from those who assert no pretensions to a religious character; as with the one we are apt to be less on our guard than the other. Avoid the world's amusements; they will eat as a canker into the very core of your spirituality. "Do not be conformed to this world," is a prohibition—"Our conversation is in heaven," is an exhortation, which should never be absent from the eye of a traveler to the heavenly city.

And why should not our conversation be in heaven? Are not its attractions many and powerful? It is a holy place, and it is the place of the holy. There is the city of the living God, the heavenly Jerusalem; an innumerable company of angels, and the general assembly and church of the first-born, which are written in heaven; God the Judge of all, the spirits of just men made perfect, and Jesus the Mediator of the new covenant. How rich is heaven! And there we, too, will shortly be. Why, then, should not our conversation be there? It will be recollected that when the high priest entered within the veil, bearing in his hands the blood of atonement and the smoking censer, the eyes of the congregation who stood without followed him to the entrance as the curtain parted, and then veiled him from their gaze. Many a thrilling heart and trembling hope followed him within that holy place, its fervent sympathies clustering around him while he presented the offerings, and made intercession for the people. And many a longing eye intently and fondly watched for his return, when, with uplifted hands, he would bless the waiting congregation. Our great High Priest has passed within the veil. As our Advocate, he fills heaven's high chancery. He loves us—remembers us—sympathizes with us—intercedes for us—and wears our names on His breastplate and His ephod. Soon He will return in person, to bless with the first-resurrection glory all those who "love His appearing." Oh! shall not our hearts be more where our most precious treasure is, where our holiest and dearest hopes center, and where we ourselves shall shortly be? The Lord grant that we may increasingly experience, that "to be spiritually-minded is life and peace;" and in order to attain to this blessed state, we must live upon the Lord Jesus—be filled with the Spirit—be often at God's confessional—and, taking up our cross daily, be pressing onward and upward—"denying all ungodliness and worldly lusts, and living soberly, righteously, and godly in this present world; looking for that blessed hope, and the glorious appearing of the great God and our Savior Jesus Christ; who gave Himself for us, that He might redeem us from all iniquity, and purify unto Himself a peculiar people, zealous of good works."

APRIL 9

Hear, O Israel: The Lord our God is one Lord and you shall love the Lord your God with all your heart, and with all your soul, and with all your might. Deut. 6:4, 5.

IN nothing has God acted more worthily of His nature, than in constituting love as the soul and essence of religion, and Himself its supreme object. In doing so, He has as much consulted the happiness of the creature as His own honor; as much our benefit as His glory. Indeed it would seem as if, in enjoining the obligation, in issuing the requirement of our motto, He had a view to our happiness beyond every other end. Apart from the honor which accrues to Him from our obedience to this precept, what advantage can He derive from our affection? Himself the infinite sea of love, full to the eternal satisfaction of His own nature, what good could arise to Him from the tribute of affection poured from every heart? But He would bring us to a more perfect enjoyment of Himself, by bringing us to love Him with a supreme affection. He who loves God, walks with God, dwells with God, is like God. He has not far to travel in order to find God. Let him look within upon his own tranquil conscience, let him wander through the illuminated chambers of his own soul, and there, in finding love, he finds God. If love is not there, neither is God there; for where love is, there is God enthroned upon the heart. "God is love; and he that dwells in love dwells in God, and God in him."

It is, then, the great characteristic of true believers, that they love God. Their love embraces each person in the Godhead. They love the Father—for to Him they are indebted for His unspeakable gift. They love the Son—for to Him they owe their redemption. They love the Spirit—for having renewed them, He dwells in them forever as His temple. Such are all the children of God. Oh the blessedness they feel in loving God in Christ! Oh the happiness that springs from this divine, this heavenly emotion, expanding, purifying, and ennobling the soul! They ascribe its possession to no motive existing in themselves; but, with the apostle, are ever ready to acknowledge, "We love Him, because He first loved us." It is true, their love to God, the Triune God, is at best but an imperfect emotion, mingling with a thousand frailties, an affection unworthy of themselves, still more deeply unworthy of Him, yet they love Him sincerely; He has drawn their hearts, has overcome them by His grace, and they are enabled to say, "Whom have I in heaven but You? and there is none upon earth whom I desire in comparison with You."

The deathlessness of love to God is a beautiful idea of Scripture. Every other grace will cease but that of love. Faith!—that precious grace which has been as the sheet-anchor of our soul in the wildest storms; which, as our compass, has steered us through the deep billows, and brought us in safety to the port; which, amid all the trials, needs, and perils of the way, was so great and so sweet a solace—when we reach the world of glory we shall need it no more, for faith must then give place to sight. Hope!—that pole-star of the soul, which cheered us with its mild luster many a weary step of our desolate journey, gilding the dark pictures of our earthly pilgrimage with its heavenly brightness, and alluring us on to the heaven from where it shone—when we reach the world of glory we shall want it no more, for hope will terminate in full fruition. But Love will live forever! It will tread with us the dark valley, it will cross with us the swelling river, and enter with us into the realms of eternal blessedness—its home, from where it came, and where it again returns. "Whether there be prophecies, they shall fail; whether there be tongues, they shall cease; whether there be knowledge, it shall vanish away." But "Love never fails," it lives forever.

APRIL 10

And of his fullness have all we received, and grace for grace. John 1:16.

THE word fullness in this passage is sometimes employed to express the idea of abundance. "The earth is the Lord's, and the fullness thereof;" that is, the abundance of the earth is the Lord's. But in this connection it has a meaning still more impressive. It signifies not only the fullness of abundance, but the fullness of redundance. The vessel is not only full to the brim, but it runs over, and rushes on in ten thousand streams to the utmost limit of man's necessities. Such a redundance of grace was required to bring God and the sinner together. The gulf which separated these two extremes of being was just that which separates the bottomless pit in hell from the highest throne in glory. No finite being could annihilate it. All the resources of wisdom, and power, and benevolence of all the angels in heaven could not bridge it. But the redundant grace that is in Christ Jesus has crossed this gulf, and God and man meet and are reconciled in one Mediator. And now from the glorious heights of pardoning grace on which he stands, the sinner can look down upon a hell deserved, but a hell escaped.

Such a redundant fullness of grace was never seen until Jesus appeared. The patriarchs and prophets saw this grace, but not as we are privileged to see it. They realized its sufficiency, but not its redundancy. The truth was revealed to them, but by degrees. The light beamed in upon their minds, but in solitary rays. The grace distilled, rather than flowed. They had the dew, rather than the showers of grace. And yet it was sufficient to meet their case. When Jehovah opened this fountain of grace to two of the greatest sinners the world ever saw, and declared that "the seed of the woman should bruise the serpent's head," dim and partial as was the discovery, it was sufficient to lift them from the dark borders of despair and of hell, into the sunny region of hope and of heaven. Thus the saints of the former dispensation saw this grace, but not so clearly as we see it. They dwelt amid the shadows, we in the full blaze of glory. They lived in the twilight of grace, but we in its meridian day. They had the law, but we have the gospel. They had grace in the hands of Moses, but we have grace in the hands of Jesus. They were the "children of the bondwoman," but we are the "children of the free-woman." They had the "spirit of bondage unto fear," but we have the "spirit of adoption " unto love. And one passage will explain the reason of this great difference: "God, who at sundry times and in diverse manners spoke in time past unto the fathers by the prophets, has in these last days spoken unto us by His Son." Spoken unto us by His Son! Behold the fullness, the redundance, the sufficiency of this grace! "The law was given by Moses, but grace and truth came by Jesus Christ."

Such, reader, is the fullness of Jesus—this Divine Vessel of grace. And now, if this grace were sufficient for God—sufficient to enable Him to extend mercy to the utmost, to sinners the vilest, and yet remain strictly just—then, I ask, is it not sufficient, my reader, for you? If God, on the basis of this grace, can come forward and extend His hand of reconciliation to you, may you not with the plea of this same grace advance and extend your hand of faith to God? If there is no difficulty or reluctance on the part of God, why should there be on the part of man? And has God ever hesitated? Has He ever refused on the footing of Christ's merits to save the penitent sinner, who, having heard that the King of heaven is a merciful King, has cast himself upon that mercy, like the servants of Benhadad, with sackcloth upon their loins, and ashes upon their head, humbly suing for life? Never! It is the delight of God, as it is His glory, to prove the power and the sufficiency of His grace in Christ Jesus, to save man to the uttermost extent of his guiltiness and woe. How overflowing with saving grace does the heart of God appear in these words: "Let the wicked forsake his way, and the unrighteous man his thoughts: and let him return unto the Lord, and He will have mercy upon him; and to our God, for He will abundantly pardon!" Oh, place your empty vessel beneath this overflowing fountain of grace! and remove it not until, in its measure, it becomes the "fullness of Him who fills all in all."

APRIL 11

Verily, verily, I say unto you, Whatever you shall ask the Father in my name, he will give it you. John 16:23

THAT God should have erected in this lower world a throne of grace, a mercy-seat, around which may gather, in clustering and welcome multitudes, the helpless, the burdened, the friendless, the vile, the guilty, the deeply necessitous—that no poor comer, be his poverty never so great, his burden never so heavy, or his case never so desperate, should meet with the refusal of a hearing or a welcome, does greatly develop and magnify the riches of His grace, His wisdom, and His love to sinners. What a God our God must be, thus to have appointed a meeting-place, an audience-chamber, for those upon whom all other doors were closed! But more than this,

That He should have appointed Jesus the door of approach to that throne—should have given His only-begotten and well-beloved Son to be the "new and living way" of access, thus removing all obstruction in the path of the soul's coming, both on the part of Himself, and on the part of the sinner; that the door should be a crucified Savior—the wounds of the Son of God—that through blood, and that blood the blood of the incarnate Deity, the guilty should approach—wonder, O heavens, and be astonished, O earth! Shall we say even more than this? For there is a yet lower depth in this love and condescension of God—that He should have sent His Spirit into the heart, the Author of prayer, inditing the petition—breathing in the soul—implanting the desire—convincing of the existing necessity—unfolding the character of God—working faith in the heart—and drawing it up to God through Jesus—seems the very perfection of His wisdom, benevolence, and grace.

It must be acknowledged by the spiritual mind that all true prayer is of the inditing of the Spirit—that He is the Author of all real approach of the soul to God. And yet how perpetually we need to be reminded of this! Prayer is one of the most spiritual employments that can possibly engage the mind. It is that holy act of the soul which brings it immediately in contact with a holy God. It has more directly to do with the "high and lofty One" than any other exercise. It is that state of mind, too, that most deeply acknowledges its dependence on God. Prayer is the expression of want—it is the desire of need, the acknowledgment of poverty—the language of dependence—the breathing of a soul that has nothing in itself, but hangs on God for all it needs. It must therefore be a highly spiritual and holy exercise. But still more so will this appear, if we consider that true prayer is the breathing of the life of God in the soul of man. It is the Spirit dwelling and breathing in him. It is the new nature pouring out its vital principle, and that into the ear of God where it came. It is the cry of the feeble child turning to the Father it loves, and in all its conscious weakness, dependence, and need, pouring out the yearnings of its full heart into the bosom where dwells nothing but love. In a word, it is God and the creature meeting and blending, in one act of blessed, holy, and eternal fellowship.

APRIL 12

God gives not the Spirit by measure unto him. John 3:34.

WE needed just such a glorious head of His Church as Jesus. Moses could not have done; Aaron could not have sufficed. We wanted a head in whom "dwelt all the fullness of the Godhead bodily." We needed One not only "filled with the Spirit," but possessing it illimitably, even without measure; with sufficient not only for Himself, but for a poor needy people, who as empty vessels should hang upon Him as their true Eliakim. In Him there was no lack of the Spirit's anointing. And oh how much of that Spirit needed He Himself in order to work out the great problem of man's recovery! How could He have accomplished it, considered in His inferior nature as man, but as He was replenished or sustained by the supernatural grace of the Spirit! As the Head of the Church, then, expect from a source so full, so rich, and so ample, all spiritual blessings. With Him is "the residue of the Spirit." He is our true Aaron, whose anointing flows down to His feet in streams of grace, adequate to the deepest necessity of the most feeble and lowly believer. To that fullness repair, nothing doubting of a welcome and a blessing. There was a sufficiency of the Spirit in Christ for Himself, and there is a sufficiency in Him for you. Come, then, and receive "grace for grace,"—grace needed by you, equal to all grace dwelling in Him.

A solemn inference from this subject is—if our blessed and adorable Lord needed the Spirit, how much more do His people! If He needed Him to strengthen, to comfort, to uphold, to teach, to anoint, how much deeper is our necessity of the same exalted blessing! He had no human sinful infirmity; there was no conflict in His soul between the antagonist principles of sin and holiness; and yet as man He was a pensioner each moment upon the sanctifying, teaching, upholding grace of the Spirit, His deity operating by this divine and glorious Agent. But our need of the same Spirit, oh how infinitely greater! We are encompassed with innumerable sinful infirmities; we have a law in our members warring against the law of our mind, and bringing us into captivity to the law of sin which is in our members. We are constantly assailed by Satan, and as constantly liable to yield. Oh with what power, and constant actings of faith, should we throw ourselves upon the Spirit! How ceaselessly should we pray to Him with all supplication, imploring His guiding, teaching, sealing, comforting grace, to help us in every time of need!

APRIL 13

In whom also after that you believed, you were sealed with that Holy Spirit of promise. Eph. 1:13.

WHAT do we understand by the sealing of the Spirit? What does the word of God teach upon the subject? There are various passages in which the same figure is employed, but which do not convey the idea we ascribe to His present operation. For example, there is a sealing spoken of in 2 Timothy 2:19: "Nevertheless the foundation of God stands sure, having this seal, The Lord knows those who are His." We think it clear that the seal here alluded to has respect to the Father's sealing His people in election with the seal of His foreknowledge, which, of course, is an operation anterior to the existence of faith in the soul, and is within Himself, and not upon them. It is, so to speak, His secret designation of His people, known especially and only to Himself. There is also a sealing spoken of in Sol. Song 8:6: "Set me as a seal upon your heart, as a seal upon your arm: for love is strong as death." Equally clear is it that this cannot refer to the work of the Spirit, but to Christ's strong and unchangeable love to His people. They are set as a seal upon His heart, the dwelling-place of love, and upon His arm, the instrument of power; unchangeable love and omnipotent power being pledged to their eternal security. As a seal set upon His heart, and worn upon His arm, they are precious to, and valued by, Him.

Nor are we to interpret the sealing under consideration to mean the extraordinary gifts of the Spirit; for it is a remarkable fact, which speaks solemnly to those who are forming a higher estimate of gifts than of graces—that the Corinthian Church, the most distinguished for its possession of the gifts of the Spirit, was at the same time most remarkable for its lack of the sanctifying graces of the Spirit. It was the most gifted, but at the same time the least holy, community gathered and planted by the apostles.

The question still recurs—what are we to understand by the sealing of the Spirit? It is that act of the Holy Spirit, by which the work of grace is deepened in the heart of the believer, so that he has an increasing and abiding conviction of his acceptance in Jesus, and his adoption into the family of God. It is a clearer and more undoubted manifestation of Christ to the soul—a larger degree of the sanctifying, witnessing, and anointing influences of the Holy Spirit—evidencing itself in a growing holiness of character. Let us not be misunderstood. We speak not of some peculiar and sudden impulse on the mind—of some immediate suggestion or revelation to the soul—some vision of the night, or voice in the air. No; we speak of a growth in the knowledge of Christ—in sanctification of heart—in holiness of life—in an increasing and abiding moral certainty of the believer's "calling and election." The Holy Spirit is both the seal and the sealer; even as Jesus was both the sacrifice and the priest. He deepens the work of grace in the heart—He witnesses to the believer that he is born of God He seals the soul to the day of redemption, and by His indwelling and anointing influences enables him to say, "I know in whom I have believed. He has loved one, and given Himself for me."

APRIL 14

Whereof the Holy Spirit also is a witness to us. Hebrews 10:15

THIS is sometimes a sudden work of the Spirit. A soul may be so deeply sealed in conversion—may receive such a vivid impression of Divine grace—such an enlarged communication of the Divine Spirit, as it never afterwards loses. It is sealed "unto the day of redemption;" and that, too, in the most simple way: in the hearing of a single sermon, the reading of a single chapter of God's word, some promise brought with the power of the Holy Spirit and sealed upon the heart; in a moment the soul is brought into the full assurance of understanding and of faith. Take for example that one precious promise which the Spirit has sealed, never to be effaced, upon many a poor sinner's softened heart—"him that comes to me I will in no wise cast out." Oh, what a sealing is this! God speaking to a poor, distressed, and disconsolate soul, assuring it of a cordial welcome and of a free pardon—that though no tongue can express its vileness and poverty, and no imagination conceive its deep sorrow, yet, coming to Jesus just as it is, it shall in no wise be cast out! Is not this an impression of the seal in the hands of the great Sealer, which is unto the day of redemption?

Sometimes it is as the Holy Spirit unfolds to the anxious soul that great truth,—that Christ is the Savior of a sinner. You have been long waiting for some reward, some gift, some price with which to come—long lingering at the edge of the fountain, preparing to enter—in other words,—waiting to feel less vile, less unworthy, in order that you may feel more welcome. And then the blessed Spirit opens to your mind that precious truth,—"Christ died for the ungodly," and that He is the mighty and willing Savior of the sinner—that no gift, no price, is asked—no previous fitness or self-preparation is necessary. Oh, what an impression of the seal is this upon a wounded heart! When the glorious announcement is brought home to the soul—a full and free pardon for a poor sinner—the blood of Jesus cleansing from all sin—is it any marvel that no change of time or circumstance can ever obliterate the impression or the remembrance of that moment from the mind? It was a sealing of pardon upon a heart which God had made soft, and which was the sure prelude to, yes, the beginning of, eternal glory.

But, in most cases, the sealing of the Spirit is a more gradual work. It is a work of time. The soul is placed in the school of deep experience—is led on step by step, stage by stage. The knowledge of self and of Christ increases—deeper views of indwelling sin are discovered—the heart's treachery is more acutely felt—the devices of Satan are better known—the mystery of God's gracious and providential dealings with His children more clearly unfolded and better understood—and all this, it may be, arrived at through a process of deep and painful, yet sanctified, discipline of the covenant—so that years may elapse before a child of the covenant attains to the full sealing of the Spirit. And yet, blessed be God, the work of regeneration is so perfect in itself—the blotting out of all a believer's sins so complete, and his justification so entire—that a saint of God dying in the first stages of the Divine life is safe forever. May we not refer to the thief upon the cross, as an example illustrating and confirming this?

APRIL 15

A bruised reed shall he not break, and smoking flax shall he not quench, until he send forth judgment unto victory. Matthew 12:20

SURELY, it is a question of all others the most interesting and important, "Am I, or am I not, a true believer in the Lord Jesus Christ?" We do not say that the state of doubt and uncertainty from which this inquiry arises necessarily invalidates the evidence of grace which already exists; nor would we have it inferred, that the question itself indicates a healthy, vigorous tone of mind. But what we affirm is, that where there exists the principle of life, and a growing acquaintance with the plague of the human heart, with a conscience increasingly tender, the question will sometimes arise—"Am I a living soul in Christ?"

In enabling us to meet and satisfy this inquiry, how kind and condescending is God the Holy Spirit! A state of uncertainty regarding one's personal salvation is not favorable to the cultivation of personal holiness. He is the most heavenly-minded, happy, and useful child of God, who, with the lowly confidence of the great apostle, can say, "I know in whom I have believed." But we must admire the love of the Spirit in providing for the necessities of the weakest state of grace. If saints of advanced stature in Christ can but little sympathize with the timidity, the fearfulness, and the weakness of the tender new believer, not so the loving, faithful Spirit of God. The smallest part is too precious to Him, to allow the neglect of His eye from it for a single moment. It is not the extent of the territory which He has subjugated to Himself in the soul, that most thrills His heart with delight—this He is sure to perfect—but it is His having at all effected an entrance, and established Himself permanently there. This is the ground of his greatest triumph, the source of His highest joy—that after all the opposition and the difficulty, He should at last have gotten Himself the victory. Is it possible, then, that the tenderest bud of grace, or the faintest glimmering of light in the soul, can be a matter of indifference to Him? Ah no! Would Titian have despised a painting, upon whose outline He had stamped the impress of his genius, because its pencilings were not complete? Would Canova have destroyed his sculpture, almost breathing with life, because its chiselings were unfinished? And will the Holy Spirit, in drawing the moral likeness of God upon the soul, in modeling the mind for heaven, slight this, His master-piece of wisdom and of power, because of its present incompleteness? No! The faintest outline of the Divine image, the roughest shaping of the Divine nature in man, presents to His eye more beauty, and symmetry, and skill, than the finest pencilings of nature, or the most perfect modelings of are. The universe of loveliness and of wonder contains nothing that can compare with it.

APRIL 16

For innumerable evils have compassed me about: mine iniquities have taken hold upon me, so that I am not able to look up; they are more than the hairs of mine head: therefore my heart fails me. Psalm 40:12

IN the more advanced stages of the Christian life, we find much into the experience of which the believer is brought, tending to cast down the people of God. Without minutely describing the many causes of soul-unrest which exist, we may group together in one view those, the most fruitful, which conspire to this abasement of the spirit. We may mention, as among the most powerful, the clinging body of sin, to which his renewed spirit is enchained, from which it sighs to be delivered, but from which death only frees it; consequently, there is the daily battle with a heart of unbelief, incessantly departing from God. Then there are the labyrinths of the desert, the straitness of the narrow way, the fears within, and the fightings without, the trials of faith, the chastisements of love, the offence of the cross, the intricacies of truth, the woundings of the world, the unkindnesses of the saints, and the varied difficulties and afflictions of the wilderness—all these create oftentimes great disquietude and despondency of soul. When to these are added the yet more painful and humbling remembrance of his sins since conversion, his stumblings and falls, his unkind requitals of God's love, the base returns which he has made, and the deep ingratitude which he has felt for all the Divine goodness, with the consequent hidings of God's face, and the withdrawments of Christ's presence, he exclaims in the bitterness of his spirit, "My soul is cast down within me;" "my heart fails me."

Ah! there is no humiliation like that which a sight and sense of sin produces, the heart laid open and the soul laid low before God. The world's bitter scorn, the creature's cold neglect, are nothing in comparison. In the one case, the heart is only mortified; in the other, it is truly humbled. The one is a feeling that has to do with man only—the other is an emotion that has to do with God. And when once the believer is solemnly conscious of acting beneath the eye of God, the gaze of other eyes affects him but slightly. Oh how little do some professors deport themselves as though they had to do only with God! How imperfectly do they look upon sin as God looks upon it! But did they live more as setting the Lord always before them, how superior would they rise to the poor opinion of their fellow-sinners! To them it would then appear a very little matter to be judged of man's judgment.

APRIL 17

God, that comforts those that are cast down. 2 Cor. 7:6

IF there is much to cast down the child of God, there is more to lift him up. If in his path to glory there are many causes of soul-despondency, of heart-sorrow, and mental disquietude, yet in that single truth—God comforts the disconsolate—he has an infinite counterbalance of consolation, joy, and hope. That "God comforts those that are cast down," His own truth declares. It is in His heart to comfort them, and it is in His power to comfort them. He blends the desire, deep and yearning, with the ability, infinite and boundless. Not so with the fondest, tenderest creature. The sorrow is often too deep and too sacred for human sympathy to reach. But what is fathomless to man is a shallow to God.

I have said, that it is in the heart of God to comfort His people. Everything that He has done to promote their comfort proves it. He has commanded His ministers to "speak comfortably" to them. He has sent forth His word to comfort them. He has laid up all comfort and consolation for them, in the Son of His love. And in addition to all this, He has given them His own Spirit, to lead them to the Divine sources of "all consolation" which He has provided. Who could comfort the disconsolate but God? Who could effectually undertake their case but Himself? He only knows their sorrow, and He only could meet it. There is not a moment in which God is not bent upon the comfort of "those that are cast clown." All His dealings with them tend to this—even those that appear adverse and contrary. Does He wound?—it is to heal. Does He cause deep sorrow?—it is to turn that sorrow into a deeper joy. Does He empty?—it is to fill. Does He cast down?—it is to lift up again. Such is the love that moves Him, such is the wisdom that guides Him, and such too is the end that is secured in the Lord's disciplinary conduct with His people. Dear reader, it is in God's loving heart to speak comfortably to your sorrowful heart. Let but the Holy Spirit enable you to receive this truth in simple faith, and your grief, be its cause and its degree what they may, is more than half assuaged. Not a word may yet be spoken by the "God of all comfort," not a cloud may be dispersed, nor a difficulty be removed; yet to be assured by the Divine Comforter that the heart of God yearns over you, and that consolation is sparkling up from its infinite depths, waiting only the command to pour its tide of joyousness into your sorrow-stricken bosom, and it is enough. Yes, I repeat it—for every reiteration of so precious a truth must still be but a faint expression of its magnitude—it is in the loving heart of God to lift up your disconsolate soul from the dust. Listen to His words—there is melody in them such as David's harp spoke not when its soft and mellow strains soothed the perturbed spirit of Saul—"I, even I, am He that comforts you." Mark with what earnestness He makes this declaration. How solicitous does he appear to impress this truth upon the heart—that to comfort His own tried saints is His sole prerogative, and His infinite delight. "I, even I, am He that comforts you."

APRIL 18

For our gospel came not unto you in word only, but also in power, and in the Holy Spirit, and in much assurance;...And you became followers of us, and of the Lord, having received the word in much affliction, with joy of the Holy Spirit. 1 Thes. 1:5, 6

THUS does the Spirit of God empty the soul, preparing it for the reception of the grace of Christ. He 'sweeps and garnishes' the house. He dislodges the unlawful inhabitant, dethrones the rival sovereign, and thus secures room for the Savior. He disarms the will of its rebellion against God, the mind of its ignorance, and the heart of its hatred. He prostrates the barrier, removes the veil, and unlocks the door, at which the Redeemer triumphantly enters. In effecting this mighty work, He acts as the Divine Forerunner of Christ. What the Baptist was to our Lord, "crying in the wilderness, Prepare you the way of the Lord," the Holy Spirit is, in heralding the entrance of Jesus to the soul. He goes before, and prepares His way. The Divinity of the Spirit furnishes Him with all the requisites for the work. He meets with difficulty, and He removes it—with obstruction, and He overcomes it—with opposition, and He vanquishes it. His power is omnipotent, His influence is irresistible, His grace is efficacious. There is no soul, however filled with darkness, and enmity, and rebellion, which He cannot prepare for Christ. There is no heart of stone which He cannot break, no brazen wall which He cannot prostrate, no mountain which He cannot level. Oh, for more faith in the power of the Holy Spirit in the soul of man! How much do we limit, and in limiting how do we dishonor, Him in His work of converting grace!

The providential dealings of God are frequently instrumental in the hand of the Holy Spirit of accomplishing this emptying process, thus preparing the soul for the reception of Christ. The prophet thus strikingly alludes to it: "Moab has been at ease from his youth, and He has settled on his lees, and has not been emptied from vessel to vessel." It was in this way God dealt with Naomi. Listen to her touching words: "I went out full, and the Lord has brought me home again empty." Thus it is that the bed of sickness, or the chamber of death, the loss of creature good, perhaps the loveliest and the dearest, has prepared the heart for Christ. The time of bereavement and of solitude, of suffering and of loss, has been the Lord's time of love. Providence is the hand-maid of grace—and God's providential dealings with man are frequently the harbingers of the kingdom of grace in the soul. Ah! how many whose glance falls upon this page may testify "Even thus has the Lord dealt with me. I was rich, and He has impoverished me. I was exalted, and He has laid me low. Not one cup only did He drain, not one vessel only did He dash to the earth, but many. He has emptied me 'from vessel to vessel.' " Happy shall you be if the result of all this emptying and humbling shall be the filling and enriching of your soul with larger communications of grace and truth from Jesus. A cloud of witnesses around you testify to this invariable principle of the Lord's procedure with His people—that He enriches by impoverishing them; strengthens by weakening them; replenishes by emptying; and exalts by laying them low.

APRIL 19

And I looked, and, lo, a Lamb stood on the mount Zion, and with him an hundred forty and four thousand, having his Father's name written in their foreheads. Rev. 14:1

DO NOT FORGET, O believer, that you are journeying to the mount of God, and will soon be there. Behold it in the distance! What wonders encircle it! What glory bathes it! The exile of Patmos, lifting a corner of the veil, has presented it to our view in the words of our motto. Oh what a spectacle of magnificence is this! There is Jesus the Lamb as it had been slain. To Hin every face is turned, on Him every eye is fixed, before Him every knee bends, and every tongue chants His praise, "Worthy is the Lamb that was slain." Around Him are gathering each moment the One Church of God, redeemed from among men. In the light and splendor of the scene all distinctions are absorbed, all minds assimilate, all hearts blend, all voices harmonize, and the grand, visible manifestation of the Unity of the Church is perfected.

To this consummation you are hastening—keep it full in view. Turn not aside, yielding to the enchanting scenes through which you pass; but forgetting the things that are behind, press forward to the mark of the prize of your high calling of God in Christ Jesus. To Mount Zion you will certainly arrive at last. Your feet shall stand upon its summit. Your voice shall blend with its music. Your heart shall thrill with its gladness. Your soul shall bathe in its glory. Oh! kindles not your spirit with ardor, and is not your heart winged with love, while the mount of God unveils its splendor to your view? Speak, Elijah! for you have reached that exaltation, and tell us what it is to be there! No, you cannot tell. You have heard its deep songs of joy—but their strains are unutterable. You have seen its ineffable glory—but that glory is unspeakable. Let but your mantle fall upon us, and a double portion of your spirit be ours, and at our departure let your chariot of fire convey us to the skies, and we will be content to wait and gaze for awhile upon the distant vision—like some early traveler pausing upon the mountain's side to admire the ascending sun, until his features and his vestments borrow the crimson glow—until, "changed into the same image from glory to glory, as by the Spirit of the Lord," we reach it at last, and delight ourselves forever amid its transcendent beams—ceasing from our conflict, and reposing from our toil, in the beatific presence of God!

APRIL 20

When the even was come, they brought unto him many that were possessed with devils: and he cast out the spirits with his word, and healed all that were sick: that it might be fulfilled which was spoken by Elijah the prophet, saying, Himself took our infirmities, and bare our sicknesses. Matthew 8:16, 17

IN one respect only may it be said, that our Divine and adorable Lord would seem to have been exempted from the physical infirmities peculiar to the nature which He so voluntarily and entirely assumed—it does not appear that He was ever, in His own person, the subject of sickness or disease. It is indeed declared by His inspired biographer, thus confirming at the same time a prediction of one of the prophets, "Himself took our infirmities, and bare our sicknesses;" but this He did in the same manner in which He bore our moral sicknesses, without any personal participation. He bore our sins, but He was Himself sinless. He carried our sicknesses, but He Himself was a stranger to disease. And His exemption from the one will explain His exemption from the other. His humanity knew no sin; it was that "holy thing" begotten by the Holy Spirit, and as stainless as God Himself. As sin introduced into our nature every kind of physical evil, and disease among the rest, our Lord's freedom from the cause necessarily left Him free from the effect. He was never sick, because He never sinned. No, He had never died, had He not consented to die. With a nature prepared and conceived totally without moral taint, there were no seeds of decay from which death could reap its harvest. Under no sentence of dissolution, death had no power to claim Him as its victim. As pure as our first parents before the fall, like them in their original state of holiness, He was naturally deathless and immortal. Had He not, by an act of the most stupendous grace, taken upon Him the curse and sin of His Church, thereby making Himself responsible to Divine justice for the utmost payment of her debt, the "bitterness of death" had never touched His lips. But even then His death was voluntary. His relinquishment of life was His own act and deed. The

Jew who hunted Him to the cross, and the Roman by whose hands He died, were but the actors in the awful tragedy. The "king of terrors" wrenched not His spirit from Him. Death waited the permission of Essential Life before he winged the fatal dart. "Jesus yielded up the spirit," literally, made a surrender, or let go His spirit. Thus violent though it was, and responsible for the crime as were its agents, the death of Jesus was yet voluntary. "I lay down lay life," are His expressive words.

The control and power of Christ over bodily disease form one of the most instructive and tender pages of His history when upon earth. We can but briefly refer the reader to a few of the different traits of the Divine Physician's grace, as illustrated by the various cures which He effected. His promptness in healing the nobleman's son, John 4:43—54. His unsolicited cure of the sick man at the pool of Bethesda, and the man with a withered hand, John 5:1—9; Mark 3:1—6. The humility and delicacy with which He heals the centurion's servant, Matt. 8:5—13. The tenderness with which He restored the widow's son, Luke 7:11—17. The simplicity with which He recovered the man born blind, John 9:1—7. The gentle touch with which He cured the man, sick of the dropsy, Luke 14:1—6. The natural and spiritual healing of the paralytic, Luke 5:17—28. The resistless compassion with which He cured the daughter of the Syrophenician woman, Mark 8:24—3O. The wisdom and the authority with which He healed the lunatic child, Luke 9:37—43. The power with which He ejected the demons from the man, permitting their entrance into the swine, Matthew 8:28—34. Truly the name of our Divine Physician is "Wonderful!" All this skill and power and feeling He still possesses; and in their exercise, in His present dealings with His suffering saints, is He glorified.

APRIL 21

And Jesus answering said unto them, Those who are whole need not a physician; but those who are sick. Luke 5:31

THAT Physician is He who spoke these words. The power of the Son of God over the moral and physical diseases of men, prove Him to be just the Physician which our circumstances require. Want we skill? He possesses it. Sympathy? He has it. Patience, tenderness, perseverance? all belong to Jesus. Wonderful Physician! No disease can baffle You, for You are Divine. No suffering can fail to move You, for You are human. Are your deep anxieties awakened, my reader, on behalf of some loved object, now pining in sickness, perhaps, to all appearance, in circumstances of extreme danger? In simple faith call in the aid of this Physician. Let the prayer of Moses for Miriam be yours, presented with the faith and urged with the importunity of the Syrophenician mother, "Heal her now, O Lord, I beseech You." "I will come and heal her," will be His reply. Deem not the case beyond His skill. Thus reasoned the sister of Lazarus: "Lord, if You had been here, my brother had not died. But I know that even now, whatever You will ask of God, God will give it You." Go in prayer and faith, and lay your sick one at His feet. Jesus is with you. One word from Him, and the disease shall vanish; one touch of His hand, and health shall be restored. He who raised Lazarus from the grave, can bring back from its brink the dear one around whose fast-waning life the veins of your heart are entwined. Ask believingly, ask submissively, ask importunately, and then leave the result with Him.

When human power has come to its end—when skill and affection can do no more—when man retires, and hope is extinguished, and the loved one is despairingly abandoned to death—then to see the Lord step forward and take the case in His hands, arresting the disease, rebuking the distemper, bringing back the glow of health to the cheek, vigor to the frame, elasticity to the limb, and brilliance to the eye, raising as from the very grave itself—oh how glorious does He appear in that chamber of sickness! Who bowed down His ear to the whisper that faintly cried for help and support? Who heard the fervent agonizing prayer that that precious life might be spared, which in another room broke from the lips of some anxious, holy wrestler—a parent, a brother, a sister, a friend, it may be? It was the Son of God! and oh how is He glorified in the recovery!

Or, if that sickness terminates in death's slumber, is He less glorified? Ask the spirit just emerged from its shattered tenement, and soaring away to its home on high—ask it as it enters the portals of heaven, the blaze of eternal glory bursting upon its view—ask it as it finds itself before the throne of God, once an earthly, polluted creature, now whiter and brighter than an unfallen angel—ask it as it rests in the bosom of its redeeming Savior, blissfully conscious of its final and eternal safety, and reposing in expectation of its complete glorification, when its reunion with the spiritual body shall take place on the morning of the first resurrection—ask, and it will testify how great was the glory brought to the Son of God, by the termination of a sickness which, while it left kindred and friends weeping around the death-bed below, demonstrated His life, and power, and love, "who has abolished death, and has brought life and immortality to light through the gospel."

APRIL 22

All Scripture is given by inspiration of God, and is profitable for doctrine, for reproof, for correction, for instruction in righteousness: that the man of God may be perfect, throughly furnished unto all good works. 2 Tim. 3:16, 17

IT has seemed good to the Holy Spirit, the Divine Author of the Bible, to embody and exhibit some of the most important spiritual and magnificent truths of His word in the form of type, symbol, and similitude. Neither His wisdom nor His love, in thus throwing a veil of apparent obscurity around revelations so momentous, can be questioned. It cannot be reasonably denied that God, who saw proper to unveil His own mind, and in a way of extraordinary relation communicate His will to man, could as easily, if so it pleased Him, not only have accompanied that revelation with the self-evident assurance that He, and no other, was the speaker; but that also He could have cleared away whatever was mysterious and obscure from each truth, causing it to stand forth, palpable and demonstrative, bathed in the splendor of its own Divine effulgence. But with a view, doubtless, of simplifying the meaning, of heightening the grandeur, and of deepening the solemnity of truth in the estimation of the human mind, this peculiar mode of conveying it is, in part, adopted.

Nor for these reasons alone. The spirit of earnest and persevering research is the spirit which a proper and successful study of the Bible demands. It is not everywhere upon the surface of God's word, that the most important instruction is found; though even there truths the most spiritual and precious are sometimes scattered, like brilliant constellations pendant from the firmament, and visible to the naked eye, or as gems detached from the ocean's cave are sometimes thrown upon the shore, and gathered up by the passing traveler. But in most cases the truth of God lies deep and invisible. A superficial and careless research will not conduct the investigator to its richest revelations. The mine must be excavated, the firmament must be explored, the ocean must be fathomed—in other words, the Scriptures must be searched with much prayer for the Spirit's teaching, and with "patient continuance," or their greatest beauties and their costliest treasures will remain concealed. "All Scripture is given by inspiration of God," and there is no type, nor symbol, nor parable, nor story, nor song, which enfolds not some profound truth, and which conveys not some deep practical lesson of wisdom, some rich word of comfort, or some precious unfolding of Jesus, the "price of which is above rubies."

APRIL 23

For the Lord will not forsake his people for his great name's sake: because it has pleased the Lord to make you his people. I Samuel 12:22

GOD rests in the immutability of His love. It is a love that knows no change in its character, and no variation in its degree. There never has been a period in which the love of God in Christ towards His people has been more or less than it is at this moment. It must have been great before conversion, because then it was that He gave His only begotten Son, that they might live through Him. Then, too, it was He sent His own Spirit to regenerate their minds, and to make them new creatures in Christ Jesus. If He thus loved them before conversion, when they were yet sinners, do you think, dear reader, that His love can be less since conversion! Impossible! God rests in the unchangeableness of His love towards His saints. Nothing can move Him from it. When He set His heart upon His people, He foresaw and foreknew all that was in them. He knew when they would revolt, when they would start aside like a broken bow, when they would startle and fall. He knew all their waywardness, folly, and ingratitude. "I knew that you would deal very treacherously," says God. And yet He loved them. Acquainted with their sin, does He not chasten it? and in chastening, does He withdraw His love from them? Listen to His own words—"If his children forsake my law, and walk not in my judgments; if they break my statutes, and keep not my commandments; then will I visit their transgressions with the rod, and their iniquities with stripes. Nevertheless my loving-kindness will I not utterly take from him, nor suffer my faithfulness to fail." What language can more strongly set forth the Lord's determination to correct the departures of His people, while yet resting in the unchangeableness of His love towards them?

If God thus rests in His love towards us, how jealous ought we to be of the fervor and fidelity of our love to Him! Ah! how inconstant, wavering, and restless have been our affections! How little have we rested in our love to Christ! Other objects have attracted us away from it; we have been as changeable as the wind, and as unstable as the sea. But let us watch over this holy affection, apart from which God takes no pleasure in our sacrifices or services. Let it be our aim to yield up whatever rivals Christ. He sacrificed all for the love He bore us; let us sacrifice all that He requires for the love we bear Him. Jesus is worthy—oh how worthy!—of our deepest, strongest, most self-consuming affection. And God, who gave us His Son, asks nothing in return but that we give Him our hearts. Let His love, then, constrain us to a more unreserved obedience, to a holier walk, to a more ardent, inseparable attachment to Him, to His people, and to His cause. Let us, in this day of easy and abounding profession—this day of papal encroachment and of popish imitation—this day of exaltation of human authority above the word of God—this day of error, of rebuke, and of blasphemy—this day of rapid and of excited action—this last solemn dispensation of the world, the events of which are rapidly ushering in the coming of the Son of man—let us, under the influence of more simple faith, more fervent love, and brightening hope, "go forth unto Jesus without the camp, bearing His reproach," resting amid our conflict and our toil, where the Father rests—where the sinner rests—where we may rest—in Jesus.

APRIL 24

Jesus said unto them, If God were your Father, you would love me: for I proceeded forth and came from God; neither came I of myself, but he sent me. John 8:42

THIS is the key to the infinite grace of God. "I am in the Father," said Christ, "and the Father in me." Glorious announcement! Collecting together all the riches of His grace, the Father places them at the disposal of His Son, and bids Him spread them out before the eyes of a fallen world. True to His covenant engagement, the Eternal Son appears, "made like unto His brethren," and announces that He has come to lift the veil, and show to us the heart of a gracious, sin-pardoning God. In declaring that the "Father Himself loves us," and that "he that had seen Him," so full of grace, "had seen the Father," He affirms, but in other words, that He is a copy, a representation of the Father. That the love, the grace, the truth, the holiness, the power, the compassion, the tenderness, that were exhibited by Him in such a fullness of supply, and were distributed by Him in such an affluence of expenditure, had their origin and their counterpart in God. Oh how jealous was He of the Divine honor! He might, had He willed it, have sought and secured His own distinction and advancement, His own interest and glory, apart from His Father's. He could, had He chosen it, have erected His kingdom as a rival sovereignty, presenting Himself as the sole object of allegiance and affection, thus attracting to His government and His person the obedience and the homage of the world. But no! He had no separate interest from His Father. The heart of God throbbed in the bosom of Jesus—the perfections of God were embodied in the person of Jesus—the purpose of God was accomplished in the mission of Jesus—the will of God was done, and the honor of God was secured, in the life and death of Jesus. "I seek not mine own will, but the will of Him that sent me," was a declaration emblazoned upon His every act.

Anxious that the worship which they offered to His deity, the attachment which they felt for his person, the admiration which they cherished for the beauty of His character and the splendor of His works, should not center solely in Himself, He perpetually pointed His disciples upward to the Eternal Father. It would seem, that such was His knowledge of His Father's grace to sinners, such His acquaintance with His heart of love, that He could find no satisfaction in the affection, the admiration, and the homage yielded to Himself, but as that affection, admiration, and homage were shared equally by His Father. With Him it was an ever-present thought—and how could He forget it?—that the Father's grace filled to overflowing this glorious vessel. He had just left the bosom of the Father, and this was well near the first announcement which broke in music from His lips, "God so loved the world, that He gave His only begotten Son, that whoever believes in Him should not perish, but have everlasting life." And as He pursued His way through the awe-struck and admiring throng, He might often be heard to exclaim, in a voice that rose in solemn majesty above their loudest plaudits, "I seek not mine own glory; I honor my Father."

APRIL 25

Grace be with you, mercy, and peace, from God the Father, and from the Lord Jesus Christ, the Son of the Father, in truth and love. 2 John 3

THE spiritual mind will at once perceive, that our object in the preceding reflections has been to place the character of God, as the "Lord God, merciful and gracious," in its own proper light. It is possible that this truth may appear to the reader, as a newly-discovered planet in the firmament of revelation. It may be to him a new truth, presenting to his eye a fresh and a more kindly view of the paternal and gracious character of God. God, the original source of grace to sinners, has, perhaps, hitherto been but a timidly received doctrine, if received at all. In the first thirstings of your newly-quickened soul, you sought and found the gentle rivulet of grace issuing from some sequestered and shaded spot in your lone path, and you "tasted that the Lord was gracious." Grateful for its refreshing, but panting for larger draughts, you coursed the rivulet to the stream, and drank yet deeper of its fullness. Not satisfied with this, but longing to explore the glorious mystery of the supply, you traced the streamlet to the "broad river," transported with joy to find that "all fullness dwelt in

Jesus," and into it you plunged. But here you have rested. Enamored of the beauty, and lost in wondering delight at the "breadth, and length, and depth, and height" of this river, you have reclined upon its green and sunny bank, forgetting that this river was but the introduction to an ocean, and that that ocean was nothing less than the heart of the Father, infinitely and eternally full of grace. Ah! little did you think, as you sipped from the rivulet, and drank from the stream, and bathed in the river of grace, that there was a depth still deeper, which, like Ezekiel's vision of the holy waters, was so deep that it "could not be passed over."

"What!" exclaims some tried believer, "is the heart of Jesus a transcript of the heart of God? Is the Father as full of forgiveness, of love, of mercy, of compassion, of tenderness, as the Son? How different from all that I had conceived Him to be! I thought of God, and was troubled. His terrors made me afraid. His dealings with me have been severe. His way has been in the whirlwind and in the storm, and his 'path in the great waters.' His judgments have been 'a great deep.' He has set a hedge about me, that I cannot pass. He has spoken to me out of the thick cloud. He answered me by fire. He has spoiled my pleasant pictures, and dashed my cup with bitter. What! is this God all that you represent Him to be? Is He so full of grace and truth? Is He my God, my loving, reconciled Father?" Yes, even so! "It pleased the Father that in Him should all fullness dwell."

Who can contemplate the work of Jesus, and not be convinced of the costliness and preciousness of this grace? How precious is the grace that pardons, that justifies, that adopts, that sanctifies, that comforts, the vilest who believe in Jesus! And yet all this Jesus does. He died for sinners. He receives sinners. He saves sinners to the uttermost. Oh, precious grace! that has opened a fountain which cleanses every stain; that has provided a robe which covers every spot; that "reigns through righteousness unto eternal life" in the soul it has renewed! Reader, have you felt the power, and tasted the sweetness, of this grace? If so, you will feel that no imagination can conceive its beauty, and that no words can express its preciousness. You will regard it as worthy of your warmest love and your highest praise. You will aim to live upon it constantly, to draw from it largely, and to magnify it holily. Nothing this side of glory will be so lovely in your eyes, or so dear to your heart, as the grace of Jesus. Ah yes! inestimably precious is it! There is more of God and of heaven, more of holiness and of happiness, unfolded and experienced in one drop of this grace, than in ten thousand worlds like this. Let others toil for wealth, or pant for glory, or plume themselves with gifts; Lord, give me your grace; this is all my salvation, and all my desire!

APRIL 26

And they shall look upon me whom they have pierced, and they shall mourn for him, as one mourns for his only son, and shall be in bitterness for him, as one that is in bitterness for his firstborn. Zech. 12:10

His this humiliation for your state reached your heart? Has this contrition for sin touched your spirit? Are you acquainted with that godly sorrow which is unto life, that repentance which needs not to be repented of? Do not think indifferently of this conviction. It is the first link in the chain of your salvation. It is the first step in your journey to the cross. No man will arise and go to Jesus, until convinced that he stands in need of Jesus. A Savior weeping, as it were, tears of blood, will only be looked upon by a sinner weeping tears of godly sorrow. A broken-hearted Savior, and a broken-hearted sinner, dwell together in the sweetest harmony. Thousands pass by the cross of Jesus, and never raise a glance towards it. And why? The problem is easy of solution. They have never experienced a heart pierced and sorrowing for sin. The veil that is upon their mind hides the cross of Christ from their view. The look of forgiveness beaming from the eye of that Divine Sufferer never meets their imploring look of sorrow and of faith. They have felt no burden of sin to lay upon Jesus—no sense of guilt to lay upon Jesus—no 'fears,' no 'changes,' no 'bands,' to lay upon Jesus—and so they pass Him blindly, coldly by. Oh awful condition! To be borne down with a load, which Jesus only can unbind; to be enchained by sins, which Jesus only can break; to be suffering from a distemper, which Jesus only can heal; to be dying a death, from which Jesus only can deliver; to be going down to a hell, whose door Jesus only can shut—and yet to remain insensible and indifferent, is appalling indeed.

Reader, if this is your state, of what are you thinking, of what are you dreaming? Of what opiate have you drunk, that you are so unconscious? By what spell are you bound, that you are so infatuated? With what delusions are you ensnared, that you are so insane? Do you imagine that your condition will always continue as it now is? Will not the fumes of that anodyne evaporate, and the world's spell be dissolved? Will not the mental hallucination vanish, and this corpse-like coldness and this grave-like darkness to all the great and momentous realities of eternity, give place to other and appalling emotions? Doubtless they will! There is fast approaching a period that will change the entire scenery of your future existence, and the relations of your present being. A sick and dying bed will impart another aspect to everything around you, and will place your character as a responsible, an accountable, and an immortal being, in a new and an awful light. Do you now anxiously inquire, "What then must I do?" The word of God supplies the answer, "Repent and be converted." Relinquish your hostility to God! Humble yourself under His mighty hand. Lay down the weapons of your rebellion before the cross. You must repent, or you cannot be converted. You must be converted, or you cannot be saved. The whole case resolves itself into this—repent or perish!

APRIL 27

Lord, I believe; help you mine unbelief. Mark 9:24

IT must be the mournful acknowledgment of every spiritual mind, that, after all the clear revealings of truth, and the deep teachings of the Holy Spirit, our views of what God is in Himself, of what He is to His people, and, we may add, of what His people are to Him, fall so far below what they ought to be. May not this disproportion of our conception of their magnitude and preciousness be traced, in a great measure, to the deficiency of our faith in the plain matter-of-fact statements of God's word? We stumble at the very simplicity of the truth. Take, for illustration, that single declaration—"God so loved the world, that He gave His only-begotten Son, that whoever believes in Him should not perish, but have everlasting life." The most unhesitating, simple belief of this, shall we say, matter-of-fact, yet astounding announcement—faith just receiving it without any qualification or demur, exactly as it is found in the Bible—will teach us more in one hour of what God in Christ is to a poor penitential believer, than a century of human teaching. The truth is, we do but half believe the word of God. We doubt, we hesitate, we reason, we cavil, we add to it, and we take from it—we receive just so much as we can understand, and reject just so much as is not palatable or clear; and the sad consequence is, God reproves our unbelief, by leaving us for a season to its painful effects.

But although we believe not, yet He remains true to every jot and tittle of His revealed truth. The imperfect credence which we give to its statements cannot invalidate His promise, nor alter the word that has gone out of His mouth. In the midst of all our slowness of heart to believe, and insensibility of heart to love, "He abides faithful." There, more immovable than the rock of the ocean, more impregnable than the battlements of heaven, firmer than the pillars of the universe, our God, our own covenant God, abides; for "He will rest in His love."

The believer in Christ should of necessity be a happy man. Though like the Master whom he loves—and loving he serves—his path in some places may be paved with flint, or fenced with briar, yet amid it all, fed from the fullness of Christ, and living upon the supply of the covenant, yes, upon the God of the covenant, he is, and he must be, a truly happy man. Beloved reader, we live below, far below, our spiritual privileges. We claim not all the blessings of our birth-right, which, in this present time-state, are ours to enjoy. And if we rise not to the experience of what God has provided and promised for us now, what marvel that we so faintly imagine, and yet more faintly realize, the glories prepared for us hereafter?

APRIL 28

O God, you know my foolishness; and my sins are not hid from you. Draw near unto my soul, and redeem it: deliver me because of mine enemies. You have known my reproach, and my shame, and my dishonor: mine adversaries are all before you. Psalm 69:5, 18, 19.

SATAN, we know, is the great accuser of the saints. And yet how insensible are we of the great power which he still exerts over the people rescued forever from his grasp. It was Satan who stood up to persuade David to number Israel; it was Satan who would have prompted God to slay Job; and it was Satan who stood at the right hand of Joshua, to condemn his soul. Thus is He ever ready to assert his charge against the people of God. Not less malignant is the world. Infidel in its principles, God-hating in its spirit, and Christ-rejecting in its whole conduct, it is no marvel that it should be the antagonist and the accuser of the saints. Sitting in judgment upon actions, the nature of which it cannot understand—interpreting motives, the character of which it cannot decide—ingeniously contriving and zealously propagating reports of evil—ever ready to defame and to detract—all who live godly in Christ Jesus must expect no mercy at its hand. Nor Satan and the world only. How often, as the history of holy Job testifies, have the saints been found the accusers of the saints (and with the deepest humiliation be it written), with an uncharitableness and censoriousness which might have kindled the world's cheek with the blush of shame. Thus does the Church herself testify, "My mother's children were angry with me." "The watchmen that went about the city found me; then smote me, they wounded me: the keepers of the wall took away my veil from me." And from whom did our blessed Lord receive His deepest wounds? Were they not from those who ranked among His friends and followers.

But what so keen and so bitter as self-reproach? Accusations proceeding from others are often most unfounded and unjust. We have felt at the time the secret and pleasing consciousness that we "suffer wrongfully." The shaft flies, but the arrow falls not more pointless and powerless than it. But far different is the accusation which the true believer brings against himself. Seeing sin where others see it not—conscious of its existence and its perpetual working, where the saints applaud, and even the world admires—he lays his hand upon his heart, his mouth in the dust, and exclaims, "I am vile! I abhor myself!" Ah! no reproaches are like those which an honest, sincere child of God charges upon himself. No accusation so true, no reproof so keen, no reproaches so bitter. Happy are they who deal much in self-condemnation. If we judged ourselves more, we should judge others less; and if we condemned ourselves more, we should be less condemned.

But what a privilege in all times of accusation, come from what quarter it may, to be alone with Jesus! With Him, when we know the charge to be untrue, to appeal to Him as an all-seeing, heart-searching, and righteous Judge, and say, "Lord, You know my principles, my spirit, my motives, my aim, and that with honesty, purity, and singleness, I have sought to walk before You." Oh it is a solace, the preciousness of which the throbbing heart may feel, but the most eloquent pen cannot describe. And when the accusation is just, and the believer feels, "Vile as I am in the eyes of others, yet more vile am I in my own eyes;" yet even then to be left alone with Jesus, self-reproved, self-condemned, is to be thrown upon the compassion of Him, "very great are whose mercies." Alone with Him, not a reproving glance darts from His eye, nor an upbraiding word falls from His lips. All is mercy, all is tenderness, all is love. There before Him the self-condemned may stand and confess; at His feet the penitent may fall and weep, and find, alone with Jesus, His arm a shield, and His bosom an asylum, within which his bleeding, panting heart may find safety and repose.

APRIL 29

In the last day, that great day of the feast, Jesus stood and cried, saying, If any man thirst, let him come unto me, and drink. John 8:37

LOOK at the false teaching of the day. What are the heretical doctrines which are now defended with such ability, and propagated with such zeal, but so many cisterns of error hewn out by man as substitutes for the fountain of revealed truth? Doctrines that sink Revelation and exalt tradition, and so deny the word of God; that ascribe regenerating grace to sacraments, and so deny the Holy Spirit; that teach the "real presence" in the Lord's Supper, and so do away with the sacrifice and atonement of Christ; that make religion to consist in a mere observance of external rites, and so deceive and ruin immortal souls; that obliterate the revealed truth of future and eternal punishment, thus weakening the power and shading the glory of God's moral government. We hesitate not to say, that these, and their kindred heresies, are the inventions of man, and designed to beguile souls from the pure fountain of truth. They are cisterns of human contrivance, which hold no water but the water of death.

Shall we find nothing in the true Church of God which would seem to indicate a proneness to substitute some object in the experience of the believer for Christ? Verily, we think so. To adduce an example, alas! but too common.—When the act of faith is substituted for the object of faith, what is this but the hewing out of a broken cistern? Whatever I put in Christ's place necessarily becomes a substitute for Christ. If I look to my faith for comfort, and peace, and evidence, instead of my faith looking to Christ for these, I exchange the Fountain for the cistern. We are now touching upon a truth of vital moment. Jesus is the fountain of all life, light, grace, and love to the believer. Faith is but the channel through which these blessings are received. And yet, who has not detected in his heart a tendency to look to faith for the evidence of his Christianity, instead of to Christ? thus making the act of believing a substitute for the object in which we believe.

You have long been pleading, as your reason for the unsettled and unhappy state of your mind, the weakness of your faith. What, I ask, is this, but the making a Savior of your faith? It was not faith that died for you—it is not faith that saves you. It is Christ, and Christ alone. Your evidences, your peace, your joy, your hope, all, all must flow from Jesus. "You have made me glad through your work," was the Psalmist's experience. And your soul also will be made glad through the atoning, finished work of Christ. That you should have found faith a broken cistern of soul-comfort, should create in you no surprise. The Lord is jealous of His glory—He will not give it to a creature, nor will He give it to a grace. Precious as that grace may be, it never can be a substitute for Christ's precious work. If by any means I exclude the sun from my garden, should I wonder that my seed did not germinate, that my flowers did not appear, and that my plants drooped and died? Surely not. And if I veil the Sun of Righteousness from my soul—if some intervening object is allowed to arrest

His beams, so that they fall not directly and warmly upon the "incorruptible seed" sown in my heart, need I wonder that it springs not forth in blossom, or that the blossom falls before it sets in fruit? But turn, O believer, from this broken cistern, to Jesus the fountain. Draw your comfort, not from the channel, but from the source where it proceeds. Stumble no longer at the weakness of your faith. Turn your eye from every object but the Lord our Righteousness, in whom you may stand before God, the object of His love and delight.

APRIL 30

Although my house do not be so with God; yet he has made with me an everlasting covenant, ordered in all things, and sure: for this is all my salvation, and all my desire, although he make it not to grow. 2 Samuel 23:5

GOD sometimes comforts the cast-down, by bringing them to rest in the fullness and stability of the covenant. David was a man of great grace, a man after God's own heart, and yet he was deeply tried. The greater the amount of precious ore which the refiner places in his furnace, the severer the test to which he subjects it. This may explain what, perhaps, to some minds is a mystery in the Divine conduct—why the most distinguished saints have ever been the most tried saints. But see how God comforted David, in the deepest trial which could wring a believing parent's heart. He had arranged, as he thought, for the best welfare of his family. God steps in, and disarranges all. Incest, treason, murder are crimes which find an entrance within his domestic circle. His children make themselves vile, and he could not restrain them. What a cloud was now resting upon his tabernacle! How bitter were the waters he was now drinking! But see how God comforted him. "Although my house do not be so with God; yet He has made with me an everlasting covenant, ordered in all things and sure; for this is all my salvation, and all my desire, although He makes it (his house) not to grow."

Believer, this covenant is equally yours. You have the same individual interest in it that David had. The "sure mercies" of the true David are yours, as they were those of "the sweet Psalmist of Israel." In the midst of domestic trial—family changes—thwarted designs—blighted hopes, God has made with you in the hands of Jesus, its Surety and Mediator, "an everlasting covenant." In it your whole history is recorded by Him who knows the end from the beginning. All the events of your life, all the steps of your journey, all your sorrows and your comforts, all your needs and your supplies, are ordained in that covenant which is "ordered in all things." While mutability is a constituent element of everything temporal—"passing away" written upon life's loveliest landscape, and upon the heart's dearest treasure—this, and this alone, remains sure and unchangeable. Let, then, the covenant be your comfort and your stay, your sheet-anchor in the storm, the bow in your cloud, upon which God invites you to fix your believing eyes; yes, all your salvation and all your desire, though He makes not domestic comfort to grow.

MAY

MAY 1

"For he is our peace, who has made both one, and has broken down the middle wall of partition between us." Ephes. 2:14

BEHIND this wall Jesus did once stand, and although thus partially obscured, yet to those who had faith to see Him, dwelling though they were in the twilight of the Gospel, He manifested Himself as the true Messiah, the Son of God, the Savior of His people. "Abraham rejoiced to see my day," says Jesus, "and he saw it, and was glad." But this wall no longer stands. The shadows are fled, the darkness is dispersed, and the true light now shines. Beware of those teachers who would rebuild this wall; and who by their superstitious practices, and legal representations of the Gospel, do in effect rebuild it. Remember that "Christ is the end of the law for righteousness to every one that believes."

It is behind "our wall" that Jesus stands—the wall which we, the new covenant saints, erect. Many are the separating influences between Christ and His people; many are the walls which we, alas! allow to intervene, behind which we cause Him to stand. What are the infidelity, I had almost said atheism, the carnality, the coldness, the many sins of our hearts, but so many obstructions to Christ's full and frequent manifestations of Himself to our souls? But were we to specify one obstruction in particular, we would mention unbelief as the great separating wall between Christ and His people. This was the wall which obscured from the view of Thomas his risen Lord. And while the little Church was jubilant in the new life and joy with which their living Savior inspired them, he alone lingered in doubt and sadness, amid the shadows of the tomb. "Except I thrust my hand into His side, I will not believe." Nothing more effectually separates us from, or rather obscures our view of, Christ than the sin of unbelief. Not fully crediting His word—not simply and implicitly relying upon His work—not trusting His faithfulness and love—not receiving Him wholly and following Him fully—only believing and receiving half that He says and commands—not fixing the eye upon Jesus as risen and alive, as ascended and enthroned, leaving all fullness, all power, all love. Oh this unbelief is a dead, towering wall between our Beloved and our souls!

And yet does He stand behind it? Does it not compel Him to depart and leave us forever? Ah no! He is there! Oh wondrous grace, matchless love, infinite patience! Wearied with forbearing, and yet there! Doubted, distrusted, grieved, and yet standing there—His locks wet with the dew of the night—waiting to be gracious, longing to manifest Himself. Nothing has prevailed to compel Him to withdraw. When our coldness might have prevailed, when our fleshliness might have prevailed, when our neglect, ingratitude, and backslidings might have prevailed, never has He entirely and forever withdrawn. His post is to watch with a sleepless eye of love the purchase of His dying agonies, and to guard His "vineyard of red wine night and day, lest any hurt it." Who can adequately picture the solicitude, the tenderness, the jealousy, with which the Son of God keeps His especial treasure? And whatever would force Him to retire—whether it be the coldness that congeals, or the fierce flame that would consume—yet such is His deathless love for His people, "He withdraws not His eyes front the righteous" for one moment. There stands the "Friend that sticks closer than a brother," waiting to beam upon them a glance of His love-enkindled eye, and to manifest Himself to them as He does not unto the world, even from behind our wall.

MAY 2

"That God in all things may be glorified through Jesus Christ, to whom be praise and dominion forever and ever. Amen." 1 Peter 4:11

God's dealings with His people in seasons of bodily sickness have this for their ultimate and great end—"the glory of God." How illustrious was the glory brought to Jesus by the sickness and death of Lazarus! Shall we contemplate it for a moment? Let us go, then, in hallowed imagination, and stand—not by the sick bed, for the mortal struggle was now over—but by the grave of Lazarus. What a halo surrounds it! It scarcely seems like the place of the dead, for Essential Life is present, and the grave is preparing at His command to yield back its prey. Wrapped in His winding-sheet, reposing in the stillness of death, lay one whom Jesus loved. "Groaning in His spirit, and troubled," He approached the spot. Behold the sensibility of the Divine Redeemer! "Jesus wept." How truly human does He appear! How like the Elder Brother! Never more so than now. Philosophy may scorn to betray emotion, and human genius might deem it beneath its dignity to weep. But the philosophy and the genius of Jesus were Divine, and imparted a dignity and a sacredness to the sensibility and benevolence of His humanity: and if it be true that by genius a tear is crystallized and exhibited to the admiration of future ages, surely the tears of sympathy and love which Jesus dropped over the new-made grave of Lazarus, will thrill the holy heart with feeling to the remotest period of time, and perpetuate their wonder through eternity. Bereaved mourner! cease not to weep! Stifle not your emotions, impede not the flow of your tears. They well up from the fountain of feeling placed in your bosom by the Son of God Himself; who, as if longing to experience the luxury of human sensibility, bowed His Deity to your nature—and wept. This only would I say, let your tears fall like the dew of heaven—gentle, noiseless, chastened; or rather, like the tears of Jesus—meek, resigned, submissive.

But not illustrious does appear His humanity only. Behold, on this occasion, how His Deity shone forth resplendent and overpowering. He who had just wept, and while yet the tear-drops lingered in His eye, with a voice of conscious, God-like power, which showed how completely Essential Life held death within its grasp, exclaimed, "Lazarus, come forth! And he that was dead came forth." Behold the spectacle, you condemners of His Divine nature—you who would pluck the diadem from His brow, and force us by your soulless, lifeless creed to a reliance upon a created Redeemer—gaze upon the wondrous scene! See the Savior bathed in human sensibility like a man—behold Him summon back the dead to life like a God! Never did the glory of His complex person—the Son of man, the Son of God—burst forth with more overpowering effulgence than at this moment. Who will deny that the sickness and death of Lazarus brought glory to the Deity of the Savior?

But what was true of this servant of Christ is also true of all the sick whom Jesus loves—their sickness is for His glory. Trace it in the origin of your sickness. It came not by accident nor by chance—words which should never find a place in the Christian vocabulary of a child of God. It was God who stretched you on that bed of languishing. By the arrangement of your heavenly Father, those circumstances transpired which resulted in your present painful visitation. You have been looking alone at second causes—I do not say that they are to be entirely excluded in attempting to unravel the mystery of the Divine procedure, for they often develop links in the chain of God's providence most harmonious and instructive—but there is such a thing as resting in second causes, and not using them rather as steps in the ladder which conducts us up to God Himself, as the first great cause of all the circumstances of our history, from our cradle to our grave. Oh how is the Lord glorified when the sinking patient whom He loves traces the mysterious and strange event which, arresting him in the midst of health and usefulness, has severed him from active life, from domestic duties, and public engagements, imprisoning him in that lone chamber of sickness and solitude, the prey of disease, and perhaps the destined victim of death—to the infinite, infallible, unerring wisdom of the Son of God!

MAY 3

"The crown is fallen from our head: woe unto us, that we have sinned!" Lam. 5:16

MAN, in his original constitution, was a glorious temple. Two facts will prove it. First, he was like God in his moral image; and second, God dwelt in him. He was in every respect worthy of such a resident. He was the holy temple of a holy God. Not a flaw was there. The entire man was holy. There was perfect knowledge in the judgment, perfect holiness in the will, and perfect love in the heart. "Holiness to the Lord" was the inscription written on every window and every door, yes, on every part of this temple. A beautiful structure was man in his original state! Well did the mighty Architect, as He gazed upon His work, pronounce it "very good."

But, behold what sin has done! Man has lost his original resemblance to God. It is true, he yet retains his spiritual, intelligent, and immortal nature; these he can never lose. But his moral likeness to God—his knowledge, purity, justice, truth, and benignity, these glorious lineaments are blotted from his soul; and darkness, impurity, desolation, and death reign there. With the obliteration of his moral resemblance, the soul has lost all love to God. More than this; there is not only the absence of love, but there is positive enmity. "The carnal mind is enmity against God," that enmity showing itself in a thousand ways; principally in its seeking to dethrone God. From his affections he has dethroned Him. To eject Him from the throne of His moral government in the universe is the great and constant aim of the carnal mind. If not so, why this perpetual war against God—against His being, His law, His will, His supreme authority to govern and reign? Why this refusal to acknowledge and obey Him? "Who is the Lord God, that I should obey Him?" Oh! there is no mystery in the case. Man has revolted from God, and having thrown off all allegiance to Him as his sovereign, he seeks to be a god to himself. Self is to him what Jehovah once was—the object of supreme delight. Having cast out God, he moves in a circle of which he himself is the center—all he does is from self, and for self. From this all the lines diverge, and to this they all again return. It needs not the argument or the illustration of a moment to show that this being the moral destitution of man, God has ceased to dwell in him. The temple polluted, defaced, and destroyed, the Divine resident has gone; and the heart, once so sweet a home of Deity, is now the dwelling-place of all sin. Another occupant has taken possession of the ruin; like ancient Babylon, it has become the den of every ravenous beast, a habitation of dragons, the impure abode of every foul, malignant passion. Reader, it is as impossible that God can make your bosom His dwelling-place, while every thought, and feeling, and passion is up in arms against Him, as it would be for Christ to dwell with Belial, or light to commingle with darkness. You must be renewed in the spirit of your mind. You must be born again.

MAY 4

"O Israel, you have destroyed yourself; but in me is your help." Hosea 13:9

IT was God's eternal and gracious purpose to restore this temple. Satan had despoiled His work—sin had marred His image—but both usurpers He would eject, and the ruin of both He would repair. Oh, what mercy, infinite, eternal, and free, was this, that set him upon a work so glorious! What could have moved Him but His own love, what could have contrived the plan but His own wisdom, and what could have executed it but His own power? In this restoration, man was no auxiliary. He could be none. His destruction was his own, his recovery was God's. He ruined himself, that ruin he could not himself repair. It was a work as far surpassing all finite power, as it was first to speak it out of nothing! Yes, the work of restoration is a greater achievement of power than was the work of creation. To repair the temple when ruined was more glorious than to create it out of nothing. In one day He made man; He was four thousand years in redeeming man. It cost Him nothing to create a soul; it cost Him His dear Son to save it. And who can estimate that cost? He met with no opposition in creating man; in re-creating him, Satan, the world, yes, man himself, is against him.

We have said that it was God's gracious and eternal purpose to restore this ruined temple. The first step which He took in accomplishing this great work was his assumption of our nature, as though He Himself would be the model from which the new temple should be formed. This was one of the profoundest acts of God's wisdom, one of the greatest demonstrations of His love. "The Word was made flesh, and dwelt among us" (marg. tabernacled among us). His human body the temple; His Godhead the indwelling Deity. Was ever a temple so glorious as this? "Immanuel, God with us." "God manifest in the flesh." Oh awful mystery! what imagination can conceive, what mind can fathom it? We can but stand upon the shore of this vast ocean of wisdom and love, and exclaim, "Oh the depth!" "Great is the mystery of godliness, God was manifest in the flesh." This was the first step towards His work of replenishing the earth with spiritual temples, to be filled now and eternally with the Divine presence and glory. The entire success and glory of His undertaking rested here. This was the foundation of the structure. He could only obey the law as He was "made of a woman;" He could only "redeem those who were under the law," as He was God in our nature. The absolute necessity, then, of His Godhead will instantly appear. Had the basis of the great work He was about to achieve been laid in any other doctrine—anything inferior, and of course less infinite, less holy, less dignified—had the foundation been laid in mere creature excellence, however exalted that excellence might be—there could have been neither strength, permanency, nor glory in the temple. It would have fallen before the first storm of temptation, and fearful would have been its destruction. God well knew at what cost the work of redemption would be achieved. He knew what His violated law demanded—what his inflexible justice required—and through what costly channel His love must flow; therefore "He laid help upon one that was mighty,"—yes, "mighty to save." And what was the secret of His might?—His absolute Deity. Take a lower view than this, and you reduce the work of Christ to nothing—you tear the soul from the body, pluck the sun from the firmament, wrench the key-stone from the arch, and the foundation from the building. But look at His work through His Godhead, and oh, how vast, how costly;' how glorious does it appear! what a basis for a poor sinner to build upon! what a resting-place for the weary soul! what faith, hope, and assurance does it inspire! how perfect the obedience, how infinitely efficacious the blood, and prevalent the intercession—all derived from the Godhead of Jesus! Glorious temple were You, blessed Son of God!

MAY 5

"Jesus answered and said unto them, Destroy this temple, and in three days I will raise it up. But he spoke of the temple of his body." John 2:19, 21.

THIS temple was to be destroyed. Jesus must die! This was the second step in the accomplishment of the great work. Thus did He announce the fact to the obtuse and incredulous Jews "Destroy this temple, and in three days I will raise it up." His death was as necessary to the satisfaction of justice, as His life of obedience had been to the fulfilling of the law. As the substitute of His people, He must yield up His life; as the Surety of the covenant, He must completely surrender Himself into the hands of Divine justice; as the Testator of His own will, there must of necessity be His death, otherwise the testament would have been of no force at all while He lived. There was no possible avenue for His escape, even had He sought it. He, or His people, must die. He must taste the bitterness of the death that was temporal, or His elect must have tasted of the bitterness of the death that was eternal. Oh yes, Jesus wished to die. Never for one moment did He really shrink from the combat. He well knew the conditions upon which He had entered into a covenant engagement in behalf of His people. He knew that the price of their pardon was His own blood, that His death was their life, and that His gloomy path through the grave was their bright passage to eternal glory. Knowing all this, and with the awful scene of Calvary full in view—the cross, the sufferings of the body, the deathly sorrow of the soul—He yet panted for the arrival of the moment that was to finish the work His Father had given Him to do.

Dear reader, how ready was Jesus thus to die! Where this eagerness? It sprang from His great love to sinners. Oh, this was it! We must go down to the secret depth of His love, if we would solve the mystery of His willingness to die. "God commends His love toward us, in that while we were yet sinners, Christ died for us." Thus was the "temple of His body" destroyed, that "through death He might destroy him that had the power of death, that is, the devil, and deliver them who through fear of death were all their life-time subject to bondage." See, dear reader, the source of your free pardon, the ground of your humble trust, the secret of your "strong consolation." It is all involved in the death of Jesus. You cannot ask too much, you cannot expect too much, you cannot repose too much at the foot of the cross. All is mercy here—all is love—all is peace. Sin cannot condemn, Satan cannot tempt, the world cannot allure, conscience cannot accuse; "there is no condemnation" to a poor soul that shelters itself beneath the cross of Jesus. Here every dark cloud withdraws, and all is sunny—here every tear is dried, but that of joy, and every voice is hushed, but that of praise.

MAY 6

"And we declare unto you glad tidings, how that the promise which was made unto the fathers, God has fulfilled the same unto us their children, in that he has raised up Jesus again." Acts 13:32, 33

GREAT stress is laid upon the doctrine of the resurrection of Christ in the word. And the child of God may be but imperfectly aware, what an essential pillar it is to his hope, and how sanctifying and comforting the blessings are that spring from its full belief. The resurrection of Jesus is the great seal to the character and perfection of His work. Yes, His work, touching its saving effects, had been nothing apart from this Divine attestation. His perfect keeping of the law, and His suffering unto death, were but parts of the vast plan, and, taken separately and distinctly, were not capable of perfecting the salvation of the Church. The apostle so reasons. "If Christ do not be risen, then is our preaching vain, and your faith is also vain. Yes, and we are found false witnesses of God; because we have testified of God that He raised up Christ; whom He raised not up, if so be that the dead rise not. For if the dead rise not, then is not Christ raised: and if Christ do not be raised, your faith is vain; you are yet in your sins. Then they also which are fallen asleep in Christ are perished." A moment's reflection will justify the conclusions which the apostle deduces from the supposition that Christ had not risen.

Our dear Lord endured the "curse of the law;" a part of that curse was death—death legal, death temporal, death eternal. He was "made a curse or us," and died. So long as He remained imprisoned in the grave, "death had dominion over Him." It had been in vain that we had looked to His obedience and sufferings for the proof of the all-sufficiency and acceptableness of His satisfaction, so long as the iron scepter of the king of terrors held Him in subjection. Oh what a momentous period were the three days that intervened between the giving up of the spirit upon the cross, and the bursting of the tomb—the salvation of the whole Church hung upon it—all who had already "fallen asleep" in Him, and all whom it was the purpose of God yet to call, were deeply interested in this one fact. But, on the third day, the destroyed temple was raised again—death had no more dominion over Him—his sting was extracted, his scepter was broken, the curse was rolled away, and the redemption of the Church was complete. "He was delivered for our offenses, and rose again for our justification."

Through the incarnation, obedience, death, and resurrection of Christ, a way was opened, by which God could again dwell with man—yes, resume His abode in the very temple that sin had destroyed, and show forth the riches and glory of His grace far more illustriously than when this temple stood in its original perfection and grandeur. Here was the foundation of every successive temple that grace was about to raise. "Other foundation can no man lay than that is laid, which is Jesus Christ." On the dignity of His person, His finished righteousness, His perfect atonement, His all-sufficient grace, and His inviolable faithfulness, believers, "as lively stones, are built up a spiritual house," for the everlasting indwelling of God the Holy Spirit.

MAY 7

"And they come unto you as the people comes, and they sit before you as my people, and they hear your words, but they will not do them: for with their mouth they show much love, but their heart goes after their covetousness." Ezek. 33:31

FEW, save those who have been taught of the Spirit, and who have accustomed themselves to analyze closely the evidences of true conversion, are aware how far an individual may go, not merely in an outward reformation of character, and an external union to Christ, but in a strong resemblance to the positive and manifest evidences of the new birth, without the actual possession of a single one. In the exception that we make, we refer to a knowledge of the truth that is not saving in its effects, is not influential in its character, and which has its place in the judgment only, assented to, approved of, and even ably and successfully vindicated; while the soul, the seat of life—the will, the instrument of holiness—and the heart, the home of love, are all unrenewed by the Holy Spirit.

Beloved reader, you cannot be too distinctly nor too earnestly informed, that there is a great difference in Divine knowledge. There is a knowledge of the truth, in the attainment of which a man may labor diligently, and in the possession of which he may look like a believer; but which may not come under that denomination of a knowledge of Christ, in allusion to which our dear Lord in His memorable prayer uses these words, "This is life eternal, that they might know You, the only true God, and Jesus Christ whom You have sent." The fatal error to which you are exposed is—oh that you may have escaped it!—the substituting a knowledge of Divine truth in the judgment, for the quickening grace of God in the heart. It is surprising how far an outwardly moral individual may go in Divine attainments—spiritual knowledge—eminent gifts—and even great usefulness; and yet retain the carnal mind, the rebellious will, the unhumbled and unbroken heart. If the volume of Divine truth had not informed us of this, and supplied us with some striking cases in proof, we should be perpetually beguiled into the belief that a head filled with rational, speculative, theoretical truth, must necessarily be connected with some degree of Divine grace in the affections. But not so. Balaam's knowledge of Divine things was deep; he could ask counsel of God, and prophesy of Christ, but where is the undoubted evidence that he "knew the grace of God in truth?" Saul prophesied, had "another spirit" given him, and asked counsel of God; but Saul's heart was unchanged by the Holy Spirit. Herod sent for John, "heard him gladly, and did many things," and yet his heart and his life were strangers to holiness. Addressing the Pharisees, the apostle employs this striking language, "Behold, you are called a Jew, and rest in the law, and make your boast of God, and know His will, and approve the things that are more excellent, being instructed out of the law:" and yet deep hypocrisy was their crying sin. Oh let no man be so deceived as to substitute knowledge for grace. Better that his knowledge of the truth should be limited to its mere elements, its first principles, and yet with it be enabled to say, "Behold, I am vile," but "He has loved me, and given Himself for me," than to possess "all knowledge," and live and die destitute of the renewing grace of God upon the heart.

MAY 8

"The Lord tries the righteous." Psalm 11:5

THE furnace works wonders for a believer. Oh that he should ever wish to be exempt from it! Indeed, it may be remarked, that real grace is inseparable from a state of trial. Where there is real faith, the Lord will try it. Where there is the true ore, the Refiner will prove it in the furnace. There is not a grace of the Spirit, but, more or less, and at one time or another, Jesus tries that grace. "The Lord tries the righteous." He tries their principles—tries their graces—tries their obedience—proves His own work—brings out the new man in all its muscular fullness—develops the nature and character of His work—and shows it to be His mighty product, and in all respects worthy of Himself. Much then as we would wish at times exemption from a state of trial, anxious for the more smooth and easy path, yet, if we are really born of God, and His grace has truly made us one of His family, like them, we have been "chosen in the furnace of affliction," and with them in the furnace, we are brought into the possession of some of the most costly blessings of our lives.

Real grace, then, is tried grace. And mark how, in the process of its trial, the blessed and Eternal Spirit more deeply seals the believer. The hour of affliction is the hour of softening. Job bore this testimony, "He makes my heart soft." The hardness of the heart yields—the callousness of the spirit gives way—the affections become tender—conscience is more susceptible. It is the season of holy abstraction, meditation, and prayer—of withdrawal from the world and from creature delights, while the soul is more closely shut in with God. The heart, now emptied, humbled, and softened, is prepared for the seal of the Spirit; and what an impression is then made—what discoveries of God's love to the soul—what enlarged views of the personal glory of Christ—of the infinite perfection of His work—of the preciousness of the atoning sacrifice—of the hatefulness of sin, and of the beauty of holiness! His own personal interest in this great work of Christ is made more clear and certain to his soul. The Spirit bears a fresh witness to his acceptance, and seals him anew with the adopting love of God. It was the Psalmist's wisdom to acknowledge, "It is good for one that I have been afflicted."

MAY 9

"The Spirit itself bears witness with our spirit, that we are the children of God." Rom. 8:16

THREE important things are involved in these words—first, the Witness—then that with which He witnesses—and lastly, the great truth to which He witnesses. First, "the Spirit itself bears witness." The great business of making known to a poor sinner his acquittal in the high court of heaven, and his adoption into the King's family, is entrusted to no inferior agent. No angel is commissioned to bear the tidings, no mortal man may disclose the secret. None but God the Holy Spirit Himself. "The Spirit itself" He that rests short of this testimony wrongs his own soul. Dear reader, be satisfied with no witness to your "calling and election" but this. Human testimony is feeble here. Your minister, your friend, schooled as they may be in the evidences of experimental godliness, cannot assure your spirit that you are "born of God." God the Eternal Spirit alone can do this. He only is competent—He only can fathom the "deep things of God,"—He only can rightly discern between His own work and its counterfeit, between grace and nature —He only can make known the secret of the Lord to those who fear Him; all other testimony to your sonship is uncertain, and may fearfully and fatally deceive. "It is the Spirit that bears witness, because the Spirit is truth." Again and yet again would we solemnly repeat it—take nothing for granted touching your personal interest in Christ—rest not satisfied with the testimony of your own spirit, or with that of the holiest saint on earth; seek nothing short of "the Spirit itself." This only will do for a dying hour.

The second thing to be observed in the declaration is—that with which He witnesses—"the Spirit itself bears witness with our spirit." It is a personal testimony—not borne to others, but to ourselves—"with our spirit." The adoption of the believer into the family of God is so great a privilege, involving blessings so immense, for beings so sinful and in all respects unworthy, that, did not their heavenly Father assure them by His own immediate testimony of its truth, no other witness would suffice to remove their doubts and quiet their fears, and satisfy them as to their real sonship. The Eternal Spirit of God descends and enters their hearts, as a witness to their adoption. He firsts renews our spirit—applies the atoning blood to the conscience—works faith in the heart—enlightens the understanding—and thus prepares the believing soul for the revelation and assurance of this great and glorious truth—his adoption into the family of God. As it is "with our spirit" the Holy Spirit witnesses, it is necessary that, in order to perfect agreement and harmony, he who has the witness within himself should first be a repenting and believing sinner. He who says that he has this witness, but who still remains "dead in sins,"—a stranger to faith in the Lord Jesus—to the renewings of the Holy Spirit—in a word, who is not born of God—is wrapping himself up in an awful deception. The witness we plead for is the holy testimony, in concurrence with a holy gospel, by a holy Spirit, to a holy man, and concerning a holy truth. There can be no discrepancy, no want of harmony, between the witness of the Spirit and the word of God. He witnesses according to, and in agreement with, the truth. Vague and fanciful impressions, visions, and voices, received and rested upon as evidences of salvation, are fearful delusions. Nothing is to be viewed as an evidence of our Divine sonship which does not square and harmonize with the revealed word of God. We must have a "Thus says the Lord," for every step we take in believing that we are the children of God. Let it be remembered, then, that the Spirit bears His testimony to believers. His first step is to work repentance and faith in the heart; then follows the sealing and witnessing operation. "In whom also, after that you believed, you were sealed with that Holy Spirit of promise."

The last particular is the great truth to which He testifies, "that we are the children of God." The Spirit is emphatically spoken of as a Spirit of adoption. "For you have not received the spirit of bondage again to fear; but you have received the spirit of adoption, whereby we cry, Abba, Father." And again, "And because you are sons, God has sent forth the Spirit of His Son into your hearts, crying, Abba, Father." Now it is the peculiar office of the Spirit to witness to the adoption of the believer. Look at the blessed fact to which He testifies—not that we are the enemies, the aliens, the strangers, the slaves, but that we are "the children of God." High and holy privilege! "The children of God!" Chosen from all eternity—"having predestinated us unto the adoption of children by Jesus Christ to Himself, according to the good pleasure of His will,"—all their iniquities laid on Jesus, their blessed Surety, justified by the "Lord our righteousness,"—called by the effectual operation of the Eternal Spirit—inhabited, sanctified, sealed by God the Holy Spirit. Oh exalted state! oh holy privilege! oh happy people! Pressing on, it may be, through strong corruptions, deep trials, clinging infirmities, fiery temptations, sore discouragements, dark providences, and often the hidings of a Father's countenance, and yet "the children of God" now, and soon to be glorified hereafter.

MAY 10

"By terrible things in righteousness will you answer us, O God of our salvation." Psalm 65:5.

DEEPER experience of the truth of God is frequently the result of sore but sanctified trial. A believer knows but imperfectly what he is in himself, or what the truth of God is to him, until placed in circumstances favorable to the development of both. The Lord will have His people, and especially the ministers of His gospel, experimentally acquainted with His truth. They shall not testify of an unknown, unfelt, and unexperienced Savior. They shall be enabled to say, "That which we have heard, which we have seen with our eyes, which we have looked upon, and our hands have handled of the word of life, declare we unto you." And more valuable and precious is one grain of the truth of God experienced in the heart than the whole system occupying a place only in the judgment. To deepen, then, their knowledge of the truth—to ground and settle them in it—to bring it out in all its practical power, a good, a covenant God often places His children in sore trial and temptation. It is in the storm and the hurricane, amid rocks and shoals, that the mariner becomes practically acquainted with his science. All that he knew before He launched his vessel on the ocean, or encountered the storm, was but the theory of the school; but a single tempest, one escape from shipwreck, has imparted more experimental knowledge than years of mere theoretical toil. So learns the believer. Oh, how theoretical and defective his views of Divine truth—how little his knowledge of his own heart—his deep corruptions, perfect weakness, little faith—how imperfect his acquaintance with Jesus—His fullness, preciousness, all-sufficiency, sympathy, until the hand of God falls upon him!—and when, like Job, messenger after messenger has brought the tidings of blasted gourds, of broken cisterns—when brought down and laid low, like him they are constrained to confess, "I have heard of You by the hearing of the ear; but now mine eye sees You. Why I abhor myself, and repent in dust and ashes."

Welcome whatever makes you more acquainted with God; despise nothing that will deepen your intimacy with God in Christ. Welcome the cross—it may be heavy; welcome the cup—it may be bitter; welcome the chastening—it may be severe; welcome the wound—it may be deep; oh! welcome to your heart whatever increases your knowledge of God; receive it as a boon sent to you from your Father; receive it as a heaven-sent message to your soul. And hearken to the voice that is in that rod: "My child, I want you to know me better; for in knowing me better you will love me better, and in loving me better you will serve me better. I send this chastening, this loss, this cross, only to draw you closer and closer to my embrace—only to bring you nearer and nearer to me." Welcome, then, whatever brings you into closer transaction, communion, and fellowship with your heavenly Father.

MAY 11

"The Comforter, which is the Holy Spirit." John 14:26

IN no one aspect does the happy tendency and, we may add, the indispensable necessity of the discipline of the covenant more manifestly appear, than that through this channel mainly is the believer brought into communion with, and into enjoyment of, the tenderness and sympathy of the Spirit. The wisdom, the faithfulness, and the power of the Spirit, the soul has been brought to acknowledge and experience in conversion; but to know the Spirit as a Comforter, to experience His tenderness and sympathy, His kindness and gentleness, we must be placed in those peculiar circumstances that call it into exercise. In a word, we must know what sorrow is, to know what comfort is: and to know what true comfort is, we must receive it from the blessed and Eternal Spirit, the Comforter of the Church.

The God and Father of His people foreknew all their circumstances. He knew that He had chosen them in the furnace of affliction, that this was the peculiar path in which they should all walk. As He foreknew, so He also fore-arranged for all those circumstances. In the eternal purposes of His wisdom, grace, and love, He went before His Church, planning its history, allotting its path, and providing for every possible position in which it could be placed; so that we cannot imagine an exigency, a trial, a difficulty, or a conflict, but is amply provided for in the covenant of grace. Such is the wisdom and such the goodness of God towards His covenant family!

The great provision for the suffering state of the believer is the Holy Spirit—the special, the personal, and abiding Comforter of the Church. It was to this truth our dear Lord directed the sorrowing hearts of His disciples, when, on the eve of His return to His kingdom, He was about to withdraw from them His bodily presence. His mission on earth was fulfilled, His work was done, and He was about to return to His Father and to their Father, to His God and to their God. The prospect of separation absorbed them in grief. Thus did Jesus mark, and thus too He consoled it. "But now I go my way to Him that sent me; and none of You asks me, Where go you? But because I have said these things unto you, sorrow has filled your heart. Nevertheless I tell You the truth; it is expedient for you that I go away for if I go not away, the Comforter will not come unto you; but if I depart, I will send Him unto you." Mark the mindset of the disciples; it was a season of deep sorrow. Then observe, how Jesus mitigated that sorrow, and chased away the dark cloud of their grief, by the promise of the Comforter—assuring those who the presence and abiding of the Spirit as a Comforter would more than recompense the loss of His bodily presence. What the Spirit then was to the sorrowing disciples, He has been in every successive age, is at the present moment, and will continue to be to the end of time—the personal and abiding Comforter of the afflicted family of God.

MAY 12

"Christ, who is our life." Coloss. 3:4

THE renewed man is a living soul, in consequence of his union with the life of Christ. We too little trace the life which is in us to the life which is in Jesus. The Spirit Himself could not be our life apart from our union to Christ. It is not so much the work of the Spirit to give us life, as to quicken in us the life of Christ. The apostle thus briefly but emphatically states it—"Christ, who is our life." Hence we see the relation and the fitness of the second Adam to the Church of God. In consequence of our federal union to the first Adam, we became the subjects of death—he being emphatically our death. And in consequence of our covenant union to the second Adam, we become the subjects of life—He being emphatically "our life." Hence it is said, "The second Adam is a quickening spirit."

The headship of Christ, in reference to the life of His people, is written as with the point of a diamond in the following passages:—"In Him was life;" "The Son quickens whom He will:" "The dead shall hear the voice of the Son of God, and those who hear shall lave;" "I am the resurrection and the life: he that believes in me, though he were dead, yet shall he live;" "He that eats me, even he shall live by me." Now this life that is in Christ becomes the life of the believer in consequence of his union with Christ. "You are dead, and your life is hid with Christ in God;" "I am crucified with Christ, nevertheless I live; yet not I, but Christ lives in me." And what is the crowning act of Christ as the life of His people? What but His resurrection from the dead? "We are risen with Christ;" "You are also risen with Him;" "That I may know the power of His resurrection." This doctrine of the Lord's resurrection is the pivot upon which the whole system of Christianity hinges. He is risen, and in virtue of this, His people are partakers of a resurrection-life to eternal glory. It is utterly impossible that they can perish, for they have already the resurrection-life in their souls. Their own resurrection to everlasting life is pledged, secured, antedated, in consequence of the risen Christ being in them the hope of glory. Thus is Christ the life of His people. He is the life of their pardon—all their iniquities are put away by His blood. He is the life of their Justification—His righteousness gives them acceptance with God. He is the life of their sanctification—His grace subdues the power of the sins, the guilt of which His blood removes. He is the life of their joys, of their hopes, of their ordinances; the life of everything that makes this life sweet, and the life to come glorious.

MAY 13

"Because I live, you shall live also." John 14:19

THE divine life of a believer, from its very necessity, is deathless. The life of Adam was never so secure, even when he lifted his noble brow in spotlessness to God. The new life is more secure in a state of imperfection, than his was in a state of innocence. He stood in his own righteousness, upheld by his own power, and yet He fell. But we are more secure, because we stand in the righteousness, and are kept by the power, of God. His life was hidden in himself; our life is hidden in Christ, and is as secure in Christ as Christ's is in God. It is truly remarked by Charnock, that "Adam had no reserve of nature to supply nature upon any defect;" but out of Christ's fullness we receive grace upon grace. How much more ready are we to complain against this small measure of grace, than to praise God for the weakest grace, and to thank him for an inexhaustible source, on which we may at all times fall back. The believer ever has a reserve of grace. His resources may often be exhausted, but he has a stock in Christ's hand, and which, for the wisest end, is kept solely in Christ's hands, upon which he is privileged at any moment to draw. Well is it that that supply of grace is not all in our own hands, else it would soon be wasted; and well is it that it is not in angels' hands, else they would soon be weary with our continual coming. But the covenant was made with Christ, He being the Mediator as well as the Surety; and in Him it pleased the Father that all fullness should dwell. Thus, in His hands the Father has entrusted the keeping of His weakest child—even your soul, beloved, though you are the weakest of the weak. An infant as much belongs to the family as the most matured member. Its place in the parent's heart is as strong, and its claim upon its share of the patrimony is as valid. So is it with the feeblest child of God.

And most faithfully does our Lord Jesus discharge His office. Is the Church a garden? Jesus repairs early to the vineyard, to see "whether the tender grapes appear, and the pomegranates bud." Is it a flock? Jesus "feeds His flock like a shepherd: he gathers the lambs with His arm, and carries them in His bosom." Can any imagery more affectingly set forth the tenderness not towards weak grace—the weak lamb carried, not on the shoulders, not in the arms, but in the bosom of the Shepherd? Yes, there is one image, the most expressive and tender in the universe of imagery—a mother's love for her infant. Does God compare His love to this? Hearken words: "Can a woman forget her sucking child, that she should not have compassion on the son of her womb? Yes, they may forget, yet will I not forget you." Oh that you would, in the simplicity of faith, press this precious truth to your trembling, doubting, fearful heart. Nothing does the Holy Spirit seem to take such pains in comforting and strengthening, as real grace in its greatest weakness. Would He indulge our weak faith? Oh no! But while He would have us sue for the highest degrees, He would yet watch over the lowest degree of grace in the soul.

MAY 14

"Why gird up the loins of your mind, be sober, and hope to the end for the grace that is to be brought unto you at the revelation of Jesus Christ." 1 Peter 1:13

ALL things and all events point us to, and are leading us towards, eternity. Oh how we absorb in our present sufferings and light afflictions the thought of the coming death—the coming grave—the coming judgment—the coming heaven—the coming hell! Our sojourn here is but brief. We flit away like the shadow across the sun-dial. We weep today, we are wept for to-morrow. Today we are toiling, and fighting, and suffering; and anon, if believers in Jesus, we are with Him, and "are come unto Mount Zion, and unto the city of the living God, the heavenly Jerusalem, and to an innumerable company of angels, to the general assembly and church of the first-born, which are written in heaven, and to God the Judge of all, and to the spirits of just men made perfect, and to Jesus the Mediator of the new covenant, and to the blood of sprinkling, that speaks better things than that of Abel."

Christ will soon appear in the clouds of heaven. "The coming of the Lord draws near." "The Lord is at hand." Let us hew out no more cisterns off earthly good; but following the stream of the Lord's love—deepening and widening as it ascends—let us rise to the fountain-head in glory; having our conversation in heaven, and our affections on things above, where Christ sits—and from where He will come again—at the right hand of God. "Drink, yes, drink abundantly, O beloved," of this river, is your Lord's loving invitation. You cannot take to it too many vessels, nor vessels too empty. The precious "fountain opened to the house of David, and to the inhabitants of Jerusalem," is "for sin and uncleanness." Then, as sinners, plunge into it, "wash and be clean." Think not that you are alone in your grief, as cisterns of creature-good thus broken. A "cloud of witnesses" surrounds you, all testifying that the fled joy of earth gives place to the full and permanent bliss of heaven; that Jesus now turns His people's sorrow into joy, by the sustaining power of faith and the sweet discoveries of love; and that He will perfect that joy when He brings them to drink of the "pure river of water of life, clear as crystal, proceeding out of the throne of God, and of the Lamb."

MAY 15

"For I have satiated the weary soul, and I have replenished every sorrowful soul." Jer. 31:25

His preeminent fitness for this peculiar and difficult office is apparent. His identity with their very nature describes Him as well calculated to address Himself to their case. Of the nature thus oppressed and weary He in part partook. But for this, so infinitely removed had He been from their condition, He had been incapable of meeting its peculiar necessity. Absolute Deity could not, through the medium of sympathy, have conveyed a word of comfort to the weary. There had been wanting, not the power to relieve, but the mode of relieving, the oppressed and sorrowful heart. There had been needed the connecting and transmitting chain—the heavenly highway of thought, of feeling, and of sympathy—between these extremes of being, the loving heart of God and the desolate heart of man. Unacquainted with grief, untouched by sorrow, unbeclouded by care, unaffected by weariness, an absolute God could not possibly offer the support and the condolence which sympathetic feeling alone could give, and which a jaded spirit, a sorrow-touched, care-oppressed, and sin-beclouded soul demanded.

Nor could angels afford the help required. The only burden which they know is the burden of love; the only weariness they feel is the weariness of ever-burning devotion and zeal. It is this which gives strength to their wings, and swiftness to their flight. They are represented as "hearkening to the voice of the Lord," ready to speed their way on some embassy of mercy and love. In fulfilling this their ministry, their eye never slumbers, their pinions never droop. But we needed a nature so constituted as to enter into, and as it were become a part of, the very weariness it sought to relieve. Look at Jesus! "Behold the man!" With weariness in every form He was intimate; He knew what bodily weakness was. Do you not love to linger in pensive thoughtfulness over that touching incident of His life which describes Him as sitting fatigued upon Jacob's well? "Jesus, being wearied, sat thus on the well." Picture Him to your eye! See the dust upon His sandals, for He had walked forty miles that day—the sweat upon His brow, the air of languor upon His countenance, and the jaded expression in His eye! Do we deify His humanity? No. It was real humanity—humanity like our own. It is our joy, our boast, our glory, our salvation, that He was really man, as He was truly God.

Consider, too, what He endured for man, from man. This was no small part of the weariness of our nature into which He entered. How soon did He come to the end of the creature! Alas! the creature has an end, and sooner or later God brings us to it—and in the exercise, too, of the tenderest love of His heart. When most He needed its sheltering protection, He found the creature a withered gourd—and He bore His sorrow alone. And when He repaired to it for the refreshing of sympathy, He found it a broken cistern—and He panted in vain. Where were His disciples now? He was in trouble, but there was no one to help; He was in the storm, but no one would know Him; refuge failed Him, no man cared for His soul; He was in sorrow, but no bosom proffered its pillow; He was accused, but no tongue was heard in His defense; He was scourged, but no arm was lifted to repel; He was condemned, but no one vindicated His innocence, nor sought to arrest His progress to the cross! Oh how fully did Jesus realize the creature's nothingness, and so enter into His people's condition of weariness!

MAY 16

"Preaching peace by Jesus Christ (he is Lord of all)." Acts 10:36.

LET us turn our attention to the subject-matter of our Lord's address to the weary. What does He speak to them? Some would reply, the law. No; but the law of God never spoke a word of comfort to the weary. It was not designed for such. Its very nature forbids it. It can anathematize, alarm, and wound; but not a solitary word of consolation and soothing can it address to a soul weary and heavy-laden with sorrow and with guilt. But it is the glorious gospel of the blessed God that the Lord Jesus speaks to His weary ones. It was designed and framed especially for them. Its very nature fits it for such. Every word is an echo of the love of God's heart. Every sentence is fraught with grace, mercy, and truth. The word which Jesus speaks is just the word the weary want. It unfolds a free pardon, complete acceptance, perfect reconciliation with God, and all-sufficient grace to perfect this work in holiness. It bids me as a sinner approach just as I am; my poverty, my vileness, my guilt, my utter destitution forming no just hindrances to my salvation, because His atoning work has made it a righteous thing in God to justify the guilty, and a gracious act in Jesus to save the lost. Yes, He condescends to assure me in that word of a free-grace gospel, which He speaks with a tongue so eloquent, that I honor Him in accepting His proffered boon, and that I glorify Him by trusting my soul into His Almighty hands.

The Lord Jesus speaks at the present time to the weary. We need constantly to bear in mind the immutability of our Lord; that "Jesus Christ is the same yesterday, and today, and for ever." That all that He ever has been—and oh! what has He not been!—He is at this moment. What countless numbers are now bathing their souls in the bliss of heaven, whose tears were once dried, whose fears were once quelled, whose burden was once removed, by those precious words spoken in season—"Come unto me, all you that labor and are heavy laden, and I will give you rest"! Oh could they, bending now from their thrones, but speak to us, they would testify what substance, what reality, what sweetness, what power, and what charm they once found in them; and they would bid every weary spirit, every weeping penitent, every tried saint, believe and press the promise to their heart. But a dearer, a lovelier, and a better than they bids you receive it. Jesus Himself speaks to you: "Come unto me—and I will give you rest." All that He was in their happy experience, He will be in yours. The grace that made them what they once were, and what they now are, is sufficient for you. Go, and lay your weariness on Christ. Ask not, "Will He bear my burden." He bears every burden brought to Him. Not one poor weary, heavy-laden sinner does He turn away. You are perhaps a mourning penitent—He will receive you. You are perhaps a vile outcast—He will welcome you. He says He will, and He cannot deny Himself; it is impossible that He should lie.

MAY 17

"And Jacob was left alone; and there wrestled a man with him until the breaking of the day. And when he saw that he prevailed not against him, he touched the hollow of his thigh; and the hollow of Jacob's thigh was out of joint, as he wrestled with him. And he said, Let me go, for the day breaks. And he said, I will not let you go, except you bless me." Genesis 32:24-26

NEVER was there a conflict of so illustrious a nature, and of so strange a result, between powers so dissimilar and extreme. The incarnate God, as if to demonstrate His own Divine power, and at the same time to make the victory of human weakness over infinite might more illustrious and palpable, touches the wrestling patriarch, and he is a cripple! Then at the moment of his greatest weakness, when taught the lesson of his own insufficiency, that flesh might not glory in the Divine presence, Omnipotence retires as if vanquished from the field, and yields the palm of victory to the disabled but prevailing prince. And why all this? To teach us the amazing power of prayer, which the feeblest believer may have when alone with Jesus.

No point of Christian duty and privilege set before you in this work will plead more earnestly and tenderly for your solemn consideration than this. It enters into the very essence of your spiritual being. This is the channel through which flows the oil that feeds the lamp of your spiritual life. Dimly will burn that lamp, and drooping will be your spiritual light, if you are not used to be much alone with Jesus. Every feeling of the soul, and each aspect of Christian endeavorr, will be measurably affected by this woeful neglect. He who is but seldom with Jesus in the closet will exhibit, in all that he does for Jesus, but the fitful and convulsive movements of a mind urged on by a feverish and unnatural excitement. It is only in much prayer—that prayer secret and confiding—that the heart is kept in its right position, its affections properly governed, and its movements correctly regulated. And are there not periods when you find it needful to leave the society of the most spiritual—sweet as is the communion of saints—to be alone with Jesus? He Himself has set you the example. Accustomed at times to withdraw from His disciples, He has been known to spend whole nights amid the mountains' solitude, alone with His Father.

Oh the sacredness, the solemnity of such a season! Alone with God! alone with Jesus! no eye seeing, no ear hearing, but His; the dearest of earthly being excluded, and no one present save Jesus only, the best, the dearest of all! Then, in the sweetest and most unreserved confidence, the believer unveils his soul, and reveals all to the Lord. Conscience is read—motives are dissected—principles are sifted—actions are examined—the heart is searched—sin is confessed—iniquity is acknowledged, as could only effectually be done in the presence of Jesus alone. Is there, among all the privileges of a child of God, one in its costliness and its preciousness surpassing this?

MAY 18

"Not as though I had already attained, either were already perfect: but I follow after, if that I may apprehend that for which also I am apprehended of Christ Jesus. Brethren, I count not myself to have apprehended: but this one thing I do, forgetting those things which are behind, and reaching forth unto those things which are before, I press toward the mark for the prize of the high calling of God in Christ Jesus." Philip. 3:12-14

OH holy resolve of a regenerate man! Here is the springing up of the well of living water in the heart. Here is the turning of the soul to God. See how the fountain rises! See how the flame ascends! It is the mighty energy of God the Holy Spirit, drawing the soul upward, heavenward, Godwards.

Nothing more strikingly and truly proves the reality, we would say the divinity, of the work within, the vital principle of grace implanted in the heart of the regenerate, than the growing energy and holy tendency that ever accompany it. It is the property of that which has life in itself to increase—to multiply itself. The seed cast into the earth will germinate. Presently will appear the tender sprout, this will advance to the young sapling, and this in time to the gigantic tree, with its overshadowing branches, and richly laden with fruit. Obeying the law of its nature, it aspires to that perfection which belongs to it. It must grow. Nothing can prevent it, but such a wound as will injure the vital principle, or cutting it down entirely. The life of God in the soul of man contains the principle of growth. He that is not advancing—adding grace to grace, strength to strength—fruitful in every good word and work—increasing in the knowledge of God, of His own heart, of the preciousness, fullness, and all sufficiency of Jesus, and in Divine conformity, "growing up into Christ in all things,"—has great reason to suspect the absence of the Divine life in his soul. There may be much that marks a resemblance to the new birth, there may be the portrait finely executed, the marble statue exquisitely chiseled, but there is not the living man, "the new creature." We can expect no increase of perfection in a finished picture or in a piece of statuary; that which has not life in it cannot grow. This is self-evident. An individual may look like a believer, and even die with a false peace, like that of the righteous, and all the while retain his dwelling among the tombs.

Let no dear child of God write hard and bitter things against himself, as he reads this last sentence. Let him not come to any hasty, unbelieving, doubting, and God-dishonoring conclusions. What are you to yourself?—worthless—vile—empty? What is Jesus to you?—precious—lovely—all your salvation and all your desire? What is sin to you?—the most hateful thing in the world? And what is holiness?—the most lovely, the most longed for? What is the throne of grace to you?—the most attractive spot? And the cross?—the sweetest resting-place in the universe? What is God to you?—your God and Father—the spring of all your joys—the fountain-head of all your bliss—the center where your affections meet? Is it so? Then you are born again—then you are a child of God—then you shall never die. Cheer up, precious soul! the day of your redemption draws near. Those low views of yourself—that brokenness, that inward mourning, that secret confession, that longing for more grace, more devotedness, more love to God, does but prove the existence, reality, and growth of God's work within you. God the Holy Spirit is there, and these are but the fruits and evidences of His indwelling. Look up, then, beloved reader, and let the thought cheer you—that soul never perished, that felt itself to be vile, and Jesus to be precious.

MAY 19

"And we desire that every one of you do show the same diligence to the full assurance of hope unto the end." Heb. 6:11.

THE doctrine of an assured belief of the pardon of sin, of acceptance in Christ, and of adoption into the family of God, has been, and yet is, regarded by many as an attainment never to be expected in the present life; and when it is expressed, it is viewed with a suspicion unfavorable to the character of the work. But this is contrary to the Divine word, and to the concurrent experience of millions, who have lived and died in the full assurance of hope. The doctrine of assurance is a doctrine of undoubted revelation, implied and expressed. That it is enforced as a state of mind essential to the salvation of the believer, we cannot admit; but that it is insisted upon as essential to his comfortable and holy walk, and as greatly involving the glory of God, we must strenuously maintain. Else why these marked references to the doctrine? In Colossians 2:1, 2, Paul expresses "great conflict" for the saints, that their "hearts might be comforted, being knit together in love, and unto all riches of the full assurance of understanding," etc. In the Epistle to the Hebrews, 10:22, he exhorts them, "Let us draw near with a true heart, in full assurance of faith;" with similar language in our motto. To crown all, the apostle Peter, 2nd Epistle 1:10, thus earnestly exhorts, "Why the rather, brethren, give diligence to make your calling and election sure." We trust no further proof from the sacred word is required to authenticate the doctrine. It is written as with a sunbeam, "the Spirit itself bears witness with our spirit, that we are the children of God."

It is the duty and the privilege of every believer diligently and prayerfully to seek the sealing of the Spirit. He rests short of his great privilege, if he slights or undervalues this blessing. Do not be satisfied with the faint impression which you received in conversion. In other words, rest not content with a past experience. Many are satisfied with a mere hope that they once passed from death unto life; and with this feeble and, in many cases, doubtful evidence they are content to pass all their days, and to go down to the grave. Ah, reader, if you are really converted, and your soul is in a healthy, growing, spiritual state, you will want more than this; and especially, too, if you are led into deeper self-knowledge—a more intimate acquaintance with the roughness of the rough way, the straightness of the straight path—you will want a present Christ to lean upon and to live upon. Past experience will not do for you, save only as it confirms your soul in the faithfulness of God. "Forgetting those things that are behind," you will seek a present pardon, a present sense of acceptance; and the daily question, as you near your eternal home, will be, "How do I now stand with God?—is Jesus precious to my soul now?—is He my daily food?—what do I experience of daily visits from and to Him?—do I more and more see my own vileness, emptiness, and poverty; and His righteousness, grace, and fullness?—and should the summons now come, am I ready to depart and to be with Christ?" As you value a happy and a holy walk—as you would be jealous for the honor and glory of the Lord—as you wish to be the "salt of the earth," the "light of the world"—to be a savor of Christ in every place—oh seek the sealing of the Spirit. Rest not short of it—reach after it—press towards it: it is your duty—oh that the duty may be your privilege then shall you exclaim with an unfaltering tongue, "Abba, Father," "My Lord, and my God!"

MAY 20

"Until the appearing of our Lord Jesus Christ: which in his times he shall show, who is the blessed and only Potentate, the King of kings, and Lord of lords; Who only has immortality, dwelling in the light which no man can approach unto; whom no man has seen, nor can see: to whom be honor and power everlasting." Amen. 1 Tim. 6:14-16

STRONG is the testimony of the Holy Spirit in the word to the essential Deity of our blessed Lord. And if He has laid such amazing stress upon it, surely it should be a solemn matter with us how we think of and treat it. The great, the grand glory of Immanuel is His essential glory—the glory of His Godhead. It is only in this light that we can approach Him with the hope of pardon and acceptance. It is then we talk of Him as a Mediator—it is then we view Him as the Sin-bearer of His people—it is then we contemplate Him as their Surety, their Righteousness, their covenant Head. In vain we speak of His atoning blood, of His finished righteousness, of His mediatorial fullness, if we look not up to Him in the "glory He had with the Father before the world was." This it is that imparts such efficacy to His work, and throws such surpassing luster around it. And what is the witness of the Spirit to this doctrine? It is this; that all the names, the perfections, the works, and the worship proper only to Deity belong to Christ—thus proclaiming Him with a loud voice to be, what He really is—Jehovah Jesus.

Reader, ponder the testimony. Jesus of Nazareth, the anointed Savior of poor sinners, is emphatically styled the "great God," Titus 2:13; the "mighty God," Isa. 9:6; the "only wise God," Jude 25; the "true God," 1 John 5:20; the "only Lord God," Jude 4. The name Jehovah peculiarly belongs to God: it is never in a solitary instance applied to a mere creature. "I am Jehovah; that is my name." And yet the very name is ascribed to Jesus by the Holy Spirit, "This is the name whereby He shall be called, Jehovah our Righteousness." He is then Jehovah Jesus, "God over all, blessed for evermore." Could testimony be more clear and decisive? O precious truth on which to live—O glorious rock on which to die! Jesus is Jehovah He is "Immanuel, God with us"—"God manifest in the flesh." Hold fast to this truth, reader. Let nothing weaken your grasp upon it. It is your plank, your life-boat, your ark, your all. This gone, all goes with it! You will need it when you come to die—in that solemn hour when all else fails you—when sin in battle-array rises before you, and you think of the holiness of a holy God—then you will want a rock to stand upon; and as the Spirit leads you to Jesus the Rock, testifies to your soul of His blood, witnesses to His Godhead, unfolds Him in His essential glory, you shall be enabled to shout "Victory! victory!" as you pass safely and triumphantly over Jordan. The blood that speaks peace will be felt to be efficacious—and the righteousness that justifies will be seen to be glorious—and the Rock that sustains will be felt to be firm and immovable, just as the blessed Glorifier of Christ witnesses to the truth of His Deity. Oh then to see the Lawgiver in the character of the Law-fulfiller—to behold the God-man obeying, suffering, dying—and therefore the law honored, justice satisfied, and the Father well pleased—truly may the believing soul adopt the triumphant language of the apostle, and take up H is challenge—"Who is he that condemns? it is Christ that died." Dear reader, set a high value on the doctrine of our Lord's Deity—guard it with a jealous eye, pray to be established in its full experimental belief; for the more you see of the dignity of His person, the more you will see of the glory of His work.

MAY 21

"And for this cause he is the mediator of the new testament, that by means of death, for the redemption of the transgressions that were under the first testament, they which are called might receive the promise of eternal inheritance." Heb. 9:15

VIEWED in its proper aspect, the humanity of our Lord will be found to occupy a place in the scheme of salvation, as important and essential to its accomplishment as His Deity; that the humanity was pure humanity, and the Deity absolute Deity, while the mysterious union of the two, in the person of the Lord Jesus, constituted Him the proper and the "one Mediator between God and man." Glorious is this aspect of our Lord's complex person; full and clear is the testimony of the Spirit to its truth. Where Christ speaks of Himself as inferior to the Father—as having received "glory from the Father,"—as receiving "life from the Father,"—of "the Father being greater than He,"—He must invariably be regarded as alluding to Himself in His mediatorial office only, and not in His Divine character. He is equal to the Father in nature, subordinate to Him only in office. On this truth hinges all the glory and efficacy of redemption.

It was, then, essential to His fitness as the Surety and Mediator of His covenant people, that He should be "bone of their bone, and flesh of their flesh." That forasmuch as the children are partakers of flesh and blood, He also Himself likewise took part of the same; "it behooved Him to be made like unto His brethren." The nature of His office, and the success of his undertaking, required that the union of every Divine and human perfection should meet and center in Him. He was to be the middle person between God and man. He was to bring together these two extremes of being—the Infinite and the finite. He was to mediate for the offended Creator and the offending creature. How could He possibly accomplish this great and peculiar work, without a union of the two natures—the Divine and the human? Jehovah could admit of mediation only by one of equal holiness and glory, and man could negotiate in this great business of reconciliation but with one "in all points (sin excepted) like canto himself." Behold this wondrous union in the person of Jesus. As man, he was made under the law—honoring it in its precepts by His obedience, and in its penalty by His sufferings. As God, He imparted a dignity to that obedience, and a virtue to those sufferings, which rendered them eternally efficacious in the salvation of men, glorious in the sight of angels, and infinitely satisfactory to law and to justice.

Beloved reader, stand not aloof from the pure humanity of your blessed Lord. It was humanity that obeyed, that bled, and that died for you. Cling to the doctrine of His Deity. It was God in the man that rendered His obedience meritorious for your justification, and His death effectual for your redemption. Oh glorious person of the God-man Mediator! What a foundation is here laid for a poor condemned sinner to build upon! What a "new and living way" to God is opened—what a wide door to His very heart! He may come now, and feel that not a perfection of Jehovah is trampled upon in His coming—that not an iota of His law is dishonored in His salvation—but that the law appears in its richest luster, and every perfection shines in its resplendent glory, in the full and free redemption of a sinner through the blood and righteousness of the Son of God. Is it any wonder that over the door of mercy should be written in letters of brightness that might dazzle an angel's eye, "Whoever believes in Him shall not perish, but have everlasting life"?

MAY 22

Therefore, behold, I will allure her, and bring her into the wilderness, and speak comfortably unto her. Hosea 2:14

How does God comfort those who are cast down? His method is various. He adapts the comfort to the sorrow. He first writes the sentence of death upon all comfort out of Himself. If you have been accustomed to scrutinize narrowly God's way of dealing with you, you will often have marked this peculiar feature—that before He has unsealed the fountain, He has cut off the spring. In other words, He has suspended all human channels of comfort, preparatory to the fulfillment of his own exceeding great and precious promise—"I, even

I, am He that comforts you." It was thus He dealt with His Church of old, as described in our motto. In that wilderness, as a "woman of a sorrowful spirit," she is brought; in that wilderness, she is separated from her companions; yet in that dreary, lonely wilderness, the God of all comfort speaks to her heart. Then follows the song of the Lord in the strange land—the music of the wilderness—"And she shall sing there, as in the days of her youth, and as in the day when she came up out of the land of Egypt." Overlook not this process. It may be painful, humiliating, and trying to faith; but the issue, like all the conduct of our heavenly Father, will be most blessed and holy. Is He now, in your case, writing the sentence of death upon all creature-comfort? Does no eye pity you, no heart feel for you, no tongue address you, and is no hand outstretched to rescue you? Look now for God; for He is on the way, in this the time of the creature's failure, Himself to comfort you.

Take heed that it is God, and not man, who comforts you—that your consolation is Divine, and not human. It may be the duty of your minister, and the privilege of your friend, to speak a promise to the ear, and to spread out before you the riches of Divine comfort in the word; but it is the prerogative of the Holy Spirit alone to apply the promise, and to give a heartfelt possession of those comforts. Jealous of His love to you, and of the glory that belongs to Himself, God will delegate the office and commit the power of lightening the burden of your oppressed spirit, of soothing the sorrow of your disconsolate heart, to no created hand. "As one whom his mother comforts, so will I comfort you." Beware, then, of a creature-comfort and of a false peace. Let no one comfort you but God Himself, and let nothing give you peace but the peace-speaking blood of Jesus. A wound may be covered, and yet not be healed; a promise may be spoken, and yet not be applied. To the "God of all comfort," then, repair in your grief. To the precious blood of the Incarnate God go with your burden of sin. Oh! how welcome will you be, coming just as you are! How sacred will be your sorrow to His heart, how eloquent your pleadings to His ear, and how precious in His sight the simple child-like faith, that severs you from all other dependences, and leads you to Him alone for comfort! Then will you exclaim—and not David's harp could discourse sweeter music—"My heart trusted in Him, and I am helped. You have turned for me my mourning into dancing you have put off my sackcloth, and girded me with gladness; to the end that my glory may sing praise to you, and not be silent. I love the Lord, because He has heard my voice and my supplications. Because He has inclined His ear unto me, therefore will I call upon Him as long as I live."

MAY 23

"Verily, verily, I say unto you, The hour is coming, and now is, when the dead shall hear the voice of the Son of God: and those who hear shall live." John 5:25

THE condition from which the renewed man passes is that of death. This was his Adamic, or natural state. The sinner is by law dead; the curse is upon him, and condemnation awaits him. No, he is now condemned. "He that believes not is condemned already." As in a state of grace heaven is commenced below, so in a state of nature hell is commenced below. Grace is the beginning of glory, and nature is the beginning of condemnation. The one has in it the element of eternal happiness; the other has in it the element of eternal woe.

But the believer in Jesus is one who has "passed from death unto life." The Spirit of God has breathed into him the breath of life, and He has become a living soul. What an amazing truth is this! We see into what a new and holy life the believing sinner has passed. Quitting forever the low sensual life, he enters upon the exalted life of every believer—the life of faith in the Son of God. He has now learned to lean upon Jesus, his righteousness and his strength, his consolation and his support. He is happy in sorrow, joyful in tribulation, strong in weakness, as by faith he leans upon Christ. What a life, too, is the life of communion with God, springing from his life of oneness with Christ! The believer now holds communion with essential life, with essential holiness, with essential love. The holy breathing of his soul is the fellowship of Christ below with the Father above. It is the one life in heaven and on earth. What is prayer to you, my reader? Is it communion? Is it fellowship? Does God meet you, and open His heart to you? Are you appreciative that you possess His ear? Is prayer the element in which your soul lives? Do you make every circumstance an occasion of prayer? As soon as sorrow comes, do you take it to the Lord's heart? As soon as burdening care comes, do you take it to the Him? As soon as conscience is beclouded, do you take it to the Lord's blood? As soon as the inward corruption rises, do you take it to the Lord's grace? This, beloved, is the life of faith. Mistake not the nature of prayer. True prayer is never more eloquent and prevailing than when breathed forth in real desires, and ardent longings, and groans that cannot be uttered. Sighs, and words, and tears, flowing from a lowly, contrite heart, have a voice more powerful and persuasive than the most eloquent diction that ever clothed the lips of man. Oh to be led by the Spirit more perfectly into a knowledge of the nature and the power of prayer! for this is the grand evidence of our spiritual life. "Behold, he prays."

MAY 24

"For whatever is born of God overcomes the world: and this is the victory that overcomes the world, even our faith." 1 John 5:4

How does victory over the world mark one born of God? It proves it in this way. That which overcomes the world must be superhuman, of almighty power. It cannot be anything of the world, nor can it be of the flesh; for the flesh has no power over the flesh, and the world will never oppose itself. The flesh loves itself; and the world is too fond of power, quietly and unresistingly to yield its dominion. What then is that which overcomes the world? Faith is the conquering grace—this it is that gives the victory—this it is that crushes this tremendous foe. And what is faith but the "gift of God," and the work of the eternal Spirit in the soul? So that He who possesses that faith which is of the operation of the Spirit is "born of God;" and "whatever is born of God overcomes the world," and the instrument by which he overcomes the world is faith—"Who is he that overcomes the world, but he that believes that Jesus is the Son of God?"

And how does faith overcome the world? By leading the believer to the cross of Jesus. True faith deals with its great object, Jesus. It goes to Him in the conflict, it goes to Him when hard pressed, it goes to Him in its weakness, it goes to Him in deep distress—on Him it leans, and through Him it always obtains the victory. Of the martyrs it is recorded, that they "overcame through the blood of the Lamb;" and Paul employs similar language in describing his victory: "God forbid that I should glory, save in the cross of our Lord Jesus Christ, by whom the world is crucified unto me, and I unto the world." It is faith in Christ that gives us the victory. How could a feeble saint, with no strength or wisdom in himself, overcome so powerful and subtle an enemy as this, without supernatural aid? Never could he. Look at the world! There are its ten thousand temptations—its temptations of pleasure—its temptations of ambition—its temptations of wealth—its false religion—its temporizing policy—its hollow friendship—its empty show—its gay deceptions—its ten thousand arts to ensnare, beguile, allure, and charm; oh, how could one poor weak believer ever crush this fearful, powerful foe, but as he is "strong in the grace that is in Christ Jesus"? The cross of Christ gives him the victory. Christ has already conquered the world, and faith in His blood will enable the feeblest soul to exclaim, while the enemy lies subdued at his feet, "Thanks be unto God, which always causes us to triumph in Christ."

Reader, have you obtained the victory over the world, or has the world obtained the victory over you? One of the two is certain—either you are warring against it, or you are its passive and unresisting victim; either you are "born of God," and "have overcome the world," or you are still unregenerate, and the world has overcome you. On whose side is the victory? Perhaps you are a professor of the Lord Jesus, and yet loving the world, and conforming to its dogma, its principles, its fashions, its dress, its amusements, yes, its very religion—for it has its hollow forms of religion. Is it so? Then hear what the word of the Lord says to you: "Love not the world, neither the things that are in the world. If any man love the world, the love of the Father is not in him." Solemn declaration for you, you professors of Christ, and yet lovers of the world! You cannot love God and love the world at the same time. Do not be deceived! The outward garb will not save you. The mere name, the empty lamp—these will avail you nothing when you come to die. If the world has never been ejected from your heart—if you have never been crucified to it, then the love of God is not there; and the love of God absent, you are a stranger to the new birth.

MAY 25

"For the invisible things of him from the creation of the world are clearly seen, being understood by the things that are made, even his eternal power and Godhead; so that they are without excuse: Because that, when they knew God, they glorified him not as God, neither were thankful; but became vain in their imaginations, and their foolish heart was darkened." Romans 1:20-21

WE cannot forget that the God of revelation is the God of nature—that in exploring this vast territory, we trespass upon the domain of no foreign potentate, we invade no hostile kingdom, we tread no forbidden ground. The spiritual mind, fond of soaring through nature in quest of new proofs of God's existence, and fresh emblems of His wisdom, power, and goodness, exults in the thought that it is his Father's domain he treads. He feels that God, his God, is there; and the sweet consciousness of His all-pervading presence, and the impress of His great perfections which everywhere meets his eye, overwhelm his renewed soul with wonder, love, and praise. Oh the delight of looking abroad upon nature, under a sense of pardoning, filial love in the soul, when enabled to exclaim, "This God is my God." Let it not therefore be supposed that nature and revelation are at war with each other. A spiritual mind may discover a close and beautiful relation and harmony between the two. The study of God in His external operations is by no means discouraged in His word. "The heavens declare the glory of God; and the firmament shows His handiwork. Day unto day utters speech, and night unto night shows knowledge." And in the first verse of our motto, the apostle refers to the rejection of this source of evidence by the heathen.

But if natural theology has its advantages, it also has its limitations. It must never be regarded as taking the place of God's word. It may just impart light enough to the mind to leave its atheism "without excuse," but it cannot impart light enough to convince the soul of its sinfulness—its guilt—its exposure to the wrath of a holy God, and its need of such a Savior as Jesus is. All this is the work of the eternal and blessed Spirit; and if my reader is resting his hope of heaven upon what he has learned of God and of himself in the light of nature only—a stranger to the teaching and operations of the Holy Spirit upon his mind—he is awfully deceiving himself. Natural religion can never renew, sanctify, and save the soul. A man may be deeply schooled in it as a science—he may investigate it thoroughly—defend it ably and successfully, and even, from the feeble light it emits, grope his dark way to the great edifice of revelation—but beyond this it cannot conduct him: it cannot open the door, and admit him to the fullness of the gospel therein contained. It may go far to convince him that the word of God is true, but it cannot "open the book and loose the seals thereof," to disclose to the mind its rich and exhaustless treasures. Oh no! another and a diviner light must shine upon his soul; another and a more powerful hand must break the seals. That light, that hand, is God the Holy Spirit. He only can make the soul acquainted with this solemn truth, "The heart is deceitful above all things, and desperately wicked." He only can explore this dark chamber of imagery, and bring to light the hidden evil that is there. He only can lay the soul low in the dust before God at the discovery, and draw out the heart in the humiliating confession—"Behold, I am vile!" He only can take of the blood of a precious Savior, and the glorious righteousness of the God-Man Mediator, and, working faith to receive it, through this infinitely glorious medium seal pardon and acceptance, and peace upon the conscience. Oh you blessed and loving Spirit! this is Your work, and Your alone. Your to empty, Your to fill; Your to lay low, Your to exalt; Your to wound, Your to heal; Your to convince of sin, and Your to lead the soul, all sinful, guilty, and wretched as it is, to the precious blood of Jesus—"the fountain opened for sin and uncleanness." You shall have the praise, and wear the CROWN!

MAY 26

"O God, you have taught me , from my youth: and hitherto have I declared your wondrous works. You, which have showed me great and sore troubles, shall quicken me again, and shall bring me up again from the depths of the earth. You shall increase my greatness, and comfort me on every side." Psalm 71:17, 20, 21.

A CAREFUL reader of David's history cannot but be impressed with the early discipline into which this eminent servant of God was brought. He had scarcely slain Israel's vaunting foe, while yet the flush of victory was upon his youthful brow, and the songs of applause were resounding on his ear, when he found himself placed in a position of the keenest trial and most imminent peril. The jealousy of Saul at the unbounded popularity of the youthful warrior, in whom he at once beheld a rival in his people's affection, if not a successor to the throne, instantly dictated a most oppressive and murderous policy. From that moment the king sought his life. And thus from being the deliverer of the nation, whom he had saved with his arm—an idol of the people, whom he had entranced with his exploit, David became a fugitive and an exile. Thus suddenly and darkly did the storm-cloud rise upon his bright and flattering prospects.

Two deeply spiritual lessons may be gathered from this history. How rapidly, in the experience of the child of God, may a season of prosperity and adulation be followed by one of trial and humiliation! It is, perhaps, just the curb and the correction God sends to check and to save us. We can ill sustain too sudden and too great an elevation. Few can wear their honors meekly, and none apart from especial and great grace. And when God gives great grace, we may always expect that He will follow it with great trial. He will test the grace He gives. There is but a step from the "third heaven" to the "thorn in the flesh." Oh, the wisdom and love of God that shine in this! Who that sees in the discipline a loving and judicious Father, would cherish one unkind rebellious thought?

Another lesson taught us is, that our severest and bitterest trials may be engrafted upon our dearest and sweetest blessings. It was David's popularity that evoked the storm now beating upon him. The grateful affection of the people inspired the envy and hatred of the king. How often is it thus with us! God bestows upon us blessings, and we abuse them. We idolize the creature He has given, and cling too fondly to the friend He has bestowed—settle down too securely in the nest He has made—inhale too eagerly the incense offered to our rank, talents, and achievements—and God often adopts those very things as the voice of His rebuke, and as the instruments of our correction. Thus may our severest trials spring from our sweetest mercies. What a source of sorrow to Abraham was his loved Isaac; and to Isaac was his favored Jacob; and to Jacob was his precious Joseph; and to Jonah was his pleasant gourd! And what deep spiritual truth would the Holy Spirit teach us by all this?—to seek to glorify God in all our blessings when He gives them; and to enjoy all our blessings in God, when He takes then away.

MAY 27

"The Lord has done great things for us; whereof we are glad. Those who sow in tears shall reap in joy." Psalm 126:3, 5

TURN we again to David. What would be the result of his review in after-years of the early and severe discipline in which the God of love placed him? Would He not, when his great enemy was laid low, and He had come to the throne, awaken his harp to the sweetest praise and thanksgiving, for the schooling of trial in the morning of life? Oh yes, when binding his sacrifice upon the horns of the altar, or administering the kingdom, he would think of the cave of Adullam, and of the wilderness of Ziph; and as he recounted all the way God had led him, and remembered the deep lessons he had learned in those seasons of deep trial, with what a swelling heart and tuneful voice would he exclaim, "Blessed is the man whom You chasten, O Lord, and teach him out of Your law; that You may give him rest from the days of adversity, until the pit be dug for the wicked."

What an echo to its truth does this sweet strain awaken in many a heart! We, too, can praise God for trial. We, too, can thank God for sorrow. It has been to us, though a painful, yet a much needed and a most blessed school. The cave and the wilderness have been heavenly places on earth. True, it may be, the sorrow early came. It distilled its bitter into our cup, and flung its shadow upon our path, when that cup was so sweet and that path was so bright with life's young dream of joy; yet it was well for us that we bowed to the yoke in our youth, it was good for us that we were early afflicted. The lessons which we have been taught, the truths which we have learned, the preciousness of the Savior which we have experienced, the love of God which we have felt, the sweetness in prayer we have tasted, and the fitness for labor we have derived, all, all testify, as with one voice, to the unutterably precious blessings that flow through the channel of early, sacred, and sanctified sorrow.

Dear reader, painful and sad as may be the path you now are treading, fear not; the issue will be most glorious. The seed you are sowing in tears shall yield you a golden harvest of joy. Adversity is the school of heaven. And in heaven—where no sorrow chafes, where no tears flow, where no blight withers, where no disappointment sickens, and where no change or coldness chills, wounds, and slays—the sweetest praises will be awakened by the recollection of the early and sanctified sorrows of earth. Thus the moral beauty of the redeemed soul here, and its inconceivable glory hereafter, will be found to have been deepened by those very circumstances that threatened to deface and becloud it.

MAY 28

"Brethren, if a man be overtaken in a fault, you which are spiritual, restore such an one in the spirit of meekness; considering yourself, lest you also be tempted." Gal. 6:1

THE duty of brotherly admonition and reproof is a perfectly legitimate exercise of Christian love. It may be found the most difficult, but the result will prove it to be the most holy and precious operation of this grace. The Church of God is one family, linked together by ties and interests the closest, the holiest, and the tenderest. It is natural, therefore, that each member should desire for the others the utmost perfection of Christian attainment, and must feel honored or dishonored, as the case may be, by the walk and conversation of those with whom the relationship is so close. In Christian friendship, too, the same feeling is recognized. We naturally feel anxious to see in one whom we tenderly love the removal of whatever detracts from the beauty, the symmetry, and the perfection of Christian character. Here, then, will the duty of brotherly admonition and reproof find its appropriate sphere of exercise. Few things contribute more to the formation of Christian character, and to the holy walk of a church, than the faithful, Christ-like discharge of this duty. It is true it requires no ordinary degree of grace in him who administers, and in him who receives, the reproof. That in the one there should be nothing of the spirit which seems to say, "Stand by, I am holier than you," nothing to give needless pain or humiliation, but the utmost meekness, gentleness, and tenderness; and that in the other, there should be the tractable and humble mind, that admits the failing, receives the reproof, and is grateful for the admonition. "Let the righteous smite me," says David, "it shall be a kindness; and let him reprove me, it shall be an excellent oil." Thus, while this duty is administered and received in the spirit of the meek and lowly Jesus, the church will be kindly affectioned one to another, knit together in love, and growing up into that state in which she will be without spot, or wrinkle, or any such thing.

True Christian love will avoid taking the seat of judgment. There are few violations of the law of love more common than those rash and premature judgments, which some Christians are ever ready to pronounce upon the actions, the principles, and the motives of others. And yet a more difficult and delicate position no Christian can be placed in than this. To form a true and correct opinion of a certain line of conduct, we must often possess the heart-searching eye of God. We must be intimately acquainted with all the hidden motives, and must be fully in possession of all the concomitant circumstances of the case, before we can possibly arrive at anything like an accurate opinion. Thus, in consequence of this blind, premature pre-judgment, this rash and hasty decision, the worst possible construction is often put upon the actions and the remarks of others, extremely unjust, and deeply wounding to the feelings. But especially inconsistent with this love, when small unessential differences of opinion in the explanation of scriptural facts, and consequent nonconformity in creed and discipline, are constructed into rejection of the faith once delivered to the saints, and made the occasion of hard thoughts or of unkind and severe treatment. Let us then hear the Lord's words, "Judge not, that you do not be judged;" and the apostle's, "Why do you judge your brother? or why do you set at nothing your brother? for we shall all stand before the judgment-seat of Christ."

MAY 29

"Why are you cast down, O my soul? and why are you disquieted within me? Hope you in God: for I shall yet praise him, who is the health of my countenance, and my God." Psalm 42:11

In all His dispensations—the severest and the darkest—have faith in God. This is, perhaps, one of the greatest achievements of faith. To believe in God when He smiles, to trust in Him when conscious of His nearness, to have faith in Him when the path is flowery and pleasant, were an easy task. But to have faith in Him when "He holds back the face of His throne, and spreads His cloud upon it; to love Him when He frowns; to follow Him when He withdraws; to cleave to Him when He would seem to shake us off; to trust in Him when His arm is raised to slay—this were faith indeed. And yet all this the faith of God's elect can achieve. If not, of what value is it? Of what possible use to the mariner would be the compass which would only work in the day, and not in the night? which only served to steer the vessel in light winds, and not in rough gales? Faith is the believing soul's compass, guiding it as truly and as certainly to the heavenly port through the wildest tempest as through the serenest calm. To change the figure, faith is that celestial telescope which can pierce the thickest haze or the darkest cloud, descrying suns and stars glowing and sparkling in the far distance. It can discern God's smile under a frown; it can read His name to be "love" beneath the dark dispensation; it can behold the Sun of Righteousness beaming through the interstices of gloomy clouds; and now and then it can catch a glimpse of the harbor itself, with the towering turrets and golden spires of the "new Jerusalem" glittering in the distance. Oh, it is a wonderful grace, the precious faith of God's elect!

Is God dealing with you now in a way of deep trial, of dark providence, mysterious to your mind, and painful to your heart? Is He even chastening you for your backslidings, correcting you for your sins? Still "have faith in God." Sensible appearances, second causes, cannot in the least degree affect the ground of your faith which is God Himself—His immutable nature, His unchangeable love, His eternal purpose, His everlasting covenant, His own Divine and glorious perfections. Believe that you are in His heart, and that your interests are in His hands. Have faith in His wisdom to guide, in His love to direct, in His power to sustain, in His faithfulness to fulfill every promise that now relates to your best welfare and happiness. Only believe in God—that all things in His disposal of you, in His transactions with you, are working together for our present and eternal good. All that He expects and requires of you now is to have faith in Him. The cloud may be dark, the sea tempestuous, but God is in the cloud, and "the Lord sits upon the flood." Even now it is the privilege of your faith to exclaim, "My soul, hope you in God. He is my God; I will trust, and not be afraid."

Oh, what inspiring words are these—"hope you in God!" I hesitate not to say, my reader, you may hope in God. Though your case may seem desperate, to your eye cheerless and hopeless, not merely too intricate for man, but too unworthy for God—yet you may hope in God. Take your case to Him, hoping against hope, and believing in unbelief. Will He close His heart against you? Never! Will He repel you when you fly to Him? Never! It is not in the heart of God, no, nor is it in His power, to do so. Take hold of His strength—I speak it humbly, reverentially—and you have overcome God. You disarm Him of the instrument and of the power to punish you; you have laid your hand of faith upon the strength of His love, and have made peace with Him. You cannot cherish a hope too sanguine, nor exercise a faith too implicit in God, hopeless, cheerless, and extreme as your case may be. Impossible! God never appears so like Himself, as in the season of the believer's darkness and suffering. At the very moment in which he sees the least of God, God appears the most what He is. The tenderest unfoldings of His heart are in sorrow, the brightest exhibitions of His character are in darkness, and the most glorious displays of His wisdom, power, and grace are seen gleaming through the mist.

MAY 30

"Whoever eats my flesh, and drinks my blood, has eternal life; and I will raise him up at the last day. For my flesh is food indeed, and my blood is drink indeed. He that eats my flesh, and drinks my blood, dwells in me, and I in him." John 6:54-56

FROM where do the ordinances derive their efficacy and power, but from the vitality of the Redeemer's blood? There could be no life, for instance, in the ordinance of the Lord's Supper but as that institution presented in a lively picture to the faith of the recipient the life-blood of the Savior. With what clearness and solemnity has He Himself put forth this truth, in the verses of our motto; thus declaring that he who in lowly and simple faith drinks of the blood of Jesus, partakes of the life of Jesus, because the life of Jesus is in the blood. Should the eye of an unconverted soul light upon this page, or should it arrest the attention of an unbelieving and therefore an unworthy recipient of the ordinance, let that individual seriously ponder these solemn words of Jesus—"Except you eat the flesh of the Son of man, and drink His blood, you have no life in you." The ordinance has no life of itself; the mere symbol possesses no spiritual vitality whatever; it cannot impart life, nor can it sustain life. But the life in the ordinance flows from the exercise of faith, through this medium, with the life-blood of Jesus. Therefore, if you rest only in the symbol, if in this ordinance you partake not by faith of the blood of Jesus, your soul is destitute of spiritual life. In the words of Jesus Himself, "You have no life in you."

But oh what life does the believing communicant find in the atoning blood! what food, that refreshment, what nourishment! Is it any wonder that Jesus should be to Him the chief among ten thousand, and that the blood of Jesus should be the most precious thing in the universe? If the death of Jesus is his life, what must the life of Jesus be! If the humiliation of Jesus is his honor, what must the exaltation of Jesus be! If the cross of Jesus is his glory, what must the throne of Jesus be! If Jesus crucified is his boast, what must be Jesus glorified!

"If, when we were enemies, we were reconciled by the death of His Son, much more, being reconciled, we shall be saved by His life."

Reader, is the blood of Jesus the life of your soul? So momentous is this truth, bear with me in pressing it upon your attention. Believe me when, with all affection and solemnity, I say that Your religion, your creed, your profession, are lifeless if they are not vivified, pervaded, and animated by the blood of the Son of God. God have no dealings with you in this great matter your salvation, but through the blood. He cannot "reason" with you about your sins of "crimson" and of "scarlet" dye, but on the footing of the blood. He cannot meet you for one moment in any other character than as a "consuming fire," but as He meets you at, and communes with you from above the mercy-seat sprinkled with blood. The blood of atonement is everything to God in the way of satisfaction, of glory, and of honor; and should be everything to you in the way of acceptance, pardon, and communion. There is not a moment in which God's eye of complacence is withdrawn from the blood of His Son in the perpetual acceptance of the believer; and there should not be a moment in which our eye of faith, in every circumstance of our daily walk before Him, should not also be upon this "blood of sprinkling, that speaks better things than that of Abel."

MAY 31

"I drew them with cords of a man, with bands of love." Hosea 11:4

THE word of God teaches us, that "a soft answer turns away wrath." And, again, it is said, "By long forbearing is a prince persuaded, and a soft tongue breaks the bone." It was by kindness that David calmed down the enraged temper of Saul, obtaining thus a two-fold victory—a victory over himself; and a victory over the wrathful king. Kindness is the great law of the Divine government; and in man is the strongest element of human power. How does God overcome an evil; is it not by good? And based upon this is a like precept enforced upon us: "If your enemy hunger, feed him; if he thirst, give him drink: for in so doing you shall heap coals of fire on his head. Do not be overcome of evil, but overcome evil with good." There is no weapon so powerful as kindness. It is by the love of the cross the enmity of the carnal mind is subdued, and its inbred evils overcome; and would we be exquisitely severe to the faults and delinquencies of the erring and the hardened, we must be exquisitely kind. The very severity of love will more quickly and effectually subdue, win, and reclaim, than all the harsh, cruel treatment, unfeeling upbraiding, and bitter threats, that sternness ever invented. The human heart expands to the looks, and words, and actions of human kindness and sympathy; just as the wild rose and the delicate flower nurtured in our gardens open to the light and warmth of the morning sun.

We should remember this in our walks and labors of benevolence. Brought, as we sometimes are, into contact with extreme cases of guilt and crime, we should not overlook the material we yet possess, with which to repair the fallen structure. No heart should be considered too polluted—no mind too dark—no character too debased—for the power of God, working by human instrumentality, to restore. The surface may present to the eye the iron features of a hardened and a reckless character; nevertheless, there are springs of thought and feeling and memory, beneath that repulsive surface, which, if touched by a skillful and a delicate hand, will unlock the door of the heart, and admit you within its most sacred recesses. Thus with gentleness and kindness you may soften the most hardened, disarm the most ferocious, calm the most violent, and attain complete possession of a mind that has long resisted and repelled every other subduing influence. The true disciple of Christ, like the beloved John, who leaned on the bosom of Jesus, and felt and imbibed the warmth of its gentleness, tenderness, and love, will ever desire to exhibit the loving, sympathizing, forgiving spirit of his Lord and Master, from whose lips no words of harshness ever breathed.

JUNE

JUNE 1

"Howbeit you are just in all that is brought upon us; for you have done right, but we have done wickedly." Neh. 9:33

IT would be incorrect to suppose that the chastisements of our heavenly Father were in themselves pleasant and desirable. They are no more so than the physician's recipe, or the surgeon's lancet. But as in the one case, so in the other, we look beyond the medicine to its sanative qualities, we forget the bitterness of the draught in its remedial results. Thus with the medicine of the soul—the afflictions sent and sanctified by God. Forgetting the bitter and the pain of God's dealings, the only question of moment is, what is the cause and what the design of my Father in this? The answer is—our deeper sanctification.

This is effected, first, by making us more thoroughly acquainted with the holiness of God Himself. Sanctified chastisement has an especial tendency to this. To suppose a case. Our sense of God's holiness, previously to this dispensation, was essentially defective, unsound, superficial, and uninfluential. The judgment admitted the truth; we could speak of it to others, and in prayer acknowledge it to God; but still there was a vagueness and an indistinctness in our conceptions of it, which left the heart cold, and rendered the walk uneven. To be led now into the actual, heart-felt experience of the truth, that in all our transactions we had to deal with the holy, heart-searching Lord God, we find quite another and an advanced stage in our journey, another and a deeper lesson learned in our school. This was the truth, and in this way Nehemiah was taught. "Howbeit you are just (holy) in all that is brought upon us; for you have done right, but we have done wickedly." Oh blessed acknowledgment! Do not think that we speak unfeelingly when we say, it were worth all the discipline you have ever passed through, to a have become more deeply schooled in the lesson of God's holiness. One most fruitful cause of all our declensions from the Lord will be found wrapped up in the crude and superficial views which we entertain of the character of God, as a God of infinite purity. And this truth He will have His people to study and to learn, not by sermons, nor from books, not from hearsay, nor from theory, but in the school of loving chastisement—personally and experimentally. Thus beholding more closely, and through a clearer medium, this Divine perfection, the believer is changed more perfectly into the same moral image. "He for our profit, that we might be partakers of His holiness."

The rod of the covenant has a wonderful power of discovery. Thus, by revealing to us the concealed evil of our natures, we become more holy. "The blueness (that is, the severity) of a wound cleanses away evil." This painful discovery often recalls to memory past failings and sins. David went many years in oblivion of his departure from God, until Nathan was sent, who, while he told him of his sin, with the same breath announced the message of Divine forgiveness. Then it was the royal penitent kneeled down and poured forth from the depths of his anguished spirit the fifty-first Psalm—a portion of God's word which you cannot too frequently study. "I do remember my sin this day," is the exclamation of the chastened sufferer. Thus led to search into the cause of the Divine correction, and discovering it—perhaps after a long season of forgetfulness—the "blueness of the wound," the severity of the rod, "cleanses away the evil;" in other words, more deeply sanctifies the soul. "Show me why you contend with me."

JUNE 2

"For you, O God, have proved us: you have tried us, as silver is tried." Psalm 66:10

FAITH has its trials, as well as its temptations. Affliction is a trial of faith; sorrow in any of its multitudinous forms is a trial of faith; the delay of mercy is a trial of faith; the promise unfulfilled is a trial of faith; the prayer unanswered is a trial of faith; painful providences, mysterious dispensations, straitened circumstances, difficulties, and embarrassments, all are so many trials of faith, commissioned and designed by God to place the gold in the crucible, and the wheat in the sieve, that both may be purified and tried. Ah, is it no trial of the believer's faith, when the foundation upon which it rests is assailed? Is it no trial of faith to have distorted representations of God presented to its eye, dishonoring thoughts of God suggested to the mind, unbelieving apprehensions of Jesus, His love, His grace, and His works, foisted upon the heart? To entertain for one moment the idea that God is unfaithful to His word, or that in His dealings He is arbitrary and unkind? that Jesus is not what He represents Himself to be, an all-sufficient Savior of the lost, the healer of the broken in heart, the tender, gentle Savior, not breaking the bruised reed, but supporting it, not quenching the smoking flax, but fanning it? Oh yes, these to a holy mind are painful trials of faith, from which the tender conscience shrinks, and the sensitive heart recoils.

It is only true grace that is really tried. No man puts mere dross into his furnace, or mere chaff into his sieve. All his toils and pains-taking would go for nothing, for it would come forth in its nature unaltered and unchanged—the dross would still be dross, and the chaff would still be chaff. Now the Lord tries, and Satan tempts, nothing but genuine grace. It is the wheat, and not the tares, that is made to pass through the fiery trial. Thus do afflictions and trying dispensations prove tests of a man's religion. When there is nothing but tinsel in a profession of Christianity, the fire will consume it; when there is nothing but chaff, the wind will scatter it. The furnace of temptation and the flail of affliction often prove a man's work of what sort it is, long before the discovery is made in a world where no errors can be corrected, and when it will be too late to rectify mistakes. Thus it is that so many professors, who have not the root of the matter in themselves, but endure for awhile, are offended and fall away when tribulation or persecution arises because of the word.

And why is the "wheat" thus sifted? why is so Divine and precious a grace subjected to a process so humiliating and severe? Certainly not because of any intrinsic impurity in the grace itself. All the graces of the Spirit, as they proceed from God, and are implanted in the heart, are pure and holy; as essentially free from sin as the nature from where they flow. But in consequence of the impurity of the heart, and the defilement of the nature in which they are deposited—the body of sin and death by which they are encased—they become mixed with particles of earthliness and carnality, the fine gold with dross, and the pure wheat with chaff. To purify and separate the graces of the Holy Spirit from these things, so foreign to their nature, the Lord permits these temptations, and sends these trials of faith.

Not only may the faith of a child of God be severely assailed, but there are times when that faith may greatly waver. Is this surprising? No, the greatest wonder is, that with all these severe shocks, through which it passes, it does not entirely fail. Nothing but the Divinity that dwells within that grace keeps it. Were it not Divine and incorruptible, fail entirely it must. Look at Abraham—on one occasion in the strength of faith offering up his son, and on another occasion in the weakness of faith denying his wife! Look at David—in the strength of faith slaying Goliath, and in the weakness of faith fleeing from Saul! Look at Job—in the strength of faith justifying God in the severest of His dealings, and in the weakness of faith cursing the day that He was born! Look at Peter—in the strength of faith drawing his sword and smiting a servant of the high priest's, and in the weakness of faith forced by a little maid to deny the Lord whom he had but just defended! Oh! the wonder of wonders is, that there remains a single grain in the sieve, or a particle of metal in the furnace, or a solitary spark in the ocean—that all is not utterly scattered, consumed, and annihilated! Nothing but the power of God and its own incorruptible and imperishable nature, preserve it.

JUNE 3

"Behold, he prays." Acts 9:11

WHAT a precious fruit of the renewed heart is true prayer! If there is a single exercise of the soul that places the fact of its regeneracy beyond a doubt, it is this. Prayer, that comes as holy fire from God, and that rises as holy incense to God—prayer, that takes me, with every want and infirmity, with every sin and sorrow, to the bosom of the Father, through the smitten bosom of the Son—prayer, that sweetens my solitude, that calms my perturbed spirit, that weakens the power of sin, that nourishes the desire for holiness, and that transports the soul, by anticipation, beyond the region of winds, and storms, and tempests, into the presence of God, where all is sunshine and peace—oh what a wondrous privilege is this!

That there is much of awful mystery yet to be unraveled, in relation to this holy exercise of the soul, we readily admit. How prayer operates upon God, we know not. That it can effect any alteration in His purpose, or change His will, or afford Him information, no one for a moment supposes. And yet, that it should be an ordained medium by which finite weakness seems to overcome Infinite strength, a human will seems to turn the Divine will, and man's shallow mind seems to pour knowledge into the fathomless mind of God—that it should arrest a threatened judgment, remove an existing evil, or supply a present want—is a marvel in which, like all others of Divine revelation, I submit my reason to my faith, receiving and adoring what my reason cannot, unless I were God, perfectly comprehend. The only solution which we have of this mystery of prayer is contained in these words: "He that searches the hearts knows what is the mind of the Spirit, because He makes intercession for the saints according to the will of God;" the Holy Spirit thus inditing just that petition which is in harmony with the purpose, will, and love of Him who is emphatically the hearer and the answerer of prayer. What a volume might be composed on the subject of prayer, and yet the half would not be told! A compilation of its achievements would of itself be the work of the longest life. Blessed are they who can enter into the spirit of these words—"I give myself unto prayer." "It is good for me to draw near unto God." "Pray without ceasing." "Praying always with all prayer." "If we ask anything according to His will, He hears us; and if we know that He hears us, whatever we ask, we know that we have the petitions that we desired of Him." Have you, reader, this fruit? Then restrain not prayer before God.

JUNE 4

"They are of those that rebel against the light." Job 24:13

So far from cooperating with the Spirit in the new creation, the natural man presents every resistance and opposition to it. There is not only a passive aversion to, but there is an active resistance of, the work. The stream of man's natural inclinations runs counter to all holiness. A strong and steady current has set in against God and all that God loves. The pride of reason, the perverseness of the will, the enmity of the mind, the heart's love of sin, all are up in arms against the entrance of the Holy Spirit. Satan, the great enemy of God and man, has been too long in quiet and undisturbed possession of the soul, to resign his dominion without a strong and a fearful struggle to maintain it. When the Spirit of God knocks at the door of the heart, every ally is summoned by the "strong man armed" to "quench the Spirit," and bar and bolt each avenue to his entrance. All is alarm, agitation, and commotion within. There is a danger of being dispossessed, and every argument, persuasion, and contrivance must be resorted to, in order to retain the long-undisputed throne. The world is summoned to throw out its most enticing bait—ambition, wealth, literary and political distinction, pleasure in her thousand forms of fascination and power—all are made to pass, as in review, before the mind. The flesh, exerts its influence—the love of sin is appealed to, affection for some long-cherished lust, some long-indulged habit, some "fond amusement," some darling taste—these, inspired with new vigor, are summoned to the rescue. Thus Satan, the world, and the flesh are opposed to the Father, the Son, and the Spirit, in the great work of spiritual regeneration. Oh let no individual be so deceived as to believe, that when God the Eternal Spirit enters the soul, He finds the temple swept, and garnished, and prepared for His reception—that without the exercise of His own omnipotent and irresistible power, the heart bounds to welcome Him, the reason bows submissively to His government, and the will yields an instant and humble compliance. Oh no! if He that is in the regenerate were not greater and more powerful than he that is in the world, such is the enmity of the heart to God, such the supreme control which Satan exerts over the whole empire of man, God would be forever shut out, and the soul forever lost. See how clearly regeneration is proved to be the work of the Spirit. God has written it as with a sunbeam, "that we are His workmanship," and that the Eternal Spirit is the mighty agent.

JUNE 5

"For they being ignorant of God's righteousness, and going about to establish their own righteousness, have not submitted themselves unto the righteousness of God." Rom. 10:3

WHAT is man's own righteousness, the best that he ever made, but the hewing out of a created cistern, in the place of the infinite fountain? His obedience, at best, must be but a partial and an imperfect one; and, failing in a single point, entails eternal despair. "For whoever shall keep the whole law, and yet offend in one point, he is guilty of all." But not only is it a shallow and contracted, it is also a "broken cistern." It can hold no water of life or of peace, of consolation f or of joy. In vain his spirit, tormented with guilt and agitated with fear, repairs to it for satisfaction and repose—it supplies it not. Let a man, for example, who is thus seeking salvation by the law, take the holiest day in the calendar of his life; let it be as free as it is possible for a fallen creature to make it from sin; let it be filled up with religious duties and services—it closes, and the curtains of night have drawn around him. Reposing on his pillow, he throws forward a glance into the eternal world—he thinks of the holy God, of the righteous law, of the solemn judgment, and the question, "What if this night I should be summoned to stand before my Judge!—what if to-morrow's sun should rise upon my corpse, and I, a departed spirit, should be mingling with the dread realities of an unseen world?"—and he trembles and turns pale. What! has not his best obedience, his holiest day, his strictest observance, brought peace to his conscience and quietness to his soul? What! does no bright hope of glory play around his pillow, and no loving, peaceful view of God cradle him to rest? Ah, no! He has "forsaken the fountain of living waters, and has hewed him out a cistern, a broken cistern, that can hold no water," and his night closes in upon him with the drapery of hopeless gloom.

To you, reader, is this solemn word now sent. Ah! while your eye has been scanning this page, has there not been in your heart the secret conviction of its truth? You have forsaken the righteousness of God, and for years have you been digging into the law, hoping thus to find in its strictest observance some well-spring of life and peace to your soul. But all your toil has been in vain, and all your time misspent. And why? because "by the works of the law should no man living be justified." As true peace only flows through the channel of justification by faith, turning your back upon that channel, there is, there can be, no peace for your soul. Oh that this voice, now sounding in faithfulness on your ear, might awaken you to a sense of your delusion and your folly, and win you to the "good and the right way." Oh that you might be persuaded to abandon the implements of a self-wrought righteousness, with which you have so long fruitlessly labored, and just as you are—poor, guilty, vile, helpless, and hopeless—betake yourself to the "righteousness of God, which is by faith of Jesus Christ." The law is a "broken cistern;" it holds no sweet waters of salvation, it gives out no streams of peace. But the Lord Jesus is a living fountain. He is the "end of the law for righteousness to every one that believes." He has brought in a new and an "everlasting righteousness," for the full justification of poor sinners, such as you. Abandon at once and forever the broken cistern of a creature-righteousness—too long has it allured but to deceive you—and repair to the fountain of a Divine righteousness, which never has and never will deceive a believing sinner. Drink, oh drink, from this life-giving fountain. Here are peace, joy, confidence, and hope. Clothed in this righteousness, you can look your sins in the face, and death in the face, and fear nothing.

JUNE 6

"The righteous shall be in everlasting remembrance." Psalm 112:6

HOW great the power and charm of a holy life! The world is replete with beauty. There is beauty in nature, beauty in art, beauty in countless forms; but there is no beauty like "the beauty of holiness." The brightness which gleams through a good man's life outshines the sun in its meridian splendor. The world, too, is mighty in its forces. There is the power of intellect, of learning, and of genius, the power of wealth, of influence, and of rank; but there is no power so commanding and so effective as the power of holiness. The power it wields is omnipotent for the achievement of good. And a more precious and enduring legacy parental affluence and affection cannot bequeath to posterity, than the record of a life traced by the sanctifying influence of faith, the achievements of prayer, and the endowments of holiness. Such a life is a living demonstration of the Divinity of the Bible, and does more to confirm its veracity, and spread its truths through the world, than all that has ever been spoken or written on the evidences of Christianity.

How measureless the loss of such saints of God! To their family and friends, to the Church of Christ and the world, the withdrawal forever from earth of their living piety, fervent prayers, holy conversation, and consistent example, is a serious and far-reaching calamity. And yet they still live among us, not in our hearts and memories only, but in the undying influence of a holy life. "The righteous shall be in everlasting remembrance." The grave hides them from sight, but not from memory. Neither the green turf nor the salt wave can bury the still surviving and still molding recollections of the holy dead. In the embalmed remembrance of their graces, their prayers, and their actions, they still live to guide, stimulate, and cheer us in our homeward march. Nor do we cease to live with them. They remember and love us still. Bearing their friendships with them to the skies, purified, sublimated, and enlarged, they yet think of us, yearn over us, and pant to have us with them there, with a tenderness of interest, and an intensity of affection, such as they never felt on earth. For anything that we know, they still hover around our people, encompassing our path to the abodes of bliss. Angels are ministering agents to the heirs of salvation; and may we not suppose that many of the glorified spirits of "just men made perfect" are gifted with a like embassy? "They serve Him day and night in His temple;" and who will say that it may not enter essentially into that service for the Lord, to administer in some unknown way to their former companions in tribulation, and the expectant sharers of their glory? But until we rejoin them in the home of the Father, we should think of them but to follow their holy example, to gather encouragement from their faith and patience, to learn lessons from their failings, and to take up and carry forward the work of the Lord, which dropped from their dying hands; until we, too, are summoned to rest from our labors, and receive our reward.

JUNE 7

"For now the see through a glass, darkly; but then face to face: now I know in part; but then shall I know even as also I am known." 1 Cor. 13:12

THE expansion and perfection of the intellectual faculties will result in a consequent enlargement and perfection of knowledge; and this is no inferior element of the future happiness of the redeemed. All that is gracious and sanctifying in the soul of the believer has its basis in a certain degree of spiritual knowledge. The mind is the medium through which the first communications of the Spirit are received. A knowledge of ourselves has led to a knowledge of Christ; and a knowledge of Christ has laid the foundation of all the joy, and peace, and hope, the soul has experienced. And as our spiritual knowledge increases—the mind becoming more and snore informed in Divine truth, there is a corresponding and proportioned increase of the blessing which an experimental acquaintance with the truth yields.

Now, if this be so here, what must it be in the glorified state? Think we not that it will greatly augment the happiness, and heighten the glory, of the saints in heaven, that in their enlarged mental capacity, in the fullest development of their intellectual powers, they shall be enabled to take a wider range of thought? That they shall compass a greater knowledge of God, and see infinitely more of the glory and drink infinitely deeper of the love of Christ, than the most exalted angel in heaven? If in the present school of God—often the school of deep trial, as we advance from truth to truth, knowing more of Jesus, and increasing in the knowledge of God, we grow more holy and more happy; our peace flowing like a river, and our righteousness as the waves of the sea; our confidence in God strengthening, and our affections cleaving more closely to the Savior—what, we ask, will be the glory deepening around us, when all the present obstructions and impediments to our advancement in spiritual knowledge are removed, and our intellectual faculties, then unclouded and unfettered, expand their long-folded wings, to sweep an infinite circle of intelligence—knowing even as we are known? If our progress in spiritual knowledge is an accession to our happiness here, what hereafter will be the felicity ever expanding our glorified souls through the medium of an enlarged mind, illimitable as its range of thought, and pure and transparent as the atmosphere it traverses? Deem it not, then, O expectant of heaven! an inferior element of the glory that awaits you, that your intellectual enjoyment, perfect in its nature, shall ever be augmenting in its degree. "Then shall the righteous shine forth as the sun in the kingdom of their Father," and "then shall we know even as also we known."

JUNE 8

"They are without fault before the throne of God." Rev. 14:4

A STILL higher element of future glory will be perfect holiness. The very utterance of the thought seems to awaken music in the soul. Seeing Christ as He is, and knowing Him as we are known, we also shall be like Him. Perfected in holiness! Oh, what a conception! what a thought! No more elements of evil working like leaven in the soul. No more traces and fetters of corruption. No more evil heart of unbelief, perpetually departing from God. No more desperate depravity. No more sin warring within, and no more temptation assailing from without. All is perfect holiness now! The outline of the Divine image is complete, for the believer has awakened in the finished likeness of his Lord. The spirit of the just man is made perfect. Is there not enough in this anticipation to make us long to be there? What now shades your spirit, and embitters your joy; suffuses your eyes with tears, and inflicts the keenest pang? Not adversity, nor sickness; not changed affection, nor blighted hopes; not the shaded landscape of life, nor the hollow falling of the earth as the grave closes from your view the heart's precious treasure. Oh, no, not these! It is the sin that dwells in us! Extirpate all sin, and you have erased all sorrow. Complete the grace, and you have perfected the glory. You then have chased all sadness from the heart, and have dried all tears from the eye. That glory will be the glory of unsullied purity. Nothing of sin remains save its recollection, and that recollection but heightens our conception of the preciousness of the blood that shall have effaced every stain, and of the greatness and sovereignty of that grace which shall have brought its there. "Let the saints be joyful in glory," for their battle with sin is over. "These are they which follow the Lamb wherever He goes. These were redeemed from among men, being the first-fruits unto God and to the Lamb. And in their mouth was found no guile: for they are without fault before the throne of God."

"We through the Spirit wait for the hope of righteousness by faith." We wait the Bridegroom's coming. We wait the descent of the chariot. We wait the Father's summons to our home. We wait the Master's call to our rest. We wait the uncaging of the spirit, that it may fly. The desire to depart is ardent, but patient. The longing to be with Christ is deep, but submissive. For the full realization of a hope so sublime, so precious, and so sure, we can patiently wait. The theater of suffering is the school of patience; "And patience works experience, and experience hope;" and hope, in the depth of the trial and in the heat of the battle, looks forward to the joy of deliverance and to the spoils of victory. It is well remarked by Calvin, that "God never calls His children to a triumph, until He has exercised them in the warfare of suffering." Thus all who shall eventually wear this palm must now wield the sword. For the consummation of this hope, then, let us diligently labor, meekly suffer, and patiently wait. Living beneath the cross, looking unto Jesus, toiling for Jesus, testifying for Jesus, and cultivating conformity to Jesus, let us be always ready to give a reason of the hope that is in us; and be always ready to enter into the joy and fruition of that hope, the substance and security of which is—"Christ in you the hope of glory."

JUNE 9

"Not every one that says unto me, Lord, Lord, shall enter into the kingdom of heaven; but he that does the will of my Father which is in heaven. Many will say to me in that day, Lord, Lord, have we not prophesied in your name? and in your name have cast out devils? and in your name done many wonderful works? And then will I profess unto them, I never knew you: depart from me, you that work iniquity." Matthew 7:21-23

OUR blessed Lord foresaw and forewarned men of this evil, that an outward profession of the Gospel may exist, and yet the heart be a stranger to its power. Let His words—searching and solemn as though now uttered from the judgment-seat—sink down into our ears. If, in the days of our Lord, and of His faithful and vigilant apostles—the days when a public profession of attachment to Christ was to mark a man for the cross and the stake—if in their days, and under these circumstances, there were found those who could take refuge in a mere outward profession, is it astonishing that now, when it costs a man nothing to profess Christ, but rather adds to his worldly influence and emolument, thousands should run upon this quicksand, and make shipwreck of their souls? Oh, it is no marvel.

There may be in an individual's frame of mind and outward conduct much that bears a strong affinity and resemblance to many of the positive evidences of the new birth, without a single step towards that state having been taken. There may be, as regards the state of mind, a deep and clear knowledge of Divine truth, a strongly enlightened judgment, and a sound and scriptural creed. There shall be a strong attachment to, and a zealous maintenance of, some of the distinguishing doctrines of grace—even a desire to hear of Christ, and an ability to judge between sound and unsound, savory and unsavory preaching, and all the while the heart shall be encased in the hardness of impenitence and unbelief—a stranger to the regenerating influence of the Spirit of God. Do not misinterpret our meaning. We speak not anything against a true, spiritual, and experimental acquaintance with Divine truth. We do not forget that there can be no faith in Christ, without some knowledge of Christ. The very existence of faith in the heart implies the existence of, and an acquaintance with, the object of faith—the Lord Jesus. We speak not against an enlarged possession of Divine knowledge. It would be well for the Church of Christ, and would greatly promote her stability and real spirituality, were the standard of Divine knowledge more elevated in her midst. It would screen her from much of the unsound theology and false philosophy, which threaten her purity and her peace. It cannot, with perfect truth, be said—touching an elevated and spiritual taste and thirst for experimental truth—that "wisdom and knowledge are the stability of our times." Much of the prevalent religion is characterized by "itching ears," 2 Tim. 4:3;—habit of change, Proverbs 24:21;—unstableness, 2 Peter 3:16;—affected by "every wind of doctrine," Eph. 4:14; and which, in its influence, is "barren and unfruitful," 2 Peter 1:18. Were there a more diligent and prayerful study of God's word—a more regular and constant attendance upon a stated ministry (if that ministry be found productive of spiritual benefit), connected with frequent seasons of retirement, consecrated to meditation, self-examination, and secret prayer, there would be less of that superficial Christianity which marks the many in this day of high and universal profession. We want more depth of knowledge—more spirituality—more experience—more of the life and power of true godliness; in a word, more of the anointing and sanctifying influences of the Holy Spirit in the Church.

JUNE 10

"My spirit has rejoiced in God my Savior." Luke 1:47

THE regenerate soul possesses and acknowledges a new Savior. How glorious, suitable, and precious is Jesus to him now! Not so formerly. Then He had his saviors, his "refuges of lies," his fatal confidences many. Jesus was to him as "a root out of a dry ground, having no form nor loveliness." It may be, He denied His Deity, rejected His atonement, scorned His grace, slighted His pardon and His love. Christ is all to him now. He adores Him as the "mighty God, the everlasting Father, the Prince of peace;" as "over all, God blessed forever;" as "God manifest in the flesh;" as stooping to the nature of man, becoming bone of our bone, and flesh of our flesh; as offering Himself up, the "propitiation for our sins;" as dying "the just for the unjust." His righteousness is glorious, as "justifying from all things,"—His blood is precious, as "cleansing from all sin,"—His fullness of grace is valued, as "supplying all need." Oh how surpassingly glorious, inimitably lovely, and unutterably precious is Jesus to a renewed soul!

Truly He is a new Savior. "Other lords" he has renounced; "refuges of lies" He has turned his back upon; "false Christs" He no longer follows. He has found another and a better Savior, Jesus, the mighty God, the Redeemer of sinners; the "end of the law for righteousness to every one that believes." All is new to his recovered sight: a new world of glory has beamed on his mind; Jesus the Lamb is the light and glory thereof. Never did he suppose there was such beauty in His person, such love in His heart, such perfection in His work, such power and such willingness to save. That blood, which was trampled under foot, is now precious. That righteousness, which was scorned, is now glorious. That name, which was reviled, is now as music to the soul, yes, "a name that is above every name."

Jesus is his only Savior. Not an allowed confidence has he out of Christ. The covenant of dead works he has renounced. The Spirit, having brought him out of and away from it, has led him into the covenant of grace, the substance and stability and glory of which is Jesus. On the broad basis of Immanuel's finished, atoning work he rests his whole soul; and the more he presses the foundation, and the more he leans upon the corner-stone, the stronger and the more able to sustain him does he find it. True, a self-righteous principle he feels closely adhering to him all his journey through the wilderness. When he prays, it is there; when He labors, it is there; when he reflects, it is there: he detects it when suspicion of its existence would be most at rest. But in the sober moments of his judgment, when prostrate beneath the cross, and looking up to God through Jesus, this principle is searched out, abhorred, confessed, and mourned over; and with the eye of faith upon a suffering Savior, the language of his expanding heart is,

"Other refuge have I none,
Hangs my helpless soul on You."

JUNE 11

"Partakers of the heavenly calling." Heb. 3:1

WHAT are some of the attributes of this calling? It is holy. "Who has saved us, and called us with an holy calling." They who are the subjects of this call desire to be holy. Their direst evil is sin. It is, in their experience, not a silken chain, but a galling fetter, beneath whose weight they mourn, and from whose bondage they sigh to be delivered. It is a high and heavenly calling. "I press toward the mark for the prize of the high calling of God in Christ Jesus." "Partakers of the heavenly calling." How does this calling elevate a man—his principles, his character, his aims, his hopes! It is emphatically a "high vocation." So heavenly is it, too, it brings something of heaven into the soul. It imparts heavenly affections, heavenly joys, and heavenly aspirations. It leads to heaven. Could he look within the veil, each called saint would see a prepared mansion, a vacant throne, a jeweled crown, a robe, and a palm, all ready for the wearing and the waving, awaiting him in glory. Thus it is a call from heaven, and to heaven. It is an irrevocable calling. "The gifts and calling of God are without repentance." God has never for a moment repented that He chose, nor has the Savior repented that He redeemed, nor has the Spirit repented that He called any of His people. Not all their wanderings, nor failures, nor unfruitfulness have ever awakened one regret in the heart of God that He has called them to be saints. "I knew that You would deal very treacherously." "Then will I visit their transgression with the rod, and their iniquity with stripes. Nevertheless my loving-kindness will I not utterly take from him; nor suffer my faithfulness to fail." "Faithful is He that calls you."

Nor must we overlook the Divine sovereignty, which appears so illustrious in this special calling. All ground of human boasting is removed, and God has secured to Himself, from eternity, the entire glory of His people's salvation. So conspicuously appears the sovereignty of God in this effectual calling, that all creature-glory is annihilated. And if it be asked by the disputers of this truth, why one is called and another is left?—why Jacob, and not Esau?—why David, and not Saul?—why Cornelius the Gentile, and not Tertullus the Jew?—why the poor beggars in the highway, and not the bidden guests? why the woman who washed with her tears the Savior's feet, and not Simon, in whose house the grateful act was performed?—the answer is, "He will have mercy upon whom He will have mercy." To this acquiescence in the sovereignty of the Divine will our Lord was brought, when He beheld the mysteries of the Gospel veiled from the wise of this world: "I thank You, O Father, Lord of heaven and earth, that You have hid these things from the wise and prudent, and have revealed them unto babes. Even so, Father: for so it seemed good in Your sight." To this precious truth let us bow; and if the efficacious grace of God has reached our hearts, let us ascribe its discriminating choice to the sovereign pleasure of that Divine and supreme will, which rules over the armies of heaven and among the inhabitants of earth, and to which no creature dare say, "What do you?"

JUNE 12

"Now to him that is of power to establish you according to my gospel, and the preaching of Jesus Christ." Romans 16:25

THE Holy Spirit breathed the spiritual life in the soul, and He keeps, and nourishes, and watches over it. Let it not be supposed that there is anything in this life that could keep itself. There is no principle in Divine grace that can keep it from decline and decay. If it do not be watched over, nourished, sustained, and revived perpetually by the same omnipotent power that implanted it there, it is liable to constant decline. What experienced child of God has not felt this? Where is the believer that has not been made, solemnly and painfully, to learn it? That there is not a grace of the Spirit in him, but that grace needs, at times, greatly invigorating—not a particle of faith, but it needs strengthening—not a lesson, but he needs to re-learn—not a precept, but requires to be re-written upon his heart. Now this is the work of the ever-watchful, ever-loving, ever-faithful Spirit. He watches over, with a sleepless, loving eye, the work He has wrought in the soul. Not a moment but He has His eye upon it. By night and by day—in summer and in winter—when it decays, when it revives, He is there its guardian and its protector—its author and its finisher.

And how does He nourish it? Spiritually. As the life is spiritual, so the support is spiritual. "As new-born babes, desire the sincere milk of the word, that you may grow thereby." "Nourished up in the words of faith and of good doctrine." How does He nourish it? By leading the soul to Jesus, the substance of all spiritual truth. By unfolding His fullness of all grace, and strength, and sanctification. By leading constantly to His blood and righteousness. By teaching the believer the sweet lesson of living out of himself, his convictions, his enjoyments, his fruitfulness—upon Christ, and Christ alone. What is there in a child of God, in his best estate, that can supply adequate nourishment and support for this principle of Divine life? He has no resources within himself. He cannot live upon evidences—how soon they are clouded! He cannot grow upon enjoyment—how soon it is gone! He cannot find nourishment in any part of the work of the Spirit within him, precious and glorious as that work is. Christ is the "true bread," that sustains the life of God in the soul of man. Jesus said, "I am the living bread which came down from heaven: if any man eat of this bread, he shall live forever." Again, "As the living Father has sent me, and I live by the Father: so He that eats me, even he shall live by me." The renewed soul only lives as it lives on Jesus—it only advances, grows, and "Brings forth much fruit," as it draws its vigor, its nourishment, its support, and fruitfulness simply and entirely from Christ. These again are His words, "Abide in me, and I in you. As the branch cannot bear fruit of itself except it abide in the vine; no more can you, except you abide in me."

Dear reader, long, it may be, have you been looking to yourself for nourishment, for strength, for comfort, and for fruitfulness. And the more you have looked within yourself, the more emptiness, poverty, and barrenness have you discovered. And now, the blessed Spirit, the nourisher, as He is the author, of the life within you, may give you such a new and enlarged view of Jesus as you have never had before. It may be, He will unfold to your soul such a fullness in Him—strength for your weakness, wisdom for your folly, grace for every corruption, tenderness and sympathy for every trial—as will bring you out of your bondage, introduce you into a "large room," and cause you to exclaim, "Thanks be unto God for His unspeakable gift." Thus does the Spirit nourish and sustain the work He has wrought in the soul. He leads to Jesus.

JUNE 13

"You ask, and receive not, because you ask amiss, that you may consume it upon your lusts." James 4:3

A believer may urge a request that is in itself wrong. The mother of Zebedee's children did so, when she asked the Lord that her two sons might sit, the one on His right hand, and the other on the left, in His kingdom. Who does not mark the self that appears in this petition? Although it was a mother's love that prompted it, and, as such, presents a picture of inimitable beauty, and one exquisitely touching to the feelings, yet it teaches us that a parent, betrayed by his love for his child, may ask that of God which is really wrong in itself. He may ask worldly distinction, honor, influence, wealth for his child, which a godly parent should never do; and this may be a wrong request, which God, in His infinite wisdom and love, withholds. This was the petition of the mother, which our Lord saw fit to deny. Her views of the kingdom of Christ were those of earthly glory. To see her children sharing in that glory was her high ambition; which Jesus promptly but gently rebuked. Let a Christian mother ask for spiritual blessings for her children, and whatever else is needful the Lord will grant. Let converting, sanctifying, restraining grace be one and the constant petition presented at the footstool of mercy, and then she cannot ask too much, or press her suit too frequently or too fervently.

To allude to another illustration of our remark it was wrong in Job to ask the Lord that he might die. "Oh that I might have my request " (are his words), "and that God would grant me the thing that I long for! Even that it would please God to destroy me; that He would let loose His hand, and cut me off!" It was an unwise and sinful petition, which the Lord in great mercy and wisdom denied him. Truly "we know not what we should pray for as we ought." What a mercy that there is One who knows!

A child of God may ask for a wise and good thing in a wrong way. There may be no faith in asking, and no sense of God's freeness in bestowing. No filial approach—going as a child—as one pardoned—"accepted in the Beloved,"—as one dear to the heart of God. There may be no honoring of the Father in Himself—no honoring of Him in the Son—no honoring of the Blessed Spirit. There may be no resting upon the cross—no pleading of the atoning blood—no washing in the fountain—no humble, grateful recognition of the "new and living way" of access. There may be a want of lowliness in the mind—brokenness in the spirit—sincerity in the heart—reverence in the manner—sobriety in the words. There may be no confession of sin—no acknowledgment of past mercies—no faith in the promised blessing. How much there may be in the prayer of a dear child of God that operates as a blight upon his request, that seems to close the ear and the heart of God! But oh, to go to Him with filial confidence—sweet faith—love flowing from a broken heart—to go to Him as the people of His choice—dear to Him as the apple of His eye—viewed each moment in His Son—and who would, for the love He bears us, undeify Himself, if that would be for our real good, and His own glory. Did He not once empty Himself of His glory—did He not become poor—did He not humble Himself—did He not take upon Him human nature, all for the love He bore His people? That was approaching so near, in appearance, the cessation of Deity, that, as we gaze upon the spectacle, we wonder what another step might have produced! We seem to think He could not have gone further without ceasing to be God. Behold the broad basis, then, on which a child of God may approach Him in prayer. His love, oh how immense! it is past finding out!

JUNE 14

"As you have sent me into the world, even so have I also sent them into the world." John 17:18

NOT into the solitude of the desert—not into the calm but selfish repose of the domestic circle—not into the hallowed but restricted fellowship of the Church—but into the world—encircling them, for a season, by its vanity, and subjecting them to its trials. And what is their mission? That they should love the world? comport with the world? fraternize with the world? Oh, no! not for this were they sent into it. An object more worthy of His wisdom who sends, and more in harmony with their high calling who are sent, is before them. They are sent into the world that their lives should be a constant, uncompromising, and solemn protest against its vanities and its sins.

Mark again the words of Christ, in our motto "As you have sent me into the world, even so have I also sent them into the world." Christ was commissioned to testify of the world, that the works thereof were evil. He came to labor for the world—to bless the world—to honor His Father in the world. It was the glory of the world that the Son of God was sent into it—that He made it for awhile the place of His temporary abode, and the scene of His stupendous redemption. It was the glory of the earth, that He trod upon its turf. It was the glory of the ocean, that He sailed upon its bosom. It was the glory of the sun, that it beamed upon His head. It was the glory of the air, that it fanned His brow. It was the glory of the waters, that they quenched His thirst. It was the glory of the flowers, that they perfumed His path. It was the glory of the sky, that it spread above Him its blue canopy. What planet has been so honored as this? What world so visited, so distinguished, so blest? Such is the Christian's pattern. Why has Christ placed you in the position you now occupy? Why are you begirt with so much folly, and trial, and danger? You are converted in the midst of the world—your family is in the world—your associates are in the world—your calling is in the world. Why is it so? Even that, like your Lord and Master, you might, by your unworldly, heavenly life, testify of the world that the works thereof are evil, and only evil, and evil continually.

Saints of God, have close relations and intimate dealings with your Elder Brother. Repose in Him your confidence, yield to Him your affections, consecrate to Him your service. He regards you with ineffable delight. With all your interests He is identified, and with all your sorrows He sympathizes. He may, like Joseph, at times speak roughly to His brethren, in the trying dispensations of His providence; yet, like Joseph, He veils beneath that apparent harshness a brother's deep and yearning love. Seek a closer resemblance to His image; to which, ever remember, you are predestined to be conformed. In order to this, study His beauty, His precepts, His example; that "with open face, beholding as in a glass the glory of the Lord, you may be changed into the same image, from glory to glory, even as by the Spirit of the Lord."

JUNE 15

"Ourselves also, which have the first-fruits of the Spirit." Romans 8:23

THE figurative allusion is to a familiar law of the Jewish economy. It will be recollected that, under the Levitical dispensation, the Lord commanded that the first-fruits, in the form of a single sheaf, should be sickled and waved before him by the priest; and that this wave-offering was to be considered as constituting the herald, or the pledge, of the ripened and full harvest. And not only should it be an earnest and a pledge, but it should represent the nature and character of the fruit which, before long, in luxuriant abundance, would crowd with its golden sheaves, amid shouts of gladness, the swelling garner. When, therefore, it is said that believers in Jesus have the "first-fruits of the Spirit," the meaning clearly is, that they have such communications of the Spirit now, as are a pledge and foretaste of what they shall possess and enjoy in the great day of the coming glory. "In whom also after that you believed, you were sealed with that Holy Spirit of promise, which is the earnest of our inheritance, until the redemption of the purchased possession, unto the praise of His glory."

We remark, in general terms, that if we are believers, then are we partakers of that grace which is the earnest of glory. Do we partake of the grace of life? It is the same life which beats in the souls of the glorified. In us its pulsations are faint and fluctuating; in them they are deep and constant—yet the life is the same. And if we have the spirit of life dwelling in us now, then have we the first-fruits of the life which is to come. Have we the spirit of adoption? What is it but the earnest and the seal of our certain reception into our Father's house? The love to God which overflows our hearts, the yearnings of those hearts to be at home, are the first-fruits of our consummated and glorified sonship. Thus might we travel the entire circle of the Christian graces, which form, sanctify, and adorn the Christian character; illustrating the truth, that each grace wrought by the Spirit in the heart, on earth, is the germ of glory in heaven, and that the perfection of glory will be the perfection of each grace. The present character and tutelage of the child of God are preparatory to a higher state of being—yes, they are essential parts of that being itself. Oh, it is a holy and inspiriting thought, that every development of grace, and every aspiration of holiness, every victory of faith, every achievement of prayer, and every gleam of joy in the soul here below, is the earnest-sheaf of the golden ears of happiness and glory garnered for the saints on high. "He that goes forth and weeps, bearing precious seed, shall doubtless come again with rejoicing, bringing his sheaves with him." Have yore the "first-fruits of the Spirit"? Guard them with tender, sleepless care. Nature, in her richest domain, yields no such fruits or flowers as these. Employ all the means and appliances within your reach, to keep verdant and fruitful the sacred garden of your soul. Unveil it to the sun's light, the gentle showers, and the soft gales of heaven. Let your incessant prayer be, "Awake, O north wind; and come, you south; blow upon my garden, that the spices thereof may flow out. Let my beloved come into his garden, and eat his pleasant fruits." Oh, guard those precious "first-fruits"! Soon the glory they foreshadow will be revealed. The autumnal tints are deepening, the golden ears are ripening, the reaper's sickle is preparing, and before long we shall join in the song of the angels' harvest-home, "Grace, grace unto it!"

JUNE 16

But this man, after he had offered one sacrifice for sins for ever, sat down on the right hand of God; from henceforth expecting until his enemies be made his footstool. Heb. 10:12, 13

AND what was that sacrifice? It was God's own Son, "who gave Himself for us," "when He had by Himself purged our sins." By this sacrifice He "condemned sin in the flesh." The word never implies simply to destroy or remove. Consequently the present and entire destruction of sin in the believer, was not the condemnation secured by the sacrifice of Christ. But in two senses we may understand the word. First, He bore the condemnation and punishment of sin, and thus forever secured our pardon. Secondly, and chiefly, He actually so condemned sin in His own material actually body, that it lost the power of condemning His spiritual body, the Church. So that neither sin, nor the consequence of sin, can ever lay the believer under condemnation. Thus, while sin condemned Jesus as the Surety, Jesus condemned sin as the Judge, assigning it to its own dark and changeless doom. That, therefore, which itself is condemned, cannot condemn. Thus it is that the last song the believer sings is his sweetest and his most triumphant—"O death! where is your sting?" Sin being condemned, pardoned, and forever put away, death, its consequent and penalty, is but a pleasing trance into which the believer falls, to awake up perfected in God's righteousness. Let us, in deep adoration of soul, admire God's illustrious method of meeting the impotence of the law. How suitable to us, how honoring to Himself! Relinquishing all thought of salvation by the works of the law, let us eagerly and gratefully avail ourselves of God's plan of justification. Let our humble and believing hearts cordially embrace His Son. If the law is powerless to save, Christ is "mighty to save." If the law can but terrify and condemn, it is to drive us into Christ, that we might be justified by faith in Him. In Him there is a full, finished, and free salvation. We have but to believe, and be saved. We have but to look, and live. We have but to come, and be accepted. Disappointed of our hope in the law, and alarmed by its threatenings pealing in our ears louder than seven thunders, let us flee to Jesus, the "hiding place from the wind, and the covert from the tempest."

There is no condemnation in Christ Jesus. All is peace, all is rest; all is security there. The instant that a poor trembling sinner gets into Christ, he is safe to all eternity. Nor can he be assured of safety one moment, out of Christ. Repair, then, to the Savior. His declaration is—"him that comes unto me I will in no wise cast out." None are rejected but those who bring a price in their hands. Salvation is by grace; and not to him that works, but to him that believes, the precious boon is given. The turpitude of your guilt, the number of your transgressions, the depth of dour unworthiness, the extent of your poverty, the distance that you have wandered from God, are no valid objections, no insurmountable difficulties, to your being saved. Jesus saves sinners "to the uttermost"—to the uttermost degree of guilt—to the uttermost limit of unworthiness—to the uttermost extent of time. And not only let us look to Christ for salvation, but also for strength. Is the law weak? "Christ is the power of God." He is prepared to perfect His strength in our weakness. And the felt conviction of that weakness will be the measure of our strength. Without Him we can do nothing; but strong in His might, we can do all things. "In the Lord have I righteousness and strength."

JUNE 17

"He says to him again the second time, Simon, son of Jonas, loves you me? He says unto him, Yes, Lord, you know that I love you." John 21:16

"God is love," and the expression of that love is the sending His own Son into the world, to achieve what the law, in its weakness, could not do. Was ever love like this? "God so loved." And was Jesus willing to engage in the embassy? Did He voluntarily clothe Himself in our rags, stoop to our poverty, consent to be arrested and thrown into prison for us? Was He made a curse that He might deliver us from the curse? Did judgment pass upon Him, that we might be saved from the wrath to come? Oh here is infinite, boundless love! Then let Him have in return our love; it is the least that He can ask, or we can make. Let it be a hearty, cordial, obedient, increasing love. Alas! it is but a drop, when it should be an ocean. It is but a faint spark, when it should be a vehement flame.

How should our best affection flow out toward Him who assumed, and stills wears, our nature! What an attractive, winning object is the Incarnate God, the God-man Mediator! Fairer than the children of men, the chief among ten thousand, the altogether lovely, He is the wonder and admiration, the beloved and the song, of all heaven. Why should He not be equally so of all earth? Did the Son of God take up our rude and suffering nature, and shall we be loth to take up His lowly and despised cross, and follow hard after Him? Forbid it, Lord! Forbid it, you precious Savior! What humiliation, what abasement, can be too much for us, the sinful sons of men, when You, the sinless Son of God, did so abase and humble Yourself! Let Your love constrain us to stand firm to You, to Your truth, and to Your cause, when the world despises, when friends forsake, when relatives look cold, and all seem to leave and forsake us. And as You did condescend to be made in the likeness of our human and sinful nature, oh conform us to the likeness of Your Divine and holy nature. As You were a partaker with us, make us partakers with You. As You were made like unto us, in what was proper to man, make us like You, in what is proper to God. And as You did come down to our sinful and dim earth, lift us to Your pure and bright heaven!

What a privilege is nearness to Christ! Yet, dear and precious as it is, how sadly is it overlooked! We may trace this, in some degree, to the believer's oversight of his oneness with Christ. Yet to forget this truth is to forget that He lives. As the branch has one life with the vine, the graft one life with the tree, so he that is united to Christ, and grafted into Christ, has one life with Christ. Go where he may, he is one with Christ. Be his circumstances what they may, he is one with Christ. And as he is in Christ, so Christ is in him. And if Christ be in him, dwelling in him, living in him, walking in him, so also is Christ in every event, and incident, and circumstance of his history. He cannot look upon the darkest cloud that overhangs his path, but he may say, "Christ is in my cloud; Christ is in my sorrow; Christ is in my conflict; Christ is in my need; Christ is all to me, and Christ is in all with me."

JUNE 18

"Once have I sworn by my holiness that I will not lie unto David." Psalm 89:35.

HOLINESS is an essential perfection of God: it is an inseparable part of His being. To conceive of a God infinite in essence, divine in majesty, almighty in power, wise in counsel, and eternal in duration, and yet destitute of holiness, infinite, essential purity—to suppose such a Being possessed of the least contagion of moral evil, would be to portray to the imagination—in reverence be it written—an infinite monster! We should picture Him before us arrayed with infinite power, wisdom, and duration, and yet wanting in that perfection which tempers, chastens, and beautifies all, and which makes Him truly what His word reveals Him to be—a God of love. A denial of His being would not be a crime so fearful, nor involve guilt of deeper dye, than would be a denial of His holiness. He who refuses to acknowledge that God is immaculately holy breathes a more tremendous libel against God than the atheist, who, standing in the midst of ten thousand overwhelming demonstrations of His existence, yet impiously declares there is no God!

How rich and palpable are the Scripture proofs—rather say, revelations and unfoldings—of God's holiness. One or two must suffice. That is a sublime and conclusive one uttered by the lips of the veiled cherubim—"And one cried unto another, and said, Holy, holy, holy, is the Lord of hosts: the whole earth is full of His glory. And the posts of the door moved at the voice of Him that cried, and the house was filled with smoke." Was there no other Divine perfection, which they might have thus extolled? Oh yes! Jehovah was infinitely wise, infinitely powerful, and infinitely good; but holiness was the greatest and grandest of all; and so they cry, "holy, holy, holy, is the Lord of hosts!" thus breathing forth their adoration to the holy Triune God.

Again, in the words of our motto, "Once have I sworn by my holiness that I will not lie unto David." Why did not God swear by His veracity, by His wisdom, or by His power? Because He was about to enunciate a great truth to the house of David; and with a view of imparting to that truth its greatest force, solemnity, and beauty, He swears by His holiness. As if He did say "Holiness is my most illustrious perfection, my grandest attribute; and by it I swear that I will make good my word, that I will not lie unto David." For as "men, verily swear by the greater," so God swears by His holiness, His greatest perfection and highest glory. Oh, you saints of the Most High, who, standing in the region of doubt, and enshrouded by dark providences, are led to ask, "Will God make good the promise upon which He has caused my soul to rest?"—look at this great truth—God has sworn by His holiness that He will not lie, and you have the warrant and the encouragement to trust in God, to confide in His word, and to resign yourself and all your interests into His fatherly, faithful, though chastening hands. By this solemn oath He has bound Himself to make good to the letter His every precious promise.

JUNE 19

"And that you put on the new man, which after God is created in righteousness and true holiness." Eph. 4:24

TAKE another view of this subject. Holiness is the image which God transfers from Himself to the renewed creature. God, in regeneration, draws upon the soul of man His own moral portrait. And what is the image of Himself which He thus transfers, glorious and imperishable, to the renewed mind? Is it His wisdom? No! Is it His truth? No! Is it His love? No! It is His holiness! as if He would say, "I will draw my image upon the renewed man, and it shall be that which is my glory, my beauty, my grandest perfection; and in making the creature holy, I will make him like myself." How strikingly has the Holy Spirit brought out this truth in the words of our motto: "And that you put on the new man, which after God is created in righteousness and true holiness;" a truth worthy of our profoundest study. In nothing does the renewed soul so closely resemble God, as in holiness. May the Lord, the Spirit, write this truth deeply upon our heart!

But how has God manifested His holiness? He has not only revealed the fact in His word, but He has exhibited its perfection in various ways. Its most palpable, awful, and strident demonstration is in the cross of His Son Jesus Christ. Behold the redemption which He has wrought; contemplate this the most stupendous of God's works, and where else will you find such a demonstration of God's holiness, as that which the cross of the incarnate God exhibits? Not all the vials of judgment that have ever been poured out or that ever will be—not the flaming furnace in the conscience of the ungodly—not the irretrievable vengeance of God against the angels who kept not their first estate—not all the woe and suffering of the condemned in hell, convey any adequate idea of the holiness of God, compared with the death of His own beloved Son. There hung the holy, spotless Lamb of God! He had never sinned; there had never been the slightest hostility of His will to His Father's; He had never harbored one treason thought against Jehovah, but had "always done those things which pleased Him." Yet we behold Him exhausting the cup of Divine wrath, His human soul scathed by the lightning-stroke of Divine justice, and His sinless body bruised, and wounded, and slain. What do we learn from the spectacle, but that God was so righteous, so holy, He could not pass by the iniquity of the Church, but as He punished it with the utmost severity in the person of its Surety. And what was the perfection of God, the contemplation of which in the hour of His agony upheld Him? In prophetic language He tells us—"My God, my God, why have You forsaken me? why are You so far from helping me, and from the words of my roaring? Oh my God, I cry in the day-time, but You hear not; and in the night season, and am not silent. But You are holy." This was the truth which gave His agitated soul rest, beneath its overwhelming pressure. He saw God so holy in His withdrawal, so holy in the billows which went over His soul, so holy in taking vengeance for His people's sins, that He bowed His head in meek acquiescence to the Divine will: "But You are holy."

JUNE 20

"It is God that justifies." Rom. 8:33

IT would appear that there are two links in this marvelous chain—the purpose of God, and its final consummation; both so remote and invisible, as to bring the mind to a calm, unquestioning belief in certain doctrines of God's word, which may more properly belong to the "deep things of God." But while the two extremes of this chain of truths must for the present be left invisibly locked in God's hand; there are certain intermediate and visible links, upon which if the perplexed and inquiring reader lay hold, he shall be saved, though all the rest remains wrapped in the profoundest mystery—like its Divine Author, dwelling in lone and unapproachable grandeur. It is not essential to our salvation that we lift the veil of that awful mystery, and penetrate the depths of a past predestination, and a future glory; but it is essential to our salvation that we are called of God, and that by God we are justified. We may arrive at heaven without fathoming the awful profound of the one extreme, and with but twilight views of the magnificence spreading over all the other; but we cannot get to heaven without the Spirit's grace and Christ's righteousness. Grasp in faith, and receive into your heart, these two central and essential truths, and they will by and by lift you into a sunnier region, where all the rest will stand forth, clear and transparent, bathed in the noontide splendor of heaven's own glory.

"It is God that justifies." We believe that by many this cardinal doctrine of God's justification is but imperfectly understood, and but indistinctly seen in its results. The lofty position of security in which it places the believer, the liberty, peace, and hope, into which it brings him, are points dim and obscure in the spiritual vision of many. We also believe that much of the weak, sickly Christianity of numbers is traceable, in a great measure, to the crude and gloomy conceptions they form of God, produced by not clearly seeing the interest which he felt, and the initiatory part which he took, in the great matter of our justification. Let our faith but trace the act of our justification to God, and we have placed ourselves upon a vantage-ground of the boldest defiance to all our enemies. Survey the truth in this light for a moment. Against whom have you sinned? Adopting David's confession, you exclaim, "Against You, You only, have I sinned." Having sinned against God, from God, then, you looked for the condemnation. You had violated His law, and from the lips of the Lawgiver you waited the sentence. When, lo! He declares Himself on your side. Descending as from His tribunal, He comes and stands in your place, and avows Himself your Justifier. "It is God that justifies." Upon you, a culprit, trembling at His bar, He throws His own righteousness, "which is unto all, and upon all those who believe;" and from that moment you are justified. Shall we, then, be indifferent to the part the Father took in the great question of our acceptance? Shall we cherish the shy and suspicious thought of God, as if He looked coldly at us, and felt that in pleading for His mercy, we were infringing upon His righteousness? Oh, no! Away with such thoughts of God! He it is who pronounces the act of your acquittal, and from His lips sound the glorious words, "No condemnation!" "It is God that justifies."

JUNE 21

"Who shall lay anything to the charge of God's elect?" Romans 8:33

WHO in heaven; who on earth; who in hell? God will not; sin cannot; Satan dare not. Who? If there be in this wide universe an accuser of those whom God has justified, let him appear. There is none! Every mouth is closed. "Who shall lay anything to the charge of God's elect?" If there remain a sin unpardoned, a stain uneffaced, a precept unkept, by the Mediator of His Church, let it appear. But there is none! The work of Christ is honorable and glorious. It is a finished work. And on the basis of this complete atonement, God, while He remains just, is the justifier of him that believes. Oh, embrace this truth, you who, in bitterness of soul, are self-accused and self-condemned before God! Satan could accuse, and the world could accuse, and the saints could accuse, but more severe and true than all, is the self-accusation which lays your mouth in the dust, in the deepest, lowliest contrition. Yet, as a poor sinner, looking to Jesus, resting in Jesus, accepted in Jesus; who shall lay anything legally to our charge, since it is God—the God against whom you have sinned—who Himself becomes your Justifier? May you not, with all lowliness, yet with all holy boldness, challenge every foe, in the prophetic words of Christ Himself-"He is near that justifies me: who will contend with me?"

This truth is an elevating, because a deeply sanctifying one. It exalts the principles, and these, in their turn, exalt the practice of the Christian. The thought that it is God who justifies us at an expense to Himself so vast, by a sacrifice to Himself so precious, surely is sufficiently powerful to give the greatest intensity to our pantings, and fervency to our prayers, for conformity to the Divine image. Deep sorrows, and sore trials, and fiery temptations we may have, and must have, if we ever enter the kingdom; but, what is sorrow, what is trial, what is temptation, if they work but in us the fruits of righteousness, fit us more perfectly for heaven, and waft us nearer to our eternal home? Press, in humble faith, this precious truth to your heart; for God has forgiven all, and has cancelled all, and has forgotten all, and is your God forever and ever. "No weapon that is formed against you shall prosper; and every tongue that shall rise against you in judgment you shall condemn. This is the heritage of the servants of the Lord, and their righteousness is of me, says the Lord."

JUNE 22

"Every one that loves him that begat loves him also that is begotten of him." 1 John 5:1

THE feeling here referred to is a love to the saints, as saints. Whatever natural infirmities we may discover in them, whatever different shades of opinion they may hold to us, and to whatever branch of the Christian Church they may belong, yet the feeling which is to establish our own divine relationship is a love to them as brethren. Irrespective of all dissonance of creed, of denomination, of gifts, of attainment, of rank, of wealth, of nation—when we meet in a Christian professor the image of Christ, the family-likeness, our love will prompt us immediately to recognize that individual as a believer in Jesus, and to acknowledge him as a brother in the Lord. And what are the grounds of my affection? I may esteem his character, and prize his gifts—may admire his talents, and feel there is an assimilation of disposition, of taste, and of judgment—but my Christian love springs from an infinitely higher and holier source. I love him because the Father is in him, because the Son is in him, because the Holy Spirit is in him. I love him because he is an adopted child of the same family; a member of Christ, and of the same body; and a temple of the same Holy Spirit. I love him that is begotten, because I love Him that begat. It is Christ in one believer, going out after Himself in another believer. It is the Holy Spirit in one temple, holding fellowship with Himself in another temple. And from hence it is that we gather the evidence of our having "passed from death unto life." Loving the Divine Original, we love the human copy, however imperfect the resemblance. The Spirit of God dwelling in the regenerate soul yearns after the image of Jesus, wherever it is found. It pauses not to inquire to what branch of the Christian Church the individual resembling Him belongs; that with which it has to do is the resemblance itself.

Now, if we discover this going out of the heart in sweet, holy, and prayerful affection, towards every believer in Christ—be his denominational name what it may—the most to those who most bear the Savior's image—then have we the

Spirit of Christ dwelling in us. A surer evidence we cannot have. There is the affection which surmounts all the separating walls of partition in the Church, and in spite of sects, and parties, and creeds, demonstrates its own divine nature and heavenly birth, by its blending with the same affection glowing in the bosom of another. And where this love to the brethren exists not at all in any Christian professor, we ask that individual, with all the tenderness of affection consistent with true faithfulness, where is the evidence of your union with the body of Christ? You have turned away with hardness of heart, and with frigidity of manner, if not with secret disdain, from one whom God loves, whom Christ has redeemed, and in whom the Holy Spirit dwells, because he belonged not to your sect. Yes, you have turned away with coldness and suspicion from Christ Himself! How can you love the Father, and hate the child? What affection have you for the Elder Brother, while you despise the younger? If you are a living branch of the same vine, can you, while cherishing those feelings which exclude from your affection, from your sympathies, and from your fellowship, other Christians, more deeply wound Jesus, or more effectually grieve the Holy Spirit of God, by whom they are "sealed unto the day of redemption"? Perhaps you have long walked in darkness and uncertainty, as to the fact of your own personal adoption into the family of God. Anxious fear and distressing doubt have taken the place of a holy assurance, and a peaceful persuasion that you were one of the Lord's people. In laboring to trace this painful state of mind to its cause, did it ever occur to you, that your lack of love towards all saints, especially towards those of other branches of the same family, has, in all probability, so grieved the Spirit of adoption, that he has withheld from your own soul that clear testimony, that direct witness, by which your interest in the covenant love of God, and your union with Christ, would have been clearly made known to you? You have grieved that same Spirit in your brother, who dwells in you, and upon whom you are so dependent for all your sweet consolation and holy desires; and He has suspended the light, and peace, and joy of your own soul.

JUNE 23

"Then came Peter to him, and said, Lord, how often shall my brother sin against me, and I forgive him? until seven times? Jesus says unto him, I say not unto you, Until seven times: but, Until seventy times seven." Matthew 18:21-22

IF there is a single exercise of divine grace in which, more than in any other, the believer resembles God, it is this. God's love to man is exhibited in one great and glorious manifestation, and a single word expresses it—forgiveness. In nothing has He so gloriously revealed Himself as in the exercise of this divine prerogative. Nowhere does He appear so like Himself as here. He forgives sin, and the pardon of sin involves the bestowment of every other blessing. How often are believers called upon thus to imitate God! And how like him in spirit, in affection, and in action do they appear, when, with true greatness of soul and with lofty magnanimity of mind, they fling from their hearts, and efface from their memories, all traces of the offence that has been given, and of the injury that has been received! How affecting and illustrious the example of the expiring Redeemer! At the moment that His deepest wound was inflicted, as if blotting out the sin and its remembrance with the very blood that it shed, He prayed, as the last drop fell, and as the last breath departed, "Father, forgive them." How fully and fearfully might He have avenged Himself at that moment! A stronger than Samson hung upon the cross. And as He bowed His human nature and gave up the spirit, He could as easily have bowed the pillars of the universe, burying His murderers beneath its ruins. But no! He was too great for this. His strength should be on the side of mercy. His revenge should wreak itself in compassion. He would heap coals of fire upon their heads. He would overcome and conquer their evil, but He would overcome and conquer it with good: "Father, forgive them."

It is in the constant view of this forgiveness that the followers of Christ desire, on all occasions of offence given, whether real or imaginary, to "forgive those who trespass against them." Themselves the subjects of a greater and diviner forgiveness, they would be prompt to exercise the same holy feeling towards an offending brother. In the remembrance of the ten thousand talents from whose payment his Lord has released him, he will not hesitate to cancel the hundred pence owing to him by his fellow-servant. Where, then, will you find any exercise of brotherly love more God-like and divine than this? In its immediate tender, its greatest sweetness and richest charm appear. The longer it is delayed, the more difficult becomes the duty. The imagination is allowed to dwell upon, and the mind to brood over, a slight offence received, perhaps never intended, until it has increased to such magnitude as almost to extend, in the eye of the aggrieved party, beyond the limit of forgiveness. And then follows an endless train of evils—the wound festers and inflames; the breach widens; coldness is manifested; malice is cherished; every word, look, and act is misinterpreted; the molehill grows into a mountain, the little rivulet swells into an ocean, until happiness and peace retire from scenes so uncongenial, and from hearts so full of all hatred and strife. But how lovely in its appearance, and how pleasurable in the feelings it enkindles, is a prompt exercise of Christian forgiveness! Before the imagination has had time to distort, or the wound to fester, or ill-minded people to interfere, Christian love has triumphed, and all is forgiven!

How full of meaning is our blessed Lord's teaching on this point of Christian duty, in our motto! It behooves us prayerfully and constantly to ponder His word. True love has no limits to its forgiveness. If it observes in the bosom of the offender the faintest marks of regret, of contrition, and of return, like Him from whose heart it comes, it is "ready to forgive," even "until seventy times seven." Oh who can tell the debt we owe to His repeated, perpetual forgiveness? And shall I refuse to be reconciled to my brother? Shall I withhold from him the hand of love, and let the sun go down upon my wrath? Because he has trampled upon me, who have so often acknowledged myself the chief of sinners, because he has slighted my self-importance, or has wounded my pride, or has grieved my too sensitive spirit, or, it is possible, without just cause, has uttered hard speeches, and has lifted up his heel against me, shall I keep alive the embers of an unforgiving spirit in my heart? Or rather, shall I heap coals of fire upon his head, not to consume him with wrath, but to overcome him with love? How has God my Father, how has Jesus my Redeemer, my Friend, dealt with me? Even so will I deal with my offending brother. I will not even wait until he comes, and acknowledges his fault. I will go to him, and tell him that at the mercy-seat, beneath the cross, with my eye upon the loving, forgiving heart of God, I have resolved to forgive all, and will forget all.

JUNE 24

"And the ransomed of the Lord shall return, and come to Zion with songs and everlasting joy upon their heads: they shall obtain joy and gladness, and sorrow and sighing shall flee away." Isaiah 35:10

THE absence of all evil will be an eminent feature of the coming glory. Take the long catalogue of ills we suffer here—the cares that corrode, the anxieties that agitate, the sorrows that depress, the bereavements that wound, the diseases that waste, the temptations that assail—in a word, whatever pains a sensitive mind, or wounds a confiding spirit; the rudeness of some, the coldness of others, the unfaithfulness and heartlessness of yet more; and as you trace the sad list, think of glory as the place where not one shall enter. All, all are entirely and eternally absent. "God shall wipe away all tears from their eyes; and there shall be no more death, neither sorrow, nor crying, neither shall there be any more pain: for the former things are passed away."

The presence of all good will take the place of the absence of all evil. And in the foreground of this picture of glory we place the full, unclouded vision of Jesus. This is the Sun that will bathe all other objects in its beams. We see Him now through faith's telescope, and how lovely does He appear! Distant and dim as is the vision, yet so overpowering is its brightness, as for a moment to eclipse every other object. How near He is brought to us, and how close we feel to Him! Encircled and absorbed by His presence, all other beings seem an intrusion, and all other joys an impertinence. Reposing upon His bosom, how sweetly sounds His voice, and how winning His language: "O my dove, that are in the clefts of the rock, in the secret places of the stairs, let me see your countenance, let me hear your voice; for sweet is your voice, and your countenance is lovely." These are happy moments. But how transient, and how brief their stay! Some earthly vapor floats athwart our glass, and the bright and blissful vision is gone—veiled in clouds, it has disappeared from our view! But not lost is that vision; not withdrawn is that object. As stars that hide themselves awhile, then appear again in brighter, richer luster, so will return each view we have had of Christ. The eye that has once caught a view of the Savior shall never lose sight of Him forever. Long and dreary nights may intervene; the vision may tarry as though it would never come again, yet those nights shall pass away, that vision shall return, and "we shall see Him as He is." And if the distant and fitful glimpses of the glorified Christ are now so ravishing, what will the ecstatic and overpowering effect of the full unclouded vision be, when we shall see Him face to face?

JUNE 25

"After this I beheld, and, lo, a great multitude, which no man could number, of all nations, and kindreds, and people, and tongues, stood before the throne, and before the Lamb, clothed with white robes, and palms in their hands; And cried with a loud voice, saying, Salvation to our God which sits upon the throne, and unto the Lamb." Rev. 7:9-10

WITH the unveiled sight of the glorified Redeemer, will be associated the certain reunion and perfected communion of all the glorified saints. We are far from placing this feature of glory in an obscure distance of our picture of heavenly happiness. A source of so much pure and hallowed enjoyment now, surely will not be wanting nor be more limited hereafter. It is a high enjoyment of earth, that of sanctified relationships and sacred friendships. The communion of renewed intellect, the union of genial minds, and the fellowship of loving and sympathizing hearts, God sometimes kindly vouchsafes, to smooth and brighten our rough and darks path to the grave. But death interposes and sunders these precious ties. And are they sundered forever? Oh, no! We shall meet again all from whom in faith and hope we parted—whom we loved in Jesus, and who in Jesus have fallen asleep. "For we believe that through the grace of our Lord Jesus Christ we shall be saved even as they." Heart-breaking as was the separation, it was not final, nor will it be long. The time-piece we wear upon our people reminds us at each second, that the period of our reunion is nearing. Yes! we shall meet them again, in closer and purer friendship. They wait and watch for our coming. Do not think that they forget us: that cannot be; and thinking of us, they love us still. The affection they cherished for us here death did not chill; they bore that affection with them from the earthly to the heavenly home; and now, purified and expanded, it glows with an intensity unknown, unfelt before. Heavenly thought is immortal. Holy love never dies. Meeting, we shall know them again; and knowing, we shall rush into their warm embrace, and sever from them—never! "I would not have you to be ignorant, brethren, concerning those who are asleep, that you sorrow not, even as others which have no hope. For if ace believe that Jesus died and rose again, even so them also which sleep in Jesus will God bring with him." What a soothing, sanctifying thought—what a heaven-attracting hope is this!

In our anticipations of the coming glory, we must not overlook the glorified body of the saints. The first resurrection will give back this "vile body," so changed that it shall be "fashioned like unto Christ's glorious body." We have two examples of what this "glorious body" of our Lord is. The first was at His transfiguration, when the "fashion of His countenance was altered, and His face did shine as the sun, and His clothing was white as the light." The second was when He appeared to John in Patmos, arrayed in such glory that the apostle says, "When I saw Him, I fell at His feet as dead." Fashioned like unto Christ's glorious body, will be the glorified bodies of the saints. No deformity, no wrinkle, no defect whatever, shall mar its beauty. "It is sown in corruption; it is raised in incorruption: it is sown in dishonor; it is raised in glory: it is sown in weakness; it is raised in power: it is sown a natural body; it is raised a spiritual body. And as we have borne the image of the earthly, we shall also bear the image of the heavenly." "We shall be like Him, for we shall see Him as He is."

JUNE 26

"Why, beloved, seeing that you look for such things, be diligent that you may be found of him in peace, without spot, and blameless." 2 Peter 3:14

IS not the anticipation of the coming glory most sanctifying? Ought it not to have so powerful an influence upon our minds, as to lessen the value of the things that are seen and temporal, and enhance the value of those which are unseen and eternal? We are at present in a state of nonage—children under tutors and governors. But before long we shall attain our full age, and shall be put in possession of our inheritance. And because we are children, we are apt to think as children, and speak as children, and act as children—magnifying things that are really small, while diminishing those that are really great. Oh, how little, mean, and despicable will by and by appear the things that now awaken so much thought, and create so much interest! Present sorrows and joys, hopes and disappointments, gains and losses—will all have passed away, leaving not a ripple upon the ocean they once agitated, nor a footprint upon the sands they once traversed.

Why, then, allow our white garments to trail upon the earth? If glory is before us, and so near, why so slow in our advance to meet it? Why so little of its present possession in our souls? Why do we allow the "Bright and Morning Star" to sink so often below the horizon of our faith? Why, my soul, so slow to arrive at heaven, with heaven so full in view? Oh, to press our pillow at night, composed to slumber with this sweet reflection—"Lord, if I open my eyes no more upon the rising sun, I shall open them upon that risen Sun that never sets—awaking in Your likeness." Oh, to be looking for, and hastening unto, the coming of the Lord; that blessed hope, that glorious epiphany of the Church, which shall complete, perfect, and consummate the glorification of the saints!

How should the prospect of certain glory stimulate us to individual exertion for Christ! What a motive to labor! With a whole eternity of rest in prospect, how little should we think of present toil and fatigue for the Savior! Shall we, then, be indolent in our Master's cause? Shall we in selfishness wrap our graces as a mantle around us, and indolently bury our talents in the earth? Shall we withhold our property from the Lord, complaining that the calls of Christian benevolence are so many, the demands so pressing, and the objects so numerous? Oh, no! It cannot, it must not be. Let us live for Christ—labor for Christ—suffer for Christ—and, if needs be, die for Christ—since we shall, before long and forever, be glorified with Christ. And who can paint that glory?

JUNE 27

"For before his translation he had this testimony, that he pleased God." Heb. 11:5

BEHOLD the character of those with whom God is pleased. They are a spiritual people, and God, who is a Spirit, must love and delight in that which harmonizes with His own nature. Faith may be feeble, grace may be limited, and knowledge may be defective; yet, if there be just that strength of faith that travels to, and leans upon, the sacrifice of Jesus, and just that measure of love that constrains to a sincere, though imperfect, obedience, with just that extent of knowledge that discerns Christ to be the Savior of a poor lost sinner, then, there is one who is pleasing to God.

They are also an accepted people, and therefore their people are pleasing to Him. The delight of the Father in the person of His Son reveals to us the great secret of His marvelous delight in us. "This is my beloved Son, in whom I am well pleased." Blessed truth to those who see enough defilement and imperfection in their best doings, to cover them with eternal confusion and shame!—who, after the most spiritual performances, are constrained to repair in penitence and confession to Him, who bears the iniquity of His people's holy things. Sweet truth to fall back upon in all the failures and flaws we are perpetually discerning in our works, in our motives, and our ends—blots not appearing upon the surface, but visible to the microscopic eye of faith, which sees material for self-condemnation, where others, in their fond and blind affection, approve and applaud. If God, my Father, is well pleased in His Son, then is it a truth, strictly inferential, that He is well pleased in me whom He beholds in His Son. But not their people only, their offerings also are equally pleasing to God. "I will accept you" (the person first), "with your sweet savor" (the offering next). Their preceptive walk likewise pleases Him. Is the obedience of the child, springing from love, a pleasing and acceptable offering to a parent's heart? Ah! how imperfectly are we aware of the beauty and fragrance there are to God in a single act of filial, holy obedience, the fruit and offering of a divine and deathless affection!

How great and exalted the heavenly calling of the Christian! Aim to walk worthy of it. Debase it not by allying it with a carnal mind. Impair not your spiritual life by enchaining it to spiritual death. Let the friendships which you cultivate, and the relationships of life which you form, be heavenly in their nature, and eternal in their duration. Seek to please God in all things. Rest not where you are, even though you may have attained beyond your fellows. Let your standard of heavenly-mindedness do not be that of the saints, but of Christ. Study not a copy, but the original. High aims will secure high attainments. He is the most heavenly, and the happiest, who the most closely resembles his Divine Master.

Be much in your closet. There is no progress in spiritual-mindedness apart from much prayer: prayer is its aliment, and its element. But leave not your religion there; let it accompany you into the world. While careful not to carry your business into your religion—thus secularizing and degrading it—be careful to carry your religion into your business—high integrity, holy principle, godly fear—thus imparting an elevation and its concerns. Be the man of God wherever you are. Let these solemn words be held in vivid remembrance—"I have created you for my glory. I have formed you for my praise. You are my witnesses, says the Lord."

JUNE 28

"Jesus wept." John 11:35

PERHAPS to some whose tearful eye may glance on these pages, the most touching and endearing chapter in our Lord's life of varied and affecting incident is that which portrays Him in Bethany's house of mourning, and bending over the grave of Lazarus—thus illustrating His peculiar sympathy with the bereaved. It would seem as if Jesus loved to visit the haunts of human woe. "Lord, if You had been here, my brother had not died," were words bursting from the lips of the two bereaved sisters, which seemed to chide the delay of an interposition, which might have averted their sad calamity. And why that delay? Would it not seem as if one reason was, that the cup of woe was not yet brimmed, and thus the time for the richest display of His human sympathy and Divine power had not yet come? But when death had invaded that happy circle, had cast its shadow over the sunny home, and the sorrow of bereavement was now bursting each heart—lo! Jesus appears, gently lifts the latch, and enters. And who has passed within that dark abode of grief? The Creator of all worlds, the Lord of angels and of men, robed in a real, a suffering, and a sympathizing humanity, to mingle with the daughters of sorrow.

Returning from the house of mourning, we follow Him to the grave. Groaning in spirit, He asks, "Where have you laid him?" And then it is written—and oh, never were words more full of meaning—"Jesus wept!" The incarnate God in tears! Oh marvelous sympathy! such as earth never before saw, and such as heaven in astonishment looked down to see. But why did Jesus weep? Was such an expression of sensibility in keeping with the occasion? Was He not about to recall His friend to life again? And did He not know, that before the sun had declined an hour, He should have robbed death of his victim, and the grave of its prey, restoring gladness to those bereaved sisters, and the sunshine of joy to that desolate home? Most assuredly. And yet "Jesus wept!" Oh, it was sympathy! Those tears were the outgushing of a sensibility He could not repress, nor wished to conceal. Moved by His own loss, He was yet more deeply moved with the loss of Martha and Mary. He stood at that grave, as though He were the chief mourner, upon whom the brunt of the calamity had fallen; and there were no tears flowing at that moment like His. He wept, because He was human—He wept, because He was bereaved—He wept, because others wept. It was a sympathetic emotion, that now agitated to its center his whole soul. Behold Him who makes His people's sorrows all His own!

Bereaved one! that speaking, weeping Brother was born for your adversity! Though now in glory, where no tears are shed, He still sympathizes with the sorrows of the bereaved on earth—yes, sympathizes with yours. Into all the circumstances of your present calamity—the irreparable loss it has entailed, the deep void it has created, the profound grief it has awakened, the painful changes it involves, the sable gloom with which, to your bedimmed eye, it enshrouds all the future of life—He fully enters. And though, when the storm-cloud of Divine vengeance was darkling above His head, Gethsemane and Calvary full in view, not a nerve quivered, nor a tear fell—yet, lo! He comes and weeps with you, and breathes the soothing balmy influence, of a human sympathy over the scene and the sadness of your sorrow. Christian mourner! the weeping One of Bethany is near you! Christ is with you, Christ is in your sorrow.

JUNE 29

"Choosing rather to suffer affliction with the people of God, than to enjoy the pleasures of sin for a season." Hebrews 11:25.

THE believer should never fail to remember that the present is, by the appointment of God, the afflicted state to him. It is God's ordained, revealed will, that His covenant children here should be in an afflicted condition. When called by grace, they should never take into their account any other state. They become the disciples of the religion of the cross—they become the followers of a crucified Lord—they put on a yoke, and assume a burden: they must, then, expect the cross inward and the cross outward. To escape it is impossible. To pass to glory without it, is to go by another way than God's ordering, and in the end to fail of arriving there. The gate is strait, and the way is narrow, which leads unto life; and a man must become nothing, if he would enter and be saved. He must deny himself—he must become a fool that he may be wise—he must receive the sentence of death in himself, that he should not trust in himself. The wise man must cease to glory in his wisdom, the mighty man must cease to glory in his might, the rich man must cease to glory in his riches, and their only ground of glory in themselves must be their insufficiency, infirmity, poverty, and weakness; and their only ground of glory out of themselves must be, that "God so loved the world, that He gave His only begotten Son, that whoever believes in Him should not perish, but have everlasting life."

The believer in Jesus, then, must not forget that if the path he treads is rough and thorny, if the sky is wintry, if the storm is severe, and the cross He bears is heavy, that yet this is the road to heaven. He is but in the wilderness, why should He expect more than belongs to the wilderness state? He is on a journey, why should he look for more than a traveler's fare? He is far from home, why should He murmur and repine that he has not all the rest, the comfort, and the luxuries of his Father's house? If your covenant God and Father has allotted to you poverty, be satisfied that it should be your state, yes, rejoice in it. If bitter adversity, if deep affliction, if the daily and the heavy cross, be your portion, yet, breathe not one murmur, but rather rejoice that you are led into the path that Jesus Himself walked in, to "go forth by the footsteps of the flock," and that you are counted worthy thus to be one in circumstance with Christ and his people.

JUNE 30

"Save me, O God, by your name, and judge me by your strength. Hear my prayer, O God; give ear to the words of my mouth. For strangers are risen up against me, and oppressors seek after my soul: they have not set God before them. Selah. Behold, God is mine helper: the Lord is with those who uphold my soul." Psalm 54:1-4

WHERE was David now? "In the wilderness of Ziph, in a wood." With not a follower or companion, this favorite of the nation was a homeless wanderer, hunted like a partridge upon the mountain by the bloodthirsty king. But oh, the deep teaching of which he would now be the subject! The nothingness of earthly glory—the emptiness of human applause—the poverty of the creature—the treachery of his own heart—in a word, the vapid nature and utter insufficiency of all earthly good, would be among the many holy and costly lessons he would now learn. Nor this alone. Driven from man, he would now be more exclusively and entirely shut in with God. In his happy experience, that wilderness would be as a peopled world, and that wood as a blooming paradise. From the profound depths of its solitude and stillness, there would ascend the voice of prayer and the melody of praise. The wilderness of Ziph would be another Patmos, all radiant with the glorious and precious presence of Him, who laid his right hand upon the exiled Evangelist, and said, "Fear not, I am He that lives."

See we no fore-shadowing of Jesus here? Oh yes; much, we think. Nor is this strange, since David was preeminently a personal type of Christ. There were periods in our Lord's brief and humiliating history on earth, when, indeed, He seemed for awhile to ride upon the topmost wave of popular favor. After some stupendous prodigy of His power, or some splendid outgushing of His benevolence, sending its electric thrill through the gazing and admiring populace, He would often become the envy and the dread of the Jewish Sanhedrin. Jealous of His widening fame and growing power, they would seek to tarnish the one by detraction, and to arrest the other by His death. Escaping from their fury, He would betake Himself to the fastnesses of the rock, and to the solitude of the desert—but, alas! with no human sympathy to strengthen His hands in God. Oh, how strangely has Jesus trodden the path, along which He is leading His saints to glory!

Is there nothing analogous to this in the experience of the faithful? Who can witness for the Lord Jesus—conceive some new idea of doing good—occupy some prominent post of responsibility and power—or prove successful in some enterprise of Christian benevolence—and while thus winning the admiration and applause of the many, not find himself an object of the unholy envy and vituperation of a few? "Woe unto you when all men shall speak well of you!" Thus may an active, zealous, successful Christian be crucified between human idolatry on the one hand, and creature jealousy on the other. Well, be it so, if self be slain, and God is glorified. The great secret, however, to learn here is, entire deadness to both. Going forward in the work of the Lord, as judgment dictates, as conscience approves, and as Providence guides—dead to human applause, and indifferent to human censure; ever taking the low place, aiming at the Lord's glory, and seeking the honor that comes from God only—this is happiness. Oh, to live and labor, to give and to suffer, in the meek simplicity of Christ, and with eternity full in view! The Lord grant us grace so to live, and so to die!

JULY

JULY 1

"Abide in me, and I in you. As the branch cannot bear fruit of itself, except it abide in the vine; no more can you, except you abide in me." John 15:4

The union of the believer with Jesus, and the consequent fruitfulness, is a glorious truth: the Holy Spirit, in His word, has laid great stress upon it. It is spoken of as a being in Christ—"Every branch in me." "If any man be in Christ, he is a new creature." "So we, being many, are one body in Christ." "Those who are fallen asleep in Christ." But in what sense are we to understand this being "in Christ"? To be in Christ truly, spiritually, vitally, is to be in that eternal covenant of grace made with Christ, as the Surety and Mediator of His people; one of the number spoken of as the Lord's "peculiar treasure;"—"For the Lord has chosen Jacob unto himself, and Israel for His peculiar treasure;" and concerning whom the Holy Spirit declares that they are elected in Christ—"Blessed be the God and Father of our Lord Jesus Christ, who has blessed us with all spiritual blessings in heavenly things in Christ: according as He has chosen us in Him before the foundation of the world, that we should be holy and without blame before Him in love." To be in Christ truly, is to stand accepted in His righteousness, to be justified by Him freely from all things; it is to be brought to the knowledge of our own vileness, insufficiency, and guilt; to be made to cast aside all self-dependence, that is, all works of human merit, and to come as the thief on the cross came, without any allowed confidence in anything of self, but as a poor, helpless, ruined, condemned sinner, all whose hope of pardon and acceptance is through the free mercy of God in Christ Jesus. To be in Christ is to be the subject of a living, holy, influential principle of faith; it is to be brought into the blessed state thus described by the apostle as his own—"I am crucified with Christ: nevertheless I live; yet not I, but Christ lives in me; and the life which I now live in the flesh I live by the faith of the Son of God, who loved me, and gave Himself for me." To be in Christ is to be one with Him; it is to be a member of His mystical body, of which He is the spiritual Head: and the Head and members are one. It is to have Christ dwelling in the heart—"Christ in you the hope of glory." Yes, it is to dwell in the heart of Christ; it is to rest there in the very pavilion of His love, to abide there every moment, to be sheltered there from all evil, and to be soothed there under all sorrow. Oh blessed state of being in Christ! Who would not experience it? Who would not enjoy it? "There is therefore now no condemnation to those who are in Christ Jesus, who walk not after the flesh, but after the Spirit."

These are the living branches, united to the true vine, which bear fruit. From their union to the living vine their fruit comes—"From me is your fruit found." "As the branch cannot bear fruit of itself, except it abide in the vine, no more can you, except you abide in me." And oh, what precious fruit does such a living branch bear! The broken heart—the contrite spirit—the mourning over sin—the low, abasing, humbling views of self—the venturing by faith on a full, mighty, willing Savior—the going out of self, and resting in His all-atoning work and all-satisfying righteousness. This is followed by a progressive advance in all holiness and godliness, the fruits of faith which are by Jesus Christ abounding, and proving the reality of the wondrous change—the close walk with God—the submission of the will in all things to His—the conformity of the life to the example of Jesus—the "power of His resurrection" felt—the "fellowship of His sufferings," known—and "conformity to His death," marking the entire man.

These are some of the fruits of a truly regenerate soul. The Holy Spirit testifies, that the "fruit of the Spirit is in all goodness, and righteousness, and truth;" and still more minutely, as consisting of "love, joy, peace, patience, gentleness, goodness, faith, meekness, temperance."

JULY 2

"O the depth of the riches both of the wisdom and knowledge of God!" Romans 11:33

Behold this wisdom, as it shines in the recovery of lost and ruined man by Christ. Here is a manifestation infinitely transcending in greatness and glory the first creation of man in holiness. In the first creation, God had nothing to undo; no dilapidated temple to take down, no occupant to dispossess, no ruin to repair, no rubbish to remove, no enemy to oppose. But in the re-creation of man, how vastly different! The beautiful temple is a ruin—dilapidated and fallen. God is ejected; another and an antagonist occupant dwells in it, and enmity to its Creator is written in letters of darkness upon every part and over every inlet. In rebuilding this structure, all things were to be created anew. "Behold," says God, "I create a new thing in the earth." It was a new and profounder thought of infinite wisdom, unheard, unseen before. Fallen man was to be raised—lost man was to be recovered—sin was to be pardoned—the sinner saved, and God eternally glorified. Now were the treasures of wisdom, which for ages had been hid in Christ, brought forth. Infinite wisdom had never developed such vast wealth, had never appeared clothed in such glory, had never shone forth so majestic, so peerless, and Divine. Oh, how must angels and archangels have wondered, admired, and loved, as this brighter discovery of God burst in glory upon their astonished vision–as this new temple of man rose in loveliness before their view!

The greatest display of infinite wisdom was in the construction of the model upon which the new temple, regenerated man, was to be formed. This model was nothing less than the mysteriously constituted person of the Son of God. In this, its highest sense, is "Christ the wisdom of God." Here it shone forth in full-orbed majesty. Gaze upon the living picture! Look at Immanuel, God with us—God in our nature—God in our accursed nature—God in our tried nature—God in our sorrowful nature—God in our suffering nature—God in our tempted nature—yet untouched, untainted by sin. Is not this a fathomless depth of Divine wisdom? To have transcended it, would seem to have transcended Deity itself.

The next step in the unfolding of this Divine wisdom is the spiritual restoration of man to a state corresponding in its moral lineaments to this Divine and perfect model. This is accomplished solely by "Christ crucified, the wisdom of God." And here, again, does the glory of God's wisdom shine in the person and work of Jesus. Every step in the development of this grand expedient establishes His character as the "only wise God," whose "understanding is infinite;" while it augments our knowledge, and exalts our views of the Lord Jesus, as making known the Father. Here was a way of salvation for perishing sinners, harmonizing with every perfection of Jehovah, sustaining the highest honor of His government; bringing to Him the richest glory, and securing to its subjects, as the rich bequest of grace, happiness eternal, and inconceivably great. Oh, how truly did God here "work all things after the counsel of His own will"! How has He "abounded towards us in all wisdom and prudence"! In Jesus' sacrificial obedience and death we see sin fully punished, and the sinner fully saved–we see the law perfectly honored, and the transgressor completely justified–we see justice entirely satisfied, and mercy glorified to its highest extent–we see death inflicted according to the extreme tenor of the curse, and so vindicating to the utmost the truth and holiness of God; and yet life, present and eternal life, given to all whom it is the purpose and grace of the Father to save. Tell us, is not Jesus the great glory of the Divine wisdom?

JULY 3

"For we who live are always delivered unto death for Jesus' sake, that the life also of Jesus might be made manifest in our mortal flesh. We having the same spirit of faith, according as it is written, I believed, and therefore have I spoken; we also believe, and therefore speak." 2 Corinthians 4:11, 13

What is the life of faith which the believer lives, but a manifestation of the life of the Lord Jesus? The highest, the holiest, the happiest life lived below, is the life of faith. But nature contributes nothing to this life. It comes from a higher source. It is supernatural—it is opposed to nature. It springs from the life "hid with Christ in God." "I am crucified with Christ, nevertheless I live; yet not I, but Christ lives in me; and the life which I now live in the flesh, I live by the faith of the Son of God." Here is a glorious manifestation of the life of Jesus. If we desire any evidence that Jesus is risen, that He is alive again, and that He is the life of the soul, here it is! See the faith of a child of God sifted as wheat, yet not one grain falling to the ground—tried as gold, yet not one particle lost—though in the flame, yet never consumed. And why? Because Christ lives in the soul. Dear believer! your faith may be sharply tempted—severely tried—but never, never shall it quite fail; for Jesus lives in you, and lives in you forever. Oh blessed trial of faith, that manifests in, and endears to, you the life of Jesus! It is the precious trial of "precious faith,"—a faith which the more deeply it is tried, the more deeply it manifests the risen life of its Divine "Author and Finisher."

And what, too, are all the supports of the believer in seasons of trial, suffering, and bereavement, but so many manifestations of the life of the Lord Jesus? What is our path to glory, but the path of tribulation, of suffering, and of death? Our Lord and Master, in the expression of His wisdom and love, forewarns us of this—"In the world you shall have tribulation." And His apostles but echo the same sentiment, when they affirm that it is "through much tribulation we must enter the kingdom." But the life of our risen Lord is daily manifested in us. This it is that keeps the soul buoyant amid the billows, strong in faith, joyful in hope, soaring in love. Thus is Jesus the life of every grace, the life of every promise, the life of every ordinance, the life of every blessing; yes, of all that is really costly and precious to a child of God, Jesus is the substance, the glory, the sweetness, the fragrance, yes, the very life itself. Oh! dark and lonely, desolate and painful indeed were our present pilgrimage, but for Jesus. If in the world we have tribulation, in whom have we peace?—in

Jesus! If in the creature we meet with fickleness and change, in whom find we the "Friend that loves at all times"?—in Jesus! When adversity comes as a wintry blast, and lays low our comforts, when the cloud is upon our tabernacle, when health, and wealth, and influence, and friends are gone—in whom do we find the covert from the wind, the faithful, tender "Brother born for adversity?"—in Jesus! When temptation assails, when care darkens, when trial oppresses, when bereavement wounds, when heart and flesh are failing, who throws around us the protecting shield, who applies the precious promise, who speaks the soothing word, who sustains the sinking spirit, who heals the sorrow, and dries the tear?—Jesus! Where sin struggles in the heart, and guilt burdens the conscience, and unbelief beclouds the mind, whose grace subdues our iniquities, whose blood gives us peace, and whose light dispels our darkness?—Jesus! And when the spark of life wanes, and the eye grows dim, and the mind wanders, and the soul, severing its last fetter, mounts and soars away, who, in that awful moment, draws near in form unseen, and whispers in words unheard by all but the departing one, now in close communion with the solemn realities of the invisible world—"Fear not; I am the resurrection and the life: he that believes in me, though he were dead, yet shall he live; and whoever lives and believes in me shall never die"?—still, it is Jesus!

JULY 4

"It is the Spirit that quickens, the flesh profits nothing: the words that I speak unto you, they are spirit, and they are life." John 6:63

The Spirit of God undertakes the achievement of a stupendous work. He enters the soul, and proposes to restore the empire of grace, the reign of holiness, and the throne of God. He engages to form all things anew; to create a revolution in favor of Christ and of heaven. He undertakes to change the heart, turning its enmity into love; to collect all the elements of darkness and confusion, educing from them perfect light and perfect order; to subdue the will, bringing it into harmony with God's will; to explore all the recesses of sin, turning its very impurity into holiness; in a word, to regenerate the soul, restoring the Divine image, and fitting it for the full and eternal enjoyment of God in glory. Now, in accomplishing this great work, what instrumentality does He employ? Passing by all human philosophy, and pouring contempt upon the profoundest wisdom and the mightiest power of man, He employs, in the production of a work in comparison with which the rise and the fall of empires were as infants' play, simply and alone, the "truth as it is in Jesus."

With this instrument He enters the soul—the seat of the greatest revolution that ever transpired. He moves over the dark chaos, without form and void, and in a moment a world of immortal beauty bursts into view. He overshadows the soul, and a vital principle is imparted, whose stream of existence, once commenced, flows on with the eternity of God Himself. How divine, yet how natural, too, the process! In the lapses of human thought, in the overtasked powers of the human intellect, how often is the mind impaired and shattered by the severe process through which it passes! But here is a revolution which touches every faculty of the soul, which changes all the powers of the mind; and yet, so gentle, so persuasive, and so mild, is the Spirit's operation, that, so far from deranging the power or disturbing the balance of the intellect, it develops resources, awakens energies, and inspires strength, of which until now it knew not its possession. "The entrance of Your word gives light; it gives understanding unto the simple."

And to what shall we turn for the secret of this? To the gospel, so replete with the glory of Jesus—that gospel, the substance of which is the incarnate God; the theme of which is Christ crucified—that gospel which testifies of His Godhead, which declares His manhood, which unfolds the union of both in the person of a glorious Redeemer; and which holds Him up to view, mighty, and willing to save to the uttermost. Oh, how sanctifying and comforting is the truth which testifies of Jesus! It has but to point to Him, and, clothed with the energy of the Spirit, the strongest corruption is subdued, the deepest grief is soothed. Of what value or efficacy is all our knowledge of the truth, if it lead us not to Jesus; if it expand not our views of His glory; if it conform not our minds to His image; if it increase not our love to His person, and if it quicken not our obedience to His commands, and our zeal for His cause; and mature us not, by a progressive holiness, for the enjoyment of His beatific presence?

JULY 5

"Faith which works by love." Galatians 5:6

Love is that grace of the Spirit that brings faith into active exercise; and faith, thus brought into exercise, brings every spiritual blessing into the soul. A believer stands by faith; he walks by faith; he overcomes by faith; he lives by faith. Love is therefore a laboring grace—"God is not unrighteous to forget your work and labor of love, which you have showed towards His name." There is nothing indolent in the nature of true love; it is not an inert, sluggish principle: where it dwells in the heart in a healthy and vigorous state, it constrains the believer to live not to himself, but unto Him who loved and gave Himself for him; it awakes the soul to watchfulness, sets it upon the work of frequent self-examination, influences it to prayer, daily walking in the precepts, acts of kindness, benevolence, and charity, all springing from love to God, and flowing in a channel of love to man.

The Holy Spirit distinguishes love as a part of the Christian armor—"Let us, who are of the day, be sober, putting on the breastplate of faith and love." Without ardent and increasing love to God, the believer is but poorly armed against his numerous spiritual and ever aggressive foes; but what a breastplate and helmet is this in the day of battle! Who can overcome a child of God, whose heart is overflowing with Divine love? What enemy can prevail against him thus armed? He may be, and he is, in himself, nothing but weakness; his foes many and mighty; hemmed in on every side by his spiritual Philistines; and yet, his heart soaring to God in love, longing for His presence, panting for His precepts, desiring, above and beyond all other blessings, Divine conformity! Oh, with what a panoply is he clothed! No weapon formed against him shall prosper; every "fiery dart of the adversary" shall be quenched, and he shall "come off more than a conqueror, through Him who has loved him."

In a word, love is immortal; it is that grace of the Spirit that will never die. This is not so with all the kindred graces: the period will come when they will no more be needed. The day is not far distant, when faith will be turned into sight, and hope will be lost in full fruition; but love will never die; it will live on, and expand the heart, and tune the lip, and inspire the song, through the unceasing ages of eternity. "Whether there be prophecies, they shall fail; whether there be tongues, they shall cease; whether there be knowledge, it shall vanish away;" but love never fails; it is an eternal spring, welled in the bosom of Deity: heaven will be its dwelling-place, God its source, the glorified spirit its subject, and eternity its duration.

JULY 6

"The Spirit of the Lord God is upon me; because the Lord has anointed me to preach good tidings unto the meek; he has sent me to bind up the broken-hearted, to proclaim liberty to the captives, and the opening of the prison to them that are bound." Isaiah 61:1

We can with difficulty realize, as the eye traces this evangelical declaration, that we are reading the prophecy, and not its fulfillment; the shadowy writings of the Old, and not the noontide revelation of the New Testament; so luminous with the gospel, so fragrant with the name, so replete with the work of JESUS is it. Oh, what tidings of joy and gladness are here to the heart-broken, burdened captive! Could announcements be more suited to his case, more appropriate to his circumstances, more soothing to his heart? Here, from the very heart of the Bible, Jesus Himself speaks. And never, in the days of His flesh, when preaching from the mountain or in the synagogue, were sweeter sounds uttered from His lips than these. This was the work that was before Him—to seek and to save lost sinners, to save them as sinners, to rend asunder their chains, to deliver them from their captivity, and to introduce them into the glorious liberty of the sons of God.

The quiet, lowly, unostentatious character of Jesus, blending with the most exquisite tenderness of heart, the pen of the evangelical prophet with equal vividness and beauty portrays—"He shall not cry, nor lift up, nor cause His voice to be heard in the street. A bruised reed shall He not break, and the smoking flax shall He not quench." Was not the entire life of our Lord in exact harmony with this prophetical portrait? Did not the glory of His lowly life, which Isaiah saw with a prophet's far-reaching eye, illumine, as with a living light, every step and every act of His history? Verily it did! Truly might He say, "Learn of me; for I am meek and lowly in heart." The most sublime miracles, the most stupendous exertions of power, and the most brilliant displays of philanthropy, on which a self-aggrandizing man would have established successfully his claims to profound and universal homage, He only referred to as sustaining the glory of His Father in His Divine mission; while all earthly honor and temporal power that might have accrued separately to Himself, He utterly rejected, veiling His own person in the deep folds of that humility which clothed Him as a garment. Shrinking from the intense gaze of a delighted multitude, and from the murmuring breath of popular applause, He would vanish as in a moment from the scene of His benevolence, either to lavish His boundless compassion on other and more wretched objects of suffering and woe, or to hide Himself amid the gloom and solitude of the desert. Never was humility like Your, you meek and lowly Lamb of God! Subdue this hated self in us—lay low this pride—suppress these inward risings, and draw, in fairer and deeper lines, Your own image on our souls!

JULY 7

"Buried with him in baptism, wherein also you are risen with him through the faith of the operation of God, who has raised him from the dead. And you, being dead in your sins and the uncircumcision of your flesh, has he quickened together with him; having forgiven you all trespasses." Colossians 2:12, 13

Is Jesus alive? then the saints of God are a risen people. What a glorious character is theirs! Mystically they are risen with Christ from the tomb, and spiritually they are risen from the grave of death and sin to newness of life. One of the most fruitful causes of a feeble Christianity is the low estimate the believer forms of his spiritual character. Were this higher, were it more proportioned to our real standing, our responsibility would appear in a more solemn light, our sense of obligation would be deeper, and practical holiness of a high order would be our more constant aim. Ours is a glorious and exalted life. Our standing is higher, infinitely higher, than the highest angel; our glory infinitely greater than the most glorious seraph. "Christ is our life." "We are risen with Christ." By this we are declared to be a chosen, an adopted, a pardoned, a justified, and a quickened people. This is our present state; this is our present character. We bear about with us the life of God in our souls. As Jesus did bear about in His lowly, suffering, tempted, and tried humanity the hidden essential life; so we, in these frail, sinful, bruised, dying bodies, enshrine the life derived from a risen Head—the hidden life concealed with Christ in God. What an exalted character, what a holy one, then, is a believer in Jesus! Herein lie his true dignity and his real wealth—it is, that he is a partaker of the Divine nature, that he is one with the risen Lord. All other distinctions, in comparison, vanish into insignificance, and all other glory fades and melts away. Poor he may be in this world, yet is he rich in faith, and an heir of the kingdom; for he has Christ. Rich he may be in this world, titled and exalted, yet, if Christ is in his heart, that heart is deeply sensible of its native poverty—is lowly, child-like, Christ-like.

If this is our exalted character, then how great our responsibilities, and how solemn our obligations! The life we now live in the flesh is to be an elevated, a risen, a heavenly life. "If you be risen with Christ, seek those things which are above, where Christ sits on the right hand of God. Set your affection on things above, not on things on the earth. For you are dead, and your life is hid with Christ in God." What is the holy state here enjoined?—heavenly-mindedness. On what ground is it enforced?—our resurrection with Christ. As a risen people, how heavenly-minded, then, ought we to be! How incompatible and incongruous do groveling pursuits, and carnal joys, and earthly ambitions appear, with a life professedly one and risen with the incarnate God! But even here much heavenly wisdom is needed to guide in the narrow and difficult way. To go out of the world—to become as a detached cipher of the human family—to assume the character, even in approximation, of the religious recluse—the gospel nowhere enjoins. To relinquish our secular calling, unless summoned by God to a higher and more spiritual service in the church—to relax our diligence in our lawful business—to be indifferent to our personal interests and responsibilities—to neglect our temporal concerns, and to be regardless of the relative claims which are binding upon us, are sacrifices which a loyal attachment to our heavenly King does not necessarily demand; and, if assumed, are self-inflicted; and, if made, must prove injurious to ourselves and displeasing to God.

But to be heavenly-minded, in the true and Scripture sense, is to carry our holy Christianity into every department of life, and with it to elevate and hallow every relation and engagement. There is no position in which the providence of God places His saints, for which the grace of Jesus is not all-sufficient, if sincerely and earnestly sought. Nor is there any sphere or calling, to which the life of Jesus in the soul may not impart dignity, luster, and sacredness. Christianity, through all grades, and classes, and occupations, is capable of diffusing a divine, hallowing, ennobling influence, transforming and sanctifying all that it touches. Blessed and holy are they who know it from personal and heartfelt experience!

JULY 8

"Do not be anxious about anything, but in everything, by prayer and petition, with thanksgiving, present your requests to God." Philippians 4:6

It must be admitted that the believer requires constant exhortation to the sweet and precious privilege of communion with his heavenly Father—that he needs to be urged by the strongest arguments and the most persuasive motives to avail himself of the most costly and glorious privilege this side of glory. Does it not seem like pleading with a man to live?—reminding him that he must breath, if he would maintain life? Without the exercise of prayer, we tell a child of God, he cannot live; that this is the drawing in of the Divine life, and the breathing of it forth again; that the spiritual nature requires constant supplies of spiritual nourishment; and that the only evidence of its healthy existence is its constant rising towards God. We tell him, Cease to pray, and your grace withers, your vigor decays, and your comfort dies.

Observe how prayer, as a duty, is enjoined in God's word—"Call upon me in the day of trouble; I will deliver you, and you shall glorify me." As though the Lord had said, "Call upon me when all is dark, when all is against you. I speak not now of the day of prosperity, of the sunny hour, when your soul prospers, when all things go smooth with you, and the sky above you is cloudless, and the sea beneath you is unruffled; but call upon me in the day of trouble, the day of want, the day of adversity, the day of disappointment and of rebuke, the day when friends forsake, and the world frowns upon you, the day of broken cisterns and withered gourds—call upon me in the day of trouble, and I will deliver you." Observe, too, how our dear Lord enjoined this precious duty upon His disciples—"You, when you pray, enter into your closet, and, when you have shut your door, pray to your Father which is in secret." And observe how He also encouraged it—"Verily, verily, I say unto you, whatever you shall ask the Father in my name, He will give it you." In harmony with this, is the sweet exhortation of the apostle—"Do not be anxious about anything, but in everything, by prayer and petition, with thanksgiving, present your requests to God." And what a striking unfolding of the true nature of prayer does the same writer give us in another passage—"Praying always with all prayer and supplication in the Spirit, and watching thereunto with all perseverance and supplication for all saints." The apostle James bears the same testimony—"If any of you lack wisdom, let him ask of God, that gives to all men liberally, and upbraids not, and it shall be given him."

But we take higher ground than this; we urge the exercise of prayer, not merely as a solemn duty to be observed, but also as a precious privilege to be enjoyed. Happy is that believer, when duties come to be viewed as privileges. What! is it no privilege to have a door of access ever open to God? is it no privilege when the burden crushes to cast it upon One who has promised to sustain? When the corruptions of an unsanctified nature are strong, and temptations thicken, is prayer no privilege then? And when perplexed to know the path of duty, and longing to walk complete in all the will of God, and, as a child, fearing to offend a loving Father, is it then no privilege to have a throne of grace, an open door of hope? When the world is slowly stealing upon the heart, or when that heart is wounded through the unkindness of friends, or is bleeding under severe bereavement, is it then no privilege to go and tell Jesus? Say, you poor, you needy, you tried, you tempted souls! say, if prayer is not the most precious and costly privilege this side heaven.

JULY 9

"He shall baptize you with the Holy Spirit." Mark 1:8

"Neither will I hide my face any more from them; for I have poured out my Spirit upon the house of Israel, says the Lord God." Ezekiel 39:29

In a more enlarged communication of the Holy Spirit's gracious influence lies the grand source and secret of all true, spiritual, believing, persevering, and prevailing prayer; it is the lack of this that is the cause of the dullness, and formality, and reluctance, that so frequently mark the exercise. The saints of God honor not sufficiently the Spirit in this important part of His work; they too much lose sight of the truth, that of all true prayer He is the Author and the Sustainer, and the consequence is, and ever will be, self-sufficiency and cold formality in the discharge, and ultimate neglect of the duty altogether. But let the promise be pleaded, "I will pour upon the house of David, and upon the inhabitants of Jerusalem, the spirit of grace and of supplication;" let the Holy Spirit be acknowledged as the Author, and constantly sought as the Sustainer, of this holy exercise; let the saint of God feel that he knows not what he should pray for as he ought, that the Spirit itself makes intercession for us with groanings which cannot be uttered, and that God knows the mind of the Spirit, because He makes intercession for the saints according to His will; and what an impulse will this give to prayer! what new life will it impart! what mighty energy, what unction, and what power with God! Seek, then, with all your blessings, this, the richest, and the pledge of all, the baptism of the Spirit; rest not short of it. You are nothing as a professing man without it; your religion is lifeless, your devotion is formal, your spirit is unctionless; you have no moral power with God, or with man, apart from the baptism of the Holy Spirit. Seek it, wrestle for it, agonize for it, as transcendently more precious than every other mercy. Submerged in His quickening and reviving influences, what a different Christian will you be! How differently will you pray, how differently will you live, and how differently will you die! Is the spirit of prayer languishing? is its exercise becoming irksome? is closet-devotion abandoned? is the duty in any form becoming a task? Oh, rouse you to the seeking of the baptism of the Spirit! This alone will revive the true spirit of prayer within you, and this will give to its exercise sweetness, pleasantness, and power. God has promised the bestowment of the blessing, and He will never disappoint the soul that seeks it.

JULY 10

"Ought not Christ to have suffered these things, and to enter into his glory?" Luke 24:26

As the faithful servant of the everlasting covenant, it was proper, it was just, it was the reward of His finished work, that Christ's deepest humiliation on earth should be succeeded by the highest glory in heaven. "For the joy that was set before Him,"—the joy of His exaltation, with its glorious fruits—"He endured the cross, despising the shame, and is set down at the right hand of the throne of God." How proper, how righteous does it appear, that the crown of His glory should follow the cross of His humiliation! Toilsome and faithful had been His life; ignominious and painful had been His death. From both there had accrued to God—is now, and will yet be accruing, through the countless ages of eternity—a revenue of glory, such as never had been His before. He had revealed the Father gloriously. Drawing aside the veil as no other hand could do, He caused such Divine glory to beam forth, as compelled every spotless spirit in heaven to cover Himself with His wings, and fall prostrate in the profoundest humility and homage.

The glorious perfections of God!—never had they appeared so glorious as now. The mediatorial work of Jesus had laid a deep foundation, on which they were exhibited to angels and to men in their most illustrious character. Never before had wisdom appeared so truly glorious, nor justice so awfully severe, nor love so intensely bright, nor truth so eternally stable. Had all the angels in heaven, and all creatures of all worlds, become so many orbs of divine light, and were all merged into one, so that that one should embody and reflect the luster of all, it would have been darkness itself compared with a solitary beam of God's glory, majesty, and power, as revealed in the person and work of Immanuel. Now it was fit that, after this faithful servitude, this boundless honor and praise brought to God, His Father should, in return, release Him from all further obligation, lift Him from His humiliation, and place Him high in glory. Therefore it was that Jesus poured out the fervent breathings of His soul on the eve of His passion: "I have glorified You on the earth; I have finished the work which You gave me to do: I have manifested Your name, and now, O Father, glorify You me."

The ascension of Jesus to glory involved the greatest blessing to His saints. Apart from His own glorification, the glory of His church was incomplete—so entirely, so identically were they one. The resurrection of Christ from the dead was the Father's public seal to the acceptance of His work; but the exaltation of Christ to glory was an evidence of the Father's infinite delight in that work. Had our Lord continued on earth, His return from the grave, though settling the fact of the completeness of His atonement, could have afforded no clear evidence, and could have conveyed no adequate idea, of God's full pleasure and delight in the person of His beloved Son. But in advancing a step further—in taking His Son out of the world, and placing Him at His own right hand, far above principalities and powers—He demonstrated His ineffable delight in Jesus, and His perfect satisfaction with His great atonement. Now it is no small mercy for the saints of God to receive and to be well established in this truth, namely, the Father's perfect satisfaction with, and His infinite pleasure in, His Son. For all that He is to His Son, He is to the people accepted in His Son; so that this view of the glorification of Jesus becomes exceedingly valuable to all who are "accepted in the Beloved." So precious was Jesus to His heart, and so infinitely did His soul delight in Him, He could not allow of His absence from glory a moment longer than was necessary for the accomplishment of His own purpose and the perfecting of His Son's mission; that done, He showed His Beloved the "path of life," and raised Him to His "presence, where is fullness of joy," and to "His right hand, where there are pleasures for evermore. "

JULY 11

"I have surely heard Ephraim bemoaning himself thus; You have chastised me, and I was chastised, as a bullock unaccustomed to the yoke: turn you me, and I shall be turned; for you are the Lord my God. Surely after that I was turned, I repented; and after that I was instructed, I smote upon my thigh: I was ashamed, yes, even confounded, because I did bear the reproach of my youth." Jeremiah 31:18, 19

The divine life in the soul of man is indestructible—it cannot perish; the seed that grace has implanted in the heart is incorruptible—it cannot be corrupted. So far from trials, and conflicts, and storms, and tempests impairing the principle of holiness in the soul, they do but deepen and strengthen it, and tend greatly to its growth. We look at Job; who of mere man was ever more keenly tried?—and yet, so far from destroying or even weakening the divine life within him, the severe discipline of the covenant, through which he passed, did but deepen and expand the root, bringing forth in richer clusters the blessed fruits of holiness. Do you think, dear reader, the divine life in his soul had undergone any change for the worse, when, as the result of God's covenant dealings with him, he exclaimed—"I have heard of You by the hearing of the ear, but now mine eye sees You: why I abhor myself, and repent in dust and ashes?" No, the pruning of the fruitful branch impairs not, but rather strengthens and renders more fruitful the principle of holiness in the soul.

It is the will of God that His people should be a fruitful people. "This is the will of God, even your sanctification,"—the sanctification of a believer including all fruitfulness. He will bring out His own work in the heart of His child; and never does He take His child in hand with a view of dealing with him according to the tenor of the covenant of grace, but that dealing results in a greater degree of spiritual fruitfulness. Now, when the Lord afflicts, and the Holy Spirit sanctifies the affliction of the believer, is not this again among the costly fruit of that discipline, that self has become more hateful? This God declared should be the result of His dealings with His, ancient people Israel, for their idolatry—"They shall loathe themselves for the evils which they have committed in all their abominations." And again—"Then shall you remember your ways, and all your doings wherein you have been defiled; and you shall loathe yourselves in your own sight, for all your evils that you have committed." To loathe self on account of its sinfulness, to mortify it in all its forms, and to bring it entirely into subjection to the spirit of holiness, is, indeed, no small triumph of Divine grace in the soul, and no mean effect of the sanctified use of the Lord's dispensations. That must ever be considered a costly mean that accomplished this blessed end. Beloved reader, is your covenant God and Father dealing with you now? Pray that this may be one blessed result, the abasement of self within you, the discovering of it to you in all its deformity, and its entire subjection to the cross of Jesus.

JULY 12

"Herein is love, not that we loved God, but that he loved us, and sent his Son to be the propitiation for our sins." 1 John 4:10

It is a self-evident truth, that as God only knows, so He only can reveal His own love. It is a hidden love, veiled deep within the recesses of His infinite heart; yes, it seems to compose His very essence, for, "God is love,"—not merely lovely and loving, but love itself, essential love. Who, then, can reveal it but Himself? How dim are the brightest views, and how low the loftiest conceptions, of the love of God, as possessed by men of mere natural and speculative knowledge of divine things! They read of God's goodness, even in nature, with a half-closed eye, and spell it in providence with a stammering tongue. Of His essential love—His redeeming love—of the great and glorious manifestation of His love in Jesus, they know nothing. The eyes of their understanding have not been opened; and "God, who commanded the light to shine out of darkness," has not as yet "shined into their hearts, to give the light of the knowledge of the glory of God in the face of Jesus Christ."

But God has declared His own love—Jesus is its glorious revelation. "In this was manifested the love of God toward us, because that God sent His only begotten Son into the world, that we might live through Him." Oh, what an infinite sea of love now broke in upon our guilty and rebellious world, wafting in upon its rolling tide God's only begotten Son! That must have been great love—love infinite, love unsearchable, love passing all thought—which could constrain the Father to give Jesus to die for us, "while we were yet sinners." It is the great loss of the believer that faith eyes with so dim a vision this amazing love of God in the gift of Jesus. We have transactions so seldom and so unbelievingly with the cross, that we have need perpetually to recur to the apostle's cheering words, written as if kindly and condescendingly to meet this infirmity of our faith—"He that spared not His own Son, but delivered Him up for us all, how shall He not with Him also freely give us all things!"

But, behold God's love! See how He has inscribed this glorious perfection of His nature in letters of blood drawn from the heart of Jesus. His love was so great, that nothing short of the surrender to the death of His beloved Son could give an adequate expression of its immensity. "For God so loved the world, that He gave His only begotten Son." Here was the greatest miracle of love—here was its most stupendous achievement—here its most brilliant victory—and here its most costly and precious offering. Seeing us fallen, obnoxious to the law's curse, exposed to its dreadful penalty, guilty of innumerable sins, and deserving of as many deaths, yet how did it yearn to save us! How did it heave, and pant, and strive, and pause not, until it revealed a way infinitely safe for God and man; securing glory to every Divine attribute in the highest degree, and happiness to the creature, immense, unspeakable, and eternal.

JULY 13

"And all mine are your, and your are mine; and I am glorified in them." John 17:10

The manifested glory of Christ in His church is clearly and manifestly stated in the sublime prayer of our Lord. Addressing His Father, He claims with Him—what no mere creature could do—a conjunction of interest in the church, based upon an essential unity of nature. What angel in heaven could adopt this language, what creature on earth could present this claim—"All your are mine"? It would be an act of the most daring presumption; it would be the very inspiration of blasphemy: but when our Lord asserts it—asserts it, too, in a solemn prayer addressed on the eve of His death to His Father—what does it prove, but that a unity of property in the church involves a unity of essence in being? There could be no perfect oneness of the Father and the Son in any single object, but as it sprang from a oneness of nature. The mutual interest, then, which Christ thus claims with His Father refers in this instance specifically to the church of God. And it is delightful here to trace the perfect equality of love towards the church, as of perfect identity of interest in the church. We are sometimes tempted to doubt the perfect sameness, as to degree, of the Father's love with the Son's love; that, because Jesus died, and intercedes, the mind thus used to familiarize itself with Him more especially, associating Him with all its comforting, soothing, hallowing views and enjoyments, we are liable to be beguiled into the belief that His love must transcend in its strength and intensity the love of the Father. But not so. The Father's love is of perfect equality in degree, as it is in nature, with the Son's love; and this may with equal truth be affirmed of the "love of the Spirit." "He that has seen me," says Jesus, "has seen the Father." Then he that has seen the melting, overpowering expressions of the Redeemer's love—he that has seen Him pouring out His deep compassion over the miseries of a suffering world—he that has seen His affectionate gentleness towards His disciples—he that has seen Him weep at the grave of Lazarus—he that has followed Him to the garden of Gethsemane, to the judgment-hall of Pilate, and from thence to the cross of Calvary—has seen in every step which He trod, and in every act which He performed, a type of the deep, deep love which the Father bears towards His people. He that has thus seen the Son's love, has seen the Father's love. Oh, sweet to think, the love that travailed—the love that toiled—the love that wept—the love that bled—the love that died, is the same love, in its nature and intensity, which is deep-welled in the heart of the TRIUNE GOD, and is pledged to secure the everlasting salvation of the church. "God was in Christ, reconciling the world unto Himself." "In this was manifested the love of God toward us, because that God sent His only begotten Son into the world, that we might live through Him."

JULY 14

"And not only so, but we glory in tribulations also: knowing that tribulation works patience." Romans 5:3

By a patient endurance of suffering for His sake, the Redeemer is greatly glorified in His saints. The apostle—and few drank of the bitter cup more deeply than he—presents suffering for Christ in the soothing light of a Christian privilege. "Unto you it is given in the behalf of Christ, not only to believe on Him, but also to suffer for His sake." "But if you be reproached for the name of Christ, happy are you;" for thereby Christ is glorified in you. Believer, suffering for Christ, rejoice, yes, rejoice that you are counted worthy to suffer shame for His sake. What distinction is awarded you! What honor is put upon you! What a favored opportunity have you now of bringing glory to His name; for illustrating His sustaining grace, and upholding strength, and Almighty power, and infinite wisdom, and comforting love! By the firm yet mild maintenance of your principles, by the dignified yet gentle spirit of forbearance, by the uncompromising yet kind resistance to allurement, let the Redeemer be glorified in you! In all that you suffer for righteousness' sake, let your eye be immovably fixed on Jesus. In Him you have a bright example. "Consider Him that endured such contradiction of sinners against Himself, lest you be wearied and faint in your mind." Remember how, for your redemption, He "endured the cross, despising the shame," and, for your continual support, "is set down at the right hand of the throne of God."

Remember, too, that it is one peculiar exercise and precious privilege of faith, to "wait patiently for the Lord." The divine exhortation is, "Commit your way unto the Lord; trust also in Him; and He shall bring it to pass." "Rest in the Lord, and wait patiently for Him." This patience of the soul is the rest of faith on a faithful God; it is a standing still to see His salvation. And the divine encouragement is, that in this posture will be found the secret of your real power. "In quietness and in confidence shall be your strength." Be watchful against everything that would mar the simplicity of your faith, and so dim the glory of Jesus; especially guard against the adoption of unlawful or doubtful measures, with a view to disentanglement from present difficulties. Endure the pressure, submit to the wrong, bear the suffering, rather than sin against God, by seeking to forestall His mind, or to antedate His purpose, or by transferring your interests from His hands to your own.

Oh, the glory that is brought to Jesus by a life of faith! Who can fully estimate it? Taking to Him the corruption, as it is discovered—the guilt, as it rises, the grief, as it is felt—the cross, as it is experienced—the wound, as it is received; yes, simply following the example of John's disciples, who, when their master was slain, took up his headless body, and buried it, and then went and poured their mournful intelligence in Jesus' ear, and laid their deep sorrow on His heart; this is to glorify Christ! Truly is this "precious faith," and truly is the "trial of our faith precious," for it renders more precious to the heart "His precious blood," who, in His person, is unutterably "precious to those who believe."

JULY 15

"Yet it pleased the Lord to bruise him; he has put him to grief: when you shall make his soul an offering for sin, he shall see his seed, he shall prolong his days, and the pleasure of the Lord shall prosper in his hand." Isaiah 53:10

In the person and work of Christ the holiness of God is revealed with equal power and luster. It is only through this medium that we possess the most clear and perfect demonstration of this divine and awful perfection. Where was there ever such a demonstration of God's infinite hatred of sin, and His fixed and solemn determination to punish it, as is seen in the cross of Christ? Put your shoes from off your feet; draw near, and contemplate this "great sight." Who was the sufferer? God's only-begotten and well-beloved Son! His own Son! In addition to the infinitely tender love of the Father, there was the clear knowledge of the truth, that He, who was enduring the severest infliction of His wrath, was innocent, guiltless, righteous—that He, Himself, had never broken His law, had never opposed His authority, had never run counter to His will; but had always done those things which pleased Him. At whose hands did He suffer? From devils? from men? They were but the agents; the moving cause was God Himself. "It pleased the Lord to bruise Him; He has put Him to grief." His own Father unsheathed the sword: He inflicted the blow: He kindled the fierce flame: He prepared the bitter cup. "Awake, O sword, against my shepherd, and against the man that is my fellow, says the Lord of hosts: smite the shepherd." "The cup which my Father has given me, shall I not drink it?" "My God, my God, why have you forsaken me?" And what were the nature and degree of His sufferings? Imagine, if we can, what must have been the outpouring of God's wrath upon the whole church for all the sins of that church, through eternity! Can you compute the amount of her transgressions? can you conceive the degree of her punishment? can you measure the duration of her woe? Impossible! Then, who can tell what Jesus endured, when standing in the place and as the Surety of His church, in the solemn hour of atonement, and in the day of God's fierce anger? Never had God so manifested before, and never will He so manifest again, His essential holiness—His spotless purity—the inconceivable heinousness of sin—His utter hatred of it—and His solemn purpose to punish it with the severest inflictions of His wrath; never did this glorious perfection of His being blaze out in such overwhelming glory, as on that dark day, and in the cross of the incarnate God. Had He emptied the vials of His wrath full upon the world, sweeping it before the fury of His anger, and consigning it to deserved and eternal punishment, it would not have presented to the universe so vivid, so impressive, and so awful a demonstration of the nature and glory of His holiness, of His infinite abhorrence of sin, and the necessity why He should punish it, as He has presented in the humiliation, sufferings, and death of His beloved Son. What new and ineffably transcendent views of infinite holiness must have sprung up in the pure minds even of the spirits in glory, as, bending from their thrones, they fixed their astonished gaze upon the cross of the suffering Son of God!

JULY 16

"Nevertheless I have somewhat against you, because you have left your first love." Revelation 2:4

Should the humiliating truth force itself upon you, my dear reader—"I am not as I once was; my soul has lost ground—my spirituality of mind has decayed—I have lost the fervor of my first love—I have slackened in the heavenly race—Jesus is not as He once was, the joy of my day, the song of my night—and my walk with God is no longer so tender, loving, and filial, as it was,"—then honestly and humbly confess it before God. To be humbled as we should be, we must know ourselves; there must be no disguising of our true condition from ourselves, nor from God; there must be no framing of excuses for our declensions: the wound must be probed, the disease must be known, and its most aggravating symptoms brought to view. Ascertain, then, the true state of your affection towards God; bring your love to Him to the touchstone of truth; see how far it has declined, and thus you will be prepared to trace out and to crucify the cause of your declension in love. Where love declines, there must be a cause; and, when ascertained, it must be immediately removed. Love to God is a tender flower; it is a sensitive plant, soon and easily crushed; perpetual vigilance is needed to preserve it in a healthy, growing state. The world's heat will wither it, the coldness of formal profession will often nip it: a thousand influences, all foreign to its nature and hostile to its growth, are leagued against it; the soil in which it is placed is not genial to it. "In the flesh there dwells no good thing;" whatever of holiness is in the believer, whatever breathing after Divine conformity, whatever soaring of the affections towards God, is from God himself, and is there as the result of sovereign grace. "That which is born of the flesh is flesh; and that which is born of the Spirit is spirit." What sleepless vigilance, then, and what perpetual culture are needed, to preserve the bloom and the fragrance, and to nourish the growth, of this celestial plant. Search out and remove the cause of the decay of this precious grace of the Spirit; rest not until it is discovered and brought to light: should it prove to be the world, come out from it, and be you separate, and touch not the unclean thing; or the power of indwelling sin, seek its immediate crucifixion by the cross of Jesus. Does the creature steal your heart from Christ, and deaden your love to God?—resign it at God's bidding; He asks the surrender of your heart, and has promised to be better to you than all creature love. All the tenderness, the deep affection, the acute sympathy, the true fidelity, that you ever did find or enjoy in the creature, dwells in God, your covenant God and Father, in an infinite degree. He makes the creature all it is to you. Possessing God in Christ, you can desire no more—you can have no more. If He asks the surrender of the creature, cheerfully resign it; and let God be all in all to you.

JULY 17

"I acknowledged my sin unto you, and mine iniquity have I not hid. I said, I will confess my transgressions unto the Lord, and you forgave the iniquity of my sin." Psalm 32:5

This is just what God loves—an open, ingenuous confession of sin. Searching and knowing, though He does, all hearts, He yet delights in the honest and minute acknowledgment of sin from His backsliding child. Language cannot be too humiliating; the detail cannot be too minute. Mark the stress He has laid upon this duty, and the blessing He has annexed to it. Thus He spoke to the children of Israel, that wandering, backsliding, rebellious people—"If they shall confess their iniquity, and the iniquity of their fathers, with their trespass which they trespassed against me, and that also they have walked contrary unto me; and that I also have walked contrary unto them, and have brought them into the land of their enemies; if then their uncircumcised hearts be humbled, and they then accept of the punishment of their iniquity; then will I remember my covenant with Jacob, and also my covenant with Isaac, and also my covenant with Abraham will I remember; and I will remember the land." Truly may we exclaim, "Who is a God like unto You, that pardons iniquity, and passes by the transgression of the remnant of His heritage! He retains not His anger forever, because He delights in mercy." And how did the heart of God melt with pity and compassion when He heard the audible relentings of His Ephraim! "I have surely heard Ephraim bemoaning himself thus: You have chastised me and I was chastised, as a bullock unaccustomed to the yoke: turn me, and I shall be turned; for You are the Lord my God." And what was the answer of God? "Is Ephraim my dear son? is he a pleasant child? for since I spoke against him, I do earnestly remember him still; therefore my affections are troubled for him: I will surely have mercy upon him, says the Lord." Nor is the promise of pardon annexed to confession of sin unfolded with less clearness and consolatoriness in the New Testament writings. "If we confess our sins, He is faithful and just to forgive us our sins, and to cleanse us from all unrighteousness." How full, then, the blessing, how rich the consolation connected with an honest, heart-broken confession of sin! How easy, and how simple too, this method of return to God! "Only acknowledge your iniquity." It is but a confession of sin over the head of Jesus, the great sacrifice for sin. Oh, what is this that God says? "Only acknowledge your iniquity!" Is this all He requires of His poor wandering child? This is all! "Then," may the poor soul exclaim, "Lord, I come to You. I am a backslider, a wanderer, a prodigal. I have strayed from You like a lost sheep. My love has waxed cold, my steps have slackened in the path of holy obedience, my mind has yielded to the corrupting, deadening influence of the world, and my affections have wandered in quest of other and earthly objects of delight. But, behold, I come unto You. Do You invite me? Do You stretch out Your hand? Do You bid me approach You? Do You say, 'Only acknowledge your iniquity?' Then, Lord, I come; in the name of Your dear Son, I come; restore unto me the joy of your salvation.'" Thus confessing sin over the head of Jesus, until the heart has nothing more to confess but the sin of its confession—for, beloved reader, our very confession of sin needs to be confessed over, our very tears need to be wept over, and our very prayers need to be prayed over, so defaced with sin is all that we do—the soul, thus emptied and unburdened, is prepared to receive anew the seal of a Father's forgiving love.

JULY 18

"Whatever you shall ask in my name, that will I do, that the Father may be glorified in the Son." John 14:13

In the matter of prayer, ever cultivate and cherish a kindly, soothing view of God in Christ. Without it, in this most solemn and holy of all transactions, your mental conceptions of His nature will be vague, your attempts to concentrate your thoughts on this one object will be baffled, and the spiritual character of the engagement will lessen in tone and vigor. But meeting God in Christ, with every perfection of His nature revealed and blended, you may venture near, and in this posture, and through this medium, may negotiate with Him the most momentous matters. You may reason, may adduce your strong arguments, and throwing wide the door of the most hidden chamber of your heart, may confess its deepest iniquity; you may place your "secret sins in the light of His countenance;" God can still meet you in the mildest luster of His love. Drawing near, placing your tremulous hand of faith on the head of the atoning sacrifice, there is no sin that you may not confess, no want that you may not make known, no mercy that you may not ask, no blessing that you may not crave, for yourself, for others, for the whole church. See! the atoning Lord is upon the mercy-seat, the golden censer waves, the fragrant cloud of the much incense ascends, and with it are "offered the prayers of all saints upon the golden altar which is before the throne." Jesus is in its midst—

"Looks like a Lamb that has been slain,
And wears His priesthood still."

"Having therefore, brethren, boldness to enter into the holiest by the blood of Jesus, and having an High Priest over the house of God, let us draw near." Open all your heart to God through Christ, who has opened all His heart to you in Christ. Remember that to bring Himself in a position to converse with you, as no angel could, in the matter that now burdens and depresses you, He assumed your nature on earth, with that very sorrow and infirmity affixed to it; took it back to glory, and at this moment appears in it before the throne, your Advocate with the Father. Then hesitate not, whatever be the nature of your petition, whatever the character of your need, to "make known your requests unto God." Coming by simple faith in the name of Jesus, it cannot be that He should refuse you. With His eye of justice ever on the blood, and His eye of complacency ever on His Son, Himself loving you, too, with a love ineffably great, it would seem impossible that you should meet with a denial.

Yield your ear to the sweet harmony of the Redeemer's voice, "Verily, verily, I say unto you, Whatever you shall ask the Father in my name, He will give it you. Hitherto have you asked nothing in my name; ask, and you shall receive, that your joy may be full."

JULY 19

"For God, who commanded the light to shine out of darkness, has shined in our hearts, to give the light of the knowledge of the glory of God in the face of Jesus Christ." 2 Corinthians 4:6

That God was under any obligation or necessity to reveal Himself to man, is an idea that cannot for a moment be seriously entertained. It will follow, then, that such a revelation of Himself, His mind and will, to fallen creatures, having been made, it must be regarded as an astounding act of His sovereign mercy, irrespective of any claim whatever arising from the creature man. The source where it originates must be entirely within God Himself.

The only full and perfect revelation of the glory of God is seen in the Lord Jesus; and apart from a spiritual and experimental knowledge of the Son there can be no true, adequate, and saving knowledge of the Father. "No man has seen God at any time; the only begotten Son, which is in the bosom of the Father, he has declared Him." The vast importance of a correct knowledge of God is a truth which finds an assent in well-near every judgment. Every awakened conscience desires it; every believing mind admits it; every tried soul feels it. It lies at the basis of salvation; it forms the material of happiness; it supplies the true motive to holiness; it is the ground-work and the prelude of future and eternal glory.

As all knowledge of God out of Christ is defective and fallacious, examine closely, and in the light of the revealed word, the source and character of your professed acquaintance with the nature, character, and perfections of God. Ponder seriously this solemn declaration of Christ Himself. "No man knows the Son, but the Father; neither knows any man the Father, save the Son, and he to whomsoever the Son will reveal Him." Has your knowledge of God overwhelmed you with a sense of your sinfulness? Have you caught such a view of the Divine purity, the immaculate holiness of His nature, as to compel you to exclaim, "Woe is me! for I am undone, because I am a man of unclean lips,...for mine eyes have seen the King, the Lord of Hosts; why I abhor myself, and repent in dust and ashes?" Has your study of His law forced upon your mind the deep and solemn conviction that you are a fallen, ruined, lost, guilty, condemned sinner, at this moment lying under the wrath of God, and exposed to future and everlasting destruction from the presence of the Lord, and the glory of His power? Has it laid you beneath the cross of Christ? Has it brought you to His blood and righteousness for pardon and acceptance? Has it led you utterly to renounce all self-trust, self-confidence, self-boasting, and to accept of Jesus, as "made of God unto you wisdom, and righteousness, and sanctification, and redemption"? If it has not wrought this for you, your knowledge of God is but as "sounding brass or a tinkling cymbal." "This," says Christ, "is life eternal, that they might know You, the only true God, and Jesus Christ, whom You have sent." If you know not the Son, you know not the Father. "No man knows the Father, but he to whom the Son shall reveal Him,"—Jesus Himself has declared. Consider well the mercy of having transactions with such a God, in such a Christ. A God so holy and just, so good and wise, in a Christ so truly human, so spotless, so near, so dear and precious! God in Christ! Oh the immensity of the truth! Oh the glory of the revelation! That God reconciled, one with the believer; all His feelings love, all His thoughts peace, and all His dealings parental; each perfection harmonizing in the most perfect agreement with all the others, to secure the highest amount of good here, and of happiness unspeakable and eternal hereafter.

JULY 20

"I pray with all my heart; answer me, Lord! I will obey your principles. I cry out to you; save me, that I may obey your decrees. I rise early, before the sun is up; I cry out for help and put my hope in your words. I stay awake through the night, thinking about your promise." Psalm 119:145-148

To be heavenly-minded, in the true and scriptural sense, is to carry our holy Christianity into every department of life, and with it to elevate and hallow every relation and engagement. There is no position in which the providence of God places His saints, for which the grace of Jesus is not all sufficient, if sincerely and earnestly sought. Nor is there any sphere, however humble, or calling, however mean, to which the life of Jesus in the soul may not impart dignity, luster, and sacredness. Christianity, through all grades, and classes, and occupations, is capable of diffusing a divine, hallowing, and ennobling influence, transforming and sanctifying all that it touches. Blessed and holy are they who know it from personal and heartfelt experience.

But "if we be risen with Christ," what is it to seek those things which are above, and to set our affections not on things on the earth? In other words, what is true heavenly-mindedness? It involves the habitual and close converse with God. The life of the soul can only be sustained by constant and ceaseless emanations from the life of God. There must be a perpetual stream of existence flowing into it from the "Fountain of Life." And how can this be experienced but by dwelling near that Fountain? Of no practical truth am I more deeply and solemnly convinced than this, that elevated spirituality—and, oh, what a blank is life without it!—can only be cultivated and maintained by elevated communion. The most holy, heavenly-minded, devoted, and useful saints have ever been men and women of much prayer. They wrestled with God secretly, and God wrought with them openly; and this was the source which fed their deep godliness, which supplied their rich anointing, and which contributed to their extensive and successful labors for Christ. Thus only can the life of God in the soul of man be sustained. Other duties, however spiritual—other enjoyments, however holy—other means of grace, however important and necessary, never can supply the place of prayer. And why? because prayer brings the soul in immediate contact with Christ, who is our life, and with God, the Fountain of life. As the total absence of the breath of prayer marks the soul "dead in trespasses and sins," so the waning of the spirit of prayer in the quickened soul as surely defines a state in which all that is spiritual within is "ready to die." Let nothing, then, rob you of this precious mean of advancing your heavenly-mindedness—nothing can be its substitute.

The believer should correctly ascertain the true character of his prayers. Are they lively and spiritual? Are they the exercises of the heart, or of the understanding merely? Are they the breathings of the indwelling Spirit, or the cold observance of a form without the power? Is it communion and fellowship? Is it the filial approach of a child, rushing with confidence and affection into the bosom of a Father, and sheltering itself there in every hour of need? Examine the character of your devotions; are they such as will stand the test of God's word? will they compare with the holy breathings of David, and Job, and Solomon, and the New Testament saints? Are they the breathings forth of the life of God within you? Are they ever accompanied with filial brokenness, lowliness of spirit, and humble and contrite confession of sin? See well to your prayers! "The Lord is far from the wicked: but He hears the prayer of the righteous." "The Lord is near unto all those who call upon Him, to all that call upon Him in truth."

JULY 21

"Hide your face from my sins, and blot out all mine iniquities. Create in me a clean heart, O God; and renew a right spirit within me. Cast me not away from your presence; and take not your Holy Spirit from me. Restore unto me the joy of your salvation; and uphold me with your free Spirit." Psalm 51:9-12

All religion that excludes as its basis the state of mind portrayed in these words is a shell without a pearl, a body without a spirit. It has ever been a leading and favorite scheme of Satan to persuade men to substitute the religion of man for the religion of God. The religion of man has assumed various forms and modifications, always accommodating itself to the peculiar age and history of the world. But we have observed that the religion of man—be its form what it may—has ever kept at the remotest distance from the spiritual; everything that brought the mind in contact with truth, and the conscience and the heart into close converse with itself and with God, it has studiously and carefully avoided; and thus it has evaded that state and condition of the moral man which constitutes the very soul of the religion of God—"the broken and contrite heart."

The state of holy contrition described in these words of David mark an advanced stage in the experience of the spiritual man; a stage which defines one of the most interesting periods of the Christian's life—the Divine restoring. David was a backslider. Deeply and grievously had he departed from God. But he was a restored backslider, and, in the portion we are now considering, we have the unfoldings of his sorrow-stricken, penitent, and broken heart—forming, perhaps, to some who read this page, the sweetest portion of God's word. But of the truth of this we are quite assured, that in proportion as we are brought into the condition of godly sorrow for sin, deep humiliation for our backslidings from God, our relapses, and declensions in grace, there is no portion of the sacred word that will so truly express the deep emotions of our hearts, no language so fitted to clothe the feelings of our souls, as this psalm of the royal penitent: "Have mercy upon me, O God, according to Your loving-kindness: according unto the multitude of Your tender mercies blot out my transgressions. Wash me thoroughly from my iniquity, and cleanse me from my sin. For I acknowledge my transgressions; and my sin is ever before me. Against You, You only, have I sinned, and done this evil in Your sight: that You might be justified when You speak, and be clear when You judge." Thus upon the altar of God he lays the sacrifice of a broken heart, and seems to exclaim, "Wretch that I am, to have forsaken such a God, to have left such a Father, Savior, and

Friend! Has He ever been unto me a wilderness—a barren land? Never! Have I ever found Him a broken cistern? Never! Has He ever proved to me unkind, unfaithful, untrue? Never! What! did not God satisfy me, had not Jesus enough for me, did not a throne of grace make me happy, that I should have turned my back upon such a God, should have forsaken such a bosom as Christ's, and slighted the spot where my heavenly Father had been so often used to meet and commune with me? Lord! great has been my departure, grievous my sin, and now most bitter is my sorrow—here at Your feet, upon Your altar, red with the blood of Your own sin-atoning sacrifice, I lay my poor broken, contrite heart, and beseech You to accept and heal it."

"Behold, I fall before Your face;
My only refuge is Your grace.
No outward forms can make me clean;
The leprosy lies deep within."

Such is the holy contrition which the Spirit of God works in the heart of the restored believer. Brought beneath the cross, and in the sight of the crucified Savior, the heart is broken, the spirit is melted, the eye weeps, the tongue confesses, the bones that were broken rejoice, and the contrite child is once more clasped in his Father's forgiving, reconciled embrace. "He restores my soul," is his grateful and adoring exclamation. Oh what a glorious God is ours, and what vile wretches are we!

JULY 22

"Yes, everything else is worthless when compared with the priceless gain of knowing Christ Jesus my Lord. I have discarded everything else, counting it all as garbage, so that I may have Christ" Philippians 3:8

Endeavor to enrich and enlarge your mind with more spiritual apprehensions of the personal glory, love, and fullness of Christ. All soul-declension arises from the admission of things into the mind contrary to the nature of indwelling grace. The world—its pleasures, its vanities, its cares, its varied temptations—these enter the mind, disguised in the shape often of lawful undertakings and duties, and draw off the mind from God, and the affections from Christ. These, too, weaken and deaden faith and love, and every grace of the indwelling Spirit: they are the foxes that spoil the vines; for our "vines have tender grapes." The world is a most hurtful snare to the child of God. It is impossible that he can maintain a close and holy walk with God, live as a pilgrim and a sojourner, wage a constant and successful warfare against his many spiritual foes, and at the same time open his heart to admit the greatest foe to grace—the love of the world. But when the mind is preoccupied by Christ, filled with contemplations of His glory, and grace, and love, no room is left for the entrance of external allurements; the world is shut out, and the flesh is shut out, and the fascinations of sin are shut out; and the soul holds a constant and undisturbed fellowship with God, while it is enabled to maintain a more vigorous resistance to every external attack of the enemy. And oh! how blessed is the soul's communion, thus shut in with Jesus! "Behold, I stand at the door and knock: if any man hear my voice, and open the door, I will come in to him, and will sup with him, and he with me." "I would come in," says the dear Lamb of God, "and dwell in you, and take up my abode with you, and sup with you, and you with me." This is true fellowship! And oh, sweet response of His own Spirit in the heart, when the believing soul exclaims—"When You said, Seek you my face; my heart said unto You, Your face, Lord, will I seek!" Enter, You, precious Jesus; I want none but You; I desire no company, and would hear no voice, but Your; I will have fellowship with none but You. Let me sup with You; yes, give me Your own flesh to eat, and Your own blood to drink! Ah! dear Christian reader, it is because we have so little to do with Jesus—we admit Him so seldom and so reluctantly to our hearts—we have so few dealings with Him—travel so seldom to His blood and righteousness, and live so little upon His fullness—that we are compelled so often to complain, "My leanness, my leanness!" But if we "be risen with Christ, seek those things which are above, where Christ sits on the right hand of God:" let us seek to know Christ more, to have more spiritual and enlarged comprehensions of His glory, to drink deeper into His love, to imbibe more of His Spirit, and conform more closely to His example.

JULY 23

"Will you not revive us again; that your people may rejoice in you?" Psalm 85:6

A fresh baptism of the Holy Spirit forms the great secret of all personal revival. This a declining soul needs more than all beside. Possessing this in a large degree, he possesses every spiritual blessing; it includes and is the pledge of every other. Our dear Lord sought to impress this, His last consoling doctrine, upon the drooping minds of His disciples: His bodily presence in their midst, He taught them, was to be compared with the spiritual and permanent dwelling of the Spirit among them. The descent of the Holy Spirit was to bring all things that He had taught them to their remembrance; it was to perfect them in their knowledge of the supreme glory of His person, the infinite perfection of His work, the nature and spirituality of His kingdom, and its ultimate and certain triumph, in the earth. The descent of the Spirit, too, was to mature them in personal holiness, and more completely fit them for arduous and successful labor in His cause, by deepening their spirituality, enriching them with more grace, and enlarging them with more love; and fully did the baptism of the Holy Spirit, on the day of Pentecost, accomplish all this: the apostles emerged from His influence, like men who had passed through a state of re-conversion; and this is state you must pass through, if you would experience a revival of God's word in your soul—you must be filled again by the Holy Spirit. Nothing short of this will quicken your dying graces, and melt your frozen love, and restore your backsliding heart. You must be baptized afresh with the Spirit; that Spirit whom you have so often and so deeply wounded, grieved, slighted, and quenched, must enter you anew, and seal, and sanctify, and re-convert you. Oh, arise, and pray and agonize for the outpouring of the Spirit upon your soul; give up your lifeless religion, your form without the power, your prayer without communion, your confessions without brokenness, your zeal without love. And oh, what numerous and precious promises cluster in God's word, all inviting you to seek this blessing! "He shall come down as rain upon the mown grass; as showers that water the earth." "Come, let us return unto the Lord; for He has torn, and He will heal us; He has smitten, and He will bind us up. After two days will He revive us; in the third day He will raise us up, and we shall live in His sight. Then shall we know, if we follow on to know the Lord: His going forth is prepared as the morning; and He shall come unto us as the rain, as the latter and former rain unto the earth." Seek, then, above and beyond all other blessings, the renewed baptism of the Holy Spirit. "Be filled with the Spirit;" seek it earnestly—seek under the deep conviction of your absolute need of it—seek it perseveringly—seek it believingly: God has promised, "I will pour out my Spirit upon you;" and asking it in the name of Jesus you shall receive.

JULY 24

"We also joy in God through our Lord Jesus Christ, by whom we have now received the atonement." Romans 5:11

Not a single perfection of God can a believing mind view in Christ, but it smiles upon him. Oh! to see holiness and justice, truth and love, bending their glance of sweetest and softest benignity upon a poor trembling soul, approaching to hide itself beneath the shadow of the cross! What a truth is this! All is sunshine here. The clouds are scattered, the darkness is gone, the tempest is hushed, the sea is a calm. Justice has lost its sting, the law its terror, and sin its power: the heart of God is open, the bosom of Jesus bleeds, the Holy Spirit draws, the Gospel invites, and now the weary and the heavy-laden may draw near to a reconciled God in Christ. Oh, were ever words sweeter than these, "God was in Christ, reconciling the world unto Himself, not imputing their trespasses unto them." "Whom God has set forth to be a propitiation through faith in His blood." "He is able to save to the uttermost those who come unto God by him"?

God in Christ is the covenant God of His people. He is their God; their tender, loving, condescending Father. They may lose for a while the sight and the enjoyment of this truth, but this contravenes it not; it still remains the same, unchangeable, precious, and glorious. Nothing can rob them of it. In the tempest let it be the anchorage of your faith; in darkness the pole-star of your hope. Let every circumstance—the prosperity that ensnares, and the adversity that depresses, the temptation that assails, and the slight that wounds—endear to your believing soul this precious thought—"God reconciled, God at peace, God a Father in Christ, is my God forever and ever, and He will be my guide even unto death." If to view God in Christ is a comforting truth, it is also a most sanctifying truth. Why has God revealed Himself in Jesus? To evince the exceeding hatefulness of sin, and to show that nothing short of such a stupendous sacrifice could remove it, consistently with the glory of the Divine nature and the honor of the Divine government. Each sin, then, is a blow struck at this transcendent truth. The eye averted from it, sin appears a trifle; it can be looked at without indignation, tampered with without fear, committed without hesitation, persisted in without remorse, confessed without sorrow. But when Divine justice is seen, drinking the very heart's blood of God's only Son in order to quench its infinite thirst for satisfaction—when God in Christ is seen in His humiliation, suffering, and death—all with the design of pardoning iniquity, transgression, and sin, how fearful a thing does it seem to sin against this holy Lord God! How base, how ungrateful appears the act, in view of love so amazing, of grace so rich, and of glory so great! Cultivate a constant, an ardent thirst for holiness. Do not be discouraged, if the more intensely the desire for sanctification rises, the deeper and darker the revelation of the heart's hidden evil. The one is often a consequent of the other; but persevere. The struggle may be painful, the battle may be strong, but the result is certain, and will be a glorious victory—VICTORY, through the blood of the Lamb!

JULY 25

"Looking for that blessed hope, and the glorious appearing of the great God and our Savior Jesus Christ." Titus 2:13

Let us now contemplate the appropriate and spiritual posture in which it behooves all, and especially Christ's church, to be found in view of so glorious and near an event as the second coming of Jesus. For "behold the Lord comes, with ten thousand of his saints." Faith in the doctrine of a coming Savior is the basis of a holy posture of expectation. Without a belief of this truth, there can be no looking for this blessed hope. "When the Son of man comes, will He find faith"—in this doctrine—"on the earth?" No, it is to be feared that many in the church will be found sadly wanting here. They had believed in the coming of death, but they had not believed in the coming of Him who "abolished death." They had expected with trembling the "king of terror," but had not expected with joy the "King of glory." They had hoped to go to Christ, but they had not hoped that Christ would come to them. But the "glorious appearing" of Jesus, and not the death of the saints, is the "blessed hope" of the church of God. On this one grand event the eye of faith is bade to rest, as the pole-star of the soul, "until the day-star arise in your hearts." And how much more soothing to a believing mind is such an object of faith than the terrific monster—Death! To look up upon the "bright and morning Star," and not down in to the misty vault of the grave—to anticipate the glorious coming of the great Captain of my salvation, and not the gloomy and subtle approach—perhaps by slow and lingering steps—of the "last enemy of my being—to hope for the coming of the Conqueror, and not to live in dread expectation of the foe—surely is more strengthening to faith, animating to hope, and stimulating to love.

Faith, thus firmly grasping the doctrine that reveals, will inspire the hope that expects the event. The child of God, first believing it, will then be found looking for it. Resembling the faithful and affectionate wife, who frequently retires to read over the letters of her long-absent and far-distant husband, lingering with especial interest and delight over the assurances of his certain and speedy return to her again, love will constrain you to dwell upon the promise—"I go to prepare a place for you. And if I go to prepare a place for you, I will come again and receive you unto myself; that where I am, you may be also." Thus a quickening power and holy exercise are given to these sister graces of the Spirit, faith, hope, and love. Faith believes it; hope expects it; love desires it.

With this firm belief in the doctrine of the Lord's coming, the truth itself will be found an eminently influential one. Is it asked, of what practical use is this blessed hope to the church of God? We answer, "much every way." Chiefly in the emptiness and nothingness to which it reduces all worldly glory, and in the holy elevation which it gives the believer above all sublunary enjoyments. And is this no great attainment in holiness? The grand duty of the believer is to live above the world: he is not of the world, even as Christ was not of it. But we require powerful motives to influence us to this. We are moved by motive, and the religion of Jesus is preeminently a religion of motive. The certain and speedy coming of Christ to glorify His church, oh, what a motive is here! Were you to rise in the morning impressed with this truth, how sweetly would it carry you through the day!—how effectually would it dim the luster of the world's pomp, deaden its joys, soothe your sorrows, dry your tears, lighten your burdens, reconcile you to poverty, to crosses, to losses, yes, to whatever your Lord ordains! You would feel, "What have I do with the world's vanities, its smiles, and its glories? I am waiting, expecting, looking, hoping, praying, for that blessed hope, the appearing of my Redeemer." Oh, what an eminent Christian would you be! What a burning and shining light! What vigorous faith, what lively hope, what fervent love, what a holy living for God, for Christ, and for eternity, would henceforth distinguish you!

JULY 26

"And take the sword of the Spirit, which is the word of God." Eph. 6:17

The Bible was given not as a text-book of human science, but as a divine revelation of God's will. It was designed, not to make skillful disputants or dry theologians, but converted sinners and holy Christians; not to inform the judgment merely, but to renew and sanctify the heart. Above all blessings, then, seek in the study of the Bible large degrees of the grace, influence, and teaching of the Holy Spirit; apart from this, the Word of God, with all the human subsidiary aid you can bring to its investigation, will remain but as a sealed book—an unrolled scroll. Remember, there is a gracious influence and operation of the Holy Spirit separate from, though in harmony with, the written word. Without that influence, you cannot understand the Bible, nor will its revelations come to you with a quickening, saving power. "The letter kills, but the Spirit makes alive." Dishonor and grieve not the Spirit by supposing that He brings to bear upon the mind no other influence than that which the mere letter of the written word contains. There are those who hold this doctrine, to the leanness of their souls, and to the denial of the Spirit. If this doctrine were true, how came it to pass that our Lord, the great Prophet of His people, promised that, on His departure to glory, He would send the Comforter, the Spirit of truth, who should guide us into all truth? If the written word were enough, why promise such a guide? why send the Holy Spirit? why enjoin upon us to ask His bestowment, and to seek His teaching! Oh! it is alone the Spirit that quickens! It is the Spirit alone that unseals the word! It is the Spirit that takes of the things of Christ, and shows them unto us! The word is the "sword of the Spirit;" He it is who makes the word effectual. Without the wielding of His arm, polished as is its blade, and sharp its edge, and fine its point, and beautiful its ornament, it yet is but a passive and a powerless weapon—it pierces not, it wounds not, it slays not; there is no "dividing asunder of soul and spirit, and of the joints and marrow;" nor is there any "discernment of the thoughts and intents of the heart." You have, perhaps, hitherto been baffled and confounded in your at tempts to understand the Scriptures. But have you not come to the study of God's word as to a mere human production? Instead of humbly bringing the word to the teaching of the Spirit, have you not proudly brought it to your reason? Have you not attempted to fathom the fathomless, to measure the illimitable, to know what God has not made known, to comprehend what He has not revealed, even hidden purposes, mysteries, and modes, which must ever remain concealed in His own infinite mind, forgetting that "secret things belong to God"? Trace then your embarrassment and difficulty in understanding the sacred word to its real cause, and see if it may not be found to exist in a secret pride of intellect, and in a consequent restraining of prayer for the direct teaching of the Holy Spirit. Oh, let our fervent petition from this moment be—"Teach me, O Lord! You who alone teach to profit! Open my eyes, that I may behold wondrous things out of Your law! Waiting upon You, eternal, creating Spirit, would I daily be found seeking as a little child, as a humble learner, that 'anointing which teaches of all things.'"

JULY 27

"Look unto me, and be you saved, all the ends of the earth; for I am God, and there is none else." Isaiah 45:22

A true spiritual beholding of the Lord Jesus, in the great matter of our eternal salvation, requires that we look from every other object that would divide our attention, to Him alone. We must look from ourselves. This is, perhaps, the most common and insidious object that comes between the eye of the soul and Jesus. When God was ejected from the heart of man, self vaulted into the vacant throne, and has ever since maintained a supremacy. It assumed two forms, from both of which we are to look, in looking savingly to Jesus. We must look from righteous self; from all works of righteousness which we can perform—from our almsgivings, from our charities, from our religious observances, our fastings, and prayers, and sacraments—from all the works of the law, by which we are seeking to be justified; from all our efforts to make ourselves better, and thus to do something to commend ourselves to the Divine notice, and to propitiate the Divine regard; from all this we must look, if we rightly look unto Jesus, to be saved by His righteousness, and by His alone. The noble language of the apostle must find an echo in our hearts—" What is more, I consider everything a loss compared to the surpassing greatness of knowing Christ Jesus my Lord, for whose sake I have lost all things. I consider them rubbish, that I may gain Christ and be found in him, not having a righteousness of my own that comes from the law, but that which is through faith in Christ--the righteousness that comes from God and is by faith."

We must equally, too, look unto Jesus from unrighteous self. Our sins, and transgressions, and iniquities—red as crimson, countless as the sands, and towering as the Alps—are not for one moment to intercept or obscure our looking unto Jesus for salvation. Jesus is a Savior, as His precious name signifies. As such, He came to save us from our sins, be those sins never so great for magnitude, or infinite for number. It is impossible that we can look unto Jesus, and feel the joy of His salvation flowing into our hearts, while at the same time we are looking at the number and the turpitude of our sins. We must not look at the sin and at the Savior at the same time; but beholding by faith Him who "bore our sins in His own body on the tree," who was "made a sin-offering for us," who was "wounded for our transgressions, and was bruised for our iniquities," who shed His precious blood that the guiltiest may be cleansed and the vilest saved, and between whom and the penitent sinner, though he were another Manasseh, another Saul of Tarsus, another dying malefactor, no transgression and no crime can interpose an effectual barrier, we shall see the exceeding greatness and sinfulness of sin in a clearer and more searching and solemn light than we possibly could, viewing it apart from the cross. Look unto Jesus, then, from your sins: their magnitude and their number interpose no difficulty, and form no real discouragement to your immediate approach to Christ. No argument based upon your unworthiness can avail to exclude you from an interest in His great salvation. He came into the world to save sinners, even the chief. It is His work, it is His joy, it is His glory to save sinners. For this He exchanged heaven for earth, relinquished the bosom of His Father for the embrace of the cross. He was never known to reject a poor sinner that came to Him; He has never refused to take within His sheltering side, to hide within His bleeding bosom, the penitent that sought its protection, fleeing from the condemnation of the law to the asylum of the cross. "Whoever comes unto me, I will in no wise cast out." With such a declaration as this, flowing from the lips of Jesus, who can refuse to look from the greatness of his own sin and guilt, to the greatness of His love, the greatness of His grace, the greatness of His salvation, "who came into the world to save sinners"?

JULY 28

"I sleep, but my heart wakes, it is the voice of my beloved that knocks, saying, Open to me, my sister, my love, my dove, my undefiled: for my head is filled with dew, and my locks with the drops of the night." Song of Solomon 5:2

"I sleep, but my heart wakes." Here was the existence of the divine life in the soul, and yet that life was on the decline. The church knew that she had fallen into a careless and slumbering state, that the work of grace in her soul was decaying, that the spirit of slumber had come over her; but the awful feature was, she was content to be so. She heard her Beloved knock; but, so enamored was she with her state of drowsiness, she gave no heed to it—she opened not to him. Her duty would have been instantly to have aroused herself from her sleep, and admitted her Lord. A believer may fall into a drowsy state of soul, not so profound as to be entirely lost to the voice of his Beloved speaking by conscience, by the word, and by providences: and yet so far may his grace have decayed, so cold may his love have grown, and so hardening may have been his declension, he shall be content that this should be his state. Oh, alarming symptom of soul-declension, when the indulgence of sloth and self is preferred to a visit from Jesus!

Then observe, that when she did arise, Christ had withdrawn Himself. "I opened to my Beloved, but my Beloved had withdrawn Himself, and was gone; my soul failed when He spoke. I sought Him, but I could not find Him; I called Him, but He gave me no answer." Weary with waiting so long, and wounded by her cold repulse, He withdrew His sensible, loving presence, and left her to the consequences of her sad departure. The Lord never withdraws Himself from His people willingly: He is never actuated by an arbitrary impulse of His will. Such is His delight in His people, such His love towards them, and such the joy He derives from their fellowship, that He would walk with them all the day long, and sun them with the unclouded light of His countenance. But when He hides Himself for a little moment, He is driven from their embrace by their lukewarmness of heart and unkind resistance of His love. Possessing a tender heart Himself, the slightest indifference discoverable in His child wounds it; an ocean of love Himself, the least lukewarmness in the love of His people causes Him to withdraw. And yet this momentary withdrawal is not a judicial, but a fatherly, loving correction, to bring them to a knowledge and confession of their state. "I will go and return to my place, until they acknowledge their offence, and seek my face: in their affliction they will seek me early."

There is yet one more remarkable feature in the state of the church, too instructive to pass by unnoticed; we allude to the persuasion she felt, that though the divine life in her soul was at a low ebb, still Christ was hers, and she was Christ's. "I sleep, but my heart wakes: it is the voice of my Beloved that knocks." In the worst frame that can affect a true child of God, there is always some indication that the divine life in the soul is not quite extinguished. In the darkest hour, there is that in the nature of true grace, which emits some scintillation of its essential glory; in its greatest defeat, that which asserts its divinity. Just as a king, though deposed from his throne and driven into exile, can never entirely divest himself of the dignity of his regal character; so real grace, though often severely tried, sharply assailed, and sometimes momentarily defeated, can never sink its character, nor relinquish its sovereignty. Mark the proof of this in the case of the apostle Paul: "Now then it is no more I that do it, but sin that dwells in me. For the good that I would I do not: but the evil which I would not, that I do. Now if I do that I would not, it is no more I that do it, but sin that dwells in me." And so the church expresses it, "I sleep, but my heart wakes." In her most drowsy, slothful state, she could not forget that she was still her Beloved's, and that her Beloved was hers. Glorious nature, and blessed triumph of the life of God in the soul of man!

JULY 29

"And he saw that there was no man, and wondered that there was no intercessor; therefore his arm brought salvation unto him; and his righteousness, it sustained him." Isaiah 59:16

How frequently, clearly, and solemnly does the Holy Spirit unfold this great truth in His word, that salvation is entirely in and of God, irrespective of all worth, worthiness, or power of the creature; and that as the salvation of His covenant people is supremely and solely His own work, so in every respect it is infinitely worthy of Himself. God can do nothing but what harmonizes with His own illimitable greatness; He can never act below Himself. All the productions of His creative power in nature, all the events of His directive wisdom in providence, bear the impress, from the smallest to the greatest, of His "eternal power and Godhead." But in salvation it is supremely and preeminently so. Here, the whole Deity shines; here, the entire Godhead is seen; here, Jehovah emerges from the veiled pavilion of His greatness and glory, and by one stupendous exercise of power, and by one august act of grace, and by one ineffable display of love—before which all other revelations of His glory seem to fade away and well-near disappear—walks abroad among men in His full-orbed majesty. "And I heard a great voice out of heaven, saying, Behold, the tabernacle of God is with men, and He will dwell with them, and they shall be His people; and God Himself shall be with them, and be their God." This glorious "tabernacle" that is "with men," what less is it than the manifestation of Jesus in our own nature—God manifest in the flesh? Truly may we say, "His glory is great in our salvation." Is He the only wise God?—His salvation must needs be the most profound result of that wisdom. Is He most holy?—His salvation must be holy. Is He just?—His salvation must be just. Is He gracious?—so must be His salvation. It bears the imprint of every attribute; it embodies in its nature the manifestation of every perfection. No other conception of His wisdom, no other product of His power, no other revelation of His greatness, gives any adequate conception of God, but the cross of His beloved Son. Salvation, with all the blessings it involves, originated in the very heart of Jehovah. Where could the thought else have originated, of saving a guilty world, and saving it in such a way, and at such a sacrifice? It was a stupendous thought—even that of saving, of showing mercy to rebellious man. The bare idea of exercising love towards the apostate race was in itself so mighty, that God alone could have conceived it. But when the plan of salvation is viewed—when the method of mercy is contemplated—when the sacrifice, "the price of pardon," is weighed—that sacrifice, His only-begotten and well-beloved Son—that price, His own most precious blood; oh the grandeur of the thought! It was fit only to have originated with God, and is in every view worthy of Himself. "God commends His love towards us, in that while we were yet sinners Christ died for us. Much more then, being now justified by His blood, we shall be saved from wrath through Him."

JULY 30

"Therefore I love your commandments above gold; yes, above fine gold. Therefore I esteem all your precepts concerning all things to be right; and I hate every false way." Psalm 119:127, 128

To the true believer there is glory, harmony, and excellence in spiritual truth. Every part to Him is precious—no portion undervalued. In whatever form it presents itself, whether doctrinal or preceptive—with whatever tone it speaks, whether it rebukes or comforts, admonishes or cheers, he welcomes it as God's own eternal truth, more precious to him than gold, yes, than much fine gold. In His eye it is a perfect system; dismember it of any one part, and you mar its beauty. It is a sovereign panacea; take out of it any single ingredient, and you impair its efficacy. He must have it with no doctrine dissevered, with no precept diluted, with no institution perverted. He can consent to no compromise; he has bought the truth, and the truth he cannot sell. Not only does he feel bound to watch it with a jealous and vigilant eye, because it is God's own truth, but he loves it for its perfect adaptation to his own case. It has disclosed to him his sinfulness, and has revealed to him a "fountain open for sin." It has led him in his ruin, helplessness, poverty, and condemnation, to the cross, and there introduced him to a Savior all-sufficient and willing to repair that ruin, assist that helplessness, enrich that poverty, and remove that condemnation. Is it any marvel that to such an individual God's revealed truth should be precious? that he should guard it vigilantly, and love it ardently?

This leads us to revert to the close and important yet much forgotten connection which exists between a clear, spiritual perception of God's truth, and a holy, humble, and close walk with God. The two can never be separated. A distant and careless walk not only veils the mind to the glory of the truth, but hardens the heart to the power of the truth. The world in the heart, guilt upon the conscience, and unmortified sin in the life, have a fearful and certain tendency to petrify the moral sensibilities, and render powerless the sword of the Spirit. Let not such a professor of Christ wonder that appeals the most thrilling, truths the most solemn, and motives the most persuasive, all, all are disarmed of their force in his case. Let him not be amazed that, with an enlightened judgment, and a scriptural creed, and a spotless orthodoxy, he knows nothing of the holy spiritual actings of the life of God in the soul; and that he does but hang a lifeless, sapless, withered branch upon the vine, ready to be removed at the husbandman's bidding. Let him not be astonished that there is no close and fervid fellowship with the Father and His dear Son

Christ Jesus—that his prayers are cold and formal, the habitual frame of his mind earthly and sensual—and that all taste and desire for the "communion of saints," and for a spiritual searching ministry, should have become extinct in his soul—this is no marvel. The greater wonder would be if it were otherwise; that if, while living in a state of distance from God—the ordinances neglected, and sin unmortified—the Father and the Son should yet draw near and manifest themselves, and so make known that secret which peculiarly belongs to those that fear Him. But oh, to have Christ in the heart!—this, this is the truth of God experienced. Call you it enthusiasm? Blessed enthusiasm!—we exult in it, we glory in it. Let the formalist, let the man of notional religion, let the mere professor, call it what he may, deride it as he will; we admire the grace, and adore the love, and extol the power, which has formed "Christ within us the hope of glory." Reader, be satisfied with nothing short of this.

JULY 31

"Forasmuch then as the children are partakers of flesh and blood, he also himself likewise took part of the same." Hebrews 2:14

The Divine compassion and sympathy could only be revealed by the incarnation of Deity. In order to the just exhibition of sympathy of one individual with another, there must be a similarity of circumstances. The like body must be inhabited, the same path must be trod, the same, or a similar, sorrow must be felt. There can be no true sympathy apart from this. A similarity of circumstances is indispensably necessary. See, then, the fitness of Christ to this very purpose. God took upon Him our nature, in order to bear our griefs, and carry our sorrows. Here we enter into the blessedness that flows from the human nature of Christ. As God merely, He could not endure suffering, nor weep, nor die; as man only, He could not have sustained the weight of our sin, grief, nor sorrow. There must be a union of the two natures to accomplish the two objects in one person. The Godhead must be united to the manhood; the one to obey, the other to die; the one to satisfy Divine justice, the other to sympathize with the people in whose behalf the satisfaction was made. Let not the Christian reader shrink from a full and distinct recognition of the doctrine of our Lord's humanity; let it be an important article of his creed, as it is an essential pillar of his hope. If the Deity of Jesus is precious, so is His humanity; the one is of no avail in the work of redemption apart from the other. It is the blending of the two in mysterious union that constitutes the "great mystery of godliness."

Approach, then, the humanity of your adorable Lord: turn not from it. It was pure humanity—it was not the form of an angel He assumed; nor did He pause in His descent to our world to attach Himself to an order of intelligent being, if such there be, existing between the angelic and the human. It was pure humanity, bone of our bone and flesh of our flesh, which He took up into intimate and indissoluble union with His Deity. It was humanity, too, in its suffering form. Our Lord attached Himself to the woes of our nature; He identified Himself with sorrow in its every aspect. This was no small evidence of the love and condescension of Jesus. To have assumed our nature, this had been a mighty stoop; but to have assumed its most humiliating, abject form, this surpasses all our thoughts of His love to man.

It was necessary that our Lord, in order to sympathize fully with His people, should not only identify Himself with their nature, but in some degree with their peculiar circumstances. This He did. It is the consolation of the believer to know, that the Shepherd has gone before the flock. He bids them not walk in a path which His own feet have not first trod and left their impress. As the dear, tender, ever-watchful Shepherd of His sheep, "He goes before them;" and it is the characteristic of His sheep, that they "follow Him." If there were a case among His dear family, of trial, affliction, or temptation, into which Jesus could not enter, then He could not be "in all points" the merciful and sympathetic High Priest. View the subject in any aspect, and ascertain if Jesus is not fitted for the peculiarity of that case. Beloved reader, you know not how accurately and delicately the heart of Jesus is attuned to yours, whether the chord vibrates in a joyous or a sorrowful note. You are perhaps walking in a solitary path; there is a peculiarity in your trial—it is of a nature so delicate, that you shrink from disclosing it even to your dearest earthly friend; and though surrounded by human sympathy, yet there is a friend you still want, to whom you can disclose the feelings of your bosom—that friend is Jesus. Go to Him—open all your heart; do not be afraid—He invites, He bids you come. "For in that He Himself has suffered being tempted, He is able to support those who are tempted."

AUGUST

AUGUST 1

"So then, after the Lord had spoken unto them, he was received up into heaven, and sat on the right hand of God." Mark 16:19

The circumstance of the Lord's ascension and exaltation meets with frequent and marked allusion in the word of God. The Holy Spirit has attached to the fact the greatest weight. The writings of the Old Testament frequently and distinctly speak of it. Thus, in Psalm 47:5, "God is gone up with a shout; the Lord with the sound of a trumpet." It is impossible to misunderstand the obvious allusion of these words. He came down as God; He went up as "God manifest in the flesh." The ascension was worthy of His Deity. It was royal and triumphant. He went up as a "great King," and as a mighty Conqueror, "leading captivity captive." Attended by a celestial escort, and amid the shouts and acclamations of all the heavenly hierarchy, He passed within the portals of glory. The demand was made, the challenge was given, the answer was returned: "Lift up your heads, O you gates; and be you lift up, you everlasting doors; and the King of glory shall come in. Who is this King of glory? The Lord strong and mighty—the Lord mighty in battle. Lift up your heads, O you gates; even lift them up, you everlasting doors; and the King of glory shall come in. Who is this King of glory? The Lord of hosts, He is the King of glory." Yes, our Immanuel, God with us, is "gone up with a shout;" the Lord, JEHOVAH-JESUS, "with the sound of a trumpet." And although no echo of the heavenly minstrelsy was heard on earth, and the cloud which received Him veiled His receding form from the gaze of His disciples, hiding from the view the deepening glory which encircled His ascending flight, yet all heaven reverberated with the song, and grew resplendent with the majesty of His entrance within its gates.

The scene and the circumstances of our Lord's ascension were of thrilling interest, and deeply spiritual in their meaning. The period, which it is important distinctly to specify, was just forty days after His resurrection; thus affording ample time to establish, by the most irrefragable proof and tangible evidence, this master-fact of His history. Not only did He take this occasion to answer all the reasonings, and resolve all the doubts, of His still incredulous disciples, but He crowded into this brief space of time instructions the most needed, precious, and momentous to the well-being of His church. Drawing closer around Him, as if by the new and more powerful attraction of His risen body, His devoted apostles—the future builders of His spiritual temple—He proceeds to renew their divine commission to preach the gospel, widening it to the exigencies of the world that gospel was intended to bless. Opening their understandings more perfectly to understand the Scriptures, He cleared and enlarged their view of His Divine nature, the spiritual character of His kingdom, and the offices, ordinances, and discipline which were to be observed in each gospel-constituted section of His church. Thus, even after His atoning work was finished, and the great seal of heaven was affixed to it, our adorable Lord was still engaged in His Father's business, still intent upon promoting His glory, and the eternal welfare of His people. Oh, what love was the love of our Immanuel!

Let us now ascend in spirit with Jesus, and contemplate the glory of His exaltation. His entrance into heaven was the signal for the full development of His mediatorial power and glory. This was the promise of His Father, and this the reward of His death. "I have set my King upon my holy hill of Zion." "Unto the Son He says, Your throne, O God, is for ever and ever." "I appoint unto you," says Christ, "a kingdom, as my Father has appointed unto me." Thus His exaltation at the right hand of the Father was His full induction into His mediatorial kingdom. Now was He exalted "heir of all things"—now were "all things put under His feet"—now "all power in heaven and on earth was given to Him;" and from that moment that He touched the crown, and grasped the scepter, and the government was placed upon His shoulder, His truth was to advance, and His kingdom widen, with ever-growing power, until, supplanting all error, and subduing all kingdoms, He was to reign "King of kings and Lord of lords."

AUGUST 2

"Let us lift up our heart with our hands unto God in the heavens." Lamentations 3:41

Prayer is the spiritual pulse of the renewed soul; its beat indicates the healthy or unhealthy state of the believer. Just as the physician would decide upon the health of the body from the action of the pulse, so would we decide upon the spiritual health of the soul before God, by the estimation in which prayer is held by the believer. If the soul is in a spiritually healthy, growing state, prayer will be vigorous, lively, spiritual, and constant; if, on the contrary, the heart is wandering, and love waxes cold, and faith is decaying, the spirit and the habit of prayer will immediately betray it.

The spirit of prayer may decline in the believer, and he may not at once be sensible of it. The form and the habit of prayer may for a while continue—but the spirit of prayer has evaporated, and all is coldness and dullness—the very torpor and frigidity of death! But of what real worth is the habit of prayer, apart from the spirit of prayer? Just what this planet would be without the sun, or the body without the living, animating, breathing soul—what but a cold, lifeless form? Yes, and a believer may be beguiled into this lamentable state, and not a suspicion of its existence be awakened; he may observe his accustomed habit, and use his empty form, and not suspect that all is cold and breathless as death itself. Oh, it is not the rigidly-observed form that God looks at; nor is it great volubility, and eloquent fluency, and rich sentiment, and splendid imagery, and rounded periods, that God regards: far from this; a man may not be able to give expression to his deep emotion in prayer, his thoughts may find no vehicle of utterance, language may entirely fail him; and yet the spirit of prayer may glow in his breast—and this—the true language of prayer—finds its way to the ear and to the heart of God. Reader, look well to the state of your soul; examine your prayers; see that you have not substituted the cold form for the glowing spirit—the mere body for the soul. Real prayer is the breathing of God's own Spirit in the heart: have you this? It is communion and fellowship with God: know you what this is? It is brokenness, contrition, confession, and that often springing from an overwhelming sense of His goodness and His love shed abroad in the heart: is this your experience? Again, we repeat it, look well to your prayers; test them, not by the natural or acquired gift which you may possess—this is nothing with God; but test them by the real communion you have with God—the returns they make to your soul.

There should be the searching out and the removal of that which hinders prayer. Many things weaken true prayer: unsubdued sin—unrepented sin—unpardoned sin (we mean the secret sense of it upon the conscience)—worldly-mindedness—light and trifling conversation, vain disputations—much and frequent communion either with unconverted individuals, or cold and formal professors—all these combined, or any single one, will, if suffered to prevail, unfit the mind for converse with God, and cause a decay of the spirit of prayer in the soul. Regard that as injurious which touches the devotional frame of your mind, which abridges the hour of prayer, and removes the fine edge of its holy enjoyment.

AUGUST 3

"And many other signs truly did Jesus in the presence of his disciples, which are not written in this book: but these are written, that you might believe that Jesus is the Christ, the Son of God; and that believing you might have life through his name." John 20:30, 31

All the value and efficacy of the atoning blood is derived solely and entirely from the dignity of the person who sheds it. If Christ do not be absolutely and truly what the word of God declares, and what He Himself professes to be, the true God, then, as it regards the great purpose for which His atonement was made, namely, the satisfaction of Divine Justice, in a full and entire sacrifice for sin, it were utterly valueless. We feel the vast and solemn importance of this point; it is of the deepest moment—it is the key-stone of the arch, sustaining and holding together every part of the mighty fabric. Our examination of the claims of Christ to proper Deity cannot be too close; we cannot too rigidly scrutinize the truth of His Godhead; Jesus Himself challenges investigation. When personally upon earth, carrying forward the great work of redemption, on all occasions, and by all means, He announced and proved His Deity. Thus was He used to declare it—"I and my Father are one." "Verily, verily, I say unto you, before Abraham was, I AM." "I come forth from the Father, and am come into the world; again, I leave the world and go to the Father." Thus was He used to confirm it—"I have greater witness than that of John; for the works which the Father has given me to finish, the same works that I do, bear witness of me that the Father has sent me." "If I do not the works of my Father, believe me not; but if I do, though you believe not me, believe the works; that you may know and believe that the Father is in me, and I in Him." Our blessed Lord saw and felt the importance of a full belief in the doctrine of His Godhead. If the foundation of our faith were not laid deep and broad in this, He well knew that no structure, however splendid in its external form, could survive the storm that will eventually sweep away every lying refuge. And what, to the believing soul, is more animating than the full unwavering conviction of the fact, that He who bore our sins in His own body on the tree was God in our nature? that He who became our surety and substitute was Jehovah Himself—"God manifest in the flesh?" that, as God, He became incarnate—as God, He obeyed, and as God-man, He suffered the penalty? What deep views does this fact give of sin! what exalted views of sin's atonement! Pray, dear reader, that the blessed and eternal Spirit may build you up in the belief of this truth. It is a truth on which we can live, and on no other can we die. That Satan should often suggest suspicions to the mind respecting the veracity of this doctrine we can easily imagine. That a dear saint of God should at times find his faith wavering in its attempts to grasp this wondrous fact, "the incarnate mystery," we marvel not. It is the very basis of his hope; is it surprising that Satan should strive to overturn it? Satan's great controversy is with Christ. Christ came to overthrow his kingdom, and He did overthrow it. Christ came to vanquish him, and He triumphed. This signal and total defeat Satan will never forget. To regain his kingdom he cannot. To recover what he has lost he knows to be impossible. Therefore his shafts are leveled against Christ's members; and the doctrine, to them most essential and precious—the doctrine of Christ's Godhead—is the doctrine most frequently and severely assailed. Let no believer sink in despondency under this severe temptation. Let him look afresh to the cross, afresh to the atoning blood, and faith in Him, whose word stilled the angry waves of the Galilean lake, and whose look prostrated to the ground the soldiers sent to His arrest, will give Him the victory.

AUGUST 4

"For as the sufferings of Christ abound in us, so our consolation also abounds by Christ." 2 Corinthians 1:5

Christian reader, we suppose you to be no stranger to grief; your heart has known what sorrow is; you have borne, perhaps for years, some heavy, painful, yet concealed cross. Over it, in the solitude and silence of privacy, you have wept, agonized, and prayed. And still the cross, though mitigated, is not removed. Have you ever thought of the sympathy of Christ? Have you ever thought of Him, as bearing that cross with you?—as entering into its peculiarity, its minutest circumstance? Oh, there is a fiber in His heart that sympathizes, there is a chord there that vibrates, to that grief of yours. That cross He is bearing with you at this moment; and although you may feel it to be so heavy and painful, as to be lost to the sweet consciousness of this, still it rests on Him, as on you; and were He to remove His shoulder but for a moment, you would be crushed beneath its pressure. "Then why, if so tender and sympathizing, does He place upon me this cross?" Because of His wisdom and love. He sees you need that cross. You have carried it, it may be, for years: who can tell where and what you would have been at this moment, but for this very cross? What evil in you it may have checked; what corruption in you it may have subdued; what constitutional infirmities it may have weakened; from what lengths it has kept you; from what rocks and precipices it has guarded you; and what good it has been silently and secretly, yet effectually, working in you all the long years of your life—who can tell but God Himself? The removal of that cross might have been the removal of your greatest mercy. Hush, then, every murmur; be still, and know that He is God; and that all these trials, these sufferings, these untoward circumstances, are now working together for your good and His glory.

And what would you know, may we not ask, of Jesus—His tenderness, and love, and sympathizing heart—but for the rough and thorny path along which you have been thus led? The glory and fullness, the preciousness and sympathy of Christ are not learned in every circumstance of life. The hour of prosperity, when everything passes smoothly on—providences smiling—the heart's surface unruffled—the gladsome sunlight of creature-happiness gilding every prospect with its brightness—this is not the hour, nor these the circumstances, most favorable to an experimental acquaintance with Christ. It is in the dark hour of suffering—the hour of trial and of adversity, when the sea is rough, and the sky is lowering, and providences are mysterious, and the heart is agitated, and hope is disappointed—its bud nipped, and its stem broken, and creature comfort and support fail—oh, then it is the fullness, and preciousness, and tenderness of Jesus are learned. Then it is the heart loosens its hold on created objects, and entwines itself more fondly and more closely around the Incarnate Son of God. Blessed Jesus! You Brother born for our every adversity! did You take our nature into union with Your own? And can You, do You, weep when we weep, and rejoice when we rejoice? O You adorable Son of God! we stand amazed, and are lost in this love, this condescension, and this sympathy of Your. Draw our hearts to Yourself; let our affections rise and meet in You, their center, and cling to You, their all.

AUGUST 5

"Knowing that Christ being raised from the dead dies no more; death has no more dominion over him." Romans 6:9

The resurrection of Christ was the consummation of His glorious victory. Until this moment, the Redeemer had all the appearance of one vanquished in the great fight. He was left slain upon the battle-field. Indeed it would appear that He had really endured a momentary defeat. He was now under the dominion of death; and as death was the consequence and penalty of sin, so long as He was subject to its power, He still lay beneath the sins of His people. Cancelled although they were by the blood He had just shed, the great evidence of their remission did not and could not transpire until the resurrection had passed. What gloom now enshrouded the church of God! The Sun of Righteousness was setting in darkness and in blood; and with it was descending into the tomb, the hopes of patriarchs and prophets, of seers and apostles. The "king of terrors" had laid low his illustrious victim; and the cold earth had closed upon His sacred body, mangled and lifeless. Oh, what a victory did hell and sin, death and the grave, now seem to have achieved! But the "triumphing of the wicked is short." In three days the tomb, at the mighty fiat of Jehovah, unveiled its bosom, and yielded back its Creator and Lord. The Sun of Righteousness ascended again in cloudless glory and peerless majesty, to set no more forever. The church of God, now "begotten again unto a lively hope by the resurrection of Jesus Christ from the dead," arose from the dust, and put on her beautiful garments. Now was the scene changed. His enemies, no longer wearing even the semblance of victory, were overthrown and vanquished. Hell was disappointed, and its gates forever closed against the redeemed. Sin was thrown to an infinite distance, and "death had no more dominion over him, God having loosed its pains, because it was not possible that He should be holden of it." He rose a mighty and an illustrious Conqueror. And all this conquest, let it not be forgotten, was achieved in behalf of a chosen and a beloved people. It was our battle that He fought, it was our victory that He won. Therefore, called though we are to "wrestle against principalities and against powers," and exhorted though we are to "take unto us the whole armor of God," we are yet confronted with enemies already vanquished. It would seem as though we were summoned, not so much to go out upon the field of battle, as upon the field of conquest; not so much to combat with the foe, as to gather up the spoils of victory. For what is every successful conflict with our spiritual adversaries—what is every corruption mortified—what is every temptation resisted—what is every sin overcome—but a showing forth the great victory already won by the Captain of our salvation? Every triumph of the Holy Spirit in the heart of a regenerate man is a display of the triumph of Him who, in hanging on the cross, and in rising from the grave, "spoiled principalities and powers, and made a show of them openly, triumphing over them in it."

AUGUST 6

"Not by works of righteousness which we have done, but according to his mercy he saved us, by the washing of regeneration, and renewing of the Holy Spirit; which he shed on us abundantly through Jesus Christ our Savior." Titus 3:5, 6

The conversion of a sinner to God is a convincing and precious evidence that Jesus is alive. In the regeneration wrought in the soul by the Holy Spirit, the life of Jesus is imparted. He breathes into the soul morally dead the breath of life, and it becomes a living soul. Until, in the exercise of His distinct office, this Divine Person of the adorable Trinity convinces of sin, quickens and brings the soul to Christ for acceptance, risen with Christ though that soul mystically is, it yet remains totally dead to, and insensible of, its great privilege—an utter stranger to that new life which springs from oneness with the "second Adam." The new nature which the Eternal Spirit now imparts is nothing less than the creation of the life of Christ in the soul; yes, even more than this, it is the bringing of Christ Himself into the soul to dwell there the "hope of glory" through time, and glory itself, through eternity.

Here, then, is an evidence that Jesus is alive, to a renewed mind the most convincing and precious. Thus quickened by the Eternal Spirit, believers become temples of Christ. Jesus lives in them. "I in them." "Know you not that Christ is in you?" "Christ lives in me." "Christ in you the hope of glory." Thus every believer is a living witness that Jesus is alive, because he bears about with him the very life of Jesus. By the indwelling of the Spirit, and realized by faith, Christ abides in the believer, and the believer abides in Christ. "I in them, and you in me, that they may be made perfect in one; that they also may be one in us."

We have already stated that this glorious entrance of Christ within the soul transpires at the period of the new birth. What, then, is every new conversion, every fresh trophy of redeeming grace, but a new manifestation to the universe of the life of Jesus? I see the sinner pursuing his mad career of folly, rebellion, and guilt. Suddenly he is arrested, I see him bowed to the earth, his heart broken with sorrow, his spirit crushed beneath the burden of sin. He smites upon his breast; acknowledges his transgression, confesses his iniquity, deplores it in the dust. Presently I see him lift his eye, and rest it upon a bleeding Savior; he gazes, wonders, believes, adores—is saved! By whom is this miracle of grace wrought?—The Spirit has descended to testify that Jesus is alive. That newly-converted soul, so lately dead in sins, but now quickened with Christ—that sinner but recently dwelling among the tombs, whom no human power could tame, now sitting at the feet of Jesus, clothed and in his right mind—demonstrates that Christ is in heaven, and is alive, for evermore. Oh, it is the heaven-descending life of Jesus. Show me, then, a soul just passed from death unto life, and I will show you an evidence that Jesus is alive at the right hand of God.

AUGUST 7

"And if they be bound in fetters, and are held in cords of affliction; then he shows them their work, and their transgressions that they have exceeded. He opens also their ear to discipline, and commands that they return from iniquity." Job 36:8-10

The very discipline which a covenant God employs with His child proves the existence and reality of grace in the soul. It is not the lifeless branch that He prunes, it is not the spurious one that He puts in the furnace. When He takes His child in hand to deal with him, it is with a view of drawing forth the grace which He has first implanted in the soul. The very trial of faith supposes the existence of faith; and the trial of any one grace of the Spirit supposes the previous indwelling of that grace in the believer. No man goes to a dry well to draw water from it; no man goes to a bank, in which he has made no previous deposit, to draw money from it. When God, the spiritual husbandman of the church, comes into His garden, and walks amid the "trees of righteousness," and in His sovereignty marks one here and another there for discipline, for pruning, whom does He select for this blessed purpose, but the trees which He has Himself planted? Jesus has declared that every plant which His heavenly Father has not planted shall be rooted up! And have we not often seen the solemn fulfillment of this threatening in the case of graceless professors?—the first blast of temptation has carried them away. God, perhaps, has brought them into deep trial; the storm of adversity has fallen upon them; death has snatched away the "desire of their eyes with a stroke;" riches have taken wings and flown away; character has been assailed; temptations have overtaken them; and what has been their end? We look for their religion—it has fled away like the chaff of the threshing-floor before the sweeping hurricane; their profession—it is all gone; their prayers—they have evaporated into empty air. The solemn "place of the holy," that knew them, knows them no more; the furnace tested the ore, and it proved nothing but tin; and so it will be with every plant that our heavenly Father has not planted; and so with all the wood, hay, and stubble, built upon an outward acknowledgment and profession of Christ.

But the true child of the covenant the Lord tries; and there is that in every believer, yes, the most eminent child of God—eminent for his holy and close walk—that needs trying. We cannot always see the necessity of the discipline; we wonder often why such a believer is so constantly and, in a sense, so severely dealt with. But what says God?—"I, the Lord, search the heart." Here is the secret revealed; the hidden evil of that holy man of God we could not discover. The powerful corruptions that dwelt in his heart—which he, in a degree, knew, and mourned over, and confessed daily before the Lord—were concealed from our eye; and while we were judging from outward appearance, the Lord was probing and searching the heart, and, for the subjugation of the evil that He discovered there, was thus disciplining His beloved child.

Afflicted believer, do not forget that it is "whom the Lord loves He chastens;" and again He declares, "Whom I love I rebuke and chasten." Then thank Him for the sanctified trial, that weans you from earthly things, that deadens your heart to every rival of Christ, and that imparts an upward spring to faith, hope, and love. Not one unkind thought is there in the heart of the God that now chastens you. True, He may have cut off all your earthly springs, He may lead you down into the deep valley of abasement; yet still is He love, and nothing but love. Could you look into His heart, not a spring would be found dwelling, nor a pulse beating there, that would not speak of love to you at this very moment. All that He seeks with regard to yourself is your increased fruitfulness; and to promote your real sanctification is to promote your real happiness. In all God's dealings with His covenant people, He seeks their greatest good, their highest happiness, and in nothing more manifestly than in this does he show the intense love which dwells in His heart towards them.

AUGUST 8

"We love him, because he first loved us." 1 John 4:19

All love to God in the soul is the result of His love to us; it is begotten in the heart by His Spirit: He took the first step, and made the first advance—"He first loved us." Oh heart-melting truth! The love of God to us when yet we were sinners, who can unfold it? what mortal tongue can describe it? Before we had any being, and when we were enemies, He sent His Son to die for us; and when we were far off by wicked works He sent His Spirit to bring us to Him in the cloudy and dark day. All His dealings with us since then—His patience, restoring mercies, tender, loving, faithful care, yes, the very strokes of His rod—have but unfolded the depths of His love towards His people; this is the love we desire you to be filled with. "The Lord direct your hearts into the love of God." Draw largely from this river—why should you deny yourselves? There is enough love in God to overflow the hearts of all His saints through all eternity; then why not be filled? "The Lord direct your hearts into the love of God;" stand not upon the brink of the fountain, linger not upon the margin of this river; enter into it—plunge into it; it is for you—poor, worthless, unworthy, vile, as you feel yourself to be, this river of love is yet for you! Seek to be filled with it, that you may know the love of Christ, which passes knowledge, and that your heart, in return, may ascend in a flame of love to God.

Deal much and closely with a crucified Savior. Here is the grand secret of a constant ascending of the affections to God. If you do find it difficult to comprehend the love of God towards you, read it in the cross of His dear Son. "In this was manifested the love of God towards us, because that God sent His only begotten Son into the world, that we might live through Him. Herein is love, not that we loved God, but that He loved us, and sent His Son to be the propitiation for our sins." Dwell upon this amazing fact; drink into this precious truth; muse upon it, ponder it, search into it, pray over it, until your heart is melted down, and broken, and overwhelmed with God's wondrous love to you, in the gift of Jesus. Oh, how will this rekindle the flame that is ready to die in your bosom! how it will draw you up in a holy and unreserved surrender of body, soul, and spirit! Do not forget, then, to deal much with Jesus. Whenever you detect a waning of love, a reluctance to take up the daily cross, a shrinking from the precept, go immediately to Calvary; go simply and directly to Jesus; get your heart warmed with ardent love by contemplating Him upon the cross, and soon will the frosts that gather round it melt away, the congealed current shall begin to flow, and the "chariots of Amminadab" shall bear your soul away in communion and fellowship with God.

AUGUST 9

"Know you not that you are the temple of God, and that the Spirit of God dwells in you." 1 Corinthians 3:16

The believer may cherish an imperfect consciousness of the indwelling of the Spirit in his heart, and in this sense may the Holy Spirit of God be grieved. For the Holy Spirit effectually to call, renew, sanctify, and take possession of the soul, make it His temple, His permanent dwelling-place; and yet for that soul to entertain inadequate views of this great truth, forget who is dwelling with, and in him, slight his heavenly guest, and go out and come in, and live and act, as if he were not a temple of the Holy Spirit—what can be more dishonoring to the blessed and Eternal Spirit! Oh that this momentous truth should even for a single moment be lost sight of by the believer! That he should be the dwelling-place of the Most High, "the High and Lofty One that inhabits eternity, whose name is Holy," the residence of the Holy Spirit, and yet entertain a feeling or a thought not in perfect harmony with so great a fact, does indeed show the necessity of the apostolic admonition, "Grieve not the Spirit of God."

When, too, the Spirit's still small voice is unheeded, and His gentle constraints are not yielded to, there is a slight put upon His work of a very grievous nature. The abiding Indweller of the saints of God, the Spirit, is perpetually speaking to, admonishing, leading, drawing, and constraining the soul; His great work there is to teach, to sanctify, to shield, to check, and to comfort the believer. Every holy shrinking from sin, every firm resistance of its power, every victory achieved over its motions, every aspiration after holiness, and every feeble desire to walk in the way of filial obedience to, and sweet communion with, God, is the fruit of the indwelling Spirit in the heart. How grieving, then, to that Spirit, when this loving voice of His, and these gentle constraints of His, are overlooked, stifled, disregarded, and slighted by the soul He so tenderly loves, and so faithfully watches over! Grieve not thus the Holy Spirit of God. In all His dealings with you, He seeks but your real good; He aims to deepen His own work in your hearts; He seeks but to promote your holiness, and to mature your soul for the joys and the companionship of the saints in light. Yet more; He desires your true happiness—He would draw you off from carnal things, He would allure you from objects of sense and sin, and open to you springs of higher and purer enjoyment, and lead you into fairer and greener pastures; this would He do by unfolding to you what you possess in Jesus, in the covenant of grace, and in a covenant God. Let your ear, then, be open to the persuasive voice of the Spirit, and follow promptly and implicitly His secret and gentle leadings.

AUGUST 10

"Look to yourselves, that we lose not those things which we have wrought, but that we receive a reward. Whoever transgresses, and abides not in the doctrine of Christ, has not God. He that abides in the doctrine of Christ, he has both the Father and the Son." 2 John 8, 9

Dear reader, in whose righteousness do you at this moment stand? Is it all profession merely? Startle not at the question—turn not from it; it is for your life we ask it. Do you wonder that such a scrutiny into the ground of your hope should be made? Are you astonished at the solemn fact implied in this question? Do not be so. Many have lived in the outward profession—have put on Christ in the external garb—have talked well of Him—have been baptized in His name—given liberally for His cause, and, after all, have gone into eternity holding up the empty lamp! Oh, marvel not, then, that we repeat the question—in whose righteousness do you at this moment stand? Mere profession will not save your soul; your being found mingling among the wise virgins will not secure you an admittance with them into heaven; your talking respectfully of Jesus will avail you nothing; your church membership, your liberality, your spotless morality, your regular attendance on the sanctuary, all, all are in vain, without the justifying righteousness of the God-man upon you. What do you know of the broken heart and the contrite spirit? What do you know of the healing blood of Jesus? What do you know of a sense of pardon and acceptance? What do you know of the witness of the Spirit? What do you know of a humble, low, abasing view of yourself? What do you know of a holy and a close walk with God? What do you know of communion and fellowship with the Father and His dear Son? In a word, what do you know of yourself as a helpless, ruined sinner; and of Jesus, as a rich, able, and present Savior? Ponder these solemn questions. The hand that pens them trembles with awe as it traces this page. This is a day of great profession—a day of great ingathering into the church—a day when much chaff must necessarily be gathered with the wheat. It solemnly behooves, then, each professing member of Christ's church, of every name and denomination, narrowly to scrutinize his motives, deeply to prove his heart, and closely and habitually to examine the foundation on which he is building for eternity. Thus shall he walk, if he be an adopted child, in the sweet and holy realization of his pardon and acceptance; thus shall he experience the blessedness of "the man whose transgression is forgiven, whose sin is covered;" and thus, too, shall he constantly be "a vessel unto honor, sanctified, and meet for the Master's use, and prepared unto every good work."

AUGUST 11

"These things have I written unto you that believe on the name of the Son of God; that you may know that you have eternal life, and that you may believe on the name of the Son of God." 1 John 5:13

No imagination can fully depict, nor language adequately describe, the importance of this life, the grandeur of its nature and destiny, and the necessity of its progression and its manifestations. Reader, the world without you teems with sentient existence. All is life, activity, and progress. There is vegetable life, and animal life, and rational life. To this may be added a species of moral life maintained by many, developed and embodied in religious forms, observances, and sacrifices. But there is a life as infinitely superior to all these, as the life of Him whose mind conceived the towering pyramid is to that of the little insect that flutters its brief hour in the sun-beam, and then vanishes forever. It is the life of God in the soul of man. Deep planted in the center of his spiritual nature, lodged within the hidden recesses of his deathless mind, diffusing its mysterious but all-pervading and renovating influence through the judgment, the will, the affections, and linking his being with a future of glory, which "eye has not seen, nor ear heard, neither has it entered into the heart of man to conceive"—the world rushes on, and knows not its existence, and sees not its glories, and heeds not its joys—so deeply veiled from human eye, ay, and so far removed from human power, is the spiritual life "hidden with Christ in God." Reader, there is a religion towering as far above your religion of merit, and of works, and of forms, as the heavens are above the earth, even as the spiritual life of God is above the sensual life of man. It is the religion of a renewed mind, of a renovated heart, of a conquered will, of a soul, all whose sanctified faculties are consecrated to the glory of God here, and are destined to the enjoyment of God hereafter. Have you thus "passed from death unto life"? Have the avenues of the heart, closed and barred against the admission of Christ, been thrown open? Has the fearful alienation, and the withering curse, and the deep guilt, which portrays to you God as an enemy, and which arms all the powers of your soul against Him as His foe, been revealed, felt, and deplored? Has the captive spirit been disenthralled, the prey taken from the mighty, the power of the destroyer broken, and the soul awakened from its deep slumber to listen to its Creator speaking in tones of mercy, and in thoughts of love? Has light, emanating from the abodes of glory—invisible to others—dawned upon the midnight of your moral desolation? Has a voice speaking from the throne of heaven—unheard by others—startled your spirit in its deep trance, and dispelled its floating dreams? Has a hand, mighty and unseen, riven the chain, thrown open the dungeon, and led you forth to liberty and joy, to life and immortality? In a word, has another and a diviner life, descending from God, and begotten within you by the Spirit, and unfolding to your view a heaven of brightness, full of purity, and fragrance, and song, been communicated to your soul, thus creating you a new creature, and constituting you an "heir of God, and a joint heir with Christ Jesus"? If so, then you may adopt the language of Paul, and exultingly exclaim, "I live, yet not I, but Christ lives in me." Oh, deem not this a vain thing, for it is your life!

AUGUST 12

"That you may be blameless and harmless, the sons of God, without rebuke, in the midst of a crooked and perverse nation, among whom you shine as lights in the world." Philippians 2:15

Christian influence begins with the first grain of grace, the first throb of life, the first beam of light, the first tear of godly sorrow, the first glance of faith—but its impressions and its results are as lasting as eternity. Solemn thought! The holy, gracious influence of a good man stretches far into the invisible world. But consider his present influence; his sphere, be it what it may, is just what God has made it—but in that sphere, be it limited or boundless, he is God's "salt," designed to preserve and to transform, by the holy influence which he exerts, the community in which he dwells. What a blessing is that Christian! Be the relation what it may that binds him to society—a husband, a wife, a parent, a child, a brother, a sister, a friend—he shines as a light in the circle in which he moves. That little spark which glows in his bosom may light the steps of some benighted wanderer to eternity; that measure of grace, diffusing its fragrance through his soul, may cheer and invigorate some tried and drooping spirit; that degree of spiritual knowledge which he possesses may confirm some waverer, or guide some anxious and perplexed seeker after truth. The holy and commanding influence which God has given him may, with its power, awe and subdue the mightiest agent of evil; or with its smile, cheer and encourage the weakest and lowliest effort of good. Blessed of God, he is a blessing to man. Of course we are describing the character and influence of a spiritually-minded Christian—of the influence exerted by one in whom the spiritual life is in a healthy, vigorous, active state. Such a believer is an incalculable blessing in any sphere in which he may move; we feel, when we converse with him, that we are in the presence of a true Christian, that we are holding communion with one who is used to hold communion with God, one who dwells near the cross, who lives beneath the anointing blood, who walks humbly with God, who lives as: "beholding Him who is invisible." There is that in him which bespeaks the gracious man—there is an echo to your voice, a response to your thought, a vibration to your touch, which rebounds upon your own soul with thrilling effect. You have caught the contagion of his holiness—his example has rebuked you, his zeal has quickened you, his love has melted you, his faith has invigorated you, his grace has refreshed you, his smile has gilded the dark cloud that, perhaps, hung around your spirit, his word has fallen balmy and healing upon your sorrowing, bleeding heart—and the secret of all is, he is "a sweet savor of Christ" to your soul. Seek, then, dear reader, to "let your light so shine before men, that they may see your good works, and glorify your Father which is heaven."

AUGUST 13

"For if, when we were enemies, we were reconciled to God by the death of his Son, much more, being reconciled, we shall be saved by his life." Romans 5:10

God in Christ is the covenant God of His people. He is their God; their tender, loving, condescending Father. They may lose sight and enjoyment of this for a time, but this contravenes it not; it still remains the same, unchangeable, precious, and glorious reality. Nothing can rob them of it. In the tempest let it be the anchorage of your faith, in darkness the pole-star of your hope. Let every circumstance—the prosperity that ensnares, and the adversity that depresses, the temptation that assails, and the slight that wounds—endear to your believing soul this precious thought, "God reconciled—God at peace—God a Father in Christ is my God forever and ever, and He will be my guide even unto death."

This thought is in the highest degree soothing, comforting, and encouraging. It seems to introduce us into the very pavilion of God's heart. There, curtained and shut in, we may repose in perfect peace. Not a single perfection can a believing mind view in Christ but it smiles upon him. Oh! to see holiness and justice, truth and love, bending their glance of sweetest and softest benignity upon a poor, trembling soul, approaching to hide itself beneath the shadow of the cross! What a truth is this! All is sunshine here. The clouds are scattered, the darkness is gone, the tempest is hushed, the sea is a calm. Justice has lost its sting, the law its terror, and sin its power: the heart of God is open, the bosom of Jesus bleeds, the Holy Spirit draws, the gospel invites, and now the weary and the heavy-laden may draw near to a reconciled God in Christ. Oh, were ever words sweeter than these, "God was in Christ, reconciling the world unto Himself, not imputing their trespasses unto them." "Whom God has set forth to be a propitiation, through faith in His blood." "He is able to save to the uttermost those who come unto God by Him."

If to view God in Christ is a comforting truth, it is also a most sanctifying truth. Why has God revealed Himself in Jesus? To evince the exceeding hatefulness of sin, and to show that nothing short of such a stupendous sacrifice could remove it, consistently with the glory of the Divine nature, and the honor of the Divine government. Each sin, then, is a blow struck at this transcendent truth. The eye averted from it, sin appears a trifle; it can be looked at without indignation, tampered with without fear, committed without hesitation, persisted in without remorse, gloried in without shame, confessed without sorrow. But when Divine justice is seen drinking the very heart's blood of God's only Son in order to quench its infinite thirst for satisfaction—when God in Christ is seen in His humiliation, suffering, and death, all with the design of pardoning iniquity, transgression, and sin, how fearful a thing does it seem to sin against this holy Lord God! How base, how ungrateful, appears the act, in view of love so amazing, of grace so rich, and of glory so great! Cultivate a constant, an ardent thirst for holiness. Do not be discouraged, if the more intensely the desire for sanctification rises, the deeper and darker the revelation of the heart's hidden evil. The struggle may be painful, the battle may be strong, but the result is certain, and will be a glorious victory—VICTORY, through the blood of the Lamb!

AUGUST 14

"When the Son of man shall come in his glory, and all the holy angels with him, then shall he sit upon the throne of his glory." Matthew 25:31

Surpassing in glory all that the eye has ever seen, or the imagination has ever conceived, will be the second personal appearing of the Son of God. A perfect contrast will it present to His first advent. Then He appeared a king, but disguised in the form of a servant, without a retinue, without the insignia of royalty, without visible glory, His throne a cross, His crown the thorns, His scepter a reed. But His second coming will be in perfect contrast with this. He will now have thrown off the garment of humiliation, and will appear clad with the robe of majesty, the King acknowledged and adored.

In the first place, He will appear in the glory of the Father. "The Son of man shall come in the glory of His Father." As the representative of the Father, He appeared in the flesh: "He that has seen me, has seen the Father." But when He appears the second time, it will be with a clearer, brighter manifestation of the Father's glory; He will come as the Father's equal—as His own beloved Son, and with all the glory which the Father gave Him as the mediator of His church. This will contribute immensely to the splendor of the scene. The Father's glory and the Son's glory will now be seen to be one glory. All His former claims to a oneness with the Father, to a perfect equality with Him in essential dignity, will now be made good. How gloriously will shine out the Father's love, the Father's grace, the Father's wisdom, when the Son of God appears in the clouds of heaven with great glory and majesty! Exalted and precious as had been our previous view of the Father, methinks it will appear as nothing compared with the revelations which at that moment will burst in overwhelming power on the soul.

But more especially will He appear in His own personal glory. "The Son of man shall come in His glory." He will come in the glory of His Divine nature. His Deity will now be unveiled, unclouded, and undenied, the "God over all, blessed for evermore." He will appear as the "Great God, even our Savior." The question of His Deity will be set at rest forever. Will men deny it now? Will they refuse Him divine honor? Will they withhold from Him divine worship? Will they now lift their puny hands, and pluck the crown of Godhead from His brow? No! "At the name of Jesus every knee shall bow, and every tongue shall confess that Jesus Christ is Lord, to the glory of God the Father." Angels will laud Him, saints will crown Him, devils fear Him, His enemies will bow to Him; every tongue shall confess His Deity. His own glory will shine out to the confusion of His foes, and to the admiration of His friends.

But He will also appear in the glory of His human nature. This was concealed beneath the cloud of sin and sorrow, when He was on earth. Although it was holy, spotless, flawless, yet it was humbled, bruised, and trodden under foot. But He will "appear the second time without sin unto salvation," that same humanity now robed in glory, and exalted in dignity. Especially will the glory of His priestly character now burst forth; and like the Jewish high priest, who, after he had offered the sacrifice, entered the holy of holies, taking in his hands the blood of atonement, then when he had sprinkled the blood upon the mercy-seat, put on his gorgeous robes, and appeared again to bless the congregation; so Jesus, our great High Priest, having offered Himself a sacrifice, and having entered within the veil with His own blood, will appear the second time, robed in majesty and glory, to bless His people, and to take them to Himself forever.

Angels and saints will contribute to the glory of the scene. The celestial beings who sang His natal song, and who escorted Him back to heaven, with ten thousand times ten thousand, and thousands of thousands more, will now throng His descending way. Clustering around still nearer to His person will be the ransomed church, the "holy city, new Jerusalem, coming down from God out of heaven, prepared as a bride adorned for her husband." And as she nears the new earth, the future scene of her rest and glory, a "great voice out of heaven" will be heard, saying, "Behold the tabernacle of God is with men, and He will dwell with them, and they shall be His people, and God Himself shall be with them, and be their God. And God shall wipe away all tears from their eyes: and there shall be no more death, neither sorrow, nor crying, neither shall there be any more pain; for the former things are passed away." Oh, blessed hope and glorious appearing of the great God our Savior, when He "shall come to be glorified in His saints, and to be admired in all those who believe"!

AUGUST 15

"My Father, which gave them me, is greater than all; and no man is able to pluck them out of my Father's hand. I and my Father are one." John 10:29, 30

The doctrine of Christ's pre-existence affords a most exalted and satisfactory view of the nature, glory, and stability of that covenant of grace entered upon by the infinitely glorious people of the triune God in behalf of the church. This covenant must be rich in its promises of mercy, seeing that it is made by Jehovah Himself, the fountain of all holiness, goodness, mercy, and truth, whose very name is "love." It must be glorious, because the Second Person in the blessed Trinity became its surety. It must be stable, because it is eternal. It must meet all the circumstances of a necessitous and tried church, because it is "ordered in all things." It must be sure, seeing its administration is in the hands of an infinitely glorious Mediator, who died to secure it, rose again to confirm it, and "ever lives" to dispense its blessings, as the circumstances of His saints require. How animating are the words which direct the believer to the fullness of this precious covenant: "Incline your ear, and come unto me: hear, and your soul shall live; and I will make an everlasting covenant with you, even the sure mercies of David." And when the children of the covenant are brought by the converting grace of the Holy Spirit into this visible relation, what says God concerning them? "I will make an everlasting covenant with them, that I will not turn away from them, to do them good; but I will put my fear in their hearts, that they shall not depart from me." And what is the precious blood of Jesus, but the "blood of the New Testament," the "blood of the everlasting covenant," deriving all its value, efficacy, and preciousness from the personal dignity and pre-eternal glory of Him who shed it?

The eternal love, grace, and fullness of Christ to His church spring from this glorious truth. Is the eternity of Christ's being a doctrine of revealed truth? equally so is the doctrine of the eternity of His love, with all the streams of blessing of which it is the spring-head. The love of Jesus runs parallel with His being; and as that is from all eternity to all eternity, so is His love towards the church which He has purchased with His own blood. "I have loved you," says the Lord, "with an everlasting love." "Blessed be the God and Father of our Lord Jesus Christ, who has blessed us with all spiritual blessings in heavenly places in Christ: according as he has chosen us in Him before the foundation of the world, that we should be holy, and without blame before Him in love." Hard though this truth is to be believed by some, yet in the clearer light of heaven will every child of God see that electing love brought Him there, and but for which He had been lost forever.

Call you this doctrine of Christ's pre-existence a dry, speculative, and uninfluential article of faith? Oh, no! it is manna and fatness to him that believes it with his heart, while it supplies him with the most powerful and persuasive motive to a holy, godly life. On this truth, experimentally and practically received, he can live; and on it in the simple exercise of faith, he, can die. More precious is it to him than gold, yes, than much fine gold, since it endears to his soul the incarnate God, sustains him in his conflicts, comforts him in his trials, strengthens his aspirations for Divine conformity, and will, in the final hour, and amid the swellings of Jordan, enable him to exclaim, "Thanks be to God for His unspeakable gift!"

AUGUST 16

"Watch you therefore, and pray always, that you may be accounted worthy to escape all these things that shall come to pass, and to stand before the Son of man." Luke 21:36

How closely and beautifully has our dear Lord connected together these two important Christian duties—"Watch and pray!" The one as necessary as the other is sublime. Watchfulness implying uncertainty as to time; prayer expressive of an earnest desire to be found in an appropriate attitude for the event. "Therefore, be you ready also; for in such an hour as you do not think, the Son of man comes." "Behold, I come as a thief. Blessed is he that watches, and keeps his garments." Surely if our affections were supremely fixed on Jesus—were He to us as the "chief among ten thousand," and did we really feel in our hearts the sentiment which our lips so often utter, "Whom have I in heaven but You? and there is none upon earth that I desire beside You," the return of our Lord would be to us a matter of most delightsome expectation and wearisome desire. Our earnest prayer would oftener be, "Why are Your chariot-wheels so long in coming? Come, Lord Jesus, come quickly!"

Dear reader, are you prepared for the coming of the Lord? Are you ready to enter in with Him to the marriage supper? Are you a professor? Have you grace-renewing, humbling, sanctifying, Christ-exalting grace in your heart? Is your preparation one of principle, one of habit? Will it abide the searching scrutiny of that day? Examine and see. Take nothing for granted, in deciding a matter so solemn, and involving interests so momentous. Christ must be all in all to you—the entire ground-work and fabric of your salvation. Mere notions of truth—external membership with the church—sacraments—regular attendance upon means—punctilious observance of days, and forms, and ceremonies, in themselves are no fit preparation for this awful event. As the fruit of a living faith in Jesus, they are valuable; but standing alone, without repentance towards God and faith in the Lord Jesus Christ, they are the wood, the hay, the stubble which the last fire will consume.

Believer in Jesus! the day of your redemption draws near! The Lord is at hand. Behold, the Judge stands at the door. The days we live in are eventful—the times are perilous. The signs, thickening and darkening around us, are deeply and fearfully significant. We are standing on the eve of events perhaps more awful than the world has ever seen. A period of glory for the church, brighter than has yet shone upon her, and a period of woe to the world, more dark than has yet cast its shadows upon it, seems rapidly approaching. Then, "let us not sleep as do others, but let us watch and be sober." "And that, knowing the time, that now it is high time to awake out of sleep; for now is our salvation nearer than when we believed. The night is far spent, the day is at hand." "Watch you, therefore: for you know not when the Master of the house comes; at even, or at midnight, or at the cock-crowing, or in the morning: lest coming suddenly, He find you sleeping." Oh, to blend the steady thought of our Redeemer's coming with every present duty, privilege, and effort, how would it hallow, cheer, and dignify us, consecrating by one of the most solemn motives the lowliest work of faith and the feeblest labor of love!

Thus, too, would there be a growing preparedness of mind for the judgments which are yet to come upon the earth. "For there shall be great tribulation, such as was not since the beginning of the world to this time, no, nor ever shall be." "Men's hearts failing them for fear, and for looking after those things which are coming on the earth; for the powers of heaven shall be shaken. And then shall they see the Son of man coming in a cloud, with power and great glory. And when these things begin to come to pass, then look up, and lift up your heads; for your redemption draws near."

AUGUST 17

"Having made known unto us the mystery of his will, according to his good pleasure which he has purposed in himself; that in the dispensation of the fullness of times he might gather together in one all things in Christ, both which are in heaven, and which are on earth; even in him." Ephesians 1:9, 10

That we have a partial discovery of God, His wisdom, and power, and goodness, in creation, is not enough to satisfy a mind convinced that God is holy, to quiet a conscience convicted of sin, and to soothe a heart bowed with godly grief. The grand inquiries with such a soul are, "How can I be just with God? How can I satisfy His justice, appease His wrath, and propitiate His regard? How may I know that He is my God, my reconciled Father? How may I be assured that He loves, has pardoned, and accepted me, and that I shall be with Him forever?" Traverse in imagination the extent of creation, wander over the most beautiful landscape, pluck the most fragrant flower, glide upon the surface of the fairest lake, scale the highest mountain, soar to the furthermost star, still the momentous question rushes back upon the mind, "How may I stand with acceptance before this holy Lord God?" Poor anxious searcher for peace, all nature unites in testifying, "It is not in me! it is not in me!"

The knowledge of God derived from His law must also necessarily be partial and shadowy. It is true, the holiness of God is discovered in its precepts; and the justice of God is inferred from its threatenings; but the law can never be more or less than what the Holy Spirit has declared it to be—the "ministration of condemnation." As a fallen creature, revolving the great matter of the soul's salvation, it can afford no satisfactory reply to the great question, "What must I do to be saved?" It breathes not a sound of mercy to a poor sinner; not one kind, soothing, saving accent falls from its lips. It speaks of death, but not of life; of condemnation, but not of salvation. It asserts the authority, reflects the holiness, and denounces the vengeance of God; but not one beam of hope springing from His mercy, His grace, or His love, does it throw upon the gloomy path of a soul passing on to judgment, bowed beneath the terrors of the Lord. Reader! are you seeking salvation by the law? Alas for you! How can that save which but condemns? How can that give life, which in its nature and design is but the minister of death? Mount Sinai is no refuge for your soul, poor guilty, condemned, heart-broken sinner. Get you down from the mount, before you are consumed. Abandon, as utterly futile and deceptive, all your legal expectations of acceptance, and betake yourself to the one only refuge of your guilty soul—the cross of the incarnate God.

We are now conducted to the consideration of the great point. We have seen that upon an extensive scale a great and fatal experiment had been made by man to know God and happiness. That God existed he had every demonstrative proof. The same evidence which authenticated His being, proved Him to possess great and glorious attributes; and the manner in which these attributes were displayed gave some insight into his character; "so that they are without excuse." Wearied as the creature was with a laborious, and dispirited with a fruitless research, God, in the depths of infinite mercy and wisdom, takes the work of salvation into His own hands. He sends His only-begotten and well-beloved Son into the world, and declares Him to be the perfect revelation of Himself to man. On this important truth Jesus Himself laid great stress. "Have I been so long time with you, and yet have you not known me, Philip? He that has seen me has seen the Father; and how say you then, Show us the Father? Believe you not that I am in the Father, and the Father in me? The words that I speak unto you I speak not of myself; but the Father that dwells in me, He does the works."

The great revelation of the Godhead, Jesus, is equally the revelation of all the perfections of the Godhead. Is "God only wise"? Jesus is the glory of that wisdom—"Christ, the wisdom of God." He is the master-piece of Divine wisdom; its highest manifestation; its most perfect, finished production. We trace the lesser forms of wisdom in nature; we ascend a scale higher in providence; we reach the summit in grace. Here we launch into a boundless immensity, and, overwhelmed with its greatness, can but exclaim, "Oh the depth of the riches, both of the wisdom and knowledge of God!"

AUGUST 18

"Blotting out the handwriting of ordinances that was against us, which was contrary to us, and took it out of the way, nailing it to his cross." Colossians 2:14

THE atonement of the blessed Redeemer was a full and entire blotting out of the sins of the believer. Need we say anything upon the vast importance of this truth? Need we say how closely it stands connected with the peace, the sanctification, and the eternal glory of the sinner that builds on Christ? The phraseology which the Holy Spirit employs in announcing the doctrine of Divine forgiveness confirms the statement we have made—"I have blotted out, as a thick cloud, your transgressions, and, as a cloud, your sins: return unto me, for I have redeemed you." Where would be the constraining-power of the motive to "return to God," but on the ground of a full and entire blotting out of all sin? This it is that subdues, overcomes, and wins back God's wandering child. This it is that abases the soul, deepens the conviction of its vileness, makes the sin of departure, of ingratitude, of rebellion, so abhorred, when, on the broad basis of a full and free blotting out of sin, God bids the soul "return"—"I have blotted out all your sins, therefore return. Though you have gone after other lovers—though you have departed from me, forgotten, and forsaken me, yet have I blotted out, as a thick cloud, your transgressions: return, for I have redeemed you." Again, "In those days, and in that time, says the Lord, the iniquity of Israel shall be sought for, and there shall be none; and the sins of Judah, and they shall not be found." "He will turn again, He will have compassion upon us; He will subdue our iniquities; and You will cast all their sins into the depths of the sea." What an astounding truth is contained in these two passages! In the one it is declared, that if the iniquity of Israel, and the sin of Judah, be sought for, they shall not be found. So entire was the blotting out, so glorious was the work of Jesus, so perfect His obedience, that if the eye of God's holy law searches—and where can it not penetrate?—it cannot discover them. In the other, it is declared, that, so fathomless are the depths of that sea of atoning blood, which Christ has poured out, that in it are cast, never to be found again, all the sins of the believer. So that the trembling soul may exclaim, "You have, in love to my soul, delivered it from the pit of corruption; for You have cast all my sins behind Your back."

Look up, you saints of God, who are disconsolate through fear of condemnation. See all your sins charged to the account of your mighty Surety. Yes, see them all laid upon Him as your substitute. See Him bearing them away—sinking them in the ocean of His blood—casting them behind His back. Look up and rejoice! Let not the indwelling of sin, the remains of corruption, cause you to overlook this amazing truth—the entire blotting out of all your sins, through the atoning blood of your adorable Immanuel. It is truth, and it is your privilege to live in the holy enjoyment of it. Fully received into the heart by the teaching of the Holy Spirit, its tendency will be of the most holy, sanctifying, abasing character. It will weaken the power of sin—it will draw up the heart in pantings for Divine conformity—it will deaden the influence of the objects of sense—expel the love of the world and of self—impart tenderness to the conscience, and cause the soul to go softly—"walking worthy of the Lord, unto all pleasing, being fruitful in every good work, and increasing in the knowledge of God."

AUGUST 19

"And he is before all things, and by him all things consist. And he is the head of the body, the church: who is the beginning, the first-born from the dead; that in all things he might have the preeminence." Colossians 1:17, 18

In this striking and beautiful passage, Jesus is declared to be before all created things; could this be true, if He Himself were a created being? Christ is either created, or He is uncreated. He is a creature, or the Creator. If a mere creature, then it were absurdity to suppose Him creating all things; for He must have been created before He could create: then He could not have been before all created things. If, too, He were a mere creature, how could He uphold all things? for He would need an upholding power for Himself. No mere creature ever has, or ever can, sustain itself. The angels could not, for they fell. Adam could not, for he fell. And Christ could not have sustained Himself in the solemn hour of atonement, when standing beneath the mighty load of His people's sins, had He not been more than creature—the uncreated Jehovah. His humanity did indeed tremble, and shudder, and shrink back; but, upborne by His Godhead, secretly, invisibly, yet effectually sustained by His Deity, He achieved a complete triumph, made an end of sin, and brought in a new and everlasting righteousness. If, too, He were a creature only, how could He give spiritual life to the dead, and how could He sustain that life when given? All spiritual life is from Christ, and all spiritual life is sustained by Christ—"Christ who is our life"—the life of the soul, the life of pardon, the life of justification; the life of sanctification, the life of all the Christian graces—the life of all that now is, and the life of all that is to come. Glorious truth this, to the saint of God!

Turn to our blessed Lord's conference with the Jews, in which He asserts His eternal existence: "Jesus said unto them, Verily, verily, I say unto you, Before Abraham was, I am." What a consoling view do we derive of Christ, from this revealed attribute of His nature! Is He eternal ?—then His love to His people is eternal; His love to them being coeval with His very being. It is not the love of yesterday or of to-day—it is the love of eternity: its spring-head is His own eternal existence. Is He eternal?—then must He be unchangeable too: His precious love, set upon them from all eternity, can never be removed: having given them Himself, Himself He will never take away. Blessed thought! He may blight earthly hopes, He may break up earthly cisterns, He may wither earthly gourds; He may send billow upon billow, breach upon breach, but never, never will He take Himself from the people of His love. Dear reader, you may be conscious of many and great departures; this single view of your Father's unchangeableness may recall to your recollection backslidings many and aggravated; forgetfulness, ingratitude, unkindnesses without number; murmurings, rebellion, and unbelief. Still does God, your God, say to you, "Though you have dealt so with me, though you have forgotten me, though your name is rebellious, yet do I love you still. Return unto me, and I will return unto you." What a soul-humbling, heart-melting thought is this! Does your Father love your sins? No! Does He look complacently on your wanderings? No! He hates your sins, and He will follow your wanderings with His chastising rod; but He loves your person, beholding you in the Beloved, fully and freely accepted in the glorious righteousness of Jesus, who is the same "yesterday, today, and forever." If this truth, dear reader, be broken up to your soul by the blessed and eternal Spirit, the effect will be most holy and abasing. The legitimate tendency of all spiritual truth is sanctifying. Hence our blessed Lord prayed that the truth might be the medium through which His people should be sanctified. "Sanctify them through your truth." And hence the apostle reasons, "Christ also loved the church, and gave Himself for it. That He might sanctify and cleanse it with the washing of water, by the word." That God's truth has been and is abused by wicked and ungodly men, is no argument against the truth. They abuse it to their own condemnation; they turn it from its right and legitimate use to their own loss. Still the truth stands firm in its peerless dignity and holy tendency, and when unfolded to the understanding, and laid upon the heart by the Holy Spirit, Christ's prayer is answered in the progressive sanctification of the soul.

AUGUST 20

"Therefore by the deeds of the law there shall no flesh be justified in his sight: for by the law is the knowledge of sin. But now the righteousness of God without the law is manifested, being witnessed by the law and the prophets; even the righteousness of God which is by faith of Jesus Christ unto all and upon all those who believe." Romans 3:20-22

Thus does Paul triumphantly establish the perfect freeness and unconditional character of a sinner's acceptance with God. By "the deeds of the law," he has reference to those many and fruitless efforts to obey the law which men in a state of nature are found so zealously to aim at. Are you striving, dear reader, to conform to the requirement of this holy, this inflexible law of God? Let me assure you, that all these strivings, all these works, all this toiling, is worse than worthless in God's holy sight; they are sinful—they proceed from an unregenerate nature, from an unrenewed, unsanctified heart—they flow not from faith and love; and therefore, the heart being thus a fountain of corruption, every stream that branches from it must partake of the foulness of the source from where it flows. Let the failure of the past suffice to teach you that this holy law you can never keep. Let your formal prayers, your lifeless religion, your vows forsworn, your resolutions broken, all confirm the solemn declaration of the apostle: "by the deeds of the law there shall no flesh be justified in His sight." Again: "For by the law is the knowledge of sin." Accompanied by the Spirit of God, it discloses to the soul the sinfulness of the heart and life, and brings it in guilty and self-condemned before God. Now, how is it possible that the law can ever be an instrument of life and an instrument of death to a sinner? It is utterly impossible that it can be. It never yet gave spiritual life to the soul—it never yet emancipated the soul from its thraldom—it never yet conducted it to Jesus—it never yet whispered liberty and peace. It can and does condemn—it can and does curse—and this is the utmost extent of its prerogative. Oh, then, resign all the hope you fondly cherish of life, peace, and acceptance by "the deeds of the law," and betake yourself to Him who has, by His most precious blood, "redeemed us from the curse of the law, being made a curse for us."

Having established the incapacity of the law to justify the sinner, the apostle then proceeds to unfold the glory, fitness, and freeness of that righteousness which can and does justify the soul before God. He takes up and argues two important points—the nature of the righteousness, and the instrument by which it is received. With regard to the first, he declares it to be "the righteousness of God"—and nothing but "the righteousness of God" can justify a soul in the sight of God. It must not be the righteousness of angels, nor the righteousness of Adam, nor the righteousness of Moses—it must be the righteousness of God in our nature. Away with every other refuge—away with every other covering; and let not the reader dream of entering with acceptance into the presence of a holy and heart-searching God, clad in any other righteousness than that which the adorable Immanuel wrought out. In this righteousness the believing sinner is safe, and safe forever; take him for a moment out of this righteousness, and he is lost, and lost forever!

The instrument by which this divine righteousness is received is the second point established by the apostle. He clearly proves it to be by faith. Thus: "Even the righteousness of God, which is by faith of Jesus Christ unto all and upon all those who believe." How perfectly does this statement of the instrument or medium by which the blessings of pardon and justification are received into the soul harmonize with every other portion of God's word! Thus, for instance—"By Him all that believe are justified from all things." "Believe in the Lord Jesus Christ, and you shall be saved." "God so loved the world, that He gave His only begotten Son, that whoever believes in Him should not perish, but have everlasting life." Oh see, disconsolate soul, the freeness of the gift! "To him that believes"—not to him that works, not to him that deserves, not to the worthy, but "to him that believes." "Where is boasting, then? It is excluded. By what law? Of works? No, but by the law of faith. Therefore we conclude that a man is justified by faith (in Christ) without the deeds of the law."

AUGUST 21

"Herein is my Father gloried, that you bear much fruit; so shall you be my disciples." John 15:8

This "much fruit" is often found mostly in those with whom the Lord mostly deals. He has created His people for His own glory, and this He will secure to Himself in their abundant fruitfulness. This is why the most illustrious saints have ever been the most deeply tried, severely pruned: their great fruitfulness sprang from their great afflictions. And yet, beloved, the Lord deals with His saints according to His holy sovereignty; not by one line, or in one path, does He always conduct them. Is God smiling upon you? does the summer sun shine? is your sea smooth and flowing? does the "south wind" blow upon you? See, then, that you walk humbly with God; "Do not be high-minded, but fear." If God in His providence has elevated you a little in the world, you have need to besiege His throne for great grace to keep your spirit low in the dust before Him. Do your fellows admire your talents, extol your gifts, applaud your works, and court your society? oh, how closely, and softly, and humbly ought you now to walk with God! That breath of adulation that lighted upon you will prove a blight upon your graces, if you go not upon your knees before God; that flattering word which fell upon your ear will prove as the fly in the apothecary's ointment to your soul, if you get not closer down at the foot of the cross. Let every circumstance and state take you there; whether the north wind or the south wind blows, whether the dark cloud of adversity gathers over you, or the sunshine of prosperity beams upon you—still let your posture ever be low before the Savior's cross: nothing can harm you there. See that the season of outward prosperity is the season of your soul's fruitfulness; see that every mercy takes you to God; convert every new blessing into a fresh motive for living, not unto yourself, but unto Him from whom the blessing came.

And if you are constrained to take your worst frames to Christ, your sins as they rise, your weakness as you are conscious of it, your corruptions as they discover themselves, even so shall you be a fruitful branch of the true Vine. In the very act of going, just as he is, to Christ, the believer brings forth fruit. For what marks the frame of the soul thus traveling up to the cross, but self-distrust, self-abasement, deep conceptions of its own nothingness, high views of Christ's sufficiency? And is not this precious and costly fruit? I know of none more so.

And let the fruitful believer anticipate the approaching period of his translation to a more genial and healthy soil. In heaven, the home of the saints, there will be nothing to blight the flower of grace; no frosts of winter, no burning heat of summer, no crushing storms, no sweeping tempests; the former things will all have passed away, and a new heaven and a new earth, in which dwells righteousness, shall have succeeded them. Happy hour of his release! Here he is a "lily among thorns;" there he will be a tree of righteousness, on which the storm will never rise, on which the sun will never set.

AUGUST 22

"Turn, O backsliding children, says the Lord; for I am married unto you." Jeremiah 3:14

Let the Christian reader call to mind the period and the circumstances of his first espousals to Jesus. If there ever was a blissful period of your life—if a spot of verdure in the remembrance of the past, on which the sunlight ever rests—was it not the time, and is it not the place where your heart first expanded with the love of Jesus? You have, it may be, trod many a thorny path since then; you have traveled many a weary step of your pilgrimage—have buffeted many storms, have waded through many deep afflictions, and fought many severe battles, but all have well-near faded from your memory; but the hour and the events of your "first love," these you never have forgotten, you never can forget. Oh ever to be loved, ever to be remembered with deep songs of joy, with adoring gratitude to free and sovereign grace, the period when the chains of your bondage were broken—when your fettered soul broke from its thraldom, and sprang into the liberty of the sons of God—when light discovered your darkness, and that darkness rolled away before its increasing luster—when the Spirit wounded you, then healed that wound with the precious balm of Gilead—when He gave you sorrow, then soothed that sorrow by a view of the crucified Lamb of God—when faith took hold of Jesus, and brought the blessed assurance into the soul, "I am my beloved's, and my beloved is mine;" and when Jesus whispered—oh, how tender was His voice!—"Your sins, which were many, are all forgiven you; go in peace." Blissful moment! Oh that the Lord should ever have reason to prefer the charge, "you have left your first love."

It is an affecting and humbling truth that the grace of love in a child of God may greatly and sadly decline. We speak, let it be remembered, not of the destruction of the principle, but of the decline of its power. This spiritual and influential truth cannot be too frequently nor too strongly insisted upon—that though faith, and love, and hope, and zeal, and their kindred graces may greatly decline in their vigor, fervor, and real growth, yet that they may entirely fail even in their greatest decay, or severest trial, the Word of God assures us can never be. To believe the opposite of this is to deny their Divine origin, their spiritual and immortal character, and to impeach the wisdom, power, and faithfulness of God. Not a grain of the true wheat can ever be lost in the sifting, not a particle of the pure gold in the refining. Remember, that though your love has waxed cold, the love of your God and Father towards you has undergone no diminution—not the shadow of a change has it known. What an encouragement to return to Him again! Not one moment has God turned His back upon you, though you have turned your back upon Him times without number. His face has always been towards you; and it would have shone upon you with all its melting power, but for the clouds which your own waywardness and sinfulness have caused to obscure and hide from you its blessed light. Retrace your steps and return again to God. Though you have been a poor wanderer, and have left your first love—though your affections have strayed from the Lord, and your heart has gone after other lovers—still God is gracious and ready to pardon; He will welcome you back again for the sake of Jesus, His beloved Son, in whom He is well pleased; for this is His own blessed declaration—"If his children forsake my law, and walk not in my judgments; if they break my statutes, and keep not my commandments; then will I visit their transgressions with a rod, and their iniquity with stripes. Nevertheless my loving-kindness will I not utterly take from him, nor suffer my faithfulness to fail."

AUGUST 23

"To whom God would make known what is the riches of the glory of this mystery among the Gentiles; which is Christ in you, the hope of glory." Colossians 1:27

The believer in Jesus is a partaker of the Divine nature. He is "born of the Spirit;" Christ dwells in him by faith; and this constitutes his new and spiritual life. It is not so much that the believer lives, as that Christ lives in him. Thus the apostle expresses it: "I am crucified with Christ: nevertheless I live; yet not I, but Christ lives in me." Do we look at the history of Paul as illustrative of the doctrine? Behold the grand secret of his extraordinary life. He lived unreservedly for Christ; and the spring of it was, Christ lived spiritually in him. This it was that rendered him so profound in wisdom, rich in knowledge, bold in preaching, undaunted in zeal, unwearied in toil, patient in suffering, and successful in labor—Christ lived in him, and this forms the high and holy life of every child of God—"Christ who is our life." To Him, as the covenant head and mediator of His people, it was given to have life in Himself, that He might give eternal life to as many as the Father had given Him. Christ possesses this life, Christ communicates it, Christ sustains it, and Christ crowns it with eternal glory. A peculiar characteristic of the life of God in the soul is, that it is concealed. "Your life is hid with Christ in God." It is a hidden life. Its nature, its source, its actings, its supports, are veiled from the observation of men. "The world knows us not." It knew not Jesus when He dwelt in the flesh, else it would not have crucified the Lord of life and glory. Is it any wonder that it knows Him not, dwelling, still deeper veiled, in the hearts of His members? It crucified Christ in His own person, it has crucified Him in the people of His saints, and, if power were given, would so crucify Him yet again. And yet there is that in the divine life of the believer which awakens the wonderment of a Christ-rejecting world. That the believer should be unknown, and yet well known—should die, and yet live—should be chastened, and yet not killed—sorrowful, yet always rejoicing—poor, yet making many rich—having nothing, and yet possessing all things—is indeed an enigma, a paradox to a carnal mind; yes, there are moments when the believer is a mystery to himself. How the divine life in his soul is sustained in the midst of so much that enfeebles, kept alive surrounded by so much that deadens, the glimmering spark not extinguished, though obscured, amid the billows—to drop all figure—how his soul advances when most opposed, soars when most hardened, rejoices when most afflicted, and sings the sweetest and the loudest when the cross presses the heaviest, and the thorn pierces the deepest, may well cause him to exclaim, "I am a wonder to others, but a greater wonder to myself!" But, if the nature and the supports of the divine life in the soul are hid, not so are its effects, and these prove its existence and reality. There is that in the honest, upright walk of a child of God which arrests the attention and awakens the surprise of men, who, while they hate and despise, cannot but admire and marvel at it.

Yet another characteristic of the divine life in the soul is its security. "Your life is hid with Christ in God." There, nothing can touch it: no power can destroy it. It is "hid with Christ," the beloved Son of the Father, the delight, the glory, the richest and most precious treasure of Jehovah: still more—it is "hid with Christ in God"—in the hand, in the heart, in the all-sufficiency, yes, in the eternity of God. Oh the perfect security of the spiritual life of the believer! No power on earth or in hell can move it. It may be stormed by Satan, assaulted by corruption, scorned by men, and even, in the moment of unbelief and in the hour of deep trial, its existence doubted by the believer himself; yet there it is, deep lodged in the eternity of God, bound up in the heart and with the existence of JEHOVAH, and no foe can destroy it. "I give unto them eternal life, and they shall never perish, neither shall any man pluck them out of my hand." Let the sheep and the lambs of the "little flock" rejoice that the Shepherd lives, and that because He lives they shall live also.

AUGUST 24

"For the Lord will not cast off forever: but though he cause grief, yet will he have compassion according to the multitude of his mercies. For he does not afflict willingly, nor grieve the children of men." Lam. 3:31-33

Oh! what emptying, what humbling are necessary in order to make room for the lowly Lamb of God in the heart of a poor believing sinner! And for years after the first reception of Jesus, are this emptying and humbling needed. If it were not so, would our dear Lord discipline as He does? Would He cut off this and that dependence? would He take us off of creature trust, and that sometimes in the most painful way? Oh no! by these means He seeks to establish Himself in our affections—He would have our whole hearts. And when thus unhinged from earthly trust, when emptied of confidence in self, when deprived of earthly comforts—oh how unutterably precious does Jesus become! Then do we see Him to be just the Jesus we want, just the Savior that we need; we find in Him all that we ever found in the creature, and infinitely more—wisdom, strength tenderness, and sympathy, surpassing all that men or angels ever felt, or could possibly feel for us. Then it is His blood and righteousness are endeared; then we fly to His fullness of all grace; and then the tender, bleeding branch takes a firmer hold on its stem, and henceforth looks only to it for all its vigor, its nourishment, and its fruit. "As the branch cannot bear fruit of itself, except it abide in the vine, no more can you, except you abide in me." Ah! beloved reader, if you are His child, He will cause you to know it, and will endear Himself to you as such. And this is seldom done, save in the way of severe discipline. Shrink not from it, then. All the good that the Lord ever takes from you, He returns ten thousand-fold more in giving Himself. If you can say, "the Lord is my portion," then what more do you, can you, want? And remember, too, the Lord will deprive you of nothing that was for your real good. He is the judge of what is best for you—not yourself. We are but imperfect judges of what tends best to our spiritual or temporal benefit. That which we may deem absolutely essential to both, the Lord in His wisdom and love may see proper to remove; and as frequently, that the removal of which we had often besought the Lord, He may see fit to retain. Thrice Paul prayed for the removal of his infirmity, and thrice the Lord denied his request: but the denial was accompanied by a promise, calculated to soothe into sweet acquiescence every feeling of the apostle—"My grace," said the Lord, "is sufficient for you." Let it ever be remembered by the tried believer, that supporting grace, in the season of trial, is a greater mercy than the removal of the trial itself. The Lord Jesus did seem to say to His servant, "I see not that it would be for your good to grant your prayer, but I will enable you to bear the infirmity without a murmur: I will so support you, so manifest my strength in your weakness, my all-sufficiency in your nothingness, that you shall not desire its removal." "Lord," he might have replied, "this is all that I desire. If You in Your wisdom and love do see fit still to afflict me, I am in Your hands to do with me as seems good in Your sight. The continuance of the trial will but prove the strength of Your grace, and the tenderness and sympathy of Your heart." After this, we hear no more of Paul's thorn in the flesh: the grace of the Lord, doubtless, proved all-sufficient for him.

AUGUST 25

"Blessed be the God and Father of our Lord Jesus Christ, who has blessed us with all spiritual blessings in heavenly places in Christ." Ephesians 1:3

Our blessed Redeemer is glorified in being the covenant Head of all blessing to His people. He is our true Joseph, with all the treasures which a Father's love can bestow, or which the covenant of grace provides, placed in His hands and at His disposal. It has "pleased the Father" to constitute Him the Head of the church, and that in Him, as such, "all fullness should dwell." He, too, is our true spiritual Eliakim, of whom it is sweetly prophesied, "And they shall hang upon Him all the glory of His Father's house, the offspring and the issue; all vessels of small quantity, from the vessels of cups, even to all the vessels of flagons." Who sustains, as a "nail fastened in a sure place," all the glory of the church, but Jesus? In Christ the church is chosen. In Christ it is preserved. In Christ it lives. In Christ it is pardoned. In Christ it is justified. In Christ it is sanctified. In Christ it will be glorified. Thus does all the glory of the spiritual house hang on Christ—He is its foundation, He is its cornerstone; in Him "fitly framed together, it grows up a holy temple in the Lord," and He will be the top-stone, which shall be brought forth on the day of its completion, amid the shoutings of "Grace, grace unto it."

On Him, too, hang the "vessels" of the house, the "vessels of cups and the vessels of flagons;" the small and the great, the young and the old, the feeble and the strong, all the saints hang on Jesus, and Jesus supports and supplies all. See how the "vessels of cups, the vessels of small quantity," hang upon Him, and how He supplies them. "And, behold, there came a leper, and worshiped Him, saying, Lord, if You will, You can make me clean. And Jesus put forth His hand, and touched him, saying, I will; be you clean. And immediately his leprosy was cleansed." "And one of the multitude answered and said, Master, I have brought unto You my son, which has a dumb spirit...and ofttimes it has cast him into the fire, and into the waters, to destroy him: but if You can do anything, have compassion on us, and help us. Jesus rebuked the foul spirit, saying unto him, You dumb and deaf spirit, I charge you come out of him, and enter no more into him." "And he said unto Jesus, Lord, remember me when You come into Your kingdom. And Jesus said unto him, Verily I say unto you, Today shall you be with me in paradise." Behold, how these "vessels of small quantity" hang on Jesus; and behold, how He sustains and fills them. They are but as "vessels of cups"—their knowledge is defective, their grace is limited, their experience but shallow, their faith but small, and they themselves but little—oh! how little, who can tell?—in their own eyes; yet coming thus to Jesus' grace, exclaiming,

"Other refuge have I none,
Hangs my helpless soul on You."

He receives them, He welcomes them, He bears them up, He supplies them, He fills them; He rejoices in their feeble grace, He despises not their little strength, He crowns their weak faith, He grants them the utmost desire of their hearts. Oh, what a Jesus is our Jesus! Were ever such gentleness, tenderness, and skill manifested towards the "bruised reed and the smoking flax"? Dear reader, are you a vessel of "small quantity"? It may be that, through the infirmities that encompass you, the trials that oppress you, the temptations that assail you, the clouds that surround you, you can receive Christ's fullness but in a limited degree; truth is understood but partially, there being doctrines, perhaps, hard to be understood, and precepts still harder to be obeyed. Christ's grand atonement, His one perfect obedience, His great and finished work, the sprinkling of His blood upon the conscience, the completeness of a believing soul in His righteousness, and the consequent "peace and joy in the Holy Spirit," but little known. Yet, feeling your own vileness, and Christ's sufficiency and preciousness, and constrained to hang on Him solely and exclusively, as all your salvation and all your desire; though you can receive but a "small quantity" of knowledge, of grace, and of love, you are yet a "vessel of gold" in His house, and Jesus bears you on His heart, sets you as a seal upon His arm, and presents you each moment before God complete in Himself.

But there are also in this house "vessels of flagons"—the larger vessels—saints of deep grace, of profound knowledge. Hear one of them exclaim, "I am crucified with Christ: nevertheless I live; yet not I, but Christ lives in me: and the life which I now live in the flesh, I live by the faith of the Son of God, who loved me, and gave Himself for me." Oh how abundantly did this beloved apostle drink of the "river of God"! How deeply did he sink into the ocean of Christ's fullness! How high did he soar into the beatific presence of God, until, sweeping the heavens with his expanded pinions, all the treasures that sparkle there seemed gathered into his soul. Yet, a large vessel though he was, in himself he was poor, vile, and empty, counting himself as the "chief of sinners," esteeming himself "less than the least of all saints," and ascribing all that he was as a renewed man to the "grace of God." In this his poverty, vileness, and emptiness, he hung with the small vessel, solely, entirely, on Christ. The thief saved at the last moment, and Paul, the great apostle of the Gentiles, side by side, hung on Jesus. "Of His fullness have all we received, and grace for grace." Both were pardoned by the same blood, both were justified by the same righteousness, both were filled from the same source, and both are now in glory, chanting the same song, and together casting their crowns before the throne. Thus is Jesus made the "Head over all things to His church;" and His church becomes in all its members, be they small or great, "the fullness of Him that fills all in all." Thus is Christ glorified in them,—what finite mind can compute the revenue of glory thus accruing to the Redeemer through His saints!

AUGUST 26

"The hour is coming, in the which all that are in the graves shall hear his voice, and shall come forth." John 5:28, 29

"But how are the dead raised up?" That there is much of sublime mystery associated with this event, we readily admit. But its very mystery endears Him to the soul, "who has abolished death" (or, rendered it of none effect), "and has brought life and immortality to light by the gospel." Thus is this mystery explained: "It is sown in corruption; it is raised in incorruption: it is sown in dishonor; it is raised in glory: it is sown in weakness; it is raised in power: it is sown a natural body; it is raised a spiritual body. Behold, I show you a mystery. We shall not all sleep; but we shall all be changed, in a moment, in the twinkling of an eye, at the last trumpet: for the trumpet shall sound, and the dead shall be raised incorruptible, and we shall be changed. For this corruptible must put on incorruption, and this mortal must put on immortality." Yes, this very body, as much redeemed by the precious blood of the incarnate God as the deathless principle it enshrines, shall rise again! and by what power? The power of Omnipotence! "He that raised up Christ from the dead, shall also quicken your mortal bodies by His Spirit that dwells in you." Every entombed saint of God is an entombed temple of the Holy Spirit. Think of this, and tread lightly, as you carry it to the grave. You bear a temple of the Holy Spirit! Precious is the dust, and hallowed the urn that contains it. And shall that temple lie in ruins forever? God forbid! Oh, it is a mighty and a glorious work to resuscitate, remold, and reoccupy this dilapidated structure!—to gather from the four winds of heaven every particle of the scattered dust—to bring bone to bone, and sinew to sinew—to invest the re-formed skeleton with a covering more soft and delicate than an infant's—to summon back its former occupant, and then to lift it to glory, outliving, in its deathlessness, the stars of heaven, and outshining in its brilliancy the brightest angel before the throne. Oh, it is a stupendous work! But, stupendous as it is, it transcends not in its mightiness the power of God. Oh, we deal too faintly with the almightiness of Jehovah! We limit the power of the Holy One of Israel. Bring but this power to bear upon the doctrine of the resurrection, and all its mystery is explained, and all its difficulty vanishes. On this divine perfection rested the faith of Abraham, who, in obedience to God's command, bound his child upon the altar, and took the knife to slay him, "believing that God was able to raise him up again, even from the dead." Shall it, then, be thought a thing incredible, that God should raise the dead? The difficulties of summoning together every atom of dust, borne though it may have been by the winds to the furthermost parts of the earth, or strewn upon the waves of the sea—of distinguishing what element belonged to each individual, and appropriating to each his own—of clothing the framework with a new and a deathless nature, and animating it with the same human soul which it contained in the long years of its humiliation, oh, how do they vanish before one touch of Omnipotence! What! shall He who at first formed man out of the dust, and breathed into him the breath of life—shall He at whose fiat world on world started into being, each one, for anything that we know, teeming with a population partaking of His likeness, and sharing in His immortality—shall He who "upholds all things by the word of His power," who "takes up the isles as a very little thing," who "holds the winds in His fist, and the waters in the hollow of His hand," who "has His way in the whirlwind and in the storm, and the clouds are the dust of His feet"—shall He be perplexed and baffled when He comes to unlock the world's charnel-house, quickening, and summoning to His bar, each slumbering occupant? Oh, it will be a stupendous and a glorious work! but reason and revelation unite in ascribing it to Him as worthy of His infinite greatness, majesty, and glory.

AUGUST 27

"And now I am no more in the world, but these are in the world, and I come to you. Holy Father, keep through your own name those whom you have given me." John 17:11

In the Redeemer's exaltation we have the strongest pledge of His continued sympathy, support, and deliverance in all our trials and temptations. It is delightful to the believing mind to reflect, that in passing from the scene of His humiliation to that of His glory, and in the spiritual change which His body must have undergone, thus to fit it for the region which flesh and blood cannot inherit, His humanity lost none of the tender sympathies of our nature which so closely clung to Him when upon earth. The same compassionate nature—the same loving heart—the same deep sympathy with all our sorrows, and the same outstretched hand to relieve them, distinguish the glorified state of the precious Son of God! Do you think that, though dwelling in yon region of light, and holiness, and joy, and glory, He has forgotten the days of His humiliation—the "strong crying and tears"—the "wormwood and the gall"? No! He has them still in remembrance. And can He forget the church in the wilderness—His tried and suffering people? Never! Hark how He prays for them: "I pray for them; I pray not that you should take them out of the world, but that you should keep them from the evil." "As you have sent me into the world, even so have I also sent them into the world." Yes, He forgets not that His church is yet in the world—a polluting, persecuting, harassing world, demanding all the infinite resources of His sympathy and might. Oh how sweet and holy is the thought, that, having passed within the veil though He has, there is still a chain of the closest sympathy suspended from the glorified Redeemer on the throne, touching the most lowly and tried of the redeemed on earth! How can Jesus forget that He still bears our nature, a part of our very being?—the "head so full of bruises," the body so scarred, reminding Him of the suffering state of the church below, and pleading with a power which omnipotence itself cannot resist, for the support, comfort, and deliverance of every tried and tempted member of that body. "Seeing then, that we have a great High Priest, that is passed into the heavens, Jesus the Son of God, let us hold fast our profession. For we have not an high priest which cannot be touched with the feeling of our infirmities."

Thus, through the channel of our glorified Redeemer, what immense and varied blessings may the believer expect and receive! "Exalted a Prince and a Savior, to give repentance unto Israel, and forgiveness of sins," will He not with these costly mercies freely give us all things? What an open door is here for a humble suppliant, bowed with sorrow, and pressed with want! Do you think that He can close His heart, or withdraw His hand, or falsify His promise? Ah, no! our Jesus in His exaltation is more mindful of His people in their low estate than the chief butler, in His advancement, was of Joseph imprisoned in the dungeon. He thinks of us still—He speaks a good word for us to His Father—bends upon us each moment a glance of the most ineffable love, with whose expression infinite compassion sweetly blends. Nor is there a moment in which He is not exerting Himself on our behalf, hedging up the way of one believer, and opening the way of another; strengthening the tried faith of some saints, and soothing the deep sorrows of others. Oh, see what costly blessings are bound up in the exaltation of Jesus! All sanctification to make us holy—all love to make us happy—all wisdom to guide—all grace to uphold—and all glory to crown. "Let us therefore come boldly unto the throne of grace, that we may obtain mercy, and find grace to help in time of need."

AUGUST 28

"But now being made free from sin, and become servants of God, you have your fruit unto holiness and the end everlasting life." Romans 6:22

The Word of God means by Gospel justification, the imputation of Christ's infinite and finished righteousness to a repenting, believing sinner; the making over of His perfect obedience in behalf of His church to him that believes. Christ obeyed not for Himself, but for His church. And on the ground of His obedience—His obedience or righteousness imputed to them, in the same manner in which their sins were imputed to Him—they stand before God, the holy, the heart-searching God, fully and freely "justified from all things." "For He has made Him to be sin for us, who knew no sin, that we might be made the righteousness of God in Him."

What consideration shall we urge upon the Christian reader why he should welcome this truth of God's word? Shall we say his sanctification is intimately connected with it? and what an argument should this be with a child of God! To be holy—to be like God—to be conformed entirely to the will and image of Christ—to have the temper, the taste, the principles, the daily walk, all like our blessed Immanuel, who is "the chief among ten thousand, the altogether lovely"—oh! can a believer aspire to a more lofty aim? And this righteousness, this infinite, this divine, this finished righteousness, received in the heart by the power of God the Holy Spirit, broken up to the soul, lived upon daily, will promote all this: "In Your righteousness shall they be exalted." The righteousness of Christ has a most exalting tendency; it exalts a believer's view of God, of His character and perfections; it exalts his view of Jesus, His person, work, and love; it exalts the believer himself, it takes him out of himself, above and beyond himself; it exalts his principles, his practice, his affections, and conforms him to Christ. Shall we say his happiness is intimately connected with it? And where is the believer that does not desire to walk happily with God? This is the attainment the world are eagerly in search of—but the believer in Christ is its only possessor; he has found it, and found it in Jesus; he has found it in a renunciation of self-righteousness, and in a humble reception of Christ; and there is no happiness worthy of the name, that is sought and found out of Jesus. What true happiness can the heart feel while it is unrenewed, its sins unpardoned, the soul unjustified, and therefore under condemnation, and exposed to the wrath of a holy and just God? Oh, dream not of happiness, reader, until you have gone as a repenting sinner to the cross of Christ; until the atoning blood has been applied to your conscience, and the Spirit bears His witness to your adoption.

If this, and this only, is the source of all true happiness, then the more constantly and closely the believer realizes his full and complete acceptance in the Beloved, the greater must his happiness be. You may be a son or a daughter of affliction; in this furnace you may be chosen, and through this furnace it may be the Lord's holy will you should pass all your days. You may be a child of poverty, possessing but little of this world's comforts, lonely, neglected, despised; yet oh, look up! you are precious in God's sight—dear to Him as the apple of His eye. His heart yearns over you with more than a mother's exquisite fondness for her child, because He has loved you with an everlasting love, and, to the praise of the glory of His grace, has accepted you in the Beloved. Realize this, and though rough and thorny may be your path, and fiery the furnace, and deep your poverty, and lonely your situation, you shall experience a peace and a happiness to which the world around you is an utter stranger. "Therefore being justified by faith, we have peace with God through our Lord Jesus Christ. By whom also we have access by faith into this grace wherein we stand, and rejoice in hope of the glory of God."

AUGUST 29

"For to this end Christ both died, and rose, and revived, that he might be Lord both of the dead and living." Romans 14:9

Thus is it clear that Jesus is the God of providence. The government of all worlds and of all creatures, according to the prediction of prophecy, is upon His shoulders. Is not this thought full of rich comfort and consolation to the experienced believer? Jesus is the God of providence. All your steps, dear reader, if you are His, are ordered and directed by Him—by Him who is God in your nature—by Him who loved you unto the death—by Him who is your Elder Brother, your Prophet, Priest, and King. Oh how tranquillizing to the soul in the hour of its deepest sorrow and bereavement, to know that it is sheltered in the hollow of those very hands which were once pierced for us!—that Christ has blended with His mediatorial character His providential government—that the Redeemer, who died to save, is the God who lives to sway the scepter! It has been well remarked, that Providence was intended to be the handmaid to Grace, but that Grace only can unfold the steps of Providence. It is only the experimental believer who can clearly discern the movements of an invisible hand in all the affairs and incidents of life. He has learned to acknowledge the Lord in all his ways, and to commit to His disposal all his steps. And He who thus guides and governs is the Mediator—the Christ who obeyed, suffered, and died in our behalf. Oh consoling thought! Christian reader, ponder this! What are your present circumstances? Are you persecuted for Jesus' sake? Listen to His own cheering words—"Marvel not if the world hate you, for you know that it hated me before it hated you." "In the world you shall have tribulation; but be of good cheer, I have overcome the world." Are you in circumstances of want?—what does He say?—"Take no thought for your life, what you shall eat, or what you shall drink; nor yet for your body, what you shall put on. Is not the life more than food, and the body than clothing? Behold the fowls of the air: for they sow not, neither do they reap, nor gather into barns, yet your heavenly Father feeds them. Are you not much better than they?" "But seek you first the kingdom of God and His righteousness, and all these things shall be added unto you." Are you perplexed to know the path of duty?—longing to know the way the Lord would have you walk?—this is His promise, "Call upon me in the day of trouble, and I will deliver." "Commit your way unto the Lord; trust also in Him, and He shall bring it to pass." Are you sore pressed by temptation?—see how the Holy Spirit would lead you to the sympathy and tenderness of Jesus—"He took not on Him the nature of angels, but He took on Him the seed of Abraham. Why in all things it behooved Him to be made like unto His brethren, that He might be a merciful and faithful High Priest in things pertaining to God, to make reconciliation for the sins of the people. For in that He Himself has suffered being tempted, He is able to support those who are tempted." "For we have not an High Priest which cannot be touched with the feeling of our infirmities, but was in all points tempted like as we are, yet without sin. Let us therefore come boldly unto the throne of grace, that we may obtain mercy, and find grace to help in time of need." Are you oppressed by present or anticipated trials? Hearken again to His dear voice—"Let not your hearts be troubled; you believe in God, believe also in me." Whatever may be the dark and gloomy aspect of things around you, yet Jesus does all things well—and all things, however adverse, and apparently severe, yet all things are working for your present and ultimate good.

AUGUST 30

"I have chosen you in the furnace of affliction." Isaiah 48:10

With what is the Divine will, as stated in these words, connected, respecting the afflictions of the believer? Is it with the circumstances of time? Is it since they were brought into existence that God determined upon the circumstances that should surround them, and the path they should tread? Oh no! The trying circumstance, the heavy affliction, stands connected with the great and glorious doctrine of God's eternal, sovereign, and unconditional election of His people. They were "chosen in the furnace"—chosen in it before all time—chosen in it from all eternity—chosen in it when He set His heart upon them, entered into an everlasting covenant with them, and took them to be His "chosen generation, His royal priesthood, His holy nation, His peculiar people." Oh, thus to trace up every affliction that comes from God to His eternal choice of His people; to see it in the covenant of grace; to see it connected with His eternal purpose of salvation—thus viewed, in connection with His eternal love, in what a soothing light does it place the darkest dispensation of His providence.

But there is another thought in the passage equally blessed. "I have chosen you"—in what? in prosperity?—no: in the bright summer's day? —no: in the smooth and flowery paths of worldly comforts?—no. "I have chosen you in the furnace of affliction." The furnace of affliction!—is this according to our poor finite ideas of love and tenderness? Oh no! Had we been left to choose our own path, to mark out our own way, it had been a far different one from this. We should never have thought of affliction as a source of blessing. But God's thoughts are higher than our thoughts, and His ways above our ways.

The path of affliction, along which the believer walks, is the path of God's own appointment; and walking in this path, he comes into the possession of rich and varied blessings not found in any other. This is a truth much forgotten, especially by the young Christian, who has just set out on his pilgrimage. To his eye now opened to the new world into which grace has introduced him, all seems fair and lovely; "The love of his espousals" is the one theme of his heart. He thinks not that all, now so fair, will soon change; that the summer sea will be lashed by angry billows; that the sky will look dark and threatening; that the fragile bark will be tossed from billow to billow, and that the port will be lost to sight. How needful, then, that this important truth, "through much tribulation we must enter the kingdom," should be ever kept in view. In looking into God's word, we find it full and decisive on this point: "And I will bring the third part through the fire, and will refine them as silver is refined, and will try them as gold is tried." "Behold, I have refined you, but not with silver; I have chosen you in the furnace of affliction." Our Lord's own testimony harmonizes with this declaration—"in the world you shall have tribulation." As though He had said, Expect nothing less: it is a world of sorrow, and while in it you shall have tribulation. It is your lot. It is the way of my appointment—it is the path I have ordained you to walk in. It is the path I have trod myself; and I leave you an example that you should follow my steps. "In the world you shall have tribulation, but in me you shall have peace." And so taught His apostles. They went forth confirming the souls of the disciples, and exhorting them to continue in the faith; and that we must "through much tribulation enter into the kingdom of God."

From the declarations of God's word, let us pass to consider the examples. The entire histories of the Old and New Testament saints present to us a people "chosen in the furnace of affliction." Paul inquires, "What son is there whom the Father chastens not?" He seems to throw out a challenge—"Where is the exception to this principle of the Divine procedure? Where is the child taken into God's family, where is the adopted son, who has never felt the smartings of the rod—whom the Father chastens not?" More than this. Let it not be supposed that the feeblest of God's saints—those who have the least measure of grace and strength, who find the ascent difficult, and whose advance is slow and tardy—are those whom the Lord most frequently and sharply afflicts. Oh no! In looking into the word of truth—in reading the memoirs of God's ancient saints, it will be found that those whom He blessed most, who were the most distinguished for some eminent grace of the Spirit, some mighty exploit of faith, some great act of devotedness, were those whom He most deeply afflicted. "The branch that bears fruit, He purges it, that it may bring forth more fruit." Let the histories of Abraham, Jacob, Moses, Job, and David testify. Let Paul's thorn in the flesh speak. And what is the testimony?—that the most eminent of God's saints are the most afflicted. Their eminence grew out of their afflictions. Like their blessed Lord, they were perfected through suffering. They became thus strong in faith, holy in life, close in their walk, devoted in the service of their Master, by the very discipline through which they passed. They were eminently holy, because eminently tried.

AUGUST 31

"What man of you, having an hundred sheep, if he lose one of them, does not leave the ninety and nine in the wilderness, and go after that which is lost, until he find it? And when he has found it, he lays it on his shoulders, rejoicing." Luke 15:4, 5

Here is the gentleness of the shepherd—"he lays it on his shoulders." Too feeble itself to walk, too exhausted in its wanderings to return, the gentle shepherd, having sought and found it, "lays it on his shoulders, rejoicing." Touching picture of the Savior's gentleness in restoring a backsliding soul! What but infinite gentleness is seen in the restoring of Peter? It was but a look—not a word fell from the lips of the Savior—not an unkind rebuke, not a harsh upbraiding word did He breathe; yet that look so full of love, so full of gentleness, so full of forgiveness, did seem to say, "I am going to die for you, Peter: all this and more I suffer for you; will you, can you, deny me?" That look, so touching, so melting, so eloquent, and so forgiving, reached the heart of the backsliding apostle, melted it, broke it, and sent him from the judgment-hall weeping bitterly. There was no expression in the look which Jesus bent upon Peter, but love. Let this truth be fixed in the heart of every backsliding believer. The Lord restores the soul gently. The moment He discovers to it its sin, He conveys some token of His pardoning mercy; the balm is applied the moment the wound is given; the remedy is at hand the moment the distemper is discovered. There is a tenderness, an unutterable tenderness, in the heart and hand, in the mercy and the method of the Lord's recovery of His child, which only He can feel. See it in the case of David. How did God bring his sin to remembrance? By the chastising rod? by heavy judgment? by severe expressions of displeasure? No; none of these were His messengers: but He sent a kind, tender, faithful prophet to discover to him his awful backsliding; and the astounding words, "You are the man," had scarcely died away upon his ear, before he pours in this healing balm, "The Lord also has put away your sin, you shall not die." Oh, what gentleness, what tenderness, are thus shown in the Lord's restorings of His wandering child! From whom could this have been expected but from Him whose nature and whose name is love—from whom, but Him who could thus speak to His backsliding Ephraim—"Is Ephraim my dear son? is he a pleasant child? for since I spoke against him, I do earnestly remember him still; therefore my affections are troubled for him: I will surely have mercy upon him, says the Lord." This is an outgushing of tenderness towards a poor, returning, backsliding soul, which could only have had its dwelling-place in the heart of Jehovah.

All real return of a backsliding soul is through Jesus. Jesus is God's great door of approach to His throne. No other entrance will conduct us to the golden scepter; no other will bring us to the holy of holies. Thus has the Holy Spirit unfolded this truth—"Having therefore, brethren, boldness to enter into the holiest by the blood of Jesus, by a new and living way, which He has consecrated for us, through the veil, that is to say, His flesh; and having an High Priest over the house of God; let us draw near." Oh blessed door of return for a poor, backsliding, heart-broken believer!—a crucified Savior, in whom God is well pleased, and for whose sake He can receive the sinner, and put away his sin, can welcome the backslider, and heal his backsliding.

SEPTEMBER

SEPTEMBER 1

"And the angel of the Lord appeared unto him in a flame of fire out of the midst of a bush: and he looked, and, behold, the bush burned with fire, and the bush was not consumed. And Moses said, I will now turn aside, and see this great sight, why the bush is not burned. And when the Lord saw that he turned aside to see, God called unto him out of the midst of the bush, and said, Moses, Moses. And he said, Here am I. And he said, Draw not near here: put off your shoes from of your feet, for the place whereon you stands is holy ground. Moreover he said, I am the God of your father, the God of Abraham, the God of Isaac, and the God of Jacob. And Moses hid his face; for he was afraid to look upon God." Exodus 3:2-6

This type—a type it doubtless is—is radiant with the glory of Christ. It shadows forth Christ in the mysterious constitution of His complex person, and in the great work for the accomplishment of which he became so constituted.

The first point demanding our attention is the Divine manifestation. That Jehovah was here revealed, the evidence is most conclusive. When Moses turned aside to see the great sight, "God called unto him out of the midst of the bush." It was no mere vision that he saw, no hallucination of the mind had come over him; he could not be deceived as to the Divine Being in whose immediate and solemn presence he then stood. How awe-struck must have been his mind! how solemn his impressions! how sacred his thoughts! But if further proof were needed, the declaration of God Himself sets the question of the Divine appearance at rest—"I am the God of your father, the God of Abraham, the God of Isaac, and the God of Jacob." No truth could be more clearly established.

But in which person of the sacred and adorable Three, it may be asked, did God thus appear? We have every scriptural reason to believe that it was JEHOVAH-JESUS; that it was a manifestation anticipative of His future appearance in the flesh, of the Godhead of Christ. Thus, then, the type sets forth the glory of the Divine person of our dear Lord. How solemn, and yet how delightful to the mind, and establishing to our faith, is the truth, that the same God who under the old dispensation, on so many occasions, in so many gracious and glorious ways, and in so many remarkable and undoubted instances, appeared to the ancient believers, is He who was born in Bethlehem, who lived a life of obedience to the law, and died an atoning death upon the cross; the Savior, the Surety of His people! What reality does it give to the salvation of the saints! Beloved, remember at all times, the same Jehovah who spoke from the midst of the flaming bush, and said, "I am the God of Abraham, the God of Isaac, and the God of Jacob," speaks to you from the cross and in the Gospel, and says, "Come unto me, all you that labor and are heavy-laden, and I will give you rest." Oh "glorious Gospel of the blessed God!"

The second point of consideration in this remarkable type, as setting forth the glory of Immanuel, is the symbol in which He appeared. It is full of instruction. And what symbol did our Lord select in which to embody His Deity? Did He choose some tall cedar of Lebanon, or some majestic oak of the forest? No; but a bush—the most mean and insignificant, the most lowly and unsightly of all trees—was to enshrine the Godhead of Him whom the heaven of heavens cannot contain. And what is the truth it conveys? Oh, most glorious and precious. It points to the incarnate glory of the Son of God—the lowliness and lowliness of His nature. Referring again to the type, it will instantly appear that the unveiled, unclouded, and unembodied glory of Jehovah would have appalled and overwhelmed with its ineffable brightness the awe-stricken and astonished man of God. He could not have looked upon God and lived. "There shall no man see me and live," says the Lord. It was therefore proper, yes, it was merciful that all the manifestations of God to His people in the old dispensation should be through the medium of objects on which the eye could look without pain, and on which the mind could repose with out fear. Veiled in a cloud, or embodied in a bush, God could approach the creature with condescending grace, and reveal His mind; the creature could approach God with humble confidence, and open his heart. How kind and condescending in Jehovah to subdue and soften the splendor of His majesty, thus attempting it to the weak vision of mortal and sinful man!

But this was typical of that more wondrous and stupendous stoop of God in the new dispensation. All the subdued and obscure manifestations of the Godhead in the former economy were but the forecasting shadows of the great mystery of godliness then approaching; and possessed no glory, by reason of the glory that excels. But mark the condescending grace, the deep abasement, the infinite lowliness of the Son of God. When He purposed to appear in an inferior nature, what form of manifestation did He assume? Did He embody His Godhead in some tall archangel? Did He enshrine it in some glowing seraph? No! "For verily He took not on Him the nature of angels; but He took on Him the seed of Abraham." He lowered Himself to our mean and degraded nature—He selected our fallen, suffering, sorrowing, tempted humanity—He takes into union with Deity a creature, not of the highest rank and beauty, but a spirit dwelling in a temple of flesh; yes, not merely the inhabitant of the temple, but He unites Himself with the temple itself: for the "Word was made flesh, and dwelt among us;" and even this flesh not connected with its state of primeval glory, but associated with all the humbling, though sinless, infirmities of its fallen condition. Behold, too, the lowliness of Christ in the world's eye. In Him it sees no glory, and traces no beauty; His outward form of humiliation veils it from their view. He is to them but as a "root out of the dry ground, having no form nor loveliness."

SEPTEMBER 2

"And the angel of the Lord appeared unto him in a flame of fire out of the midst of a bush: and he looked, and, behold, the bush burned with fire, and the bush was not consumed." Exodus 3:2

There is yet another part of this significant type to be considered, equally important and rich in the view it conveys of the glory of Jesus in His work. "And he looked, and, behold, the bush burned with fire, and the bush was not consumed." The symbol of fire was expressive of the holiness and justice of God. It is thus frequently employed—"The Lord your God is a consuming fire." "And the sight of the glory of the Lord was like devouring fire." "Our God is a consuming fire." But that which formed the greatest wonder,—which riveted the eye, and attracted and enchained the feet of Moses to the spot, was the bush unconsumed. "And Moses said, I will NOW TURN aside, and see this great sight, why the bush is not burned."

But a more marvelous and stupendous spectacle meets us in the cross of Christ—Jesus enduring the fire of His Father's wrath; wrapped in the flame of His justice, and yet unconsumed! Let us turn aside from all inferior objects, and for a while contemplate this "great sight." It is indeed a great sight! The Son of God is bound upon the altar as a "burned-offering"—a sacrifice for sin. The fire of Divine justice descends to consume Him; holiness in fearful exercise heaps on its fuel, and the flame and the smoke ascend in one vast column before the throne of the Eternal, "an offering and a sacrifice to God for a sweet-smelling savor." But behold the astonishment! Jesus suffering, and yet rejoicing! dying, and yet living! consuming, and yet unconsumed! These prodigies marked the offering up of our great High Priest upon Calvary. The dark billows of sorrow rolled over the human soul of Christ, but the Godhead remained calm and peaceful, its tranquility unruffled by a wave of grief, its sunshine undimmed by a cloud of darkness. He thus passed through all these throbs, and throes, and agonies of death, descended into the grave, rose again, lived, and still lives, the Fountain of life to the created universe. Behold the GOD! Say you, He is a mere creature? Preposterous thought! Mad conception! Soul-destructive belief! Had He been less than Divine, suffering as He did for sin, the devouring fire would have consumed Him in its quenchless flame.

To a heart-broken sinner, how attractive and glorious is this spectacle of an almighty Redeemer, sustaining the wrath, and suffering the justice of God for transgression! Mourning soul! turn aside, and behold yet again this "great sight." "Put off your shoes from off your feet, for the place whereon you stands is holy ground." Lay aside your fleshly reasoning, your carnal views of self-justification, self-salvation, and human power. Put off all your fleshly ideas of God, of His grace, and of His goodness; divest yourself of all your unbelieving and hard thoughts of His power, willingness, and readiness to save you. Thus prepared, approach—gaze—wonder—and adore! No one can stand on this holy ground, but he who stands on his own nothingness; none are welcome here but the poor, the empty, the bankrupt, and the vile. Are you all this? is this your case? Then draw near! God will speak from amid the flame of the sacrifice, and say to you, "Fear not!"

Dear tried and suffering reader, do you resemble this burning bush? Are you in the fire, passing through the furnace? Does some strong temptation assail you—some sore trial oppress you—some deep sorrow wound you? He who dwelt in the bush, dwells in you! and He who kept the bush unconsumed amid the flame, will keep you! Let your greatest care and deepest solicitude be to "glorify God in the fires." Be more prayerful for sustaining and sanctifying grace, than for the removal of your trial. This will bring richer glory to God. Beseech your Father that the flame may not be extinguished until the alloy is consumed, and the tried gold has come forth reflecting more vividly from its surface the image of Jesus—your soul partaking more deeply of the Divine HOLINESS.

SEPTEMBER 3

"Behold the Lamb of God." John 1:36

In the deep study of the holiness of the law, and the strictness of Divine justice, what a suitable and glorious object for the alarmed and trembling spirit to look upon, is He who came to honor that law, and to satisfy that justice! Are you agitated by thoughts of the Divine holiness, and your own impurity?

Do you tremble as you contemplate God's determination to punish sin, by no means clearing the guilty? Look unto Jesus, and let your trembling subside into the calmness with which His whisper stills the tempest. He has become "the end of the law for righteousness, to every one that believes." His atonement, while it vindicates the majesty of the Father's government, spreads its mighty shield around the Father's child, and thus protected, neither the thunder of the law nor the flaming sword of justice can reach him. Oh! the blessedness of looking, by faith, to Jesus, from the wrath and the condemnation justly due to our transgressions; to see all that wrath and condemnation borne by Him who wept and bled in the garden, who languished and died upon the tree; to see Jesus, with the keys of all authority and power suspended from His girdle, closing up our hell, and opening wide our heaven. In the season of solitude and sorrow, Christian reader, when thoughts of God's holiness mingle with views of your sinfulness, and fears of Divine wrath blend with the consciousness of your just deserts, darkening that solitude, and embittering that sorrow, oh! turn and fix your believing eye upon the Divine, the suffering, the atoning Savior, and peace, composure, and joy will lull your trembling spirit to rest. You are not sick, nor in solitude, nor in sorrow, because there is wrath in God; for all that wrath was borne by your redeeming Surety. You are so—oh, that you could believe it!—because God is love. It must be, since Jesus so bore away the curse and the sin, that God now brims the cup He emptied with a love that passes knowledge. "My son, despise not the chastening of the Lord, neither be you weary of His correction: for whom the Lord loves He corrects, even as a father the son in whom he delights.

In every position of life, our privilege is to look unto Jesus. God can place us in no circumstances, be they humble or exalted, in which we may not repair to Christ for the wisdom and the strength, the grace and the consolation, those circumstances demand. It is our mercy to know that God adapts Himself to every position of His saints. He knows that in times of prosperity, the feet of His saints are apt to slide; and that in times of adversity, they are often pierced and wounded. Thus, in the smooth path, as in the rough, Jesus is to be the one object to which the eye is raised, and upon which it rests. If He exalts you, as He may do, to any post of distinction and responsibility, look unto Jesus, and study the self-annihilation and lowliness of His whole life. If He lays you low, as in His dealings with His people He often does, from the depth of your humiliation let your eye look unto Jesus, who reached a depth in His abasement infinitely beneath your own; and who can descend to your circumstances, and impart the grace that will enable you so to adapt yourself to them as to glorify Him in them. Thus you will know both how to abound, and how to suffer need.

In each season of affliction, to whom can we more appropriately look than to Jesus? He was preeminently the man of sorrows and acquainted with grief. If you would tell your grief to one who knew grief as none ever knew it—if you would disclose your sorrow to one who sorrowed as none ever sorrowed—then in your affliction turn from all creature sympathy and support, and look to Jesus: to a tenderer bosom, to a deeper love, to a more powerful arm, to a more sympathizing friend, you could not take your trial, your affliction, your sorrow. He is prepared to embosom Himself in your deepest grief, and to make your circumstances all His own. So completely and personally is He one with you, that nothing can affect you that does not instantly touch Him. Tender to Him are you as the apple of His eye. Your happiness, your reputation, your labors, your necessities, your discouragements, your despondencies, all pass beneath His unslumbering notice, and are the objects of His tenderest love and incessant care. If Jesus, then, is willing to come and make, as it were, His home in the very heart of your sorrow, surely you will not hesitate in repairing with your sorrow to His heart of love.

SEPTEMBER 4

"But none says, Where is God my Maker, who give songs in the night?" Job 35:10

Who but God could give songs in the night? No saint on earth, no angel in heaven, has power to tune our hearts to a single note of praise in the hour of their grief; no, nor could any creature above or below breathe a word of comfort, of hope, or of support, when heart and flesh were failing. Who but the incarnate God has power enough, or love enough, or sympathy enough, to come and embosom Himself in our very circumstances—to enter into the very heart of our sorrow—to go down into the deepest depth of our woe, and strike a chord there that, responding to His touch, shall send forth a more than angel's music? It is God who gives these songs. He is acquainted with your sorrows: He regards your night of weeping: He knows the way that you take. He may be lost to your view, but you cannot be lost to His. The darkness of your night-grief may veil Him from your eye, but the "darkness and the light are both alike to Him." Then repair to Him for your song. Ask Him so to sanctify your sorrow by His grace, and so to comfort it by His Spirit, and so to glorify Himself in your patient endurance of it, and so to make you to know the why of your trial, and your trial so to answer the mission on which it was sent, as will enable you to raise this note of praise—"You have turned for me my mourning into dancing: You have put off my sackcloth, and girded me with gladness; to the end that my glory may sing praise to You, and not be silent."

In giving you a throne of grace, God has given you a song, methinks, one of the sweetest ever sung in the house of our pilgrimage. To feel that we have a God who hears and answers prayer—who has done so in countless instances, and is prepared still to give us at all times an audience—oh! the unutterable blessings of this truth. Sing aloud then, you sorrowful saints; for great and precious is your privilege of communion with God. In the night of your every grief, and trial, and difficulty, do not forget that in your lowest frame you may sing this song—"Having boldness to enter into the holiest by the blood of Jesus, by a new and living way, I will draw near, and pour out my heart to God." Chant, then, His high praises as you pass along, that there is a place where you may disclose every need, repose every sorrow, deposit every burden, breathe every sigh, and lose yourself in communion with God—that place is the blood-besprinkled mercy-seat, of which God says, "There will I meet with you, and I will commune with you."

Ah! but perhaps you exclaim, "Would that I could sing! I can weep, and moan, and even trust, but I cannot rejoice." Yes, but there is One who can give even you, beloved, a song in the night. Place your harp in His hands, all broken and unstrung as it is, and He will repair and retune it; and then, breathing upon it His Spirit, and touching it with His own gentle hand, that heart, that was so sad and joyless, shall yet sing the high praises of its God. How much of God's greatness and glory in nature is concealed until the night reveals it! The sun is withdrawn, twilight disappears, and darkness robes the earth. Then appears the brilliant firmament, studded and glowing with myriads of constellations. Oh the indescribable wonder, the surpassing glory, of that scene! But it was the darkness that brought it all to view; thus is it in the Christian's life. How much of God would be unseen, how much of His glory concealed, how little should we know of Jesus, but for the night-season of mental darkness and of heart-sorrow. The sun that shone so cheeringly has set; the grey twilight that looked so pensively has disappeared; and just as the night of woe set in, filling you with trembling, with anxiety, and with fear, a scene of overpowering grandeur suddenly bursts upon the astonished eye of your faith. The glory of God, as your Father, has appeared—the character of

Jesus, as a loving tender Brother, has unfolded—the Spirit, as a Comforter, has whispered—your interest in the great redemption has been revealed—and a new earth redolent with a thousand sweets, and a new heaven resplendent with countless suns, has floated before your view. It was the darkness of your night of sorrow that made visible all this wonder and all this glory; and but for that sorrow how little would you have known of it. "I will sing of mercy and of judgment: unto You, O Lord, will I sing."

Suffering, sorrowful believer! pluck your harp from your willow, and, with the hand of faith and love, sweep it to the high praises of your God. Praise Him for Himself—praise Him for Jesus—praise Him for conversion—praise Him for joys—praise Him for sorrows—praise Him for chastenings—praise Him for the hope of glory—oh praise Him for all! Thus singing the Lord's song in a strange land, you will be learning to sing it in diviner sounds—

"With those just spirits that wear victorious palms,
Hymns devout, and holy psalms
Singing everlastingly."

"And they sing the song of Moses, the servant of God, and the song of the Lamb, saying, Great and marvelous are Your works, Lord God almighty; just and true are Your ways, O King of saints. Who shall not fear You, O Lord, and glorify Your name? for You only are holy: for all nations shall come and worship before You."

SEPTEMBER 5

"These things said Elijah, when he saw his glory, and spoke of him." John 12:41

It will be observed, that John affirms of Isaiah that he saw the glory of Christ. The glory of the Redeemer has ever been an object visible to the spiritual eye. What the evangelist here records of the prophet, he also avows of himself and his fellow-disciples. "And the Word was made flesh, and dwelt among us, and we beheld His glory." Here is a point of vital moment, entering deeply into the very soul of experimental Christianity. May the Spirit of all truth give us a clear and solemn perception of it! If a man sees not the glory of Christ, we hesitate not to say of him, that with regard to all other spiritual objects he is totally blind—he is yet a stranger to the illuminating grace of the Holy Spirit. To see the Redeemer's glory, the eye must be spiritual; a spiritual object being only discerned by a spiritual organ. Hence the apostle prays in behalf of the

Ephesian Christians, "That the God of our Lord Jesus Christ, the Father of glory, may give unto you the Spirit of wisdom and revelation in the knowledge of Him: that the eyes of your understanding being enlightened." And enlightened by the Spirit of God, the believer beholds the glory of Jesus. Brought to see no glory in himself, yes, nothing but deformity in that on which the eye once so complacently rested, the glory of the Redeemer, as it is reflected in His person, in His atoning blood and justifying righteousness, His infinite fullness of grace to pardon and to sanctify, fills now the entire scope of his moral vision, and lifts his soul in admiring and adoring thoughts of the holiness and love of God!

More than this, such is its transforming influence, he comes to be a partaker, in a degree, of that very glory which has arrested his eye and ravished his heart. On him the glory of the Lord has shone, the Sun of Righteousness has risen—he rises from the dust, and shines arrayed in garments of light from Christ's reflecting light. A sight of Jesus assimilates the soul to His Spirit; a contemplation of His beauty transforms the believer more and more into "the child of the light;" and thus perpetually "looking unto Jesus," the path he treads kindles and glows with an increasing effulgence, until its luster expands into perfect cloudless day. "We all, with open face beholding as in a glass the glory of the Lord, are changed into the same image, from glory to glory, even as by the Spirit of the Lord." The medium through which the spiritual eye beholds the glory of Christ is faith. It is a hidden glory until the Eternal Spirit imparts this mighty principle to the soul. The eye of reason cannot discern it—the eye of intellect and of sense cannot behold it—it remains a veiled thing, "dark with excessive brightness," until God the Holy Spirit utters His voice, "Let there be light." "Abraham," says Christ, "rejoiced to see my day; and he saw it, and was glad." At that remote period, how did he see it?—by faith. Through the long and dreary vista of advancing ages he saw the day dawning, the sun rising. By faith he beheld Jesus approaching. He saw His blood, His righteousness, and His own interest there, "and he was glad." Oh yes, a sight of Jesus by faith—be it distant and dim, be it shadowy and imperfect—fills the soul with ineffable gladness, lights up its onward way, sweetens its solitude, enlivens its loneliness, and soothes it amid its deepest sorrows.

Isaiah not only beheld the glory of Christ, but he also "spoke of it." He could not but speak of that which he saw and felt. And who can behold the glory of the Redeemer, and not speak of it? Who can see His beauty, and not extol it—who can taste His love, and not laud it? "Come," will be the invitation, "see a man who told me all things that ever I did: is not this the Christ?" The church of old, as her eye wandered over the beauties of her Lord, broke forth in expressions of wonder and praise; and, after particularizing and extolling these beauties, she then exclaims, as if all language were exhausted, "Yes, He is altogether lovely. This is my beloved, and this is my friend." "In His temple does every one speak of His glory." Yes, the saints of the Most High must speak of the King in His beauty. They are constrained to show forth His praise, and tell of His love and loveliness, who is to them more precious than the gold of Ophir; yes, dearer than life itself. The Pharisee may murmur, the worldling may scorn, and the cold-hearted professor may rebuke; yet, "if these should hold their peace," who have been redeemed by His most precious blood, and who are looking forward to His second appearing, as an event which shall conform them to His likeness, "the stones would immediately cry out."

SEPTEMBER 6

"And, having made peace through the blood of his cross, by him to reconcile all things unto himself; by him, I say, whether they be things in earth, or things in heaven. And you, that were once alienated and enemies in your mind by wicked works, yet now has he reconciled." Colossians 1:20, 21

Only trust the salvation of Christ—He would have us commence with what He has constituted the central truth of the gospel—the cross. God has made it the focus of His glory—for around no object do such wonders and glories gather as the cross of Christ—and He would have us make it the central fact of our faith. What a sure ground of trust for a poor sinner is here—the great and complete salvation of the Lord Jesus! Here God Himself rests; for He has confided all His glory to Christ, whom "He has made strong for Himself." And surely if the work of Jesus were sufficient to uphold the moral government and secure the eternal honor of God, there need be no demur, no hesitation on the part of the sinner, there to place his entire trust for forgiveness and acceptance. Sinner as you are, here is a salvation worthy of your confidence. "Christ died for the ungodly." "He was wounded for our transgressions, He was bruised for our iniquities." "Through His blood we have redemption, even the forgiveness of our sins." "By Him all that believe are justified." The great debt of Divine justice Christ has paid. His resurrection from the dead by the glory of the Father is His complete discharge, and now, "whoever will, may come and drink of the water of life freely." To each guilt-stricken, heart-broken, sorrow-burdened, weary sinner Jesus says, "Only trust me." Beloved reader, no partial trust must this be. Your foothold on every other foundation must give way—your grasp upon every other support must loosen—your clinging to duties, to works, to self, in every form, must yield—and your whole, implicit, sole trust for salvation must be in the one atonement which God has provided, in the one salvation which Christ has finished, in the only name given under heaven whereby we must be saved. "Neither is there salvation in any other: for there is none other name under heaven given among men, whereby we must be saved."

Never was there before—nor has there been since—nor ever will be again—such ancient, marvelous, stupendous love as the love of Jesus. It is the astonishment of heaven, it is the wonder of angels, and, in their best, holiest, and most self-abased moments, it is the marvel of saints on earth, and will be, through eternity, their study and their praise. His condescending stoop to our nature—His descent from heaven's glory to earth's lowliness—His bearing our sins—His endurance of our curse—His suffering our penalty—His exhaustion of our bitter cup—His resurrection from the grave, and His ascent into heaven, are facts which speak, louder and sweeter than an angel's trumpet, the love of Christ to His church. "Husbands, love your wives, even as Christ also loved the church, and gave Himself for it." But not only was Jesus the unveiler of His own heart, but He came to unveil the heart of God. He came, not to inspire the heart of God with an affection for man, but to make known a love already and from eternity existing. He, who only knew the secret love of God's heart, came to reveal that love, its only revealer, and its most precious gift. Christ is God's love embodied—God's love speaking, God's love acting, God's love weeping, God's love dying, God's love inviting. Blessed truth, that he whose arms of faith embrace Christ, in and through Christ also embrace the Triune Jehovah. The Lord Jesus would have us trust His love when it wears the disguise of displeasure—when, changing its appearance and its tones, it looks and speaks threatening and unkind. What a harsh disguise did Joseph wear to his brethren; and yet beneath it there never heat a more loving, tender, or kinder heart than his. Such is our Jesus—the Brother who has saved us from famine and from death, and has done for us more than Joseph did for his brethren—has died for us. Let us trust this love. Trust it when veiled—trust it when it threatens to slay—trust it when it appears to frown—trust it when even we cannot trace it; still, oh, still let us trust in Jesus' love, when, to our dim sight, it would seem never to smile or speak to us again. The time may come, or the circumstances may arise, that shall put to the utmost test our confidence in the Savior's love. When it shall say to us, "Can you make this sacrifice—can you bear this cross for me?" oh, blessed if your heart can reply, "Lord, relying upon Your grace, trusting in Your love, I can—I will—I do!"

SEPTEMBER 7

"Holding faith, and a good conscience, which some having put away, concerning faith have made shipwreck." 1 Timothy 1:19

Faith is an essential part of the spiritual armor: "Above all, taking the shield of faith, with which you shall be able to quench the fiery darts of the wicked." Faith is also spoken of as the believer's breastplate: "But let us, who are of the day, be sober, putting on the breastplate of faith." There is not a moment, even the holiest, but we are exposed to the "fiery darts" of the adversary. The onset, too, is often at a moment when we least suspect its approach; seasons of peculiar nearness to God, of hallowed enjoyment—"for we wrestle not against flesh and blood, but against principalities, against powers, against the rulers of the darkness of this world, against spiritual wickedness in high places"—are frequently selected as the occasion of attack. But, clad in this armor—the shield and the breastplate of faith—no weapon formed against us shall prosper; no "fiery dart" shall be quenched, and the enemy shall be put to flight. Faith in a crucified, risen, conquering, exalted Savior—faith in a present and ever-living Head—faith eyeing the crown glittering, and the palm waving in its view, is the faith that overcomes and triumphs. Faith, dealing constantly and simply with Jesus, flying to His atoning blood, drawing from His fullness, and at all times and under all circumstances looking unto Him, will ever bring a conflicting soul off more than conqueror. "This is the victory that overcomes the world, even our faith. Who is He that overcomes the world, but he that believes that Jesus is the Son of God?"

Faith is a purifying grace: "Purifying their hearts by faith." It is a principle holy in its nature and tendency: he is most holy who has most faith; he who has least faith is most exposed to the assaults of his inbred corruptions. If there is in any child of God a desire for Divine conformity, for more of the Spirit of Christ, more weanedness, and crucifixion, and daily dying, this should be his ceaseless prayer—"Lord, increase my faith." Faith in Jesus checks the power of sin, slays the hidden corruption, and enables the believer to "endure as seeing Him who is invisible."

Nothing, perhaps, more secretly and effectually militates against the vigor of a life of faith, than the power of unsubdued sin in the heart. Faith, as we have just seen, is a holy indwelling principle; it has its root in the renewed, sanctified heart; and its growth and fruitfulness depend much upon the progressive richness of the soil in which it is embedded: if the noxious weeds of the natural soil are allowed to grow and occupy the heart, and gain the ascendancy, this celestial plant will necessarily droop and decay. In order to form some conception of the utter incongruity of a life of faith with the existence and power of unmortified sin in the heart, we have but to imagine the case of a believer living in the practice of unsubdued sin. What is the real power of faith in him? where is its strength? where are its glorious achievements? We look for the fruit of faith—the lowly, humble, contrite spirit—the tender conscience—the traveling daily to the atoning blood—the living upon the grace that is in Christ Jesus—the carrying out of Christian principle—crucifixion to the world—patient submission to a life of suffering—meek resignation to a Father's discipline—a constant and vivid realization of eternal realities—we look for these fruits of faith, but we find them not. And why? Because there is the worm of unmortified sin feeding at the root; and, until that is slain, faith will always be sickly, unfruitful, and "ready to die."

A looking off of Christ will tend greatly to the weakening and unfruitfulness of faith. It is said, that the eaglet's eye becomes strong through the early discipline of the parent; placed in such a position when young, as to fix the gaze intently upon the sun, the power of vision gradually becomes so great, as to enable it in time to look at its meridian splendor without uneasiness, and to observe the remotest object without difficulty. The same spiritual discipline strengthens the eye of faith; the eye grows vigorous by looking much at the Sun of Righteousness. The more constantly it gazes upon Jesus, the stronger it grows; and the stronger it grows, the more glory it discovers in Him, the more beauty in His person, and perfection in His work. Thus strengthened, it can see things that are afar off—the promises of a covenant-keeping God, the hope of eternal life, the crown of glory; these it can look upon and almost touch. "Faith is the substance of things hoped for, the evidence of things not seen." O precious, costly grace of the Eternal Spirit! who would not possess you? who would not mortify everything that would wound, enfeeble, and cause you to decay in the soul?

SEPTEMBER 8

"And our hope of you is steadfast, knowing, that as you are partakers of the sufferings, so shall you be also of the consolation." 2 Corinthians 1:7

Affliction and poverty are the distinctive features of the saints of God under the new dispensation; affluence and exemption from great suffering were probably those of the saints of the former economy. The character of the gospel economy is unique. It is the dispensation of suffering, the economy of the cross. The suffering of the old dispensation was more in type, and shadow, and symbol; that of the new is the great, the dark filling-up of the outline of the picture. The Son of God suffered—the Son of God died! And Christianity derives all its efficacy, and the Christian dispensation all its character, and the Christian all his glory, from this single, this wondrous fact.

Tracing affliction and suffering, whatever its nature, to God as the first great Cause, faith calmly acquiesces and says, "It is well." From nothing does the believer find it more difficult to disengage his mind, in the first blow of his affliction, than second causes. The reasoning of the bereaved sisters of Bethany finds its corresponding frame of mind in almost every similar case. "Lord, if you had been here, my brother had not died!" But with second causes the child of God has nothing to do. Second causes are all by the appointment and under the control of the First Cause. They are but the agents God employs, the means which He selects, to accomplish His own eternal purpose. "He Himself has done it," is the voice of His word, and faith responds, "It is well." Rise, then, above the circumstances of your calamity, and rest in the Lord, from whom your affliction proceeds.

Child of adversity! can you say, "It is well," now that God may have taken from you health, friends, riches, earthly comforts, and creature supports? It must be well, since providence and not accident, God Himself has done it. But weep not, do not be cast down, all is not gone. God is still your God and Father, Christ is still your Friend and Brother, the Spirit is still your Comforter and Guide, the covenant is still your inexhaustible supply, the promises are still left you, and all these losses and trials are working together for your good. God will not leave you in this time of adversity. In Him let your faith be filial, implicit, unwavering. If you honor Him, by trusting Him now, He will honor your trust by and by. Give yourself to prayer, you will find it a sweet outlet to your full and burdened heart; all will yet be well. Stand still, and let God solve His own deep problems; and you will then see how much infinite love, and wisdom, and faithfulness, and goodness was enfolded in this dark, distressing calamity.

Sick one! "it is well." Is it true—can it be? you doubtfully inquire. Yes, it is, and must be so, since He who loves you has permitted, no, has sent this sickness. His wisdom cannot err, His love cannot be unkind. God's ways are not as our ways, nor His thoughts as our thoughts. He works His purposes of mercy and love towards us in a way often directly opposite to all our reasoning and plans. This sickness may appear to you a heavy calamity; the result may prove an untold blessing. Sanctified by the Spirit's grace, that bed of suffering, that couch of weakness, those wearisome days, and long sleepless nights, shall teach you truth, and realize to you promises, and bring your soul so near to God, and so endear the Savior to your heart, as shall constrain you to exclaim, "Lord, it is well!" "Commune with your own heart upon your bed, and be still." "Let patience have her perfect work, lacking nothing." And suppose this should be unto death—will not that be well? What! not to be released from a body of infirmity and sin? Not to go home, and take possession of your glorious inheritance! Not to go and see Christ in His glory, and be reunited to those who have gone before, and mingle with prophets, and apostles, and martyrs, and be as they are—perfected in holiness and love? Oh, yes! it will be far better to depart and be with Christ, if He sees fit. Tremble not to cross the flood. Our true Joshua has paved the path with precious stones—the doctrines, truths, and promises of His word—upon which your faith may plant its feet, and so to pass over dry-shod into the heavenly Canaan. The bitterness of death is passed, to all who believe in Jesus.

Saints of the Most High! over these broken waters of a sinful, sorrowful, toilsome life we shall soon have passed, and standing upon the "sea of glass," with the harp of God in our hand, there shall be reflected from its tranquil bosom the glory, and there shall breathe from every string the praise, of our God in having done all things well. Oh, what harmony shall we then see in every discrepancy, what pardon, what tenderness, and love, and gentleness, and forethought in every stroke of His hand, and in every event of His providence! The mystery of God will be finished, and God will be all in all.

SEPTEMBER 9

"Having loved his own which were in the world, he loved them unto the end." John 13:1

Dear reader, ever trust in the sympathy of Christ. The blessing of creature-sympathy we would not undervalue. The word of God does not. The Scriptures of truth enjoin and encourage it; yes, command it. "Look not every man on his own things, but every man also on the things of others." "If one member suffer, all the members suffer with it." We believe it to be no small evidence of grace, and to assimilate in no little degree with the mind that was also in Christ Jesus, to "weep with those that weep." And yet so enamored of it may we be, so look and cling to it, as to be insensible to the higher, purer, deeper sympathy of Christ. The power of human sympathy—like everything created—must necessarily be limited. A Christian brother or sister has so much personal trial, anxiety, and pressure of his own, the marvel is that a single chord of a heart, all whose strings are stretched to such tension on its own account, can emit a solitary note of real sympathy with our grief. Let us, then, be thankful to God for the smallest measure of true human sympathy. But there is no limit, no fathom, to the sympathy of Jesus. It is real, human, most tender, boundless, fathomless. It enters into all our sorrows, and, with a penetration and delicacy indescribable, it insinuates itself into all the shades and peculiarities of our sorrow. It even enters into our infirmities. Infirmities into which others cannot enter, and still more, with which we can ill bear ourselves, Jesus sympathizes with. Infirmities of temperament—infirmities of constitution—infirmities of habit—infirmities of education—infirmities of position—bodily, mental, and spiritual infirmities—there is One who enters deeply into all! He has borne them all—bears them still. Commiserating the feebleness of our nature—for it is still the robe He wears in heaven—He patiently bears with us, tenderly deals with us, and gently soothes, supports, and sustains us. "For we have not a High Priest which cannot be touched with the feeling of our infirmities; but was in all points tempted like as we are, yet without sin. Let us, therefore, come boldly unto the throne of grace, that we may obtain mercy, and find grace to help in time of need." In this sympathy Jesus would have us confide. And if upon your opening path there falls the forecasting shadow of some approaching sorrow—if the sky is lowering, and the surge is swelling—meet it by a renewed appeal to the anticipated compassion and intercession of Christ. JESUS!—what a plenitude of sympathy, tenderness, and grace is in that name! Run into it, and you shall be safe from the coming storm. And when the darkling sorrow comes—the rose-hue of health paling—blossoms falling—flowers withering—hope expiring—fame, fortune, friends, like the orient tints of evening, fading one by one away, remember that in JESUS you have a Brother born for your adversity, a Friend who loved you in eternity—loved you on the cross—loves you on the throne—and will love you unto the end. He will make the cloud His chariot—will walk upon your stormy waters—and will say, "Peace, be still!"

SEPTEMBER 10

"Go and proclaim these words toward the north, and say, Return, you backsliding Israel, says the Lord; and I will not cause mine anger to fall upon you; for I am merciful, says the Lord, and I will not keep anger forever." Jeremiah 3:12

Where is the heart, deeply conscious of its backsliding, that can resist the power of language like this? Here is the warrant for your return—God's own free invitation! You need no more. What if Satan discourages, what if your sins plead against you, what if guilt, and unbelief, and shame combine to impede your way, if God says, "Return!"—that is sufficient for you. You need no more; if He is willing to receive you back, to pardon your sins, to forget your base ingratitude, to heal your backslidings, and restore your soul, you have the broad warrant to return, in the face of all opposition and discouragement. Yet again, the cheering invitation runs—"Only acknowledge your iniquity that you have transgressed against the Lord your God." "Turn, O backsliding children, says the Lord, for I am married unto you." "I will heal their backsliding, I will love them freely; for mine anger is turned away from him."

The character of God is such as encourages the return of a backsliding soul. In the invitations He has given, He urges them upon the ground of what He is: "Return, you backsliding Israel, says the Lord; and I will not cause mine anger to fall upon you: for I am merciful, says the Lord." Oh, touching, soul-subduing, heart-melting argument—"Return unto me, for I am merciful!" Merciful to receive you, merciful to pardon you, merciful to heal you. Oh, the boundless mercy of God in Christ towards a soul returning from its wanderings! Will not this draw you? Again: "I have blotted out as a thick cloud your transgressions, and as a cloud your sins; return unto me, for I have redeemed you." "Return, for I have blotted out your transgressions— return, for I have put away your sins: return, for I have redeemed you. The work is already done—the pardon has already gone forth—the backsliding has already been forgiven; then linger not, but return, for I have redeemed you." Here, on the broad basis of the Lord's free and full pardon, the wandering soul is urged to return. Truly may the apostle say, "If we confess our sins, He is faithful and just to forgive us our sins, and to cleanse us from all unrighteousness."

Thus is the character of God, as a merciful, sin-pardoning God, held out in the word as a motive and an encouragement to return. This is just the view of God which you need. In yourself, you see everything to discourage, everything to forbid your return; but God comes forth, and vindicates His own gracious character, unfolds His own love, and, in accents most encouraging and persuasive, addresses Himself to His wandering child, and says, "Return, you backsliding Israel, for I am merciful."

In the parable of the prodigal son, we have the character of God towards a returning soul truly and beautifully drawn. The single point we would now advert to is the posture of the father on the approach of his child. What was that posture?—the most expressive of undiminished love, of yearning tenderness, of eagerness to welcome his return. Thus is it described: "And when he was a great way off, his father saw him, and had compassion, and ran, and fell on his neck, and kissed him." All this is God to you, dear returning soul! He is on the eager watch for your first movement towards Him; He is looking as with outstretched neck for the first sign of your soul's return, for the first sound of your footsteps, for the first relentings of your heart: yes, even more than this—or this were nothing—He sends His own Spirit to work that return in your soul, to break your heart, to rouse your slumbering spirit, to draw you, win you to His arms. This is your God—the God whom you have forsaken, from whose ways you have declined, but who in the very extremity of your departure has never withdrawn His eye of love one moment from you.

SEPTEMBER 11

"But those things, which God before had showed by the mouth of all his prophets, that Christ should suffer, he has now fulfilled." Acts 3:18

Our adorable Lord was a sufferer—the Prince of sufferers—the Martyr of martyrs. None had ever suffered as He; no sorrow was ever like His sorrow. Scarcely had He touched the surface of our sin-accursed earth, before the cup of suffering was placed to His lips. The deep fountain of human woe, stirred to its very center, poured in upon His soul its turbid streams from every source and through every channel. Human malignity seized upon Him as its victim, and mingled the first draught that He tasted. Linked though He was by the strongest sympathies to our nature, descending though He had, to elevate, sanctify, and save him, man yet ranked himself among His first and deadliest foes. Oh that condescension and love to our race so profound should have met with a requital so base!

The necessity of Christ's sufferings is the chief point that arrests the mind in contemplating this subject. In His wayside conversation with the two disciples journeying to Emmaus, our Lord clearly and emphatically pronounced this characteristic of His passion—"Ought not Christ to have suffered?" The following considerations would seem to justify this plea of necessity.

The sufferings of Christ were necessary in order to accomplish the eternal purpose and counsel of God. To suppose that His sufferings were contingent, originating in the circumstances by which He was surrounded, is to take a very low and defective view of truth. But the light in which the Scripture presents the doctrine of a suffering Redeemer is that which gives the most exalted view of redemption, and reflects in the richest manner the glory of the Triune God. The truth we have now advanced, the apostle Peter embodies in his awakening discourse on the day of Pentecost, and which truth the Holy Spirit employed in the conversion of three thousand souls—"Him being delivered by the determinate counsel and foreknowledge of God, you have taken, and by wicked hands have crucified and slain." Our Lord Himself confirms this doctrine when he says, "The Son of man goes, as it was determined." Dear reader, behold the fountain-head, where arise all those precious streams of covenant mercy which flow into your soul—the electing love of God, which constrained Him to present His beloved Son as an atoning Lamb for the slaughter, from before the foundation of the world! Oh! that must be infinite love—vast love—costly love—unchangeable love—which had its existence in the heart of God towards you from all eternity. Oh, repair with humility and gladness to this holy and blessed truth. Welcome it joyfully to your heart as God's truth, from which you may not, you dare not turn, without robbing your soul of immense blessing, and incurring fearful responsibilities. And when by faith you stand beneath the cross, and gaze upon its glorious Sufferer, remember that in His death were fulfilled the eternal purpose and counsel of the Triune Jehovah; and that to predestination—rejected and hated as this truth is by some—you owe all that is dear and precious to you as a ransomed expectant of glory.

To fulfill the types and to make good the prophecies concerning Him, it was necessary that Jesus should suffer. The Levitical dispensation and the prophetical Scriptures point steadily to Jesus; they are replete with Christ crucified. He who reads and investigates them with his eye turned from Jesus will find himself borne along upon a rapid stream of prophetic annunciation he knows not where, and involved in a mass of ceremonial usages to him perfectly chaotic and unintelligible, "without form and void." But with the Spirit of God opening the spiritual eye, and moving upon the word, a flood of light is poured upon every page, and every page is seen to be rich with the history and effulgent with the glory of a suffering Messiah. Thus does our Lord assert this truth—"Think you that I cannot now pray to my Father, and He shall presently give me more than twelve legions of angels? But how then shall the Scriptures be fulfilled, that thus it must be?" Again, "But all this was done that the Scriptures of the prophets might be fulfilled." It was necessary, therefore, that Christ should humble Himself—should be a man of sorrows—should drink deep the cup of suffering, and should be lifted upon the cross, in order to authenticate the Divine mission of Moses, to establish the consistency of the Jewish dispensation, to vindicate the truth of the prophets, to fulfill the counsel of the Lord, and thus to verify His own most blessed word.

SEPTEMBER 12

"Endeavoring to keep the unity of the Spirit in the bond of peace. There is one body, and one Spirit, even as you are called in one hope of your calling." Ephesians 4:3,4

The unity of the mystical church of God consists not in a unity of creed. A higher, a diviner, and more enduring principle united her than this. Ardently as it should be desired, and fervently as it should be prayed for, that the promised day of millennial blessedness might speedily come, when the "watchmen shall see eye to eye," when from every battlement in Zion the silver trumpets shall emit one sweet harmonious sound, yet, even then, not more essentially will the church of God be one than she is now. True, her unity will be more visible, her divisions will be healed, her bleeding wounds will be staunched, her internal conflicts will have ceased; "Ephraim shall not envy Judah, and Judah shall not vex Ephraim more;" and the harsh sounds of strife, now so loud and discordant, shall be lost in the sweet strains of peace and love floating from every lip; yet is the church at this moment essentially one and indivisible. Not, then, in a unity of creed or of ecclesiastical polity does the real unity of the church consist, but in the "unity of the Spirit"—unity sustained by the "bond of peace." She has been baptized, not into one form of church government, nor into one system of doctrinal truth, but "by one Spirit we are all baptized into one body, whether we be Jews or Gentiles, whether we be bond or free; and have all been made to drink of the same Spirit." The "one Spirit" regenerating all the children of God, fashioning alike their hearts, uniting them by a living faith to the Head, equally dwelling in, teaching and guiding, comforting and sanctifying them, demonstrates the perfect oneness of Christ's body. And thus, then, when an individual crosses our path in whom the Spirit of Jesus breathes, who betrays a union to the Head, and who speaks the language and bears the image of the Father, and a resemblance to the one family, be his climate and color, be his name and minor points of creed what they may, it becomes our solemn duty, as it is our great privilege, to extend to him the recognition, and to greet him with the tender and holy affection of the one brotherhood. In the Lord's eye he is a member of His body and he should be so in ours. And if, refusing to own the relationship, we withdraw the hand of Christian love, we render our own regeneration doubtful, we wound, and grieve, and deny the Spirit in him. It is written—yes, it is written by the pen of the Holy Spirit, "Whoever believes that Jesus is the Christ, is born of God: and every one that loves Him that begat, loves him also that is begotten of Him."

I would recur to what may be considered one of the most fruitful and painful causes of the defective Christian union which so much mars the beauty and impairs the moral power of the church of God in our day. I allude to the great distance from Christ which characterizes the spiritual walk of so many believers. The effect of this upon the operation of Christian love is obvious. A distance of spirit from the Head leads to distance in spirit from the members of the body. As with the beams of the sun, the farther they recede from their center, the wider are they separated from each other; so is it with the "children of the light." Each believer is a solar beam—an emanation from the Sun of Righteousness. The more remote he lives from Christ—the center of the soul—the wider will he be alienated in affection and in spirit from the members of Christ. His eye less simply and constantly looking unto Jesus, his sense of union to, and communion with, Him weakened, love waning, faith declining, there will, of necessity, be a lessening attachment to the church of Christ. But the converse, oh, how precious! The rays of light reflected back to the sun, meeting and rejoicing in their center, meet and rejoice in themselves. So with the saints. Drawn closer to Jesus—our wandering steps retraced—restored by those sanctifying unfoldings of the cross which the Spirit delights to impart, the eye of penitence and faith, swimming though it be in tears, once more turned on Christ, love rekindled in the heart—oh how will the affections, in their fondest and holiest power, go forth towards "all them who love our Lord Jesus Christ in sincerity!" His image will be their passport to our hearts; His name will secure their welcome to our homes.

SEPTEMBER 13

"Christ also loved the church, and gave himself for it." Ephesians 5:25

Our Lord Jesus Christ suffered most voluntarily. In this consisted greatly the perfection of His sacrifice. His penal death had proved of no atoning efficacy but for this willing obedience, and the Divine merit that was in it. It would have been unjust in justice to have inflicted punishment upon an innocent and unwilling person. The full and free concurrence of His own will was essential to the perfection of His sacrifice. Yes, had it not been most free, and acting in perfect harmony with His Father's consent, our sins could not have been imputed to, the punishment inflicted upon Him. Entering, then, most freely into a bond to cancel the mighty debt, it was righteous in God, it was just in justice, and it invested the throne of the eternal Jehovah with surpassing glory, to arrest, in default of the debtor, the Surety, and to exact from Him the uttermost payment.

And here, my reader, is the great point to which we are aiming to bring you—the wonderful love of Jesus in so willingly suffering, "The just for the unjust." Oh, how readily did He humble Himself, and become obedient unto death, even the death of the cross! "I delight to do your will, O my God: yes, your law is within my heart." "I have a baptism to be baptized with, and how am I straitened until it be accomplished!" "Who gave Himself for us." "Christ also has loved us, and has given Himself for us." This is the spring of all that He has done, for, "Christ has loved us." Constrained by this, He gave Himself as the Son of God, and as the Son of man—His soul and body, His life and death, yes, all that He possessed in heaven and on earth, He freely gave for us. What was there above or below—in His previous state of glory, or subsequent state of humiliation—that He retained? What part of the price did He withhold? When He could give no less—for all angels and all men would not have sufficed—and when He could give no more, He gave Himself. Ah! this made His "offering and sacrifice to God a sweet-smelling savor." And still it perfumes the oblation, and sends it up each moment fragrant and acceptable before the throne of the Holy One. Oh, surpassing love of Jesus! With the burden of sin—the fire of justice—the wrath of God—the ridicule of man—the malignity of devils—the sorrows of Gethsemane—the pains of Calvary, and the sea of His own blood, all, all in vivid prospect before Him, He yet went forward, loving not His own life unto the death, because He loved ours more. Oh, let your heart bend low before this amazing love. Yield to its sweet and attractive influence; let it draw you from yourself, from the creature, from all, to Him. Are you wounded? Does your heart bleed? Is your soul cast down within you? Is your spirit within you desolate? Still Jesus is love, is loving, and loves you. He has suffered and died for you; and, were it necessary, He would suffer and die for you yet again. Whatever blessing He sees good to take from you, Himself He will never take. Whatever stream of creature love He sees fit to dry, His own love will never fail. Oh, can that love fail—can it cease to yearn, and sympathize, and soothe, and support, which brought Jesus from heaven to earth to endure and suffer all this for us? Be still, then, lie passive and low—drink the cup, and let the surrender of your sin, your obedience, and yourself to Him be as willing and as entire as was the surrender of Himself for you. Then shall you, in a blessed degree, be "able to comprehend with all saints what is the breadth, and length, and depth, and height, and know the love of Christ, which passes knowledge, filled with all the fullness of God."

SEPTEMBER 14

"Your throne, O God, is forever and ever: the scepter of your kingdom is a right scepter. You loves righteousness, and hate wickedness: therefore God, your God, has anointed you with the oil of gladness above your fellows." Psalm 45:6, 7

The Divine anointing of the Lord Jesus Christ, constituting an important feature of His official glory, and opening a channel of the most costly blessing to the church, forms a distinct and sacred theme of the prophetical writings. "The Spirit of the Lord God is upon me, because the Lord has anointed me." "And there shall come forth a rod out of the stem of Jesse, and a Branch shall grow out of his roots: and the Spirit of the Lord shall rest upon him." This anointing was upon the Redeemer, in infinite richness and fragrance. "God gives not the Spirit by measure unto Him." As essentially Jehovah, He needed it not; but as the great High Priest, and the mediatorial head of His "church, which is His body, the fullness of Him that fills all in all," it was necessary that the anointing oil should be upon Him in its utmost plenitude. As one with Him, all the members alike participate. "It is like the precious ointment upon the head, that ran down upon the beard, even Aaron's beard: that went to the skirts of his garment;" even to the lowest believer. Ah! and he that lies the lowest, obtains the most of this "precious ointment," as it descends from Jesus; the hand of faith, that touches but the hem of His garment, receives from Him who was "anointed with the oil of gladness above his fellows." Dear reader, are you professedly one with Jesus and His saints? then seek, oh, diligently seek, a large and still larger degree of this holy and fragrant anointing. Rest not short of it. Be not satisfied to proceed another step without it. Do not be content with a mere profession, having a name to live, yet lacking all the essential evidences of real life, while discovering many of the fearful attributes of actual death.

The possession of this anointing of the Holy Spirit will decide the momentous and perhaps, with you, doubtful question of your union with Christ. Men will take knowledge of you, that you have been with Jesus, and learned of Him. Your life will be a reflection, faint at best, yet a reflection of His holy life. You will bear some resemblance to the "altogether lovely" One; your spirit will breathe His meekness; your demeanor will be stamped with His gentleness; your whole conversation will be seasoned with His grace; all your "garments will smell of myrrh, and aloes, and cassia out of the ivory palaces;" an unction will pervade your prayers, a power irresistible will accompany your labors, and in every place you will be a sweet savor of Christ, blessed and a blessing.

SEPTEMBER 15

"Christ Jesus; who, being in the form of God, thought it not robbery to be equal with God: but made himself of no reputation, and took upon him the form of a servant, and was made in the likeness of men: and being found in fashion as a man, he humbled himself, and became obedient unto death, even the death of the cross." Philippians 2:6-8

There could have been no restoration and no satisfaction to law and justice, but in the humiliation of the Son of God. The very necessity of the case demanded it. The Divine government had been dishonored—that dishonor could only be removed by the humiliation of one equal in dignity, holiness, and glory—even an infinite Being. The humiliation of every angel in heaven would not have effaced a single stain of its reproach, nor have restored a single beam of its glory. The law of God had been humbled—justice demanded, as a price of its reparation, the humiliation of the Lawgiver Himself. The incarnate God did humble Himself, and became obedient unto death, even the death of the cross. Thus it was Jesus "restored that which He took not away." He restored holiness to the law—satisfaction to justice—dignity to the Divine government—honor to God, and happiness and immortality to man. "Then I restored that which I took not away." Oh, what stable foundation is thus laid for the full salvation of every believer.

The humiliation of the Redeemer opens a fountain of infinitely great and ever-glorious grace. Nothing could we have known of the glory of His person, nothing of the character of God, and all the things of His hidden love must have remained forever sealed, had He not so humbled Himself. His coming forth, invested not with the dazzling robes of His infinite Majesty, but wearing our degraded nature, descending to our state of deep abasement—yes, sinking infinitely deeper than we—throws open a treasury of grace as rich in its glory, and ample in its supply, as were the dark humiliation and deep poverty which made it ours. Here is glory springing from His abasement—it is the "glory of His grace;" "We beheld His glory, full of grace." This fullness of grace in Jesus includes all that a poor sinner needs, all that a necessitous believer requires, all that the glory of God demanded. Here is the grace of pardon in all its fullness—the grace of justification in all its fullness—the grace of sanctification in all its fullness—the grace of consolation in all its fullness—the grace of strength in all its fullness. "It pleased the Father, that in Him should all fullness dwell." Grace is poured into His lips, and gracious words proceed from His lips. Hearken! "Come unto me, all you that labor and are heavy laden, and I will give you rest." Hearken again! "Him that comes unto me, I will in no wise cast out." Does He not bind up the broken heart? Does He not preach glad tidings to the meek? Does He not "satisfy the hungry soul, and satiate the weary soul with goodness"? Has He ever sent the poor empty away? Was He ever known to turn His back upon one humble comer drawing near, bowed with guilt, disconsolate with sorrow, oppressed with trial? Never! never! Oh, it is with infinite delight—delight, the depth of which we can form no conception—that He welcomes poor sinners. He thinks of His own humiliation for sin—He remembers His own sorrows and tears, agonies and death, and throwing Himself, as it were, into the very center of a bosom storm-tossed with godly grief, He seeks to soothe and hush it to a calm. And how does He allay the tempest? He pours the oil of His own love upon the waves; He sprinkles the conscience with that blood which cleanses from all sin, and bids the soul go in peace. Dear reader, where least we should have expected it, Jesus is set before us the "door of hope," even in the deep valley of His humiliation. "I will give the valley of Achor for a door of hope." The gospel of this precious promise is found in the wondrous theme we are now contemplating—the humiliation of the incarnate God. To that humiliation we must sink; into that valley we must descend. Convinced of sin—separated from all self-reliance and creature trust—emptied, humbled, laid low in the dust before God, we shall then find Jesus to be the "door of hope" set open for us in the deep and dark valley of our poverty, hopelessness, vileness, and abasement. Just the Door we need, is

Jesus. A door to a Father's forgiving heart, a door to God's reconciled love; a door to the sweetest, closest, holiest fellowship and communion; a door into heaven itself; a door so wide, that the greatest sinner may enter—so free, that the penniless may come.

SEPTEMBER 16

"Do not be faithless, but believing." John 20:27

When any grace of the Spirit is in a sickly and declining state, an effect so painful must originate in a cause that needs to be searched out: the great difficulty in a backsliding soul is to bring it to the spiritual and needed duty of self-scrutiny. But as the cure of any disease, or the correction of any evil, depends upon the knowledge of its cause, so does the revival of a declining believer closely connect itself with the discovery and removal of that which led to his declension. Declining believer! what is the cause of your weak faith? Why is this lovely, precious, and fruitful flower drooping, and ready to die? What has dimmed the eye, and paralyzed the hand, and enfeebled the walk of faith? Perhaps it is the neglect of prayer: you have lived, it may be, days, and weeks, and months, without communion with God; there have been no constant and precious visits to your closet; no wrestling with God; no fellowship with your Father. Marvel not, beloved, that your faith languishes, droops, and fades. The great marvel is, that you have any faith at all; that it is not quite dead, plucked up by the root; and, but for the mighty power of God, and the constant intercession of Jesus at His right hand, it would long since have ceased to be. But what will revive it?—an immediate return to prayer; revisit your closet; seek your forsaken God. Oh how can faith be revived, and how can it grow, in the neglect of daily, secret, and wrestling prayer with God? The Eternal Spirit laying this upon your heart, showing you your awful neglect, and breathing into you afresh the spirit of grace and supplication, will impart a new and blessed impulse to faith.

Perhaps you have been misinterpreting the Lord's providential dealings with you; you have been indulging in unbelieving, unkind, unfilial views of your trials, bereavements, and disappointments: you have said, "Can I be a child, yet be afflicted thus? can He love me, yet deal with me so?" Oh, that thought! Oh, that surmise! Could you have looked into the heart of your God when He sent that trial, caused that bereavement, blew upon that flower, and blasted that fair design, you would never have murmured more: so much love, so much tenderness, so much faithfulness, so much wisdom would you have seen, as to have laid your mouth silent in the dust before Him. Wonder not that, indulging in such misgivings, interpreting the covenant dealings of a God of love in such a light, your faith has received a wound. Nothing, perhaps, more tends to unhinge the soul from God, engenders distrust, hard thoughts, and rebellious feelings, than thus to doubt His loving-kindness and faithfulness in the discipline He is pleased to send. But faith, looking through the dark cloud and anchoring itself on the Divine veracity and the unchangeable love of God, is sure to strengthen and increase by every storm that beats upon it.

Is it the enchantment of the world that has seized upon your faith? has it stolen upon you, beguiled you, caught you with its glitter, overwhelmed you with its crushing cares?—come out from it, and be separate; resign its hollow friendships, its temporizing policy, its carnal enjoyments, its fleshly wisdom, its sinful conformity. All these becloud the vision, and enfeeble the grasp of faith. Would you be "strong in faith, giving glory to God"?—then yield obedience to the voice which with an unearthly tongue exclaims to every professing child of God, "Do not be conformed to this world; but be you transformed by the renewing of your mind, that you may prove what is that good, and acceptable, and perfect will of God."

Is it the indulgence of unbelieving fears touching your interest in Christ? Yield them, and let the wind scatter them. There is no ground for the doubts and unbelief of a child of God; there may be much in himself to cast him down, but nothing in which he professes to believe; nothing in Christ, nothing in the work of Christ, nothing in the word of God, calculated to beget a doubt or a fear in the heart of a poor sinner; on the contrary, everything to inspire confidence, strengthen faith, and encourage hope. Does his sin plead loud for his condemnation? the voice of Immanuel's blood pleads louder for his pardon. Does his own righteousness condemn?—the righteousness of Christ acquits. Thus there is nothing in Christ to engender an unbelieving doubt in a poor convinced sinner. Himself he may doubt—he may doubt his ability to save himself—he may doubt his power to make himself more worthy and acceptable—but never let him doubt that Christ is all that a poor, lost, convinced sinner needs. Let him not doubt that Jesus is the Friend of sinners, the Savior of sinners, and that He was never known to cast out one who in lowliness and brokenness of heart sought His compassionate grace. Oh seek, reader, more simple views of Jesus; clearer views of His great and finished work; take every doubt as it is suggested, every fear as it rises, to Him; and remember that whatever of vileness you discover in yourself that has a tendency to lay you low, there is everything in Jesus calculated to lift you from the ash-heap, and place you among the princes.

SEPTEMBER 17

"Let the word of Christ dwell in you richly in all wisdom." Col. 3:16

The diligent and prayerful reading of God's holy word is a great means of increasing and promoting a spiritual mind. This, I fear, is not an element in the life of many. It defines a duty sadly and, to a great extent, totally neglected. The tendency of the age is to substitute the writings of man for the Book of God. Let them come but with the robe of religion gracefully thrown around them, and whether they assume the form of history, or story, or song, they are devoured by the professing multitude, who would deem their true spirituality beyond question! But the Divine life of the soul is not to be fed and nourished by the discoveries of science, nor the axioms of philosophy, nor the brilliance of genius, nor the dreams of a poetical imagination. It ascends to a higher and a diviner source; it aspires towards the nourishments of its native climate. The bread that comes down from heaven, and the water that flows, pure as crystal, from beneath the throne of God and the Lamb, can alone nourish and refresh. Jesus is its sustenance; and the gospel, as it unfolds Him in His glory and grace, is the spiritual storehouse from where its daily food is drawn. To this it retreats,—pressed with hunger, or panting with thirst, weary and exhausted, drooping and faint, and it finds its doctrines and its precepts, its promises and its admonitions, its exhortations and revelations, a "a feast of fat things, a feast of wines on the lees; of fat things full of marrow,..." And thus refreshed and satisfied, the grateful soul adoringly exclaims, "Your words were found, and I did eat them; and Your word was unto me the joy and rejoicing of my heart." Truly did Jesus testify, "Verily, verily, I say unto you, Except you eat the flesh of the Son of man, and drink His blood, you have no life in you;" evidently and solemnly implying, that if there exists no appetite for spiritual food, there is lacking the great evidence of the life of God in the soul. A mere semblance of life, an informed judgment, a "fair show" of religion "in the flesh," can content itself with anything short of the spiritual aliment contained in God's word. But the Divine life of a quickened soul, while it disdains no auxiliary to its spiritual advance, can yet feed on nothing but Divine food. The "flesh and the blood of Immanuel can alone meet and satiate its hunger and thirst. It is from heaven, and its satisfaction must be heavenly; it is from God, and its nourishment must be Divine. Jesus, and Jesus alone, received into the heart, rested in, and lived upon by faith, is the food of a believing man. Nothing but Christ—"Christ all" in Himself, and Christ "in all," means "in all" ordinances, "in all" channels, "in all" seasons, sustains a soul whose "life is hid with Christ in God." Do you see the importance and feel the gravity of this truth? It is a great and solemn one! Except by faith you "eat the flesh and drink the blood of the Son of man, you have no life in you!" Nothing short of Christ—Christ's righteousness, Christ's atonement, Christ's flesh and blood, Christ in us, Christ without us, Christ risen, Christ alive at the right hand of God, yes, "Christ all and in all"—can meet the deep, immortal necessities of your soul. You need all that Christ is in the matter of pardon, and justification, and sanctification, and wisdom, and redemption. If anything less than Jesus had sufficed, if an expedient less magnificent, or if an expenditure less costly, had answered for God and man, then less would save you. But since the incarnate God alone is the Savior of a poor, lost sinner, see that you detract not from, or add to, this salvation by any works of human merit.

Be exhorted, then, to an intimate acquaintance with God's holy word, as supplying a powerful help to the progress of the soul in deep spirituality. And if your time for reading is limited, limit it to one book, and let that one book be—the BIBLE. Let it be the companion of your hours of solitude; the solace in your seasons of sorrow; the store-house in all your necessities; the man of your counsel in all your doubts and perplexities. Then will your blessed experience resemble that of the psalmist: "Your word have I hid in mine heart, that I might not sin against You. This is my comfort in my affliction: for Your word has quickened me. Your word is a lamp unto my feet, and a light unto my path. I rejoice at Your word, as one that finds great spoil."

SEPTEMBER 18

"In the year that king Uzziah died I saw also the Lord sitting upon a throne, high and lifted up, and his train filled the temple. Above it stood the Seraphim: each one had six wings; with twain he covered his face, and with twain he covered his feet, and with twain he did fly. And one cried unto another, and said, Holy, holy, holy, is the Lord of hosts; the whole earth is full of his glory. And the posts of the door moved at the voice of him that cried, and the house was filled with smoke. Then said I, Woe is me! for I am undone; because I am a man of unclean lips; and I dwell in the midst of a people of unclean lips: for mine eyes have seen the King, the Lord of hosts." Isaiah 6:1-5

What an august revelation of the glory of Christ's Godhead was this which broke upon the view of the lowly prophet! How instructive is each particular of His beatific vision! Mark the profound humility of the seraphim—they veiled with their wings their faces and their feet. They were in the presence of Jesus. They saw the King in His beauty, and covered themselves.

But the effect of this view of our Lord's divine glory upon the mind of the prophet is still more impressive: "Then said I, Woe is me! for I am undone; because I am a man of unclean lips...for mine eyes have seen the King, the Lord of hosts." What prostrated his soul thus low in the dust? What filled him with this self-abasement? What overwhelmed him with this keen sense of his vileness? Oh, it was the unclouded view he had of the essential glory of the Son of God! And thus will it ever be. The beaming forth of Christ's glory in the soul reveals its hidden evil; the knowledge of this evil lays the believer low before God with the confession, "I abhor myself. Woe is me! for I am undone." Beloved, let this truth be ever present to your mind, that as we increasingly see glory in Christ, we shall increasingly see that there is no glory in ourselves. Jesus is the Sun which reveals the pollutions and defilements which are within. The chambers of abomination are all closed until Christ shines in upon the soul. Oh, then it is these deep-seated and long-veiled deformities are revealed; and we, no longer gazing with a complacent eye upon self, sink in the dust before God, overwhelmed with shame, and covered with confusion of face. Holy posture! Blessed spectacle!—a soul prostrate before the glory of the incarnate God! All high and lofty views of its own false glory annihilated by clear and close views of the true glory of Jesus. As when the sun appears, all the lesser lights vanish into darkness, so when Jesus rises in noontide glory upon the soul, all other glory retires, and He alone fixes the eye and fills the mind. "With twain they covered their faces, and with twain they covered their feet." Their own perfections and beauty were not to be seen in the presence of the glory of the Lord. How much more profound should be the humility and self-abasement of man! Have we covered ourselves—not with the pure wings of the holy cherubim, but with sackcloth and ashes before the Lord? Have we sought to veil—not our beauties, for beauty we have none—but our innumerable and flagrant deformities, even the "spots upon our feasts of charity," the sins of our best and holiest things; and, renouncing all self-glory, have we sunk, as into nothing before God? Oh, we are yet strangers to the vision of Christ's glory, if we have not. If the constellation of human gifts and attainments, distinctions and usefulness, on which unsanctified and unmortified self so delights to gaze, have not retired into oblivion, the Sun of Righteousness has yet to rise upon our souls with healing in His wings.

SEPTEMBER 19

"But now when Timothy came from you unto us, and brought us good tidings of your faith and charity, and that you have good remembrance of us always, desiring greatly to see us, as we also to see you: therefore, brethren, we were comforted over you in all our affliction and distress by your faith: for now we live, if you stand fast in the Lord." 1 Thessalonians 3:6-8

Oh, it is a lovely and a holy sight, the strong attachment of a pastor and a church! Earth presents no spectacle of moral beauty surpassing it; and angels, bending from their thrones in heaven, must gaze upon it with new ecstasy and delight. We would not breathe a word, or pen a sentence, tending to mar the symmetry, or shade the beauty, or impair the strength of such a union. This only would we say to the church—receive your pastor reverently and gratefully, as the Lord's messenger, esteem him very highly in love for his work's sake; yet hold him infinitely subordinate to Christ, and with a loose and gentle grasp. If heavenly-minded, and the channel of blessing to your souls, he is the Lord's gift, and as such only is he to be regarded. All that he possesses, really valuable, is from Jesus—his gifts, his acquirements, his grace, his usefulness, his moral loveliness, and even those minor attractions of person and address, which, if possessed, may, without much holy caution, but strengthen the heart's idolatry, and shade the infinite loveliness of Christ, came from God, are the bestowments of His undeserved mercy, and were intended but to lead you up to Himself, the source from where they proceed. Then lend your ear and yield your heart to the needed exhortation, as it bears upon this point, "Set not your affection on things on the earth." Cherish a devout and grateful spirit for the precious and invaluable gift of a holy, affectionate, and useful minister; but rest not in him short of Jesus. Give to him his proper place in your affections and thoughts—a place infinitely beneath the adorable Son of God, God's "unspeakable gift." He is not his own, nor yours, but the Lord's. And He, whose he is and whom he serves, may, in the exercise of His infinite wisdom and sovereign will, and, I may add, tender love, suspend for awhile his labors, or transfer him to another section of the vineyard, or, which would be more painful, crumble the earthen, though beautiful, vessel to dust, and take the precious treasure it contained to Himself. Still, Christ is all, He is your all; and, as the chief Shepherd and Bishop of His church, He will never take Himself from her. The happy secret of retaining our mercies is to receive and enjoy Christ in them; to turn every blessing bestowed into an occasion of knowing, and loving, and enjoying more of Jesus, apart from whom, poor indeed were the most costly blessing. Blessed indeed would our blessings then be! Leading our affections up to God; giving us a deeper insight into a Father's love; laying us lower in the dust at His feet; filling the spirit with secret contrition and tender brokenness, the heart with adoring love, the mouth with grateful praise; endearing the channel through which it descends, and the mercy-seat at which it was sought and given; encouraged and stimulated by the gift, to devote person, time, influence, and property, more simply and unreservedly, to the glory of God; then should we keep a longer possession of our sanctified blessing, nor fear the thought, nor shrink from the prospect, of its removal; or, if removed, we should be quite satisfied to have God alone as our portion and our all.

SEPTEMBER 20

"The Holy Spirit was not yet given; because that Jesus was not yet glorified." John 7:39

Our adorable Lord, as He approached the termination of His sojourn on earth, went more fully into the work of the Spirit, than at any former period of His ministry, laying especial stress on this truth, that His own personal residence on earth in permanent conjunction with the presence of the Spirit, was a union not to be expected by the church. Why such an arrangement might not have been made, we proceed not to inquire. Sufficient should be the answer to this, as to all questions involving the sovereignty of the Divine will—"Even so, Father, for so it seemed good in Your sight." But the promise to which He directed the eye of His disciples, and with which He sought to soothe their sorrow in the prospect of His personal withdrawal from the church, was the descent of the Holy Spirit in an enlarged degree, and in continuous outpouring to the end of the Christian dispensation. This event, dependent upon, and immediately to follow, that of His inauguration in His heavenly kingdom, is thus alluded to by our Lord—"Nevertheless, I tell you the truth: it is expedient for you that I go away; for if I go not away, the Comforter will not come unto you; but if I depart, I will send Him unto you."

The descent of the Holy Spirit upon the church in His most enlarged degree, and for the highest and most gracious ends, rendered the glorification of the Head necessary and expedient. Holding in His hands, not only the keys of hell and of death, but of all the fullness of God, all the riches of the covenant, all the treasures of His Father, He could only dispense these blessings in His exalted state. As it was necessary in the case of Joseph—a personal type of our glorious Redeemer—that he should be exalted to the office of prime-minister in Egypt, in order to possess dignity, authority, and power to dispense the riches of Pharaoh, so was it expedient that the great Antitype should assume a mediatorial exaltation, with a view of scattering down mediatorial blessings upon His people. The delay of this event was the only barrier to the outpouring of the Spirit upon the church. "The Holy Spirit was not yet given, because that Jesus was not yet glorified." Now here, second to Himself, was the gift of gifts—the donation of the Holy Spirit, the greatest God could give, the richest man could receive—suspended upon the single fact of the Redeemer's ascension to glory. It would seem as if the baptism of the church by the Spirit was an event especially reserved to signalize the enthronement of the Son of God in His mediatorial kingdom. God would demonstrate how great was the glory of Jesus in heaven, how perfect was the reconciliation which He had effected between Himself and man, how spiritual was that kingdom which He was about to establish in the earth, the foundation of which His own hand had laid—and how full, and immense, and free were the blessings ready to be bestowed upon all who, in poverty of spirit, and sincerity of heart, and fervency of soul, should seek them, by opening the windows of heaven, and pouring down the Holy Spirit in all His converting, life-giving, sanctifying, and comforting grace. And oh, how must this Divine and Eternal Spirit—occupying as He did a personal existence in the glorious Trinity, possessing equal glory, honor, and love with the Father and the Son, as equally engaged in securing the salvation of a chosen people—how must He have rejoiced at the consummation of an event which permitted Him to give full vent to the overflowing fountain of His heart's grace and love over a church which He was about to renew, sanctify, and dwell in through eternity! "The love of the Spirit" pleaded eloquently for the exaltation of Jesus.

SEPTEMBER 21

"And you said, I will surely do you good." Genesis 32:12

God, in the administration of His all-wise, all-righteous, all-beneficent government, has night seasons as well as day—seasons of darkness as well as seasons of light—and in both He must be contemplated, studied, and known. As the night reveals glories in the firmament, which the day concealed, so dark dispensations of Divine Providence bring to the believer's eye, as viewed through the telescope of faith, glories in the character and wonders in the government of Jehovah, which the milder and brighter displays of Himself had veiled from the eye. Oh, beloved, how scanty were our experience of God—how limited our knowledge of His love, wisdom, and power—how little should we know of Jesus, our best Friend, the Beloved of our souls, did we know Him only in mercy, and not also in judgment—were there no lowering skies, no night of weeping, no shady paths, no rough places, no cloud-tracings, no seasons of lonely sorrow, of pressing need, and of fierce temptation. "In the way of Your judgments, O Lord, have we waited for You; the desire of our soul is to Your name, and to the remembrance of You."

Nor should we overlook the full play and exercise of faith which occurrences, to us dark, discrepant, and mysterious, call into operation. Faith in God is the most precious, wondrous, and fruitful grace of the Holy Spirit in the renewed soul. Its worth is beyond all price. Its possession is cheap at any cost. One saving view of Jesus—one dim vision of the cross—one believing touch of the Savior—a single grain of this priceless gold—millions of rubies were as nothing to it. Then were its exercise and trial good. And but for its trial how uncertain would it be! Were there no circumstances alarming in the aspect they assume—somber in the form they wear—rude in the voice they utter—events which threaten our happiness and well-being—which seem to dry our springs, wither our flowers, blight our fruits, and drape life's landscape in gloom—how limited would be the sphere of faith! It is the province of this mighty grace to pierce thick clouds, to scale high walls, to walk in the dark, to pass unhurt through fire, to smile at improbabilities, and to master impossibilities. As the mariner's compass guides the ship, coursing its way over the ocean, as truly and as safely in the starless night as in the meridian day, so faith—the needle of the soul—directs us safely, and points the believer in his right course homewards as truly, in the gloomiest as in the brightest hour. Oh, how little are we aware of the real blessings that flow to us through believing! God asks of us nothing but faith; for where there is faith in the Lord Jesus there is love—and where there is, love there is obedience—and where there is obedience there is happiness—and where there is happiness, the soul can even rejoice in tribulation, and sit and sing sweetly and merrily in adversity, like a bird amid the boughs whose green foliage the frost has nipped, and the autumnal blast has scattered.

It is God's sole prerogative to educe good from seeming evil—to order and overrule all events of an untoward nature, and of a threatening aspect, for the accomplishment of the most beneficent ends. This He is perpetually doing with reference to His saints. The Spirit of love broods over the chaotic waters, and life's dark landscape appears like a new-born existence. The curse is turned into a blessing—the discordant notes breathe the sweetest music. You marvel how this can be. What is impossible with man is more than possible with God. Often in your silent musings over some untoward event in your life, sad in its nature, and threatening in its look, have you asked, "What possible good can result from this? It seems utterly opposed to my interests, and hostile to my happiness. It appears an unmixed, unmitigated evil." Be still! Let not your heart fret against the Lord and against His dealings—all things in your history are for your good—and this calamity, this affliction, this loss, is among the "all things." The extraction of the curse from everything appertaining to the child of God converts everything into a blessing. Christ has so completely annihilated the curse by obedience, and has so entirely put away sin by suffering, nothing is left of real, positive evil, in the dealings of God with His church. Jesus, because His love was so great, did all, endured all, finished all; and it is not only in the heart of God, but it is in the power of God—a power exerted in alliance with every perfection of His being—to cause all events to conspire to promote our present and eternal happiness. I cannot see how God will work it, or when He will accomplish it, but assured that I am His pardoned, adopted child, I can calmly leave the issue of all things in my life with Him; confident that, however complicated may be the web of His providence, however hostile the attitude or discouraging the aspect of events, all, all under the government and overruling will of my Heavenly Father are working together for my good. The result, then, of this matter, my God, I leave with You.

"Your ways, O Lord, with wise design,
Are framed upon Your throne above,
And every dark and bending line
Meets in the center of Your love."

What is there of good we need, or of evil we dread, which God's heart will withhold, or His power cannot avert? Oh, it is in the heart of our covenant God to lavish every good upon us—to "withhold no good thing from those who walk uprightly." Lord, lead us into Your love—Your love infinite, Your love unfathomable, Your love hidden and changeless as Your nature!

SEPTEMBER 22

"This is my blood of the new testament, which is shed for many for the remission of sins." Matthew 26:28

The atoning blood of Christ possesses a pardoning efficacy. Through this blood, God, the holy God—the God against whom you have sinned, and whose wrath you justly dread, can pardon all your sins, blot out all your transgressions, and take from you the terror of a guilty conscience. Oh what news is this! Do you doubt it? We know it is an amazing fact, that God should pardon sin, and that He should pardon it, too, through the blood of His dear Son, yet take His own word as a full confirmation of this stupendous fact, and doubt no more—"The blood of Jesus Christ His Son cleanses us from all sin." Oh yes—blessed declaration! it cleanses us from all sin—"all manner of sin." We ask not how heavy the weight of guilt that rests upon you; we ask not how wide the territory over which your sins have extended; we inquire not how many their number, or how aggravated their nature, or how deep their dye; we meet you, just as you are, with God's own declaration, "the blood of Jesus Christ cleanses from all sin." Many there are who can testify to this truth. "Such were some of you," says the apostle, when writing to the Corinthian converts, who had been fornicators, idolaters, adulterers, effeminate, thieves, covetous, drunkards, revilers, extortioners; "such were some of you, but you are washed." In what had they washed?—where were they cleansed? They washed in the "fountain opened to the house of David, and the inhabitants of Jerusalem, for sin and uncleanness." To this fountain they came, guilty, vile, black as they were, and the blood of Jesus Christ cleansed them from all sin. Mourning soul, look up—the fountain yet is open, and open too for you. Satan will seek to close it—unbelief will seek to close it—yet it is ever running, ever overflowing, ever free. Thousands have plunged in it, and emerged washed, sanctified, and saved. To this fountain David, and Manasseh, and Saul, and Peter, and Mary Magdalene, and the dying thief, and millions more, came, washed, and were saved; and yet it has lost nothing of its sin-pardoning, sin-cleansing efficacy—sovereign and free as ever! Oh say not that you are too vile, say not that you are too unworthy! You may stand afar from its brink, looking at your unfitness, looking at your poverty, but listen while we declare that, led as you have been by the Holy Spirit to feel your vileness, for just such this precious blood was shed, this costly fountain was opened.

This "blood of the new testament" is peace-speaking blood. It not only procured peace, but when applied by the Holy Spirit to the conscience, it produces peace—it gives peace to the soul. It imparts a sense of reconciliation: it removes all slavish fear of God, all dread of condemnation, and enables the soul to look up to God, not as "a consuming fire," but as a reconciled God—a God in covenant. Precious peace-speaking blood, flowing from the "Prince of Peace!" Applied to your heart, penitent reader, riven asunder as it may be with godly sorrow, it shall be as a balm to the wound. Sprinkled on your conscience, burdened as it is with a sense of guilt, you shall have "beauty for ashes, the oil of joy for mourning, the garment of praise for the spirit of heaviness."

It is through simply believing that the blood of Christ thus seals pardon and peace upon the conscience. Do not forget this. "Only believe," is all that is required; and this faith is the free gift of God. And what is faith? "It is looking unto Jesus;" it is simply going out of yourself, and taking up your rest in the finished work of the Lord Jesus Christ—this is faith. Christ has said, that "He saves to the uttermost all that come unto God by Him;" that He died for sinners, and that He saves sinners as sinners: the Holy Spirit working faith in the heart, lifting the eye off the wound, and fixing it on the Lamb of God, pardon and peace flow like a river in the soul. Oh, stay not then from the gospel-feast, because you are poor, penniless, and unworthy. See the provision, how full! see the invitation, how free! see the guests—the poor, the maimed, the lame, the blind! Come then to Jesus just as you are. We stake our all on the assertion, that He will welcome you, that He will save you. There is too much efficacy in His blood, too much compassion in His heart for poor sinners, to reject you, suing at His feet for mercy. Then look up, believer, and you shall be saved; and all heaven will resound with hallelujahs over a sinner saved by grace!

SEPTEMBER 23

"In a little wrath I hid my face from you for a moment; but with everlasting kindness will I have mercy on you, says the Lord your Redeemer." Isaiah 54:8

Many are the seasons of spiritual darkness, and sensible withdrawments of God's presence, through which the believer is often called to pass. Seasons, during which his hope seems to have perished; and God, as he believes, has forgotten to be gracious; seasons, during which he cannot look up as a pardoned sinner, as a justified soul, as an adopted child, and say, "Abba, Father!" All is midnight gloom to his soul. And while God seems to have withdrawn, Satan instantly appears. Taking advantage of the momentary absence of the Lord, for let it be remembered, it is not an actual and eternal withdrawal—he levels his fiery darts—suggests hard thoughts of God—tempts the soul to believe the past has been but a deception, and that the future will develop nothing but darkness and despair. Satan, that constant and subtle foe, frequently seizes, too, upon periods of the believer's history, when the providences of God are dark and mysterious—when the path, along which the weary pilgrim is pressing, is rough and intricate, or, it may be, when he sees not a spot before him, the way is obstructed, and he is ready to exclaim with Job, "He has fenced up my way that I cannot pass, and he has set darkness in my paths." Or with Jeremiah, "He has hedged me about that I cannot get out." Let it not then be forgotten by the soul that walks in darkness and has no light, that the providential dealings of a covenant God and Father, which now are depressing the spirits, stirring up unbelief, and casting a shade over every prospect, may be seized upon by its great enemy, and be appropriated to an occasion of deep and sore temptation. It was thus he dealt with our blessed Lord, who was in all points tempted as His people, yet without sin. And if the Head thus was tempted, so will be, the member—if the Lord, so the disciple. And for this very end was our blessed Lord thus tempted, that He might enter sympathetically into all the circumstances of His tried and suffering people—"For in that He Himself has suffered being tempted, He is able to support those who are tempted."

But a momentary sense of God's withdrawal from the believer affects not his actual security in the atoning blood; this nothing can disturb. The safety of a child of God hinges not upon a frame or a feeling, the ever-varying and fitful pulses of a believing soul. Oh no! the covenant rests upon a surer basis than this; the child of the covenant is sealed with a better hope and promise. He may change, but his covenant God never; his feelings may vary, but his Father's love never veers: He loved him from all eternity, and that love extends to all eternity. As God never loved His child for anything He saw, or should see, in that child; so His love never changes for all the fickleness, sinfulness, and unworthiness, He daily and hourly discovers. Oh where would the soul fly but for this truth? When it takes into account the sins, the follies, the departures, the flaws of but one week—yes, when it reviews the history of but one day, and sees enough sin in a single thought to sink it to eternal and just perdition—but for an unchangeable God, to what consolation would it resort?

SEPTEMBER, 24

"Much more then, being now justified by his blood, we shall be saved from wrath through him." Romans 5:9

What forms the great security of the believer? what, but the atoning blood? This, and this only. The Father, beholding His child in His beloved Son, washed and clothed, pardoned and justified, can "rest in His love, and joy over Him with singing." The atonement guarantees his eternal safety. What formed the security of Noah and his family, when the deluge of God's wrath descended upon an ungodly world?—the ark in which God had shut him in. What formed the security of the children of Israel in Egypt, when the destroying angel passed through the camp, waving in his hand the weapon of death?—the blood of the paschal lamb, sprinkled on the lintel and door-posts of their dwellings; and where this sacred sign was seen, into that house he dared not enter, but passed on to do the work of death where no blood was found. Exactly what the ark was to Noah, and the blood of the lamb was to the children of Israel, is the atoning blood of Christ to the believing soul. It forms his eternal security. Reader, is that blood applied to you? Are you washed in it? Is it upon you at this moment? Precious blood! precious Savior who shed it! precious faith that leads to it! how it washes away all sin—how it lightens the conscience of its burden—heals the heart of its wound—dispels the mist, and brings down the unclouded sunshine of God's reconciled countenance in the soul! Oh, adore the love and admire the grace that opened the fountain, and led you to bathe, all guilty, polluted, and helpless as you were, beneath its cleansing stream! and with Cowper let us sing,—

"E'er since by faith I saw the stream
Your flowing wounds supply,
Redeeming love has been my theme,
And shall be until I die."

Surely the Christian will ever strive to live near this fountain—the only spot where his soul shall flourish. As the gentle flower which blooms unseen by the side of some veiled spring is, from the constant moisture it receives, always beautiful and fragrant, so is that believing soul the most fruitful, holy, spiritual, and devoted, who daily dwells by the side, yes, in the "fountain opened for sin and uncleanness." We see not how a child of God can be fruitful otherwise. A sweet and abiding consciousness of pardon and acceptance is essential to spiritual fruitfulness. The great impelling motive to all gospel obedience is the love of Christ in the heart. David acknowledged this principle when he prayed, "I will run the way of Your commandments, when You shall enlarge my heart." The apostle admits it when he says, "the love of Christ constrains us." In order to walk as an obedient child, to bear the daily cross, to delight in the precepts as in the doctrines of God's truth, the atoning blood must be realized. How easy and how sweet will then become the commandments of the Lord: duties will be viewed as privileges, and the yoke felt to be no yoke, and the cross to be no cross.

No believer can advance in the divine life, wage a daily war with the innumerable foes that oppose him, and be fruitful in every good work, who is perpetually in search of evidence of his adoption. We need all our time, all our energies, all our means, in order to vanquish the spiritual Philistines who obstruct our way to the heavenly Canaan: we have none to send in search of evidences, lest while they have gone the Bridegroom comes. Oh, then, to know that all is right; the thick cloud blotted out—the soul wrapped in the robe of righteousness—ready to enter in to the marriage supper of the Lamb. To die will be quite enough; to face and grapple with the king of terrors will be sufficient employment for the spirit struggling to be free: no time, no strength, no energy then to search for evidences. Let not the professor of Christ leave the "sealing" of his pardon and acceptance to that fearful hour; but let him earnestly seek it now, that when he comes to die he may have nothing to do but to die; and that will be quite enough.

SEPTEMBER 25

"And he said to them all, If any man will come after me, let him deny himself, and take up his cross daily, and follow me. For whoever will save his life shall lose it: but whoever will lose his life for my sake, the same shall save it." Luke 9:23, 24

The life of our adorable Lord was a life of continuous trial. From the moment He entered our world He became leagued with suffering; He identified Himself with it in its almost endless forms. He seemed to have been born with a tear in His eye, with a shade of sadness on His brow. He was prophesied as "a man of sorrows and acquainted with grief." And, from the moment He touched the horizon of our earth, from that moment His sufferings commenced. Not a smile lighted up His benign countenance from the time of His advent to His departure. He came not to indulge in a life of tranquility and repose; He came not to quaff the cup of earthly or of Divine sweets—for even this last was denied Him in the hour of His lingering agony on the cross. He came to suffer—He came to bear the curse—He came to drain the deep cup of wrath, to weep, to bleed, to die. Our Savior was a cross-bearing Savior: our Lord was a suffering Lord. And was it to be expected that they who had linked their destinies with His, who had avowed themselves His disciples and followers, should walk in a path diverse from their Lord's? He Himself speaks of the incongruity of such a division of interests: "The disciple is not above his Master, nor the servant above his Lord. It is enough for the disciple that he be as his Master, and the servant as his Lord." There can be no true following of Christ as our example, if we lose sight of Him as a suffering Christ—a cross-bearing Savior. There must be fellowship with Him in His sufferings. In order to enter fully and sympathetically into the afflictions of His people, He stooped to a body of suffering: in like manner, in order to have sympathy with Christ in His sorrows, we must, in some degree tread the path He trod. Here is one reason why He ordained, that along this rugged path His saints should all journey. They must be like their Lord; they are one with Him: and this oneness can only exist where there is mutual sympathy. The church must be a cross-bearing church; it must be an afflicted church. Its great and glorious Head sought not, and found not, repose here: this was not His rest. He turned His back upon the pleasures, the riches, the luxuries, and even the common comforts of this world, preferring a life of obscurity, penury, and suffering. His very submission seemed to impart dignity to suffering, elevation to poverty, and to invest with an air of holy sanctity a life of obscurity, need, and trial.

We have seen, then, that our blessed Lord sanctified, by His own submission, a life of suffering; and that all His followers, if they would resemble Him, must have fellowship with Him in His sufferings. The apostle Paul seems to regard this in the light of a privilege. "For unto you," he says, "it is given in behalf of Christ, not only to believe on Him, but also to suffer for His sake." It seems, too, to be regarded as a part of their calling. "For even hereunto were you called: because Christ also suffered for us, leaving us an example, that you should follow His steps." Happy will be that afflicted child of God, who is led to view his Father's discipline in the light of a privilege. To drink of the cup that Christ drank of—to bear any part of the cross that He bore—to tread in any measure the path that He trod, is a privilege indeed. This is a distinction which angels have never attained. They know not the honor of suffering with Christ, of being made conformable to His death. It is peculiar to the believer in Jesus—it is his privilege, his calling.

SEPTEMBER 26

"Jesus said unto him, If you will be perfect, go and sell that you have, and give to the poor, and you shall have treasure in heaven: and come and follow me. But when the young man heard that saying, he went away sorrowful: for he had great possessions." Matthew 19:21, 22

There cannot, perhaps, be a position, however peculiar and difficult, in which the believer may be placed, but he will find that Jesus, either by precept or example, has defined the path in which he should walk. The subject of this meditation pointedly and solemnly addresses itself to the rich. Circumstanced as you are by the providence of God, you have need closely and prayerfully to ascertain how, in your situation, Jesus walked. One of the peculiar snares to which your station exposes you is high-mindedness, and consequent self-trust and complacency. But here the Lord Jesus presents Himself as your example. He, too, was rich; creating all things, He possessed all things. The Creator of all worlds, all worlds were at His command. Yet, amazing truth! in the days of His humiliation, He was as though He possessed not—"Though He was rich, yet for our sakes He became poor." In view of such an illustrious pattern, what is your duty? Simple and obvious. You are in a degree to become poor, by devoting your substance to the glory of God. To amass wealth, for the purpose of hoarding it, is contrary to the spirit of the gospel, and is opposed to the teaching and example of Christ. It is a sin, an awful, a soul-periling sin. Your property is a talent, for which, as a steward, you are as certainly and as solemnly accountable to God as for any other. It is, perhaps, the one talent that He has given you. What if you bury it in covetousness and parsimony, or in a prodigal expenditure and self-indulgence, refusing to relax your grasp of it to promote His cause and truth, who became poor to enrich us, how will you meet His scrutiny and His glance when the judgment is set, and He demands an account of your stewardship? Nor is it a small, though perhaps a solitary talent. Bestowed upon but few, the obligation becomes the greater to consecrate it unreservedly to the Lord. And how can you withhold it in view of the claims which crowd upon you on either hand? What! are you at a loss for a channel through which your benevolence might flow? Are you inquiring, "How shall I devote my property to God? In what way may this, my one talent, best answer the end for which it is bestowed?" Cast your eye around you—surely you cannot long hesitate. Survey the map of Christian missions—is there no part of Christ's kingdom languishing through an inadequacy of pecuniary support? Is there no important enterprise impeded in its course of benevolence by the lack of funds? No useful society discouraged and crippled through the narrowness and insufficiency of its resources? Is there no important sphere of labor in your vicinity neglected, no spot in the moral wilderness entirely untilled, because the means to supply an effective agency have been lacking? Is there no faithful, hard-working minister of Christ within your knowledge and your reach, combating with straitened circumstances, oppressed by poverty, and toiling amid lonely care, embarrassment, and anxiety, studiously and delicately screened from human eye, which it is in your power to alleviate and remove? Is there no widow's heart you could make to sing for joy? no orphan, whose tears you could dry? no saint of God tried by sickness, or need, or imprisonment, from whose spirit you could lift the burden, and from whose heart you could chase the sorrow, and from whose feet you could strike the fetter? Surely a world of need, and woe, and suffering is before you, nor need you yield to a moment's hesitation in selecting the object around which your charity should entwine.

Here, then, is your example. Jesus became poor, lived poor, and died poor. Dare you die a rich man—an affluent professor? I beseech you ponder this question. If your Lord has left you an example that you should follow His steps, then you are called upon to become poor, to live poor, even to die poor for Him. Especially are you exhorted to rejoice in that, by the grace of God, you are made low. That in the midst of so much calculated to nourish the pride and lofty independence of the natural heart, you have been made to know your deep spiritual poverty, and as a sinner have been brought to the feet of Jesus. By that grace only can you be kept low. Here is your only security. Here wealth invests its possessor with no real power or greatness. It confers no moral or intellectual glory. It insures not against the inroad of evil. It throws around no shield. It may impart a measure of artificial importance, authority, and influence in the world's estimation; beyond this, what is it? Unsanctified by Divine grace, it entails upon its unhappy possessor an innumerable train of evils. As a Christian man, then, exposed to the snares of even a moderate degree of worldly prosperity, your only security is in drawing largely from the "exceeding riches of Christ's grace;" your true wealth is in the fear of God ruling in your heart, in the love of Christ constraining you to "lie low in a low place;" to bear the cross daily; to walk closely, obediently, and humbly with God; employing the property with which He has entrusted you as a faithful steward; your eye ever "looking unto Jesus" as your pattern. You "know the grace of our Lord Jesus Christ"—the rich, the amazing, the sovereign, the free grace of Jesus, to which you owe all that is precious and glorious in the prospect of eternity—let this grace, then, accomplish its perfect work in you, by leading you to glory only in Jesus, to yield yourself supremely to His service, and to regard the worldly wealth God has conferred upon you as valuable only as it promotes His kingdom, truth, and glory, who "though rich, for your sakes became poor, that you, through His poverty, might be made rich."

SEPTEMBER 27

"Be merciful unto me, O God, be merciful unto me: for my soul trusts in you: yes, in the shadow of your wings will I make my refuge, until these calamities be overpast. I will cry unto God most high; unto God that performs all things for me." Psalm 57:1, 2

The exercise of faith strengthens, as the neglect to exercise, weakens it. It is the constant play of the arm that brings out its muscular power in all its fullness; were that arm allowed to hang by its own side, still and motionless, how soon would its sinews contract, and its energy waste away! So it is with faith, the right arm of a believer's strength; the more it is exercised, the mightier it becomes; neglect to use it, allow it to remain inert and inoperative, and the effect will be a withering up of its power. Now when gloomy providences, and sharp trials and temptations, thicken around a poor believing soul, then is it the time for faith to put on its strength, and come forth to the battle. God never places His child in any difficulties, or throws upon him any cross, but it is a call to exercise faith; and if the opportunity of its exercise passes away without improvement, the effect will be a weakening of the principle, and a feeble putting forth of its power in the succeeding trial. Do not forget, that the more faith is brought into play, the more it increases; the more it is exercised, the stronger it becomes.

Some of the choicest mercies of the covenant brought into the experience of the believer, come by a travail of faith: it maybe a tedious and a painful process; faith may be long and sharply tried, yet the blessings it will bring forth will more than repay for all the weeping, and suffering, and crying, it has occasioned. Do not be surprised, then, at any severe trial of faith; be sure that when it is thus tried, God is about to bring your soul into the possession of some great and perhaps hitherto unexperienced mercy. It may be a travail of faith for spiritual blessing; and the result may be a deepening of the work in your heart, increase of spirituality, more weanedness from creature-trust, and more child-like leaning upon the Lord; more simple, close, and sanctifying knowledge of the Lord Jesus. Or, it may be a travail of faith for temporal mercy, for the supply of some need, the rescue from some embarrassment, the deliverance out of some peculiar and trying difficulty; but whatever the character of the trial of faith be, the issue is always certain and glorious. The Lord may bring His child into difficult and strait paths, He may hedge him about with thorns so that he cannot get out, but it is only to draw the soul more simply to repose in Himself; that, in the extremity, when no creature would or could help, when refuge failed, and no man cared for his soul, that then faith should go out and rest itself in Him who never disowns His own work, but always honors the feeblest exhibition, and turns His ear to the faintest cry. "Out of the depths have I cried unto You, O Lord. Lord, hear my voice; let Your ears be attentive to the voice of my supplication." "In my distress I called upon the Lord, and cried unto my God: He heard my voice out of His temple, and my cry came before Him, even into His ears." "O magnify the Lord with me, and let us exalt His name together. I sought the Lord, and He heard me, and delivered me from all my fears." "This poor man cried, and the Lord heard him; and saved him out of all his troubles." Here was the severe travail of faith, and here we see the blessed result. Thus true is God's word, which declares that "weeping may endure for a night, but joy comes in the morning."

The trial of faith is a test of its degree. We know not what faith we possess, until the Lord calls it into exercise; we may be greatly deceived as to its nature and degree; to walk upon the stormy water may be thought by us an easy thing; to witness for Christ, no hard matter: but the Lord brings our faith to the test. He bids us come to Him upon the water, and then we begin to sink; He suffers us to be assailed by our enemies, and we shrink from the cross; He puts our faith to the trial, and then we learn how little we possess.

SEPTEMBER 28

"But we see Jesus, who was made a little lower than the angels for the suffering of death, crowned with glory and honor." Hebrews 2:9

There was an honoring, but not a glorifying of our humanity, when the Son of God assumed it. Its union with the Deity—its fullness of the Spirit—its spotless holiness—its deep knowledge of, and intimate fellowship with, God—conspired to invest it with a dignity and honor such as no creature had ever before, or ever shall again attain. But not until its ascension into heaven was it glorified. Oh, through what humiliation did it pass, what indignity did it endure, when below! What sinless weaknesses, imperfections, and frailties clung to it! It hungered, it thirsted, it labored, it sorrowed, it wept, it suffered, it bled, it died! "The poor man's scorn, the rich man's ridicule," what indignities did it endure! It was scourged, it was bruised, it was mocked, it was smitten, it was spit upon, it was nailed to the tree, it was pierced, it was slain! Oh, what eye, but that of faith, can, through all this degradation, behold the person of the incarnate God?

But now "we see Jesus, who was made a little lower than the angels, for the suffering of death, crowned with glory and honor." Even after His resurrection, it must be acknowledged that a change, approximating to that state of glory, had already passed over Him. So transformed was He, that even His disciples, when they saw Him, knew Him not. What, then, must be the glory that encircles Him now that He has passed within His kingdom, and is exalted at the right hand of God, "far above all heavens, that He might fill all things"! John, during his banishment at Patmos, was favored with a view of His glorified humanity, and thus describes its dazzling appearance—"I saw seven golden candlesticks; and in the midst of the seven candlesticks one like unto the Son of man, clothed with a garment down to the foot, and girt about the breasts with a golden girdle. His head and His hairs were white like wool, as white as snow; and His eyes were as a flame of fire, and His feet like unto fine brass, as if they burned in a furnace; and His voice as the sound of many waters. And He had in His right hand seven stars; and out of His mouth went a sharp two-edged sword; and His countenance was as the sun shines in his strength. And when I saw Him, I fell at His feet as dead. And He laid His right hand upon me, saying unto me, Fear not; I am the first and the last: I am He that lives, and was dead; and, behold, I am alive for evermore, Amen; and have the keys of hell and of death." Sublime description of the "glory and honor" which now crown the exalted humanity of our adorable Redeemer! Did the awe-stricken and prostrate evangelist entertain any doubt of the glorious person who thus appeared to him? that doubt must all have vanished the moment he felt the "right hand" of Jesus laid upon Him, and heard His own familiar voice saying unto him, "Fear not." Oh, what a tangible evidence and what a near view did he now have of the exalted and glorified humanity of his Lord! At that instant he saw Him to be divine, and he felt Him to be human!

Yes! the very tabernacle of flesh in which He dwelt, the identical robe of humanity that He wore, He carried up with Him into heaven, and sat down with it upon the throne. There it is, highly exalted. There it is, above angels, and higher than saints, in close affinity and eternal union with the Godhead. There it is, bathing itself in the "fullness of joy," and drinking deeply of the satisfying "pleasures" which are at God's "right hand for evermore." Oh, what must be the holy delight which the human soul of Jesus now experiences! Sin presses upon it no more; sorrow beclouds it no more; the hidings of God's face distress it no more; infirmity clings to it no more: it exults in the beams of God's unveiled glory, and it swims in the ocean of His ineffable love. If the vision upon Mount Tabor was so glorious—if the splendors there encircling that form which yet had not passed through the scenes of the crucifixion, the resurrection, and the ascension, were so overpowering—if the attractions of that spot were so great, and the ecstasy of that moment was so ravishing—what, oh, what must be the glory, the joy, the bliss of heaven, where we shall no longer see Him "through a glass darkly," but "as He is," and "face to face"!

SEPTEMBER 29

"For if the blood of bulls and of goats, and the ashes of an heifer sprinkling the unclean, sanctifies to the purifying of the flesh: how much more shall the blood of Christ, who through the eternal Spirit offered himself without spot to God, purge your conscience from dead works to serve the living God?" Hebrews 9:13, 14

But for a crucified Savior, there could be no possible return to God; in no other way could He, consistently with the holiness and rectitude of the Divine government, with what He owes to Himself as a just and holy God, receive a poor, wandering, returning sinner. Mere repentance and humiliation for and confession of sin could entitle the soul to no act of pardon. The obedience and death of the Lord Jesus laid the foundation and opened the way for the exercise of this great and sovereign act of grace. The cross of Jesus displays the most awful exhibition of God's hatred of sin, and at the same time the most august manifestation of His readiness to pardon it. Pardon, full and free, is written out in every drop of blood that is seen, is proclaimed in every groan that is heard, and shines in the very prodigy of mercy that closes the solemn scene upon the cross. Oh blessed door of return, open and never shut to the wanderer from God! how glorious, how free, how accessible! Here the sinful, the vile, the guilty, the unworthy, the poor, the penniless may come. Here, too, the weary spirit may bring its burden, the broken spirit its sorrow, the guilty spirit its sin, the backsliding spirit its wandering. All are welcome here. The death of Jesus was the opening and the emptying of the full heart of God; it was the outgushing of that ocean of infinite mercy that heaved, and panted, and longed for an outlet; it was God showing how He could love a poor guilty sinner. What more could He have done than this? what stronger proof, what richer gift, what costlier boon could He have given in attestation of that love? Now, it is the simple belief of this that brings the tide of joy down into the soul; it is faith's view of this that dissolves the adamant, rends asunder the flinty rock, smites down the pyramid of self-righteousness, lays the rebellious will in the dust, and enfolds the repenting, believing soul in the very arms of free, rich, and sovereign love. Here, too, the believer is led to trace the sin of his backsliding in its darkest lines, and to mourn over it with his bitterest tears—

"Then beneath the cross adoring,
Sin does like itself appear;
When the wounds of Christ exploring,
I can read my pardon there."

If the Lord has restored your soul, dear reader, remember why He has done it—to make you hate your sins. He hates them, and He will make you to hate them too; and this He does by pardoning them, by sprinkling the atoning blood upon the conscience, and by restoring unto you the joys of His salvation. And never is sin so sincerely hated, never is it so deeply deplored, so bitterly mourned over, and so utterly forsaken, as when He speaks to the heart, and says, "Your sins are forgiven you, go in peace." As though He did say, "I have blotted out your transgressions, I have healed your backslidings, I have restored your soul; that you may remember and be confounded, and never open your mouth any more because of your shame, when I am pacified toward you for all that you have done, says the Lord God."

If your heavenly Father has restored your soul, not only has He done it from the spring of His own unchangeable love, but that which has prevailed with Him was the power of the sweet incense of the Redeemer's blood before the mercy-seat. Moment by moment does this fragrant cloud go up, bearing as it ascends all the circumstances of all the Israel of God. There is not only the blood already sprinkled on the mercy-seat, which has satisfied Divine justice, but there is the constant pleading of the blood, by Jesus, the Priest, before the throne. Oh precious thought, oh comforting, encouraging truth, for a soul retreading its steps back to God! Of its own it has nothing to plead but its folly, its ingratitude, its wretchedness, and its sin; but faith can lay its trembling hand upon this blessed truth—faith can observe Jesus clothed in His priestly garments, standing between the soul and God, spreading forth His hands, and pleading on behalf of the returning believer the merits of His own precious obedience and death. And thus encouraged, he may draw near and touch the scepter: "If any man sin, we have an Advocate with the Father, Jesus Christ the righteous." "Christ is not entered into the holy places made with hands, which are the figures of the true; but into heaven itself, now to appear in the presence of God for us.

SEPTEMBER 30

"Then said Jesus to those Jews which believed on him, If you continue in my word, then are you my disciples indeed; and you shall know the truth, and the truth shall make you free." John 8:31, 32

In proportion to a believer's simple, filial, and close walk with God, will be his deep and spiritual discoveries of truth. "If any man will do His will, he shall know of the doctrine whether it be of God." The more steadily he walks in God's light, the clearer will he see the light. The nearer he lives to the Sun of Righteousness, the more entirely will he be flooded with its glory, and the more vividly will he reflect its brightness. The more simply and entirely the believing soul lives on Christ, the more enlarged, experimental, and practical will be his ideas of all truth. The central fact of the Bible is, Christ crucified. From this, as their center, all the lines of truth diverge, and to this, as by a common attraction, they all again return. To know Christ, then—to know Him as dwelling in the heart by His own Spirit —is to have traversed the great circle of spiritual truth. What is His own testimony? "He that has seen me, has seen the Father." "I am the Father's great revelation. I have come to make Him known. To unveil His attributes, to illustrate His law, to pour forth the ocean fullness of His love, and to erect one common platform on which may meet in holy fellowship God and the sinner—the two extremes of being. Learn of me; I am the way, the truth, and the life."

Not only will a spiritual perception of the beauty and fitness of the truth be the result of a close and filial communion with God, but the assurance that God's word is truth, and not fiction, will increase. And to be thoroughly established in this is no small attainment. To know that God's word is true—to cherish no doubt or hesitancy—to give Him full credit for all that He has said—to repose by simple faith upon the promise, and on the faithfulness of Him that has promised—is a blessing earnestly to be sought, and, when found, diligently to be kept.

To quote the striking words of the apostle, "He that believes on the Son of God has the witness in himself." He has the inward witness to the truth. He needs no outward demonstration. He is in possession of a sort of evidence to the truth of God's word which scepticism cannot shake, because it cannot reach it. He may not be able to define the precise nature of his evidence; his reply to the unbelieving objector is, "It must be felt to be known, it must be experienced to be understood. This evidence is not the result of a labored process of thought.

I arrived not at it by mathematical reasoning. I was convinced by the Eternal Spirit of sin, fled to Christ, ventured my all upon Him, and now I know of a surety that God's blessed word is truth." And not more completely was his sophistry confuted, who attempted to disprove the doctrine of motion, by his opponent immediately rising and walking, than a humble, spiritual, though unlettered believer may thus put to silence the foolishness and ignorance of men. Their sophistry he may not be able to detect, their assertions he may not be able to disprove, yet by a walk holy and close with God he may demonstrate to the unbelieving universe that Jehovah's word is true.

Christian professor! are you one of Christ's true disciples, following Him closely, or are you walking at a distance from Him? A distant walk will as certainly bring darkness into the soul, with its painful attendants—unbelief—loss of evidence—hard thoughts of God—slavish fear—as if an individual were to close every inlet of a habitation to the rays of the sun, and sit down amid the gloom and obscurity with which He has enshrouded Himself. There is no true spiritual light but that which beams from the Sun of Righteousness, and to this every inlet of the soul must be open. To enjoy this light, then, a believer must dwell near the Sun—he must live close to Christ; he must live the life of daily faith upon Him—he must look away from himself to Jesus—he must walk worthy of the Lord unto all pleasing—he must be found prayerful and diligent in the means; while, rising above them, he draws all his life, light, and peace from the God of the means. Oh, what losers are they who walk as Peter walked—at a distance from their Lord; what seasons of endearing communion—what tokens of love—what visits of mercy they rob themselves of! What losers are they who neglect the means of grace—closet prayer—church fellowship—the communion of saints—the blessed ordinances of baptism and the Lord's supper—these channels, through which a covenant God conveys such untold blessings into the soul of His dear child; for "The secret of the Lord is with those who fear Him;" and to fear Him is not to dread Him as a slave, but as a child to walk in all the commandments and ordinances of the Lord blameless. "Oh, send out Your light and Your truth; let them lead me, let them bring me unto Your holy hill and to Your tabernacles. Then will I go unto the altar of God, unto God my exceeding joy: yes, upon the harp will I praise You, O God, my God."

OCTOBER

OCTOBER 1

"The law of the Lord is perfect, converting the soul." Psalm 19:7

Emanating from a Being infinitely perfect in every moral perfection, it follows as a natural sequence from this truth, that the law, designed to be a transcript of what God is—a copy of Himself—must be in every respect a most perfect law. How could it be otherwise? Is it rational to suppose that a Being of infinite holiness, wisdom, and goodness would form a rule for the government of moral creatures, that would fail to place before their eye the loftiest standard of excellence, and that should not demand and secure their supreme obedience and happiness? It follows, then, that the law being essentially and perfectly holy, all its requirements must be equally so. It cannot change, nor compromise, nor soften down either the nature or the outline or the enforcement of a single enactment. It demands of every creature the profoundest homage, the most implicit obedience, and the most perfect love. In requiring this, the creature shall have no ground for impeaching the Divine goodness. He shall have no reason for alleging of God that He is harsh and austere. As if fearful of perplexing the mind with a multitude of enactments, our Lord has presented one precept of the law, the perfect keeping of which resolves itself into a virtual fulfillment of all—"Jesus said unto him, You shall love the Lord your God with all your heart, and with all your soul, and with all your mind. This is the first and great commandment."

Who but an infinitely wise Lawgiver could have embodied all the requisitions of an extended code in a single one? What an unfolding of the wisdom of God is here! In securing to Himself the supreme love of His creatures, He wins a willing obedience to every precept of His law. Such is the all-commanding, all-constraining power of love to God! Employing no other than this gentle and persuasive motive, God asks your intellect—your time—your service—your rank—your substance—your person—your life—your all. In demanding this complete surrender, His law stands forth, in view of all created intelligences, as a rule worthy of Him from whom it emanates. Oh yes! it is a most righteous law.

OCTOBER 2

"But we speak the wisdom of God in a mystery, even the hidden wisdom, which God ordained before the world unto our glory." 1 Corinthians 2:7

There is much of deep mystery in revelation. God, considered both in Himself and in His operations, is a mystery stretching far beyond the most sublime power of finite reason. "Can you by searching find out God? can you find out the Almighty unto perfection?" and of His operations may we not exclaim with the inspired penman, "Lo! these are parts of His ways; but how little a portion is heard of Him!" Christ, too, is the great "mystery of godliness." Whether His complex person is regarded—the union of the Divine and human natures in one—or whether we look at His work—His obedience and death constituting a full atonement to Divine justice in behalf of the sins of His people—it must be acknowledged a depth too profound for human thought adequately to fathom. What can poor finite reason accomplish here? What beams can its feeble, flickering light cast upon this world of mystery? And if ever it stands forth invested in its own native impotence, it is when it sits in judgment upon the doctrines and facts of revelation, discarding or retaining such only as are intelligible to its dwarfish capacity. "Which things," says the apostle, "the angels desire to look into." Mark his expressions! He represented not these celestial beings of purity and intellect as scaling the heights and diving into the depths of redemption's mystery, but "which things the angels desire"—scarcely dare—but "desire to look into." And yet for a fallen and unrenewed mind to sit in judgment upon God's truth can only be exceeded in its temerity by the depravity which prompts it.

If the truth of God, in its doctrines and facts, is a mystery incomprehensible to unrenewed reason, what shall we say of the truth as experienced in the heart? If reason cannot understand the vast framework of truth, how can it comprehend the secret power by which it operates? The very fact, that to be understood it must be experienced, accounts for the difficulty. The transforming operation of the Holy Spirit upon the mind—giving it a new bias, new inclinations, turning its darkness into light, and kindling its enmity into love; the life of God in the soul, creating the man anew in Christ Jesus—that life which is hidden, ever productive of a holy life that is seen—its hopes and its fears, its defeats and its triumphs—the causes which operate to deaden it, and the spiritual nourishment by which it is supported—all, all is incomprehensible to human reason. Truly "the world knows us not."

The cause of this incapacity of reason, in its natural state, to comprehend spiritual and experimental truth is its corruption and perversion by sin. Sin has impaired our mental faculties—enslaved, clouded, and debased our reason. We open God's word, and it declares that since the fall the nature of man has been corrupt, and his reason blind; his understanding darkened, and his heart, the seat of his affections, polluted: "having the understanding darkened, being alienated from the life of God through the ignorance that is in them, because of the blindness of their heart." The natural man, while in that state, so far from being able to explore the wide domain of spiritual truth, hates and flees from it when proposed to his consideration, "receiving not the things of the Spirit of God, they being foolishness unto him." This being the state of man, God's word consequently declares it necessary that, before spiritual truth can be understood, he should be "transformed by the renewing of his mind;" that he should be restored to that sound mind, and enlightened understanding, and spiritual discernment, with which his nature was endowed when it came originally from the hand of God; in a word, that he should be born again, created anew in Christ Jesus; that old things should pass away, and that all things should become new. Then, and then only, will he be able to understand the "truth of God in a mystery."

OCTOBER 3

"But they had heard only, That he which persecuted us in times past, now preaches the faith which once he destroyed. And they glorified God in me." Galatians 1:23, 24

In the conversion of His people—their translation from nature to grace—the Redeemer is glorified. This is the first step to a manifest glorifying of Christ in His called saints. Conversion is the commencement of an endless revenue of glory to Christ. To behold a poor sinner living a life of practical enmity to God, hatred to Jesus, rebellion against the Divine government, and willful and determined hostility to the one glorious plan of salvation—perhaps a blasphemer, a persecutor, and injurious—now changed, now conquered, now sitting at the feet of Jesus, "clothed and in his right mind," oh, is there no glory thus brought to the grace of Christ Jesus? To see him translated out of darkness into God's marvelous light, emancipated from the power of sin and Satan, and made the Lord's free-man—the rebellious will conquered, the hard heart subdued, the proud spirit humbled, the hatred turned into love, and the long roving mind now finding its center of rest and fountain of happiness in a reconciled

God—oh! is there no crown of glory placed on the head of Jesus in all this. Say, you angelic spirits, bending over the mercy-seat in deep contemplation of its awful mysteries of incarnate grace and dying love—whose eyes glisten with new effulgence, and whose bosoms expand with new joy, over one sinner that repents—do you see no glory deepening around the Son of God, as each vessel of mercy is called in, emptied of self, and filled with Jesus? Oh, how are the power, the wisdom, the grace, the love of the Redeemer glorified, and God through Him, by every new accession thus made to the number of the redeemed! Aim to be instrumental of bringing one soul to receive the Lord Jesus as all its salvation, and you bring more glory to His name than were a thousand worlds like this to start into being at your fiat. "Those who be wise shall shine as the brightness of the firmament; and those who turn many to righteousness as the stars forever and ever."

In what a solemn and responsible position is every believer placed! "You are my witnesses, says the Lord." "I have created him for my glory." "You are my servant, O Israel, in whom I will be glorified." Then how "very jealous for the Lord of hosts" should we be! How vigilant, lest in any degree, or in any way, we withhold from Christ the glory due unto Him! There are many ways by which we may be betrayed into this grievous sin—a careless walk—unmortified sin—self-indulgence—a light and volatile spirit—a neglect of means—a distant walk with God—coldness of love towards the saints; but especially mixing up with, and indulging in, a sinful conformity to the world—its fashions, its pleasures, its literature, its religion! Christian reader, put the question fairly, honestly, and closely to your conscience—"Do I bring glory to Christ? Is my Redeemer magnified in me before the world and the church?" Oh, aim for a high standard! Do not be an ordinary Christian. "Herein is my Father glorified, that you bear much fruit; so shall you be my disciples." Thank God for the little, but, oh, aim for the "much fruit"—strong faith, ardent love, self-consuming zeal, unreserved obedience, holy, entire, and supreme surrender. Come, drawn by grace, constrained by love, attracted by the glory and the preciousness of Jesus—come now to that one "altar which sanctifies both the giver and the gift;" and as you lay yourself upon it, body, soul, and spirit, exclaim with the apostle, "Christ shall be magnified in my body, whether it be by life or by death." The solemn vow is taken! The holy surrender is made! It is seen, it is heard, it is ratified in heaven! May you be so strengthened from above, "that the name of our Lord Jesus Christ may be glorified in you, and you in Him, according to the grace of God and the Lord Jesus Christ."

OCTOBER 4

"But now is Christ risen from the dead, and become the first fruits of them that slept." 1 Corinthians 15:20

The resurrection of Christ is the pledge and earnest of the glorious resurrection of the believer. This great event—the crowning bliss of the church—has long been as a star of hope, on which the eye of faith has loved to gaze. Who does not recognize the doctrine of the resurrection, and trace the yearning of his soul for this glorious event, in the expressive and touching words of Job?—"There is hope of a tree, if it be cut down, that it will sprout again, and that the tender branch thereof will not cease. Though the root thereof wax old in the earth, and the stock thereof die in the ground; yet through the scent of water it will bud, and bring forth boughs like a plant." How strikingly and beautifully significant is this figure of the resurrection! His faith grafted upon the doctrine, see how his heart longed for the arrival of the event—"Oh that You would hide me in the grave, that You would keep me secret, until Your wrath be past; that You would appoint me a set time, and remember me! If a man die, shall he live again? All the days of my appointed time" (not the appointed time of his death, as some interpret it, but of his resurrection, for this is the event he is now anticipating), "will I wait until my change come. You shall call"—oh! how sweetly will fall the sound of the archangel's trumpet upon the ear of those who sleep in Jesus!—"You shall call, and I will answer: You will have a desire to the work of Your hands." But, if possible, in terms yet more distinct and glowing, the holy patriarch announces his faith in this doctrine, and expresses his ardent longing for this event—"I know that my Redeemer lives, and that He shall stand at the latter day upon the earth: and though after my skin worms destroy this body, yet in my flesh shall I see God; whom I shall see for myself, and mine eyes shall behold, and not another; though my reins be consumed within me."

The hope to which the resurrection of the Lord has begotten the believer is termed by the apostle a "lively," or, as it may be rendered, a "living hope." Its life springs from the resurrection-life of Christ, just as the same glorious event imparts quickening to the whole Christian economy. "Blessed be the God and Father of our Lord Jesus Christ, which, according to His abundant mercy, has begotten us again unto a lively hope, by the resurrection of Jesus Christ from the dead." Thus the believer, and he alone, can adopt the language of his Lord, as he resigns his body to the dust—and oh! Let it be the epitaph of all who sleep in Jesus—"MY FLESH ALSO SHALL REST IN HOPE." A living hope, based upon the resurrection of Jesus, smooths his suffering pathway to the tomb; hope dissipates its gloom, and kindles within its somber recesses an immortal radiance; and hope—the beacon of the sepulcher—throws its bright beams across the dark waters of eternity, revealing in all its glory an "inheritance incorruptible and undefiled, and that fades not away." Observe how closely the two events—the resurrection of Jesus, and that of the believer—are interwoven one with the other. "Now is Christ risen from the dead, and become the first-fruits of those who slept." "Every man in his own order: Christ the first-fruits; afterwards they that are Christ's at His coming." What was the meaning of the first sheaf, which, under the law, was commanded to be presented before the Lord in His temple? Was it not to be considered as an earnest, a pledge, and a pattern of the future harvest, ripening for the sickle? So was the resurrection of Jesus Christ from the dead. In like manner He burst from the grave, the "first-fruits," the earnest, the pledge, and the pattern of a future and a glorious harvest. As surely as He rose, so surely shall all His people rise. As certainly as the first golden sheaf has been presented in the temple, and waved before the throne of God, as certainly shall the "blade, the ear, and the full corn in the ear" be sickled in and gathered home, "and not the least grain fall upon the earth." "For if we believe that Jesus died and rose again, even so them also which sleep in Jesus will God bring with Him."

OCTOBER 5

"Yet made we not our prayer before the Lord our God, that we might turn from our iniquities, and understand your truth. Therefore has the Lord watched upon the evil, and brought it upon us: for the Lord our God is righteous in all his works which he does." Daniel 9:13, 14

All backsliding has its commencement in the neglect of prayer: it may date its beginning at the throne of grace. The restraining of prayer before God was the first step in departure; and the first step taken, and not immediately retraced, was quickly succeeded by others. Reader, do you tremble at the possibility of ever becoming a backslider? do you dread the thought of wounding Jesus, then restrain not prayer before God; vigilantly guard against the first symptom of declension in this holy exercise, or if that symptom has already appeared, haste you to the dear Physician, who alone has power to arrest its progress, and heal your soul.

A distant walk from God will super-induce distant thoughts of God, and this is no light consequence of the soul's declension in the spirit and habit of prayer. If the simple axiom be true, that the more intimate we become with any object, the better we are prepared to judge of its nature and properties, we may apply it with peculiar appropriateness to our acquaintance with God. The encouraging invitation of His word is, "Acquaint now yourself with God, and be at peace." Now, it is this acquaintance with God that brings us into the knowledge of His character as a holy, loving, and faithful God; and it is this knowledge of His character that begets love and confidence in the soul towards Him. The more we know of God, the more we love Him: the more we try Him, the more we confide in Him. Let the spiritual reader, then, conceive what dire effects must result from a distant walk with God. When He appears in His corrective dealings, how will those dealings be interpreted in the distant walk of the soul? As of a covenant God? as of a loving Father? No, far from it. They will receive a harsh and unkind interpretation, and this will neutralize their effect: for in order to reap the proper fruit of the Lord's dealings with the soul, it is necessary that they should be viewed in the light of His faithfulness and love. The moment they are otherwise interpreted, the soul starts off from God, and wraps itself up in gloomy and repulsive views of His character, and government, and dealings. But this will assuredly follow from a distant walk. Oh guard against a declension in prayer; let there be no distance between God and your soul!

Do not forget that the season of trial and of bereavement is often the sanctified occasion of a revival of prayer in the soul. The Lord has marked your wanderings, He has had His eye upon the declension of your soul. That voice, always so pleasant to His ear, has ceased to call upon Him; and now He would recover you; He would hear that voice again, and how will He effect it? He causes you to "pass under the rod," sends some sore trial, lays on you some weighty cross, brings trouble and sorrow into your soul, and then you cry unto Him, and do besiege the mercy-seat. Oh how eagerly is God sought, how attractive and how precious does the throne of grace become, when the soul is thus led into deep waters of trial! No longer silent, no longer dumb, the believer calls upon God, pleads with "strong crying and tears," wrestles and agonizes, and thus the slumbering spirit of prayer is stirred up and revived in the soul. Oh sweet affliction, oh precious discipline, that brings back the wandering soul to a closer and a holier walk with God!

Again we exhort the believer—guard against the least declension in prayer; let the first unfavorable symptom that appears alarm you, go to the Lord in your worst frames; stay not from Him until you get a good one. Satan's grand argument to keep a soul from prayer is—"Go not with that cold and insensible frame; go not with that hard and sinful heart; stay until you are more fit to approach God!" and listening to this specious reasoning, many poor, distressed, burdened, longing souls have been kept from the throne of grace, and consequently from all comfort and consolation. But the gospel says—"Go in your very worst frames;" Christ says—"Come just as you are;" and every promise and every example but encourages the soul to repair to the cross, whatever be its frame or condition.

OCTOBER 6

"Many are the afflictions of the righteous: but the Lord delivers him out of them all." Psalm 34:19

How many and diversified are the peculiar trying circumstances of God's dear family! Each heart has its own sorrow—each soul bears its own cross; but Jesus is enough for all—He has sympathy for each and all His suffering people. Are you suffering from pining sickness? are your days wearisome, and your nights sleepless, from the inroads of disease? Then there is sympathy in Christ for you: for it is written, "Himself took our infirmities, and bore our sicknesses." He remembers that you are but dust—and we doubt not, His blessed body knew what languid days and sleepless nights were. Oh, then, think of Jesus. That disease that wastes—that pain that racks—that debility that unnerves you, Jesus knows full and sympathetically. True, He is now beyond all physical feelings, yet His tender heart sympathizes still.

Are you suffering from temporal poverty? Are sources on which you depended broken up? Friends on whom you have leaned removed? Does want stare you in the face? And are you at a loss to know from where the next supply may come? Even here, my brother, even here, my sister, can Jesus sympathize with you. He, like you, and like the greater part of His people, was poor in this world's goods. No home sheltered, no daily-spread table provided for Him; He was a poor, homeless, houseless, friendless wanderer. The foxes had holes, and the birds had nests, but Jesus had not where to lay His blessed head—that head that ached and bled for you. Take your poverty to Him—take your needs to Him. Let the principle of faith now be exercised. Has He died for your soul—has He pardoned your sins—has He given you Himself, then will He not with Himself freely give you all things necessary for your temporal comfort, while yet a pilgrim upon earth? Take your poverty and your want simply and directly to Jesus; He has an ear to hear your cry, a heart to sympathize with your case, and a hand to supply all your need. Then again we say, take your needs simply and directly to Christ.

Has death entered your domestic circle, plucking from it some precious and valued member? Has He put lover and friend far from you, leaving the heart to weep in silence and sadness over the wreck of hopes that were so bright, and over the rupture of ties that were so tender? Oh, there is sympathy in Christ for this! Jesus knew what it was to weep over the grave of buried love—of friendship interred; He knew what it was to have affection's ties broken, leaving the heart wounded and bleeding. He can enter into your sorrow, bereaved reader; yes, even into yours. See Him at the tomb of Lazarus—see Him weep—"behold how He loved him." What! do you repair to the grave of the dear departed one to weep, and Jesus not sympathize with you? Let not unbelief close up this last remaining source of consolation—the tender sympathy of Christ. He can enter into those tears of yours: the heart's desolateness, loneliness, and disappointment are not unknown and unnoticed by our blessed Immanuel. And why has the Lord dealt thus with you? why has He torn the idol from its temple? why has He emptied the heart, and left it thus lonely and desolate? Oh why, but to prepare that temple for Himself; why, but to pour into its emptiness the full tide of His own precious love and sympathy. For this, beloved, has He been, and, it may be, is now dealing with you. That heart belongs to Him—He bought it at a costly price; it belongs to Him—He vanquished it by the omnipotence of His Spirit; it belongs to Him—He sealed it with His precious blood. And He would have you know this, too, by deep and sweet experience. He would have you know how He has loved you, and loves you still; He would have you know that you are His—His by eternal election—His by gift—by purchase—by conquest—by a covenant that all your departures, all your unfaithfulness, all your unworthiness, all the changing scenes through which you pass, shall never and can never alter. All this it is His will you should experience. Then bow with submission to the discipline; as a weaned child, sit you at His feet, adopting His own blessed words, "Not my will, but Your be done."

OCTOBER 7

"But God commends his love towards us, in that, while we were yet sinners, Christ died for us." Romans 5:8

From what other and higher source could the atonement have proceeded, if not from the very heart of God? And from His heart it did proceed. And not more freely does the sun pour forth its streams of light, and not more freely does the air fan with its refreshing influence, and not more freely does the ocean-billow heave, than the atonement flows from the heart of God! "God is love;" and the seat of that love is His heart. Towards a sinner standing in the righteousness of His Son, that heart is love, and nothing but love. Not an unkind thought lodging there; not a repulsive feeling dwelling there; all is love, and love of the most tender character. Yes, we dare affirm, that towards His chosen people there never has been, and there never will be, one thought of unkindness, of anger, of rebuke in the heart of God: from eternity it has been love, through time it is love, and on through eternity to come it will be love. What! are not their afflictions, their chastisements, the rough and thorny path they tread, proofs of God's displeasure? What! is that individual loved of God, whom I see yonder bearing that heavy and daily cross; against whom billow after billow dashes, to whom messenger after messenger is sent; whose gourds are withered in a night, and whose fountains are all broken in a day; who is poor, feeble, and dependent; what! is that individual beloved of God? Go and ask that afflicted saint; go and ask that cross-bearing disciple; go and ask that son and daughter of disease and penury; and they will tell you, their Father's dealings with them are the most costly proofs of His love: that instead of unkindness in that cross, there was love; instead of harshness in that rebuke, there was tenderness; and that when He withered that gourd, and broke up that cistern, and removed that earthly prop, it was but to pour the tide of His own love in the heart, and satiate the soul with His goodness. Oh, dear cross! oh, sweet affliction! thus to open the heart of God; thus to bring God near to the soul, and the soul near to God.

Let it not be forgotten that the atonement had its origin in the heart of God; it follows, then, that it must be free. Does the sun need bribing in order to shine? does the wind need persuasion in order to blow? does the ocean-wave need argument in order to roll? is the sun-light purchased? is the air purchased? is the water that flows from the fountain purchased? Not less free is the love of God, gushing from His heart, and flowing down through the channel of the cross of Christ, to a poor repenting, believing sinner, without works, without merit, without money, without price, without a previous fitness. Convictions do not merit it; repentances do not merit it; tears do not merit it; faith does not merit it. Pardon to the chief of sinners—forgiveness to the vilest of the vile—the blotting out of sins of the deepest dye—the justification and acceptance of the most unworthy—all, free as the heart of God can make it. The hungry and the thirsty, the poor and the penniless, the weary and the heavy-laden, may come to the gospel provision, for the heart of God bids them welcome.

The objects contemplated in the special and gracious design of the atonement establish its perfect freeness beyond all question. Who are they? Are they spoken of as the worthy, the righteous, the deserving, the rich, the noble? The very reverse. They are sinners, ungodly, unworthy. "When we were yet without strength, in due time Christ died for the ungodly." And see how our blessed Lord confirms this statement: "I am not come to call the righteous (that is, the self-righteous—those who were righteous in their own estimation, and despised others), but sinners to repentance." And who did He save when upon earth? Were they the worthy or the most unworthy? were they the righteous or sinners? Take the case of Saul of Tarsus. His own description of his previous character will certainly be believed: "which was before a blasphemer, and a persecutor, and injurious." And yet he "obtained mercy:" and why? "That in me Jesus Christ might show forth all long-suffering, for a pattern to them who should hereafter believe on Him to life everlasting." If Saul of Tarsus, then, obtained mercy—obtained it as a sinner of the deepest dye—obtained it fully, freely, aside from all human merit—penitent reader, so may you.

OCTOBER 8

"But to him that works not, but believes on him that justifies the ungodly, his faith is counted for righteousness." Romans 4:5

Faith has to do with the understanding and the heart. A man must know his lost and ruined condition before he will accept of Christ; and how can he know this, without a spiritually enlightened mind? What a surprising change now passes over the man! He is brought, by the mighty power of the Holy Spirit, to a knowledge of himself. One beam of light, one touch of the Spirit, has altered all his views of himself, has placed him in a new aspect; all big thoughts, his affections, his desires, are diverted into another and an opposite channel; his fond views of his own righteousness have fled like a dream, his high thoughts are humbled, his lofty looks are brought low, and, as a broken-hearted sinner, he takes his place in the dust before God. Oh wondrous, oh blessed change! to see the Pharisee take the place, and to hear him utter the cry, of the Publican—"God be merciful to me a sinner!"—to hear him exclaim, "I am lost, self-ruined, deserving eternal wrath; and of sinners the vilest and the chief." And now the work and exercise of faith commences; the same blessed Spirit that convinced of sin presents to the soul a Savior crucified for the lost—unfolds a salvation full and free for the most worthless—reveals a fountain that "cleanses from all sin," and holds up to view a righteousness that "justifies from all things." And all that He sets the poor convinced sinner upon doing to avail himself of this, is simply to believe. To the momentous question, "What shall I do to be saved?" this is the only reply—"Believe in the Lord Jesus Christ, and you shall be saved." The anxious soul eagerly exclaims—"Have I then nothing to do but to believe?—have I no great work to accomplish, no price to bring, no worthiness to plead?—may I come just as I am, without merit, without self-preparation, without money, with all my vileness and nothingness?" Still the reply is, "Only believe." "Then, Lord, I do believe," exclaims the soul in a transport of joy; "help my unbelief." This, reader, is faith—faith, that wondrous grace, that mighty act of which you have heard so much, upon which so many volumes have been written, and so many sermons have been preached; it is the simple rolling of a wounded, bleeding heart upon a wounded, bleeding Savior; it is the simple reception of the amazing truth, that Jesus died for the ungodly—died for sinners—died for the poor, the vile, the bankrupt; that He invites and welcomes to His bosom all poor, convinced, heavy-laden sinners. The heart, believing this wondrous announcement, going out of all other dependencies and resting only in this—receiving it, welcoming it, rejoicing in it, in a moment, all, all is peace. Do not forget, reader, that faith is but to believe with all the heart that Jesus died for sinners; and the full belief of this one fact will bring peace to the most anxious and sin-troubled soul.

OCTOBER 9

"That you may know how you ought to behave yourself in the house of God, which is the church of the living God, the pillar and ground of the truth." 1 Timothy 3:15

God has been graciously pleased to appoint His church the great conservator of His truth, and His truth the especial medium of sanctification to His church; there is a close and beautiful relation between the two. The church may be compared to the golden lamp which contains the sacred oil, which, in its turn, feeds the flame of its light and holiness. The church is to guard with a jealous and vigilant eye the purity of the truth, while the truth is to beautify and sanctify the ark which preserves it. Thus there is a close relation, and a reciprocal influence, between the church of Christ and the truth of God.

Every individual believer in Jesus is himself a subject, and therefore a witness, of the truth; he has been quickened, called, renewed, and partially sanctified through the instrumentality of God's revealed truth: "Of His own will begat He us with the word of truth." "For the truth's sake which dwells in us." "You are my witnesses, says the Lord." Here is unfolded one of the most solemn and affecting truths touching the character and individual responsibility of a child of God. He is a subject of truth, he is a repository of the truth, and he is a witness for the truth; yes, he is the only living witness to the truth which God has on earth. The world he lives in is a dark, polluted, God-blaspheming, Christ-denying, truth-despising world. The saints who have been called out of it according to His eternal purpose and love, and by His sovereign, distinguishing, and free grace, are the only lights and the only salt in the midst of this moral darkness and corruption. Here and there a light glimmers, irradiating the gloomy sphere in which it moves; here and there a spot of verdure appears, relieving the arid and barren desolation by which it is surrounded. These are the saints of the Most High, the witnesses of the Divine character, the omnipotent power, and the holy tendency, of God's blessed truth. Let the saints of God, then, solemnly weigh this affecting fact, that though the written word and the accompanying Spirit are God's witnesses in the world, yet they are the only living exemplification of the power of the truth, and, as such, are earnestly exhorted to be "blameless and harmless, the sons of God without rebuke, in the midst of a crooked and perverse nation, among whom you shine as lights in the world." Let them be careful to maintain good works, and so walk in all the holiness of the truth they profess; let them see that by no carelessness of deportment, by no want of integrity, by no worldly conformity, yes, by no inconsistency whatever, they bring a slur upon the holy doctrines they avowedly maintain and love; but let them show that, with the truth in their judgments, they possess grace in the heart, and unspotted holiness in the life.

OCTOBER 10

"Our backslidings are many; we have sinned against you." Jer. 14:7

All spiritual declension in the true believer necessarily implies the actual possession of grace. We must not lose sight of this truth. Never, in the lowest condition of the believer, does Christ deny His own work in the soul. "You have a little strength," are His heart-melting words to the backsliding church in Sardis. Oh, what a gracious, patience Savior is ours! But let us briefly trace this melancholy state to some of its causes, that we may be better able to point out its appropriate remedy.

The first cause undoubtedly is, the unguarded state of the soul. A Christian living in the daily neglect of self-examination must not marvel if, at a certain period of his religious course, he finds himself trembling upon the brink of gloomy despondency, his evidences gone, his hope obscured, and all the past of his Christian profession appearing to his view as a fearful delusion. But here let me suggest the cure. Examine before God the real state of your soul. Ascertain where you have lost ground. Retrace your way. Look honestly and fairly at your condition. Discouraging and repelling as it may appear, look it fully in the face, and lay it open before God exactly as it is, in the spirit and language of the Psalmist: "Search me, O God, and know my heart; try me, and know my thoughts; and see if there be any wicked way in me, and lead me in the way everlasting."

The grieving of the Spirit of God is a most fruitful cause of spiritual relapse. We have yet much to learn of our entire dependence upon the Holy Spirit, and of our eternal obligation to Him for all the blessings of which He is the author and the conveyancer. What themes for grateful contemplation to the spiritual mind are the love of the Spirit—the faithfulness of the Spirit—the tenderness of the Spirit—the patience of the Spirit! And yet in the long catalogue of the believer's backslidings, not the least is his grieving this Holy Spirit of God. But there is a remedy. Seek that Spirit whom you have driven from your presence; implore His return: beseech Him for Jesus' sake to revisit you, to breathe His reviving influence as of old upon your soul. Then will return the happy days of former years, the sweet seasons of your early history, and you shall "sing as in the days of your youth, and as in the day when you came up out of the land of Egypt."

"Return, O holy Dove, return,
Sweet messenger of rest;
I hate the sins that made You mourn,
And drove You from my breast."

Distance from the cross contributes greatly to a state of spiritual declension. Retiring from beneath its shelter and its shade, you have left the region of safety, light, and peace, and, wandering over the mountains of sin, worldliness, and unbelief, have lost yourself amid their darkness, solitude, and gloom. Turning away from the cross of Jesus, you have lost the view you once had of a sin-pardoning, reconciled Father; and judging of Him now by His providences and not by His promises, and contemplating Him through the gloomy medium of a conscience unsprinkled with the blood of Christ, you are disposed to impeach the wisdom, the faithfulness, and the love of all His conduct towards you. But listen to the remedy. Yield yourself afresh to the attractions of the cross. Return, return to it again. No burning cherubim nor flaming sword guards its avenue. The atoning blood there shed has opened the way of the sinner's approach, and the interceding High Priest in heaven keeps it open for every repentant prodigal. Return to the true cross. Come and sit down beneath its grateful shade. Poor, weary wanderer! there is life and power, peace and repose, for you still in the cross of Christ. Mercy speaks from it, God smiles in it, Jesus stands by it, and the Holy Spirit, hovering above it, is prepared to reveal it to you afresh, in all its healing, restoring power.

OCTOBER 11

"He was led as a sheep to the slaughter; and like a lamb dumb before his shearer, so opened he not his mouth: in his humiliation his judgment was taken away: and who shall declare his generation? for his life is taken from the earth." Acts 8:32, 33

In the person of the Son of God, the two extremes of being—the infinite and the finite—meet in strange and mysterious, but close and eternal union. The Divine came down to the human—Deity humbled itself to humanity. This was humiliation indeed! It was not the creature descending in the scale of creation, but it was the Creator stooping to the creature. "God was manifest in the flesh." "He humbled Himself." Oh, it is an amazing truth! So infinitely great was He, He could thus stoop without compromising His dignity, or lessening His glory.

But, if possible, a step lower did He seem to descend. Thus in prophetic language did he announce it: "I am a worm and no man." What astounding words are these! Here was the God-man sinking, as it were, in the depths of abasement and humiliation below the human. "I am a worm, and no man!" In the lowliness which marked His external appearance, in the estimation in which He was held by men, in the contemptuous treatment which He received from His enemies, the trampling of His glory in the dust, and the crushing of His person on the cross, would seem in His own view to have robbed Him, not only of His glory as God, but even to have divested Him of His dignity as man! "I am a worm, and no man!" Oh, here is glory—glory surpassing all imagination, all thought, all power of utterance! He who bent His footsteps along this flinty path, He who sunk thus low, was Jehovah, the "mighty God, the everlasting Father, the Prince of Peace." Wonder, O heavens, and be astonished, O earth! Lowliness and majesty, humiliation and glory, how strangely were they blended in You, O incarnate God!

Our nature, in its depressed and bruised condition, constituted no small feature in the abasement of the Son of God. That He was "holy, harmless, undefiled, and separate from sinners," is an undeniable truth we cannot too distinctly affirm, or too earnestly maintain. The least doubt about the perfect sinlessness of the human nature of our Lord tends to weaken the confidence of faith in the atonement, and so to enshroud in darkness the hope of the soul. As a single leak must have sunk the ark beneath the waves, so the existence of the slightest taint of sin in Jesus would have opened an inlet through which the dark billows of Divine wrath would have rolled, plunging both Himself and the church He sustained in eternal woe. But that "holy thing" that was begotten of the Holy Spirit knew not the least moral taint. He "knew no sin," He was the sacrificial "Lamb without spot." And because He presented to the Divine requirement a holy, unblemished, and perfect obedience and satisfaction, we who believe are "made the righteousness of God in Him."

But His taking up into subsistence with His own our nature in its fallen condition, comprehends the sinless infirmities and weaknesses with which it was identified and encompassed. When I see my Lord and Master bowed with grief and enduring privation, when I behold Him making the needs and sorrows and sufferings of others His own, what do I learn but that He was truly a "man of sorrows and acquainted with grief"? Is there any spectacle more affecting, than thus to behold the Incarnate God entering personally and sympathetically into all the humiliations of my poor, bruised, vile nature, and yet remaining untouched, untainted by its sin?—taking my weaknesses, bearing my sicknesses, sorrowing when I sorrow, weeping when I weep, touched with the feeling of my infirmities, in all points tempted like as I am.

OCTOBER 12

"Then Jesus spoke again unto them, saying, I am the light of the world: he that follows me shall not walk in darkness, but shall have the light of life." Jn. 8:12

Are you, my reader, a searcher of this life? Are you breathing for it, panting after it, seeking it? Then be it known to you, that He who inspired that desire is Himself the life for which you seek. That heaving of your heart, that yearning of your spirit, that "feeling after God, if haply you may find Him," is the first gentle pulsation of a life that shall never die. Feeble and fluctuating, faint and fluttering, as its throbbings may be, it is yet the life of God, the life of Christ, the life of glory in your soul. It is the seedling, the germ of immortal flower; it is the sunshine dawn of an eternal day. The announcement with which we meet your case—and it is the only one that can meet it—is, "THIS MAN RECEIVES SINNERS." Oh joyful tidings! Oh blessed words! Yes, he receives sinners—the vilest—the meanest—the most despised! It was for this He relinquished the abodes of heavenly purity and bliss, to mingle amid the sinful and humiliating scenes of earth. For this He quitted His Father's bosom for a cross. For this He lived and labored, suffered and died. "He receives sinners!" He receives them of every name and condition—of every stature and character and climate. There is no limit to His ability to pardon, as there is none to the sufficiency of His atonement, or to the melting pity of His heart. Flee, then, to Jesus the crucified. To Him repair with your sins, as scarlet and as crimson, and His blood will wash you whiter than snow. What though they may be as clouds for darkness, or as the sand on the sea-shore for multitude; His grace can take them all away. Come with the accusations and tortures of a guilty conscience, come with the sorrow and relentings of a broken heart, come with the grief of the backslider, and with the confession of the prodigal; Jesus still meets you with the hope-inspiring words—"Him that comes unto me, I will in no wise cast out." Then, "return unto the Lord, and He will have mercy upon you; and to our God, for He will abundantly pardon!"

OCTOBER 13

"Who are kept by the power of God through faith unto salvation." 1 Pet.1:5

This salvation takes in all the circumstances of a child of God. It is not only a salvation from wrath to come—that were an immeasurable act of grace—but it is a present salvation, anticipating and providing for every exigency of the life that now is, including deliverance from all evil, help in all trouble; comfort in all sorrow, the supply of all want, and through all conflicts, assaults, and difficulties, perfect safety and final triumph. The present and certain security of the believer is provided for in the covenant of grace, made sure in Jesus the covenant Head, and revealed in the glorious covenant plan of salvation. May the Holy Spirit unfold to us this great and consoling truth, that in the midst of all their weakness, waywardness, and tendency to wander, the Lord is the keeper of His people, and that they whom He keeps are well and eternally kept.

The Lord could not in truth be said to be the keeper of His people, if there were anything of self-power in the believer, any ability to keep himself—if he were not weakness, all weakness, and nothing but weakness. Of this the believer needs to be perpetually put in remembrance. The principle of self-confidence is the natural product of the human heart; the great characteristic of our apostate race is a desire to live, and think, and act independently of God. What is the great citadel, to the overthrow of which Divine grace first directs its power? what is the first step it takes in the subjection of the sinner to God? what, but the breaking down of this lofty, towering, independent conceit of himself, so natural to man, and so abhorrent to God? Now, let it be remembered, that Divine and sovereign grace undertakes not the extraction of the root of this depraved principle from the heart of its subjects. The root remains to the very close of life's pilgrimage; though in a measure weakened, subdued, mortified, still it remains; demanding the most rigid watchfulness, connected with ceaseless prayer, lest it should spring upward, to the destruction of his soul's prosperity, the grieving of the Spirit, and the dishonoring of God. Oh how much the tender, faithful discipline of a covenant God may have the subjection and mortification of this hateful principle for its blessed end, who can tell? We shall never fully know until we reach our Father's house, where the dark and, to us, mysterious dealings of that loving Father with us here below shall unfold themselves in light and glory, elevating the soul in love and praise!

What a confirmation are the histories of God's most eminent saints to this most important truth,—that the creature, left to itself, is pure weakness! If the angels in their purity, if Adam in his state of innocence, fell in consequence of being left, in the sovereign will of God, to their own keeping, what may we expect from a fallen, sinful, imperfect creature, even though renewed? What has God's word declared regarding the power of a regenerate man to keep himself? How affecting are these declarations—"Having no might;" "Without strength;" "Weak through the flesh;" "Out of weakness were made strong"! Could language more forcibly set forth the utter weakness of a child of God? And what are their own acknowledgments?—"The Lord is the strength of my life;" "Hold You me up, and I shall be safe;" "Hold up my goings in Your paths, that my footsteps slip not;" "Yet not I, but the grace of God which was with me;" "By the grace of God I am what I am." And what are the examples? Look at the intemperance of Noah, the unbelief of Abraham, the adultery and murder of David, the idolatry of Solomon, the self-righteousness of Job, the impatience of Moses, the self-confidence and weakness of Peter. Solemn are these lessons of the creature's nothingness; affecting these examples of his perfect weakness!

But why speak of others? Let the reader, if he is a professing child of God, pause and survey the past of his own life. What marks of perfect weakness may he discover, what evidences of his own fickleness, folly, immature judgment, may he trace, what outbreakings of deep iniquity, what disclosures of hidden corruption, what startling symptoms of the most awful departure and apostasy from God, does the review present! And, this, too, let it be remembered, is the history of a believer in Jesus, a renewed child of God, a partaker of the Divine nature, an expectant of eternal glory! Holy and blessed are they who, relinquishing all their fond conceit of self-power and self-keeping, shall pray, and cease not to pray, "Lord, hold You me up, and I shall be safe!" "Let him that thinks he stands, take heed lest he fall."

OCTOBER 14

"Being filled with the fruits of righteousness, which are by Jesus Christ, unto the glory and praise of God." Philippians 1:11

There is a perpetual proneness to seek our fruitfulness from anything save a close, spiritual, and constant dealing with the cross of Jesus: but as well might we expect the earth to clothe itself with verdure, or the tree to blossom, and the blossom ripen into fruit, without the sun's genial warmth, as to look for fruitfulness in a regenerate soul, without a constant dealing with the Lord Jesus Christ; for just what the sun is to the kingdom of nature, Jesus the Sun of righteousness is to the kingdom of grace—the blessed source of all its verdure, fragrance, and fruitfulness. Then, let all your expectations be centered here. No real good can come to you, no healing to your spirit, no fruitfulness to your soul, from a perpetual living upon convictions of sin, legal fears, or transient joys; the Divine life can derive no nourishment from these. But live upon the atoning blood of Jesus—here is the fatness of your soul found; this it is that heals the wound, wins the heart, and hushes to repose every fear of condemnation; this it is that enables a poor sinner to look full at God, feeling that justice, holiness, truth, and every Divine perfection are on his side. It is the blood of Jesus, applied by the Spirit, that moistens each fibre of the root of holiness in the soul, and is productive of its fruitfulness; this it is that sends the warm current of life through every part of the regenerate man, quickening the pulse of love, and imparting a healthy and vigorous power to every act of obedience. And when the spiritual seasons change—for it is not always springtime with the soul of a child of God—when the summer's sun withers, or the autumnal blast scatters the leaves, and winter's fiercer storm beats upon the smitten bough, the blood and righteousness of Christ, lived upon, loved, and cherished, will yet sustain the Divine life in the soul, and in due season the spring blossom and the summer fruit shall again appear, proving that the Divine life of a believer is "hid with Christ in God." Then shall be said of you, as was said of the church by her Beloved: "The winter is past, and the rain is over and gone; the flowers appear on the earth, the time of the singing of birds is come, and the voice of the turtle is heard in our land. The fig-tree puts forth her green figs, and the vines with the tender grape give a good smell. Arise, my love, my fair one, and come away." Then let your heart respond, "Awake, O north wind, and come, you south, blow upon my garden, that the spices thereof may flow out."

Let the believer be aware how he despises what little fruitfulness the Lord the Spirit may have given him: there is danger of this. But it is a mercy that the Lord does not regard your estimate of a fruitful state; else, were He to judge us as we do ourselves; were He to despise His own work as we too frequently do, it would indeed go hard with us. But He does not: that which we have often thought unworthy of His notice, He has looked down upon with the greatest delight. See, then, that you despise not what the Lord has done in you. Any desire of the heart for Christ, any secret brokenness, any godly sorrow over indwelling sin, any feeble dying to self and leaning on Jesus, is the gracious work of the Holy Spirit, and must not be undervalued or unacknowledged. A truly humble view of one's self is a most precious fruit of the Spirit; perhaps, more than any other state of mind. That bough most heavily laden with fruit hangs nearest the ground. It is no unequivocal mark of great spiritual fruitfulness in a believer, when tenderness of conscience, contrition of spirit, low thoughts of self, and high thoughts of Jesus, mark the state of his soul. "Who has despised the day of small things?"—not Jesus.

OCTOBER 15

"He looks upon men, and if any say, I have sinned, and perverted that which was right, and it profited me not; he will deliver his soul from going into the pit, and his life shall see the light." Job 33:27, 28

Let the child of God be encouraged to take all his sins to his heavenly Father. Have you sinned? Have you taken a single step in departure from God? Is there the slightest consciousness of guilt? Go at once to the throne of grace; stay not until you find some secret place for confession—stay not until you are alone; lift up your heart at once to God, and confess your sin with the hand of faith upon the great, atoning Sacrifice. Open all your heart to Him. Do not be afraid of a full and honest confession. Shrink not from unfolding its most secret recesses—lay all bare before His eyes. Do you think He will turn from the exposure? Do you think He will close His ear against your breathings? Oh no! Listen to His own encouraging, persuasive declarations—"Go and proclaim these words towards the north, and say, Return, you backsliding Israel, says the Lord; and I will not cause mine anger to fall upon you: for I am merciful, says the Lord; and I will not keep anger forever. Only acknowledge your iniquity that you have transgressed against the Lord your God." "I will heal their backsliding; I will love them freely; for mine anger is turned away from him." Oh, what words are these! Does the eye of the poor backslider fall on this page? And as he now reads of God's readiness to pardon—of God's willingness to receive back the repenting prodigal—of His yearning after His wandering child—feels his heart melted, his soul subdued, and, struck with that amazing declaration, "Only acknowledge your iniquity," would dare creep down at His feet, and weep, and mourn, and confess. Oh! is there one such now reading this page? then return, my brother, return! God—the God against whom you have sinned—says, "Return." Your Father—the Father from whom you have wandered—is looking out for the first return of your soul, for the first kindlings of godly sorrow, for the first confession of sin. God has not turned His back upon you, though you have turned your back upon Him. God has not forgotten to be gracious, though you have forgotten to be faithful. "I remember you"—is His own touching language—"the kindness of your youth, the love of your espousals." Oh! then, come back; this moment, come back; the fountain is still open—Jesus is still the same—the blessed and eternal Spirit, loving and faithful as ever—God ready for pardon: take up, then, the language of the prodigal and say, "I will arise and go to my Father, and will say unto him, Father, I have sinned against heaven and in Your sight, and am no more worthy to be called Your son." "If we confess our sins, He is faithful and just to forgive us our sins, and to cleanse us from all unrighteousness."

The blessings that result from a strict observance of daily confession of sin are rich and varied. We would from the many specify two. The conscience retains its tender susceptibility of guilt. Just as a breath will tarnish a mirror highly polished, so will the slightest aberration of the heart from God—the smallest sin—leave its impression upon a conscience in the habit of a daily unburdening itself in confession, and of a daily washing in the fountain. Going thus to God, and acknowledging iniquity over the head of Immanuel—pleading the atoning blood—the conscience retains its tenderness, and sin, all sin, is viewed as that which God hates, and the soul abhors.

This habit, too, keeps, so to speak, a clear account between God and the believer. Sins daily and hourly committed are not forgotten; they fade not from the mind, and therefore they need not the correcting rod to recall them to remembrance. For let us not forget, God will eventually bring our sins to remembrance; "He will call to remembrance the iniquity." David had forgotten his sin against God, and his treacherous conduct to Uriah, until God sent the prophet Nathan to bring his iniquity to remembrance. A daily confession, then, of sin, a daily washing in the fountain, will preserve the believer from many and, perhaps, deep afflictions. This was David's testimony—"I acknowledged my sin unto You, and mine iniquity have I not hid. I said, I will confess my transgression unto the Lord, and You forgave the iniquity of my sin."

OCTOBER 16

"By faith Abraham, when he was called to go out into a place which he should after receive for an inheritance, obeyed; and he went out, not knowing where he went." Hebrews 11:8

The entire spiritual life of a child of God is a life of faith—God has so ordained it; and to bring him into the full and blessed experience of it, is the end of all His parental dealings with him. If we desire to see our way every step of our homeward path, we must abandon the more difficult though more blessed ascent of faith; it is impossible to walk by sight and by faith at the same time—the two paths run in opposite directions. If the Lord were to reveal the why and the why of all His dealings—if we were only to advance as we saw the spot on which we were to place our foot, or only to go out as we knew the place where we were going—it then were no longer a life of faith that we lived, but of sight. We shall have exchanged the life which glorifies, for the life which dishonors God. When God, about to deliver the Israelites from the power of Pharaoh, commanded them to advance, it was before He revealed the way by which He was about to rescue them. The Red Sea rolled its deep and frowning waves at their feet; they saw not a spot of dry ground on which they could tread; and yet this was the command to Moses— "Speak unto the children of Israel that they go forward." They were to "walk by faith, not by sight." It had been no exercise of faith in God, no confidence in His promise, no resting in

His faithfulness, and no "magnifying of His word above all His name," had they waited until the waters cleaved asunder, and a dry passage opened to their view. But, like the patriarchs, they "staggered not at the promise of God through unbelief; but were strong in faith, giving glory to God." Have little to do with sense, if you would have much to do with faith. Expect not always to see the way. God may call you to go out into a place, not making known to you where you go; but it is your duty, like Abraham, to obey. All that you have to do is to go forward, leaving all consequences and results to God: it is enough for you that the Lord by this providence says, "Go forward!" This is all you may hear; it is your duty instantly to respond, "Lord, I go at Your bidding; bid me come to You, though it be upon the stormy water."

"Having begun in the Spirit," the believer is not to be "made perfect in the flesh;" having commenced his divine life in faith, in faith he is to walk every step of his journey homewards. The moment a poor sinner has touched the hem of Christ's garment, feeble though this act of faith be, it is yet the commencement of this high and holy life of faith; even from that moment the believing soul professes to have done with a life of sense—with second causes—and to have entered upon a glorious life of faith in Christ. It is no forced application to him of the apostle's declaration: "I am crucified with Christ; nevertheless I live, yet not I, but Christ lives in me; and the life which I now live in the flesh, I live by the faith of the Son of God."

OCTOBER 17

"These words spoke Jesus, and lifted up his eyes to heaven, and said, Father, the hour is come; glorify your Son, that your Son also may glorify you: as you have given him power over all flesh, that he should give eternal life to as many as you have given him." John 17:1, 2

The certain glorification with Jesus of every believer is a truth as much involving the honor of God, as it does the present comfort and future happiness of the church. The opposite sentiment—the possibility of a child of God falling short of eternal glory (a doctrine, let it be observed, at total variance with the entire Scriptures of truth), by unhinging the soul from God, and throwing it back completely upon itself, must necessarily lead to low and dishonoring views of the Divine character; while it begets in the mind a spirit of bondage, and a sense of the most painful apprehension, both equally inimical to a healthy and fruitful Christianity. But the most solemn, I may say awful, light in which the doctrine of the believer's final insecurity presents itself is, that it casts a thick veil over the glory of Immanuel. It touches every perfection of his being. Oh could the dear saints of God, thus tossed in the troubled sea of doubt, and thus agitated with a "fearful looking for of judgment and fiery indignation," but be brought to see how the Jesus whom they love is wounded, dishonored, and shorn of His glory by this unscriptural tenet, would they not unhesitatingly renounce it as leading to a result so fearful? Can that, I earnestly ask, be a doctrine of Divine revelation, which tends in the slightest degree to shade the glory of Christ? If one of those given to Him of His Father—one whose sins He carried, whose curse He bore, whose soul He has renewed by the grace of His Spirit—were permitted finally and eternally to perish, where would be His glory? where the glory of His truth? where the glory of His power? where the glory of His love? where the glory of His work? Gone! Every perfection of His Divine being would be impeached, and every beam of His Divine glory would be tarnished.

But all shall be brought safely to heaven. Hark, how distinctly and authoritatively He pleads for this, their crowning blessing, when on the eve of His mysterious passion, and about to spring from His cross to His throne. "Father, I will that they also whom You have given me be with me where I am; that they may behold my glory." Sublime prayer!—comprehensive and tender petition! How did the Head long to have with Him, where He was, each member of His body! Having had fellowship with Him in His humiliation, it was His desire that they should have fellowship with Him in His glory. And this He asks not as a gift, but claims as a right. In virtue of His covenant engagement with the Father, His full satisfaction to Divine justice, His perfect obedience to the Divine law, His finished redemption of His people, He reverently bows at the mercy-seat, and pours out His full soul, and unburdens His loving heart, in the most sublime petition that ever ascended from mortal lip: "Father, I will that they also whom You have given me be with me where I am." And mark the reason why—"that they may behold my glory." Consummation of glory!—overflowing cup of bliss!—height of perfect holiness! Was it the parting charge of Joseph to His brethren—"You shall tell my father of all my glory in Egypt, and of all that you have seen; and you shall haste and bring down my father here"? Our Joseph, with love infinitely more intense, desires that all His brethren be brought to heaven, that they may behold His glory there—the glory of His unveiled Deity—the glory of His glorified humanity—and the glory to which, as Mediator, His Father has advanced Him.

OCTOBER 18

"But not as the offence, so also is the free gift. For if through the offence of one many be dead, much more the grace of God, and the gift by grace, which is by one man, Jesus Christ, has abounded unto many." Romans 5:15

From the want of clear and spiritual views of the freeness of the atonement, the perfectly unconditional bestowment of the blessings of pardon and justification, many are kept, even among those "called to be saints," from entering fully into the liberty and peace of the gospel. They have been convinced of their need of Christ; they have been made to hunger and thirst for pardon and acceptance; they have been brought, it may be, through a deep "law-work of the soul," to stand as on the very borders of the land that flows with milk and honey; but looking more to themselves, and less to Christ—lingering on its edge, while the river flows so richly and so freely at their feet, waiting for some condition to be performed, some fitness to be experienced, or some price to bring—they are kept back from those rich and untold blessings which a drawing nearer to Jesus would assuredly bring into their possession.

Where will be found more distinct and glorious views of the atonement—its nature, design, and freeness—than are found in the Old Testament writings? This is the testimony to the perfect freeness of the gift: "Ho! Everyone that thirsts, come you to the waters; and he that has no money, come you, buy and eat; yes, come, buy wine and milk, without money and without price." Behold the freeness of the rich and inestimable blessing! "Without money—without price." The simple meaning of which is—without worthiness, without fitness, without condition. So that the most unworthy, the most vile, the most penniless, may come and drink water freely out of the wells of salvation. This is the language of God by the mouth of His prophets. What a gospel then is here revealed! How full the supply! How free the gift! And if this was the language of God under the obscure exhibition of the gospel, what must be His free welcome to poor sinners under the full revelation of the gospel? Now that Christ has come, and the atonement has been made, and the fountain has been opened, and the invitation has gone out, can we suppose that the blessing of pardon will be less freely bestowed? Again—"The Spirit of the Lord is upon me; because the Lord has anointed me to preach good tidings unto the meek: He has sent me to bind up the broken-hearted, to proclaim liberty to the captives, and the opening of the prison to those who are bound." Note the expressions as descriptive of the characters to whom our blessed Lord came—"broken-hearted"—"captives"—"those who are bound." Where was the worthiness here? What price with which to purchase their redemption had these bound and broken-hearted captives? See, then, how the glorious atonement received its stamp of freeness, even under the legal dispensation. Come we now to the clearer revelations of the new dispensation.

Take those remarkable words—"And when they had nothing to pay, he frankly forgave them both." Oh sweet expression! "Nothing to pay". Entirely bankrupt. Poor, wretched, penniless, bereft of all—nothing to pay, and yet frankly forgiven; that is, fully, freely, agreeably forgiven—with all the heart of God. But one hear another— "And the Spirit and the bride say, 'Come.' And let him that hear say, 'Come.' And let him that is athirst come. And whoever will, let him take the water of life freely." See how the last words that linger in sweet vibration on the ear, as the blessed canon of Scripture closes, are, "the water of life—freely"!

OCTOBER 19

"But I would not have you to be ignorant, brethren, concerning those who are asleep, that you sorrow not, even as others which have no hope." 1 Thessalonians 4:13

It is a magnificent and expressive image this by which Christianity presents to the bereaved mind the departure of brethren in Christ. They are not dead, they are asleep. The question instantly arises—What is it which, in the experience of the believer, has so materially changed the aspect of death? What is it that invests this solemn, this fearful crisis of our being with so softened and mitigated a character? What is it that throws around the pillow of the expiring saint an air of repose so sacred, so peaceful, and serene? The ATONEMENT of the Son of God alone supplies the answer. The influence of His death, and the power of His resurrection, have changed, in the case of all believers in Christ, the entire character and aspect of death. The Savior, by dying, conquered death. Plucking his pale crown from his brow, hurling him from his towering throne, snapping in twain his proud scepter, and with His own blood washing away the venom of his dart. Lo! Death is no more the "king of terrors" to those who believe. Entering within his gloomy palace—there slumbering awhile—then returning victorious the "Resurrection and the Life"—henceforward to the Christian to depart is not to die, but—to sleep!

And what is that sleep? No unconsciousness of the soul is it! No intermediate state of dreamy insensibility—of cold, silent torpidity of spirit, waiting the voice of the archangel and the trumpet of God to dissolve its slumber. The believer sleeps; but it is the sleep of the body, and not of the soul. "Absent from the body," in the full, unclouded, unimpaired consciousness, intelligence, and joyousness of the spirit, he is "present with the Lord." Death to him is but a change of place; not of state. As the natural sleep of the body is not the extinction, nor even the momentary suspension, of the soul's intellectual faculties—for who has not experienced that some of the profoundest thoughts and most sublime soarings of the imagination have been those which have played around the pillow of midnight slumber, like gleams of summer lightning upon the lurid night?—so, in like manner, when death has sealed in profound unconsciousness the material senses, the immaterial and the immortal is expatiating amid the glories and the wonders of the spiritual world, as it springs from star to star and from sun to sun—and thus sleep becomes the gentle and expressive emblem of the Christian's death. They "sleep in Jesus," who is the "Resurrection and the Life;" how, then, can it be possible that the soul is unconscious, since it is in union—personal, changeless union—with Him who, in His office as Mediator, has said, "Because I live, you shall live also"?

The death-sleep of the believer is a season of complete bodily and mental repose. How precious is this prospect to the child of God! lighting up even the grim visage of the last foe with a smile of pleasantness. We naturally attach the idea of rest to sleep. What a rest remains even in the grave for the people of God! "There the wicked cease from troubling, and there the weary be at rest." Who so wearied as the believer in Jesus? With him the world is a toilsome desert—life a scene of conflict and of trial—the travel to heaven a pilgrimage arduous, self-denying, and lonely. We have to contend with principalities and powers, to conflict with foes visible and invisible, to subdue indwelling sin, and repel outward temptation. Then there are the "many afflictions" which belong to the "righteous," the trials peculiar and sore with which the Lord in love tries His people. In the midst of all this, and superadded as an element of weariness yet more potent, there is often the drooping of faith, the chill of love, the obscured evidences, the beclouded hope, the withdrawal of the Divine presence, the suspension of the sensible comforts and consolations of the Holy Spirit; all conspiring to make this a weary land. Thus the soul of the believer is frequently cast down within him because of the way. But "the sleep of a laboring man is sweet;" and such is the sleep in Jesus of the believer, the Christian laborer. In view of this truth, how chastened and cheered should be our sorrow when visiting the graves of the holy dead. Not a wavelet disturbs their calm repose. No painful sufferings, no convulsive throes, no affrighting dreams; no mental wanderings, no confused sounds, no fantastic fancies disturb their peaceful slumber. The world is rushing on, as before, in turmoil, sin, and conflict—the war-cry, the martial music, the sigh of sorrow, and the wail of agony are heard—but not a spent echo mars their placid rest. The body reposes in the tomb, the soul in the Paradise of God, and over their graves is heard a voice, saying, "Blessed are the dead which die in the Lord from henceforth; yes, says the Spirit, that they may rest from their labors; and their works do follow them."

OCTOBER 20

"Though he were a Son, yet learned he obedience by the things which he suffered; and being made perfect, he became the author of eternal salvation unto all those who obey him." Hebrews 5:8, 9

The basis or cause of the completeness of Christ's atonement arises from the infinite dignity of His person: His Godhead forms the basis of His perfect work. It was this that gave perfection to His obedience, and virtue to His atonement: it was this that made the blood He shed efficacious in the pardon of sin, and the righteousness He wrought out complete in the justification of the soul. His entire work would have been wanting but for His Godhead. No created Savior could have given full satisfaction to an infinite law, broken by man, and calling aloud for vengeance. An obedience was required, in every respect equal in glory and dignity to the law that was violated. The rights of the Divine government must be maintained, the purity of the Divine nature must be guarded, and the honor of the Divine law must be vindicated. To accomplish this, God Himself must become flesh; and to carry this fully out, the incarnate God must die! Oh, depth of wisdom and of grace! Oh, love infinite, love rich, love free!—

"Not to be thought on, but with tides of joy;
Not to be mentioned, but with shouts of praise."

The pardon of a believer's sins is an entire pardon. It is the full pardon of all his sins. It were no pardon to him, if it were not an entire pardon. If it were but a partial blotting out of the thick cloud—if it were but a partial canceling of the bond—if it were but a forgiveness of some sins only, then the gospel were no glad tidings to his soul. The law of God had brought him in guilty of an entire violation. The justice of God demands a satisfaction equal to the enormity of the sins committed, and of the guilt incurred. The

Holy Spirit has convinced him of his utter helplessness, his entire bankruptcy. What rapture would kindle in his bosom at the announcement of a partial atonement—of a half Savior—of a part payment of the debt? Not one throb of joyous sensation would it produce. On the contrary, this very mockery of his woe would but deepen the anguish of his spirit. But go to the soul, weary and heavy-laden with sin, mourning over its vileness, its helplessness, and proclaim the Gospel. Tell him that the atonement which Jesus offered on Calvary was a full satisfaction for his sins;—that all his sins were borne and blotted out in that awful moment;—that the bond which Divine justice held against the sinner was fully cancelled by the obedience and sufferings of Christ, and that, appeased and satisfied, God was "ready to pardon." How beautiful will be the feet that convey to him tidings so transporting as this! And are not these statements perfectly accordant with the declarations of God's own word? Let us ascertain. What was the ark symbolical of, alluded to by the apostle, in the ninth chapter of his Epistle to the Hebrews, which contained the manna, Aaron's rod, and the tables of the covenant, over which stood the cherubim of glory shadowing the mercy-seat? What, but the entire covering of sin? For, as the covering of the ark did hide the law and testimony, so did the Lord Jesus Christ hide the sins of His chosen, covenant people—not from the eye of God's omniscience, but from the eye of the law. They stand legally acquitted. So entire was the work of Jesus, so infinite and satisfactory His obedience, the law of God pronounces them acquitted, and can never bring them into condemnation. "There is therefore now no condemnation to those who are in Christ Jesus; who walk not after the flesh, but after the Spirit." "Who is he that condemns? It is Christ that died, yes rather, that is risen again, who is even at the right hand of God, who also makes intercession for us."

OCTOBER 21

"Why say my people, We are lords; we will come no more unto you? Can a maid forget her ornaments, or a bride her attire? yet my people have forgotten me days without number." Jeremiah 2:31, 32

When God becomes less an object of fervent desire, holy delight, and frequent contemplation, we may suspect a declension of Divine love in the soul. Our spiritual views of God, and our spiritual and constant delight in Him, will be materially affected by the state of our spiritual love. If there is coldness in the affections, if the mind grows earthly, carnal, and selfish, dark and gloomy shadows will gather round the character and the glory of God. He will become less an object of supreme attachment, unmingled delight, adoring contemplation, and filial trust. The moment the supreme love of Adam to God declined, the instant that it swerved from its proper and lawful center, he shunned converse with God, and sought to embower himself from the presence of the Divine glory. Conscious of a change in his affections—sensible of a divided heart, of subjection to a rival interest—and knowing that God was no longer the object of his supreme love, nor the fountain of his pure delight, nor the blessed and only source of his bliss—he rushed from His presence as from an object of terror, and sought concealment in Eden's bowers. That God whose presence was once so glorious, whose converse was so holy, whose voice was so sweet, became as a strange God to the rebellious and conscience-stricken creature, and, "absence from You is best," was written in dark letters upon his guilty brow.

And where this difference? Was God less glorious in Himself? Was He less holy, less loving, less faithful, or less the fountain of supreme bliss? Far from it, God had undergone no change. It is the perfection of a perfect Being that He is unchangeable, that He can never act contrary to His own nature, but must ever be, in all that He does, in harmony with Himself. The change was in the creature. Adam had left his first love, had transferred his affections to another and an inferior object; and, conscious that he had ceased to love God, he would sincerely have veiled himself from His presence, and have excluded himself from His communion. It is even so in the experience of a believer, conscious of a declension in his love to God. There is a hiding from His presence; there are misty views of His character, misinterpretations of His dealings, and a lessening of holy desire for Him: but where the heart is right in its affections, warm in its love, fixed in its desires, God is glorious in His perfections, and communion with Him the highest bliss on earth. This was David's experience—"O God, You are my God; early will I seek You: my soul thirsts for You, my flesh longs for You in a dry and thirsty land where no water is; to see Your power and Your glory, so as I have seen You in the sanctuary. Because Your loving-kindness is better than life, my lips shall praise You."

Not only in the declension of Divine love in the soul, does God become less an object of adoring contemplation and desire, but there is less filial approach to Him. The sweet confidence and simple trust of the child is lost, the soul no longer rushes into His bosom with all the lowly yet fond yearnings of an adopted son, but lingers at a distance; or, if it attempts to approach, does so with the trembling and the restraint of a slave. The tender, loving, child-like spirit that marked the walk of the believer in the days of his espousals—when no object was so glorious to him as God, no being so loved as his heavenly Father, no spot so sacred as the throne of communion, no theme so sweet as his free-grace adoption—has in a great degree departed; and distrust, and legal fears, and bondage of spirit have succeeded it. All these sad effects may be traced to the declension of filial love in the soul of the believer towards God.

OCTOBER 22

"Sanctified by the word of God." 1 Timothy 4:5

It is the natural tendency of Divine truth, when received into the heart, to produce holiness. The design of the whole plan of redemption was to secure the highest holiness and happiness of the creature; and when the gospel comes with the power of God unto the salvation of the soul, this end is preeminently secured. The renewed man is a pardoned man; the pardoned man becomes a holy man; and the holy man is a happy man. Look, then, at God's word, and trace the tendency of every doctrine, precept, promise, and threatening, and mark the holy influence of each. Take the doctrine of God's everlasting love to His people, as seen in their election to eternal life. How holy is the tendency of this truth! "Blessed be the God and Father of our Lord Jesus Christ, who has blessed us with all spiritual blessings in heavenly places in Christ; according as He has chosen us in Him before the foundation of the world, that we should be holy and without blame before Him in love." Let not my reader turn from this glorious doctrine, because he may find it irreconcilable with others that he may hold, or because the mists of prejudice may long have veiled it from his mind; it is a revealed doctrine, and therefore to be fully received; it is a holy doctrine, and therefore to be ardently loved. Received in the heart by the teaching of the Holy Spirit, it lays the pride of man in the dust, knocking from beneath the soul all ground for self-glorying, and expands the mind with the most exalted views of the glory, grace, and love of Jehovah. He who receives the doctrine of electing love in his heart by the power of the Spirit, bears about with him the material of a holy walk; its tendency is to humble, abase, and sanctify the man.

Thus holy, too, is the revealed doctrine of God's free, sovereign, and distinguishing grace. The tendency of this truth is most sanctifying: for a man to feel that God alone has made him to differ from another—that what he has, he has received—that by the free, distinguishing grace of God he is what he is—is a truth, when experienced in the heart, surely of the most holy influence. How it lays the axe at the root of self! how it stains the pride of human glory, and hushes the whispers of vain boasting! It lays the renewed sinner where he ought ever to lie, in the dust; and places the crown, where it alone ought to shine, bright and glorious, upon the head of sovereign mercy. "Lord, why me? I was far from You by wicked works; I was the least of my Father's house, and, of all, the most unworthy and unlikely object of Your love and yet Your mercy sought me—Your grace selected me out of all the rest, and made me a miracle of its omnipotent power. Lord, to what can I refer this, but to Your mere mercy, Your sovereign and free grace, entirely apart from all worth or worthiness that You did see in me? Take, therefore, my body, soul, and spirit, and let them be, in time and through eternity, a holy temple to Your glory."

All the precepts, too, are on the side of holiness. "If you love me, keep my commandments;" "Be you holy, for I am holy;" "Come out of the world and be you separate, and touch not the unclean thing.'" "God has not called us unto uncleanness, but unto holiness;" "That you might walk worthy of the Lord unto all pleasing, being fruitful in every good work, and increasing in the knowledge of God." Holy precepts! May the eternal Spirit engrave them deep upon our hearts.

Not less sanctifying in their tendency are the "exceeding great and precious promises" which the word of truth contains. "Having, therefore these promises, dearly beloved, let us cleanse ourselves from all filthiness of the flesh and spirit, perfecting holiness in the fear of God."

Thus holy and sanctifying are the nature and the effect of Divine truth. It is in its nature and properties most holy; it comes from a holy God and whenever and wherever it is received in the heart, as the good and incorruptible seed of the kingdom, it produces that which is in accordance with its own nature—HOLINESS. As is the tree, so are the fruits; as is the cause, so are the effects. It brings down and lays low the high thoughts of man, by revealing to him the character of God; it convinces him of his deep guilt and awful condemnation, by exhibiting the Divine law; it unfolds to him God's hatred of sin, His justice in punishing and His mercy in pardoning it, by unfolding to his view the cross of Christ; and taking entire possession of the soul, it implants new principles, supplies new motives, gives a new end, begets new joys, and inspires new hopes—in a word, diffuses itself through the whole moral man, changes it into the same image, and transforms it into "an habitation of God through the Spirit."

OCTOBER 23

"Remember therefore from where you are fallen, and repent, and do the first works." Revelation 2:5

Let the backsliding believer be brought to this first step. "Remember from where you are fallen"—revert to your past history, your former spiritual state—remember your first sorrow for sin, the first joy of its pardon—remember the spring-tide of your first love—how precious Jesus was, how glorious was His person, how sweet was His cross, how fragrant was His name, how rich was His grace—remember how dear to you was the throne of grace, how frequently you resorted to it, regarding it of all spots on earth the most blessed—remember how, under the anointings of adopting love, you walked with God as with a Father—how filial, how close, how holy was your communion with Him—remember the seasons of refreshing in the sanctuary, in the social meeting, in the closet; how your soul did seem to dwell on the sunny sides of glory, and you longed for the wings of a dove that you might fly to your Lord; remember how, publicly and before many witnesses, you put off sin and put on Christ, and; turning your back upon the world, took your place among the followers of the Lamb—remember how holy, and circumspect, and spotless your walk, how tender was your conscience, how guileless was your spirit, how humble and lovely your whole deportment. But what and where are you now? Oh, remember from where you are fallen! Think from what a high profession, from what an elevated walk, from what holy employments, from what hallowed joys, from what sweet delights, and from what pleasant ways have you declined!

But in the exhortation given to the backsliding church at Ephesus, there is yet another instruction equally applicable to the case of all wanderers from the Lord: "Repent, and do the first works." How can a departing soul return without repentance? by what other avenue can the prodigal reach his Father's heart? Repentance implies the existence and conviction of sin. Ah! is it no sin, beloved reader, to have turned your back upon God? is it no sin to have lost your first love, to have backslidden from Jesus, to have transferred your affections from Him to the world, or to the creature, or to yourself? is it no sin to go no more with the Shepherd, and to follow no more the footsteps of the flock, and to feed no more in the green pastures, or repose by the side of the still waters? Oh yes! it is a sin of peculiar magnitude; it is a sin against God in the character of a loving Father, against Jesus in the character of a tender Redeemer, against the Holy Spirit in the character of a faithful Indweller and a Sanctifier; it is a sin against the most precious experience of His grace, against the most melting exhibitions of His love, and against the most tender proofs of His covenant faithfulness.

Repent, then, of this your sin. Think how you have wounded Jesus afresh, and repent; think how you have requited your Father's love, and repent; think how you have grieved the Spirit, and repent. Humble yourself in dust and ashes before the cross, and through that cross look up again to your forgiving God and Father. The sweet promise is, "They shall look upon Him whom they have pierced, and shall mourn for Him as one mourns for his only son."

OCTOBER 24

"My tongue shall sing aloud of your righteousness." Psalm 51:14

If we cannot sing of Jesus and of His love in the night of our pilgrimage, of what, of whom, then, can we sing? As all music has its ground-work—its elementary principles—so has the music of the believing soul. Jesus is the basis. He who knows nothing experimentally of Jesus has never learned to sing the Lord's song. But the believer, when he contemplates Jesus in His person dignity, glory, and beauty—when he regards Him as God's equal—when he views Him as the Father's gift—as the great depository of all the fullness of God, can sing, in the dark night of his conscious sinfulness, of a foundation upon which he may securely build for eternity. And when too, he studies the work of Jesus, what material for a song is gathered here! when he contemplates Christ as "made of God unto him wisdom, righteousness, sanctification, and redemption;" when he views the atoning blood and righteousness which present him moment by moment before God, washed from every stain, and justified from every sin, even now he can sing the first notes of the song they chaunt in higher strains above: "Unto Him that loved us, and washed us from our sins in His own blood, and has made us kings and priests unto God and His Father; to Him be glory and dominion, forever and ever. Amen." Oh! yes, Jesus is the key-note—Jesus is the ground-work of the believer's song.

Is it a season of heart-ploughing, of breaking up of the fallow ground, of deeper discovery of the concealed plague? Still to turn the eye of faith on Jesus, and contemplate the efficacy of His blood to remove all sin, and the power of His grace to subdue all iniquity, oh, what music in the sad heart does that sight of Him create! "My soul does magnify the Lord, and my spirit has rejoiced in God my Savior."

In giving you a throne of grace, God has given you a song, methinks one of the sweetest ever sung in the house of our pilgrimage. To feel that we have a God who hears and answers prayer—who has done so in countless instances, and is prepared still to give us at all times an audience—oh! the unutterable blessedness of this truth. Sing aloud, then, you sorrowful saints, for great and precious is your privilege of communion with God. In the time of your every grief, and trial, and difficulty, do not forget that, in your lowest frame, you may sing this song—"Having boldness to enter into the holiest by the blood of Jesus, by a new and living way, I will draw near, and pour out my heart to God." Chaunt, then, His high praises as you pass along, that there is a place where you may disclose every want, repose every sorrow, deposit every burden, breathe every sigh, and lose yourself in communion with God; that place is the blood-besprinkled mercy-seat, on which God says, "There will I meet with you, and I will commune with you."

OCTOBER 25

"So also Christ glorified not himself to be made an high priest; but he that said unto him, You are my Son, today have I begotten you." Hebrews 5:5

The Atonement of Christ is of infinite value and efficacy. If Christ were a mere creature, if He claimed no higher dignity than Gabriel, or one of the prophets or apostles, then His atonement, as it regards the satisfaction of Divine justice, the honoring of the law, the pardon of sin, the peace of the conscience, and the salvation of the soul, would possess no intrinsic efficacy whatever. It would be but the atonement of a finite being—a being possessing no superior merit to those in whose behalf the atonement was made. We state it, then, broadly and unequivocally, that the entire glory, dignity, value, and efficacy of Christ's precious blood which He shed for sin rests entirely upon the Deity of His person. If the Deity of Christ sinks, the atonement of Christ sinks with it; if the one stands, so stands the other. How strong are the words of Paul, addressed to the Ephesian elders: "Take heed therefore unto yourselves, and to all the flock over which the Holy Spirit has made you overseers, to feed the church of God which He has purchased with His own blood." How conclusive is this testimony! The blood that purchased the church was Divine. It was indeed the blood of Christ's humanity—for His human nature alone could suffer, bleed, and die—yet deriving all its glory, value, and efficacy from the union of the human with the Divine nature. It was the blood of the God-man, Jehovah Jesus—no inferior blood could have sufficed. The law which Adam, our federal head, broke, before it could release the sinner from its penalty, demanded a sacrifice infinitely holy, and infinitely great: one equal with the

Father—the dignity of whose person would impart infinite merit to His work, and the infinite merit of whose work would fully sustain its honor and its purity. All this was found in the person of Christ. In His complex person He was eminently fitted for the mighty work. As God, He obeyed the precepts and maintained the honor of the law; as man, He bore its curse and endured its penalty. It was the blending as into one these two natures; the bringing together these extremes of being, the finite and the infinite, which shed such resplendent luster on His atonement, which stamped such worth and efficacy on His blood. Dear reader, treat not this subject lightly, deem it not a useless speculation; it is of the deepest moment. If the blood of Christ possess not infinite merit, infinite worth, it could never be efficacious in washing away the guilt of sin, or in removing the dread of condemnation. When you come to die, this, of all truths, if you are an experimental believer, will be the most precious and sustaining. In that solemn hour, when the curtain that conceals the future parts, and eternity lets down upon the view the full blaze of its awful realities—in that hour, when all false dependencies will crumble beneath you, and sin's long catalogue passes in review before you—oh, then to know that the Savior on whom you depend is God in your nature—that the blood in which you have washed has in it all the efficacy and value of Deity—this, this will be the alone plank that will buoy up the soul in that awful moment, and at that fearful crisis. Oh precious truth this, for a poor believing soul to rest upon! We wonder not that, fast anchored on this truth, amid circumstances the most appalling, death in view, wearing even its most terrific aspect, the believer in Jesus can survey the scene with composure, and quietly yield his spirit into the hands of Him who redeemed it.

OCTOBER 26

"That in the ages to come he might show the exceeding riches of his grace in his kindness toward us through Christ Jesus. For by grace are you saved through faith; and that not of yourselves: it is the gift of God." Ephesians 2:7, 8

It was no little kindness in our God, that as one saving object, and one alone, was to engage the attention and fix the eye of the soul, through time and through eternity, that object should be of surpassing excellence and of peerless beauty. That He should be, not the sweetest seraph nor the loveliest angel in heaven, but His own Son, the "brightness of His glory, the express image of His person." God delights in the beautiful; all true beauty emanates from Him;

"He has made all things beautiful." How worthy of Himself, then; that in providing a Savior for fallen man, bidding him fix the eye of faith supremely and exclusively upon Him, that Savior should unite in Himself all Divine and all human beauty; that He should be the "chief among ten thousand, the altogether lovely." Adore the name, oh! praise the love of God, for this. In looking to Jesus for salvation, we include each Divine Person of the glorious Trinity. We cannot look unto Jesus without seeing the Father, for Christ is the revelation of the Father. "He that has seen me," says Christ, "has seen the Father." Nor can we contemplate Jesus exclusive of the Holy Spirit, because it is the Spirit alone who imparts the spiritual eye that sees Jesus. Thus, in the believing and saving view a poor sinner has of Jesus, he beholds, in the object of his sight, a revelation of each separate Person of the ever blessed Trinity, engaged in devising and accomplishing his eternal salvation. Oh! what a display of infinite love and wisdom is here, that in our salvation one object should arrest the eye, and the that object should embody an equal revelation of the Father, who gave Jesus, and of the Holy Spirit of truth, who leads to Jesus, and that that object should be the loveliest being in the universe. God has deposited all fullness in Christ, that we might, in all need, repair to Christ. "Looking unto Jesus," for our standing before God—for the grace that upholds and preserves us unto eternal life—for the supply of the Spirit that sanctifies the heart, and meets us for the heavenly glory—for each day's need, for each moment's support—in a word, "looking unto Jesus," for everything. Thus has God simplified our life of faith in His dear Son. Severing us from all other sources, alluring us away from all other dependencies, and weaning us from all self-confidence, He would shut us up to Christ above, that Christ might be all and in all.

For the weakness of faith's eye remember that Christ has suitably provided. His care of, and His tenderness towards, those whose grace is limited, whose experience is feeble, whose knowledge is defective, whose faith is small, are exquisite. He has promised to "anoint the eye with eye-salve, that it may see," and that it may see more clearly. Repair to Him, then, with your case, and seek the fresh application of this divine unguent. Be cautious of limiting the reality of your sight to the nearness or distinctness of the object. The most distant and dim view of Jesus by faith is as real and saving as if that view were with the strength of an eagle's eye. A well-known example in Jewish history affords an apposite illustration: the wounded Israelite was simply commanded to look to the brazen serpent. Nothing was said of the clearness of his vision or the distinctness of his view; no exception was made to the dimness of his sight. His eye might possibly be blurred, the phantoms of a diseased imagination might float before it, intercepting his view; no, more, it might already be glazing and fixing in death! Yet, even under these circumstances, and at that moment, if he but obeyed the Divine command, and looked towards, simply towards, the elevated serpent, distant and beclouded as it was, he was immediately and effectually healed. Thus is it with the operation of faith. Let your eye, in obedience to the gospel's command, be but simply raised and fastened upon Jesus, far removed as may be the glorious object; and dim as may be the blessed vision, yet then "looking unto Jesus," you shall be fully and eternally saved: "Being justified freely by His grace, through the redemption that is in Christ Jesus: whom God has set forth to be a propitiation through faith in His blood."

OCTOBER 27

"The Lord gave, and the Lord has taken away; blessed be the name of the Lord." Job 1:21

Bereaved Christian, God has smitten, and the stroke has fallen heavily. The blessing you thought you could the least spare, and would be the last to leave you, God your Father has taken. Why has He done this? To show you what He can be in your extremity. It may be difficult for faith, in the first moments of your calamity, to see how it can be well to be thus afflicted; but be still and wait the issue. Banish from your mind every hard thought of God, stifle in your breast every rebellious feeling, suppress upon your lip every repining word, and bow meekly, submissively, mutely, to the sovereign, righteous will of your Father. The blessings, like spring flowers blooming on the grave over which you weep, that will grow out of this affliction, will prove that God never loved you more deeply, was never more intent upon advancing your best interests, never thought more of you, nor cared more for you, than at the moment when His hand laid your loved one low. Receive the testimony of one who has tasted, ay, has drunk deeply, of the same cup of grief which your Father God now mingles for you. Let us drink it without a murmur. It is our Father's cup. As a father pities his children, so does He pity us even while He mingles and presents the draught. It is bitter, but not the bitterness of the curse; it is dark, but not the frown of anger; the cup is brimmed, but not a drop of wrath is there! Oh, wondrous faith that can look upon the beautiful stem broken; the lovely, promising flower, just unfolding its perfection, smitten; the toils and hopes of years, and in a moment, extinguished, and yet can say—"It is well!" Go, now, you precious treasure! God will have my heart, Christ would not I should be satisfied with His gift of love, but that I should be satisfied with His love without the gift. "You only are my portion, O Lord." The world looks dreary, life has lost a charm, the heart is smitten and withered like grass, some of its dearest earthly affections have gone down into the tomb, but He who recalled the blessing is greater and dearer than the blessing, and is Himself just the same as when He gave it. Jesus would be glorified by our resting in, and cleaving to, Him as our portion, even when the flowers of earthly beauty, and the yet more precious fruits of spiritual comfort and consolation wither and depart. Satan would suggest that we have sinned away our blessings and forfeited our comforts, and that therefore the Lord is now hiding His face from us, and in anger shutting up His tender mercies. But this is not really so; He is hiding the flowers, but not Himself. In love to them, He is transferring them to His garden in heaven; and in love to us, He thus seeks to draw us nearer to His heart. He would have us knock at His door, and ask for a fresh cluster. We cherish our blessings, and rest in our comforts, and live upon our frames and feelings, and lose sight of and forget Him. He removes those who we might be always coming to Him for more. Oh, matchless love of Jesus!

But the place where the clearest view is taken of the present unfathomable dispensations of God, and where their unfolding light and unveiling glory wake the sweetest, loudest response to this truth—"He has done all things well"—is heaven. The glorified saint has closed his pilgrimage; life's dark shadows have melted into endless light; he now looks back upon the desert he traversed, upon the path he trod, and as in the full blaze of glory each page unfolds of his wondrous history, testifying to some new recorded instance of the loving-kindness and faithfulness of God, the grace, compassion, and sympathy of Jesus, the full heart exclaims—"He has done all things well." The past dealings of God with him in providence now appear most illustrious to the glorified mind. The machinery of Divine government, which here seemed so complex and inexplicable, now appears in all its harmony and beauty. Its mysteries are all unraveled, its problems are all solved, its events are all explained, and the promise of the Master has received its utmost fulfillment, "What I do you know not now but you shall know hereafter." That dispensation that was enshrouded in such mystery; that event that flung so dark a shadow on the path; that affliction that seemed so conflicting with all our ideas of God's infinite wisdom, truth, and love; that stroke that crushed us to the earth—all now appears but parts of a perfect whole; and every providence in his past history, as it now passes in review, bathed in the liquid light of glory, swells the anthem—"HE HAS DONE ALL THINGS WELL!"

OCTOBER 28

"For God has not appointed us to wrath, but to obtain salvation by our Lord Jesus Christ." 1 Thessalonians 5:9

Salvation is God's greatest work; in nothing has He so manifested forth His glory as in this. He embarked all His infinite resources, and staked all His Divine honor, in the accomplishment of this work so dear to His heart—the salvation of His church. The universe is full of His beauty, but myriads of worlds, on a scale infinitely more vast and magnificent than this, could give no such idea of God as the salvation of a single sinner. Salvation required the revelation and the harmony of all the Divine perfections. Creation affords only a partial view of God. It displays His natural but not His moral attributes. It portrays His wisdom, His goodness, His power; but it gives no idea of His holiness, His justice, His truth, His love. It is but the alphabet, the shadow of God. These are parts of His ways, and how little of Him is known! But in the person of Immanuel, in the cross of Christ, in the finished work of redemption, God appears in full-orbed majesty. And when the believing soul surveys this wondrous expedient of reconciling all the interests of heaven, of uniting all the perfection of Jehovah in the salvation of sinners by the blood of the cross—"Mercy and truth meeting together, righteousness and peace kissing each other"—it exclaims in full satisfaction with the salvation of God—"Oh the depth of the riches both of the wisdom and knowledge of God!"

The anxious question of an awakened soul, as it bears its weight of sin to the cross, is, "Is the salvation of the Lord Jesus a work commensurate with my case? Will it meet my individual condition as a sinner? May I, in a deep conviction of my guiltiness, venture my soul upon Jesus? Am I warranted, without a work of my own, apart from all my merit or my demerit, to believe in Christ and indulge the hope that I shall be saved?" The Bible, in brief but emphatic sentences, answers these inquiries. "Believe in the Lord Jesus Christ, and you shall be saved." "Him that comes unto me I will in no wise cast out." "By grace are you saved." "If by grace, then it is no more of works." "You are complete in Him." The Holy Spirit giving the inquirer a possession of these declarations, working the faith that receives the Lord Jesus into the heart, the believing soul is enabled to say, "I see that it is a salvation for sinners—for the vilest, the poorest, the most unworthy. I came to Christ, and was received; I believed in Him, rested in Him, and I am saved. Christ is mine, His salvation is mine, His promises are mine, His advocacy is mine, His heaven is mine."

Dear reader, is your soul saved? Are you converted by the Spirit of God?

Everything else in comparison is but as the bubble that floats down the stream. This busy life will soon cease; its last thought, and care, and anxiety will yield to the great, the solemn realities of eternity. Are you ready for the result? Are you in a state of pardon, of justification, of peace with God through Christ? How is it with your soul? Will it be well with you in death, well with you after death, well with you at the judgment-seat of Christ? Have you come to the Lord Jesus as a Savior—to His blood for cleansing, to His righteousness for acceptance, to His cross for shelter, to Himself for rest? Have you fled as a sinner to Jesus as the Savior? Look these questions, I beseech you, fairly, fully in the face, and answer them in your own conscience, and as in view of that dread tribunal at whose bar you will soon be cited. What if you should prosper in temporals, and be lean in spirituals! What if you should pamper the body, and starve the soul! What if you should gain the world—its riches, its honors, its pleasures—and be yourself through eternity a castaway! To die in your sins, to die without union to Christ, to die unreconciled to God, tremendous will be the consequences; so dire will be your condition, so fearful and interminable your sufferings from the wrath of a holy and righteous God, it would have been good for you never to have been born. The unrighteous will be "punished with everlasting destruction, from the presence of the Lord, and from the glory of His power."

But there is hope! Does this page meet the eye of a penitent mourner—one whose heart is smitten with godly grief for sin? Be it known you, that the sacrifice of a broken heart and of a contrite spirit God will not despise. Despise it! oh, no! It is the precious, holy fruit of His Spirit in your soul, and in His eye it is too holy, too costly, too dear to be despised. Bring to Him that broken heart, and Jesus will bind it up, heal and fill it with joy, and peace, and hope. It was His mission to receive and save sinners—it is His office to receive and save sinners—it is His delight and glory to receive and save sinners; and if you will but approach Him, exactly as you are, He will receive and save you.

OCTOBER 29

"I delivered unto you first of all that which I also received, how that Christ died for our sins according to the Scriptures; and that he was buried, and that he rose again the third day according to the Scriptures." 1 Cor. 15:3, 4

What are some of the great truths confirmed by the resurrection of Jesus, and in the belief of which the believer is built up, by this glorious and life-inspiring doctrine? They are many and vast. Indeed, it would not be too much to affirm of the entire system of Divine truth, that it depended mainly for its evidence upon the single fact of Christ's resurrection from the dead. In the first place, it establishes the Bible to be the revelation of God. If the types which shadowed forth, and the prophecies which predicted, the resurrection of the Lord, received not their substance and their fulfillment in the accomplishment of that fact, then the Scriptures were not true, the types were meaningless, and the predictions were false. For thus do they unite in setting forth this glorious and precious truth. First, as it regards the types. What was the receiving back of Isaac after he had been laid upon the altar, and the knife raised to slay him, but the shadowing forth of Christ's resurrection? As the binding of him upon the wood prefigured the sacrificial death of Christ, so the unbinding of him from altar, and his surrender to his father the third day from the time that he received the command to sacrifice him, prefigured the risen life of Christ. Significant type! radiant with the glory of a Jesus! In the one part we see Him dying, the other part we see Him rising. The one shadows forth His atoning sacrifice, the other His risen glory. And here did the mind of Abraham rest. His towering faith rose above the type; he looked beyond the shadow. His soul embraced a crucified and a risen Lord. Strong in the exercise of a prospective faith, he beheld before him as vividly, and he reposed in as firmly, a dying and a living Redeemer, as did John when the sweet voice broke upon his ear, "I am He that lives and was dead." "By faith Abraham, when was tried, offered up Isaac…Accounting that God was able to raise him up even from the dead; from where also he received him in a figure."

The type of the slain and the living goat embodies in vivid outline the same essential doctrine. Aaron was commanded to kill the goat of the offering, and bring his blood within the veil. But upon the head of the live goat he was to place both his hands, and confess over him all the iniquities of the children of Israel, and then to send him away by the hand of a fit man into the wilderness. "And he shall let go the goat in the wilderness." Our adorable Lord was the glorious substance of this expressive type. Both parts met and were realized in Him. "He was delivered for our offenses, and rose again for our justification."

The prophetic Scriptures are equally as explicit in setting forth the resurrection of Christ. "My flesh also shall rest in hope. For You will not leave my soul in hell, neither will You suffer Your Holy One to see corruption." "You are my Son, this day have I begotten You." "I will make an everlasting covenant with you, even the sure mercies of David." Now mark how these portions of the prophetic Scriptures are quoted by the apostle Paul, and strictly applied by him to the resurrection of Christ. Acts 13: "But God raised Him from the dead: and He was seen many days of those who came up with Him from Galilee to

Jerusalem, who are His witnesses unto the people. And we declare unto you glad tidings, how that the promise which was made unto the fathers, God has fulfilled the same unto us, their children, in that He raised up Jesus again; as it is also written in the second Psalm, You are my Son, this day have I begotten you. And as concerning that He raised Him up from the dead, now no more to return to corruption, He said this wise, I will give you the sure mercies of David. Why He says also in another Psalm, You shall not suffer Your Holy One to see corruption. For David, after he had served his own generation by the will of God, fell on sleep, was laid unto his fathers, and saw corruption; but He, whom God raised again, saw no corruption." How brightly does the doctrine of a risen Savior shine throughout this remarkable portion of God's holy word! Truly the life of Jesus is the life of the Scriptures. Again, "Your dead men shall live, together with my dead body shall they arise." "I know that my Redeemer lives." Thus does the resurrection of Christ from the dead confirm the truth of God's holy word. The types find their substance, and the prophets their fulfillment, in Him who was emphatically the "plague of death, and the destruction of the grave."

OCTOBER 30

"What think you of Christ?" Matthew 22:42

Reader, what do you think of Christ? Do you see beauty, surpassing beauty, in Immanuel? Has His glory broken upon your view?—has it beamed in upon your mind? Has a sight of Jesus, seen by faith, cast you in the dust, exclaiming, "I have heard of You by the hearing of the ear: but now mine eye sees You; why I abhor myself, and repent in dust and ashes"? Your honest reply to these searching questions will decide the nature and the ground of your present hope for eternity. On the confines of that eternity you are now standing. Solemn consideration! It is of infinite moment, then, that your views of the Son of God should be thoroughly examined, sifted, and compared with the inspired word. A crown now lowered on your brow, a kingdom stretched at your feet, a world gained and grasped, were as infant's baubles, compared with the tremendous interests involved in the question, "What think you of Christ?" And what do you think of Him? Is He all your salvation and all your desire? Have you laid sinful self and righteous self beneath His cross? and in all your poverty, nakedness, and vileness, have you received Him as made of God unto you "wisdom and righteousness, sanctification and redemption"? Does His glory dim all other glory; and does His beauty eclipse all other beauty in your eye? Can you point to Him and say, in the humble confidence of faith and joy of love, "This is my Beloved, and this is my Friend"? Eternal God! but for the righteousness of Your Son, I sink in all my pollution! but for the atoning blood of Immanuel, I perish in all my guilt! Holy Father, look not on me, but behold my shield, look upon the face of Your anointed! and when Your glory passes by—the glory of Your majesty, Your holiness, and Your justice—then put me in the cleft of the rock, and cover me with Your hand while You pass by.

Cultivate frequent and devout contemplations of Christ and of His glory. Immense will be the benefit accruing to your soul. The mind, thus preoccupied, filled, and expanded, will be enabled to present a stronger resistance to the ever-advancing and insidious encroachments of the world without. No place will be found for vain thoughts and no desire or time for carnal enjoyments. Oh, how crucifying and sanctifying are clear views of the glory of Immanuel! how emptying, humbling, and abasing! With the patriarch we then exclaim, "I abhor myself, and repent in dust and ashes." And with the prophet, "Woe is me! for I am undone; because I am a man of unclean lips. Mine eyes have seen the King." And with the apostle, "God forbid that I should glory, save in the cross of our Lord Jesus Christ, by whom the world is crucified unto me, and I unto the world." Oh, then, aim to get your mind filled with enlarged and yet expanding views of the glory of Christ. Let it, in all the discoveries it affords of the Divine mind and majesty, be the one subject of your thoughts, the one theme of your conversation. Place no limit to your knowledge of Christ. Ever consider that you have but read the preface to the volume, you have but touched the margin of the sea; stretching far away beyond you, are undiscovered beauties, and precious views, and sparkling glories, each encouraging your advance, inviting your research, and asking the homage of your faith, the tribute of your love, and the dedication of your life. Go forward, then! The glories that yet must be revealed to you in a growing knowledge of Jesus, what imagination can conceive, what pen can describe them! "You shall see greater things than these," is the promise that bids you advance. Jesus stands ready to unveil all the beauties of His person, and admit you into the very arcana of His love. There not a chamber of His heart that He will not throw open to you; not a blessing that He will not bestow upon you; not a glory that He will not show to you. You shall see greater things than you have yet seen—greater depths of sin in your fallen nature shall be revealed—deeper sense of the cleansing efficacy of the atoning blood shall be felt—clearer views of your acceptance in the Beloved—greater discoveries of God's love—and greater depths of grace and glory in Jesus shall be enjoyed. Your "peace shall flow like a river, and your righteousness as the waves of sea." Sorrow shall wound you less deeply; affliction shall press you less heavily; tribulation shall affect you less keenly: all this, and infinitely more, will result from your deeper knowledge of Jesus. Ah, wonder not that the apostle exclaimed, "Doubtless, and I count all things but loss for the excellency of the knowledge of Christ Jesus my Lord. That I may know Him, and the power of His resurrection, and the fellowship of His sufferings, being made conformable unto His death." "Then shall we know, if we follow on to know the Lord."

OCTOBER 31

"And the Lord said, I have surely seen the affliction of my people which are in Egypt, and have heard their cry by reason of their taskmasters; for I know their sorrows; and I am come down to deliver them out of the hand of the Egyptians, and to bring them up out of that land unto a good land and a large, unto a land flowing with milk and honey." Exodus 3:7, 8

But a greater work, a mightier and more glorious deliverance, did our Almighty Redeemer come down to effect. To this the Spirit of Christ which was in the prophet Isaiah testified: "The Spirit of the Lord God is upon me; because the Lord has anointed me to preach good tidings unto the meek; He has sent me to bind up the broken-hearted, to proclaim liberty to the captives, and the opening of the prison to those who are bound." The Lord saw from heaven the affliction of His chosen people which were in Egypt—the land of spiritual darkness, bondage, and oppression: He heard their cry by reason of their hard task-masters; He knew their sorrows, and He came down to deliver and to bring them out of that land into a good land—a large place—a land truly flowing with milk and honey. Oh, from what a land of gloom, from what an iron furnace, and from what a hard oppressor, has Jesus delivered His people! He has rescued them from a state of nature, and brought them into a state of grace—from ignorance of God, of Christ, and of themselves, in which the fall had involved them—from the guilt of sin, and the condemnation of the law—from the captivity and tyranny of Satan, and from their hard and oppressive servitude. And, oh, into what a land of rest, blessedness, and plenty has He brought them! Into covenant relationship with God, as His adopted children—into a state of pardon and acceptance—into the enjoyment of His love and presence; to know God as their reconciled Father—to know their oneness with Jesus their exalted Head, and their union with the body as its members—to a state of most holy and blessed liberty, as chosen, called, and adopted saints. Into the experience of all these blessings has a greater than Moses brought us. "When the fullness of the time was come, God sent forth His Son, made of a woman, made under the law, to redeem those who were under the law, that we might receive the adoption of sons." Let then, "give thanks unto the Father, which has made us meet to be partakers of the inheritance of the saints in light: who has delivered us from the power of darkness, and has translated us into the kingdom of His dear Son," "even Jesus, which delivered us from the wrath to come."

And how shall we set forth the love of our Redeemer—the deep and precious love of Christ? Persuasion did not induce Him to undertake our redemption. Compulsion did not bring Him to the cross. His own love constrained Him. Love for His church, His bride, bore Him on its soft wings, from the highest throne in glory to the deepest abasement on earth. How forcibly and touchingly was His love depicted in His bearing, when on the eve of suffering!—"Jesus, therefore, knowing all things that should come upon Him, went forth." He not only knew that death awaited Him, but with equal prescience He knew all the circumstances of ignominy with which that death would be attended. The storm, the outskirts of which had already touched Him, was now thickening and darkening, each moment concentrating its elements of destruction, and preparing for the tremendous outburst. Yet He went forth, as if eager to meet its central horrors, not with the fame-panting spirit of Achilles, when he hastened to the Trojan war, knowing that he should fall there; but with the irresistible power and constraint of His own love, which would have nerved Him for a thousand deaths, had His Father's law demanded, and the salvation of His church required it. "Christ also has loved us, and has given Himself for us an offering and a sacrifice to God, of a sweet-smelling savor." Truly is Jesus, our Great Deliverer, "counted worthy of more glory than Moses."

NOVEMBER

NOVEMBER 1

"Now if I do that I would not, it is no more I that do it, but sin that dwells in me." Romans 7:20

The entire testimony of God's word, and the stories of all the saints recorded in its pages, go to confirm the doctrine of indwelling sin in a believer. The Lord has wisely, we must acknowledge, ordained it, that sin should yet remain in His people to the very last step of their journey; and for this He has graciously provided His word as a storehouse of promises, consolations, cautions, rebukes, admonitions, all referring to the indwelling sin of a believer. The covenant of grace—its sanctifying, strengthening, invigorating, animating provision, all was designed for this very state. Yes, the gift of Jesus—all His fullness of grace, wisdom, strength, and sympathy—His death, resurrection, ascension, and advocacy—all was given with an especial view to the pardon and subjection of sin in a child of God. Perfect holiness, entire sinlessness, is a state not attainable in this life. He who has settled down with the conviction that he has arrived at such a stage has great reason to suspect the soundness, or at least the depth, of his real knowledge of himself. He, indeed, must be but imperfectly acquainted with his own heart, who dreams of perfect sanctification on this side of glory. With all meekness and tenderness, I would earnestly exhort such an individual to review his position well—to bring his heart to the touchstone of God's word—to pray over the seventh chapter of the Epistle to the Romans, and to ascertain if there are not periods when the experience of an inspired apostle, once "caught up to the third heaven," will not apply to him—"I am carnal, sold under sin,"—the "sin that dwells in me." The writings and the preaching of men—mistaken views of truth—yes, I would add, even what was once a sincere and ardent desire for sanctification—either of these, or all combined, may have led to the adoption of such a notion as sinless perfection, the nature and tendency of which are to engender a spirit of human pride, self-trust, self-complacence; to throw the mind off its guard, and the heart off its prayerful vigilance, and thus render the man an easy prey to that subtle and ever-prowling enemy, of whose "devices" (and this is not the least one) no believer should be "ignorant."

Oh yes, sin, often deep and powerful, dwells in a child of God. It is the source of his greatest grief, the cause of his acutest sorrow. Remove this, and sorrow in the main would be a stranger to his breast. Go, ask yon weary, dejected, weeping believer the cause of his broken spirit—his sad countenance—his tears. "Is it," you inquire, "that you are poor in this world?" "No." "Is it that you are friendless?" "No." "Is it that worldly prosperity shines not upon you—your plans blasted—your circumstances trying—your prospects dark?" "No." "What is it, then, that grieves your spirit, clouds your countenance, and that causes those clasped hands and uplifted eyes?" "It is sin," the soul replies, "that dwells in me: sin is my burden—sin is my sorrow—sin is my grief—sin is my confession—sin is humiliation before my Father and God—rid of this, and the outward pressure would scarce be felt." Truly does the apostle say—and let the declaration never be read apart from its accompanying promise—"If we say that we have no sin, we deceive ourselves, and the truth is not in us. If we confess our sins, He is faithful and just to forgive us our sins, and to cleanse us from all unrighteousness. If we say that we have not sinned, we make Him a liar, and His word is not in us. My little children, these things write I unto you, that you sin not. And if any man sin, we have an Advocate with the Father, Jesus Christ the righteous."

NOVEMBER 2

"And all things, whatever you shall ask in prayer, believing, you shall receive." Matthew 21:22

Draw near, then, seeking soul, with boldness; not the boldness of a presumptuous, self-righteous man, but that of one chosen, called, pardoned, and justified. Draw near with the lowly boldness of a child—with the humble confidence of a son. Dear are you to your Father. Sweet is your voice to Him. Precious is your person, accepted in His Beloved. You can not come too boldly—you can not come too frequently—you can not come with too large requests. You are coming to a King, that King your Father, that Father viewing you in His beloved Son. Oh, hang not back. Stand not afar off. He now holds out the golden scepter, and says, "Come near; what is your request? Come with your temporal want. Come with your spiritual need. Ask what you will, it shall be granted you. I have an open hand, and a large heart." Is it your desire—"Lord, I want more grace to glorify You. I want more simplicity of mind, and singleness of eye. I want a more holy, upright, honest walk. I want more meekness, patience, lowliness, submission. I want to know more of Jesus, to see more of His glory, to feel more of His preciousness, and to live more simply upon His fullness. I want more of the sanctifying, sealing, witnessing, and anointing influences of the Spirit"? Blessed, holy desires! It is the Spirit making intercession in you according to the will of God; and entering into the holiest by the blood of Jesus, the Lord will fulfill the desires of your heart, even to the half of kingdom.

Watch diligently against the least declension in the spirit of prayer. If there be declension here, there will also be declension in every part and department of the work of the Spirit in your soul. It is prayer that keeps every grace of the Spirit in active, holy, and healthy exercise. It is the stream, so to speak, that supplies refreshing vigor and nourishment to all the plants of grace. It is true, that the fountain-head of all spiritual life and "grace to help in time of need," is Christ; "for it pleased the Father that in Him should all fullness dwell." And Paul's encouragement to the Philippians was, "My God shall supply all your need, according to His riches in glory by Christ Jesus." But the channel through which all grace comes is prayer—ardent, wrestling, importunate, believing prayer. Suffer this channel to be dry—permit any object to narrow or close it up—and the effect will be a withering and decay of the life of God in the soul.

Guard, then, against the slightest decline of prayer in the soul. If prayer—family prayer, social prayer, most of all, closet prayer, is declining with you, no further evidence is needed of your being in a backsliding state of mind. There may not yet have been the outward departure, but you are in the way to it—and nothing but a return to prayer will save you. Oh, what alarm, what fearfulness and trembling, should this thought occasion in a child of God, "I am on my way to an awful departure from God! Such is the state of my soul at this moment, such my present state of mind, such the loss of my spirituality, such the hold which the world has upon my affections, there is no length in sin to which I may not now go, there is no iniquity which I may not now commit. The breakers are full in view, any my poor weak vessel is heading to and rapidly nearing them." What can shield you from the commission of that sin, what can keep you from wounding Jesus afresh, what can preserve you from foundering and making shipwreck of your faith, but an immediate and fervent return to prayer. Prayer is your only safety. Prayer, for grace to help in your time of need. Prayer, for reviving grace, for quickening, restraining, sanctifying grace. Prayer, to be kept from falling, to be held up in the slippery paths. Prayer, for the lowly mind, for the contrite spirit, for the broken heart, for the soft, and close, and humble walk with God.

NOVEMBER 3

"But the God of all grace, who has called us unto his eternal glory by Christ Jesus, after that you have suffered a while, make you perfect, establish, strengthen, settle you." 1 Peter 5:10

There is a painful forgetfulness among many of the saints of God of the appointed path of believers through the world. It is forgotten that this path is to be one of tribulation; that so far from being a smooth, a flowery, and an easy path, it is rough, thorny, and difficult. The believer often expects all his heaven on earth. He forgets that whatever spiritual enjoyment there may be here, kindred in its nature to the joys of the glorified—and too much of this he cannot expect—yet the present is but the wilderness state of the church, and the life that now is, is but that of a pilgrimage and a sojourning. Kind was our Lord's admonition, "in the world you shall have tribulation:" and equally so that of the apostle, "we must through much tribulation enter into the kingdom." Affliction, in some of its many and varied forms, is the allotment of all the Lord's people. If we have it not, we lack the evidence of our true sonship; for the Father "scourges every son whom he receives." But whatever the trial or affliction is, the Holy Spirit is the Comforter. And how does He comfort the afflicted soul? In this way.

He unfolds the love of his God and Father in the trial. He shows the believer that his sorrow, so far from being the result of anger, is the fruit of love; that it comes from the heart of God, sent to draw the soul nearer to Himself, and to unfold the depths of His own grace and tenderness; that whom he "loves He chastens." And, oh, how immense the comfort that flows into a wounded spirit, when love—deep, unchangeable, covenant love—is seen in the hand that has stricken; when the affliction is traced to the covenant, and through the covenant, to the heart of a covenant God.

The Spirit comforts by revealing the end why the affliction is sent. He convinces the believer that the discipline, though painful, was yet needed; that the world was, perhaps, making inroads upon the soul, or creature love was shutting out Jesus; some indulged sin was, perhaps, crucifying Him afresh, or some known spiritual duty was neglected. The Comforter opens his ears to hear the voice of the rod, and Him who had appointed it. He begins to see why the Lord has smitten, why He has caused His rough wind and His east wind to blow; why He has blasted, why He has wounded. And now the Achan is discovered, cast out, and stoned. The heart, disciplined, returns from its wanderings, and, wounded, bleeding, suffering, seeks more earnestly than ever a wounded, bleeding, suffering Savior. Who can fully estimate the comfort which flows from the sanctified discipline of the covenant? When the end for which the trial was sent is accomplished, it may be in the discovery of some departure, in the removal of an obstruction to the growth of grace, of some object that obscured the glory of Jesus, and that suspended His visits of love to the soul, "Blessed discipline," he may exclaim, "that has wrought so much good—gentle chastisement, that has corrected so much evil—sweet medicine, that has produced so much health!"

NOVEMBER 4

"Jesus says unto her, Woman, why are you weeping?" John 20:15

In unfolding the tenderness and sympathy of Jesus, the Spirit most effectually restores comfort to the tried, tempted, and afflicted soul. He testifies of Christ especially in the sympathy of His manhood. There can be no question, that in His assumption of our nature Jesus had in view, as one important end, a closer affinity with the suffering state of His people, with regard to their more immediate comfort and support. The great end of His incarnation, we are well assured, was obedience to the law in its precept, and the suffering of its penalty. But connected with and resulting from this, is the channel that thus is open for the outflowings of that tenderness and sympathy of which the saints of God so constantly stand in need, and as constantly receive. Jesus is the "Brother born for adversity."—"It behooved Him to be made like unto His brethren, that He might be a merciful and faithful High Priest."—"In that He Himself has suffered, being tempted; He is able support those who are tempted."—"We have not an High Priest which cannot be touched with the feeling of our infirmities, but was in all points tempted like as we are, yet without sin."

Come, dear reader, what is your sorrow? Has the hand of death smitten? Is the beloved one removed? Has He taken away the desire of your eyes with a stroke? But who has done it? Jesus has done it; death was but His messenger. Your Jesus has done it. The Lord has taken away. And what has He removed?—your wife? Jesus has all the tenderness that ever your wife had. Hers was but a drop from the ocean that is in His heart. Is it your husband? Jesus is better to you than ten husbands. Is it your parent, your child, your friend, your all of earthly bliss? Is the cistern broken? Is the earthen vessel dashed to pieces? Are all your streams dry? Jesus is yet enough. He has not taken Himself from you, and never, never will. Take your bereaved, stricken, and bleeding heart to Him, and repose it upon His, once bereaved, stricken, and bleeding, too; for He knows how to bind up the broken heart, to heal the wounded spirit, and to comfort those that mourn.

What is your sorrow? Has health failed you? Has property forsaken you? Have friends turned against you? Are you tried in your circumstances? perplexed in your path? Are providences thickening and darkening around you? Are you anticipating seasons of approaching trial? Are you walking in darkness, having no light? Go simply to Jesus. He is a door ever open. A tender, loving, faithful Friend, ever near. He is a Brother born for your adversity. His grace and sympathy are sufficient for you. The life you are called to live is that of faith—that of sense you have done with. You are now to walk by faith, and not by sight. This, then, is the great secret of a life of faith—to hang upon Jesus daily—to go to Him in every trial—to cast upon Him every burden—to take the infirmity, the corruption, the cross, as it rises, simply and immediately to Jesus. You are to set Christ before you as your Example to imitate; as your Fountain to wash in; as your Foundation to build upon; as your Fullness to draw from; as your tender, loving, and confiding Brother and Friend, to go to at all times and under all circumstances. To do this daily constitutes the life of faith. Oh to be enabled with Paul to say, "I am crucified with Christ: nevertheless I live; yet not I, but Christ lives in me: and the life which I now live in the flesh, I live by the faith of the Son of God, who loved me, and gave Himself for me." Oh holy, happy, heavenly life!—the life Jesus Himself lived when below; the life all the patriarchs and prophets, the apostles and martyrs, and the spirits of just men made perfect, once lived; and the life every true-born child of God is called and privileged to live, while yet a stranger and pilgrim on the earth.

NOVEMBER 5

"Verily, verily, I say unto you, He that hears my word, and believes on him that sent me, has everlasting life, and shall not come into condemnation; but is passed from death unto life." John 5:24

Let us consider what this condition does not imply. It does not include deliverance from the indwelling of sin, nor exemption from Divine correction, nor the absence of self-accusation; still less does it suppose, that there is nothing for which the believer deserves to die. All this exists where yet no condemnation exists. The battle with indwelling evil is still waged, the loving chastisement of a Father is still experienced, the self-condemnation is still felt, and daily in the holiest life there is still transpiring that which, were God strict to mark iniquities, merits and would receive eternal woe; yet the declaration stands untouched and unimpeached—"No condemnation to those who are in Christ Jesus."

The freedom of the believer is just what it is declared to be—entire exemption from condemnation. From all which that word of significant and solemn import implies he is, by his relation to Christ, delivered. Sin does not condemn him, the law does not condemn him, the curse does not condemn him, hell does not condemn him, God does not condemn him. He is under no power from these, beneath whose accumulated and tremendous woe all others wither. The pardon of sin necessarily includes the negation of its condemnatory power. There being no sin legally alleged, there can be no condemnation justly pronounced. Now, by the sacrifice of Christ, all the sins of the church are entirely put away. He, the sinless Lamb of God, took them up and bore them away into a land of oblivion, where even the Divine mind fails to recall them. "How forcible are right words!" Listen to those which declare this wondrous fact. "I, even I, am He that blots out your transgressions for mine own sake, and will not remember your sins." "You have cast all my sins behind Your back." "Having forgiven you all trespasses." Their sins and iniquities will I remember no more." The revoking of the sentence of the law must equally annihilate its condemnatory force. The obedience and death of Christ met the claims of that law, both in its preceptive and punitive character. A single declaration of God's word throws a flood of light upon this truth: "Christ has redeemed us from the curse of the law, being made a curse for us." The sentence of the law thus falling upon Surety, who was "made under the law, that He might redeem those who were under the law," there can be no condemnation from it to those who have taken shelter in Him. Thus, then, it is evident that both sin and the law are utterly powerless to condemn a believer in the Lord Jesus Christ.

The perfection of Christ's satisfaction supplies the meritorious and procuring cause of our condemnation. No legal obedience—no personal merit or worthiness of the sinner whatever—is taken into the account of His discharge. This exalted position can only be reached by an expedient that harmonizes with the attributes of God, and thus upholds, in undimmed luster, the majesty and honor of the Divine government. God will pardon sin, and justify the sinner, but it must be by a process supremely glorifying to Himself. How, then, could a creature-satisfaction, the most perfect that man, or the most peerless that angel could offer, secure this result? Impossible! But the case, strange and difficult though it is, is met, fully, adequately met, by the satisfaction of Jesus. The Son of God became the Son of man. He presents Himself to the Father in the character of the church's substitute. The Father, beholding in Him the Divinity that supplies the merit, and the humanity that yields the obedience and endures the suffering, accepts the Savior, and acquits the sinner. Hence the freedom of the believer from condemnation: "There is, therefore, now no condemnation." It is the existence of a present condition. It is the enjoyment of a present immunity. It is the simple belief of this fact that brings instant peace to the bosom. A present discharge from condemnation must produce a present joy. Christian! there is now no condemnation for you. Be yours, then, a present and a full joy.

NOVEMBER 6

"If we confess our sins, he is faithful and just to forgive us our sins, and to cleanse us from all unrighteousness." 1 John 1:9

Deal much and closely with the fullness of grace that is in Jesus. All this grace in Christ is for the sanctification of the believer. "It pleased the Father that in Him should all fullness dwell," for the necessities of His people; and what necessities so great and urgent as those which spring from indwelling sin? Take the corruption, whatever be its nature, directly and simply to Jesus: the very act of taking it to Him weakens its power; yes, it is half the victory. The blessed state of mind, the holy impulse that leads you to your closet, there to fall prostrate before the Lord in lowliness of spirit and brokenness of heart—the humble confession of sin, with the hand of faith on the head of Jesus, the atoning sacrifice—is a mighty achievement of the indwelling Spirit over the power of indwelling sin.

Learn to take the guilt as it comes, and the corruption as it rises, directly and simply to Jesus. Suffer not the guilt of sin to remain long upon the conscience. The moment there is the slightest consciousness of a wound received, take it to the blood of Christ. The moment a mist dims the eye of faith, so that you can not see clearly the smile of your Father's countenance, take it that instant to the blood of atonement. Let there be no distance between God and your soul. Sin separates. But sin immediately confessed, mourned over, and forsaken, brings God and the soul together in sweet, close, and holy fellowship. Oh the oneness of God and the believer, in a sin-pardoning Christ! Who can know it?—He only who has experienced it. To cherish, then, the abiding sense of this holy, loving oneness, the believer must live near the fountain. He must wash daily in the brazen laver that is without; then, entering within the veil, he may "draw near" the mercy-seat, and ask what he will of Him that dwells between the cherubims.

Thank God for the smallest victory gained. Praise Him for any evidence that sin has not entire dominion. Every fresh triumph achieved over some strong and easy-besetting infirmity is a glorious battle won. No victory that ever flushed the cheek of an Alexander or a Caesar may once be compared with his, who, in the grace that is in Christ Jesus, overcomes a single corruption. If "he that rules his spirit is better than he that takes a city," then, he who masters one corruption of his nature has more real glory than the greatest earthly conqueror that ever lived. Oh, how God is glorified—how Jesus is honored—how the Spirit is magnified, in the slaying of one spiritual enemy at the foot of the cross! Cheer up, precious soul! You have every encouragement to persevere in the great business of sanctification. True, it is a hard fight—true, it is a severe and painful contest—but the victory is yours! The "Captain of your salvation" has fought and conquered for you, and now sits upon His throne of glory, cheering you on, and supplying you with all needed strength for the warfare in which you are engaged. Then, "Fight the good fight of faith, be men of courage,"—"be strong in the grace that is in Christ Jesus,"—for you shall at length "overcome through the blood of the Lamb," and be "more than conquerors [triumphant] through Him that has loved us." Here, beneath the cross, would I breathe for you the desire and the prayer once offered by the apostle of the Gentiles, in behalf of the church of the Thessalonians: "And the very God of peace sanctify you wholly; and I pray God your whole spirit and soul and body be preserved blameless unto the coming of our Lord Jesus. Christ." Amen and amen.

NOVEMBER 7

"For consider him that endured such contradiction of sinners against himself, lest you be wearied and faint in your minds." Hebrews 12:3

The assaults of the adversary contribute not a little to the sense of weariness which often prostrates a child of God. To be set up as a mark for Satan; the enemy smiting where sensibility is the keenest; assailing where weakness is the greatest; taking advantage of every new position and circumstance, especially of a season of trial, of a weak, nervous temperament, or of a time of sickness—distorting God's character, diverting the eye from Christ, and turning it in upon self—are among Satan's devices for casting down the soul of a dear believer. And then, there are the narrowness of the narrow way, the intricacies of the intricate way, the perils of the perilous way—all tending to jade and dispirit the soul. To walk in a path so narrow and yet so dangerous, that the white garment must needs be closely wrapped around; to occupy a post of duty so conspicuous, responsible, and difficult, as to fix every eye; some gazing with undue admiration, and others with keen and cold suspicion, ready to detect and to censure any slight irregularity—add not a little to the to toilsomeness of the way. Notice, also, the numerous and varied trials and afflictions which pave his pathway to heaven—his tenderest mercies often his acutest trials, his trials often weighing him to the earth—and you have the outline of a melancholy picture, of which he whose eye scans this page may be the original. Does it surprise, then, that from the lips of such a one the exclamation often rises, "Oh that I had wings like a dove! for then would I fly away, and be at rest. I would hasten my escape from the windy storm and tempest."

Remember, there will be a correspondence between the life of Christ in the soul, and the life which Christ lived when he tabernacled in the flesh. The indwelling of Christ in the believer is a kind of second incarnation of the Son of God. When Christ enters the heart of a poor sinner, He once more clothes Himself with our nature. The life which Christ lived in the days of His sojourn on earth was a life of sorrow, of conflict, of temptation, of desertion, of want, and of suffering in every form. Does He now live a different life in the believer? No; He is still tempted and deserted, in sorrow and in want, in humiliation and in suffering—in His people. What! did you think that these fiery darts were leveled at you? Did you suppose that it was you who were deserted, that it was you who suffered, that it was you who were despised, that it was you who were trodden under foot? No, my brother, it was Christ dwelling in you. All the malignity of Satan, all the power of sin, and all the contempt of the world, are leveled, not against you, but against the Lord dwelling in you. Were it all death in your soul, all darkness, sinfulness, and worldliness, you would be an entire stranger to these exercises of the renewed man.

Behold the love and condescension of Jesus! that after all He endured in His own person, He should again submit Himself to the same in the persons of His saints; that He should, as it were, return, and tread again the path of suffering, of trial, of humiliation, in the life which each believer lives. Oh, how it speaks that love which passes knowledge! How completely is Christ one with His saints! and yet, how feebly and faintly do we believe this truth! How little do we recognize Christ in all that relates to us! and yet He is in all. He is in every providence that brightens or that darkens upon our path. "Christ is all, and in all."

NOVEMBER 8

"And the Word was made flesh, and dwelt among us, (and we beheld his glory, the glory as of the only begotten of the Father,) full of grace and truth." John 1:14

Before this Vessel of grace let us pause in adoring admiration of its greatness and its beauty. It is the "great mystery of godliness." Angels are summoned to adore it. "When He brings in the first-begotten into the world, He says, And let all the angels of God worship Him." It was the profoundest conception of God's wisdom, the masterpiece of His power, and worthy of their deepest homage. Such an unveiling of the glory of God they had never gazed upon before. In the countless glories with which He had enriched and garnished the universe, there was not its symbol, nor its type. All other wonders cease to astonish, and all other beauty fades, in comparison with this, the grandest, the peerless of all. As if fathoming the utmost depth of infinity, and collecting all its hidden treasures of wisdom and power, of grace and truth, God would seem to have concentrated and embodied, to have illustrated and displayed them all, in the person of His Incarnate Son, "God manifest in the flesh." In this was found to consist the fitness of Immanuel, as the covenant Head of grace to the church. The Divine and costly treasure, no longer confided to the guardianship and ministration of a weak, dependent creature, was deposited in the hands of incarnate Deity, One whom the Father knew, His "equal," His "fellow," made strong for Himself; and thus it was secured to His church, an inexhaustible and eternal supply.

But not in His Divine nature only did the fitness and beauty of our Lord, as the one Vessel of grace, appear. His human nature, so perfect, so sinless, so replenished, enriched, and sanctified with the in-being of the Holy Spirit, conspired to render Him "fairer than the children of men."—But in what did the chief excellence and beauty of our Lord's humanity consist? Was it the glory of human wisdom, of worldly grandeur, of secular power? No; not in these! It was that which the world the least esteems, and the most hates, which formed the rich endowment of our Lord's inferior nature—the grace which dwelt within Him. The world conferred no dignity upon Christ, save that of its deepest ridicule and its bitterest scorn. In His temporal estate, He preferred poverty to wealth, obscurity to distinction, insult to applause, suffering to ease, a cross to a throne. So indigent and neglected was He, though every spot of earth was His, and all creatures were feeding from His hand, He had no nightly shelter, and often no "daily bread." How affecting to those who love the Savior, and who owe all their temporal comforts to His deprivation, and all their glory to His abasement, are expressions like these—"Jesus hungered;" "Jesus said, I thirst;" "Jesus sighed deeply in His spirit." "Jesus groaned within Himself;" "Jesus wept" "The Son of man has not where to lay His head." Thus low did stoop the incarnate God!

But in the midst of all this poverty and humiliation, God did seem to say, "I will make Him, my Son, more glorious than angels, and fairer than the children of men. I will endow Him immeasurably with my Spirit, and I will replenish Him to the full with my grace. I will anoint Him with the oil of gladness above His fellows." When He appeared in the world, and the eye of the evangelist caught the vision, he exclaimed with wondering delight, "The glory of the only-begotten of the Father, full of grace and truth." How did all that He said and did, each word and action, betray the fullness of grace that dwelt within Him! The expressions that distilled from His lips were "gracious words;" the truths He thus taught were the doctrines of grace; the works He performed were the miracles of grace; the invitations He breathed were the promises of grace; the blessings He pronounced were the gifts of grace; in a word, the blood He shed, the righteousness He wrought, the redemption He accomplished, the salvation He proclaimed, the souls He rescued, and the kingdom He promised, were the outgushings, the overflowings, the achievements, the triumphs, and the rewards of grace.

NOVEMBER 9

"Him has God exalted with his right hand to be a Prince and a Savior, for to give repentance to Israel, and forgiveness of sins." Acts 5:31

How glorious an object is this Savior, whom the gospel thus reveals! It is true His essential greatness, like the peace which He Himself gives, "passes all understanding;" yet, like that peace, He may be known, though He cannot be measured. "We may know experimentally," as Owen beautifully remarks, "that which we cannot know comprehensively; we may know that in its power and effect, which we cannot comprehend in its nature and depths. A weary person may receive refreshment from a spring, who cannot fathom the depth of the ocean from where it proceeds." That this is true of the "love of Christ, which passes knowledge," is equally true of the person of Christ Himself, whom "no man knows but the Father." Do not think that all His beauty is concealed. They, in whom it has pleased the Father to reveal His Son, "behold His glory;" they "see the King in His beauty;" the discovery of His excellence often captivates their soul, and the sense of His love often cheers their hearts; while in lively faith and joy they exclaim, "I am my Beloved's, and my Beloved is mine."

Take one more view of Him, who is the "chief among ten thousand." Look at His sinless yet real humanity; without a single taint, yet sympathizing with all the conditions of ours: afflicted in our afflictions; tempted in our temptations; infirm in our infirmities; grieved in our griefs; "wounded for our transgressions, bruised for our iniquities;" and now that He is in glory, still cherishing a brother's heart, bending down His ear to our petitions, ever standing near to catch our sighs, to dry our tears, to provide for our needs, to guide us by His counsel, and afterwards to receive us to glory. Oh what a Savior is Jesus Christ! Wonder not, my readers, that when He is known, all other beings are eclipsed; that when His beauty is seen, all other beauty fades; that when His love is felt, He becomes supremely enthroned in the affections; and that to know Him more is the one desire of the renewed mind, and to make Him more known is the one aim of the Christian life.

What glorious tidings, too, does the gospel announce! Take the doctrine of pardon, the very mention of which thrills the soul with gladness. Pardon through the blood-shedding of God's dear Son; for "all manner of sin," and for the chief of sinners! What myriads have gone to glory, exulting with their expiring breath in those melodious words, "the blood of Jesus Christ His Son cleanses us from all sin." Is there no music in this declaration, to the ear of a sin-burdened soul? And when the called children of God behold in that blood of Immanuel the sea which has drowned all their sins, the fountain which has cleansed all their guilt, the source of their reconciliation, the cause of their peace, and the ground of their access—is not the gospel a joyful sound to their ears? And yet how few live in the full enjoyment of this truth—"You will cast all my sins behind Your back." "You have forgiven all their iniquity." "I have blotted out as a cloud your transgression, and as a thick cloud your sins." Precious truth! Since God has spoken it, faith exclaims, "I believe it. On this I can live holily, and on this I can die happily."

NOVEMBER 10

"Beloved, let us love one another: for love is of God; and every one that loves is born of God, and knows God." 1 John 4:7

It were as much a libel upon the religion of Jesus to represent it as destroying the instincts of our sympathetic nature, as it were a dim conception of the Divine power of that religion, to suppose that it does not increase, to an intensity and tenderness almost infinite, the depth and power of those instincts. It is generally admitted, that, compared with the Christian economy, the Old Dispensation was characterized by many essential and palpable features of terror and harshness and that those who lived under its sway would naturally imbibe the spirit of the economy to which they belonged. Yet, oppressive as appear to have been many of its laws, unfeeling many of its requirements, and harsh the spirit of its whole economy, we find in that dispensation some of the most real, tender, and touching exhibitions of sympathy springing from holy hearts, recorded in the Bible. Who, as he wanders amid the vine-clad but deserted hills of Palestine, with a heart of cultivated affections, and an ear attuned to plaintive sounds, does not regard it as the sacred home of sensibility—its valleys and its mountains still vocal with the sighings of sympathy and the lamentations of love? There would still seem to vibrate the touching tones of Jacob, pouring forth the tenderness of his soul, for his beloved Rachel, and for his darling son. There, too, would seem yet to linger the mournful requiem of David for the fallen sovereign whom he venerated, for the faithful friend whom he loved, and for the unhappy son whose untimely death he deplored. Could sympathy be portrayed in a picture more vivid, or embodied in words more heart-subduing, than this: "And the king was much moved, and went up to the chamber over the gate, and wept: and as he went, thus he said, O my son Absalom, my son, my son Absalom! would God I had died for you, O Absalom, my son, my son!" Such is a recollection of Palestine. And who can thus think of that hallowed land, and not associate with it all that is elevating, grateful, and touching in sympathy!

But another and a more sympathetic economy has succeeded. Christianity is the embodiment, the incarnation of love. It not only inculcates, but it inspires, it not only enjoins, but it originates, the most refined sensibility of soul. Sympathy is no by-law of Christianity, it is the embodied essence of all its laws; and Christianity itself is the embalmed sympathies of Him, in whom dwelt bodily the fullness of Divine and Essential Love. If the ancient economy, with all its coldness, harshness, and severity, dedicated its temples and tuned its lyres, lent its holy oracles and consecrated the very scenes and scenery of nature, to the highest, noblest, and purest sympathies of the soul; surely the gospel will not frown or pour contempt upon the feelings, emotions, and breathings, which the law held precious and sacred. Oh no! the religion of Jesus is the religion of love. It is the school of the affections; and it is only here that they are fully developed, sanctified, and trained. To love man as man should be loved, God must be the first and supreme object of our love.

NOVEMBER 11

"Why the rather, brethren, give diligence to make your calling and election sure: for if you do these things, you shall never fall: for so an entrance shall be ministered unto you abundantly into the everlasting kingdom of our Lord and Savior Jesus Christ." 2 Peter 1:10, 11

The doctrine of an assured belief of the pardon of sin, of acceptance in Christ, and of adoption into the family of God, has been, and yet is, regarded by many as an attainment never to be expected in the present life; and when it is expressed, it is viewed with a suspicion unfavorable to the character of the work. But this is contrary to the Divine word, and to the concurrent experience of millions who have lived and died in the full assurance of hope. The doctrine of assurance is a doctrine of undoubted revelation, implied and expressed. That it is enforced as a state of mind essential to the salvation of the believer, we cannot admit; but that it is insisted upon as essential to his comfortable and holy walk, and as greatly involving the glory of God, we must strenuously maintain. Else why these marked references to the doctrine? In Col. 2:1, 2, Paul expresses "great conflict" for the saints, that their "hearts might be comforted, being knit together in love, and unto all riches of the full assurance of understanding." In the Epistle to the Hebrews, 7:11, he says, " We desire that every one of you do show the same diligence to the full assurance of hope unto the end." In chap. 10:22, he exhorts them, "Let us draw near with a true heart, in full assurance of faith." And to crown all, the apostle Peter thus earnestly exhorts, "Why the rather, brethren, give diligence to make your calling and election sure." We trust no further proof from the sacred word is required to authenticate the doctrine. It is written as with a sunbeam, "The Spirit itself bears witness with our spirit, that we are the children of God."

It is the duty and the privilege of every believer diligently and prayerfully to seek the sealing of the Spirit. He rests short of his great privilege, if he slights or undervalues this blessing. Do not be satisfied with the faint impression, which you received in conversion. In other words, rest not content with a past experience. Many are satisfied with a mere hope that they once passed from death unto life, and with this feeble and, in many cases, doubtful evidence, they are content to pass all their days, and to go down to the grave. Ah, reader, if you are really converted, and your soul is in a healthy, growing, spiritual state, you will want more than this. And especially, too, if you are led into deeper self-knowledge—a more intimate acquaintance with the roughness of the rough way, the straitness of the strait path, you will want a present Christ to lean upon, and to live upon. Past experience will not do for you, save only as it confirms your soul in the faithfulness of God. "Forgetting those things that are behind," you will seek a present pardon, a present sense of acceptance; and the daily question, as you near your eternal home, will be, "how do I now stand with God?—is Jesus precious to my soul now?—is He my daily food?—what do I experience of daily visits from and to Him?—do I more and more see my own vileness, emptiness, and poverty, and His righteousness, grace, and fullness?—and should the summons now come, am I ready to depart and to be with Christ?" As you value a happy and a holy walk—as you would be jealous for the honor and glory of the Lord—as you wish to be the "salt of the earth," the "light of the world"—to be a savor of Christ in every place—oh, seek the sealing of the Spirit. Rest not short of it—reach after it—press towards it: it is your duty—oh that the duty may be your privilege; then shall you exclaim with an unfaltering tongue, "Abba; Father," "my Lord my God!"

NOVEMBER 12

"If you then, being evil, know how to give good unto your children: how much more shall your heavenly Father give the Holy Spirit to those who ask him." Luke 11:13

God has ordained that prayer should be the great channel through which His covenant blessings should flow into the soul. If it is your anxious desire to attain this sealing influence of the Spirit, I would quote for your direction a remark of that eminent servant of Christ, Dr. Goodwin, "Be sure of this," says he, "that before God ever communicates any good to a soul, He puts that soul in a state of holiness to receive it." To confirm and illustrate this thought, let me ask—what was the state of the apostles, when the Holy Spirit descended upon them in His witnessing, anointing, and sealing influences? It is described in these words—"These all continued with one accord in prayer and supplication, with the women, and Mary the mother of Jesus, and with His brethren," Acts 1:14. What is the important lesson thus taught us? That God would have His child in a waiting, seeking, supplicating posture; and in this holy state, prepared to receive the high attainment He is ready to bestow.

Do you earnestly desire the sealing of the Spirit? "Ask, and you shall receive; seek, and you shall find." As sure as you petition for it—sincerely, humbly, believingly—seeking it in the name of Jesus, through the cross of Christ, you shall have it. The Lord the Spirit is ready to impart it to you. It is the free gift of

His love, without respect to any worth or worthiness on the part of the soul that receives it. It is a gift of grace—for the poor, the dependent, the unworthy—those that are little in their own eyes, and little in the eyes of others; and if this is your conscious state, then is it for you. And oh, the blessed results!—who can describe them? Sealed! How will all your legal fears and unbelieving doubts in a moment vanish away! your soul, so long fettered and imprisoned, shall now go free; the cross you have so long looked at, not daring to bow your shoulder to it, shall now be taken up with a cheerful mind; Christ's yoke, so long resisted, will now be easy, and His burden, so long refused, will now be light; and, with a heart enlarged with the love of Jesus, you will "run the way of His commandments," esteeming His precepts better than life. Prayer, importunate prayer, will bring the blessing we plead for into your soul. Seek it with your whole heart—seek it diligently, perseveringly. Seek it by day and by night—seek it in all the means of grace—in every way of God's appointment—especially seek it in the name of Jesus, as the purchased blessing of His atoning blood. "Ask what you will in my name," are His own encouraging words, "and it shall he granted unto you." Then ask for the sealing of the Spirit. Ask nothing less: more you do not want. Feel that you have not "attained," until you possess it—that you have not "apprehended that for which also you are apprehended of Christ Jesus," until you have "received the Holy Spirit" as a sealer.

NOVEMBER 13

"Be filled with the Spirit." Ephesians 5:18

The possession of the Holy Spirit in the fullness of His grace contributes essentially to the constitution of the spiritual mind. The antagonist of carnality is the Spirit. "If we walk in the Spirit, we shall not fulfill the lusts of the flesh." As the Spirit of God, He is the author of all that is spiritual. As the Spirit of holiness, He maintains and carries forward the work of sanctification in the soul. He it is who forms, and He it is who leads forward, the spiritual mind. The large possession of the Spirit! nothing can exceed the blessing. Without the Spirit of God, what is man? He is the mark of every fiery assault, the prey of every prowling foe—a magazine of corruption, around which a thousand sparks—sparks of his own kindling—fall. But possessing the Spirit; even in its most limited measure, what is man? A living soul—a holy being—a temple of God—an heir of glory. But suppose him possessing the Spirit in the plenitude of His grace, not partially, but "filled with the Spirit—what must be the invincibility of his might in the resistance of sin! what the potency of his shield in disarming the power of temptation! and what the eminence of his attainments in spiritual-mindedness, as a child of God! While others are girding for the conflict, or are adjusting their armor, he is covering himself with glory on the battle-field. While others are training for the race, he has well-near reached the goal. "Filled with the Spirit," he is filled with all the fruits of the Spirit. Faith is vigorous, hope is bright, love is fervent. He is mighty in the "Spirit of power, and of love, and of a sound mind."

It was this possession of the Spirit in His fullness which gave to the apostles, who until then were so timid and unbelieving, such irresistible boldness and power on the day of Pentecost. Some in their hearing exclaimed, "These men are full of new wine." But the secret was, "They were all filled with the Holy Spirit." And the hearts of the great mass to whom they preached the crucified Savior bowed before the power of their preaching, "as the trees of the wood are moved with the wind." Oh seek to "be filled with the Spirit"! then will your thirstings for God be deeper, your breathings after holiness more intense, your communion with your heavenly Father closer, and your faith in Jesus stronger. The indwelling of the Spirit is the root of all holiness; but the communication of the Spirit in the plenitude of His gracious, sanctifying, Christ-transforming influence, is the secret of an elevated tone of heavenly-mindedness. Would you repel some strong assault, or vanquish some powerful corruption, or throw off some clinging infirmity, and abide by the verdant banks and quiet waters of fellowship with the Father and with His Son Christ Jesus?—oh ask, and you shall receive, the fullness of the Spirit.

Beware of being guided by any other than the Spirit of God. The temptation is strong, and the tendency to yield to it equally so, of being biased in forming our theological views, and in modeling our Christian practice, by the profound research, the distinguished talents, the exalted piety, and admired example of men. But this must not be. It is inconsistent with the honor that belongs, and with the love that we owe, to the Spirit. A human must necessarily be a fallible guide; against the influence of whose doctrinal errors, and practical mistakes, no extent of learning, or depth of spirituality, or eminence of position on their part, can insure us. We are only safe, as we constantly and strictly follow our Divine and heavenly guide. Blessed and Eternal Spirit! to Your teaching would I bow my mind. To Your love would I yield my heart. To Your consolation would I carry my sorrows. To Your government would I resign my entire soul. "You shall guide me by Your counsel, and afterwards receive me to glory."

NOVEMBER 14

"And the Lord shall deliver me from every evil work, and will preserve me unto his heavenly kingdom; to whom be glory forever and ever. Amen." 2 Timothy 4:18

Things temporary and transient, be they sad or of joyous, pleasant or painful; indwelling sin, temporary trial, occasional temptations, the momentary suspensions of God's realized love—none of these, or any other things present; shall separate from Christ. What human foresight can predict the future of the earthly history of the child of God? What human hand can uplift the veil that conceals the events that shall yet transpire in his history, before he reaches that perfect world where there will be no future, but one eternal present? Oh, what goodness hides it from our view! But be that future what it may—shady or sunny, stormy or serene—God will stand fast to His covenant with His church, and Christ to His union with His people. Things to come, be they more terrible than things that are past, or that are now, shall not touch their interest in the Lord's love.

No elevation to which He may advance them, no height of rank, or wealth, or honor, or influence, or usefulness, shall peril their place in His love. Thus it was the Lord advanced Moses, and David, and Joseph, and Gideon; but in their elevation to worldly distinction, power, and affluence, they were kept walking humbly with God—and this was the secret of their safety. "The Lord God is my strength, and He will make my feet like hinds' feet, and He will make me to walk in mine high places." From the loftiest height to the lowest depth of adversity, God can bring His servant, yet love him still with an unchanged and deathless affection. But no depth of soul-distress, no depth of poverty, or suffering, or humiliation, shall disturb the repose, or peril the security, of a believing soul in the love of God.

If there be any other thing or being in the wide universe that wears a threatening or unkindly aspect towards the Christian, Divine power shall restrain its force, saying to the proud waves, "Thus far shall you come, and no farther." And thus all the billows, amid which the ark has for ages been tossed, shall but bear it gently and triumphantly onward to the mount of God. On that mount, beloved, where now are gathering all who have the Father's name written on their foreheads, we too, through grace, shall stand, eternally extolling the Lamb, through Him who, because He died, there is for us no condemnation from Divine justice, and through Him who, because He lives, there is for us no separation from Divine love.

NOVEMBER 15

"For the creature was made subject to vanity, not willingly, but by reason of him who has subjected the same in hope." Romans 8:20

The vanity here referred to is opposed to the state of glory in anticipation, and therefore expresses the condition of corruption and trial in the midst of which the renewed creature dwells, and to the assaults of which it is incessantly exposed. The world through which the Christian is passing to his rest may be emphatically called a state of vanity. How perpetually and forcibly are we reminded of the king of Israel's exclamation, "Vanity of vanities, all is vanity and vexation of spirit." "Surely every man walks in a vain show." His origin, the earth; his birth, degenerate; his rank, a bauble; his wealth, but glittering dust; his pomp, an empty pageant; his beauty, a fading flower; his pursuits, an infant's play; his honors, vexations of spirit; his joys, fleeting as a cloud; his life, transient as a vapor; his final home, a grave. Surely "man at his best state is altogether vanity." And what is his religion but vanity?—his native holiness, a vain conceit; his natural light, Egyptian darkness; his human wisdom, egregious folly; his religious forms, and rites, and duties, "a vain show in the flesh;" his most gorgeous righteousness, "filthy rags." In the impressive language of Scripture, of him it may be said, "That man's religion is vain." "Lord, what is man, that you take knowledge of him! or the son of man, that you make account of him!"

Truly "vanity" is inscribed in legible characters on each created good. How, then, can the renewed creature escape its influence? He is "subject to vanity," Dazzled by its glare, captivated by its fascinations, ensnared by its promises, he is often the victim of its power. But it is not a voluntary subjection on the part of the renewed creature. "For the creature was made subject to vanity, not willingly." It is not with him a condition of choice. He loves it not, he prefers it not, he glories not in it. From it he would sincerely be freed; beyond it he would gladly soar. "For we who are in this tabernacle do groan, being burdened." His prayer is, "Turn away mine eyes from beholding vanity; and quicken me in Your way." He pants for a holier and a happier state—a state more congenial with his renewed nature. Like the Israelites under the Egyptian bondage, he is a most unwilling servant, groaning beneath his galling yoke, and sighing for the glorious liberty of the children of God. Ah, yes! God has given you another will, O renewed creature! and your present subjection to this poor, vain world is an involuntary subjection of the divine nature within you. Why God should have subjected the renewed creature to vanity does not appear; we well know that He could have transferred us to heaven, the moment that He renewed us on earth. But may we not infer that in sending His people into the world, after He had called them by His grace, and; in a sense, taken them out of it—that in subjecting them for so many years to this state of vanity—He has best consulted His own glory and their good? The school of their heavenly teaching, the scene of their earthly toil, and the theater of their spiritual conflict they are kept in this world for a season; "made subject to vanity, not willingly, but by reason of Him who has subjected the same in hope."

NOVEMBER 16

"I therefore, the prisoner of the Lord, beseech you that you walk worthy of the vocation with which you are called." Ephesians 4:1

The calling here referred to is that inward, effectual calling of which the same apostle speaks in another place "Among whom are you also the called of Jesus Christ: to all that be in Rome, beloved of God, called to be saints." What a glorious vocation is this! To have heard the Holy Spirit's divine yet gentle voice in the deep recesses of the soul—to have felt the drawings of the Savior's love upon the heart—to have listened to a Father's persuasive assurance of a love that has forgotten all our enmity, forgiven all our rebellion, and that remembers only the kindness of our youth, and the love of our espousals—"called to be saints," God's holy ones—called to be sons, the Father's adopted ones—oh, this were a vocation worthy indeed of God, and demanding in return our supremest, deepest affection!

The principle upon which this call proceeds, is said to be "according to His purpose." Thus it is a calling over which we have no control, either in originating or frustrating it, and therefore there is no ground of self-boasting. "In whom also we have obtained an inheritance, being predestinated according to the purpose of Him who works all things after the counsel of His own will." It excludes all idea of merit on the part of the called. "Who has saved us, and called us with an holy calling, not according to our works, but according to His own purpose and grace, which was given us in Christ Jesus before the world began." Oh, yield your heart to the full belief and holy influence of this truth.

Does it clash with your creed?—then your creed is defective. Does it awaken the opposition of your heart?— then your heart is not right. Are you really among the "called of God"?—then ascribe it to His eternal purpose, and believe that you have no ground of boasting, in the possession of a favor so distinguished, save in the sovereign will and most free grace of the most holy Lord God who has called you. Has this call reached you, my reader? Ministers have called you—the gospel has called you—providences have called you—conscience has called you—but has the Spirit called you with an inward and effectual vocation? Have you been called, spiritually called, from darkness to light—from death to life—from sin to holiness—from the world to Christ—from self to God? Examine your heart and ascertain. It is a matter of the greatest moment that you know that you are truly converted—that you are called of God. Has the thrilling, life-inspiring music of that call sounded and reverberated through all the chambers of your soul?

Are we called? Then let us heed the earnest entreaty of the apostle, in the words of our motto, "I therefore, the prisoner of the Lord, beseech you that you walk worthy of the vocation with which you are called." Let the lowliest and the highest vocation of life be dignified and sanctified by the heavenly calling. Wherever you are, and in whatever engaged, do not forget your high calling of God. You are called to be saints; called to a separation from the world; called to a holy, heavenly life; called to live for God, to labor for Christ; and soon will be called to be with the Lord forever!

NOVEMBER 17

"Let every man be fully persuaded in his own mind. But why do you judge your brother? or why do you set at nothing your brother? for we shall all stand before the judgment seat of Christ. Let us not therefore judge one another any more; but judge this rather, that no man put a stumbling-block or an occasion to fall in his brother's way." Romans 14:5, 10, 13

The exercise of private judgment is the natural and inalienable right of every individual. Sanctified by the Spirit of God, it becomes a precious privilege of the believer. He prizes it more than riches, claims it as one of the immunities of his heavenly citizenship, and will surrender it only with life itself. Christian love will avoid infringing, in the least degree, upon this sacred right. I am bound by the law of love to concede to my brother, to its fullest extent, that which I claim for myself. I am moreover bound to believe him conscientious and honest in the views which holds, and that he maintains them in a reverence for the word, and in the exercise of the fear of God. He does not see eye to eye with me in every point of truth—our views of church government, of ordinances, and of some of the doctrines are not alike. And yet, discerning a perfect agreement as to the one great and only way of salvation—and still more, marking in him much of the lowly, loving spirit of his Master, with an earnest desire, in simplicity and godly sincerity, to serve Him—how can I cherish or manifest towards him any other than a feeling of brotherly love? God loves him, God bears with him; and Christ may see in him, despite of a creed less accurately balanced with the word of truth than mine, a walk more in harmony with the holy, self-denying, God-glorifying precepts of that truth. With an orthodoxy less perfect, there may be a life more holy. With less illumination in the judgment, there may be more grace in the heart. How charitable in my interpretation, then, how loving in my spirit, how kind and gentle in my manner, should I be towards him. How jealous, too, ought I to be, of that independence of mind, in the exercise of which he may, notwithstanding, have arrived at conclusions opposite to my own.

Cherishing these feelings, Christians who differ in judgment, will be placed in a more favorable position for the understanding of each other's views, and for the united examination of the word of God. Diversity of judgment, through the infirmity of our fallen nature, is apt to beget alienation of feeling; and consequently, the development of truth is hindered. But where harmony of affection is cultivated, there will be a greater probability of arriving at more perfect agreement in sentiment, thus walking in accordance with apostle's rule—"I beseech you, brethren, by the name of our Lord Jesus Christ, that you all speak the same thing, and that there be no divisions among you: but that you be perfectly joined together in the same mind, and in the same judgment."

NOVEMBER 18

"But the salvation of the righteous is of the Lord; he is their strength in the time of trouble. And the Lord shall help them, and deliver them: he shall deliver them from the wicked, and save them, because they trust in him." Psalm 37:39, 40

Of all the consolations which flow into the soul of the afflicted believer, not the least is that he has a covenant God to go to in prayer. What can surpass this? What could supply its place? Nothing. In no way does God more effectually comfort those that are cast down, than by drawing them to Himself. For this He has instituted prayer, sprinkled the mercy-seat with the blood of His Son, and sends the sweet promise and grace of His Spirit, to invite and draw the disconsolate to Himself. "A Christian, when he is beaten out of all other comforts, has a God to run unto. He can wrestle, and strive with God by God's own strength, can make use of His own weapons, and plead with God by His own arguments. What a happy estate is this! Who would not be a Christian, if it were but for this, to have something to rely on when all things else fail?"

Approach, then, disconsolate soul! and pour out your sorrow to God in prayer. Your God is upon the throne of grace, and "waits that He may be gracious unto you." Then "you shall weep no more: He will be very gracious unto you at the voice of your cry; when He shall hear it, He will answer you." Why are you then cast down? "Trust in God, grace will be above nature, God above the devil, the Spirit above the flesh. Be strong in the Lord; the battle is His, and the victory ours beforehand. If we fought in our own cause and strength, and with our own weapons, it were something; but as we fight in the power of God, so are we kept by that mighty power through faith unto salvation. Corruptions are strong, but stronger is He that is in us than the corruption that is in us. Our corruptions are God's enemies as well as ours; and therefore in trusting to Him, and fighting, we may be sure He will take our part against them."

In each season of casting down, ascend your watch-tower in the full expectation of an especial blessing. This would seem to be the order God: "When men are cast down, then you shall say, There is lifting up." Expect great mercies through the medium of great trials; great comforts through great sorrows; deep sanctification from deep humiliation. All the trying dispensations of God in the histories of His people are preparatory to their greater grace. It was in this school the distinguished apostle of the Gentiles was taught the greatest and holiest lesson of life. Descending from the third heaven, all fragrant with its odors, and glowing with its light, he was plunged into the deepest humiliation, in order that he might be instructed more thoroughly in that truth, which he could not experimentally have learned even in paradise itself—the sufficiency of Christ's grace to sustain the believer the deepest trial. Tried believer! suffering saint! expect an especial blessing to your soul. If Lord has led you in by the north gate, he will lead you out by the south gate. Dark though the cloud may be, and painful the path, have patience in your affliction, and God will give you a happy issue out of all your troubles. And, oh, blessed result, if sin is embittered, if holiness is sweetened, if some tyrant corruption is mortified, if communion with God is quickened, if Jesus is endeared, if your Father in heaven is glorified! "Why are you cast down, O my soul? and why are you disquieted within me? hope in God; for I shall yet praise Him, who is the health of my countenance, and my God."

NOVEMBER 19

"In whom we have redemption through his blood, even the forgiveness of sins." Colossians 1:14

The blood of Jesus is the life of our pardon and acceptance: "Whom God has set forth to be a propitiation through faith in His blood, to declare His righteousness for the remission of sins that are past through the forbearance of God—that is, the transgressions of the Old Testament saints; the life-giving blood of Jesus extending its pardoning efficacy back to the remotest period of time, and to the greatest sinner upon earth; even to him "by whom sin entered into the world, and death by sin—such is the vitality of the atoning blood of God's dear Son. And if the pardoning blood thus bore an antecedent virtue, has it less a present one? No! listen to the life-inspiring words! "In whom we have redemption through His blood, the forgiveness of sins, according the riches of His grace." Once more, "The blood of Jesus Christ His Son cleanses us from all sin. It has a present life, an immediate efficacy. The life of our pardon! Yes! the believing though trembling penitent sees all his sins cancelled, all his transgressions pardoned, through the precious blood of Jesus. Nothing but the life-blood of the incarnate God could possibly effect it. And when, after repeated backslidings, he returns again, with sincere and holy contrition, and bathes in it afresh, lo! the sense of pardon is renewed; and while he goes away to loathe himself, and abhor his sin, he yet can rejoice that the living blood of the Redeemer has put it entirely and forever away.

And what is the life of our acceptance but the blood of Immanuel? "Justified by His blood!" The robe that covers us is the righteousness of Him who is "the Lord our Righteousness;" who, when He had, had, by one act of perfect obedience to the law, woven the robe of our justification, bathed it in His own lifeblood, and folded it around His church, presenting her to His Father a "glorious church, not having spot, or any such thing." Not only is it the ground of our present acceptance, but the saints in heaven, "the spirits of just men made perfect," take their stand upon it. "Who are these," it is asked, "which are arrayed in white robes? and where came they?" The answer is, "These are they who came out of great tribulation, and have washed their robes, and made them white in the blood of the Lamb. Therefore are they before the throne of God." Thus now, pleading the justifying blood of Jesus, the believing though distressed and trembling soul may stand before God, "accepted in the Beloved." Wondrous declaration! Blessed state! Rest not, reader, until you have attained it. No, you cannot rest, until you have received by faith the righteousness of Christ.

From where, too, flows the life of spiritual joy, but from the life-giving blood of Immanuel? There can be no real joy, but in the experience of pardoned sin. The joy of the unpardoned soul is the joy of the condemned on his way to death—a mockery and a delusion. With all his sins upon him, with all his iniquities yet unforgiven, every step brings him nearer to the horrors of the second death; what, then, can he know of true joy? But when the blood of Jesus is sprinkled upon the heart, and the sense of sin forgiven is sealed upon the conscience, then there is joy indeed, "joy unspeakable, and full of glory." From where, also, flows peace—sweet, holy, divine peace—but from the heart's blood of the Prince of Peace? There can be no true peace from God, where there does not exist perfect reconciliation with God. That is a false peace which springs not from a view of God pacified in Christ, God one with us in the atonement of His Son, "speaking peace by Jesus Christ." "The blood of sprinkling speaks better things than that of Abel," because it speaks peace.

NOVEMBER 20

"In whom also we have obtained an inheritance, being predestinated according to the purpose of him who works all things after the counsel of his own will: that we should be to the praise of his glory, who first trusted in Christ." Ephesians 1:11, 12

The doctrine of predestination is well calculated to confirm and strengthen the true believer in the fact and certainty of his salvation through Christ. Feeling, as he does, the plague of his own heart, experiencing the preciousness of the Savior, looking up through the cross to God as his Father, exulting in a hope that makes not ashamed, and remembering that God the Eternal Spirit only renews those who are chosen by God the Father, and are redeemed by God the Son, this doctrine is found to be most comforting and confirming to his faith. The faintest lineaments of resemblance to God, and the feeblest breathing of the Spirit of adoption he discovers in his soul, is to him an indisputable evidence of his predestination to Divine sonship and holiness.

Another blessing accruing from the doctrine is, the sweet and holy submission into which it brings the mind under all afflictive dispensations.

Each step of his pilgrimage, and each incident of his history, the believer sees appointed in the everlasting covenant of grace. He recognizes the discipline of the covenant to be as much a part of the original plan, as any positive mercy that it contains. That all the hairs of his head are numbered; that affliction comes not out of the earth, and therefore is not the result of accident or thence, but is in harmony with God's purposes of love; and that thus ordained and permitted, must work together for good—not the least blessing resulting from this truth is its tendency to promote personal godliness. The believer feels that God has "chosen us to salvation through sanctification and belief of the truth;" that He has "chosen us that we should be holy and without blame before Him in love;" that we are "His workmanship, created in Christ Jesus unto good works, which God has before ordained that we should walk in them." Thus the believer desires to "give all diligence to make his calling and election sure," or undoubted, by walking in all the ordinances and commandments of the Lord blameless, and standing complete in all the will of God.

And what doctrine more emptying, humbling, and therefore sanctifying, than this? It lays the axe at the root of all human boasting. In the light of this truth, the most holy believer sees that there is no difference between him and the vilest sinner that crawls the earth, but what the mere grace of God has made. Such are some of the many blessings flowing to the Christian from this truth. The radiance which it reflects upon the entire history of the child of God, and the calm repose which it diffuses over the mind in all the perplexing, painful, and mysterious events of that history, can only be understood by those whose hearts have fully received the doctrine. Whatever betides him—inexplicable in its character, enshrouded in the deepest gloom, as may be the circumstance—the believer in this truth can "stand still," and, calmly surveying the scene, exclaim: "This also comes forth from the Lord of hosts, who is wonderful in counsel, and excellent in working. He who works all things after the counsel of His own will has done it, and I am satisfied that it is well done."

NOVEMBER 21

"You are fairer than the children of men: grace is poured into your lips: therefore God has blessed you forever." Psalm 45:2

"No man knows the Son, but the Father." Matthew 11:27

These two passages of God's word convey to the mind the most forcible and exalted views of the personal excellence and dignity of the Lord Jesus. The first portrays His matchless beauty, the second His incomprehensible greatness. The Psalmist doubtless refers here to the perfection of His human excellence. As man, His beauty transcends the comeliest of human beings—"fairer than the children of men." Their beauty is mixed; His is pure. Theirs is derived; His is from Himself. Theirs decays; His is imperishable. His body prepared of God, His mind filled with all the wisdom, grace, and holiness of the Spirit—He stands forth the "bright and morning star," the perfect, peerless Son of man. Oh for an eye to see and admire His excellence! and not admire only, but to imitate. Oh for grace to lie at His feet, and learn of His meekness! to lean on His bosom, and drink of His love! to set the Lord always before us, never moving the eye from this perfect model, but ever aiming to transcribe its lineaments upon our daily life! Yes! "You are fairer than the children of men!" You altogether lovely One! And as I gaze upon Your perfection, passing from beauty to beauty, my admiration increases, and my love deepens; until, in the assurance of faith, and in the transport of joy, I exclaim, "This is my Beloved, and this is my Friend."

Respecting His superior nature, not less clear and emphatic is the declaration of His essential greatness: "No man knows the Son, but the Father." Surely these words are sufficient to remove all doubt as to His Deity. Were He only man, with what truth could it be affirmed of Him, that "no man knows the Son"? It is the property of an angel, that he understands the angelic nature; and of man, that he understands the human nature. It is the perfection of God, that He only understands the nature of God. Who, then, but the Infinite can measure the infinite greatness of the Son of God? The loftiest created imagination, the mightiest human intellect, the profoundest angelic research, falls infinitely short of what He is. The Father alone knows the Son, because He is of the same nature and mind with the Father. Beware of holding this doctrine lightly. A more important one—one more glorious or more precious—asks not the confidence of your faith. Hold it fast, even as the vessel in the storm clings to its anchor. This gone, the next mountain wave drives you upon the quicksand of doubt and perplexity, and then where are you? Consider how important must be that single truth, on which the value, the preciousness, and the efficacy of all other truths depend. Such a truth is the Godhead of Christ.

NOVEMBER 22

"For the law of the Spirit of life in Christ Jesus has made me free from the law of sin and death." Romans 8:2

The interpretation we propose for the adoption of the reader is that which regards the "law of the Spirit of life," as describing the gospel of Christ, frequently denominated a "law"—and emphatically so in this instance, because of the emancipation it confers from the Mosaic code, called the "law of sin and death," as by it the knowledge of sin, and through it death is threatened as the penalty of its transgression. But in what sense is the believer free from this deadly law? As a covenant he is free from it. The believer's union to Christ frees him from the condemnatory power of this law. He looks not to it for life; he rests not in it for hope; he renounces it as a saving covenant, and under the influence of another and a higher obligation—his union to Christ—he brings forth fruit unto God. Was ever liberty so glorious as this—a liberty associated with the most loving, cordial, and holy obedience? Not a single precept of that law, from whose covenant and curse he is released by this act of freedom, is compromised. All its precepts, embodied and reflected in the life of Christ—whose life is the model of our own—appear infinitely more clear and resplendent than ever they appeared before. The obedience of the Lawgiver infinitely enhanced the luster of the law, presenting the most impressive illustration of its majesty and holiness that it could possibly receive.

The instrument to whose agency this exalted liberty is ascribed is the "law of the Spirit of life in Christ Jesus." The term law is forensic; though not infrequently used in God's word to designate the gospel of Christ; indicating it in the text, as the great instrument by which this freedom is obtained. The gospel is the law which reveals the way of salvation by Christ. It is the development of God's great expedient of saving man. It speaks of pardon and adoption, of acceptance and sanctification, as all flowing to the soul through faith in His dear Son. It represents God as extending His hand of mercy to the vilest sinner; welcoming the penitent wanderer back to His home, and once more taking the contrite rebel to His heart. It is also a quickening law—emphatically the "law of the Spirit of life." What numbers are seeking sanctification from the "law of sin," and life from the "law of death"! But the gospel speaks of life. Its doctrines—its precepts—its promises—its exhortations—its rebukes—its hopes—are all instinct with spiritual life, and come with quickening power to the soul. "The words that I speak unto you," says Jesus, "they are spirit and they are life." Oh, there is life in the gospel, because it is the "law of the Spirit of life in Christ Jesus." It testifies of "Christ who is our life." It declares that there is no spiritual life but in Him. And although "the letter kills," working alone, yet in the hands of the Spirit it gives life. Thus clothed with the energy of the Holy Spirit, the gospel proves a "savor of life unto life," to all who believe in it to the saving of the soul.

Believer; a holy, filial, joyful liberty is your birthright. It is the liberty of a pardoned and justified sinner; of a reconciled, adopted child; of one for whom there is "now no condemnation." Yet how few of God's people walk in the full enjoyment of this liberty! How few pray, and love, and confide, as adopted children! Oh, sons of God, rise to this your high and heavenly calling! Your freedom was purchased at a high price—undervalue it not. It is most holy—abuse it not. It binds you by the strongest obligations to yield yourselves unto God, as those that are alive from the dead. Be these the breathings of our soul: "Lord! my sweetest privilege is obedience to You; my highest freedom wearing Your yoke—my greatest rest bearing Your burden. Oh, how love I Your law after the inward man! I delight to do Your will, O my God!"

NOVEMBER 23

"Now our Lord Jesus Christ himself; and God, even our Father, which has loved us, and has given us everlasting consolation and good hope through grace, comfort your hearts, and establish you in every good word and work." 2 Thessalonians 2:16, 17

Upon the subject of comfort great stress is laid in the sacred word. It is clearly God's revealed will that His people should be comforted. The fullness of Christ, the exceeding great and precious promises of the word, the covenant of grace, and all the dealings of God, bear upon this one point, the comfort and consolation of the saints. A brief reference to the Divine word will convince us of this. This is the very character He Himself bears, and this is the blessed work He accomplishes. Thus, "Blessed be God, even the, Father of our Lord Jesus Christ, the Father of mercies, and the God of all comfort; who comforts us in all our tribulation, that we may be able to comfort those who are in any trouble by the comfort with which we ourselves are comforted of God." 2 Corinthians 1:3, 4. Kindred to this, are those striking words in Isaiah 40:1: "Comfort you, comfort you my people, says your God." This was God's command to the prophet. It was His declared will that His people should be comforted, even though they dwelt in Jerusalem, the city which was to witness the crucifixion of the Lord of life and glory. What an unfolding does this give us of Him who is the God of all comfort, who comforts us in all our tribulation, and that, too, in every place!

To comfort the saints is one important end of the Scriptures: "Whatever things were written aforetime were written for our learning, that we through patience and comfort of the Scriptures might have hope." Romans 15:4. And thus the exhortation runs—"Comfort the feeble-minded." "Why comfort yourselves together, and edify one another, even as also you do." "Then we which are alive and remain shall be caught up together with them in the clouds, to meet the Lord in the air; and so shall we ever be with the Lord. Why comfort one another with these words." Thus has the Holy Spirit testified to this subject, and thus is it clear that it is the will, and it is in the heart, of God, that His people should be comforted.

The Spirit comforts the believer by unfolding to his eye the near prospect of the coming glory. Heaven is near at hand. It is but a step out of a poor, sinful, sorrow-stricken world, into the rest that remains for the people of God. It is but a moment, the twinkling of an eye, and we are absent from the body, and are present with the Lord. Then will the days of our mourning be ended, then sin will grieve no more—affliction will wound no more—sorrow will depress no more, and God will hide Himself no more. There will be the absence of all evil, and the presence of all good; and they who have come out of great tribulation, and have washed their robes, and made them white in the blood of the Lamb, shall take their stand before the throne of God, and shall "serve Him day and sight in His temple: and He that sits on the throne shall dwell among them. They shall hunger so more, neither thirst any more; neither shall the sun light on them, nor any heat. For the Lamb which is in the midst of the throne shall feed them, and shall lead them unto living fountains of waters: and God shall wipe away all tears from their eyes." Why, beloved in the Lord, let us comfort one another with these words, and with this prospect.

NOVEMBER 24

"And my speech and my preaching was not with enticing words of man's wisdom, but in demonstration of the Spirit and of power: that your faith should not stand in the wisdom of men, but in the power of God." 1 Corinthians 2:4, 5

True wisdom has been defined as that power which accomplishes the greatest results by the simplest means. Then, here is wisdom! To save souls from eternal death, by the "foolishness of preaching," must be regarded as the highest point to which wisdom can soar. It is recorded of the apostles, that they "so spoke, that a great multitude, both of the Jews, and also of the Gentiles believed." They presented Christ so prominently—they divided truth so skillfully—they preached with such power, point, and simplicity, that "multitudes were added to the Lord." See with what contempt they looked down upon the unsanctified wisdom and lore of this world. Addressing the Corinthians, their great leader could say, "My speech and my preaching was not with enticing words of man's wisdom, but in demonstration of the Spirit and of power." By the influence of his preaching, pagan altars were destroyed, senseless idols were abandoned, the Pantheon and the Lyceum were forsaken, and "a great company of the priests were obedient to the faith;" but it was not with the "wisdom of this world," in order that their "faith should not stand in the wisdom of man, but in the power of God."

And why may not the same results in the employment of the same means be ours? Preach we not the same gospel? Deal we not with the same intelligent and deathless minds? Draw we not our motives and our appeals from the same eternity? True, we possess neither the spirit of prophecy nor the gift of miracles. We need not. Nor did they in their grand work of converting men to God. They never, in a single instance; quickened a soul by the power of a miracle. The extraordinary gifts with which they were endowed were bestowed for another and a different purpose. The cases of our Lord and of His fore runner are strikingly in point. The ministry of Jesus, although attended by a succession of miracles the most brilliant and convincing, resulted in fewer conversions than the ministry of John, who did no miracle. To what divine agency, then, did the apostles themselves trace the extraordinary result of their preaching? To what, but the "demonstration of the Spirit"? Oh for tongues of fire to proclaim the glad tidings of the gospel! With such a Savior to make known—with such revelations to disclose—with such souls to save—with such results to expect—is it not marvelous that we should speak with any other?

The true preacher of the gospel, then, is so rightly to divide God's word, as not to confound truth with error—so discriminatingly to proclaim it, as to separate the precious from the vile— and so distinctly and prominently to hold up the cross of Christ, as to save immortal souls. The cross, the cross, must be the central exhibition of our ministry, to which every eye must be directed, and before which all the glory of man must fade. The Holy Spirit, too, must be more honored—His anointing more especially sought—His influence more earnestly insisted upon. Apart from this, no ministry, be its character in other respects what it may, has any real power. How poor a thing it is, distinguished only by its learning, genius, and eloquence; and destitute of the vital warmth, and impassioned earnestness, the soul-subduing and heart-awakening energy of the Holy Spirit! Weighed in the balance of the sanctuary, it is as light as air; estimated in view of the judgment, it is an awful mockery.

NOVEMBER 25

"And that he might make known the riches of his glory on the vessels of mercy, which he had afore prepared unto glory, even us, whom he has called, not of the Jews only, but also of the Gentiles." Romans 9:23, 24

Let us for a moment transport our thoughts to the future. The future! oh, how bright it is, and full of blessing, to the "vessels of mercy afore prepared unto glory"! The grace, ceasing on earth, is now succeeded by "an exceeding and eternal weight of glory." He who has tasted that the Lord is gracious shall assuredly see that the Lord is glorious. "How may we know," is often a trembling inquiry, "that our departed friends are with Jesus?" Were they partakers, in the most limited degree, of the grace of Jesus? then, their safety is beyond all doubt. The grace which they possessed was the seedling, the germ, the first-fruits of glory. The light which illumined their souls was the twilight dawn of heaven. It was utterly impossible that germ could die, or that light could be extinguished. It was as imperishable and as immortal as God Himself. The weak grace battled with sin, and the feeble light struggled with darkness, but both conquered at last. There they are—"standing on the sea of glass," chanting the high praises of the grace that brought them there. Yonder they are—in the Father's house, in the Savior's mansions; they conflict no more; they weep no more; they hunger and thirst no more; for He who once gave them grace, now gives them glory. "Grace is glory militant, and glory is grace triumphant; grace is glory begun, glory is grace made perfect; grace is the first degree of glory, glory is the highest degree of grace."

Lift up your heads, you, gracious souls! Heaven is before you, and your full redemption draws near. "The Lord is at hand." His coming is near. That "blessed hope" of the church, His "glorious appearing," will soon be realized, bursting upon your soul in all its blissful splendor, and then you shall be perfectly like, and forever with, the Lord. But should you go to Him, before He returns to you—for if Jesus does not come for you, He will send for you—fear not to descend the dark valley, already trodden by your Lord and Savior. Dying grace is bound up in the covenant of grace; and Jesus, full of grace, to the last moment, will be there to dispense it to your need, His left hand under your head, and His right hand embracing you.

His aged saints are the especial objects of God's loving, tender, faithful care. Lean, in all the decrepitude of years, in all the weakness, pain, and tremulousness of advanced age, in all the fears, misgivings, and becloudings of life's close, upon this Divine rod and staff. Now that you are old and grey-headed, your God will not forsake you. Rest in the faithfulness of God, lean upon the finished work of Jesus, and hope on for the glory so soon to be revealed. Let your believing prayer be, "Cast me not off in the time of old age; forsake me not when my strength fails." And God's faithful answer will be, "Even to your old age I am He; and even to hoar hairs will I carry you."

NOVEMBER 26

"Praying in the Holy Spirit." Jude 20

A more holy and solemn engagement enlists not the thoughts, and feelings, and time of the believer, than the engagement of prayer. In proportion, then, to the spirituality of a duty, will be the keen sense of the opposition it meets from either the mental or physical frailties which encompass the Christian. The apostle Paul thus defines this infirmity—"We know not what we should pray for as we ought." How shall we describe it? With what feature shall we begin? There is first the difficulty which some feel in reference to the nature of prayer. Simple as prayer is, we see how even an apostle could be perplexed, for he includes himself in this general description of the saints. Three times did he urge a petition the granting of which would have proved a curse rather than a blessing. "What am I to pray for?" is the earnest inquiry of some. "Am I to limit my requests in petitioning for spiritual blessings, or may I include in my petitions blessings that are temporal?" "What is real prayer?" is the yet more earnest question of another. "I fear mine is not true prayer. May I characterize by such a holy and significant term the cold effusions of my closet, the feeble ejaculations of the wayside, the wandering devotions of the sanctuary, the moanings of a spirit wounded, the sighs of a heart oppressed, the upward glancings of a mind beclouded, the breathings of a soul whose spiritual exercises are at times so opposite and contradictory? Is this prayer?" Then there is the infirmity of the act of prayer. The vagrancy of thought—the coldness of affection—the intrusion of low cares—the consciousness of unreal petitions, of unfelt confessions, of undesired requests—the felt oppressiveness of a distasteful task, rather than the felt luxury of a precious privilege—the slovenliness of the performance—the little solemnity of mind—all mark the infirmity which attaches to this transcendently spiritual employment.

Then as to the mode of prayer; this also is felt to be a source of painful embarrassment by some. There are many Christians who find it difficult, if not impossible, to give expression to the heart's utterances, in what is termed free prayer. Compelled, through an infirmity they cannot conquer, to restrict themselves to a liturgical form of devotion, while others pour out their souls to God in unfettered breathings, in unrestricted communion, they are, at times, perplexed to know whether they are acquainted with the reality and power of true prayer. Thus many a saint of God, whose needs are not the less real, whose desires are not the less spiritual, and whose breathings are not the less fervent and divinely acceptable, may, through this his infirmity, be much cast down and discouraged. But who, whatever be his mode of prayer, is free from some clinging infirmity, interfering with the sanctity and power of this hallowed engagement? Who is not mournfully sensible, that of all his spiritual privileges, this, his highest, most sacred and solemn, is the most encompassed with, and marred and fettered by, the deep corruptions of his fallen and depraved nature? that after all his rigid observance of the duty, his many devotional engagements, public and private, there should yet be so little felt nearness to God, so little confidential communion—in a word, so little real prayer. Oh, how much prayerless prayer do we have to mourn over! How little brokenness of heart; how little sense of sin; how faint a taking hold of the atoning blood; how imperfect a realization of God's relation to us as a Father; how little faith in His promise to hear, in His ability to aid, in His readiness to bless us! Such are some of the infirmities associated with prayer, often suggesting the gospel petition, "Lord, teach us to pray."

NOVEMBER 27

"No, in all these things we are more than conquerors through him that loved us." Romans 8:37

The apostle had enumerated certain things which, to the obscure eye of faith, and to the yet obscurer eye of sense, would appear to make against the best interests of the Christian, regarded either as evidences of a waning of Christ's love to him, or as calculated to produce such a result. He proposes an inquiry—"Who shall separate us from the love of Christ?"—and then proceeds to give the reply. That reply sets the question entirely at rest. He argues, that so far from the things which he enumerates shaking the constancy of Christ's love, periling the safety of the Christian, or shading the luster of His renown, they but developed the Savior's affection to him, more strongly confirmed the fact of his security, and entwined fresh and more verdant laurels around his brow. "No, in all these things we are more than conquerors."

"Through Him that loved us." Here is the great secret of our victory, the source of our triumph. Behold the mystery explained, how a weak, timid believer, often starting at his own shadow, is yet "more than a conqueror" over his many and mighty foes. To Christ who loved him, who gave Himself for him, who died in his stead, and lives to intercede on his behalf, the glory of the triumph is ascribed. And this is the song he chants: "Thanks be to God, which gives us the victory, through our Lord Jesus Christ." Through the conquest which He Himself obtained, through the grace which He imparts, through the strength which He inspires, through the intercession which he presents, in all our "tribulation and distress, and persecution, and famine, and nakedness, and peril, and sword," we are "more than conquerors." Accounted though we are as "sheep for the slaughter," yet our great Shepherd, Himself slain for the sheep, guides His flock, and has declared that no one shall pluck them out of His hand. We are more than conquerors, through His grace who loved us, in the very circumstances that threaten to overwhelm. Fear not, then, the darkest cloud, nor the proudest waves, nor the deepest needs—in these very things you shall, through Christ, prove triumphant. Nor shrink from the battle with the "last enemy." Death received a death-wound when Christ died. You face a conquered foe. He stands at your side a crownless king, and waving a broken scepter. Your death shall be another victory over the believer's last foe. Planting your foot of upon His prostrate neck, you shall spring into glory, more than a conqueror through Him that loved you. Thus entering heaven in triumph, you shall go to swell the ranks of the "noble army of martyrs"—those Christian heroes of whom it is recorded, "They overcame him by the blood of the Lamb."

NOVEMBER 28

"Though I speak with the tongues of men and of angels, and have not love, I am become as sounding brass, or a tinkling cymbal. And though I have the gift of prophecy, and understand all mysteries, and all knowledge; and though I have all faith, so that I could remove mountains, and have not love, I am nothing. And though I bestow all my goods to feed the poor, and though I give my body to be burned, and have not love, it profits me nothing." 1 Corinthians 13:1-3

There is no truth more distinctly uttered or more emphatically stated than this—the infinite superiority of love to gifts. And in pondering their relative position and value, let it be remembered, that the gifts which are here placed in competition with grace are the highest spiritual gifts. Thus does the apostle allude to them: "God has set some in the church, first apostles, secondarily prophets, thirdly teachers, after that miracles, then gifts of healing." Then follows the expressive declaration of our motto. In other words, "Though I were an apostle, having apostolic gifts; though I were a prophet, possessed of prophetic gifts; or though I were an angel, clothed with angelic gifts; yet, destitute of the grace of love, my religion were but as an empty sound, nothing worth." Is there in all this any undervaluing of the spiritual gifts which the great exalted Head of the church has bestowed upon His ministers? Far from it. The apostle speaks of the way of spiritual gifts as excellent, but existing alone, they cannot bring the soul to heaven. And love may exist apart from gifts; but where love is found, even alone, there is that most excellent grace, that will assuredly conduct its possessor to glory. "Grace embellished with gifts is the more beautiful; but gifts without grace are only a richer spoil for Satan."

And why this superiority of the grace of love? Why is it so excellent, so great, so distinguished? Because God's love in the soul is a part of God Himself; for "God is love." It is as it were a drop of the essence of God falling into the heart of man. "He that dwells in love, dwells in God, and God in him." This grace of love is implanted in the soul at the period of its regeneration. The new creature is the restoration of the soul to God, the expulsion from the heart of the principle of enmity, and the flowing back of its affections to their original center. "Every one that loves is born of God." Is it again asked, why the love of His saints is so costly in God's eye? Because it is a small fraction of the infinite love which He bears towards them. Does God delight Himself in His love to His church? Has He set so high a value upon it, as to give His own Son to die for it? Then, wherever He meets with the smallest degree of that love, He must esteem it more lovely, more costly, and more rare, than all the most splendid gifts that ever adorned the soul. "We love Him because He first loved us."

Here, then, is that grace in the soul of man which more than all others assimilates him to God. It comes from God, it raises the soul to God, and it makes the soul like God. How encouraging, then, to know the value which the Lord puts upon our poor returns of love to Him! Of gifts we may have none, and even of love but little; yet of that little, who can unfold God's estimate of its preciousness! He looks upon it as a little picture of Himself. He sees in it a reflection—dim and imperfect indeed—of His own image. As He gazes upon it, He seems to say—"Your parts, my child, are humble, and your gifts are few; your knowledge is scanty, and your tongue is stammering; you can not speak for me, nor pray to me in public, by reason of the littleness of your attainments, and the greatness of your infirmity; but you do love me, my child, and in that love, which I behold, I see my nature, I see my heart, I see my image, I see myself; and that is more precious to me than all besides." Most costly to Him also are all your labors of love, your obedience of love, your sacrifices of love, your offerings of love, and your sufferings of love. Yes, whatever blade or bud, flower or fruit, grows upon the stem of love, it is most lovely, and precious, and fragrant to God.

NOVEMBER 29

"But Christ being come an high priest of good things to come, by a greater and more perfect tabernacle, not made with hands, that is to say, not of this building; neither by the blood of goats and calves, but by his own blood he entered in once into the holy place, having obtained eternal redemption for us." Hebrews 9:11, 12

The work of intercession constituted an essential and a delightful part of the priestly office of our Lord Jesus. Not to atone only, but upon the ground of that atonement to base His office of advocate, and with the plea of that atonement to appear in the presence of God as an intercessor, equally entered into the engagements of Christ in behalf of His people. A moment's reference to the Levitical type will throw much light upon this part of the Savior's work. It will be recollected that the high priest, on the day of expiation, was to slay and to offer the sacrifice in the outer part of the tabernacle; after which he entered within the sanctuary, bearing in his hands the blood of atonement, and sprinkled it seven times upon and before the mercy-seat. He was then to bring a censer full of burning coals from off the altar, and his hands full of sweet incense beaten small, within the veil, and place it upon the fire before the Lord, "that the cloud of the incense might cover the mercy-seat." All this was beautifully typical of the atonement and intercession of Jesus, our great High Priest. The basis of our Lord's intercessory work is the great atonement of His own blood, with which He has fully met the claims of justice, paid to the law its extreme demands, and blotted out the handwriting that was against His people, in pronouncing their sins entirely and forever cancelled.

Upon His atonement Jesus takes His stand as an Intercessor in heaven, within which He has gone to sprinkle His blood upon the mercy-seat, and to present the incense of His infinite and precious merits. Having purged our sins, He is forever set down at the right hand of God, not in a state of inglorious ease, nor cold forgetfulness of His church on earth, but to plead as its Advocate, and to pray as its Intercessor each moment with the Father, pressing His suit on the ground of justice, and resting His petition on the basis of merit. "For Christ is not entered into the holy places made with hands, which are the figures of the true; but into heaven itself, now to appear in the presence of God for us." "He ever lives to make intercession." Look up, O you of tried faith, and behold within the veil your Savior there, clothed in His sacerdotal robes, the great High Priest of heaven's temple, the glorious Advocate of heaven's chancery, representing His church, and for each individual as for the whole body, praying the Father that the weak and tried faith of His saints might not fail. This is no image of the imagination. This is no picture of the fancy. It is a blessed and glorious reality, that our once atoning and now risen and exalted Redeemer is in heaven, bearing the breastplate upon His heart, and the ephod upon His shoulder, in which each name is set of all the tribes of Israel. Yes, poor tried and suffering believer, your name is there, written not only in the Lamb's book of life, but written in the Lamb's heart of love. In approaching God in any spiritual service, why is it that your person is an object of His complacent delight? Because Jesus presents it. Why do your prayers, imperfectly framed and faintly breathed, come up before the altar with acceptance and power? Because Jesus is in heaven, and as your pleading Advocate separates your petition from all its flaws, and as your interceding Priest purifies it from all its sin, and presents it as a "golden vial full of odor" to His Father. And when in pensive sadness you have trodden your lonely path, the spirit chafed, the heart wounded, the world desolate, and a thousand images of terror and of gloom filling the vast void, oh little did you think that within that veil, so awfully mysterious to you, there stood One—your Friend and Brother, your Advocate and Priest—who knew your secret sorrow, and who at that moment was pouring out His full heart, His whole soul, in powerful and prevalent intercession, that your tried and wavering faith might not fail.

NOVEMBER 30

"But when we are judged, we are chastened of the Lord, that we should not be condemned with the world." 1 Corinthians 11:32

How great the dignity, and how precious the privilege, of chastened believers! They are the children of God. "Behold, what manner of love the Father has bestowed upon us, that we should be called the sons of God!" Angels, bright, sinless angels, stand not so closely and endearingly related to God as they. Wonderful love of God! that He should not think it a dishonor to own them as His sons, and to call Himself their Father who by nature are the children of wrath, slaves to Satan, and the servants of sin. How great our dignity! Seek, Christian reader, to know it, to enjoy it, to live according to it. If there has been no sealing of your adoption upon the heart, give the Holy Spirit no rest until there is. If, in the holy, humble confidence of faith, there never has been an "Abba, Father," upon your lip—as one professing to be a child, and soon to be in eternity, it is time that there should be. Seek it earnestly, seek it importunately, seek it believingly, and you will have it. "You shall call me, my father." "If I then be a Father," says the same God, "where is mine honor?" Have you ever honored Him, loved Him, obeyed Him, glorified Him as your Father? Bending over you, the Spirit of adoption waits to impress the sacred seal upon your heart. Loving you, the Father yearns to clasp you to His bosom, assuring you that you are His loved, pardoned, accepted child. As the loved, then, whom the Lord rebukes and chastens, let our carriage be that of children, even as His discipline is that of a Father. Let us receive the correction with meekness, and hear the voice of the Lord with reverence, since God is parental and loving in all His conduct towards His saints.

Nor let us fail to remember, for our comfort, that all the chastisements of the children of God are on this side of heaven. Not so with the ungodly. Sinner! unconverted soul! you may laugh now, sport now, rejoice now, but remember—your chastisement is to come! your condemnation is to come! your stripes are to come! all your real woe is to come! It is coming now, it comes fast, it is near at hand, even at your door—for there is but a step between you and hell! Have you ever thought what it must be to lie down in eternal torment, what it must be to meet an angry God, to confront a despised Savior?—to take the fearful plunge, without one ray of hope, into a starless, sunless, hopeless eternity? Oh happy moment! if the Eternal Spirit so bless to your soul the perusal of this page, as to awaken you to a solemn, an honest, and earnest seeking of the Lord; to give up your procrastinations, your waiting for a more convenient season—your worldly excuses—your refuges of lies—the sparks of your own kindling in which you must lie down in sorrow—your dream of a future, a death-bed repentance; and, casting all aside, you hasten as a poor, lost, dying sinner to Christ, exclaiming, "I am a dying man! I want a Savior! I want the influence of the Holy Spirit to reveal that Savior, to lead me to that Savior, and to tell me that Savior is mine." But no future sorrow awaits the children of God beyond the grave. They are chastened now, that they may not be condemned hereafter. All to come is joy and gladness, is purity and bliss. "God shall wipe away all tears from their eyes; and there shall be no more death, neither sorrow, nor crying, neither shall there be any more pain: for the former things are passed away."

Learn from this subject that you are not less the object of God's love, because He corrects you. The suspicion has, perhaps, pressed coldly and darkly upon your heart—"He cannot love me, and force this bitter cup to my lips." Hush, that murmur! Be still, that thought! and know, O chastened child, O daughter of sorrow, that "God is love;" and, because you are His loved child, His loving correction now makes you great. Then, in the words of your suffering Head, say, "The cup that my Father has given me, shall I not drink it?"

DECEMBER

DECEMBER 1

"And now also the axe is laid unto the root of the trees: therefore every tree which brings not forth good fruit is hewn down, and cast into the fire." Matthew 3:10

It is a solemn and a veritable thought, that human character is training and molding for eternity. Nothing in the universe of matter or of mind is stationary; everything is in motion; the motion is progressive—the movement is onward. Things whose being is limited by the present state, obeying the law of their nature, advance to their maturity, and then perish. They attain their appointed and ultimate perfection, and then die. Beings destined for another, a higher, and a more enduring state, are each moment tending towards that existence for which their natures are formed, and to which they aspire. There is, innate in man, a principle which incessantly yearns for, and reaches after, a state of perfection and deathlessness. He would sincerely, at times, quench in eternal night the spark of immortality which glows in his breast. A morbid distaste of life, or a pusillanimous shrinking from its evils, or the anticipation of some impending calamity—in most cases springing from a mind diseased, and destroying the power of self-control—has tended to inspire and to strengthen this desire. But eternal sleep is beyond his reach. He sighs for it, but it heeds not his moan; he invites it, but it comes not at his bidding; he inscribes the sentiment over the charnel-house of the dead, but it changes not their estate—he may slay the mortal, but he cannot touch the immortal. The compass of his soul points on to life. The long, bleak coast of eternity, its shores washed by the rough billows of time, stretches out before him; and towards it his bark each instant tends, and to it will assuredly arrive. Such is the chain that links man to the invisible world! So interesting and important a being is he. An eternity of happiness or of misery is before him; from it he cannot escape, and for one or the other, mind is educating, and character is forming.

A truth kindred in its solemnity to this is the nearness of judgment to every unconverted individual. To his eye—its vision dimmed by other and diverse objects—it may appear far remote. Damnation may seem to linger, judgment to tarry. Sentence executed against an evil work may appear delayed. But this is an illusion of the mental eye, a deception of Satan; a lie which the treacherous and depraved heart is eager to believe. Never was a snare of the devil more successful than this. But death, judgment, and hell are in the closest proximity to man; nearer than he has any conception of. His path winds along the very precipice that overhangs the billows of quenchless flame. Let him assume what position he may, high or low, fortified or unguarded, from that position there is but one step between him and death, between death and judgment, between judgment and a fixed and a changeless destiny. As one has truly remarked, what a creature of time is eternity! Time is, in some respects, more solemn and important than eternity. The present decides the future. The future is all that the present makes it. It is troubled or serene, inviting or revolting, happy or miserable, a blessing or a curse, as time, omnipotent time, ordains it.

DECEMBER 2

"But God, who is rich in mercy, for his great love with which he loved us, even when we were dead in sins, has quickened us together with Christ (by grace you are saved;) and has raised us up together, and made us sit together in heavenly places in Christ Jesus." Ephesians 2:4-6

All real spiritual-mindedness is the offspring of a new and spiritual life in the soul. It is the effect of a cause, the consequent upon a certain condition of mind. Before a man can exercise any degree of true heavenliness, he must be heavenly. Before he can bring forth the fruits of holiness, he must be holy. Dear reader, is this your condition? Have you the life of God in your soul? Have you passed from death unto life? Is the fruit you bear the result of your engrafting into Christ? You attend upon the service of the sanctuary; you visit the abodes of the wretched; you administer to the necessities of the poor; you are rigid in your duties, and zealous in your charities; but does it all spring from faith in Christ, and from love to God? Is it from life, or for life? Oh! remember, that the spiritual-mindedness which the Bible recognizes, of which God approves, has its root in the life of God in the soul!

But in what does spiritual-mindedness consist? It is the setting of the mind upon spiritual objects. The heart is fixed on God. The bent of the soul—its desires and breathings—are towards Him. It is a firm, growing approximation of all the renewed faculties to spiritual and heavenly realities. God in Christ is the attraction of the heart. That the needle of the soul always thus steadily points to Him, we do not affirm; there are false attractions which lure the affections from God, and deaden the spirituality of the mind. To be carnally-minded brings a kind of death even into the renewed soul; but this is not his reigning, predominant state. Let God remove that false attraction, let the Eternal Spirit apply with His own quickening power some precious truth to the heart, and the wayward, tremulous needle returns to its center; the heart is again fixed on God, its exceeding joy. Oh, how holy and precious are these restorings!

Individual and close communion with Jesus, in the matter of confession of sin, and washing in the atoning blood, strongly marks the state of spiritual-mindedness. No Christian duty forms a surer test of the spiritual tone of the believer than this. The essence, the very life, of spiritual-mindedness is holiness; and the deepening of heart-holiness is the measure of our sanctity of life. Now, there can be no progress in holiness apart from a habit of frequent laying open of the heart, in the acknowledgment of sin, to Christ. The conscience only retains its tenderness and purity by a constant and immediate confession; the heart can only maintain its felt peace with God, as it is perpetually sprinkled with the blood of Jesus. The soul, thus kept beneath the cross, preserves its high tone of spirituality unimpaired, in the midst of all the baneful influences by which it is surrounded. The holy sensitiveness of the soul that shrinks from the touch of sin, the acute susceptibility of the conscience at the slightest shade of guilt, will of necessity draw the spiritual man frequently to the blood of Jesus. Herein lies the secret of a heavenly walk. Acquaint yourself with it, my reader, as the most precious secret of your life. He who lives in the habit of a prompt and minute acknowledgment of sin, with his eye resting calmly, believingly, upon the crucified Redeemer, soars in spirit where the eagle's pinion ranges not. He walks in secret with God, and "sits in heavenly places in Christ Jesus."

DECEMBER 3

"And the Lord direct your hearts into the love of God." 2 Thessalonians 3:5

Love to God is the governing motive of the spiritual mind. All desire of human admiration and applause pales before this high and holy principle of the soul. Its religion, its devotion, its zeal, its toils, its sacrifices spring from love. Love prompts, love strengthens, love sweetens, love sanctifies all. This it is that expels from the heart the rival and false claimant of its affections, and welcomes and enthrones the true. It may, at times, like the pulse of the natural life, beat languidly; yet, unlike that pulse, it never ceases entirely to beat. The love of God in the soul never expires. Fed from the source from where it emanates, the holy fire, dim and dying as it may appear at times, never goes out.

Have you this evidence of the spiritual mind, my reader? Does the love of Christ constrain you? It is the first and the chief grace of the Spirit—do you possess it? "Now abides faith, hope, and love; but the greatest of these is love." It is the main-spring, the motive power, of the spiritual mechanism of the soul; all its wheels revolve, and all its movements are governed, by it. Is this the pure motive that actuates you in what you do for God? Or, do there enter into your service and your sacrifice anything of self-seeking, of thirst for human approbation, of desire to make a fair show in the flesh, of aiming to make religion subserve your temporal interests? Oh, search your hearts, and see; sift your motives, and ascertain! Love to God—pure, unmixed, simple love—is the attribute of the spiritual mind; and, in proportion to the intensity of the power of love as a motive, will be the elevated tone of your spirituality. Nor need there be any lack of this motive power. "God is love," and He is prepared to supply it to the mind's utmost capacity. We are straitened in ourselves, not in Him. The ocean on whose margin we doubtingly, timidly stand is infinite, boundless, fathomless. The Lord is willing to direct our hearts into its depths, but we hesitate and draw back, awed by its infinite vastness, or stumbling at its perfect freedom. But to a high standard of heavenly-mindedness, we must have more of the love of God shed abroad in our hearts by the Holy Spirit, which He has given unto us. We must love Christ more.

DECEMBER 4

"For there are three that bear record in heaven, the Father, the Word, and the Holy Spirit: and these three are one." 1 John 5:7

That the doctrine of the Trinity is a truth of express revelation, we think it will not be difficult to show. We may not find the term employed to designate the doctrine in the Bible, but if we find the doctrine itself there, it is all that we ask. On opening the Bible, with a view to the examination of this subject, the first truth that arrests our attention is a solemn declaration of the Divine Unity—"Hear, O Israel, the Lord our God is one Lord." Deut. 6:4. Prosecuting our research, we find two distinct people spoken of in relation to the Godhead, under the titles of the "Son of God," and the "Holy Spirit of God," to whom are ascribed the attributes of Deity, and the qualities of a person, implying Divine personality. A step further brings us to a passage in which we find these three distinct, Divine people, associated in an act of solemn worship—"Go, teach all nations, baptizing them in the name of the Father, and of the Son, and of the Holy Spirit." What conclusion must we draw from these premises? First, that there is a unity of the Godhead; and second, that in this unity, or in this one Godhead, there is a trinity of people, or three distinct subsistences, styled the Father, the Son, and the Holy Spirit. Here, then, we have the doctrine for which we plead.

The following passage clearly teaches the same glorious truth, Matt. 3:16, 17: "And Jesus, when He was baptized, went up immediately out of the water: and, lo, the heavens were opened unto Him, and He saw the Spirit of God descending like a dove, and lighting upon Him: and, lo, a voice, from heaven, saying, This is my beloved Son, in whom I am well pleased." What a conclusive evidence is this passage of the blessed Trinity! The Father speaks from the excellent glory; the Son ascends from the water, and receives the attestation of His Father; and the Holy Spirit descends from the heavens, and overshadows Him. Here are three distinct people, to each of whom the marks of Deity are ascribed, and between whom it is impossible not to observe a bond of the closest and tenderest unity. Again, 1 Cor. 12:4-6: "Now there are diversities of gifts, but the same Spirit. And there are differences of administration, but the same Lord. And there are diversities of operations; but it is the same God who works all in all." With what a sunbeam is this glorious truth here written! How richly it glows with light peculiarly its own! That here are three distinct subsistences, who can deny? And that they are equal, who can doubt? In Gal. 4:6, "And because you are sons, God has sent forth the Spirit of His Son into your hearts, crying, Abba, Father." Again, here are three people announced in connection with the blessed act of the Father's adoption of His people. Jude 20, 21, "But you, beloved, building up yourselves on your most holy faith, praying in the Holy Spirit, keep yourselves in the love of God, looking for the mercy of our Lord Jesus Christ unto eternal life." Willfully or judicially blind must he be who sees not in these words the great truth for which we plead. And it is the glory of our land, and the joy of our hearts, to know, that from every Christian pulpit, the doctrine of the blessed Trinity is proclaimed whenever the apostolic benediction is pronounced: "The grace of our Lord Jesus Christ, and the love of God, and the communion of the Holy Spirit, be with you all. Amen."

DECEMBER 5

"And have put on the new man, which is renewed in knowledge after the image of him that created him." Colossians 3:10

One important witness which the eternal Spirit bears for Christ is, when He impresses upon the believer the image of Christ. It is the peculiar work of the Spirit to glorify Christ; and this he does in various blessed ways, but none more strikingly than in drawing out the likeness of Christ upon the soul. He glorifies Christ in the believer. He witnesses to the power of the grace of Christ in its influence upon the principles, the temper, the daily walk, the whole life of a man of God. The image of Christ—what is it? In one word, it is Holiness. Jesus was the holiness of the law embodied. He was a living commentary on the majesty and purity of the Divine law. The life He lived, the doctrines He proclaimed, the precepts He enjoined, the announcements He made, the revelations He disclosed, all, all were the very inspiration of holiness. Holiness was the vital air He breathed. Although in a world of impurity, all whose influences were hostile to a life of holiness, He yet moved amid the mass of corruption, not only untouched and untainted, but reflecting so vividly the luster of His own purity, as compelled the forms of evil that everywhere thronged His path, either to acknowledge His holiness and submit to His authority, or to shrink away in their native darkness. And this is the image the Holy Spirit seems to draw, though it be but an outline of the lineaments upon the believing soul. What a testimony He bears for Christ when He causes the image of Jesus to be reflected from every faculty of the soul, to beam in every glance of the eye, to speak in every word of the tongue, and to invest with its beauty every action of the life!

Oh that every child of God did but more deeply and solemnly feel that he is to be a witness for Jesus!—a witness for a cross-bearing Savior—a witness to the spotless purity of His life, the lowliness of His mind, His deep humility, self-denial, self-annihilation, consuming zeal for God's glory, and yearning compassion for the salvation of souls—a witness to the sanctifying tendency of His truth, the holiness of His commands, the purifying influence of His precepts, the elevating power of His example. It may not be that all these Divine characteristics center in one person, or that all these lovely features are reflected in a single character. All believers are not alike eminent for the same peculiar and exalted graces of the Spirit. It was not so in the early and palmy days of the gospel, when Jesus Himself was known in the flesh, and the Holy Spirit descended in an extraordinary degree of sanctifying influence upon the church: it would therefore be wrong to expect it now.

DECEMBER 6

"A new commandment I give unto you, That you love one another; as I have loved you, that you also love one another. By this shall all men know that you are my disciples, if you have love one to another." John 13:34, 35

There is one test—a gentle, sweet, and holy test—by which the most timid and doubting child of God may decide the genuineness of his Christian character—the evidence to which we allude is, love to the saints. The apostle John presents this as a true test. He does not say, as he in truth might have said, "We know that we have passed from death unto life, because we love God;" but placing the reality of this wondrous translation upon a lower evidence, the Holy Spirit, by the inspired writer, descends to the weakest exhibition of the grace which his own power had wrought, when he says, "We know that we have passed from death unto life, because we love the brethren." Thus so costly in God's eye would appear this heaven-born, heaven-like grace, that even the faint and imperfect manifestation of it by one saint to another, shall constitute a valid evidence of his relation to God, and of his heirship to life eternal.

Our blessed Lord, who is beautifully said to have been an incarnation of love, places the evidence of Christian discipleship on precisely the same ground; "By this shall all men know that you are my disciples, if you have love one to another." He might justly have concentrated all their affection upon Himself, and thus have made their sole and supreme attachment to Him the only test of their discipleship. But no! In the exercise of that boundless benevolence which was never happy but as it was planning and promoting the happiness of others, He bids them "love one another;" and condescends to accept of this as evidencing to the world their oneness and love to Himself.

This affection, let it be remarked, transcends all similar emotions embraced under the same general term. There is a natural affection, a humane affection, and a denominational affection, which often binds in the sweetest and closest union those who are of the same family, or of the same congregation; or who assimilate in mind, in temper, in taste, or in circumstance. But the affection of which we now speak is of a higher order than this. We can find no parallel to it; not even in the pure, benevolent bosoms of angels, until, passing through the ranks of all created intelligences, we rise to God Himself. There, and there alone, we meet the counterpart of Christian love. Believer, the love for which we plead is love to the brethren—love to them as brethren. The church of God is one family, of which Christ is the Elder Brother, and "all are members one of another." It is bound by a moral tie the most spiritual, it bears a family likeness the most perfect, and it has a common interest in one hope the most sublime. No climate, nor color, nor sect, affects the relationship. If you meet one from the opposite hemisphere of the globe, having the image of Christ, manifesting the fruits of the Spirit; who, in his walk and conversation, is aiming to cultivate the heavenly dispositions and holy habits of the gospel, and who is identifying himself with the cause of God and of truth—and you meet with a member of the one family, a brother in the Lord, one who calls your Father his Father, your Lord his Lord; and one, too, who has a higher claim upon your affection and your sympathy than the closest and the tenderest natural relation that life can command.

DECEMBER 7

"My brethren, count it all joy when you fall into diverse temptations; knowing this, that the trying of your faith works patience." James 1:2, 3

"It is good for me that I have been afflicted," has been the exclamation and the testimony of many of the Lord's covenant and tried people. It is often difficult at the moment to justify the wisdom and the goodness of God in His dealings with His saints. David found it so, when he saw with envy the prosperity of the wicked. Job found it so, when, in the hour and depth of his afflictions, he exclaimed, "You are become cruel to me: with Your strong hand You oppose Thyself against me." Jeremiah found it so, when in his affliction he said, "He has hedged me about, that I cannot get out: He has made my chain heavy." And yet, where is the furnace-tried, tempest-tossed believer, that has not had to say, "In very faithfulness has He afflicted me"? During the pressure of the trial, at the moment when the storm was the heaviest, he may have thought, "all these things are against me;" but soon he has been led to justify the wisdom and the love, the faithfulness and the tenderness, of His covenant God and Father in His dealings.

The furnace is a needed process of sanctification. If not, why has God so ordered it? If not, why is it that all His people are "chosen in the furnace of affliction"? Why do all, more or less, pass through it? The furnace is needed—it is needed to "purify the sons of Levi, and purify them as gold and silver, that they may offer unto the Lord an offering in righteousness;"—it is needed to consume the dross and the tin which adhere so closely to the precious ore, to burn up the chaff that mingles with the precious grain, to purify the heart, to refine the affections, to chasten the soul, to wean it from a poor empty world, to draw it from the creature, and to center it in God. Oh the blessed effects of this sanctified process! Who can fully unfold them? That must be blessed indeed, which makes sin more exceedingly sinful—which weans and draws away from earth—which endears Jesus, His precious blood and righteousness—and which makes the soul a "partaker of His holiness." This is the blessed tendency of the sanctified discipline of the covenant, and in this way does the Holy Spirit often sanctify the child of God.

DECEMBER 8

"But let patience have her perfect work, that you may be perfect and entire, wanting nothing." James 1:4

Are you a child of affliction, dear reader? Ah! how many whose eye falls on this question shall say, "I am the man that has seen affliction!" Dearly beloved, so too was your Lord and Master, and so too have been the most holy and eminent of His disciples. Then "think it not strange concerning the fiery trial which is to try you, as though some strange thing happened unto you: but rejoice, inasmuch as you are partakers of Christ's sufferings; that when His glory shall be revealed, you may be glad also with exceeding joy." This is the path along which all the Lord's covenant people are led; and in this path, thorny though it be, they pluck some of their choicest flowers, and find some of their sweetest fruits.

I am not addressing myself to those who are strangers to sanctified sorrow—whose voyage thus far has been over a smooth and summer sea—whose heart's affections have never been sundered, whose budding hopes have never been blighted—whose spring blossoms have never fallen, even while the fruit was beginning to appear—or whose sturdy oaks around which they fondly and closely clung, have never been stricken at their side: to such, I speak a mystery when I speak of the peculiar and costly blessings of sanctified affliction. Not so the experienced child of God, the "man that has seen affliction by the rod of His wrath." He is a witness to the truth of what I say. From this mine, he will tell you, he has dug his richest ore—in this field he has found his sweetest fruit. The knowledge of God to which he has here attained—His tender, loving, and wise dealings with His people—of His glorious character and perfections, His unchangeable love and faithfulness—his knowledge of Christ—His all-sufficiency and fullness, His sympathy and love—the knowledge of himself—his poverty, vileness, unworthiness—oh where, and in what other school, could these high attainments have been made, but in the low valley of humiliation, and beneath the discipline of the covenant of grace? thus does the Spirit sanctify the soul through the medium of God's afflictive dispensations; thus they deepen the work of grace in the heart—awaken the soul from its spiritual drowsiness—empty, humble, and lay it low—thus they lead to prayer, to self-examination, and afresh to the atoning blood; and in this way, and by these means, the believer advances in holiness, "through sanctification of the Spirit."

Blessed school of heavenly training! By this afflictive process, of what profounder teaching, what deeper purification, have we become the favored subjects! It is good for us to have been afflicted. Now have we, like our Lord, learned obedience by the things which we have suffered; and like Him, too, are being made perfect through suffering. The heart has been emptied of its self-confidence—the shrine has been despoiled of its idol—the affections that had been seduced from God, have returned to their rest—the ties that bound us to the vanities of a world, perishing in its very using, have become loosened—the engagements that absorbed our sympathies, and secularized our minds, have lost their fascination and their power—the beguiling and treacherous enjoyments that wove their spell around us, have grown tasteless and insipid—and thus by all these blessed and hallowed results of our trial, the image of the earthy has become more entirely effaced, and the image of the heavenly more deeply engraved, and more distinctly legible.

DECEMBER 9

"Remember now your Creator in the days of your youth." Eccl. 12:1

Remember Him who created you, and who created you for His glory—who fashioned your form, who endowed your mind, and who placed you in your present position in life, be it of rank and influence, or of lowliness and obscurity. Remember Him as a holy, sin-hating God, and that you stand to Him in the relation of a fallen creature, impure and unrighteous, impotent and hostile, unworthy to live, unfit to die. Remember what He must have done, and what He must do for you if ever that relation is changed, and you become a new creature, an adopted child, an heir of glory. Remember the strong and inalienable claims He has upon you—claims which He will never relax or revoke. He who commanded that the first of the ripe fruits, and creatures of the first year, to be offered to Him, bids you remember Him in the days of your youth!—your first days, and your best, while the body is in health, and the mind is vigorous, and all the faculties of the soul fit you especially for His service and His glory. Oh, remember Him now, before other things and other objects come and occupy the place which belongs to God alone.

Remember your breath is in His hands; that the axe of judgment lies at the root of the green tree as well as the dry, that the blooming flower and the young sapling are often cut down long before the stately cedar or venerable oak bows itself to the earth. Build not upon length of days; plume not yourself with the laurels which profound learning, or brilliant talent, or successful enterprise, may already have won for you. See how soon they fade upon the brow which they adorn! Think of Kirk White, and of Spencer, of Urquhart, and of McCheyne, of Taylor, of Swain, and of Griffin—those beautiful cedars of God's Lebanon—how verdant and how fragrant were the honors which went down with them to the tomb. But they early lived in the Lord, and unreservedly for the Lord—and the Lord took them early to live with Himself forever. They gave to Him the first and the best, and He took them the first to glory, and has given them the best of glory. Who would not live and die as did they?

Build, then, on nothing beneath the sky, save an immediate and undoubted interest in Christ. Until you are born again, you are in peril; until God possesses your heart, as to any real holiness, usefulness, and happiness, your life is a perfect blank. You live to yourself; and not to live to Him who created you, who upholds you, and who will soon judge you—is a poor life indeed. Oh, give to Christ the golden period of your life. Bind the early sacrifice upon the altar. Lay upon it the first-fruits; Jesus is worthy of your young affections, and of your earliest development of the mind. Oh what a treasure is Christ! To begin life with Christ in the heart, is to begin with a radiant morning—the sure prelude of a smiling day, and of a cloudless evening!

DECEMBER 10

"Jesus answered, You say that I am a king. To this end was I born, and for this cause came I into the world, that I should bear witness unto the truth. Every one that is of the truth hears my voice. Pilate says unto him, What is truth?" John 18:37, 38

"What is Truth?" Momentous question! The anxious inquiry of every age, of every church, of every lip. Pilate knows it now! And he might have known it when the question first fell from his trembling lips—for Eternal and Essential Truth stood as a criminal at his bar!

But summon the witnesses, and they shall testify what is truth. Ask the devils, who beheld His miracles and quailed beneath His power, and they will answer—"It is Jesus, the Son of God Most High." Ask the angels, who beheld His advent and announced His birth, and they will answer—"It is the Savior, who is Christ the Lord." Ask His enemies, who nailed Him to the tree, and they will answer—"Truly it is the Son of God!" Ask His disciples, who were admitted to

His confidence, and who leaned upon His bosom, and they will answer—"We believe and are sure that it is Christ, the Son of the living God." Ask the Father, testifying from the "secret place of thunder," and He will answer—"It is my beloved Son, in whom I am well pleased." Summon witnesses from the inanimate world. Ask the water blushing into wine—ask the sea calmed by a word—ask the earth trembling upon its axis—ask the rocks rent asunder—ask the sun veiled in darkness—ask the heavens robed in mourning—ask all nature agonized and convulsed, as He hung upon the tree—and all, as with one voice, will exclaim—"JESUS IS TRUTH!"

Happy are they, who, through the teaching of the Holy Spirit, receive Jesus into their hearts as the truth—believe in Him as the truth—walk in Him as the truth—and who, under the sanctifying influence of the truth, are employing their holiest energies in making Him known to others as "the way, the truth, and the life"—thus, like their Lord, "bearing witness unto the truth." In the Lord Jesus, then, as the head of the new-covenant dispensation, grace and truth essentially and exclusively dwell; and sitting at His feet, each sincere, humble disciple may receive grace out of His fullness, and be taught the truth from His lips. "The law was given by Moses, but grace and truth came by Jesus Christ." Added, to this, let us not forget that the "Spirit of truth" is promised to "guide us into all truth."

DECEMBER 11

"Obey those who have the rule over you, and submit yourselves: for they watch for your souls, as those who must give account, that they may do it with joy, and not with grief: for that is unprofitable for you. Pray for us: for we trust we have a good conscience, in all things willing to live honestly." Hebrews 13:17, 18

Oh you flocks of the Lord, you churches of Christ, you saints of the Most High, pray, pray for your ministers! No one more deeply needs, no one more affectingly asks your prayers than he. For you he toils in the study, wrestles in the closet, and labors in the pulpit. For your best welfare he consecrates his youthful vigor, his mature experience, his declining years. To you he has been the channel of untold blessing. Often has the Lord spoken through him to your oppressed heart, thoughts of peace and words of love. He has often been instrumental of removing doubt from your mind, of clearing up points of truth that were hard to be understood, and of building you up on your most holy faith. Often, too, has he been the means of endearing Christ to you, leading you to Him as a Counselor, as a Brother, as a Friend, and as a Redeemer; thus unveiling His glory to your eye, and His preciousness to your heart. Perhaps he first told you of Jesus! From his lips you heard the life-giving sound of the gospel; by him you were wounded, by him you were healed, and by his hands you were received within the pale of the Christian church. Is it an unreasonable request that he should ask especial remembrance in the petitions which you breathe to God for "all saints"? Think how often you have filled his mind with thoughtfulness, his heart with anxiety, his eyes with tears, his mouth with holy, fervent pleadings at the throne of grace. Then, will you not continue to pray for your pastor? Gratitude demands it.

Remember him not in your petitions on ordinary occasions merely, but let there be especial seasons of prayer set apart for him alone. Particularly if you know him to be passing through a season of trial, or sorrow, or mental anxiety—take him constantly and especially to the Lord. You need not know the cause of that sorrow. Proper feelings dictating, you will not wish to know. It will be enough for you that, with delicacy of perception, you have seen the shade of sadness on his brow; the look of anxiety in his eye; the expression of deep thoughtfulness upon his countenance; you will instantly take him in your heart to the Lord. And oh! who can unfold the extent of the blessing, which your prayers may thus be the channel of conveying to his soul? You may deem yourself, my reader, but an insignificant member of the flock. The grace which the Lord has given you may constrain you to think meanly of yourself, and to retire into the shade; but mean and feeble though you may be in your own eyes, yet you have power with God in prayer. See you yon little cloud sailing athwart that blue sky? it has absorbed its precious treasures from some hidden spring, and, guided by God's invisible hand, is going to unbosom itself upon some parched and thirsty spot, refreshing, gladdening, and fructifying it. The little rivulet, that flows noiseless and unseen from that shaded spot, has thus transmitted from its sequestered glen an influence felt far beyond it, and to an extent it never conceived, and never can know! Such, dear reader, may be the character, and such the results, of your intercessions in behalf of your pastor. Silver and gold you may have none to offer him; he asks not this at your hands. But your prayers you may give, and your prayers he does ask. He beseeches you, earnestly and affectingly, for the Lord Jesus Christ's sake, and for the love of the Spirit, that you strive in your prayers to God for him! And oh! the hallowing, cheering influence which those prayers may shed upon his mind—eternity alone can reveal! The return of blessing to yourself will be incalculable and immense. The moisture absorbed from the earth, returns again to the earth in grateful and refreshing showers. And thus every prayer which you in fervency and in faith breathe to heaven for your pastor, will, through him, return again in "showers of blessing" upon your own soul.

DECEMBER 12

"The mystery of the gospel." Ephesians 6:19

The apostle doubtless borrows the word from the secret rites of the heathen temples, to which none were admitted, and which none understood, but the initiated. To all others they were mysteries. Freed from its original and profane use, it is here appropriately applied to designate the nature and the doctrines of the gospel of Christ; and thus becomes, by its association, a hallowed and expressive term. Nor is this the only place in which it occurs in the same use. Thus in 1 Cor. 2:7, "We speak the wisdom of God in a mystery, even the hidden wisdom which God ordained before the world for our glory." Equally clear is it, that none are initiated into this mystery of the gospel, but those who are partakers of the second birth. For, "unless a man be born again, he cannot see the kingdom of God." It is to him a mystery. He is blind, and cannot see the glorious mysteries of this kingdom of grace. Addressing His twelve disciples, our Lord further elucidates this idea, when He reminds them of their great and gracious privilege: "Unto you it is given to know the mystery of the kingdom of God; but unto those who are without, all these things are done in parables." Still more clearly is this truth developed in His remarkable prayer, thus recorded: "In that hour Jesus rejoiced in spirit, and said, I thank You, O Father, Lord of heaven and earth, that You have hid these things from the wise and prudent, and have revealed them unto babes: even so, Father; for so it seemed good in Your sight."

If, dear reader, you have been led in any degree into the knowledge of this glorious mystery of truth, hesitate not to ascribe it to the grace of God. Unto you it has been given to know the mystery of the kingdom. The sovereignty of God has so ordered it. The learning, the intellect, the philosophy of the worldly-wise and prudent, have afforded you no help in the solution and unraveling of these divine and glorious enigmas. "But God has revealed them unto us by His Spirit: for the Spirit searches all things, yes, the deep things of God." To babes in Christ—to the lowly-minded disciple—to the learner, willing to receive the kingdom of God as a little child—God unfolds this mystery, that no flesh should glory in His presence. Oh favored, happy soul, if you, through the illuminating grace of the Holy Spirit, have been led into the mystery of the Father's love in Christ to poor perishing sinners! "Even so, Father; for so it seemed good in Your sight."

DECEMBER 13

"In the multitude of my thoughts within me your comforts delight my soul." Psalm 94:19

As a system of Divine and unfailing consolation, there is a charm in the gospel of Jesus of indescribable sweetness. Originating with that God, not only whose name and whose perfection, but whose very essence is love, and who Himself is the "God of all comfort," it must be a gospel of "strong consolation," commensurate with every conceivable sorrow of His people. Let those testify who, amid the trials and the conflicts of their pilgrimage, have thus experienced it. Indeed it is only by this test that its real character can be estimated. As we can convey no adequate idea of sound to the deaf, of color to the blind, or life to the dead, neither can we by the most elaborate reasoning or eloquent description, impart to a mind estranged from sorrow—if such there be—any proper conception of the magic power of the gospel, as a consummate system of the richest consolation and support. But let a Christian be placed in circumstances of the deepest grief and sorest trial—the bread and the water of affliction his food—the iron entering his soul—the heart bereaved—the mind perplexed—the spirit dark—all human hopes blighted, and creature cisterns failing him like a spring in the summer's drought—then let the Spirit of God, the Divine Paraclete, open this box of perfume, breathing into his soul the rich consolations, the precious promises, the strong assurances, the divine counsels, and the glowing hopes which it contains, and in a moment the light of love appears in his dark cloud, his fainting spirit revives, and all is peace. What a wondrous gospel must that be which can meet the necessities of man at every point; whose wisdom no human perplexity can baffle, and whose resources of sympathy and comfort, no case of suffering or of sorrow can exhaust.

Tried soul! repair to this unfailing spring of comfort. God speaks to you in it—it is the unsealing of the heart of Jesus—it is the still small voice of the Spirit. It speaks to you—it bids you "Cast your burden on the Lord, and He will sustain you;" "Call upon Him in the day of trouble, and He will answer you." It assures you that, amid all your perplexing cares, "He cares for you." It promises you that, for your flint-paved path, your "shoes shall be iron and brass;" and "that as your days, so shall your strength be." It tells you that "a woman may forget her nursing child, yet will not God forget you;" that in all your assaults, you "shall dwell on high, your place of defense shall be the munitions of rocks," and though hemmed in on every side by a besieging foe, and all other supplies cut off, yet "your bread shall be given you, and your water shall be sure." It invites you to lay your griefs and weep out your sorrows upon the bosom of Jesus, and so, "leaning upon your Beloved, ascend from the wilderness." Oh, to be led into the heart-felt experience of these truths, even while passing through billows of sorrow to a martyr's flames!

DECEMBER 14

"It is Christ that died." Romans 8:34

"Delivered Him up for us all." If any other expression were necessary to deepen our sense of the vastness of God's love, we have it here. Who delivered up Jesus to die? Not Judas, for money; not Pilate, for fear; not the Jews, for envy—but the Father, for love! "Him, being delivered by the determinate counsel and foreknowledge of God, you have taken, and by wicked hands have crucified and slain." In this great transaction we lose sight of His betrayers, and His accusers, and His murderers, and we see only the Father travailing in the greatness of His love to His family. And to what was He delivered? To the hands of wicked men—God's "darling to the power of the dogs." To poverty and want, to contempt and infamy, to grief and sorrow, to unparalleled suffering, and a most ignominious death. "It pleased the Lord to bruise Him, He has put Him to grief." And for whom was He thus delivered up? "For us all;" for the church purchased with His own blood. For all in that church He has an equal love, and for all He paid an equal price. Deem not yourself—poor, unlettered, and afflicted as you may be—less an object of the Father's love, or less the purchase of the Savior's merits. Oh, blessed, comforting truth! For us all! For you, who are tempted to interpret your afflictions as signals of wrath, and your sins as seals of condemnation; your poverty as the mark of neglect, your seasons of darkness as tokens of desertion, and your doubts and fears as evidences of a false hope and of self-deception; for you, dear saint of God, Jesus was delivered up.

The death of Christ formed the first of all the subsequent steps, in the working out of the great plan of the church's redemption. To this, as its center, every line of truth converged. It was as a suffering Messiah, as an atoning High Priest, as a crucified Savior, as a Conqueror, returning from the battle-field with garments rolled in blood, that the Son of God was revealed to the eye of the Old Testament saints. They were taught by every type, and by every prophecy, to look to the "Lamb slain from the foundation of the world." Christ must die. Death had entered our world, and death—the death of the Prince of Life—only could expel it. This event formed the deepest valley of our Lord's humiliation. It was the dark background—the somber shading of the picture of His life, around which gathered the light and glory of all the subsequent parts of His history.

But in what character did Christ die? Not as a martyr, nor as a model, but as a substitute. His death was substitutionary. "God has not appointed us to wrath, but to obtain salvation by our Lord Jesus Christ, who died for us." This great truth the apostle, in another place, appropriates to Himself. "The Son of God, who loved me, and gave Himself for me." Here was the personal application of a general truth. And this is the privilege of faith. There breathes not a babe in Christ, who may not lay his hand upon this glorious truth—"Christ gave Himself for me." Since Christ bore our sins, and was condemned in our place; since by His expiatory death the claims of Divine justice are answered, and the holiness of the Divine law is maintained, who can condemn those for whom He died? Oh, what security is this for the believer in Jesus? Standing beneath the shadow of the cross, the weakest saint can confront his deadliest foe; and every accusation alleged, and every sentence of condemnation uttered, he can meet, by pointing to Him who died. In that one fact he sees the great debt canceled, the entire curse removed, the grand indictment quashed—and "No condemnation to those who are in Christ Jesus," are words written as in letters of living light upon the cross.

DECEMBER 15

"Yes rather, that is risen again, who is even at the right hand of God." Rom. 8:34

This is the second part of the mediation of Christ, which the apostle assigns as a reason why none can condemn the believer. It would seem by the word "rather," that we are taught to look upon this fact of our Lord's life as supplying a still stronger affirmation of the great truth He was establishing. A few observations may make this appear. The atoning work of Christ was in itself a finished work. It supplied all that the case demanded. Nothing could possibly add to its perfection. "I have finished the work which You gave me to do." But we wanted the proof; we required that evidence of the reality and acceptance of the atonement, which would render our faith in it a rational and intelligent act. The proof lay with Him, who was "pleased to bruise Him, and put Him to grief." If God were satisfied, then the guilty, trembling sinner may confidently and safely repose on the work of the Savior. The fact of the resurrection was therefore essential, to give reality to the atonement and hope to man. Had He not returned in triumph from the grave, the sanctity of His precepts, the sublimity of His teachings, the luster of His example, and the sympathies awakened by the story of His death, might have attracted, charmed, and subdued us—but all expectation of redemption by His blood would have been a mockery and a delusion. But "this Jesus has God raised up" and, grounded on this fact, the believer's acquittal is complete. When He bowed His head and gave up the spirit, the sentence of condemnation was reversed; but when He burst the bonds of death, and appeared in the character of a victor, the believer's justification was forever sealed. "For if, when we were enemies, we were reconciled to God by the death of His Son, much more, being reconciled, we shall be saved by His life."

Here, then, lies the great security of the believer. "Delivered for our offenses, He rose again for our justification." Resting his hand of faith upon the vacant tomb of his living Redeemer, the Christian can exclaim, "Who is he that condemns? it is Christ that died, yes rather, that is risen again." Oh, to feel the power of His resurrection in our souls! Oh, to rise with Him in all the reality and glory of this His new-born life; our minds, our affections, our aspirations, our hopes, all quickened, and ascending with our living Lord. "Because I live, you shall live also."

"Who is even at the right hand of God." The exaltation of Christ was a necessary part of His mediatorial work. It entered essentially into the further continuance of that work in heaven—the scene of the intercessory part of the High Priest's office. "The right hand of God" is a phrase of expressive power and dignity. "When He had by Himself purged our sins, sat down on the right hand of the Majesty on high." "Who is gone into heaven, and is on the right hand of God; angels, and authorities, and powers being made subject unto Him." What stronger assurance has the believer that no impeachment against him can be successful than this? His Savior, his Advocate, his best Friend, is at the right hand of the Father, advanced to the highest post of honor and power in heaven. All power and dominion are His. The revolutions of the planets, and the destinies of empires, His hand guides. The government is upon His shoulders; and for the well-being, security, and triumph of His church, power over all flesh, and dominion over all worlds, is placed in His hands. Who, then, can condemn? Jesus is at the right hand of God, and the principalities and powers of all worlds are subject to His authority. Fear not, therefore, O believer! your Head and Redeemer is alive to frustrate every purpose, to resist every plot, and to silence every tongue, that would condemn you.

DECEMBER 16

"Partakers of the Holy Spirit." Hebrews 6:4

Too lax views of the Holy Spirit we may entertain, but too exalted views we cannot. The great danger is in dishonoring and grieving Him, by low thoughts of the place which He occupies in the Church of God, and of the part which belongs to Him in the salvation of man. But who can trace His operations in our Lord, and not rise from the contemplation of the subject with the deepest conviction of the necessity and the importance of possessing a large portion of the Spirit, in order to deep holiness of heart and great usefulness of life? Christian reader, accustom yourself to address the Spirit in your approach to the footstool of mercy, as a Divine and distinct person; recognizing Him in all the offices which He sustains in the great economy of grace. This will very much tend to expand your mind with exalted views of His Divine and personal glory; and, at the same time, by devoutly contemplating His all-sufficiency, will make you more thoroughly acquainted with your own deep and urgent necessity of His grace. And whatever that necessity may be, ever bear in mind the Spirit is more than equal to it.

Who can reveal Jesus to the soul, save the Spirit? As He only could work in Christ the glory which beamed forth from the Godhead through the manhood, so He only can throw that glory in upon the soul of man. Do I want the peace-speaking blood of atonement upon my conscience?—the Spirit applies it. Do I desire to know my acceptance in the righteousness of Christ?—the Spirit seals it. Do I long to see the Father revealed in the Son?—the Spirit unfolds Him. Do I need in all my trials and conflicts to see the Lord Jesus to be my comfort?—the Spirit, the Comforter, takes of the things that belong to Him, and shows them to my soul—Thus in these, and in a thousand other ways, the Spirit glorifies Christ, first in Himself, and then in His people.

To the Christian reader I would once more say—Jesus is in heaven, alive at the right hand of God, having received the promise of the Father, and is prepared to bestow the Spirit in all the plenitude of His grace on those who ask the gift at His hands. He who so fully possessed the Spirit Himself, waits to give it as richly to others. As man, Jesus knew His own need—as man, He sympathizes with yours. Do not be content, then, with asking this most precious of all boons in a stinted measure, but seek it in its fullness. You are coming to a heart that loved you unto death—that bled for you on the cross—that lives for you on the throne; that desires with all the intensity of infinite affection to pour down upon you the greatest, the richest of all blessings—His own Spirit. Do you want to gain the ascendancy over your easy-besetting sins? then, "be filled with the Spirit." Want you to hold creatures and creature-blessings in their proper place? then, "be filled with the Spirit." Want you that Jesus should be the chief in your affection? then, "be filled with the Spirit." Want you that there shall be no room in your heart for carnal joys, for worldly delights, for sinful pleasures? then, "be filled with the Spirit." Want you to have much of the element of heaven below, inspiring you with longing desires for the full fruition of heaven above? then, "be filled with the Spirit." Thus will you be a living "epistle, known and read of all men." Thus will the world "take knowledge of you that you have been with Jesus." And thus, whatever your lawful calling may be, inscribed upon yourself, your labor, your all, shall be Holiness to the Lord.

DECEMBER 17

"Lord, how is it that you will manifest yourself unto us, and not unto the world?" John 14:22

Such is the infinite majesty, and such the superlative beauty of the Lord Jesus, that were He, in our present state, to stand before us fully unveiled to the eye, overwhelmed with the effulgence of His presence we should exclaim, "Lord, temper Your glory to my feeble capacity, or enlarge my capacity to the dimensions of Your glory!" When in the days of His humiliation He stood upon Mount Tabor, in close converse with Moses and Elias, upon the decease which He was about to accomplish at Jerusalem, glowing with the grandeur of the theme, and fired with the thought of the redemption that was before Him, the veil of His humanity would seem for a moment to have dropped, and the Godhead it could imperfectly conceal shone forth with such overpowering splendor, that the disciples who were with Him fell at His feet as dead. After His ascension into heaven and His inauguration at the right hand of His Father, He again manifested forth His glory in an apocalyptic vision to John at Patmos; and again the same overpowering effects were produced: "And when I saw Him," narrates the exiled evangelist, "I fell at His feet as dead."

And yet this is the Savior "whom the nations abhor," whom men despise and reject; possessing to their eye "no form nor loveliness why they should desire

Him." This is He to whom the world He created refused a home, and whom man suffered not to live, casting Him out as an accursed thing, too vile in their view to dwell among them—fit only to die! "Oh that my head were waters, and mine eyes a fountain of tears," that I might weep, dear Lord, while meditating upon the ignominy, the insult, and the suffering to which my species subjected You. Had another order of being so insulted Your person, so mangled Your form, so requited Your love, so slighted and abhorred You, I might have wept in secret places, mourned, and afflicted my soul, and vowed eternal vengeance against Your calumniators and Your murderers—but it was hatred, ingratitude, and malignity, wearing my own nature—it was man, yes, Lord, it was I myself! But for my sin, my crime, my hell, that spotless soul of Your had known no burden, that gentle spirit no cloud, that tender heart no grief, and that sacred body no scar. And when I read the story of Your wrong—how they calumniated You, blasphemed You, scourged You, spit upon You, mocked You, smote You, and then bore You to a felon's death—I could cover me with sackcloth, bury my face in ashes, and no more cherish the sin—the hateful, the abhorred, the accursed sin, that caused it all.

But overpowering as a full unveiling of the majesty of the Lord Jesus would be to us in our present imperfect state, it yet ranks among our most prized and precious mercies, that He does at times so graciously and especially manifest Himself, as to awaken the exclamation, "This is my Beloved, and this is my Friend!" Holy and blessed are such seasons! Delighted, yet amazed, the believer inquires, "Lord, how is it that You will manifest Yourself unto us, and not unto the world?" He answers and resolves the mystery—as He does the mystery of all His dealings with us—into love. "He that loves Me shall be loved of my Father, and I will love him, and will manifest myself to him." Our experience of these divine manifestations of Christ, forms one of the strongest evidences of His indwelling in our hearts. To none but those who fear the Lord, is the mystery of His covenant revealed. "The secret of the Lord is with those who fear Him." They whose posture of soul most resembles that of the "beloved disciple," are led the deepest into the secret of God's love to us in Jesus. Their intimate acquaintance with Jesus, must bring them into a closer relation and communion with God; it must result in more perfect knowledge of Him—His glory, His mind, and His love. Blessed, but much forgotten truth—he who knows much of the Son, knows also much of the Father.

DECEMBER 18

"Knowing, brethren beloved, your election of God." 1 Thessalonians 1:4

The question has often been asked by the trembling life, "How may I be assured of an interest in the eternal purpose and everlasting love of God? By what evidence may I conclude that I am one 'whom He predestinated?'" Listen to the words of the apostle, addressed to the Thessalonian saints: "Knowing, brethren beloved, your election of God." But how did he know this? Had he read their names in the Lamb's book of life? No! See how he solves the mystery. "For our gospel came not unto you in word only, but also in power, and in the Holy Spirit, and in much assurance." By this he knew their election of God. And by a similar test you must bring the question to an issue. Has the gospel come to your heart by the Holy Spirit? In other words, have you been called by the inward call? Have you fled as a poor sinner to Christ, and is He all your salvation and all your desire? Assume the truth of nothing, take nothing for granted as to your salvation, until this is the case.

It is with the fact of your open call, and not with the fact of your secret predestination, that you have mainly to do. It is this central and visible link in the chain that you must grasp. Secret things belong to God. The things revealed belong to us. You are assuming an attitude of the most appalling temerity, in attempting to force your way into the secret counsels of the Most High, plunging into the fathomless depths of a past eternity, and intruding into those mysteries, veiled and unsearchable, upon whose awful threshold an angel's foot dare not tread. But oh, how near, how visible, how precious, the truth with which you have to do—God standing in the most impressive and winning attitude of a gracious, sin-pardoning God—inviting you; imploring you, all guilty, and burdened, and sorrowful as you are, to accept His mercy; to avail yourself of His forgiveness, to believe in His Son; and thus, by grasping the outstretched hand, by heeding the earnest call, and accepting the gracious invitation, you may set forever at rest the question of your salvation. Let the great, the all-absorbing question with you be, "What shall I do to be saved?" Postpone every other inquiry, adjourn every other debate, until this is met and fairly settled, that you are the called of God. Take hold of the full and free invitations of the gospel—and Christ, and salvation, and heaven, are yours.

And for your encouragement we would say, that the feeblest puttings forth of grace in the soul are indisputable evidences of the inward and effectual call of the Spirit. If in the springtime I mark the tender buddings of the costly plant, I rejoice, yet with trembling. The cold wind may blow, and the hoar frost may light upon those buds, and so nip and kill them, that they shall never burst into the beautiful and fragrant flower. But when I trace the buddings of grace in the heart of a poor sinner, when I observe the evidence of the Spirit's operation in the soul, I feel no misgiving, I cherish no fear, for I am assured that He who has begun the good work will carry it on, and perfect it in glory. No worm shall kill its root, no frosts shall nip its leaf, no winds shall scatter its fruit; it shall never, never be destroyed. God will complete the work to which He puts His hand. Oh, precious truth, replete with encouragement to the sorrow-stricken, sin-burdened, Christ-seeking soul! Sweeter music is not heard in heaven than these words addressed to you—"Him that comes to me I will in no wise cast out."

DECEMBER 19

"When I see the blood I will pass over you." Exodus 12:13

It will be recollected that, upon Pharaoh's refusing to release God's people from bondage, the Lord commanded the first-born in every house to be slain. It was a night of woe in the land of Egypt, long to be remembered. The only exception in this work of destruction was in favor of the children of Israel. And yet even they could not escape the judicial punishment, but in the strictest compliance with the Divine method for their safety. They were ordered on the eve of that fearful night, to take "a lamb without blemish, a male of the first year," and to "slay it, and take of the blood, and strike it on the two side-posts and on the upper door-posts of the houses; and the blood," says God, "shall be to you for a token upon the houses where you are; and when I see the blood I will pass over you! and the plague shall not be upon you to destroy you, when I smite the land of Egypt." They obeyed God. And when the angel of death sped his way through the land, smiting the first-born of each Egyptian family, he paused with solemnity and awe when he beheld the sprinkled blood—sheathed his sword, and passed on to do the work of destruction where no blood was seen.

Thus will it be with the soul who has no interest in the life-giving and the life-saving blood of Jesus! The sinner who has not this Divine and sacred sign upon him is marked for condemnation; he is under the awful sentence of death! That sentence has gone forth—the destroying angel has received his commission—the sword is drawn—the arm is uplifted—one final word from that God who has long stretched out to you His beseeching, yet disregarded hand—that God whose patience you have abused, whose mercy you have despised, whose law you have broken, whose Son you have rejected—and the stroke falls—and heaven is lost forever! Oh, fly to the atoning blood of Jesus! Not a moment is to be lost. Your only hope is there—your only protection is there—your only safety is there! "When I see the blood I will pass over you." Blessed words! Where He beholds the pure heart's blood of His own Son—so precious to Him—sprinkled upon the broken, penitent heart of a poor sinner, He will pass him over in the great outpouring of His wrath; He will pass Him over when the ungodly, the Christless, and the prayerless sinner is punished; He will pass Him over in the dread day of judgment, and not one drop of wrath will fall upon Him. Escape, then, for your life! Hasten to Christ. It may be late—your evening's sun may be setting, the shadows of eternity may be deepening around you, but you have the Divine promise—plead it in faith, and God will fulfill it in your experience—"And it shall come to pass that at evening time it shall be light." Relinquish now all the strongholds of your long rebellion against God, and Christ, and truth—give up your vain reasonings, cavilings, and excuses, and come to the Lord Jesus as a penitent, believing sinner; throw yourself upon His mercy, take hold of His blood, get beneath the covering of His righteousness, and tell Him that if He casts you off you are lost, eternally lost—and you shall be saved! "I went, and washed, and received sight."

When the chill of death is congealing the life-current of your mortal existence, and heart and flesh are failing—the world receding, eternity opening—what think you will then bring life and peace into death itself, illumine the valley, and place you in safety upon the highest wave of Jordan?—It will be the living blood of the Divine Redeemer, at that awful moment applied to the conscience by the Holy Spirit, testifying that all sin is blotted out, your person accepted, and that there is now no condemnation. "Precious blood! precious blood that has secured all this!" will be the grateful expression of your expiring lips, as your ransomed soul crosses the dark stream into the light and glory of heaven.

DECEMBER 20

"And to Jesus the mediator of the new covenant, and to the blood of sprinkling, that speaks better things than that of Abel." Hebrews 12:24

The subject lifts us to the very porch, and within the porch of heaven. And what is the great truth which it presents to our view there?—the prevalency of the life-blood of Jesus within the veil. The moment the ransomed and released soul enters glory, the first object that arrests its attention and fixes its eye is—the interceding Savior. Faith, anticipating the glorious spectacle, sees Him now pleading the blood on behalf of each member of His church upon earth. "By His own blood He entered in once into the holy place, having obtained eternal redemption for us." "For Christ is not entered into the holy places made with hands, which are the figures of the true; but into heaven itself, now to appear in the presence of God for us." There is blood in heaven! the blood of the Incarnate God! And because it pleads and prays, argues and intercedes, the voice of every sin is hushed, every accusation of Satan is met, every daily transgression is forgiven, every temptation of the adversary is repelled, every evil is averted, every want is supplied, and the present sanctification and the final glorification of the saints are secured. "Who shall lay anything to the charge of God's elect? It is God that justifies. Who is he that condemns? It is Christ that died, yes rather, that is risen again, who is even at the right hand of God, who also makes intercession for us." Draw near, you Joshuas, accused by Satan! Approach, you Peters, whose faith is sifted! Come, you tried and disconsolate! The mediatorial Angel, the pleading Advocate, the Interceding High Priest, is passed into the heavens, and appears before the throne for you. If the principle of the new life in your soul has decayed, if your grace has declined, if you have "left your first love," there is vitality in the interceding blood of Jesus, and it prays for your revival. If sin condemns, and danger threatens, if temptation assails, and affliction wounds, there is living power in the pleading blood of Immanuel, and it procures pardon, protection, and comfort.

Nor let us overlook the sanctifying tendency of the pleading blood. "These things I write unto you, that you sin not." The intercession of Jesus is holy, and for holiness. The altar of incense is of "pure gold." The advocacy of Christ is not for sin, but for sinners. He prays not for the continuance of sin, but for the putting away of sin. "The righteous Lord loves righteousness." If sensible of our sin—if mourning over our sin—if loathing and turning from our sin—we come to God through Christ, then "we have an advocate with the Father, Jesus Christ the Righteous." The odor-breathing censer is in His hand—the fragrant cloud goes up—the mercy-seat is enveloped—the Father smiles—and all once more is peace! Then, "I will arise and go to my Father, and will say unto him, Father, I have sinned against heaven, and before you, and am no more worthy to be called your son."

DECEMBER 21

"Be you also patient; establish your hearts: for the coming of the Lord draws near." James 5:8

If the apostle, in his day, could thus exhort the saints, how much stronger reason have we for believing that the "Lord is at hand!" Every movement in the providential government of God, indicates the near approach of great events. The signs of the times are significant and portentous. The abounding profession of Christianity—the advancement of human science—the increase of the papal power—the spirit of despotism, of infidelity, and of superstition, these three master principles at this moment expanding through Europe, struggling each with the other, and all with the gospel, for supremacy—and the extra-ordinary movements now going forward in reference to the return of the Jews—are heralding the approaching chariot of the King of kings. The church of God will yet pass through severe trials—"many shall be purified, and made white, and tried;" nevertheless Jesus lives, and Jesus shall reign, and the church shall reign with Jesus. Let the thought of His coming be an influential theme of meditation and joy, of hope and action.

The present is the suffering state of the church. It is through much tribulation that she is to enter the kingdom prepared for her by her coming Lord. But, amid the sorrows of the pilgrimage, the perils of the desert, the conflicts of the field, the blasphemies, the taunts, and the persecutions of the world, the pangs of disease, and the wastings of decay, we will have our "conversation in heaven, from where also we look for the Savior, the Lord Jesus Christ, who shall change our vile body, that it may be fashioned like unto His glorious body, according to the working, whereby He is able even to subdue all things unto Himself." He, "whom not having seen we love," will soon appear, and then He will chase away every sorrow, dry up every tear, annihilate every corruption, and perfect us in the beauties of holiness. Then there will be no more rising of inward corruption, no more exposure to temptation, no more solicitations of evil, and no more wounding of the bosom upon which we recline. The heart will be perfected in love; and the mind, developing its faculties, enlarging its knowledge, and yielding up itself to those "intellectual revelations, to that everlasting sun-light of the soul," which all will enjoy who love, and long for, Christ's appearing—will merge itself in the light, the glory, the holiness of the Eternal Mind. Oh that the reign of Christ may be, first, by His grace in our hearts, then we may indeed expect to reign with Him in glory. The cross below is the only path to the throne above. The crucifixion now, the glory then. The scepter in our hearts here, the crown upon our heads hereafter. Precious Jesus! hasten your coming! We love You, we serve You, we long for You, we look for You. Come, and perfect us in Your likeness.

DECEMBER 22

"But whoever has this world's good, and sees his brother have need, and shuts up his affections of compassion from him, how dwells the love of God in him? My little children, let us not love in word, neither in tongue; but in deed and in truth." 1 John 3:17, 18

Christian liberality in alleviating the necessities of the Lord's poor, is an eminent attribute of the brotherly love of the one family. The greater number of the Lord's people are "poor in this world." "I will leave in the midst of you a poor and an afflicted people, and they shall trust in the Lord." The poor the church has always with her. They are a precious legacy committed to her care by her ascended Lord.

The line of Christian duty is clear respecting them. Even in the old dispensation, we find more than a dim shadowing forth of this duty. "If your brother be waxen poor, you shall relieve him. You shall not give him your money on usury, nor lend him your victuals for increase," Lev. 25:35. "If there be among you a poor man, of one of your brethren, you shall not harden your heart, nor shut your hand from your poor brother: but you shall open your hand wide unto him, and shall surely lend him sufficient for his need. And your heart shall not be grieved (i. e. shall not begrudge the gift, but shall give cheerfully) when you give unto him," Deut. 15:7, 8,10. This duty becomes still more obligatory, and is enforced with still stronger motives, under the Christian dispensation, as in the words of our motto. Also in the apostle's command to Timothy: "Charge those who are rich in this world, that they do not be high-minded, nor trust in uncertain riches, but in the living God, who gives us richly all things to enjoy; that they do good, that they be rich in good works, ready to distribute, willing to communicate." Thus "by love we serve one another."

What holy luxury of feeling has the Lord associated with the discharge of this Christian duty! Who has not realized, in obeying this sweet and lovely precept, a blessing peculiar to itself? Who has not felt that it was "more blessed to give than to receive;" that here the greatest expenditure has always resulted in the greatest increase; and that in supplying Christ's need in His poor, tried and necessitous representatives, Christ has Himself met us in the way, with some manifest token of His gracious approval? Oh, for more love to Christ, as exhibited towards His people! To see only Christ in them—be they mean, poor, tried, or infirm, despised or reviled, sick, in prison, or in bonds, to recognize Christ in them, to love Christ in them, and to serve Christ in them. This would bring more sweet discoveries of the indwelling of Christ in our own souls. How could we show our love to Christ in another, and not feel the sunshine of His love in our own hearts? Impossible! Oh! to hear Him speak, when the case of need presents itself—"Inasmuch as you have done it unto one of the least of these my brethren, you have done it unto Me."

DECEMBER 23

"For to me to live is Christ, and to die is gain." Philippians 1:21

It will not be disputed that the true test of excellence is its nearest approach to perfection. To nothing will this rule more strictly apply, than to the Christian character. Essentially considered, there can be no difference between one believer and another. Both are equally the objects of God's love, and alike the subjects of His regenerating grace. Both stand on an equal footing of acceptance, and participate in the immunities which belong to the children of God. But it cannot be denied, nor must it be concealed, that there is a great and marked difference in the moral influence which one Christian exerts beyond another. In the measure of his grace—in the depth of his Christianity—in the vigor of his faith—in the luster of his holiness—in the glory he brings to God—and in the consequent happiness of which he is conscious—it may be truly said of the church on earth, as of the church in heaven, "one star differs from another." And to what is this variation to be traced? Undoubtedly to a difference in the tone of spiritual-mindedness. The one is the man of a low, the other of a high Christian standard. Drawing their life, light, and support from one center, they yet seem to move in widely distant orbits. The one appears nearer to the sun than the other. And thus, standing in a closer proximity to the Fountain of all grace, he draws from its fullness the more largely, and dispenses the more freely. His humble walk with God, his close adherence to Christ, his following the Lord fully, imparts a charm to his piety, a brilliance to his example, and a potency to his influence, which place him at once in the highest rank of Christian men.

The last epoch of the Christian's life—such a life as this—cannot but be peculiarly interesting and impressive: It were, perhaps, incorrect to speak of it as the most instructive part of his history. A prolonged course of unreserved consecration to Christ, the record of which would be but a continuous testimony to the truth of the Bible, the character of God, and the power of the Savior's grace in upholding and succouring, sanctifying and comforting the believer, must necessarily constitute a volume of instruction, such as the most triumphant departure could scarcely supply. If this be so, of how much greater moment, then, is it that the Christian should be solicitous how he should live, rather than forestall, by vain and fruitless speculations, the question how he shall die? It is the life, and not the death, that supplies the most satisfactory and assured evidence of real conversion. "Tell me not," says the excellent John Newton, "how a man died; rather tell me how he lived." Let but the religion of an individual be a living, practical embodiment, of the noble sentiment of Paul, "For me to live is Christ," and he need not be unduly anxious about his final change; that change, be it whatever God appoints, must be his gain. It is not always that a life of transcendent beauty—"the beauty of holiness "—is closed by a departure of corresponding interest and grandeur. As if to illustrate the importance and to enforce the lesson of a holy life as a thing of essential moment, God has sometimes disappointed a too eager, and, perhaps, too curious expectation, and has taken home His child, not in a chariot of fire, but of cloud. In other cases, however, we trace the harmony between an eminently godly life and a singularly happy death. Indeed, so strangely and beautifully alike are the two, it were difficult to decide which the most became that bright example, and which brought most honor to God—the dying life, or the living death. Both were emphatically—life in Jesus.

DECEMBER 24

"And without controversy great is the mystery of godliness." 1 Tim. 3:16

The doctrine of the Incarnation presents a gospel mystery, if possible, more astonishing than that of the Trinity. We can more easily understand that there should be three people in a unity of subsistence, than that God should be manifested in the flesh. The analogy of the one meets us everywhere; turn we the eye within ourselves, or turn we it without upon the broad expanse of God's creation—from every point of observation, a trinity of existence bursts upon our view. But, of the other, in vain we search for anything approaching to resemblance. It was a thing so unheard of and so strange, so marvelous and so unique—that there was nothing in the sublime or the rude, in the bold or the tender, of nature's varied works, to prepare the mind for, or awaken the expectation of, a phenomenon so strange, so stupendous, and so mysterious. Not that the possibility of such an event astonishes us. With Jehovah all things are possible. "Is anything too hard for me?" is a question that would seem to rebuke the first rising of such an emotion—

"A God allowed, all other wonders cease."

But we marvel at the fact itself. Its stupendousness amazes us—its condescension humbles us—its glory dazzles us—its tenderness subdues us—its love overpowers us. That the uncreated Son of God should become the created Son of man—that the Eternal Word should be made flesh and dwell with men—that He should assume a new title, entwining in the awful letters that compose His divine name, others denoting His inferior nature as man, so revealing Himself as Jehovah-Jesus! Oh wonder, surpassing thought! Before this, how are all others infinitely outshone; their luster fading away and disappearing, as stars before the advancing light.

The mystical union of Christ and His church is also declared to be one of the mysteries of the gospel. "This is a great mystery;" says the apostle, "but I speak concerning Christ and His church." That Christ and His people should be one—one as the head and the body—the vine and the branch—the foundation and the house—is indeed a wondrous truth. We cannot understand how it is; and yet so many, palpable, and gracious are the blessings flowing from it, we dare not reject it. All that a believer is, as a living soul, he is from a vital union with Christ. As the body without the soul is dead, so is a sinner morally dead without union to Jesus. Not only His life, but his fruitfulness is derived from this source. All the "beauties of holiness" that adorn his character, spring from the vital principle which his engrafting into Christ produces. He is skillful to fight, strong to overcome, patient to endure, meek to suffer, and wise to walk, as he lives on Christ for the grace of sanctification. "Without me you can do nothing." Is it not indeed a mystery that I should so be one with Christ, that all that He is becomes mine, and all that I am becomes His. His glory mine, my humiliation His; His righteousness mine, my guilt His; His joy mine, my sorrow His. Mine His riches, His my poverty; mine His life, His my death; mine His heaven, His my hell? The daily walk of faith is a continuous development of the wonders of this wondrous truth. That in traveling to Him empty, I should return from Him full. That in going to him weak, I should come away from

Him strong. That in bending my steps to Him, in all darkness, perplexity, and grief, I should retrace them all light, and joy, and gladness. Why marvel at this mystery of the life of faith? My oneness with Jesus explains it.

DECEMBER 25

"God was manifest in the flesh." 1 Timothy 3:16

Viewed as a medium of the most costly blessings to the church of God, how precious a mystery does the incarnation of our Lord appear! The union of the Divine and the human in Immanuel, is the reunion of God through the second Adam with fallen man. The first Adam severed us from the Divine nature—the second Adam reunites us. The incarnation is the grand link between these two extremes of being. It forms the verdant spot, the oasis, in the desert of a ruined universe, on which God and the sinner can meet together. Here are blended in marvelous union the gloomy clouds of human woe, and the bright beams of Divine glory—God and man united! And will you, O theist, rob me of this truth, because of its mystery? Will you yourself reject it, because reason cannot grasp it? Then might I rob you of your God (whom you ignorantly worship), because of His incomprehensibleness, not one attribute of whom can you understand or explain. No! it is a truth too precious to part with so easily. God in my nature—my God—my Brother—my Friend—my Counselor—my Guide—my Redeemer—my Pattern—my all! God in my nature, my wisdom, my righteousness, my sanctification, my redemption!

But for this heaven-descending communication, of which the patriarch's ladder was the symbol and the type, how could a holy God advance towards me, or I draw near to Him? But He takes my nature that He may descend to me, and He gives me His nature that I may ascend to Him. He stoops, because I could not rise! Oh mystery of grace, wisdom, and love! Shall I doubt it? I go to the manger of Bethlehem, and gaze upon the infant Savior. My faith is staggered, and I exclaim, "Is this the Son of God?" Retiring, I track that infant's steps along its future path. I mark the wisdom that He displayed, and I behold the wonders that He wrought. I mark the revelations that He disclosed, the doctrines that He propounded, the precepts that He taught, the magnanimity that He displayed. I follow Him to Gethsemane, to the judgment-hall, and then to Calvary, and I witness the closing scene of wonder. I return to Bethlehem, and with the evidences which my hesitating faith has thus collected, I exclaim, with the awe-struck and believing centurion, "Truly this is the Son of God!" All the mystery of His lowly incarnation vanishes, and my adoring soul embraces the incarnate God within its arms. We marvel not that, hovering over the spot where this great mystery of godliness transpired, the celestial choir, in the stillness of the night, awoke such strains of music along the plains of Bethlehem as were never heard before. They left the realms of glory to escort the Lord of glory in His advent to our earth. How gladly they trooped around Him, thronging His wondrous way, their benevolent bosoms dilating in sympathy with the grand object of His mission. And this was the angel's message to the astonished shepherds: "Fear not: for behold, I bring you good tidings of great joy, which shall be to all people. For unto you is born this day, in the city of David, a Savior, which is Christ the Lord. And suddenly there was with the angel a multitude of the heavenly host, praising God, and saying, Glory to God in the highest, and on Earth peace, good will toward men." Shall angels rejoice in the incarnation of the Son of God, and our hearts be cold and unmoved? Forbid it love, forbid it gratitude, forbid it, O my soul!

DECEMBER 26

"Now all these things happened unto them for examples: and they are written for our admonition, upon whom the ends of the world are come." 1 Corinthians 10:11

What an untold blessing to one believer may be the dealings of God with another! As "no man lives to himself," so no Christian is tried and supported, wounded and healed, disciplined and taught, for himself alone. God designs by His personal dealings with us to expound some law of His government, to convey some lesson of instruction to the mind, or to pour some stream of consolation into the heart of others. Thus the experience of one child of God may prove the channel of peculiar and immense blessing to many. God, in this arrangement, is but acting in accordance with a law of our nature of His own creating—the law of individual and reciprocal influence. No individual of the human family occupies in the world a position isolated and alone. He is a part of an integral system. He is a member of a complete and vast community. He is a link in a mighty and interminable chain. He cannot think, nor speak, nor move, nor act, without affecting the interests and the well-being, it may be, of myriads. By that single movement, in the utterance of that one thought, in the enunciation of that great truth, he has sent a thrill of sensation along an endless line of existence.

Who can tell where individual influence terminates? Who can place his finger upon the last link that vibrates in the chain of intelligent being?

What if that influence never terminates! What if that chain never ceases to vibrate! Solemn thought! In another and a remote period, in a distant and an undiscovered region, the sentiment, the habit, the feeling, once, perhaps, thoughtlessly and carelessly set in motion, has gone on working for good or for evil, owned and blessed, or rejected and cursed of heaven. Nothing can recall it; no remorse, nor tears, nor prayers, can summon it back; no voice can persuade, no authority command it to return. It is working its way through myriads of minds to the judgment-seat, and is rushing onward, onward, onward through the countless ages of eternity! Thought is immortal. Its propagation is endless. It never dies, and it never ceases to act. Borne along upon the stream of time, who can calculate the good, or compute the evil, or observe the end of a single life? My soul! aim to live in view of this solemn fact!

But especially is this true of the child of God. He belongs to a people within a people, to a church within a church, to a kingdom within a kingdom—designated as a "chosen generation, a royal priesthood, a holy nation, a peculiar people." In this separate and hidden community, there is a divine cement, an ethereal bond of union, which unites and holds each part to the whole, each member to the body, in the closest cohesion and unity. The apostle more than recognizes—he emphatically asserts—this truth when, speaking of the church of God, he describes it as the "whole body fitly joined together, and compacted by that which every joint supplies." And again, when speaking of the sympathetic influence of the church, he says, "And whether one member suffer, all the members suffer with it." And so also of the consolation. When Paul penned the letter to the church at Corinth, he was with his companions in circumstances of deep trial. He was "cast down," and disconsolate. God sought to "stay His rough wind in the day of His east wind," by sending to him an affectionate Christian minister and beloved brother. "Nevertheless," writes the apostle, in recording the fact, "God, who comforts those that are cast down, comforted us by the coming of Titus." He who wrote these words has long since been in glory; and yet the experience he then traces upon the page has been, and is still telling upon the instruction, the comfort, and the holiness of millions, and will go on telling until time shall be no more. Remember, my reader, you must quit this world, but your influence will survive you. Your character and works, when dead, will be molding the living; and they, in their turn, will transmit the lineaments and the form of a mind whose thoughts never perish, to the remotest posterity. "He, being dead, yet speaks." What an expressive epitaph! A truer sentiment, and one more solemn, never breathed from the marble tablet.

The dead never die! Their memory speaks! Their character speaks! Their works speak, and speak forever!

DECEMBER 27

"The Father loves the Son, and has given all things into his hand." John 3:35

Especially in the Lord Jesus, the Mediator of the new covenant, are all great and glorious blessings prepared and treasured up. No conception can fully grasp the greatness of that declaration, "It pleased the Father that in Him should all fullness dwell." Fullness of justification, so that the most guilty may be accepted. Fullness of pardon, so that the vilest may be forgiven. Fullness of grace, so that the most unholy may be sanctified. Fullness of strength, of consolation, and of sympathy, so that the most feeble, afflicted, and tried, may be sustained, supported, and comforted. Oh how imperfectly are we acquainted with the things which God has prepared in Jesus for those who love Him! He would seem to have laid all His treasures at our feet. We go to Pharaoh, and he sends us to Joseph. We travel to the Father—and sweet it is to go to Him!—but we forget that having made Christ the "Head over all things to the church," He sends us to Jesus. Every want has the voice of the Father in it, saying, "Go to Jesus." Every perplexity is the Father's voice—"Go to Jesus." Every trial is the Father's voice—"Go to Jesus." If it pleased the Father to prepare in Christ all these spiritual things for those who love Him, surely it must be equally pleasing to Him that I, a poor, needy, ignorant, guilty creature, should draw from this supply to the utmost extent of my need. I will, then, arise with my burden, with my sorrow, with my want, and go to Christ—and prove if His infinite willingness to give is not equal to His infinite ability to provide for me all that I need.

It was only in Christ that the Divine perfections employed in saving man could meet, and harmonize, and repose. But one object could reconcile their conflicting interests, maintain the honor of each, and unite and blend them all in one glorious expedient of human salvation, as effectual to man as it was honoring to God—that one object was God's only and beloved Son. The essential dignity of the Son of God was such, that all agreed that the rebel sinner should live, if the Divine Savior would die. Divine justice—vindicating holiness, and sustained by truth—pursued the victim of its vengeance, until it arrived at the cross. There it beheld the provision of mercy, the gift of love—God's dear Son, suspended, bleeding, dying in the room of the sinner, "giving Himself a sacrifice to God for a sweet-smelling savor"—and justice was stayed, stood still, and adored. It could proceed no further in arrest of the rebel, it had found full, ample, perfect satisfaction, and returned, exclaiming, "It is enough!" and God rested in His love. Yes! Jesus is the rest of the Father. Listen to the declaration which He loved so frequently to repeat—"This is my beloved Son, in whom I am well pleased." With what holy satisfaction, with what fond complacence and delight, does He rest in Him who has so revealed His glory, and so honored His name! How dear to His heart Jesus is, what mind can conceive, what language can express? Resting in Him, delighting in His person, and fully satisfied with His work, an object ever in His presence and in His heart, the Father is prepared to welcome and to bless all who approach Him in the name of His Son. "The Father Himself loves you, because you have loved me." Therefore Jesus could say, "Whatever you shall ask the Father in my name, He will give it you." Behold, the Father resting in His love—resting in the Son of His love—resting in the gift of His love. Approach Him in the name of Jesus, and ask what you will, "He will give it you."

DECEMBER 28

"And we know that all things work together for good to those who love God." Romans 8:28

The comprehensiveness of this privilege is boundless. "All things" under the righteous government of God must necessarily be a working out of good. "You are good, and do good." In Him there is no evil, and consequently nothing can proceed from Him that tends to evil. The passage supposes something antagonistic to the well-being of the believer, in God's conduct at times. He would appear to place Himself in an attitude of hostility to those who love Him, to stand in their path as with a drawn sword in His hand. And yet to no single truth does the church bear a stronger testimony than to this, that the darkest epochs of her history have ever been those from which her brightest luster has arisen; and that those very elements which wore an aspect so portentous and threatening, by a mutual and concurrent influence, under the guiding hand of God, have evolved purposes and plans, have developed thoughts and feelings, and have terminated in results and ends, all seeking and advancing the best welfare, the highest good, of the church of Christ.

Let us pass within the individual circle of the church. Shall we take the gloomiest and most painful circumstances in the history of the child of God? The Word declares that these identical circumstances, without a solitary exception, are all conspiring, and all working together, for his real and permanent good.

As an illustration of this, take tribulation as the starting-point. Thus says the apostle: "We glory in tribulation also: knowing that tribulation works patience"—the grace that shines with such surpassing luster in the furnace; "and patience experience"—apart from which all religious profession is vain; "and experience hope"—the pole-star of the believer voyaging homeward; "and hope makes not ashamed"—but confirms and realizes all that it expected. And yet, from where this flow of precious blessing—serene patience, vital experience, and beaming hope?—all flow from the somber cloud of tribulation! That tribulation was, perhaps, of the most mysterious character—of the most humiliating nature—of the most overpowering force—yet behold the blessings it flung from its dark bosom! Who with a finite prescience could have predicted, still less have commanded, that from a bud so bitter and unsightly, a flower so sweet and fair should have blown?—that a cloud so dark and foreboding should have unbosomed a blessing to brilliant and so precious?

DECEMBER 29

"Why seeing we also are compassed about with so great a cloud of witnesses, let us lay aside every weight, and the sin which does so easily beset us, and let us run with patience the race that is set before us." Hebrews 12:1

The Bible is rich in its illustrations of this principle of the Divine government, that all that occurs in the Lord's guidance of His people conspires for, and works out, and results in, their highest happiness, their greatest good. Take, for example, the case of Jacob. Heavy and lowering was the cloud now settling upon his tabernacle. Severe was the test, and fearful the trembling of his faith. His feet were almost gone. The sad recollections of his bereavement still hovered like clinging shadows around his memory; gaunt famine stared him in the face; and a messenger with tidings of yet heavier woe lingered upon the threshold of his door. And when those tidings broke upon his ear, how touching the expression of his grief!—"Me have you bereaved of my children: Joseph is not, and Simeon is not, and you will take Benjamin away: all these things are against me." But lo! the circumstances which to the dim eye of his faith wore a hue so somber, and an aspect so alarming, were at that moment developing and perfecting the events which were to smooth his passage to the grave, and shed around the evening of his life the halo of a glorious and a cloudless sunset. All things were working together for his good!

Joseph, too, reviewing the past of his chequered and mysterious history, arrives at the same conclusion, and confirms the same truth. Seeking to tranquilize his self-condemning brothers, he says, "But as for you, you thought evil against me; but God meant it unto good, to bring to pass, as it is this day, to save much people alive." The envy of his brethren, his being sold as a slave, his imprisonment, were all working out God's purpose and plan of wisdom and love. And yet, who could have foreseen and predicted, that from those untoward events, the exaltation, power, and wealth of Joseph would spring? Yet all things were working together for good.

Thus is it, too, in the history of the Lord's loving corrections. They are all the unfoldings of a design, parts of a perfect whole. From these dealings, sometimes so heart-crushing, what signal blessings flow! "You have chastised me, and I was chastised." And what was the result? It awoke from Ephraim this precious acknowledgment and prayer—"Surely after that I was turned, I repented; and after that I was instructed, I smote upon my thigh: I was ashamed, yes, even confounded, because I did bear the reproach of my youth." Oh, who can compute the good, the real, the permanent good, that results from the trying dispensations of God?—from the corrections of a Father's love? The things that appear to militate against the believer, unfolding their heaven-sent mission, turn out rather for the furtherance of his best welfare and his highest interest.

DECEMBER 30

"The Lord is on my side; I will not fear: what can man do unto me?" Psalm 118:6

God must be on the side of His people, since He has, in an everlasting covenant, made Himself over to be their God. In an especial manner, and in the highest degree, He is the God of His people. In the most comprehensive meaning of the words, He is for us. His love is for us—His perfections are for us—His covenant is for us—His government, extending over all the world, and His power over all flesh, is for us. There is nothing in God, nothing in His dealings, nothing in His providences, but what is on the side of His people. Enshrined in His heart, engraved on His hand, kept as the apple of His eye, God forms a mighty bulwark for His church. "As the mountains are round about Jerusalem, so the Lord is round about His people from henceforth even forever." In Christ Jesus, holiness, justice, and truth, unite with mercy, grace, and love, in weaving an invincible shield around each believer. There is not a purpose of His mind, nor a feeling of His heart, nor an event of His providence, nor an act of His government, that is not pledged to the happiness, the security, the well-being of His people. What Joshua said to the children of Israel, trembling to encounter the giants of Anak, may be truly said to every believer in view of his foes, "The Lord is with us, fear them not."

Not the Father only, but the Son of God, is also on our side. Has He not amply proved it? Who, when there was no eye to pity, and no arm to save, undertook our cause, and embarked all His grace and glory in our salvation? Who slew our great Goliath, and rescued us from Pharaoh, discharged our debt, and released us from prison? Who extinguished the fires of our hell, and kindled the glories of our heaven? Who did all this by the sacrifice of Himself? Oh, it was Jesus! Need we further proof that He is for us? Who appears on our behalf within the veil? Who sits for us as a priest upon His throne? Whose blood, first shed on Calvary, now sprinkles the mercy-seat? Who pleads, and argues, and intercedes, and prays for us in the high court of heaven? Whose human sympathy flows down in one continuous stream from that abode of glory, blending with our every trial, and suffering, and sorrow? Who is ever near to thwart our foes, and to pluck our feet from the snare of the fowler? Oh, it is Christ! And there is not a moment of time, nor a circumstance of life, in which He does not show Himself strong in behalf of His people.

And so of the Holy Spirit. Who quickened us when we were dead in trespasses and in sins? Who taught us when we were ignorant, enlightened us when we were dark, comforted us when we were distressed; and when wounded and bleeding, and ready to die, led us, all oppressed with guilt and sorrow as we were, to Jesus? Who inspired the first pulsation of life, and lighted the first spark of love; who created the first ray of hope in our soul, and dried the first tear of godly grief from our eye? Oh, it was the eternal Spirit, and He, too, is for us. Survey the record of your own history, dear reader. What a chequered life yours, perhaps, has been! How dotted the map of your journeyings, how many-colored the stones that have paved your path, how varied and blended the hues that compose the picture of your life! And yet, God constructed that map, God laid those stones, God pencilled and painted that picture. God went before you, God is with you, and God is for you. He was in the dark cloud that enshrouded all with gloom, and He was in the sunshine that gilded all with beauty. "I will sing of mercy and of judgment; unto You, O Lord, will I sing." Who has carried forward the work of grace in our souls—checking our feet, restoring our wanderings, holding up our goings, raising us when we had fallen, and establishing our feet more firmly upon the rock? Who has befriended us when men rose up against us? Who has healed all our diseases, and has filled our mouths with good things, so that our youth has been renewed list the eagle's? It was the Lord who was on our side, and not one good thing of all that He has promised has failed.

DECEMBER 31

"Father, I will that they also, whom you have given me, be with me where I am; that they may behold my glory." John 17:24

As suffering precedes glory, so glory assuredly follows suffering. Thus was it with our Lord. "Ought not Christ to have suffered these things, and to enter into His glory?" Our Lord is in glory! The head that once bowed in death, pale and bleeding, is now raised in life, encircled with a glory brighter than ten thousand suns. The humanity that was despised from the lowliness of its birth, that was mocked, and scourged, spit upon, and slain, is now, from its indissoluble union with the Deity, exalted far above principalities and powers, glorified with the glory He had with the Father before the world was. Having purged our sins, He is set down on the right hand of the Majesty on high.

To that glory which belongs to Him as the Mediator of the church, each suffering confessor of Christ shall be exalted—the body with the Head, and each part of that body with the whole. A joint-heirship of suffering, it is now a joint-heirship of glory: "We shall be glorified together" with Christ. Still the oneness is manifest, and never so clearly seen as now. Glory bathes it in its light, and eternity impresses it with its seal. It is an undimmed and changeless glory. And Christ acknowledges their right to this oneness in glory. As they were not ashamed of Him among men, He is not now ashamed of them among angels. As they linked themselves to His cross, He leads them to His throne. As they confessed Him before the world, He now confesses them before His Father: "Glorified together." Wondrous words! Elevated to His side—leaning upon His bosom—gazing on His beauty—listening to His voice—entering into His joy—at home, and forever with the Lord. Now is answered in its fullness, the prayer mingled with tears, breathed from the scene of His suffering below—"Father, I will that they also whom You have given me, be with me where I am; that they may behold my glory." Welcome the suffering, succeeded by such glory! Welcome the cross, followed by such a crown!

Let us learn to regard our present tutorage as preparatory to our future inheritance. "The heir, as long as he is a child, differs nothing from a servant, though he be lord of all; but is under tutors and governors until the time appointed of the father." Thus it is with us. But soon we shall attain our majority, and come into possession of our estate. Before long we shall have done with governors and tutors, and need no more the lessons of the school, and the discipline of suffering. Oh, let us live in its near anticipation. To the poor of Christ's flock, how animating the prospect! "Has not God chosen the poor of this world, rich in faith, and heirs of the kingdom which He has promised to those who love Him." What though straitened resources, pinching poverty, or even absolute want, be your present allotment; lift up your heads with joy, for you have a joint-heirship with Christ in a kingdom which your heavenly Father will give. Confide in its security: it is made sure to you by Divine oath; "Wherein God willing more abundantly to show unto the heirs of promise the immutability of His counsel, confirmed it by an oath." Thus inalienably is it secured. Death, which robs the earthly heir of his inheritance, puts you in possession of yours. Your estate comes not to you robed in mourning, for your Father never dies. No succession awaits you, for your inheritance is yours forever. "Blessed be the God and Father of our Lord Jesus Christ, which according to His abundant mercy has begotten us again unto a lively hope by the resurrection of Jesus Christ from the dead, to an inheritance incorruptible, and undefiled, and that fades not away, reserved in heaven for you, who are kept by the power of God through faith unto salvation, ready to be revealed in the last time."

With consolations so rich, and with a hope so glorious, let us close the year through which we have traveled, with a feeling of thanksgiving and with a song of praise. We will thank God for all the way He has led us, chequered though it may have been; and we will trust Him for life's future, dark and uncertain though it may appear. We have found Christ enough for all the past—loving, faithful, wise, He is enough for the present; and we are quite sure all that He has been He will again be—"Jesus Christ the same yesterday, today, and forever." Before another year begins, or closes, we may be with Jesus forever! "Come, Lord Jesus, come quickly!" Your love will fill our hearts, Your beauty will engage our thoughts, and Your praise will employ our tongues, through eternity.

Additional titles
by Octavius Winslow—

Available at:
www.greatchristianbooks.com

THE MISSION OF GREAT CHRISTIAN BOOKS

The ministry of Great Christian Books was established to glorify The Lord Jesus Christ and to be used by Him to expand and edify the kingdom of God while we occupy and anticipate Christ's glorious return. Great Christian Books will seek to accomplish this mission by publishing Gospel literature which is biblically faithful, relevant, and practically applicable to many of the serious spiritual needs of mankind upon the beginning of this new millennium. To do so we will always seek to boldly incorporate the truths of Scripture, especially those which were largely articulated as a body of theology during the Protestant Reformation of the sixteenth century and ensuing years. We gladly join our voice in the proclamations of— Scripture Alone, Faith Alone, Grace Alone, Christ Alone, and God's Glory Alone!

Our ministry seeks the blessing of our God as we seek His face to both confirm and support our labors for Him. Our prayers for this work can be summarized by two verses from the Book of Psalms:

"...let the beauty of the LORD our God be upon us, And establish the work of our hands for us; Yes, establish the work of our hands." —Psalm 90:17

"Not unto us, O LORD, not unto us, but to your name give glory." —Psalm 115:1

Great Christian Books appreciates the financial support of anyone who shares our burden and vision for publishing literature which combines sound Bible doctrine and practical exhortation in an age when too few so-called "Christian" publications do the same. We thank you in advance for any assistance you can give us in our labors to fulfill this important mission. May God bless you.

For a catalog of other great Christian books including additional titles by Octavius Winslow—

contact us in any of the following ways:

Made in the USA
Columbia, SC
09 March 2021